Corporate Communication

Corporate Communication

An International and Management Perspective

Otto Lerbinger

WILEY Blackwell

This edition first published 2019

Registered Office
John Wiley & Sons, Inc., 111 River Street, Hoboken, NJ 07030, USA

Editorial Office
101 Station Landing, Medford, MA 02155, USA

For details of our global editorial offices, customer services, and more information about Wiley products visit us at www.wiley.com.

Wiley also publishes its books in a variety of electronic formats and by print-on-demand. Some content that appears in standard print versions of this book may not be available in other formats.

Library of Congress Cataloging-in-Publication Data
Names: Lerbinger, Otto, author.
Title: Corporate communication : an international and management perspective / Otto Lerbinger.
Description: First Edition. | Hoboken : Wiley, [2019] | Includes bibliographical references and index. |
Identifiers: LCCN 2018019360 (print) | LCCN 2018025338 (ebook) | ISBN 9781119471363 (Adobe PDF) | ISBN 9781119471158 (ePub) | ISBN 9781119471370 (pbk.) | ISBN 9781119471363 (ePDF)
Subjects: LCSH: Business communication. | Communication in management. | Management–Technological innovations. | Business enterprises–Computer networks.
Classification: LCC HF5718 (ebook) | LCC HF5718 .L457 2019 (print) | DDC 658.4/5–dc23
LC record available at https://lccn.loc.gov/2018019360

Cover Design: Wiley
Cover Images: (front cover) © Norbert Buchholz/Alamy Stock Photo; (back cover) © OnstOn/iStockphoto

Set in 10/12 pt WarnockPro-Regular by Thomson Digital, Noida, India
Printed in Singapore by C.O.S. Printers Pte Ltd

10 9 8 7 6 5 4 3 2 1

Contents

Preface

Corporate communication is a highly recognized professional activity that enables a company to inform and influence its stakeholders, other key constituencies, and the general public. A further purpose is to interact with them in order to inform management with their concerns and insights. Moreover, the intention is to influence corporate decisions and policies to make them more compatible with the public interest and uphold a company's reputation. A steady eye is kept on a company's reputation – that valuable intangible asset that affects a company's financial value and social standing – as well as being alert to the emergence of a crisis. Should it occur, he or she helps guide management's response and directs crisis communication.

This function is typically headed by a chief communication officer (CCO), who reports to the chief executive officer (CEO). Ideally, the CCO should be a member of top management – the so-called dominant coalition. CCOs typically work for a multi-national corporation (MNC), which requires them to take an international perspective. They must be able to relate to a large number and variety of players in the global arena, which includes other MNCs, supranational and international organizations, nation states, and civil society organizations, notably non-governmental organizations (NGOs). These new international players introduce new issues facing management that reflect the understandings and misunderstandings that arise through the interactions among them. These issues are typically more complex than domestic ones.

Corporate communication draws on the entire range of communication disciplines and practices, including not only public relations but public affairs, social media, and several aspects of marketing. Public affairs is particularly important because of actions by government and advocacy groups. Social media has challenged the role of the mass media in publicity efforts. Marketing is often combined with public relations in promotional efforts. Social marketing is required when fundamental changes are sought in the behavior of consumers or citizens. All these options must be considered when developing a communication strategy.

From a management perspective, corporate communication is one of several functional departments, such as human resources and finance. Its unique purpose is to consolidate all formal internal and external communications. A CCO is sensitive to public opinion and social trends and heads an organization's issues management process. He or she identifies the most relevant issues, analyzes them, and contributes to an organization's strategic planning and policy making process.

Other titles besides corporate communication have been used by companies. Historically it was public relations, but as the relevance of neighboring communication practices or disciplines – including public affairs, social media, and marketing – was recognized, the designation of corporate communication became more appropriate. In companies that are strongly affected by government regulations and social issues, corporate affairs is a prospective title. A company that does a lot of lobbying and uses public relations and public affairs to influence public opinion is more apt to have a corporate affairs officer.

This book is intended for graduate and senior level college students of corporate communications, public relations, public affairs, social media, and marketing who want to extend their competence to the global arena and to combine the various communication practices to design strategic programs and campaigns. This extension is already a part of such courses as international public relations, global corporate communications, and global marketing communication.

Acknowledgements

I owe my knowledge to dozens of public relations professionals I have met through my professorship at Boston University's College of Communication, contacts as publisher of the weekly *pr reporter*, work with Ruder & Finn and other consulting firms, and president of the New England Chapter of Public Relations. My former students have been a major source of inspiration and, increasingly, of information.

Among my former students, several are mentioned in this book. Prominent among these is Sabrina Horn, founder and former CEO of Horn Group, a nationally recognized tech public relations agency recently acquired by global communications firm Finn Partners. She was exceptionally helpful in explaining the role of integrating social media campaigns within an overall public relations program and in reviewing the chapter on social media. Flora Hung Baeseake, senior lecturer at Massey University in Wellington, New Zealand, who has explored the importance of relationships in public relations, arranged lectures to students and faculty in Hong Kong, Macau, and Beijing. She also made it possible to address the board of directors of Guangdong Daya Bay Nuclear Power Station on the subject of crisis management.

Others from abroad are Minjung Sung, chairman of the Department of Advertising and Public Relations at Chung-Ang University in Seoul, South Korea, who taught me the subtleties of national cultures. Yi-Ru Regina Chen, an assistant professor at Hong Kong Baptist University, shared her research on the strategic management of government affairs in China. Leda Karabella, from Athens, Greece, who has held top public relations positions in companies such as BP, has been a constant adviser on public affairs, especially negotiations. Beth Boswell, managing director, Southeast Asia at the counseling firm of FleischmanHillard in Hong Kong, described healthcare public relations. Jasper Fessmann, currently earning his PhD, and now Assistant Professor in the Communications Department of the University of West Virginia described public relations in Germany and at Siemens in Berlin.

James A. Morakis, former head of international public affairs at Exxon Corporation, has been a major adviser on the strategic handling of international issues and on the intricacies of corporate diplomacy. Those reporting to him held positions in Europe, Africa, South America, Central America, the Middle East, and the Asia-Pacific region. During several once-a-year seminars with members of his staff, many issues they faced were discussed, along with optimal corporate responses.

Harold Burson, a senior public relations consultant and head of Burson Marsteller, has demonstrated that the real contribution of public relations is problem-solving. Edward L. Bernays, a knowledgeable and shrewd public relations counselor, shared many of his insights with me. Patrick Jackson, head of Jackson, Jackson & Wagner and a former president of PRSA, was a constant source of new ideas in public relations thinking. Ken Kansas, a manager of communications and public service programs at Exxon, frequently shared his thoughts in my corporate public affairs class. Mary Ann Pires, head of the Pires Group, demonstrated her expertise in community relations and corporate counseling. Jane Hiscock of the Farland Group showed the usefulness of consumer research in Europe and resistance in Japan for a woman to handle a press conference.

The value of the social sciences and humanities as key sources of public relations knowledge was demonstrated when I joined the faculty of what was originally called the School of Public Relations at Boston University. It offered the first Master's degree in public relations. Edward J. Robinson, with a PhD in psychology, wrote two influential books: *Introduction to Public Relations and Communication*, and *Public Relations and Survey Research*. Bernard Rubin, with a PhD in political science, wrote *Public Relations in the Empire State*. Albert J. Sullivan, with a background in the humanities, was co-editor with me of *Information, Influence, and Communication*. Carol Hills, who was studying for a doctoral degree in sociology, had the foresight to offer one of the first courses in international public relations.

I benefited from the lectures and seminars I gave in Australia, Bahrain, Chile, China, Colombia, England, and Pakistan by being exposed to the questions and ideas of professionals in these various countries. I also want to thank the many international students I have taught, including those in Boston University's London Internship Program (where Tobe Berkovitz and I taught Global Marketing Communication) and those at Lasell College. Its chairman of the Department of Communication, Janice Barrett, was a constant source of information about public relations and its contributing fields of organizational communications and international communications.

Finally, I want to thank all the students in my international public relations and global marketing communication classes who inspired me to write this book.

Author Biography

Otto Lerbinger, PhD, Economics Department, Massachusetts Institute of Technology, is Professor Emeritus of Public Relations at Boston University, specializing in corporate public affairs, crisis management, and international public relations. He has taught courses in Economic Behavior, Organizational Structure and Behavior, and Communication Theory. He also served as chairman of what is now the Department of Mass Communication, Advertising, and Public Relation, was Director of Research at the New York public relations firm of Ruder & Finn, and served as a consultant for several public relations firms. He is the initial designee of the Burson Marsteller public relations chair at Boston University. He has given lectures and seminars in Australia, Bahrain, Chile, China and Hong Kong, Colombia, England, and New Zealand.

Overview of the Book's Five Parts

Part I The Extended Enterprise introduces the role of this organizational function in helping to achieve organizational unity and vitalize and protect its reputation. A corporation is viewed as an extended organization with three zones: primary stakeholders, the socio-political environment, and the international arena. Furthermore, the model of stakeholder management is portrayed, which recognizes an obligation to all primary stakeholders and not only investors. One chapter deals with investors and employees, and the other with the community and consumers. The aim of corporate communication is to build fruitful and enduring relationships.

Part II Strategic Application of Communication Practices: describes five disciplines associated with corporate communication:

public relations – informing and persuading;
public affairs – building and applying power;
global marketing communication – facilitating transactions and strengthening consumer relationships;
social media and big data – expanding the ever-widening range and variety of relationships;
digital and social marketing – extending marketing practices and influencing behavior.

Part III International Perspective: discusses the status of globalization and implications of the different political, economic, social, and cultural features among countries. The relevance of the nation brand is compared with a produce brand and company brand.

Part IV Pivotal Issues Facing Management: explores the increasing relevance of these issues and applies the issues of management process. The new communication settings of science and healthcare are examined and the continuing problems of intellectual property rights and importance of science writing.

Part V Corporate Communication Contribution to Management: explains and illustrates the relevance of a management perspective. Consideration of corporate social responsibility is applied to global interactions and five ways in which corporate communication contributes to corporate governance are presented.

Participation on the executive level is more likely on the global level because of the complexity in dealing with other nations, supranational organizations, and non-governmental organizations (NGOs). Specialists such as lawyers, bankers, and international relations all play a role. But chief communication officers (CCOs) are in the advantageous position of seeing a situation as a whole because they are trained to be generalists and consider the effect on corporate goodwill and reputation. They reflect the view of Rafael Reif, president of the Massachusetts Institute of Technology (MIT), who states the institute's focus on problem-solving means that it stops "worrying about boundaries between disciplines and focus instead on what it takes to solve the problem . . ."[1]

Endnote

1 A Letter from the President, *Spectrum,* Massachusetts Institute of Technology, Fall 2015, p. 3.

Part I

The Extended Enterprise

Corporate communication is the most accepted organizational designation of public relations when used by business organizations, in contrast to the designation by government and nonprofits. The purpose of corporate communication is to strengthen communications between management and its internal and external constituencies. Professionals who conduct corporate communication activities call these constituencies *stakeholders*, while public relations professionals prefer the traditional term *publics*. Both terms refer to any group that can affect the welfare of an organization and, in turn, can be affected by it.

The definition of public relations by the Public Relations Society of America's (PRSA)refers to publics: "Public relations is a strategic communication process that builds mutually beneficial relationships between organizations and their publics."[1] Because of the early association of public relations with public opinion, an organization could go beyond the opinions of the general public and also consider the opinions of discrete groups of people, such as customers, employees, and community citizens, which were called publics.

Companies that refer to stakeholders adopt a stakeholder relations model for running their operations. This model proposes that a company not be run exclusively for the benefit of its stockholders but also to satisfy the needs of other stakeholders. The former is called the classical creed and the latter the managerial creed. The latter is called the stakeholder management approach by James R. Emshoff and R. Edward Freeman of the Wharton School's Applied Research Center. They popularized the term *stakeholders* and stated that the aim of stakeholder management is to "achieve maximum overall cooperation between the entire system of stakeholder groups and the objectives of the corporation."[2] This aim is best satisfied by viewing a company as an extended enterprise.

The Extended Enterprise

A corporation was originally defined as a group of managers and employees organized vertically by the scalar system of different levels of authority – such as president, vice president, and manager – and horizontally by specialized areas of activity, such as treasurer, engineering, human resources, and marketing. Contractual exchanges governed the relations among firm's employees, owners, and others.

A better model for corporate communication is the "extended enterprise." This approach was used by James E. Post, Lee E. Preston, and Sybille Sachs, who envisioned three zones surrounding a corporation: resources, industry structure, and socio-political setting.[3] This book adopts the

Corporate Communication: An International and Management Perspective, First Edition. Otto Lerbinger.

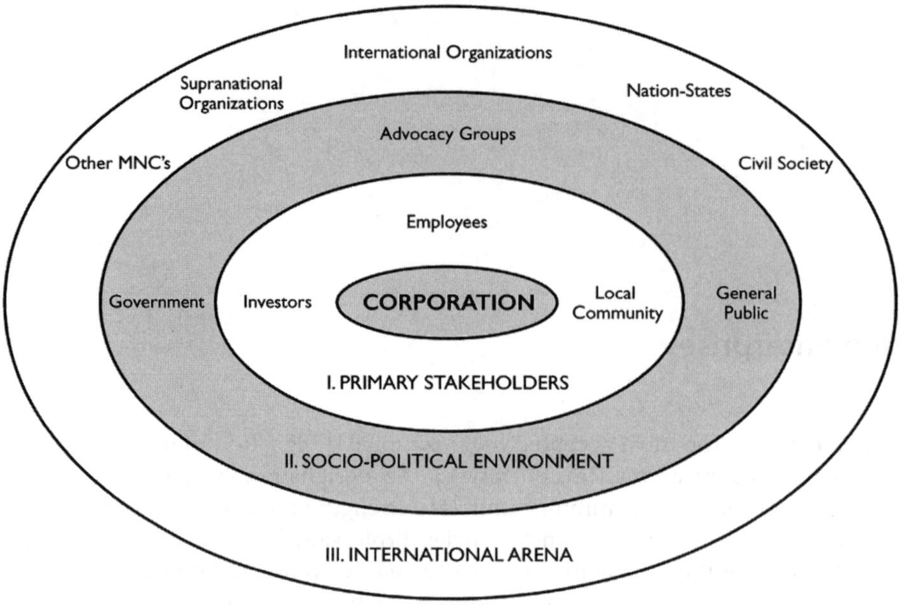

Figure 1 The extended enterprise. Prepared by Joyce Walsh.

idea of the extended enterprise but describes each zone differently to suit the needs of corporate communication. As shown in Figure 1, the three zones are as follows:

Zone 1: Primary Stakeholders. These have been the focus of public relations. They include investors who provide capital, employees who provide labor, and local communities that provide "land" and accompanying infrastructure. Collectively, they represent the economist's "factors of production."

These stakeholders are only partly reflected in a company's formal organization chart and balance sheet, which shows assets, liabilities, and capital (net worth). The organizational chart includes only managers and other employees. The balance sheet excludes employees as an asset even though they are as important as buildings and equipment that are listed.

The factors of production are paid dividends and interest. Wages, and rents from the revenue flow from consumer. It was Chester Barnard who observed in his classic *The Function of the Executive*, that customers had not been included as part of a company even though they are essential to an enterprise's success.[4] Public relations and corporate communication overcome this deficiency by recognizing all stakeholders, including consumers.

Zone 2: Socio-Political Environment. This term is used by the Public Affairs Council, a Washington, DC professional society, to define public affairs. Included are government on all levels, advocacy groups, and the general public. The attitudes and actions of these constituents constitute a company's "license to operate." The sociopolitical environment is especially important for companies that are highly regulated and are targets of advocacy groups.

Zone 3: International Arena. This zone is of special importance to global corporate communication and includes other multi-national corporations (MNCs), supranational organizations such as the United Nations, international organizations such as the World Bank and International Monetry Fund, and other nation states.

Chapters 2 and 3 of Part I discuss the stakeholder groups of Zone 1. The socio-political environment of Zone 2 is the subject of Part II's Chapter 5 on public affairs, and because this book takes an international perspective, the five chapters of Part III discuss Zone 3, the international arena.

Endnotes

1 See PRSA website on "What is Public Relations."
2 R. Edward Freeman, *Strategic Management: A Stakeholder Approach* (Boston, MA: Pitman 1984). An excellent introduction to the concept of stakeholders is James R. Eshoff and R. Edward Freeman, "Who's Butting Into Your Business?," *The Wharton Magazine*, Vol. 4, Fall 1979, pp. 44–48.
3 James E. Post, Lee E. Preston, and Sybille Sachs, "Managing the Extended Enterprise: The New Stakeholder View," *California Management Review*, Vol. 45, No. 1, Fall 2002.
4 Chester Barnard, *The Function of the Executive* (Cambridge, MA: Harvard University Press, 1938, 1962).

1

Introduction: The Domain of Corporate Communication

Corporate communication relates a company to its stakeholders, its socio-political environment, and society. It manages communications with its internal stakeholders of investors and employees, with its external stakeholders in local communities, and with governments, and society at large. Its overall mission is to improve communications and relationships within a company, enhance its reputation, and achieve harmony with society. It is an essential management function on the same organizational level as finance, human resources, and other top management activities. Its unique competence is an understanding of how business can most effectively interact with other parts of society.

"Corporate public relations" was the original name for "corporate communication." It was one of three institutional applications of public relations. It dealt with business organization while the other two dealt with government and non-profit organizations. It was important that a public relations professional in each of these sectors of society knew something about the structure of their industry, its challenges, and its problems. Those in the business sector were expected to know how a business operates, what laws and regulations govern it, how cultures among companies differ, and what events and issues affect its operations.

Business embraced public relations as a way to offset the damage to its operations and reputation by the muckracking activities of the news media against corporations. Public relations was a bulwark against growing government power and the aggressiveness of advocacy groups in civil society. The power of public relations to influence what the mass media said and to sway public opinion was attractive to business. Public relations also offered services such as issues management and the publication of social reports. Despite these accomplishments, public relations suffered because it was too closely identified with publicity and "spin" to give it sufficient credence. Many companies shunned the term and turned to the yet unblemished and distinctive term of "corporate communication."

A further reason for preferring the term corporate communication is that with the growth of communication, public relations in the popular but narrow meaning of publicity or media relations was only one part of the larger spectrum of communication practices, as outlined in Part II. Public affairs, often claimed by public relations, is treated as a separate discipline, which is evidenced in the separate professional association of the Public Affairs Council. Another practice, marketing, is considered a partner despite traditional resistance by public relations. In addition, marketing extends to digital marketing and social marketing. The latter, which seeks to change the consumption behavior of consumers, was often considered necessary to complete a marketing objective. Government and other non-businesses also found social marketing helpful. Another practice, social media, has revolutionized all communication activities, and is included as a communication practice. Corporate communication embraces all of these communication practices and disciplines, while public relations remained a separate activity.

Corporate Communication: An International and Management Perspective, First Edition. Otto Lerbinger.

Nonetheless, because the foundation of corporation communication is public relations, the two terms are often used synonymously throughout the book.

The heads of corporate communication departments are predominately called corporate communication officers (CCOs), with the rank of vice president most common.[1] Most (46%) in the US report to the CEO, but others, especially in large organizations, report to a senior vice president, who is also in charge of such other staffs as legal and marketing.[2] A CCO endeavors to be part of a company's top management group.

The competing departmental name of "corporate affairs" is increasingly used when its activities closely involve public policy, regulatory development, government/public affairs, and thought leadership. Those departments are likely to be headed by a corporate affairs officer (CAO).[3] He or she considers government relations as "the best place to sit." CAOs are more likely than CCOs to report to top management and to spend more time with the chairman and the board. CAOs argue that communication needs to be "front of mind when making business decisions."[4] In England, 42% of the FTSE 100 were members of the executive committee, with 88% of the top 50.[5]

1.1 Stakeholder Management

This scheme of an organization's extended organization presented in Part I represents the modern stakeholder management view of a corporation. Corporate communicators must be aware of all the stakeholders and other entities with whom they communicate and relate. This broader view of an organization shows how critical a deep understanding of the interface between government, business, and society is becoming.

Corporate communication helps establish and strengthen the relationships of a company with its stakeholders and society. Internally, it provides vision and values for all those who participate in the company's functioning. It is the living aspect of an organizational system. Corporate communication departments should continually work with other departments – such as human resources, finance, and marketing – to promote organizational goals and to inform management of possible problems and dissatisfactions so that corrective actions can be taken.

Externally, corporate communication relates a company to society. This relationship is essential for the effective operation of an organization and for its legitimacy and acceptance in society. It affects the endurance of the free market system within which companies operate. A company's legitimacy cannot be assumed, as fluctuations in recent decades has shown. An American Management Association survey report, *Business and Society: 1976–2000*, stated: "There is a fundamental change coming in the relationship between American business and the society it serves." More than 68% of the respondents agreed with the statement: "We have reason to be concerned whether the corporation as we know it . . . will survive into the next century . . . . The corporation itself must change, consciously evolving into an institution adapted to the new environment."[6] This new ideology was buttressed by the views of Adolf Berle and Gardner Means, who in 1933 stated in their landmark book, *The Modern Corporation and Private Property*, that the modern corporation is not only an economic but a social institution.[7]

Recent surveys, such as the Edelman Trust Barometer, confirm that the relationship between business and society remains tenuous. CCOs should view themselves as custodians of the business–society relationship. They partly do this through stakeholder relations. For example, corporate communicators work with human resources departments to keep employees informed, using the formula that good communications lead to job satisfaction, which, in turn, leads to high productivity and profitability. Similarly, by engaging in community relations, corporate communicators improve relations with local government and its institutions. By working with educational institutions, for example, they may help communities to produce more highly qualified employee recruits. Supportive efforts in marketing through consumer relationship management should lead to greater satisfaction and better sales and revenue.

1.2 Twin Goals of Corporate Communication

Corporate communication helps establish and strengthen the relationships of a company with its stakeholders and society. Second, it builds, improves, and preserves a company's reputation with stakeholders and significant entities in society.

1.2.1 Strengthening Relationships with Stakeholders

One concern of corporate communication is to strengthen the relationships of a company with its stakeholders. This concern is evidenced in the public relations roots of corporate communication. As stated in an early definition by James E. Grunig and Todd Hunt, public relations is "the management of communication between an organization and its publics."[8] Going beyond communications, one of the leading textbooks in public relations, *Effective Public Relations*, by Scott M. Cutlip, Allen H. Center, and Glen M. Broom, states that "public relations is the management function that identifies, establishes, and maintains mutually beneficial relationships between an organization and the various publics on whom its success or failure depends."[9]

Building relationships is a pivotal concern of public relations. As explained in 1984 by M.A. Ferguson, relationships are the central unit of study in public relations. She states that "not . . . the organization, nor the public, nor the communication public relations process, but relationships should be the unifying concept of public relations."[10] This is the theme of John Ledingham's *Public Relations as Relationship Management* and David Dozier's statement that "the purpose and direction of an organization (its mission) is affected by relationships with key constituents (publics) in the organization's environment."[11] Along these lines, he also states that communication is "a strategic management function (that helps) manage relationships with key publics that affect organizational mission, goals and objectives." He conceived the basis of public relations as a system of organization–public relationships.

Sociologists point out that relationships are the foundation of social systems, for they constitute the basic building block of all groups, organizations, and society that need to be considered in human interactions. As described in the jargon of sociology by Talcott Parsons, former chairman of the Social Relations Department at Harvard University, and Edward Shils of the University of Chicago, a relationship is "an organized system of interaction between ego and alter" that becomes stabilized as "they build up reciprocal expectations of each other's action and attitudes which are the nucleus of what may be called *role-expectations*." Consequently, "Alter expects ego to behave in a certain relatively specific ways, or at least within relatively specific limits."[12]

1.2.1.1 The Social Contract and Other Dimensions of a Relationship

What Parsons and Shills say is that the relationship between an organization and a specific group of stakeholders defines the social contract between them. It describes what each expects of the other and their subsequent mutual benefits. Built upon this social contract, public relations applies the following additional dimensions of a social relationship:

- Public relations preference for two-way communication, described in terms of both disclosure by a company and information inputs by stakeholders. Disclosure refers to the kinds and amounts of information a company shares with others; and information input refers to the degree of participation it invites, especially from employees but also from others, such as customers. Feedback, a response to a company's actions, is a part of such input.

- *Power relationship between a company and each stakeholder group.* How much power can a stakeholder group be expected to wield? This aspect is particularly important in employee relations as reflected in work slow-downs and labor union negotiations. It is also a critical dimension in relationships with various activist groups, such as consumers or environmentalists.
- *Privacy of stakeholders.* Although mostly focused on customer information, it also applies to employees.
- Company exercise of social responsibility to its stakeholders and to society at large.

The social contract and other aspects of a relationship are discussed in Chapters 2 and 3 in the context of a company's relationship with the key stakeholder groups of investors, employees, the community, and customers.

1.2.1.2 Evaluation of a Relationship

The relationship meaning of public relations is measured by examining the outcomes of relationships and defining them in behavioral terms. The key outcomes are:

- *Mutual satisfaction.* The needs of both a company and its stakeholders groups are met.
- *Trust.* Both the company and stakeholder groups have confidence that each will do what is expected of them and treat each other fairly.
- *Loyalty.* Both want the relationship to continue; each is committed to the other.
- *Harmony.* Both are willing to face problems and conflicts in their relationship and seek to find agreement.[13]

1.2.1.3 Trust

Of the four outcomes, trust is the most fundamental. When organizations are less known in foreign communities and nations where they operate and sell their products and services, trust replaces personal knowledge. The importance of trust is especially illustrated in medical services. Patients generally lack information and knowledge about their medical condition and must rely on their physicians for advice. But trust in physicians may be problematical. As Laurie Garrett's book, *Betrayal of Trust*, portrays, the public health capacity and responsibility in the USA, Africa, India, Russia, and around the world are declining.[14] Many doctors in the US have seemingly abandoned the Hippocratic Oath in pursuit of higher incomes and profit-making opportunities. The same may be happening more broadly in the relationship between business and society.

The dictionary meaning of trust is the "assured reliance on the character, ability, strength, or truth of someone or something."[15] Trust consists of three components: (i) integrity – the belief that an organization is fair and just; (ii) dependability – an organization will do what it says it will do; and (iii) competence – the ability to do what it says it will do.[16] Trust in a company exists when both it and stakeholder groups have confidence that each will do what is expected of them to satisfy the needs of the other and to treat each other fairly and justly. A basis for establishing trust is the willingness to share information – to be "open." Trustworthiness is one of the foundations of credibility, without which communication is impaired.

In customer relations, trust is essential when customers lack the necessary knowledge and information to judge a product or service by themselves, particularly in the complex areas of banking, finance, law, and technology. For this reason people seek information and advice from public relations professionals, who by definition are supposed to place their clients' interests ahead of their own. Trust is important in international relations because the players typically lack knowledge about one another and must therefore rely on trust. The custom of first socializing with one another in business transactions serves the purpose of learning more about the other, which may help to establish trust.

Since the collapse of Enron and other corporate scandals, Wall Street recognizes that it faces a "crisis of confidence." Business activity is severely hampered when the parties in a transaction cannot trust the information they are given. Building trust for a company is a common public relations objective. But it must be remembered that a public relations program of trust is not planned; as Jim Grunig asserts, it is the *outcome* of what is done.[17] This feature is reflected in an image ad by the *Wall Street Journal*, saying "Trust Is Something You Earn."[18]

1.2.2 Maintaining Corporate Reputation

The second goal of corporate communication is to build, improve, and preserve a company's reputation with stakeholders and significant entities in society. Reputation serves as an overall measure of a company's standing in the minds of the general public and specific publics. James Grunig and C.J. Hung define it as an intangible asset that is a valuable "composite of all of the cognitions and attitude of all stakeholders."[19] Reputation is part of a company's intangible asset called goodwill (one word), which adds to the value of a company. It is included in a company's balance sheet, which lists all the assets (anything of value owned), liabilities (anything owed), and the resultant net worth. The clearest evidence of goodwill is when a company is sold for more than its book value. The financial value of a good reputation is also reflected over time in a company's stock price. From a theoretical viewpoint, states Robyn Remke, the concept of corporate reputation involves a state of *awareness* by stakeholders, or other observers; she defines reputation as an *assessment*, and positions it as an asset.[20]

Craig Carroll provides a multi-faceted view of reputation by examining it from several perspectives: "what we really are," "what we say we are," "what we are seen to be," "what we think others see," "what the brand stands for," "what we ought to be," and "what we wish to be."[21] These different views enable a corporate communicator better to observe and measure an organization's reputation as well as to develop ways of shaping it in a desired fashion. Corporate actions strongly influence reputation, so the advice given by Davia Temin, a *Forbes* contributor, is to "strategically define who you want to be, and what you want to be known as, and then to live that definition in every interactions. If you do it right, then others will recognize your efforts and you will earn the reputation you wish to have."[22]

The most progressive companies and their CEOs know that an outcome of a corporate communication function is to elevate the importance of reputation. "If you want to be active in shaping strategy and implementing decisions, you have to report to the CEO and be at the Executive Committee table, otherwise your influence is affected."[23] Surveys of CEOs show that reputation is of increasing concern to them as they become targets of government and advocacy groups.

1.2.2.1 The Psychological Basis of Reputation

To more fully understand the significance of a company's reputation, it is helpful to examine its psychological roots. A reputation is based on the psychology of perception and attitudes – how others see and think about a company. Perception is the process by which a person becomes aware of objects, qualities, or relations by way of the sense organs. It connects the outside environment with a person's stored information and helps determine what is "seen" and what is omitted or rejected. The process of perception is analogous to crossing an international border where immigration and customs officials determine who and what is allowed to enter.

Charles Fombrun, Professor Emeritus at New York University's Stern School of Business, who has specialized in the subject of reputation, strongly focuses on the process of perception. He defines reputation as "a perceptual representation of a company's past actions and future prospects that describes the firm's overall appeal to all of its key constituents when compared with other leading rivals."[24] Although this definition sounds academic, its practical value is that it contains all the elements of a reputation: the perception of a company, its past record, its future expectations, and its appeal to constituents and comparison with its rivals.

Paul Argenti, a professor at the Amos Tuch School of Business at Dartmouth University, states that a company's brand and reputation are the foundation on which a company is built.[25] A company's reputation affects how it is treated by its various stakeholders, especially by consumers. This view also appears in Erving Goffman's *Presentation of Self in Everyday Life*, which points out that persons engage in image strategies to create favorable "terms of trade" in their dealings with others.[26] Company reputation is a "value-added" concept as seen by consumers because it provides additional assurance to whatever is known about its products or services.

A person's attitudes help both to determine what is perceived and, in a reverse process, how she or he is influenced by what is perceived. Public relations efforts are aimed at creating favorable attitudes toward a company, for example, liking it and associating favorable characteristics with it. An attitude is a precursor to behavior. The opposite is also true: by behaving in a certain way when confronted with an issue, a person's attitude is influenced. For example, if an undecided person is persuaded to sign a petition favoring recreational marijuana, that behavior will produce a positive attitude toward marijuana use. This process is explained by Leon Festinger's theory of cognitive dissonance, which states that the human tendency is to rationalize, so that when an attitude is not in sync with the parallel behavior dissonance occurs, which can then be resolved by changing either one's behavior or attitude, thus preserving consonance.[27]

1.2.2.2 Vulnerability to Crises

A crisis is any event that damages or has the potential to damage a company's reputation.[28] When in 1989 the Exxon-Valdez crashed into Bligh Reef in the pristine waters of Prince William Sound, Alaska, Exxon's reputation was severely hurt. This was a crisis of management failure that displayed its skewed values of favoring profits over safety. Other situations, such as government action, confrontations with advocacy groups, and attacks by the mass media and social media, will likely damage a company's reputation and trigger a crisis. These so-called reputational crises are becoming more frequent and worrisome.

In a recent survey of 500 biggest companies conducted by Risk Advisory Group, reputational risk was named as the most important risk to business, ahead of operational and market threats. The reason is simple, says Matthew Durdy, director at Control Risks, a leading international business risks consultancy: "In a reputational incident you get massive swings in a company's share price."[29] Furthermore, as evidenced by the demise of Arthur Andersen, the auditing firm of disgraced Enron, "a company can be forced out of business."

Companies that successfully manage their corporate reputations will secure a more sustainable future, reports Glen Peters of the *Financial Times*.[30] A company that values a good reputation is more likely to avoid behavior that harms others or the environment. But if a crisis does occur, such as a product defect, a good reputation can soften its impact because people are willing to listen to a company's explanation and give it the benefit of doubt. That is particularly true when a former relationship with injured or aggrieved people exists, for the trust in such a relationship helps soften displeasure.

An early measurement of reputation was the Opinion Corporation's well-known three dimensions:

1) *Familiarity*. How widely, if at all, an organization is known.
2) *Favorability*. The degree to which an organization liked or disliked.

3) *Attributes*. The adjectives that best describe the organization, e.g. friendly and progressive.[31]

The latter dimension of attributes allows the most detailed description of a company's reputation to be made.

1.2.2.3 Fombrun's Ingredients of a Reputation

Fombrun and Harris Interactive, a US market research company, developed a measure of reputation called the Reputation Quotient (RQ).[32] It is calculated on the basis of 20 attributes in six main categories. It measures perceptions of companies across a range of industries and stakeholder groups. The six categories of RQ are:

1) Emotional appeal—how much a company is liked and respected.
2) Products and services—perceptions of quality, innovation, value, and reliability.
3) Financial performance—competitiveness, profitability, growth prospects, and risk.
4) Vision and leadership. Does a company demonstrate clear vision, strong leadership, and an ability to recognize and capitalize on market opportunities?
5) Workplace environment. Is the company well managed? What is it like to work there? What is the quality of its employees?
6) Social responsibility. Does a company have high standards in its dealings with people, good causes, and the environment?

The 2015 Harris RQ survey, its 16th, ranked the reputations of 100 of the most visible companies in the USA. The survey states that Americans remain skeptical of Corporate America, with only one in five indicating that it has improved, while twice as many indicate it has declined. Regarding social responsibility, for example, the survey states that only five companies achieved an "excellent" rating, while 24 were rated as "poor" or "very poor."[33]

When asked to name two companies that stand out as having the best and the worst reputations overall, the list included in the survey's over 4000 respondents were Wegman's Food Market, Amazon.com, Samsung, Costco, and Johnson & Johnson. The five with the lowest ratings were Goldman Sachs, American International Group (AIG), Dish Networks, Monsanto, and Halliburton. With over a decade of experience in the field, the Harris team states it has consistently demonstrated the link between perceptions of strong corporate reputations and positive supportive behaviors toward those companies, such as product purchase or investment behavior. Moreover, it identified a strong positive relationship between change in reputation and change in market capitalization, i.e. when reputation dropped so did the value of its stocks.

Fombrun distills the analysis of corporate reputation into five simple principles: distinctiveness (among stakeholders for a product/service); focus (a single core theme); consistency (in actions and communications); identity (based on espoused principles rather than advertising or "spin"); and transparency (disclosing more information and engaging in dialogue with stakeholders). These principles offer a guide to the creation of a sound corporate reputation.

1.3 Conclusions

Corporate communication is a major management function with the overall responsibility to relate a company to its stakeholders and society and maintains its reputation. Drawing on the origins of public relations, improving relationships has become one of two major concerns of corporate communication. The sociological meaning and significance of relationships are examined, starting with the social contract between a company and those with whom it has a relationship. To be effective, corporate communicators must strengthen its relationship to top management by advising it about critical issues and trends affecting a company and about dangers to its reputation.

A company's reputation is a high concern of corporate communication. The concept of reputation is reviewed in terms of its psychological roots in the theory of perception and attitude. In so doing, the value of applying the social sciences to communication is demonstrated.

Discussion Questions

1.1. What's the relationship between corporate communication and public relations?

1.2. How is stakeholder management different from management as defined in principles of organization and management texts?

1.3. What are the twin concerns of corporate communication?

1.4. How has the fundamental relationship between American business and society changed in recent decades?

1.5. Why might it be inaccurate to say that corporate communication is concerned only with communication?

1.6. What is the social contract in a relationship? What are other dimensions of a relationship?

1.7. How are relationships evaluated?

1.8. Define reputation. What are its ingredients?

1.9. What is a crisis and how might it affect a company's reputation?

Endnotes

1 www.kornferry.com/institute/the-chief-communications-officer-2015-survey-and-findings-among-the-fortune-500#sthash.luT4Z4bm.dpuf

2 See the comprehensive article in Donald K. Wright, "The Organization of the Corporation Communication Function," in Rossella Gambetti and Stephen Quigley, editors, *Managing Corporate Communication: A Cross-Cultural Approach* (Palgrave Macmillan: 2013), pp. 73–94.

3 Ibid.

4 Jonathan Harper and Camilla Morrisby, "A Seat at the Table: The Growing Influence of the Corporate Affairs Function in FTSE 100 Companies," Spencer Stuart.com. "The Rise and Rise of the Corporate Affairs Director," *MIT, Management Today,* May 19, 2016.

5 Jonathan Harper and Camilla Morrisby, "A Seat at the Table: The Growing Influence of the Corporate Affairs Function in FTSE 100 Companies," Spencer Stuart.com.

6 American Management Association, *Business and Society: 1976–2000,* p. 1.

7 Adolf Berle and Gardner Means, *The Modern Corporation and Private Property* (New York: Macmillan, 1932).

8 James E. Grunig and Todd Hunt, *Managing Public Relations* (New York: Holt, Rinehart and Winston, 1984), p. 6.

9 Scott M. Cutlip, Allen H. Center, and Glen M. Broom, *Effective Public Relations*, 8th edition (Englewood Cliffs, NJ: Prentice-Hall, 2000), p. 6.

10 John A. Ledingham, "Explicating Relationship Management as a General Theory of Public Relations," *Journal of Public Relations Research*, 15 (2), 2003, pp. 81–198. He refers to M. A. Ferguson, "Building Theory in Public Relations: Interorganizational Relationships," Paper presented at the Association for Education in Journalism and Mass Communication, Gainesville, Florida, August 1984. See John A. Ledingham and Stephen D. Bruning, eds. *Public Relations as Relationship Management: A Relational Approach to the Study and Practice of Public Relations* (Mahwah, NJ: Lawrence Erlbaum Associations, 2000).

11 Eyun-Jung Ki, Jeong-Nam Kim, and John A. Ledingham, *Public Relations as Relationship Management* (New York: Routledge, 2015). Flora Hung also concluded, "The ultimate goal for public relations practice is building and maintaining substantive relationships with internal and external publics."

12 Talcott Parsons and Edward A. Shils, *Toward a General Theory of Action* (Cambridge, MA: Transaction Publishers, 1954), p. 19.

13 James E. Grunig and Yi-Hui Huang, "From Organizational Effectiveness to Relationship Indicators: Antecedents of Relationships, Public Relations Strategies, and Relationship Outcomes," in John A. Ledingham and Stephen D. Brunig, eds., *Public Relations as Relationship Management: A Relational Approach to the Study and Practice of Public Relations* (Mahwah, NJ: Lawrence Erlbaum Associations, 2000), pp. 23–53. Sung-Un Yang and James E. Grunig, (2005) "Decomposing Organisational Reputation: The Effects of Organisation–Public Relationship Outcomes on Cognitive Representations of Organisations and Evaluations of Organisational Performance," *Journal of Communication Management*, 9 (4), pp. 305–325.

14 Laurie Garrett, *Betrayal of Trust: The Collapse of Global Public Health* (New York: Hyperion, 2000).

15 *Webster's 7th New Collegiate Dictionary*, p. 952.

16 Morgan and Hunt (1994, K-2).

17 Sung and Grunig, op. cit.

18 October 24, 2014, p. B5. The ad continues: "It comes from 125 years of experience and an unwavering commitment to fair and unbiased reporting."

19 J.E. Grung and C.J. Hung, "The Effect of Relationships on Reputation and Reputation on Relationships: A Cognitive, Behavioral Study," Paper presented to the Public Relations Society of America Educator's Academy, Miami, Florida, 2002, p. 17.

20 Robyn Remke, "Corporate Reputation and the Discipline of Organization Communication," in Craig E. Carroll, ed., *The Handbook of Communication and Corporate Reputation* (Malden, MA: Wiley-Blackwell, 2013), p. 32.

21 Craig E. Carroll, "Corporate Reputation and the Multi-Disciplinary Field of Communication," in Craig E. Carroll, ed., *The Handbook of Communication and Corporate Reputation*, ibid., p. 4. The book is the most comprehensive review of corporate reputation.

22 Davia Temin, "Reputation Trumps All – Define Your Brand and Life It in the New Year, and Beyond," *Forbes* January 2, 2013.

23 Ibid.

24 Charles J. Fombrun, *Reputation: Realizing Value from Corporate Image* (Boston, MA: Harvard Business School Press, 1996), p. 72.

25 http://exec.tuck.dartmouth.edu/programs/open-programs/brand-and-reputation#sthash.PXBbDF6V.dpuf.

26 Erving Goffman, *The Presentation of Self in Everyday Life* (New York: Penguin Books, 1990).

27 Leon Festinger, *A Theory of Cognitive Dissonance* (Evanston, IL: Row & Pearson, 1957).

28 Definition of a crisis in Otto Lerbinger, *Managing Corporate Crises: Strategies for Executives* (Boston, MA: Barrington Press, 1986), p. 1.

29 Bob Sherwood, "Reputational Risk: Protect Your Organization's Most Important Asset," *Financial Times*, June 24, 2005.

30 Glen Peters, "Survey – World's Most Respected Companies: Why Nice Guys Finish First: Reputation Management," *Financial Times*, December 7, 1999.

31 An important finding by social psychologists is that when a person views a company as friendly, the ratings on other attributes tend to be higher.

32 Charles J. Fombrun, "Reputation: Measurable, Valuable, and Manageable." *The American Banker*, May 25, 2001.

33 2015 Harris Poll RQ Summary Report February 2015. www.harrisinteractive.com

2

Stakeholder Relations: Investors and Employees

Stakeholders comprise a basic category of a company's players. The chief ones are investors, employees, the community, and consumers. They are defined as any group of people upon which a company depends for its existence and success; they are affected by a corporation's actions and, conversely, can affect a corporation's welfare. The categories apply both domestically and to a company's foreign affiliates, but the relationships in the international arena vary in accordance with a country's socio-political and cultural characteristics. For example, state-owned enterprises (SOEs) in China wouldn't normally have investor stakeholders.

It is common to subdivide stakeholders into primary and secondary ones. The primary stakeholders fit the pattern of the relationship between business and society shown in economic books: society provides the factors of production of capital, labor, and land to business, for which it pays dividends, interest, wages, and rents in return. Business obtains the wherewithal for these payments when customers buy its products and services and produce revenue. The primary stakeholders are thus investors, labor, the community (representing land), and customers. Investors have ultimate control through their selection of the board of directors. Employees provide labor and are treated as members of a company and shown on the organizational chart, indicating that management has authority over them. The community is external to a company and neither controls the other, but the community, representing land and accompanying infrastructure, provides the physical, social, and political setting of a company. Customers provide the revenue to pay for the factors of production, including profits.

Secondary stakeholders are mainly government and civil society, which grant a company's "license to operate" by setting conditions for the operation of business.[1] Local government can exert power over a company through zoning laws and various ordinances. These secondary stakeholders are often depicted as constituting a company's socio-political environment, which is the responsibility of public affairs.

The formal identification of an organization's stakeholders can become complicated. Dejan Verčič, co-author of *The Global Public Relations Handbook*, states that "to identify stakeholders and ascertain their salience require a consideration of their influence, legitimacy of relationship with corporation, and urgency of their claim in a company."[2] He recognizes that there's some disagreement over who is a stakeholder. For example, does it include terrorists? Not everyone who is able to affect an organization is a stakeholder. Identifying company's stakeholders and becoming familiar with their particular features is a major challenge to global corporate communication.

2.1 Investor Relations

Investor relations is the most international of all stakeholder relations because investors from virtually anywhere can buy shares in a public corporation, and corporations don't restrict

Corporate Communication: An International and Management Perspective, First Edition. Otto Lerbinger.

themselves to domestic financial markets. Apple, for example, announced in September 2015 that it was joining a long list of US companies that raised funds by issuing debt in euros. It was attracted by low borrowing rates as a result of the European Central Bank's easy-money policies. In total, US non-financial companies were enabled to raise US$60.4 billion.[3]

Relationships are defined as narrow or broad. A company's relationship with investors – other than major ones – is extremely narrow. Except for annual meetings, there is seldom any personal contact between management and its stockholders and bondholders, for the social contract is expressed by specific transactions mediated by impersonal marketplaces such as stock exchanges. Furthermore, transactions are theoretically governed by rational behavior associated with the model of *economic man* and based on factual information; psychological aspects, important in public relations, are mostly ignored.

Deviations from this ideal rational model have occurred, however. An oft-mentioned example is the tulip craze in Holland in 1637 when the price of a single tulip was 10 times greater than the wages of a skilled worker. A house could be bought with one tulip.[4] As Robert Shiller's *Irrational Exuberance* states, levitating stock prices result from a blend of economics and psychology.[5] This combination is further demonstrated by the popularity of behavioral economics.[6]

2.1.1 SEC's Full and Timely Disclosure Rules

Upholding the "rational man theory," investor relations in the US is strictly guided by the Securities and Exchange Commission's (SEC) principle of full and timely disclosure. It states that everyone who is an actual or potential investor has an equal "right to know."[7] As explained by Morton J. Simon in his *Public Relations Law*, a company must provide "material business and financial facts" to investors.[8] Unlike other relationships, the meaning of material facts is explicit: it is any fact that could affect the value of a stock or bond. Examples are the departure of a CEO, the invention or development of a product (as illustrated when a pharmaceutical company discovers a "blockbuster" drug), and the acquisition or disposition of significant assets.[9]

The timing of the disclosure of material facts is critical in the financial world because in this digital age, investors can take advantage of even a split second in making a transaction. So-called insider trading by persons in or connected with a company to buy or sell securities on the basis of private information is illegal because it denies other investors an equal opportunity. The SEC continually reviews insider trading cases.

2.1.2 Feedback and Power

The feedback aspect of investor relations is evident in stockholder purchases and sales and from examining the daily record of financial transactions of stock exchanges. Moreover, stockholders in public corporations listed in stock exchanges have the opportunity to express their criticism of company performance at annual stockholder meetings and by filing proxy resolutions for changes in management policies and actions (see Chapter 17).

Institutional investors, such as the pension funds California Public Employees' Retirement System (CalPERS) and TIAA, should be distinguished from individual investors because of their considerably greater voting power. Among other institutional investors are giant fund managers such as the Vanguard Group and BlackRock Inc. They have become more assertive and often urge corporate boards to be "substantially independent of management"; they push their views harder in the boardroom.[10] A further power aspect is that investors with large security holdings can, as individuals or in combination with others, acquire commanding blocks of stock or engage in a proxy fight to gain control over a company. Sometimes proxy fights resemble political campaigns, with each side contacting stockholders (the voters) to win their support.

2.1.2.1 Mega-Deals by Big Investors

Investor relations, even by institutional investors, is dwarfed by worldwide mega-deals. By mid-September 2015 there were $3.2 trillion of deals globally during the year.[11] These deals reflect their international scope and the role of a few key investors. One of the largest is the attempt by Anheuser-Busch InBev NV to forge a global brewing juggernaut by acquiring SABMiller PLC, its chief rival.[12] Anheuser-Busch InBev is based in Belgium and is an amalgamation of at least five different companies across three continents. The company was formed in 2004 by merging AmBev and Belgium's Interbrew. In 2008 it bought Budweiser maker Anheuser-Busch Cos. for about $50 billion. Although publicly traded, it is jointly controlled by Brazilian tycoons and a group of wealthy Belgian families. Anheuser-Busch InBev is effectively controlled by a group of investors that include 3G Capital Partners LP. 3G is a small global network of the super-wealthy.[13] The two brewers together produce nearly a third of the world's beer and span hundreds of brands, including Budweiser, Corona, and Peroni.

Because of their monopolistic nature, the two brewing giants will have to seek antitrust clearance from jurisdictions around the world. Margrethe Vestger, the EU's antitrust chief, has repeatedly warned that mergers shouldn't happen at the expense or consumers. Some divestitures could be required because SABMiller has a 95.1% market share in Peru, and Anheuser-Busch InBev already has a roughly 45% market share.[14]

2.1.3 Investor Relations Activities

The typical communication activities and other tasks of investor relations include the following:

- presentations for analysts, portfolio managers, and brokers;
- field trips for analysts and portfolio managers;
- relationships with portfolio managers analysts, brokers, and individual investors;
- shareholder identification/analysis;
- presentations to the board of directors;
- preparation of standard reports – annual reports, quarterly reports, and reports on annual meetings.[15]

To communicate effectively, the investor relations officer (IRO) must be familiar with the infrastructure of the financial industry, which consists of stock exchanges, security analysts, investment bankers, and regulatory agencies such as the SEC.[16] Because of this knowledge requirement, the backgrounds of IROs have changed away from communication and toward those with a knowledge of finance.[17] They report to a chief financial officer (CFO) or treasurer.

To attract investors, companies conduct "road shows," and hold meetings. But in the US outright promotion of specific securities is prohibited by the SEC. For example, advertisements for new securities adhere to the "tombstone" format, which lists only the name of the firm and a simple statement of its business. The main goal of investor relations is to attract capital, protect the investment of stockholders and bondholders, and increase the price and value of a company's securities. To do so, the IRO must help executives build and maintain the highest standards of corporate reputation, based on solid corporate governance and ethical practices. IROs also may seek investor support on major issues such as acquisitions and mergers and various stockholder resolutions, such as climate change and variety of environmental and energy matters that may arise at annual meetings. The modern IRO therefore proactively helps build relationships with stockholders.[18]

Internationally more financial institutions are being established. For example, in November 2013, Beijing approved the first US exchange-traded funds that track stocks in mainland China, helping to open the country's capital markets to international investors. Previously, investors had to buy Chinese companies listed overseas through Hong Kong or to apply for a quota.[19] Further opening of financial markets in China occurred in November 2014 when Beijing approved a stock-trading link with Hong Kong. China allowed investment in a wide range of companies that had been largely cut off from international money. Beijing also allowed its currency, the yuan, to be traded outside the country and urged its use for trade.[20]

More international investor relations consultancies are appearing. One of them is HC International Inc., which calls itself a strategic investor relations advisor. It was recently retained by Ossen Innovation Co., Ltd, a China-based manufacturer. It will handle all facets of corporate and financial communications. Ossen is confident that HC International "will provide strong support in conveying our business model, growth strategy, competitive advantages, and value proposition to the investment community at large."[21] Another example of the internationalization of investor relations is the Annual International Investor Relations Conference, which in 2010 was held in Bahrain.[22]

2.2 Employee Relations

The basic social contract with employees is that they provide labor in exchange for wages or salaries and other benefits. Besides constituting the labor force, employees play other significant roles that should be recognized in defining the social contract with them. They may be members of a labor union that represents them in negotiating wages, hours, and conditions of employment. In their outside life, they are members of a family and a community and are citizens with the right to vote. Some companies see value in using their employees as community ambassadors to fortify their license to operate and as grassroots supporters for their political agendas.

2.2.1 Maslow's Hierarchy of Needs

Abraham Maslow's well-known hierarchy of needs serves as a useful guideline for defining the social contract. In ascending order he lists the following needs: physiological, safety, love/belonging, esteem, and self-actualization.[23] Every employer must satisfy the first two, which are usually mandated by law. The series of suicide attempts by overworked Foxconn employees in 2010 and the installation of suicide prevention nets in dormitory buildings illustrates how employee mistreatment in factories violated the first two levels.[24] With the third need, companies have learned that when they create a "feeling of belonging" employees become more productive.

Good communications, partly provided by employee relations media, help build the job satisfaction associated with being a member of an organization. A formula often mentioned is that good communications produces high job satisfaction, which in turn results in high productivity. How an employee is treated affects his or her self-esteem, which is a major outcome of employment. Self-actualization is more elusive but is helped when an employee senses that his or her full knowledge and skills are utilized on the job.

Jobs that are sent abroad to take advantage of low wages are not likely to ascend far on the hierarchy of needs. A subsistence wage may not even provide the basic physiological needs, and substandard working conditions often lack basic safety features, as fires in buildings and the collapse of others (e.g. see the Bangladesh apparel factory disaster in Chapter 16) have proven.

2.2.1.1 Concerns About Rising Income Disparities

Many explanations account for differences in employee incomes, such as the premium put on education with the rise in technology. A major question relevant to social responsibility is whether employee stakeholders are treated fairly in comparison with investors, who are inordinately favored when the goal of a corporation is to maximize profits and shareholder value. With the decline in union membership – now less than 7% of the civilian workforce in the US – the majority of workers don't have the bargaining power to gain higher wages and benefits. The globalization threat to move work abroad has kept wages low. Furthermore, since the late 1970s, their percentage increase in wages has lagged behind the increase in productivity (see Chapter 9 for further discussion).

Solutions vary and reflect economic and political ideologies. Some say that the minimum wage should be raised and that the very wealthy should pay higher income tax rates and inheritance taxes. Responding to these concerns, in early 2015, the US's largest employer, Wal-Mart announced that it would raise its minimum wage to $10 an hour by 2016. And Target announced an increase to $9 an hour in 2015.[25]

Major responsibility for employee relations is assigned to a human resources department (also known as a personnel department). This department recruits people, determines the terms of employment, administers needed skills training, and helps socialize them to become productive members of the organization. Corporate communication makes several contributions to the human resources function: (i) it has chief responsibility for employee communications beyond the immediate supervisor–employee relationship; (ii) when domestic labor is inadequate, it helps recruit overseas and migrant worker; and (iii) it assists in labor union relations and collective bargaining.

2.2.2 Employee Communications

The corporate communication function in employee communications is to help build solidarity and unity of purpose, to instill the organizational culture, and help create high morale and job satisfaction. By helping to maintain a good reputation, corporate communication also benefits employees because they gain satisfaction from knowing they work for a reputable employer.

A special feature of employee communications is that most workers are physically present on a company's premises. Daily contact between supervisors and their employees is therefore the main form of communications. Surveys show that employees generally prefer to hear company news through face-to-face encounters with their supervisors and managers rather than through formal announcements on the intranet, emails, or newsletters.

Communications in an organization can vary widely depending on a company's predominant management style. In highly bureaucratic organizations, communications are generally brief, formal, and mostly downward. Furthermore, a manager of one department is restricted from communicating with a manager of another department without first going up the chain of command to a manager in charge of both. This arrangement allows the higher-level manager to know what's going on in the departments below him or her. Departmental meetings are another common form of communication, but in an authoritarian structure members may feel inhibited from speaking freely. Some smaller firms have occasional company-wide meetings.

In the UK, a new right – the "right to ask" – has been authorized under the Information and Consultation Directive, which came into force in April 2005 among 14 000 UK companies and other organizations with more than 150 employees. Although bombarded by internal communications, employees haven't felt in touch with their companies. This requirement is expected to make employers more open and lead to more conversation.[26]

2.2.2.1 Wide Variety of Media

Companies use a wide variety of media to communicate with their employees: face-to-face communications between a supervisor and employees; formal departmental or company-wide media such as newsletters, newspapers, and videos; mass emails, electronic newsletters, and a company's external website. Loudspeakers may be used for special announcements such as fire and security warnings, and bulletin boards for legal notifications and notice of events. The three things that people most want to hear from their companies are plans for the future, the specific contribution the employee is expected to make in achieving these plans, and the extent to which they, as individuals, will benefit as a result.

Many companies use the intranet, which is a computer network that uses internet protocol technology to share information, operational systems, or computing services within an organization. The value of the intranet increases as the intangible asset of intellectual capital becomes more important. Intellectual capital refers to what people know and how they use what they know. Corporate communication professionals should help members of an organization connect with its intellectual capital. Although we think of computers as storing data and information, knowledge and wisdom reside in people. The intranet can help connect people worldwide to build and apply a company's intellectual capital.[27]

It is necessary for employers to alert their staff that internet use, email, and phone calls could be monitored as part of company acceptable use policies The warning comes on the back of a landmark ruling by the European Court of Human Rights, which ruled that the private use of company telecoms equipment and internet access could be protected under European human rights legislation if the company fails to inform the employee that their communications may be monitored. Whether an employer should monitor employee internet use, email, and phone calls is controversial. Companies generally don't, but if they do, they should inform their employees.[28]

2.2.3 Recruitment and Training of Workers

When a company experiences labor shortages of critical personnel, it must recruit from other parts of a country and, increasingly, from other countries. Shortages of technologically advanced workers in developed countries have been particularly urgent and led to "technonationalism" – a "war for talent" – when higher levels of education are required.[29]

2.2.3.1 Value of Positive Corporate Reputation

Positive images help industries and companies attract highly qualified, in-demand employees. For example the oil and gas industry as a whole, as well as individual companies and recruitment professionals, must distinguish themselves from competitors, educate prospective workers, correct misconceptions, and leverage technology to gain that critical recruitment edge.[30]

The importance of a country's reputation is illustrated by China's difficulties in labor practices when it moved some of its manufacturing to Africa because of rising labor costs at home. A survey from the Ethics Institute of South Africa showed that 46% of respondents in Africa had a negative impression of Chinese employment practices; another 55% agreed with the statement that Chinese companies in Africa use only Chinese employees. China is sometimes perceived as the continent's "new colonialist." This image of the Chinese nation state harms company–employee relations.[31]

2.2.3.2 Migrant Workers

Corporate communication can help create contacts and a conducive climate for the hiring of migrant workers. Many developed nations are experiencing labor shortages because of their slumping birth rates, longer lives, and early retirement. In Europe, Germany and Switzerland have long experienced shortages and recruited *Gastarbeiters* (guest workers) from Greece, Turkey, and other countries. In theory, they are invited when needed and sent home when no longer needed. However, the typical situation is that they are needed for long periods and become "residents."[32] Since the adoption of the Schengen Convention in Europe, national borders are open to job seekers from other European Union (EU) countries. Employers carry the burden of orienting migrant workers to their jobs, and communities have the problem of assimilating them.

The problem of swarms of people seeking entry into Europe in the summer and fall of 2015 has focused attention on the migrant problem. The question was whether Europe could accommodate hundreds of thousands of persons and families that cross their borders. They were seen mostly as a burden, not as a potential source of labor. In describing Poland's labor shortage, for example, *The Economist* noted that a hospital in Bydgoszcz in north-west Poland could fill only half of its 236 beds because of a shortage of nurses, and in the public sector Poland has five nurses per 1000 inhabitants compared with 13 in Germany. Labor shortages are common in Eastern Europe in construction, manufacturing, and technology. Two out of five firms in Poland struggle to fill vacancies, according to a survey by Manpower Group, a consultancy. Large shortages of manual workers in agriculture and construction exist, as well as a demand for carpenters, shop assistants, gardeners, and bakers.[33]

In Hungary, almost half of employers could not get the staff they needed, which was the case with 28% of employers in Slovakia and 18% in the Czech Republic. Yet when refugees surged across the EU in the summer and fall of 2015, Poland and the Czech Republic joined Hungary in refusing to accommodate them, despite the fact that some were young and educated. Cultural resistance likely counts more than economics, for Poland is 98% white and 94% Catholic, leaving many social spheres deeply insular and conservative.[34]

In contrast, Germany has already had experience hiring migrants. One company, SAP (systems application and products firm in data processing), stated that past hires "have exceeded our expectations" and that it was looking for migrants who speak English and have at least basic knowledge of information technology. As a whole, Germany had almost 1.1 million job vacancies in the second quarter of 2015.[35]

Muslim migrants in Europe have faced a backlash, especially since the killing of eight workers at the *Charlie Hebdo* satirical magazine in Paris in January 2015 and the terrorist attack in Paris on November 13, 2015, that killed 130 people and injured 368. Most country leaders, however, are asking their citizens to distinguish between terrorists and other Muslims, but protests in Leipzig, Germany, and right-wing politicians in France, such as Marine LePen, are feeding the flames. They point to "welfare tourists" whose motivation is welfare benefits rather than finding a job. Affected countries are therefore imposing more conditions and sometimes attempting to restrict the inflow of workers. Supporting these measures, the EU's top court, the Luxembourg-based European Court of Justice, stated in November 2014 that such migrants can be denied benefits.[36]

An issue from the viewpoint of migrant workers worldwide is that they are often denied basic human rights. A notorious example is the abuse of Nepalese migrants working on stadiums for the 2022 football World Cup in Qatar. They were attracted there because they could earn far more than they could at home, and their remittances make up a quarter of Nepalese GDP. But their rights were violated when their passports were confiscated, their earnings withheld, and their deaths covered up. A United Nations (UN) convention on migrant workers' rights came into force in 2003, but it has been ratified by few receivers of such workers and is largely unenforced.[37] Recognizing these abuses, some countries from which labor is recruited have taken measures to protect the rights of their workers who seek overseas employment. For example, the Philippine government requires that they must be offered a high wage, and the government sends envoys and inspectors to the main receiving countries.

2.2.4 Helping Workers Adjust to Foreign Employers

When cross-border mergers and acquisitions (M&As) occur, employers are often faced with the problem of helping employees in the acquired company to adapt to new practices. For example, a study in China showed that the "assurance of job security and the provision of training promote positive reactions among employees and improve their post-change task performance. Chinese workers had to adapt to Western management styles, characterized by liberalism, individualism, and capitalism."[38] These values were at odds with Chinese culture as characterized by Confucianism, collectivism, and socialism. It is often said that it is connections that count in China in contrast to performance in the US.

When a company acquires operations in other countries, management is advised to train employees by providing specific information and support during change. Employees have been found actively to participate in change when they are personally convinced by its rationale. This did not happen in Germany when Wal-Mart opened stores. Employees had difficulty agreeing with the company rule that requires them always to smile at customers when they come within a 3 m distance. "They thought that if customers could easily find what they wanted with low prices they would still visit our supermarket next time. Thus, what matters is not the smile but how to identify what customers want with low prices."[39]

With vocational training, Germany's apprenticeship programs have been especially effective and serve as models. One scheme consists of *Meister* schools that teach bright youngsters to become masters of a technical trade. They are often a feature in Germany's *Mittelstand* companies – middle-sized companies – with deep local roots. The strong apprenticeship system reduces unemployment, which in Germany is only 7.8% of those aged 25 or under compared with 22.1% in Sweden and 54% in Spain. These companies inspire extraordinary loyalty in their workers, keeping average annual turnover to 2.7% compared with the 30% turnover at some big American companies. Earnings of Germans with apprenticeships in 2014 were about two-thirds of the earning of those with at least a bachelor's degree.[40]

Some German multi-national companies in the US, notably BMW, Siemens, and Volkswagen, are applying the German vocational-training model to the US.[41]Siemens launched an apprenticeship program at its Charlotte, North Carolina, factory in 2011, when it partnered with a local community college to offer vocational courses in combination with on-the-job training on the shop floor. Recruiting applicants from local high schools, it spends around $180 000 per student to pay for tuition, books, and wages during the 4-year program.[42]

BMW's Spartanburg plant in South Carolina is its biggest production facility in the world, producing 1400 cars a day and sending 70% of them overseas. It too uses the apprenticeship system, training 100 apprentices at any one time. It plans to integrate digital skills in the system to empower workers for lifelong learning.[43] As General Electric's Marco Annunziata, chief economist, and executive director of global market insight, states, the winning strategy is really the connection of the education system with industry and its new technology.[44]

Employer responsibility to train workers is itself an issue. For decades US corporations have been divesting in skills development, yet they complain when they can't find skilled hires. Labor economist Paul Osterman at the Massachusetts Institute of Technology stated: "Firms have gotten lazy [about training]. They're looking for someone else, such as community colleges, for-profit schools, and online courses, to do that for them."[45]

2.2.5 Labor Unions and Collective Bargaining

Although trade union membership has been falling in Europe, it is still higher than in the US. Membership is highest, about 70% in the Nordic countries of Denmark, Sweden, and Finland;

around 30% in Germany; and 8% in France. Collective bargaining, mostly along industry lines, results in "tariff agreements" – another name for labor agreements. The inclusion of a grievance system, which is a type of feedback for employees, is standard. But collective bargaining tactics vary. France is known for calling general strikes and occasionally using such harsh measures as holding an executive hostage.

The scope of collective bargaining in labor negotiations varies among countries. The general procedure is for labor representatives to meet with company representatives to hammer out an agreement. As recommended in Roger Fisher and William Ury's *Getting to Yes*, the aim is to focus on problem solving with the goal of arriving at a mutually satisfactory agreement.[46] Public relations sometimes plays a role in protracted collective bargaining situations by using publicity and issue ads to influence public opinion. In keeping with the focus on creating sound relationships, both parties should look beyond the immediate contract terms to implications for day-to-day workplace relationships.

This model does not exist in China. Despite a 1992 trade union law and a 1994 labor law that provide unions with legal means to defend workers interests, collective bargaining is absent, and labor relations have worsened. In the highly industrialized Pearl River Delta region around Guangdong north of Hong Kong, strikes have become common. In 2014 they rose by nearly quarter to 301 in Guangdong and doubled across China compared to the previous year. Government intervention occurs.

At a recent strike in Guangdong garment factory, police entered and forced more than 100 workers to return to their jobs. "Police suppression of labor protests has become more frequent and the tactics more aggressive," said a retired trade union official in Guangdong. It is a setback for industrial relations by a government fearful of any kind of dissent. Furthermore, Chinese leaders are trying to limit foreign funding of public interest and other activist groups. For example it closed the International Center for Joint Labor Research, which was jointly established by the University of California, Berkeley, and Sun Yat-sen University to help drive scholarship and debate on industrial relations in China.[47]

An increasing number of businesses are replacing traditional grievance and arbitration systems in the workplace with alternative dispute resolution (ADR). It has drawn mixed reactions from organized labor, which has often been reluctant to give up the traditional grievance and arbitration process because ADR tends to be legalistic and expensive. To promote ADR, Cornell University has established a new Institute for the Study of Conflict Prevention and Resolution. It will also form an alliance with the accounting firm Price Waterhouse & Co., which has global fact-finding capabilities.[48]

Beyond collective bargaining, labor in Europe has obtained some substantial rights. In large companies in Germany, for example, labor leaders represent about a half of membership on supervisory boards – equivalent to boards of directors – in a system called codetermination (see Chapter 17). This is usually accompanied by works councils, which serve as "shop-floor" organizations that represent workers. These councils serve as grievance systems and complement national labor negotiations.[49]

2.2.5.1 Amazon's Experience in Germany

After Amazon entered Germany in 1998, it had to learn how to deal with the German services union, Verdi, which has 2.1 million members. The union organized an all-day strike against Amazon in Leipzig and Bad Hersfeld on the issue of how workers are categorized. Are they retail workers, as the union contends, who are paid between £11.47 and £11.94 an hour, or logistics workers, as Amazon contends, and paid £1 less. The company claims that its employees are rewarded by flexible rewards such as shares or bonuses, which couldn't be reflected in a tariff agreement. These flexible bonuses are based on performance factors. Amazon rejected the union's offer to enter labor negotiations.[50] Several employees said Amazon's lack of communication about a Polish expansion had shaken their confidence in the company and that Verdi representation could help compel Amazon to be more open.[51]

The conflict between Amazon and Verdi is symbolic of trans-Atlantic tensions between US business practices and Europe's more labor-friendly traditions. Unions are digging in to avoid losing more influence as globalized commerce expands in Europe. America's focus on financial results, say some Europeans, is eroding a social model that stresses fairness and quality of life. The US way of doing business in Germany is sometimes called by one of the most disparaging labels, "Wild West," which signifies a lack of concern for workers. It also indicates an unwillingness to consult others. Daniel Knapp, an analyst at research group IHS in London says Amazon is out of their sphere of influence completely, and when General Motors put its German unit Opel on sale (which it later canceled), union leaders and politicians complained they weren't consulted.

2.2.6 Standardization vs. Customization of Employee Relations

International employee relations faces the strategic question of which approach to adopt: whether to transfer the parent firm's human resources management practices, stick to its different affiliates (the exportive approach), or whether to let each develop its own system (the adaptive approach). One study found that worldwide consistency is favored for higher and senior level managers. But when cultural differences, labor laws, and other local differences are prominent, the adaptive approach is better.[52]

Cultural differences are important. China and other Asian countries value relationships, exemplified by the practice of *guanxi* in hiring and promoting workers, which is the opposite of the Western value of achievement. *Guanxi* is similar to particularism (see Chapter 12) whereby standards and criteria apply by virtue of a particular social relationship. The opposite of particularism is universalism, which applies the same criteria to everyone.

Another difference among companies is whether they prefer centralization or decentralization of industrial relations. Centralization is favored by some large companies whereby labor policy and negotiations are overseen by a headquarters vice president. For example, Martin (Marty) J. Mulloy, vice president of Labor Affairs at Ford Motor Company, oversees labor policy and negotiations covering the Ford's approximately 117 000 hourly employees around the world.[53]

Differences in European and US policies on vacation times and parental leave are significant but are expected to even out. In Europe, workers are guaranteed at least 20 days and as many as 35 days of paid leave; the US is the only developed country without a national paid parental leave policy.[54] One sign of moving closer to European standards is the announcement by Netflix and Microsoft that they will be adding 17 weeks of paid time off for new mothers. And Adobe Systems said it would expand paid time off for new birth mothers to 26 weeks.

2.3 Conclusions

Stakeholder relations is central to the practice of corporate communication. The relationship concept that underlies stakeholder relations fully applies to the wider application of public relations and other communication practices to new players. When a company goes abroad it must develop new relationships and do so in the context of different economic, political, social, and cultural systems (described in Part III). The building of relationships should be viewed as adding the intangible asset of social capital to a company's financial balance sheet.

The ways of interacting with stakeholders go beyond the fundamental process of communication in several ways. First is how a stakeholders group is connected with a company both as an integral part of the internal structure of a company and, in the case of labor representation in codetermination, as playing a role in corporate governance.

Second, the methods of interaction may include formal procedures such as collective bargaining with labor unions, and various methods of collaboration with non-governmental organizations (NGOs) and local communities. Finally, the review of categories of stakeholders shows the need to relate them to relevant issues. Employee relations, for example, must consider the issues of gender and human rights, and community relations must incorporate environmental issues.

The common theme of stakeholder relations is that the collective social contracts with each stakeholder group comprise a company's license to operate. The outcomes are measured by such broad indices as mutual satisfaction, loyalty and commitment, harmony, and trust.

Discussion Questions

2.1. Relationships between a company and its stakeholders can be narrow or wide. Describe those of investors, employees, and the community.

2.2. What are the international aspects of employee relations?

2.3. What, if anything, is different about community relations in another country?

2.4. Is the trust measurement of a relationship more or less important in a foreign country? Why or why not?

2.5. Explain the SEC principle of full and timely disclosure.

2.6. What are the special problems of migrant workers faced by companies?

2.7. What are the benefits of customization of employee relations policies and practices?

Endnotes

1 Witold Henisz, *Corporate Diplomacy: Building Reputations and Relationships with External Stakeholders* (Sheffield, UK: Greenleaf Publishing, 2014), pp. 22–24.

2 Krishnamurthy Sriramesh and Dejan Vercic, eds., *The Global Public Relations Handbook, Revised and Expanded Edition: Theory, Research, and Practice* (New York: Routledge, 2009), p. 852.

3 Christopher Whittall, "Apple Is Back in Euro-Bond Market," *WSJ*, September 11, 2015, p. C3.

4 The tulip craze is described in Paul Marsden, "Introduction and Summary," in Justin Kirby and Paul Marsden, eds. *Connected Marketing: the Viral, Buzz and Word of Mouth Revolution* (New York and London: Routledge, 2006), pp. xv–xvi.

5 Robert J. Schiller, *Irrational Behavior*, 3rd edition (Princeton, NJ: Princeton University Press, 2015).

6 A well-known researcher is Daniel Kahneman, a cognitive psychologist who won the Nobel Prize in economics in 2002. One of his books is *Thinking, Fast and Slow* (New York: Farrar, Strauss &

Giroux, 2011). Another well-known book is Richard H. Thaler and Cass R. Sunstein, *Nudge: Improving Decisions About Health, Wealth, and Happiness* (New Haven, CT: Yale University Press, 2008).

7 This requirement of full and timely disclosure was mandated by the US Security and Exchange Laws of 1933 and 1934 that regulate the purchase and sale of securities.

8 Morton J. Simon, *Public Relations Law* (New York: Appleton-Century-Crofts, 1969), p. 751.

9 Ibid., p. 752.

10 Kirsten Grind and Joann S. Lublin, "Vanguard and BlackRock Raise Voices," *WSJ* March 4, 2015, p. C1.

11 Tripp Mickie, Saaira Chaudhuri, and Matthew Dalton, "AB InBev Brews Plan For a Beer Behemoth," *WSJ*, September 17, 2015, pp. A1, A12.

12 Mike Esterl, "A Global Antitrust Grilling," *WSJ*, September 17, 2015, p. A12.

13 Anupreeta Das, "Brazil Tycoons Pursue Capstone for Beer Empire," *WSJ*, September 17, 2015, p. 12.

14 Esterl, op. cit.

15 Executive Alert, December 6, 1996, National Investor Relations Institute.

16 For further explanation, see Otto Lerbinger, *Corporate Public Affairs: Interacting with Interest Groups, Media, and Government* (Mahwah, NJ: Lawrence Erlbaum Associations, 2006), pp. 388–393.

17 See membership surveys of the National Investor Relations Institute.

18 Horaio Falcao, "An Open Channel of Communication Today's IRO Must Be a Good Communicator and Skilled in the Art of Negotiation," *Financial Times*, June 9, 2006, p. 1.

19 Amy Li, "Beijing Courting US Investors," *WSJ*, November 8, 2013, p. C4.

20 Daniel Inman, Chao Deng, and Wei Gu, "China Courts Foreign Investors," *WSJ*, November 11, 2014, p. A1.

21 "Ossen Innovation Retains HC International as Investor Relations Advisor," *Daily the Pak Bhanker*, February 18, 2011.

22 "Bahrain Set to Host Investor Relations Forum," *Gulf Daily News*, April 24, 2010.

23 Abraham Maslow, *Motivation and Personality* (New York: Harper and Row, 1954).

24 Aditya Chakrabortty, "The Women Who Nearly Died Making Your iPad," *The Guardian*, August 5, 2013.

25 Paul Ziobro, "Target Says It Will Raise Wages, Too," *WSJ*, March 19, 2015, p. B3.

26 Richard Donkin, *Financial Times* (London), September 29, 2005, p. 15.

27 Tom Brown, "Ringing Up Intellectual Capital," *Management Review*, Vol. 87, January 1998, pp. 47–51.

28 "Employees Must Know if Emails are Monitored," *Birmingham Post*, May 15, 2007, p. 23.

29 Peter Ford, "What's Behind Asia Moon Race?" *Christian Science Monitor*, October 25, 2007, p. 6.

30 Jill Tennant, "Reputation Matters in the Competition for Highly Qualified Workers," *World Oil*, July 2013.

31 Peer Wonacott, "China Inc. Moves the Factory Floor to Africa," *WSJ*, May 15, 2014, p. B1.

32 Vanessa Mock and Neil MacLucas, "Swiss Migration Vote Threatens Europe Ties," *WSJ*, February 11, 2014.

33 "Migrants and Labour Markets: More Vacancies than Visitors," *The Economist*, September 19, 2014, p. 47.

34 "Eastern European Attitudes: Orban the Archetype," *The Economist*, September 19, 2015, p. 48.

35 Friedrich Geiger, "Germany's Next Test: Jobs for Migrants," *WSJ*, September 16, 2015, p. A8.

36 Harriet Torry, "EU Court Blocks 'Benefit Tourism'," *WSJ*, November 12, 2014, p. A9.

37 "The Abuse of Migrants: And Still They Come," *The Economist*, April 19, 2014, p. 54.

38 Goo Hyeok Chung, Jing Du, and Jin Nam Choi, "How Do Employees Adapt to Organizational Change Driven by Cross-Bo Chun Han Wong, Chinese Labor Rifts Deepen," *WSJ*, February 10, 2015, p. A7. Goo Hyeok Chung, Jing Du, and Jin Nam Choi, "How Do Employees Adapt to Organizational change Driven by Cross-Border M&As? A Case in China," *Journal of World Business*, Vol. 49, Issue 1, January 2014, pp. 78–79.

39 Ibid., p. 83.

40 Edward P. Lazear and Simon Janssen, "Germany Offers a Promising Jobs Model," *WSJ*, September 9, 2016, p. A11.

41 Elizabeth Schulze, "US Turns to Germany to Fill Jobs," *WSJ*, September 27, 2016, p. B1; and Edward P. Lazear and Simon Janssen, "Germany Offers a Promising Jobs Model," September 9, 2016, p. A11.

42 Elizabeth Schulze, "US Turns to Germany to Fill Jobs," *WSJ*, September 27, 2016, p. B1.

43 Peter Witting, "German Apprenticeships in South Carolina," *WSJ*, May 4, 2017, p. A13.

44 "Man, Machines and Fear," *WSJ*, May 10, 2017, p. B11.

45 Lauren Weber, "Just Whose Job is it to Train Workers?" *WSJ*, July 17, 2014, p. B1.

46 Roger Fisher and William Ury, *Getting to Yes: Negotiating Agreement Without Giving In* (Boston, MA: Houghton Mifflin Company, 1981).

47 Chun Han Wong, "Chinese Labor Rifts Deepen," *WSJ*, February 10, 2015, p. A7.

48 Frank Swoboda, "New Group to Focus on Dispute Resolution; Former Presidents of AFL-CIO, Business Roundtable to Head Foundation," *Washington Post*, April 9, 1996, p. C3.

49 "German Industrial Relations: Labour's Lost Love," *The Economist*, August 3, 2013 p. 55.

50 Philip Oltermann, "Amazon Workers in Germany Strike," theguardian.com, April 17, 2014.

51 Sarah Sloat, "In Germany, Amazon Keeps Unions at Bay," *WSJ*, September 24, 2014, pp. A1, A12.

52 Maddy Janssens, "Developing a Culturally Synergistic Approach to International Human Resource Management," *Journal of World Business*, Vol. 36, Winter 2001, pp. 429–450.

53 Howard R. Stanger, Ann C. Frost, and Paul F. Clark, eds., *Collective Bargaining Under Duress: Case Studies of Major US Industries* (Urbana-Champaign, IL: University of Illinois, 2013), p. 367.

54 Steven Rattner, "Inequality in America," *International New York Times*, November 19, 2014, p. 9.

3

Stakeholder Relations: The Community and Consumers

Community and consumer stakeholders complete the list of a company's primary stakeholders. The community represents the factor of production called land. A formal definition of community relations is a "continuing participation with and within a community to maintain and enhance its environment to the benefit of both the institution and the community."[1] As stated in Nathaniel H. Sperber's *Manager's Public Relations Handbook*, "Community relations is grassroots public relations. Here is where the concept of interdependence is put to the test, and is where the company meets people face-to-face."[2] Community relations is especially important for local businesses.

Consumers are an integral part of a company as Chester Barnard, former president of the New Jersey Bell Telephone Company, observed in his landmark book, *The Functions of the Executive*.[3] He emphasized what is now obvious: that a company cannot survive without consumers. They are an integral part of an organization's system of cooperation of human activity. Consumer stakeholders complete the economic relationship between a company and society by focusing on the revenue stream. This revenue is used to pay dividends and interest to investors, wages and salaries to employees, and rent to owners of land. Consumers are the primary concern of marketing, but also involve public relations.

When interaction between a company and its consumers extends beyond transactions to relationships, the significance of consumer relations becomes apparent. In the early 1980s, the strategy of "corporate banking relationships" was inaugurated by some banks to supplement prevailing "transaction banking." The idea was to increase earnings by "maximizing the profitability of the total customer relationship over time rather than by seeking to extract the most profit from any individual product or transaction."[4] That idea is the core purpose of what is now known as consumer relationship management (CRM) discussed in this chapter.

3.1 Community Relations

Community relations deals with "land" as one of the factors of production. It can be raw land itself, resources on it, the community's infrastructure of roads and transportation, the physical places where a company is located, and its social and political institutions. Just as an employee works in the context of an organization, a corporation resides in the communities where it is headquartered and where its facilities are located. A recent article in *The Economist* reinforces the important of land. It stated, "Land, the centre of the pre-industrial economy, has returned as a constraint on growth," drawing attention, however, to "scarcity in specific places, namely, the

Corporate Communication: An International and Management Perspective, First Edition. Otto Lerbinger.

cities responsible for a disproportionate amount of the world's output." It names top cities that have become "hotbeds of innovation activity."[5]

Distinctions are made between different kinds of communities: site, fence-line, impact, and employees.[6] Fence-line communities that are immediate geographical neighbors are particularly impacted by noise, traffic pollution, and other disagreeable effects. The costs and benefits of company actions in a community will vary among different types of communities and interest groups. For example, a Walmart store will provide employment for minimum-wage workers and low prices for consumers, but may increase traffic or become a visual blight in certain neighborhoods.

Depending on the nature of a company's business, community relations may overlap with other stakeholder relations. When local citizens comprise a large part of a company's labor force, good community relations enhances employee recruitment. A community's school system, health facilities, recreational areas, and cultural resources then assume greater importance. When General Electric (GE) had a large manufacturing facility in Lynn, Massachusetts, it combined community relations and employee relations. Banks, grocery, and drug stores view the community as the source of customers.

The basic social contract between a company and the local community is broad. A community provides not only land and physical infrastructure but also a local labor supply, housing, social services, and police, fire, and other security. A company expects to be treated fairly in terms of taxes and regulations. Sometimes it looks for tax breaks and subsidies in return for providing jobs, constructing buildings, and otherwise helping a community's economic development. On the other side of the relationship, a community expects a company to be a good citizen by minimizing or preventing environmental harm, contributing money and other resources to its civil society organizations and participating in them. Through interaction, both business and the community create a form of wealth known as social capital. It is defined as the "connections among individuals – social networks and the norms of reciprocity and trustworthiness that arise from them."[7]

3.1.1 Programs and Activities

Community relations is conventionally defined as "the management function charged with interacting with local communities." It includes "all the activities that promote the interests of the company and the communities where it is located."[8] When John Browne headed the British firm BP, he expressed a clear philosophy and strategy about community relations, saying that for BP to thrive so must the communities in which it does business. Browne has insisted that the economic and social health of the villages, towns, and cities in which BP does business be a matter of central concern to the company board of directors.[9]

Participating with local chambers of commerce is an important way to advance community relations objectives because they bring together the businesses in a community to represent their collective interests. As the Greater Boston Chamber of Commerce states, "We provide leadership in creating a healthy climate for economic development and job creation. We also aspire to be a Chamber of Community as well as a Chamber of Commerce."[10] The Chamber's policy agenda included several infrastructure improvements, such as the modernization of Boston's Logan Airport, development of skilled workforce, and improving the quality of life by increasing the supply of affordable housing, supporting the arts and sciences, and promoting diversity and inclusiveness. Jim Klocke, the Chamber's executive vice president named five "economic drivers" of Boston: financial services, healthcare and life sciences, high technology, high education and consulting, and the visitor industry. In Charleston, South Carolina, the Chamber of Commerce explored ways of attracting more industry – but only clean ones![11]

3.1.1.1 Helping Build Community Infrastructure

Developed economies have abundant infrastructure. In his book on community relations, Edmund Burke lists "schools, roads, parks, recreation facilities, fire protection, police, cultural institutions, human services to protect the frail and needy, hospitals, and the like."[12] In contrast, developing countries are characterized as having meager infrastructure and inadequate housing. Non-profit organizations may also be lacking. Companies operating in such countries are burdened with providing needed infrastructure themselves. For example, Cadbury, the British multi-national corporation (MNC), which operates in more than 50 countries, found that when it opened a plant in Nigeria, it could not depend on an adequate water supply and had to drill its own well.[13]

The lack of infrastructure inhibits a country's economic growth and endangers human welfare. In India, 400 million people still have no electricity; half of Indians defecate in the open, with such dire health consequences as diarrhea (a common cause of death in developing countries, which can be arrested with zinc tablets) and encephalitis (irritation and swelling of the brain, mostly due to infection). Social investment is required for roads, fire and police protection, and sanitation facilities.

Along with lagging social problems, India has deeply entrenched inequality. Its ruling class, which is defined by caste and gender as well as education and income, has "an utter lack of interest – verging on contempt – in improving matters for the rest."[14] To address these problems, India's Tata Group invests about 30% of after-tax profits in community development programs across India.[15]

Conditions are no better in Pakistan. Asad Farid, acting president of the Islamabad Chamber of Commerce and Industry (ICCI), believes that infrastructure development plays a crucial role in economic development of a country. Lack of infrastructure has been a big hurdle in the economic progress of Pakistan, thereby putting strains on the smooth growth of trade and industrial activities. The government should involve the private sector by moving toward the public–private partnership paradigm for developing the country's infrastructure at a fast pace.[16]

3.1.2 Importance in Oil and Mining Industries

Community relations is particularly relevant in the oil and mining industries and may literally require the building of new communities. Braden Copper in Chile had to build a narrow cog rail link to remote mountain locations in the Andes and provide housing, health facilities, and other infrastructure for its employees.[17] Resource companies must locate where resources exist, which sometimes impinges on existing communities and require the relocation of residents. Newmont Mining's Ahafo gold mine in Ghana so severely affected surrounding communities that it had to resettle the people who lived or worked on the land. It initially worked with a Canadian urban planning and design firm with expertise in providing social assessment to natural resource companies. Newmont consequently built two new villages, which experienced rapid population growth. Because 97% of the people affected by the mine depended on agriculture for a living, the company helped farmers not only to re-establish their farms but also to boost production, diversify crops, and enhance access to markets.[18]

Part of Newmont's community relations efforts was to establish the Newmont Ahafo Development Foundation (NADeF).[19] Funds were allocated among member communities, favoring those that were more severely impacted by the mine. One of the lessons learned by Newmont was that some control had to be ceded to local leaders, including those in the local public sector and civil society groups. But along with giving community leaders control, Newmont had to engage in the "capacity building of stakeholders," which should be the goal of any initiative. Despite the financial costs and time, NADeF concluded "there is no initiative with a greater return in terms of removing the divide between a firm and stakeholders than one that equips stakeholders with the ability to address their most pressing concerns."[20]

Another case is Chevron in Nigeria. After a throe of violence in 2003 that forced an 18-month shutdown of its operations, Chevron realized that it had to transform its communities program. Chevron's community relations people also realized that the company shouldn't try to figure out by itself what's good for the local communities. Accordingly, said a member of the New Nigeria Foundation, a non-governmental organization (NGO), Chevron operated a cash-handout system for the community leaders. It is extremely important that "they own the process and that they own the structures in place for their development."[21]

The new process was to partner with the community in its efforts to reach out to the government, NGOs, and others in civil society. To enhance interactional trust, Chevron increased the number of channels by which its message reached stakeholders. It considered the establishment of multi-stakeholder forums moderated by someone trusted by both sides. Community development projects would be determined by a set of committees that involved Chevron, the communities, NGOs, and the government. Negotiations lasted 5 months. The company recognized the importance of hiring local contractors, concluding that "Development progress really is in the progress made by people," not in projects.[22]

3.1.3 Developing a Community Relations Program

When companies first expanded abroad, the National Foreign Trade Council, a business organization advocating a rules-based world economy, stated: "in today's complex world, it is both a social and economic responsibility of companies operating abroad to seek public acceptance in host countries."[23] A company was advised to incorporate a community relations plan in each country where substantial investment was contemplated. The overall objective was to earn the understanding and acceptance of the host community, both for the company itself and for the American business system. A specific objective was to promote a wider understanding of the ways in which the company served the community interest.

A company should carefully study community issues so that it can decide what community problems it can help support through direct help or other forms of corporate philanthropy. If the availability of adequately trained employees is a problem, a company might help local educational institutions to improve their programs with financial aid, provide staff lecturers, and make student internships available. If employees have problems of alcoholism or drug addiction, family services organizations might be supported and their help solicited. This coupling of private interests with community interests reflects the principle of strategic philanthropy whereby both a company and community benefit instead of the notion of charity.[24] The idea of forming a consortium or a public–private partnership should also be considered as a way for two or more entities among business, government, and civil society to jointly alleviate social problems.

The acceleration of mergers and acquisitions has diminished local community relations programs. An example is Boston Gas Company, which had a model community relations program, with a full time director. Several meetings with local community leaders were held annually, each attended by an equal number of community members and company managers, with the company president attending every meeting. After its acquisition by National Grid, these meetings were terminated. Its address listed on Massachusetts bills is a post office box in Newark, New Jersey.

3.2 Consumer Relationship Management (CRM)

Whereas marketing focuses on facilitating transactions and communications between sellers and buyers, consumer relationship management (CRM) explores ways to build stronger and more enduring relationships. The belief is that "the best way to sell products is to forge personal relations with consumers rather than to spend large sums on broad-brush marketing."[25] Also called relationship marketing and loyalty programs, they are global in nature. The number of research articles on this subject has tripled from 2003 to 2013, with scholars outside the US accounting for approximately 80% of this increase.[26] Marketers attempt to tailor CRM strategies to specific cultures, using the variables associated with marketing.

Microsoft has recognized the value of CRM by developing software that helps companies identify and track sales leads. Referring to customer engagement, Microsoft claims that its "Dynamic CRM" helps companies deliver exceptional customer experiences that create long-term relationships based on knowledge and trust. Its acquisition of LinkedIn Corp., with its more than 400 million mostly professional individuals, is intended to help it achieve such relationships.[27]

3.2.1 Moving from a Transaction to a Relationship

CRM expands a transaction between a seller and buyer into a full-bodied relationship. It is the opposite of the extremely narrow relationship of the economist's concept of a transaction. In such a purely economic transaction, a seller offers a product or service for sale at a given price, and the buyer either accepts or rejects the offer. If accepted, both seller and buyer are assumed to be satisfied. The law asserts that a contract has been consummated, and economists proudly proclaim that the market miracle of mutual benefit has been achieved. The encounter, however, is often anonymous and symbolized by caveat emptor – let the buyer beware.

A relationship begins when a seller gets to know more about each customer. This may involve several stages: becoming acquainted, build up, continuation, and dissolution.[28] The database of a pizza shop, for example, could show previous phone calls by a customer and what was ordered. But beyond this elementary stage, as stated in the *Handbook of Relationship Marketing*, a broader strategic view is needed. It's "putting the customer first and shifting their role of marketing from manipulating the customer (telling and selling) to genuine customer involvement (communicating and sharing the knowledge)."[29] The goal is to create trust with customers and make them loyal. They might even become supporters, advocates, and partners.[30] A relationship implies a long-term perspective in which a post-sale phase includes product stewardship, consumer education on the use of the product, and a consumer complaint system.[31]

By establishing a relationship, the seller benefits in several ways:

- Attracts sales and increase repeat sales. There is no guarantee that first-time customers will purchase again. By building loyalty and creating lifetime customers, the cost of acquiring new customers is avoided – a cost that is between six and nine times greater than keeping existing ones.
- Obtains cross-over sales. When a company establishes a relationship with its customers, they are more likely to consider giving preference to a company's other products and services. A satisfied checking book customer, for example, is more likely to seek a loan from his or her bank.
- Encourages customers to recommend products to others, which can further be stimulated by the social media.
- Makes customers less price sensitive. When loyalty becomes an outcome of a relationship, customers are less likely to switch to another company whose prices are somewhat lower.
- They may be amenable to becoming a constituent in a public affairs campaign.[32]

CRM cannot be forced, as Wells Fargo learned (see Case 2). Cross-over sales are indeed one of the benefits of CRM and sales representatives should make customers aware of a company's other products. But CRM is a process that builds on closer customer relationships; it is not another sales technique, as it was at Wells Fargo.

3.2.2 Social Contract and Consumer Rights

A company's social contract with its customers largely revolves around its recognition of consumer rights. These were institutionalized by President Kennedy's Bill of Consumer Rights, which listed the right to safety, to be informed, to choose, and to be heard. This list was expanded to include such additional rights as the right to redress (e.g. through a warranty). The right to be informed is especially important because economic theory places great emphasis on rational decision making. The Security and Exchange Commission's (SEC) principle of "full and timely disclosure" serves as a model for consumer relations in that "full" product information would enable consumers to make an informed purchase decisions.

3.2.2.1 The Dilemma of Full Disclosure

In SEC parlance, "full" disclosure refers to necessary product specifications required for rational decision making. The "timely" aspect is not relevant when products are readily available, but can be significant when supplies are short or special sales are offered. Philip Kotler refers to "informing the marketplace" and public relations refers to the two-way, symmetrical model, which implies a willingness by a company to make adjustments to its "product" to make it more acceptable and attractive to consumers.

Judging when information is "truthful" or "accurate," however, is a thorny subject and may include some of the following complications:

- *Puffery*. Exaggerating positive aspects of a product is the major "sin" in both advertising and product publicity. An extreme illustration appears in the "Case of Squeeze on Citrus Hill Orange Juice" where the Federal Trade Commission (FTC) questioned the seller's use of the word *fresh* for a container of orange juice that did not contain freshly squeezed oranges.[33] The dictionary defines fresh as "newly produced, gathered or made; hence, not stored or preserved."

  On the other hand, Bayer is legally free to say, "the world's best aspirin" and Hush Puppies can say, "The earth's most comfortable shoes." The ad rules assume that nobody would believe some of the puffs anyway. But if the "puffs" become too specific and can be measured, an advertiser may be in trouble. For example, a federal court ruled in 2000 that Papa John could not claim "Better Ingredients, Better Pizza," after Pizza Hut, which uses the slogan "Best Pizza Under One Roof" sued the competitor. It would have been legal if Papa John had simply claimed it was "better overall."[34]
- *Deceptive advertising*. This exceeds puffery. In a well-known case, the FTC challenged Kellogg's cereals on its children's advertising, which claimed that its cereal allows children to "grow" in seven different ways. Credit was wrongfully taken for the benefit of the milk in the cereal.[35] Many restrictions apply to commercial speech in advertising messages; e.g. false advertising laws, such as California's, apply.

  Advertising may not necessarily be treated as "free speech," which allows someone to say virtually anything, but must be able to back up any claims made. This distinction received prominence in the Kasky v. Nike suit of 1998, in which Marc Kasky, a San Francisco human rights activist, sued Nike, saying that its campaign to display itself as a "responsible corporate citizen" in Asia was false and that California's false-advertising laws applied. Had Kasky won, the concept of social marketing, discussed earlier, would be severely compromised.
- *Warning labels*. These commonly appear on prescription drugs, tobacco, alcohol, and contraceptives, but questions also arise with other products. For example, how much information – which in the investment world is called material *facts* – should be contained in a label for trans fats? Should a label simply state the amount of trans fats in a product, or, in addition, include the recommended "daily value," or minimum intake? Should it say "Intake of trans fats should be as low as possible?"[36]

- *Audience's knowledge and sophistication.* This factor affects the fullness of disclosure. Children are typically considered a vulnerable group because they may not possess cognitive ability to evaluate advertising. And with adults there is sometimes a need for consumer education, e.g. about pharmaceuticals.

3.2.3 Power Relationship

Consumer power is suggestively reflected in the phrase, "consumer purchasing power." When consumers refuse to buy a product, they exercise ultimate power. This power is compromised, however, depending on the degree of competition and the urgency of a need. Power is magnified if consumers are able to organize a boycott, which is one of the tools of the consumerism movement. Estimates vary as to how much time it takes for a boycott to be effective. Some companies have seen their stock price decline over a 60-day period following a boycott; others say it takes about 2 years for a boycott to be effective. The newsletter *Boycott News* reported that in 1992–1993 there were 100 ongoing boycotts in the USA. Boycotts have succeeded in sharply curtailing the use of animal testing by cosmetic firms, stopping the killing of dolphins in tuna fishing, and curtailing the selling of infant formula in poor nations.

Companies have learned to take boycotts seriously. They approach each situation by:

- finding out who called for a boycott;
- avoiding the tendency to deny the charges;
- assessing the validity of the grievance(s) and correcting behavior if necessary;
- determining how much media attention the boycott is receiving and whether well-known persons support it;
- assessing the ability and power of the boycott callers to carry out the boycott.

Some MNCs have experienced boycotts in some of their foreign markets. A notable one is the organized boycott of the Danish dairy company Arla in the Middle East in connection with cartoons published in a Danish newspaper lampooning Mohammad (see Chapter 12).

Government regulations are an increasing source or consumer power. Regulations have resulted in the need for approval of drugs and other sensitive products, prescribing of product safety features, labeling requirements for foods, and prohibiting false advertising claims, such as "fresh," and product recalls.

3.2.4 Social Responsibility to Consumers and Society

CRM requires that a company seek not only consumer satisfaction but consumer welfare. Does the promotion of sugary products lead to diabetes? Do production shortcuts make products less safe? Does excess promotion of credit cards to low-income people encourage unwise purchases?

CRM also invites a company to extend social responsibility to society as consumers become more concerned about the impact of their consumption on the environment and sustainability. What efforts should a utility company undertake to reduce energy consumption? How can a company help socially conscious consumers who want to help society? Companies may decide to engage in special consumer social responsibility programs that promote their marketing efforts while also helping social causes. Cause (or cause-related) marketing has become a major activity.

3.2.4.1 Cause Marketing

In cause marketing, a company collaborates with a non-profit organization for mutual benefit. The simplest model is when a company forms a partnership with a non-profit organization (NPO) in which the company benefits by using the name of the NPO and in exchange makes contributions to it, usually based on volume of sales generated.[37] A well-known example is American Express's 1983 campaign to fund the restoration of the Statue of Liberty. Whenever its credit card was used, one cent was donated to the fund. The campaign raised $1.7 million and American Express benefited from a 27% increase in card use and 45% increase in new card applications.[38]

Cause marketing has since grown and is broadly applied to any partnership between an NPO and company where both benefit. The relationship might be initiated by either an NPO or a company. An NPO could tell the public about its cause and a participating company or companies could benefit by publicly identifying with the cause, which enhanced its reputation for being socially responsible. However, Alan R. Andreasen, author of *Marketing Social Change: Changing Behavior to Promote Health Social Development, and the Environment,* warns that "in order to survive nonprofit organizations must develop explicit ties with for-profit corporations" and not just hope to become the lucky beneficiaries of a company's independent cause-related marketing campaign.[39]

An example is when the American Heart Association (AHA) sought to make its brand more relevant to both current and new constituents. The AHA chose to target women because heart disease is their number one killer. Carol Cone, chairman and founder of Cone, Inc., which was known for strategic cause-branding, helped develop a national campaign designed to increase awareness, change behavior, and raise funds. In a 2005 campaign she helped develop a National Wear Red Day for Women with support from Pfizer and Macy's and the participation of some 8000 corporations. The campaign generated more than 2.3 billion media impressions to increase awareness of heart disease in women and $45 million in new contributions. Corporate participants benefited through their public identification with AHA, for Cone's research showed that 82% of Americans say they have a more positive image of business when it joins hands with an NPO.[40] By selecting an issue or cause that people are highly concerned about, a company can heighten the market's awareness and acceptance of its products or services.

Another well-known program is Avon Products Inc.'s Cancer Awareness Crusade. It raised millions for community-based breast cancer programs throughout the world: US$12.5 million in Australia and New Zealand and US$815 million worldwide.[41] Joanne Mazurki, director for global corporate affairs, said, "The linchpin of this crusade has always been what we can give back to communities."[42] It's a grassroots program in that about 450 000 Avon representatives educate women about breast cancer. Its crusade partners have been the Centers for Disease Control and Prevention, the National Alliance of Breast Cancer Organizations, the National Cancer Institute, and the Young Women's Christian Association (YWCA) of the USA.

The "Canadian Breast Cancer Foundation" (CIBC) "Run for the Cure" is Canada's largest single-day fundraising event dedicated to breast cancer research, education, and awareness. CIBC, which is a leading North American financial institution that provides financial services to more than 9 million clients, is one of Canada's largest banks. Breast cancer is an appealing cause not only to its customers but its women employees, who constitute 75% of the total number of employees. In 2004, CIBC had more than 10 500 participants in the event and raised over $2.5 million for cancer research. To encourage use of its new EMT (electronic mail transfer) system, CIBC made a $1.50 donation for every transaction made in a 3-month period. The bank provided major advertising support for the event through print and television media.[43]

Cause marketing is now a global phenomenon. In the UK, 67 businesses and 64 charitable causes collaborated and undertook 82 cause-related marketing programs in 2003. In the Tesco Computers for Schools program, started in 1992, the grocer provides its customers with a voucher for every £10 spent in-store. The customers then donate the vouchers to the school of their choice, which exchanges them for brand new computer equipment. Tesco lets customers and schools make the decisions.[44]

New forms of cause-related marketing continually appear. One is to let consumers determine which cause should receive support. This feature leads to greater consumer support than those in which the company chooses the cause. For example, SunTrust Bank donated $100 to a cause chosen by consumers who opened a new checking account.[45] An important factor to consider is the fit between the cause and the firm's core business, which would occur when, for example, a book publishing company provides disadvantaged children with new books.

3.2.5 Emerging Concept of "Social CRM"

Social CRM extends traditional CRM to a further exploration of the interaction between a customer and the firm. "To fulfill customer needs, the marketer must understand how to utilise technology-enabled resources such as e-mail, Interactive Voice Response (IVR) systems, and sales force automation linked to systems for customer analytics and database marketing," states Ian Chaston of the University of Auckland.[46] IBM adopted the term to explore how the social media affects consumer relations and how to manage CRM. It conducted a survey of 1000 consumers to determine what triggers a customer to seek out a company or brand via social media. The survey sought to determine who uses social media, what sites they visit, and what drives them to engage with companies. IBM also asked 350 executives why they think consumers are engaging with them. Their stated goal was to use social media to create "consumer intimacy."

The main finding, however, is that consumers were not particularly interested in engaging with companies. Only a small percentage of consumers regularly respond to posts or author their own content. They view social media as a way to connect with friends and family, not companies. Furthermore, consumers are much more interested in gaining tangible value in exchange for their time, endorsement, and social data.[47] More company effort would be needed.

IBM proposes a social CRM strategy to enhance engagement with customers. This strategy recognizes that getting closer to customers is the overwhelming priority of CEOs and that social media are ideally suited to achieve customer engagement. Social CRM is based on meeting the personal agendas of customers while also meeting company objectives of seeking customer engagement rather than customer management. Chaston states that "the capability to exploit the interchange of information will become a key aspect of creating and sustaining customer loyalty."[48]

In examining current social media practices, the survey showed the following use of social media by companies:

74% – communicate with customers;
65% – respond to customer questions;
60% – promote events;
52% – generate sales leads;
50% – sell products and services;
48% – solicit customer reviews.

Unfortunately, businesses were found to be less inclined to capture customer insights, monitor the brand, conduct research, or solicit ideas for new products and services; only 40% did so. One of the leaders to overcome these deficiencies is IBM, which recognizes the need for a comprehensive social CRM program. The functions of marketing (52%) or marketing communications (45%) are seen as managing and implementing a social media strategy, with public relations in third place (42%).

Social CRM is still in the early stages, execution is patchy and concerns about return on investment (ROI) remain, the IBM report. What needs to be done is to move beyond isolated projects to integrated programs. This advancement requires a comprehensive strategy, as well as the operational structures to put the strategy into action. As a start, companies are mirroring consumers' stampede to social networking sites such as Facebook, LinkedIn, Orkut and QQ. A total of 79% of companies surveyed have accounts on these sites.

A model of an integrated approach is Best Buy. It developed a strategic and operational model to enable thousands of its employees throughout the enterprise to engage with customers via social media. One program, called Twelpforce, allows customers to use Twitter to send inquiries to the company, and thousands of employees, across all functions, are empowered to tweet a response if they know the answer. Best Buy also maintains multiple community forums, blogs, an idea exchange, and a Facebook presence.

An integrated approach requires a system of cross-functional governance with consolidated guidelines and policies. Best Buy manages governance through a Center of Excellence with representatives from different participating programs. It contains a Communities Team within the Customer Support function, which also facilitates social media training for all employees. This model allows each group to manage its own initiatives within the framework of a common strategy.

Establishing a social media ROI that measures the impact of social media on sales and other desired outcomes is difficult and troublesome. Most executives are not satisfied with the quality of analytics used. The main source of doubt, however, is that a third of them aren't confident in the first place that their company has the necessary social media skills to interact with customers. They see the need for more trained communicators who are savvy about social engagement. Two thirds of the executives expect that the number of such employees using social media in their jobs will increase over the next 2 years.

The majority of companies believe that social media's potential to reinvent is so promising that they are aggressively forging ahead with initiatives, despite concerns about ROI, negative brand exposure, or the lack of new strategies and support frameworks. Social CRM is a strategy for stewardship of the customer relationship, not management.

3.2.6 Privacy

Consumer relations face a dilemma: to establish a sound relationship, a company should try to understand the needs and interests of its customers, but if it goes too far it intrudes on customer privacy. This intrusion is especially pernicious when the information about its customers is shared with – or sold to – other businesses. In particular, online businesses create huge databases of consumer information which connects people's names, addresses and other personal information with data about where they go on the Web.

Public sensitivity to privacy intrusion on the internet is rising. A Pew Research Center Internet Project found that 91% of adults "agree" or "strongly agree" that consumers have lost control over how personal information is collected and used by companies. Furthermore, 80% of those who use social networking sites say they are concerned about third parties, such as advertisers or businesses, accessing the data they share on these sites. Most say they want to do more to protect their privacy, but only 24% of adults "agree" or "strongly disagree" with the statement: "It is easy for me to be anonymous when I am online."[49]

Another survey, "2014 US Consumer Data Privacy Study: Consumer Privacy Edition from TRUSTe," conducted online by Harris Interactive, shows that 92% worry about privacy online, but 55% agree with the statement, "I trust most companies with my personal information online." Although 89% also agree, "I avoid doing business with companies who I do not believe protect my privacy online."[50]

With a little monetary incentive, however, most consumers are willing to relax on privacy concerns. A *Forbes* survey showed that although about 60% say they are "very concerned" or "somewhat concerned" about privacy, they are willing to sacrifice it if they are offered 20% off "today's purchase" by filling out a customer loyalty card. This card provides merchants with a treasure trove of data.[51]

In order to protect consumers and encourage corporations to do more to protect their customers, Senate Judiciary Committee Ranking Member Patrick Leahy (D-Vt.) in April 2015 introduced the Consumer Privacy Protection Act, S1158. Its declared purpose is "To ensure the privacy and security of sensitive personal information, to prevent and mitigate identity theft, to provide notice of security breaches involving sensitive personal information, and to enhance law enforcement assistance and other protections against security breaches, fraudulent access, and misuse of personal information." A key provision requires "companies who store sensitive personal or financial information on 10,000 customers or more to meet consumer privacy and data security standards to keep this information safe, and notify the customer within 30 days of a breach."

3.3 Conclusions

The local community, seen as "land" and infrastructure, can be considered a factor of production. Thus, community relations is a major public relations activity, especially in such industries as oil and mining. The community is a source of labor and supporting infrastructure, as well as another level of government. Attention must be paid to social problems that might affect employees and the company.

Consumers are also one of a company's key stakeholders. Whereas other primary stakeholders serve as a company's factors of production, consumers provide the revenue to pay them. The elements of a relationship between a company and its customers are carefully examined: agreeing on the social contract, maintaining two-way communications systems of disclosure and feedback, recognizing power relationships, being sensitive to privacy rights, and exercising social responsibility. The goal, especially in CRM is to develop strong, enduring relationships with consumers.

Some features associated with other stakeholders can be applied to consumer relations. The SEC requirement of full and timely disclosure to investors is applied to providing consumers with full product information to allow them to make rational choices. And the equivalence of the power of employees in withholding labor is exemplified by the ability of consumers to withhold their purchasing power.

Programs such as cause marketing provide special opportunities in the exercise of social responsibility in marketing. The issue of consumer privacy is equally important and complex in consumer relations as it is in government surveillance activities. Consumers relish privacy, but the more sellers know about a buyer the better they can serve them. Ideally, a seller would like to know a buyer's location as well as needs so that a sales message can reach him or her. Privacy is invaded in many ways, as explained in the discussion of "big data" in Chapter 7.

Discussion Questions

3.1. How is a market "transaction" defined, and how does the concept of CRM differ?

3.2. What are the benefits of CRM?

3.3. To what extent does the SEC's "full and timely disclosure" rule apply to marketing?

3.4. What are the implications of advertising not being treated as free speech?

3.5. In what ways can consumers exercise power over companies?

3.6. What is "cause marketing" and what kinds of companies and NPOs can benefit from it?

3.7. What is "social CRM" and how have some companies benefited from it?

3.8. For what kinds of products is "social marketing" especially suitable?

3.9. Who besides companies have advantageously applied social marketing? Describe an example.

Case 1 General Electric – Profile of a Multi-National Corporation

GE and its CEO Jeffrey Immelt exemplify globalization. When Immelt joined GE in 1982, 80% of the company's sales occurred in the US; now 70% originate elsewhere. In the 13 years that he headed GE, revenues from abroad increased from 30% to 55%. Its revenues outside America have risen from $4.8 billion in 1980 to $65 billion in 2015.[52] It exports over $20 billion worth of goods to the world each year and its 2015 revenues totaled $117 billion It has 330 000 employees in more than 180 countries and has become woven into the global economy.

GE is increasing its presence in India as part of its localization strategy, which balances the competing demands of national leaders to build plants in their chosen locations. It is building a new $200 million locomotive plant in the infrastructure-poor city of Marhaura, India. Its reward is a $2.5 billion order for 1000 locomotives over 11 years. GE says it was helped by building a factory complex in the industrial city of Pune. There it trained a cadre of skilled workers in an automated facility, which is expected to produce about 30% of the components needed for the locomotives to be assembled in Harhaura. By so doing, GE is supporting Prime Minister Nzarendra Modi's "Make in India" platform.[53] It was already developing more than a quarter of its new healthcare products in India to take advantage of the country's frugal innovation.[54]

In China, GE supported the country's push to open more markets to Chinese companies by investing billions of dollars in risky markets from Pakistan to Egypt.[55] It fully supported China's "One Belt, One Road" foreign-policy initiative whose intention is to revive ancient trade routes by building Chinese-backed ports, pipelines, and power plants in countries along the route.[56]

In the past GE's globalization was based on outsourcing to countries with low-cost labor in large factories. Now, GE has embraced the strategy of *Ecomagination*, which, as stated in its 2015 annual report, "drives global impact by delivering cleaner and more efficient technology solutions partnerships and new business models as well as convening key stakeholders to take action." Describing itself as a Digital Industrial Company, Immelt stated: "Our theory is that every industrial company is going to have to be a digital and software company."[57]

Acquisition of France's Alstom Company

To support the strategies of Ecomagination and localization, GE's CEO Jeff Immelt realized that new skills in corporate diplomacy would be needed to acquire existing companies that complemented its business strategy. On June 25, 2014, GE offered to buy Alstom SA company for $17 billion. Alstom is in the nuclear energy, gas-turbine manufacturing and service business, and railroad businesses, which were compatible with GE's determination to build GE into a global company and to be more focused as a maker of industrial equipment. As *The Economist* reported, "The transition from being a quintessentially American firm into an increasingly global company is one of Immelt's most significant achievements."[58]

But GE couldn't just expand to another country by simply having each company's stockholders approve a deal. Immelt's plan was thwarted when the French government stepped in after discovering that talks between Alstom and GE were already at an advanced stage. France's economy minister Arnaud Montebourg, described the situation as unacceptable. He said, "French firms are not prey. However, we are prepared to make alliances enabling us to face global competition. In the last few days we have taken several initiatives, the first being to reject a fait accompli." He warned of "patriotic" concerns over a GE deal when he said on France's RTL radio he would not accept that "in three days, Alstom can decide to sell . . . a national jewel behind the backs of the employees, the government, most of the board and senior executives." The government feared the loss of a national industrial icon in the energy and transport industries, for GE sought completely to absorb Alstom's power and grid businesses.[59]

To counter GE's offer, the French government invited the German rival Siemens AG to submit a bid so that at least Alstom would be kept in European hands. After taking several weeks to prepare its bid, Siemens joined forces with the Japanese conglomerate Mitsubishi Heavy Industries Ltd. Siemens would acquire Alstom's gas-turbine manufacturing and service business and offer to negotiate another deal to combine its rail business with Alstom's larger rail unit. It invoked regional sentiments when it said it would create a "European rail champion for the world market."[60] Mitsubishi offered to buy minority stakes in Alstom's divisions that make various types of equipment for power plants. While declining to comment on the Siemens–Mitsubishi offer, French President Francois Hollande's office said he remained committed to preserving French jobs and homegrown technology that Paris deemed strategic.

Immelt personally led the campaign to influence Hollande, making three trips to the Élysée Palace to provide reassurance and offer sweeteners. By the time Siemens, in league with Mitsubishi Heavy Industries, made its own offer, GE was ready to meet all of the French government's key demands. It changed its offer by adding a 1000-job guarantee and developing partnerships that would allow French investment in some of Alstom's energy business.[61] GE also discussed the creation of a unit that would preserve French ownership of Alstom's steam turbines for nuclear power plants, which was a concern of French Economy Minister Arnaud Monteourg. Instead, GE will only buy out Alstom's gas turbine business and its steam turbine business, which lie outside of France. GE is already a world leader in production and maintenance of gas turbines, but lacks in the steam turbine area.

The end result of the agreement is that France will have a 20% stake in Alstom, making it the company's biggest shareholder. GE will acquire Alstom's gas turbine and international steam turbine business outright. But three of the units GE had sought to buy will be held in 50–50 joint ventures with Alstom. These include making power grid equipment, renewable energy products, and turbines for nuclear plants. Despite the many concessions to French nationalism, GE succeeded in advancing its current three-pronged strategy: becoming more globalized, increasing spending on research, and developing environmentally friendly products. On Saturday, June 21, Alstom's board unanimously chose GE's revised bid after Immelt again met with the French President Francois Hollande and addressed the French parliament to resolve their concerns related to, among other things, loss of jobs from France as a result of this deal.[62]

Throughout these negotiations, Alstom's Chief Executive Patrick Kron defied Siemens and his own government. He teamed up with fellow CEO Immelt who spent many days in France to head GE's negotiations. The *Wall Street Journal* commented, "The battle for Alstom . . . shows how lofty European goals can get undermined by personal and corporate rivalries . . . and the erratic conduct of governments defending national – rather than regional – interests."[63]

A year after the deal was made with France, GE still faced a review with EU antitrust regulators, who feared that the deal could lead to higher prices for large gas turbines in Europe. Immelt was willing to make the additional concession of selling intellectual property to gain approval. Under EU antitrust law, companies have to take the initiative to address the regulators concerns.[64] GE eventually offered concessions to Brussels that satisfied their concerns. Approval from US antitrust authorities was expected. In September 2015, therefore, the 8 months of wrangling over the $17 billion power-unit acquisition appeared to end.[65]

In the meanwhile, US antitrust authorities opposed another international deal whereby GE would sell its home appliance business to Electrolux AG, the appliance manufacturer headquartered in Stockholm, Sweden. The US Justice Department argued that the sale would harm competition and hurt consumers. GE, however, argued that competition for appliances is more global than critics recognize, pointing to South Korea's Samsung Electronics Co. and LG Electronics Inc. and China's Haier. The issue was resolved when GE sold its appliance business to Haier in January 2016. Haier had already diversified its production line into white, black, and brown household appliances incorporating 15 100 models of appliances in categories as wide ranging as refrigerators, freezers, wine coolers, air conditioners, washing machines, cell phones, water heaters, microwave ovens, irons, TVs, DVD players, and even computers. For GE the sale fortified Immelt's goal of concentrating entirely on heavy industry and abandoning the appliance business, even though that market generated most of the $8.4 billion in sales from GE's Appliance and Lighting Division in 2014.[66]

Immelt Responds to Changing Attitudes Toward Globalization

As explained by *The Washington Post's* Robert J. Samuelson, "the general idea of globalization was that, as countries traded with each other, their populations would become richer – in poor countries, middle classes would emerge – and nations' interests would become intertwined. The threat of major wars would recede, because middle-class societies prefer commerce to conflict. The new world order would have tensions and feuds, but they would be manageable precisely because they occurred in a context of shared interests."[67] He also said, "Immelt does not see the end of globalization, but he does see the end of the "global elite" by those who see the world only from financial centers or a website."[68]

Immelt's view of globalization was reflected in a talk he gave to MBA graduates of New York University's Stern School of Business. Saying that globalization was being attacked as never before, he said it was time for "bold pivot."[69] Excerpts of his speech more fully describe his views on the status of globalization.

> *America was at the center of globalization – quite consciously. American companies that invested in global operations were a source of pride, of jobs, of overseas influence. We became woven into the global economy . . . . Being global has helped us become more efficient, more competitive.*
>
> *These bonds have fractured. Today . . . . With globalization, it is time for a bold pivot. GE has $80 billion of revenue outside the U.S., so global growth is critical to our success. In the face of a protectionist global environment, companies must navigate the world on their own . . . . We must level the playing field, without government engagement. This requires dramatic transformation. Going forward: We will localize. In the future, sustainable growth will require a local capability inside a global footprint. GE has 420 factories around the world giving us tremendous flexibility. We used to have one site to make locomotives; now we have multiple global sites that give us market access. A localization strategy can't be shut down by protectionist politics.*
>
> *We can accelerate growth by solving local problems. In the past, every solution was viewed as a "global solution," where one size fits all. In the future, companies will impact the way the world works by innovating to solve problems with local capability . . . . Our competitive advantage is digital productivity. In the past, productivity could be achieved only through low-cost labor in large factories. In the future, manufacturing will be driven by new materials, additive techniques and digitized plants. Factories will be smaller and more flexible. Our goal is to make what we want, where we want. Workers will be more productive and more valuable.*

Immelt restructured the company for the digital age. He invested heavily in the internet of things and moved the company's headquarters to Boston to be closer to the heart of high-tech.[70] In his 2017 annual letter to investors, Immelt saw GE's competitive advantage growing because it has a superior global footprint.[71]

After 16 years as head of GE, Immelt stepped aside on August 1, 2017, to be succeeded by John Flannery, the head of GE's healthcare business.[72] Stock prices had tumbled dramatically for a variety of reasons: unrealistic financial targets, use of cash for stock repurchases, and loss from its previous insurance business. In retrospect some have questioned the Alstrom purchase saying the timing was not ideal as the market for its power unit dropped. The price for Alstrom might have been too high and the agreement to safeguard French jobs led to unexpected costs. Immelt's drive to globalize its business may have blinded him to its risks.[73] The need for sound decision making by a company does not disappear when crossing international borders.

Discussion Questions

1 How does GE exemplify a multinational corporation in the age of globalization? What measures are used?

2 Why was GE's CEO Jeffrey Immelt so determined to acquire Alstom? Why couldn't the stockholders at GE and Alstom simply vote on the matter?

3 What are the nationalistic interests of France?

4 Why did France invite other companies to bid for Alstom?

5 How did Immelt exercise corporate diplomacy to overcome opposition to the deal?

6 What is the current status of government and public attitudes toward globalization?

7 How did Immelt respond to the assault on globalization? Do you agree with him?

Case 2 Wells Fargo Misapplies CRM

Wells Fargo, the US's largest bank by market share, tried to achieve the benefits of CRM by forcing its employees to engage in illegal sales practices. Specifically, its 2015 annual report mentions the term "cross-sell" – which is one of the objectives of CRM – 20 times.[74] Employees created as many as 3.5 million accounts, using fictitious or unauthorized customer information, aggressively making referrals of products or services, and pushing to cross-sell multiple products to individual customers. A teenage daughter of one of the bank's branch managers had 24 accounts.[75] Many branch managers routinely monitored employees' progress, sometimes hourly, toward meeting sales goals.[76]

In this sales-driven culture, employees were led to move customers' money into new accounts without their knowledge. Funds were occasionally transferred from an authorized customer account to a temporary fund, which sometimes resulted in fees for insufficient funds. Another practice was to create fake email addresses to enroll unknowing or people who didn't exist in online banking services. These practices were encouraged when management established steep sales goals and attractive compensation incentives.

In July 2017, a further disclosure was made about its auto insurance practices. Customers were urged to buy auto insurance from National General Insurance, which was often more expensive than auto-insurance customers had already obtained on their own. Furthermore, the bank conceded that it had forced nearly 600 000 customers who financed their car purchases with Wells Fargo to pay for collision coverage they didn't need, resulting in 20 000 customers who had their cars wrongly repossessed.[77] Some customers were asked to obtain so-called guaranteed asset protection (GAP). About 570 000 customers who were improperly charged will get refunds of account adjustments totaling around $80 million.[78]

In November 2017 another accusation was that Wells Fargo charged some of the highest trading fees around – at least two to eight times higher than the middle market industry average, e.g. charging anywhere from 1–4% on basic transactions such as converting euros to dollars.[79] A crisis management rule was violated, namely, that all relevant aspects of a crisis should be disclosed at the beginning to avoid a string of crisis news.

As Richard Breeden, a former Securities and Exchange Commission chairman, summarized the crisis, "They have not projected a sense that how they treated their customers is an extremely important issue or that they understand why it is extremely important." He added, "The recurring themes here seem to be complacency, arrogance of being disengaged."[80]

In a review of the case, Virgil Scudder, author of *World Class Communication*, outlines the repeated neglect of explicit and repeated warnings over 5 years.[81] He said that as early as 2005 John Stumpf, the then incoming CEO, failed to take any action when some employees reported the practices to him. When a board committee became aware of the fraud, there still wasn't any action. Nor was any action taken after the City of Los Angeles filed a lawsuit against the bank in 2015 alleging the bank pressured employees to commit fraud.

Charges Brought Against Bank

On September 9, 2016, multiple law enforcement and regulatory agencies – such as the US Office of the Comptroller of the Currency, the City Attorney of Los Angeles, and the US Consumer Financial Protection Bureau brought charges against the bank and fined it $185 million. The bank did not admit or deny wrongdoing. Nor was any senior official identified as orchestrating the fraud and "widespread illegal activity."[82] Over a 5-year period, roughly 5300 (out of a total of 268 000) employees had been terminated. CEO Stumpf's explanation was that there were employees who didn't "honor" the company's values and so had to be let go. He claimed "There was no incentive to do bad things." Furthermore, he stated, "Our goal is to get it right with every customer 200% of the time. When we fall short of that goal, I feel accountable and our leadership team feels accountable – and we want all our stakeholders to know that."[83]

But many employees who were interviewed by the media explained that the reason most were fired was for not meeting sales goals. It is important to note that no mention is made of any employee survey taken by the human resources or corporate communications departments before the scandal. By not recognizing the importance of stakeholder relations with employees, top management didn't know what was going on right under their noses. And members of the board of directors, who were very inactive, were uninformed. A proxy advisory firm, Institutional Shareholder Services, subsequently advised shareholders to vote against 12 of the bank's 15 directors at the April 25, 2017 annual meeting.[84]

In an attempt to explain the scandal, the bank's top management held an hour-long telephone call to about 500 senior executives led by CEO Stumpf and President and Chief Operating Officer Timothy Sloan to rally support. Sloan said that "listening tours" had been done by Mary Mack, the new community banking head. He also said the bank planned to boost its marketing efforts after customers were ready for it and that the bank had paid for more social media advertising than usual during the interim.[85]

Wells Fargo's Crisis Management Response

In response to the fine and crisis, Wells Fargo wasted no time in placing a full-page ad in major newspapers such as the *Wall Street Journal* on September 9 titled, "To Wells Fargo Customers: Our commitment to you." The ad was unsigned. Referring to its booklet, "The Vision & Value of Wells Fargo," the ad sought to portray the illegalities as deviations from its policies. After expressing regret of "allegations that some of our retail customers received products and services they did not want," the ad states that the bank took "full responsibility for any such instances and have refunded those customers who incurred fees." It listed four improvements and told customers you "can always see all of your Wells Fargo banking relationships via our online banking services at www.wellsfargo.com."

The bank's vision and value booklet had absolutely no influence on employee behavior. Nor did higher management reinforce it. Instead it engaged in contrary behavior: its marketing officers set sales targets, checked daily on whether they were kept, and fired employees who were slack. Managers and employees who met expectations received compensation incentives.

When called to a hearing by the House Financial Services Committee on September 22, 2016, CEO Stumpf's performance was exceedingly poor and full of platitudes. He came with no concessions and his statements were lame, e.g. "If I could turn the clock back," and "I've thought about this a thousand times," "of course I wish . . . we all wish we would have done something more . . . . We will be doing everything to make it right." The Wells Fargo board moved to rescind $41 million from Stumpf's pay and $19 million from his lieutenant, former community-banking head Carrie Tolstedt.[86] Her total compensation for 2015 was $9.5 million. She had overseen retail banking during its bad behavior. At first, she was allowed to keep about $35 million in invested options, but after a 113-page report was released on April 10, 2017, a huge $47.3 million was clawed back. The report had singled her out 142 times for setting the tone for the bank's retail unit. Stumpf was also further penalized with a clawback of an additional $28 million.

Consumer Research and More Ads

The new chief marketing officer, Jamie Moldafsy, turned to opinion polls and focus groups to assess consumer and public sentiment about the bank's brand. She found that people "hadn't heard the message that we felt badly" about what had happened. She used the findings mainly to rework its ad messages.[87]

In a full-age ad, "Moving forward to make things right," on October 31, 2016, Wells Fargo outlined several specific actions.[88]

- Putting customer interests first by focusing on their financial needs, not product sales goals.
- Proactively communicating with customers, e.g. sending confirmation of new accounts.
- Full transparency of eligible accounts when enrolled in Wells Fargo Online.
- Fixing what went wrong, e.g. providing full refunds for any fees incurred through unauthorized accounts.

On December 5, 2016, another full-page ad appeared featuring its symbolic stagecoach and horses along with the theme: "We'll go wherever your business needs to go." Wells Fargo exploited its link with the overland Concord stagecoach and the fact that it at one time owned and operated the largest stagecoach company in the world. Wells Fargo considers the stagecoach and horses a living symbol of the company's heritage of service, stability, and innovation. The ad referred to a "dedicated Relationship Manager" who would "take the time to understand your business and build a team to provide a broad array of scalable offerings."

A similar ad 2 weeks later, showing two powerful horses, focused the wording to sound more like consumer relationship management, saying it assembled a "team to design and deliver strategies that help you go where you want to go. And as your needs change, our road array or services scales with you. We're with you for the long term. We're committed to your success."

An April 4, 2017 ad, headed "Thank You," summed up the steps taken by Wells Fargo to regain customer trust. Significantly it was signed by the new CEO and President Timothy J. Sloan. The steps included:

- refunding approximately $3.2 million to approximately 130 000 retail and small business accounts;
- eliminating product sales goals and changing how retail bankers are paid;
- creating a new Office of Ethics, Oversight, and Integrity;
- terminating executives linked to inappropriate sales practices and canceling all 2016 cash bonuses for eight senior leaders, including Sloan himself;[89]
- separating the roles of chairman and CEO.

These steps address the key failures of the bank and should help in the daunting process of rebuilding trust among its customers and government officials. But the long-term restoration of trust will depend on the true application of consumer relationship management.[90]

As late as April 2018 Wells Fargo faced further scrutiny about improper charges to consumers of its mortgage and auto-lending businesses. It had failed to correct the deficiencies and violations in a timely manner. It violated the crisis communication rule: "Say It Fast, Say It All, Say It Accurately."[91] By April 2018, Wells Fargo faced a fine of as much as $1 billion from the Consumer Financial Protection Bureau and Office of the Comptroller of the Currency – considerably more than the $185 million initial fine. Furthermore, citing "widespread consumer abuses," the Federal Reserve barred the bank from growing past the $ 1.95 trillion in assets it had at the end of 2017.[92]

In a two-page ad on May 7, 2018, Wells Fargo summarized the progress made in transforming the bank. It announced the names of eight new independent directors and a new independent board chair, Betsy Duke, the first female chair of a major US bank. And especially significant is reference to the elimination of its distorted consumer relationship management program consisting of its troublesome product sales goals.[93]

Discussion Questions

1 Why is CRM a suitable criterion in judging Wells Fargo's consumer relations?

2 Specifically, describe how the tenets of CRM were violated?

3 What might Well Fargo management have learned if sound employee–stakeholder relations had been exercised? What actions would such relations entail?

4 What is your judgment of CEO Stumpf, the former retail bank executive, and Carrie Tolstedt, the head of community banking?

5 How well did Stumpf respond to the crisis? How should he have responded to the House committee?

6 Was the publication of institutional ads a good idea? Was the style and content of the ads effective?

7 How does a bank create trust with its customers?

Endnotes

1 Wilbur J. Peak, "Community Relations," in Phil Lesley's *Handbook of Public Relations and Communications*, 4th edition (Chicago, IL: Probus Publishing Company, 1991), p. 117.
2 Nathaniel H. Sperber and Otto Lerbinger, *Manager's Public Relations Handbook* (Reading, MA: Addison-Wesley Publishing Company, 1982), p. 157.
3 Chester Barnard, *The Functions of the Executive* (Boston, MA: Harvard University Press, 1938).
4 Rowland T. Moriarty, Ralph C. Kimball, and John H. Gay, "The Management of Corporate Banking Relationships," *Sloan Management Review*, Vol. 24, Spring 1983, pp. 3–15.
5 "The Paradox of Soil," *The Economist*, April 4, 2015, p. 21.
6 See Edmund M. Burke *Corporate Community Relations: The Principle of the Neighbor of Choice* (Westport, CT: Quorum Books, 1999).
7 The concept is explained in Robert D. Putnam, *Bowling Alone: The Collapse and Revival of American Community* (New York: Simon & Schuster, 2000).
8 Barbara W. Altman, "Transforming Corporate Community Relations: A Management Tool for Achieving Corporate Citizenship," *Business and Society Review*, Vol. 102, No. 1, 1999, p. 46.
9 John Browne, "Addressing Global Climate Change," Stanford University, May 19, 1997.
10 Based on a personal interview with Jim Klocke, executive vice president.
11 The author spent a week interviewing local leaders for the Charleston Chamber of Commerce.
12 Burke, op. cit., p. 103.
13 Joseph Ager, *Business or Pleasures* (New York: Universe, Inc., 2006), p. 21.
14 "Indian Development: Beyond Bootstraps," *The Economist*, June 29, 2013, pp. 74–75.
15 "Tata Sauce: Emerging-Market Giants" *The Economist*, March 5, 2011, p. 83.
16 "Pakistan: Infrastructure Development vital for promotion of Business Activities-ICCI," *Right Vision News*, June 30, 2012.
17 Personal observation during visit.
18 Henisz, op. cit., pp. 64–65.

19 Ibid., p. 95.
20 Ibid., pp. 95–96.
21 Jared Diamond, *Collapse: How Societies Choose to Fail or Succeed* (New York: Penguin Group, 2011), p. 98.
22 Ibid.
23 "Community Relations Abroad," a draft statement submitted by William Baldwin, public relations director, National Foreign Trade Council, Inc., August 8, 1961.
24 Barara Ettorre, "Charity Begins at Home; Corporate Giving," *Management Review*, Vol. 84, February 1995, pp. 34–36.
25 "Schumpeter: Smart Products, Smart Makers," *The Economist*, November 21, 2015, p. 65.
26 Joshua T. Beck, Kelly Chapman, and Robert W. Palmatier, "Understanding Relationship Marketing and Loyalty Program Effectiveness in Global Markets," *Journal of International Marketing*, Vol. 23, No. 3, 2015, p. 1. Reference is to ISI Web of Science study.
27 "Why Microsoft Went All In on Linkedin," *WSJ*, June 15, 2016, p. B1.
28 B. Stern, "Advertising Intimacy: Relationship Marketing and the Services Consumer," *Journal of Advertising*, Vol. 26, 1997, pp. 7–19. He also describes the further steps of build-up, continuation, and dissolution.
29 Jagdish N. Sheth and Atul Prvatiyar, eds., *Handbook of Relationship Marketing* (Thousand Oaks CA: Sage Publications, 2000).
30 Ibid., p. 52.
31 The relationship concept starts in the post-sale phase, states Dan Steinbock. He believes that the "internet will become an instrument of maintaining a closer and abiding relationship." Dan Steinbock, *The Birth of Internet Marketing* (Westport, Ct: Quorum Books, 2000), p. 60. Emily Glazer and Christopher M. Matthews, "Prosecutors Take Up Wells," *WSJ*, September 15, 2016, p. C1.
32 T. Duncan and S. Moriarty, "A Communication-Based Marketing Model for Managing Relationships," *Journal of Marketing*, Vol. 62, 1998, pp. 1–13.
33 "Putting the Squeeze on Citrus Hill Orange Juice," Tom L. Beauchamp, *Case Studies in Business, Society, and Ethics*, 4th ed. (Upper Saddle River, NJ: Prentice Hall, 1998), pp. 59–69.
34 Noel C. Paul, "Supersize It!" *Boston Globe*, August 8, 2004, p. D5.
35 "Kellogg Cereals and Children's Television Advertising," in Beauchamp, op. cit., pp. 146–158.
36 Leila Abboud and Patricia Callahan, "Food Industry Gags at Proposed Label Rule for Trans Fats," *WSJ*, December 27, 2002, p. B1.
37 A formal definition is, "A commercial activity by which businesses and charities or causes form a partnership with each other to market an image, product or service for mutual benefit." See H. Pringle and M. Thompson, *Brand Spirit, How Cause-Related Marketing Builds Brands* (Hoboken, NJ: John Wiley & Sons, 1999). Carol Cone, who promoted cause-related marketing, adds that the goal is "to deepen trust and relationships with customers, improve corporate image and ultimately, sales, while providing benefits to the cause." Cause-Related Marketing Presentation, Cone Communications, Inc., 1997.
38 Jocelyne Daw, *Cause-Marketing for Nonprofits: Partner for Purpose, Passion, and Profits* (Hoboken, NJ: John Wiley & Sons, 2006), p. 4.
39 Alan R. Andreasen, "Profits for Nonprofits. Find a Corporate Partner," *Harvard Business Review*, November–December 1996, pp. 55–59.
40 Ibid, pp. ix–x.
41 "Million Reasons – The Avon Breast Cancer Crusade," You Tube, September 30, 2014.
42 "Avon's Grassroots PR Raises Awareness & Dollars" *PR News*, Vol. 51, April 7, 1997.
43 Daw, op. cit., pp. 109–112.
44 Ibid., p. 16.

45 Stefanie Rosen Robinson, Cagar Irmak, and Satish Jayachandran, "Choice of Cause in Cause-Related Marketing," *Journal of Marketing,* Vol. 76, July 2012, p. 126.
46 Ian Chaston, *Internet Marketing and Big Data Exploitation* (London: Palgrave Macmillan, 2015), p. 169.
47 "From Social Media to Social CRM," IBM Institute for Business Value Executive Summary.
48 Chaston, op. cit., p. 176.
49 Mary Madden, "Public Perceptions of Privacy and Security in the Post-Snowden Era," Pew Research Center, November 12, 2014.
50 https://www.trustee.com/resources/privacy-research.
51 Josh Steimle, "Survey Shows You Don't Care About Privacy as Much as You Think You Do," *Forbes,* November 7, 2014.
52 Ibid., p. 6.
53 Ted Mann and Brian Spegele, "Why GE Builds More Factories Overseas," *WSJ,* June 30, 2017, pp. A1, A9.
54 Special Report, "The Rise of the Superstars," *The Economist,* September 17, 2016, pp. 6, 10.
55 Brian Spegele, "GE Follows China Into Developing Markets," *WSJ,* October 15, 2017, p. B3.
56 Ted Mann and Brian Spegele, op. cit., p. A9.
57 "Interview: GE's Jeff Immelt," *Bloomberg Businessweek,* February 13–19, 2017, p. 23.
58 "General Electric: A Hard Act to Follow," *The Economist,* June 28, 2014, pp. 53–55.
59 Kim Willsher, "In Numbers: Hollande in Talks with GE and Siemens Over Future of Alstom," *The Guardian,* April 29, 2014, p. 27.
60 William Boston and Inti Landauro, "Siemens Moves to Derail GE Deal," *WSJ,* June 17, 2014, p. B1.
61 Adam Sage Paris, "GE Chief Speaks Hollande's Language with Pledge to Create 1000 New Jobs in France," *The Times* (London), May 29, 1014, p. 41.
62 Trefis Team, "GE Set to Expand its Power Business with Alston Acquisition," *Forbes,* June 25, 2014.
63 Stacy Melchtry, Inti Landauro, and Jan Hromadko, "France and GE, Unlikely Business Pals," *WSJ,* June 26, 2014, p. B-1. Also see *The Economist,* May 10, 2014, p.8.
64 Tom Fairless, "GE Faces Key Talks with EU Regulators," *WSJ,* May 13, 2015, p. B3, and Ted Mann, "GE Weights Concessions for Alstom Deal," *WSJ,* May 21, 2015, p. B5.
65 Tom Fairless and Ted Mann, "Regulator to Bless GE-Alstom Deal," *WSJ,* September 8, 2015, p. B1.
66 Aruna Viswanatha and Ted Mann, "GE Faces Day of Reckoning for Unit Sale," *WSJ,* October 31–November 1, 2015, p. B3.
67 Robert J. Samuelson, "We Still Need Globalization," *The Washington Post,* June 6, 2016, p. A15.
68 Ted Mann, "GE Defends Conglomerate's Global Reach," *WSJ,* February 28, 2017, p. B3.
69 Alan Murray, "GE's Immelt Signals End to 7 Decades of Globalization," *Fortune,* May 20, 2016. His entire speech is reprinted.
70 Thomas Gryta, "Why GE is Moving from the Suburbs to Boston," *WSJ,* May 17, 2017, p. R5. Also, *The Economist,* Special Report, op. cit, p. 12.
71 Ted Mann, "GE Defends Conglomerate's Global Reach," *WSJ,* February 28, 2017, p. B7.
72 Thomas Gryta, Joann S. Lublin, and David Benoit, "GE Names New CEO Amid Slump," *WSJ,* June 13, 2017, p. A1.
73 Thomas Gryta, Joann S. Lublin, and Daid Benoit, "'Success Theater' Masked Rot at GE," *WSJ,* February 22, 2018, p. A1. Also Thomas Gryta and Joann S Lubin, "Embattled GE Reshapes Board," *WSJ,* February 27, 2018, p. B1.
74 Emily Glazer, "Wells Fargo Tripped by its Sales Culture," *WSJ,* September 17–18, 2016, p. A1.
75 Emily Glazer, "Wells Slams Former Bosses' High-Pressure Sales Tactics," *WSJ,* April 11, 2017, p. A1.
76 Ibid.

77 Gretchen Morgenson and Emily Glazer, "Wells Fargo Gets New Warning," *WSJ*, November 30, 2017, p. B1.

78 Emily Glazer, "Wells Fargo Plans Refunds," *WSJ*, July 29–30, 2017, p. B10; Emily Glazer and Ryan Tracy, "Wells Could Face More Sanctions," *WSJ*, August 5, 6, 2017, p. B9.

79 Emily Glazer, "Wells Fargo Bankers, Chasing Bonuses, Overcharged Clients," *WSJ*, November 28, 2017, p. A1.

80 Emily Glazer, "Wells Fargo's Botched Crisis Management," *WSJ*, October 14, 2016, p. A1.

81 Virgil Scudder, "Anatomy of a Scandal at Wells Fargo," *The Strategist*, Winter 2016, pp. 22–23.

82 Emily Glazer, "Wells Fargo Fined for Sales Scam," *WSJ*, September 9, 2016, p. A1.

83 Emily Glazer and Christina Rexrode, "Senators Assail Wells CEO," *WSJ*, September 21, 2016, p. A1.

84 Ibid.

85 Emily Glazer, "Wells Maps a Crisis Plan," *WSJ*, October 12, 2016, p. C1.

86 Emily Glazer and Rachel Louise Ensign, "Wells Fargo's CEO Faces More Heat," *WSJ*, September 29, 2016, p. B1.

87 Emily Glazer, "The Post-Scandal Marketing Playbook," *WSJ*, May 17, 2017, p. R2.

88 Ad appeared in the *WSJ*, October 31, 2016, p. A9.

89 Emily Glazer, "Wells Fires 4 Senior Managers Over Sales Practices," *WSJ*, February 22, 2017, p. B1.

90 Emily Glazer and Joann S. Lublin, "Bank Spars With Shareholders," *WSJ*, January 30, 2017, p. B3.

91 Otto Lerbinger, *The Crisis Manager: Facing Disasters, Conflicts, and Failures* (New York: Routledge, 2012), p. 56.

92 Yuka Hayashi and Emily Glazer, "Wells Nears $1 Billion Settlement," *WSJ*, April 20, 2018, p. B1; Yua Hayashi, "Wells Lowers Net Income After Settlement," *WSJ*, April 21–22, 2018, p. B5.

93 See *WSJ*, May 7, 2018, pp. A8–A9.

Part II

Strategic Application of Communication Practices

Global corporate communication makes use of the full range of communication practices: public relations, public affairs, global marketing, social media and big data, and digital and social marketing. A suitable all-embracing term for these disciplines is "integrated communication practices." A precedent is "integrated marketing communications" (IMC), which sought to unify the various communication strategies centered around the consumer (see Chapter 6).

The strategy of applying all the communication practices to a program or campaign is reflected in the logo of "Being More" used by an affiliate of Burson-Marsteller in India. Prema Sagar, principal, and founder of Geness Burson-Marsteller, said, "Being More is a promise to provide clients with strategic counsel, ideas, and results across the spectrum of public relations, public affairs, corporate responsibility, digital, content, and crisis communication campaign for different audiences."[1]

Joseph Nye's application of *soft power* also reflects this strategy. He viewed soft power as the use of an expanded range of tools to serve as an alternative means of persuasion to coercion, military force, or economic power affairs in international relations. He defines soft power as the ability to attract and co-opt rather than coerce or use force or money as a means of persuasion. It's "getting others to want the outcomes that you want; the ability to attract."[2] He describes soft power as the use of relatively less transparent channels and the use of lobbying through powerful political and non-political organizations.

The range of communication practices available to corporate communication is shown in the objectives of each of the chapters of Part II:

- Chapter 4 – Public Relations: Influencing Public Opinion. This is the communication part of public relations that focuses on the application of publicity, media relations, and event management to inform and persuade. Beyond general public opinion, public relations influences the opinions of specific "publics," such as investors, employees, and consumers (these publics are now most frequently called stakeholders).
- Chapter 5 – Corporate Public Affairs: Exercising Power in the Socio-Political Environment. It shows how a multi-national company exercises power in its socio-political environment. It seeks to influence government policies and decisions on all levels and branches as well as advocacy groups representing such issues as the environment, human rights, poverty, and sustainability. Public affairs includes government relations, negotiations, and lobbying.
- Chapter 6 – Global Marketing Communication: Facilitating Exchanges provides an overview of marketing and the relationship to the social media, public relations, and public affairs.
- Chapter 7 – Social Media and Big Data: Extending Relationships widens an organization's relationships with all stakeholders. Major developments of digital communications are reviewed and the implications shown for public relations, public affairs, and marketing.

Corporate Communication: An International and Management Perspective, First Edition. Otto Lerbinger.

- Chapter 8 – Digital and Social Marketing: Extending Practices and Influencing Behavior expands the goal of marketing through digital relations and engages in social marketing to change the behavior of consumers and the public.

The five communication practices use similar media but to different degrees. Public relations and marketing still use mass communication, the former through publicity, and the latter through advertising. But both are now high users of social media, and marketing continues to evolve into digital marketing. Public affairs, which relies on government relations, lobbying, and negotiations, has also been affected by social media, especially Twitter, but continues to use mass media.

The application of communication practices to the design of a program or campaign is greatly enhanced through the synergy obtained from their combined contributions. Furthermore, they draw on the social sciences. The psychology of attitude change, or persuasion, is most common. Technically, persuasion properly describes symbol manipulation designed to produce action in others. Public relations professionals often fear, however, that their association with persuasion might portray them as propagandists. Yet we know that some form of influence or control over one another is an inescapable part of human living. In organizations and society persuasion is used to establish stability and harmony, as well as an instrument to exert power. Another social science, sociology, is helpful in identifying appropriate audiences in social groups and groupings. And political science explains the legislative and executive processes, as well as the actors, involved in political decision making.

Personal contacts with individuals play a large role in public relations, public affairs, and marketing. These contacts are rooted in part in the field of diplomacy. In *The Essence of Diplomacy*, Christer Jonsson and Martin Hall describe diplomacy as a regulated process of international society's communication system, with diplomats serving as messengers between nations and many of the players in the international arena. In the division of communication into mass communication and interpersonal communication, diplomacy is chiefly associated with the latter. As news commentator Edward Murrow observed, person-to-person contact – "the last three feet" – is the most important element in the communication process.[3] Modern diplomacy, however, requires communications in a wider variety of settings than face-to-face conversations between two people, with gatherings ranging from small groups and assemblies of people to large-scale conferences. Diplomacy can be defined as tact and skill in dealing with people.

The Public Relations Campaign and MARCOM

In planning and evaluating a communication campaign or program to address a specific problem or situation, corporate communicators employ two strategic tools: the public relations process and MARCOM (Marketing Communication). These communication models used in public relations and marketing are similar. Both require the following steps:

- Describe and analyze the situation, including information about the organization or client and "environmental" factors and trends.
- State objectives and show how they contribute to the organization's or client's goals.
- Identify the target audiences.
- Develop strategic approaches.
- Design the message themes, symbols, and appeals.
- Choose the media that best reach the target audiences and intermediary links to them with the designated messages.
- Evaluate effectiveness.

Evaluation is simplest and clearest in public affairs when the objective is to pass or defeat specific legislation or regulations; it's either yes or no.

Planning in marketing, public relations, and public affairs can benefit by applying the *hierarchy of effects* model. As developed by Robert J. Lavidge and Gary A. Steiner in 1961, the hierarchy consists of six steps: awareness, knowledge, liking, preference, conviction, and purchase. It is based on Everett Rogers' diffusion of innovation model, which progresses through the stages of knowledge, persuasion, decision, implementation, and confirmation.[4] It explains how over time, an idea or product gains momentum and diffuses (spreads) through a specific population or social system.

A campaign should address each of these steps and indicate which communication practices and media are used for each. For example, advertising excels in attracting attention to a product; publicity allows more information to be presented; a message reference to high credibility sources facilitates attitude change; and social media facilitates confirmation. Campaigns may encompass a total campaign or treat each level separately, e.g. Phase One would concentrate on attracting attention.

The use of campaign planning is particularly appropriate for *global* public relations in contrast to *international* public relations because it emphasizes the need for a strategy or overall perspective for programs executed in more than one nation. As stated by Gavin Anderson:

> Global public relations superimposes an overall perspective on a program executed in two or more national markets, recognizing the similarities among audiences while necessarily adapting to regional differences. It connotes a planned attitude as much as geographic reach and flexibility.[5]

Global public relations answers the question of how public relations can be practiced location by location, yet maintain a consistent overall identity and message that preserves reputation globally.

Endnotes

1 "Burson-Marsteller Comment to 'Being More' at 60," Campaign India, October 15, 2013, p. 1.
2 Joseph S·Nye, *Bound to Lead: The Changing Nature of Power* (New York: Basic Books, 1990).
3 Hans N. Tuch, *Communicating With the World* (New York: St. Martin's Press, 1990), p. 82.
4 Everett Rogers, *Diffusion of Innovations*, 3rd ed. (New York: Free Press, 1983).
5 Gavin Anderson, "A Global Look at Public Relations," in Bill Cantor, *Experts in Action*, 2nd ed. p. 413.

4

Public Relations: Influencing Public Opinion

Influencing public opinion – the opinions of individuals as well as the general public – is the most recognized function of public relations. This chapter deals with public relations in its popular meaning as publicity and media relations. Shriramesh and Verčič recognize "the power that the media have in shaping public opinion nationally and internationally" and state that "the critical linkage between media and public relations . . . has led public relations professionals to give primacy to media relations."[1] This view, however, omits the listening part of public relations, i.e. considering the interests of others, and striving for mutual benefit. The larger meaning of public relations includes communications with stakeholders (see Chapters 2 and 3) and contributing to management policy and decision making (see Part V).

In saying that public relations influences public opinion, it would be more accurate to refer to people's attitudes rather than opinions, for opinions are simply a response to questions. The psychological literature refers to attitude change and states that attitudes determine how events and issues are perceived and how those holding specified attitudes are treated.[2] Attitudes therefore are the central concern of public relations and persuasion a major activity.

Everyone knows that some form of control or influence over one another is an inescapable part of human living. Persuasion is intended to exert such influence on others and ultimately produce desired behavior.[3] To Harold Burson, a pre-eminent public relations consultant and founder and head of the highly successful and seven-decade-old firm of Burson-Marsteller, persuasion defines public relations. Significantly, he named his recent book *The Business of Persuasion*.[4] Considering opinions and attitudes as malleable, he sees his "PR programs" as achieving three objectives: "1. change these opinions and attitudes, 2. reinforce them, or 3. create opinions and attitudes where none existed." To this extent his views are consistent with the statement that the goal of public relations is persuasion. But Burson goes further by unabashedly defining persuasion as "the discipline of convincing people to do what my employer or client wanted them to do." As he points out in his book, he is totally dedicated to his clients.

Although his formula has been highly successful, it is resisted by those in public relations who don't want to be seen as "servants of power."[5] More importantly, by identifying public relations wholly with persuasion, he ignores the symmetrical aspects of communication, i.e. that the receiver of a message might influence the sender (see discussion below of four models of public relations). He thus severely constrains the definition of public relations.

In summary, persuasion is an ambiguous term because its meaning can range from outright propaganda to honest attempts to provide information. The various forms of persuasion are clarified by examining the historical connection between public relations and public opinion.

Corporate Communication: An International and Management Perspective, First Edition. Otto Lerbinger.

4.1 Historical Connection Between Public Relations and Public Opinion

Modern public relations originated in the late twentieth century when big business dominated and its selfish actions caused a public backlash. Newspapers accordingly engaged in *muckraking* against business. Fearing hostile public opinion and government regulations, business hired journalists to tell their side of the story. These former journalists were generally known as press agents who engaged in one-way communication to influence public opinion. This move led some critics of public relations, such as Vance Packard in his popular book *The Hidden Persuader*, to accuse public relations of seeking to manipulate public opinion.[6] Public relations people countered with the argument that opposing groups also have the opportunity to influence public opinion. Some of this criticism abated when public relations practitioners developed new principles of communication.

One of these practitioners was Ivy Lee, who worked for the anthracite coal industry and the Pennsylvania Railroad. He opposed the industry policy of secrecy and changed the attitude of "the public be damned" to "the public be informed."[7] His adage was "tell the truth." He declared, "In brief, our plan is, frankly and openly, on behalf of business concerns and public institutions, to supply to the press and public of the United States prompt and accurate information concerning subjects which it is of value and interest to the public to know about." James E. Grunig and Todd Hunt called Ivy Lee's approach the public information model in contrast to the former press agentry/publicity model, which was equated with propaganda.[8] Along with "the public be informed" approach, Lee created the press release, which was clearly marked to identify the source. When he later worked for Rockefeller he changed the policy of "secrecy and aloofness" to what Grunig calls the public information model.

Another proponent of the public information model was Arthur W. Page when he became vice-president of public relations at the American Telephone & Telegraph Co. in 1927.[9] He insisted on the condition that he would have a voice in policy and that the company's reputation would be based on the performance of the company. He summed up his philosophy by saying: "All business in a democratic country begins with public permission and exists by public approval. If that be true, it follows that business should be cheerfully willing to tell the public what its policies are, what it is doing, and what it hopes to do. This seems practically a duty."

Public relations was boosted during World War I when the US government recruited George Creel and his Committee on Public Information to mobilize public opinion in support of the war. Their success demonstrated the power of public relations. George Creel, Carl Byoir, and some of his group became well-known public relations professionals after the war. Among the best known is Edward L. Bernays. He called public relations the "engineering of consent" and in 1923 wrote *Crystalizing Public Opinion*, following Walter Lippmann's influential 1922 book, *Public Opinion*.[10] Bernays promoted the expression "public relations counsel."

4.1.1 The Public Relations Audit

Recognizing that public opinion is a potent force with which organizations must reckon, former Carl Byoir & Associates, once the largest public relations organization in the US, announced a new service called "The Public Relations Audit." It was described as:

- A comprehensive study of the public relations position of an organization: how it stands in the opinion of its various "publics" – stockholders, employees, customers, suppliers, the investment community, thought leaders, and the public at large.

- It points out public relations strengths and weaknesses . . . public relations asset and liabilities. It analyzes specific problems, sharpens objectives, and evaluates the adequacy of the methods being used to gain good will and patronage.
- It provides a pattern for future operations.[11]

Two steps accompany the preparation of an audit. One is to appraise a company's public nature: a public utility and a bank, for example, are more vested in public interest than a manufacturer of appliances. Similarly, the public nature is higher for a company that produces a product or service that is a biological or cultural necessary required by practically everyone in a given community or region. Such companies must show a concern for the general welfare and pay greater attention to public opinion and, therefore, public relations.

A second step is to determine what assets a company possesses to offset the power of others and promote its own public relations objectives. These assets include (i) political resources, such as the favorability of the legal climate; (ii) affective resources such as the popularity of its chief executive officer (CEO) and accumulated goodwill; (iii) cognitive resources such as its amount of newsworthy information; (iv) cultural resources such as its historical traditions, customs, and ideology; and (v) economic resources such as total revenue available and the size of the public relations budget.

Although the term "public relations audit" is no longer common, a company's standing with the public remains a critical consideration.

4.1.2 Use of Surveys in Public Relations

Public relations practitioners continually assess public opinion toward business, toward specific industries and companies, and current and emerging issues. Business wants to know its political standing compared with other power structures. In the 1950s its main political rival was labor. Now it is government, the media, and the "third sector," chiefly advocacy groups. Individual companies want to assess their reputations, which are especially important in consumer relations because they know that attitudes toward them affect sales. Positive attitudes lead to a "good reputation," which is conveniently measured by a public opinion survey.

Knowing how they stand in the eyes of the public has become a standard concern of business. Such perceptions are related to attitudes and, beyond that, to behavior. An attitude is a precursor to behavior. It indicates what a person would do when confronted with a given situation.[12] An attitude serves as a storage and transmission mechanism of a verbal expression in the present to behavior in the future. The term *opinion* is often used instead of attitude, but technically an opinion specifically refers to a response to a question on a survey.

The full scope of public relations is not completed if its meaning is restricted to changing attitudes and influencing public opinion, for ultimately the goal of communication is to influence the behavior of target audiences. It cannot be assumed that a change of opinion will necessarily lead to desired actions. A publicist must complete all of the steps in the basic communication model: deciding on the formal source, creating a message, gaining its acceptance by the selected media, reaching the target audiences, influencing their attitudes, and affecting their behavior.

Publicists often delude themselves – and their employers and clients – when they try to show proof of their effectiveness by tabulating the number of press releases sent and by listing all the media outlets that printed or broadcast their messages. But one can say "so what" if press releases and news clippings are not followed by proof that they influenced desired attitudes and behavior. For this reason some public relations professionals, notably Patrick Jackson, a former PRSA president, define their field as behavioral public relations.

Jackson described behavioral public relations as a process involving awareness, latent readiness, triggering events, preparatory or intermediate behavior, and relationship-building. All of these aspects must be employed. For example, awareness rarely leads to desired behavior; and latent readiness only occasionally. Jackson also strongly advocated three principles of public relations practice:

- That an organization must speak with one clear voice and that it must deal with substance, not only perceptions.
- That the "victory syndrome" in negotiations should be replaced by co-authorship, i.e. a collaborative approach.
- That one-on-one communication is generally preferable to mass communication, especially as a means of developing sound relationships.

Some of the earliest surveys were conducted by Gallup. For more than 70 years, states Gallup, it has built its reputation on delivering relevant, timely, and visionary research on public opinion around the world. It generally focuses on specific current issues. For example, its February 20, 2015, report was titled "Slightly More Americans See U.S. As No. 1 Military Power" and its February 25 report was "Americans Continue to See UN as a Poor Problem-Solver."

4.1.3 Current Difficulties with Surveys

Taking a public opinion poll has become more difficult and the results less reliable. Polls wrongly predicting Hilary Clinton's election victory in 2016 proved that. Gone are the days when a pollster could telephone a random sample of online telephone owners that matched the demographics of a population. Although demographic proportions might be right, the sample is no longer random. Moreover, the switch to mobile phones made such sampling costly. A 1991 federal law prohibits calling mobile phones with an auto-dialer. With sales representatives posing as researchers and phone owners screening unwanted calls and hanging up on auto-dialed calls, the number of households agreeing to participate in a poll has dropped from 36% in 1997 to 9% in 2016.[13] Research firms such as the Pew Research Center and Civis Analytics are experimenting with new methods to improve the accuracy and reliability of polls.

Public relations and marketing professionals are also rediscovering the importance of personal interviews and ethnography by visiting people in their home or work environments. They are concerned that agencies have become too infatuated with big data and aren't telling them everything they need to know. They want to assure that their samples adequately represent gender and racial diversity and come from varied socioeconomic and geographical backgrounds.[14]

But the problem of interpreting the value of public opinion findings is even more difficult in the new digital environment in which people reject the advice of experts. Economists at the American Economic Association's annual meeting in Chicago in 2017, for example, bemoaned the fact that their opinions were no longer respected by the public. For example, while economists generally support a free market system and are opposed to protectionism, polls show a falling support for free trade. An October 2016 survey by the Pew Research Center found that only 56% of Democrats and 24% of Republicans supported it.[15] They recognized a new problem: how to rebuild trust in the discipline of economics and its prescriptions.

The problem is more widespread than economics. In an article "How America Lost Faith in Expertise," Tom Nichols, professor of National Security Affairs at the US Naval War College, states that "Americans have reached a point where ignorance . . . is seen as an actual virtue." The ideal of expertise itself is challenged by "a Google-fueled, Wikipedia-based, blog-sodden collapse of any division between professionals and lay people . . . ." Americans reject the advice of experts and thereby demonstrate their independence from "nefarious elites."[16]

Public relations campaigns that in the past based the credibility of their messages on experts have to reconsider their approach.

4.1.4 The Edelman Trust Barometer

These annual surveys have become a major source of information for public relations professionals. For example, the Edelman Trust Barometer's 15th annual survey found that trust among all institutions was evaporating. The rating is linked to "the failure of key institutions to provide answers or leadership response to events such as the refugee crisis, data breaches, China's stock market downturn, Ebola in West Africa, the invasion of Ukraine, the Fédération Internationale de Football Association (FIFA) bribery scandal, Volkswagen's manipulation of emissions data, massive corruption at Petrobras, and exchange rate manipulation by the world's largest banks."[17] Edelman's 17th Trust Barometer found the disturbing fact that in 2016, trust in CEOs collapsed, blamed on their failure to lead in a void left by government. In the wake of the Trump administration's ban on immigration, people now expect them to serve as spokespersons for social justice.[18]

Richard Edelman reports that for the first time since the Great Recession, half the countries it surveyed have fallen into the "distruster" category, meaning that the overall trust among the informed public is below 50%. Included are Japan, Ireland, Sweden, Britain, and Italy. Germany was just above Italy but was placed in the "neutral" category, just below the US. In the "truster" category were the United Arab Emirates, India, Indonesia, China, Singapore, and the Netherlands.[19]

Importantly, trust in business was higher than that for government, with a 19-point difference. But although government was reported as the least trusted institution, more than half of those surveyed wanted more governmental regulation of business, especially in financial services, energy, and food. An explanation is that trust in CEOs has declined by 10 points since 2011 to only 31% in developed markets. CEOs are portrayed as taking a narrow view of their mandate in society by seeking short-term gains at a time when 81% of respondents believe that business can pursue its self-interest while doing good work for society.

4.1.5 CNBC/Burson-Marsteller Corporate Perception Indicator

Following in the tradition of appraising corporate reputations is the CNBC/Burson-Marsteller Corporate Perception Indicator. Its September 2014 global survey, which included 25 000 individuals from the general public and 1800 top executives from 25 markets, showed that only 52% of the public in developed markets have a "favorable" view of corporations, compared with 72% in emerging markets. Significantly, 45% of those in developed countries said corporations have "too much influence over government" compared with 30% in emerging economies.[20] Exposure to corporate behavior in developed countries apparently weakens public support.

Developed countries, including the US, UK, Germany, Japan, and Hong Kong, had more skeptical views than those in emerging markets, such as China, Brazil, India, Mexico, and Turkey. In the US, more than half (51%) said "strong and influential" corporations are "bad," even if they are promoting innovation and growth. In contrast, 74% of people in China embrace strong corporations as "good." Business should worry when those with greater familiarity with them develop negative views.

An important aspect of public opinion surveys is that people distinguish between power and respect. In the US, 47% of the public says CEOs are "among the most powerful people in society," but only 9% says they are "among the most respected" in society. In Germany, 43%, and in the UK, 42% agree on the power dimension, and 11% in Germany, and just 5% in the

UK agree on the respect dimension. The challenge, says the survey, is for business leaders "to show how they use their positions of power to contribute to the common good." They also want corporations to promote shared values around growth and opportunity, even as they build shareholder value.

4.1.6 Pew Research and Just Capital

Pew Research describes itself as a non-partisan fact tank that informs the public about the issues, attitudes, and trends shaping America and the world. It conducts public opinion polling, demographic research, media content analysis, and other empirical social science research. A policy of Pew Research is that it does not take policy positions. Particularly relevant to global corporate communications have been its world surveys of anti-American attitudes over several years and attitudes toward climate change.

Just Capital is a new survey organization based on the idea of a "people's index" driving more just and balanced corporate behavior. The study is called "The Research: How Does America Define Just Corporate Behavior?"[21] It seeks to rank the performance of America's largest 1000 companies on issues deemed to be most important by the public. The major findings are that across traditional political ideologies and income levels, most Americans believe that corporate behavior is headed in the wrong direction; that corporations have become less ethical just over the past decade; and that corporations should do a better job balancing the needs of all stakeholders, especially employees, customers, communities, and the environment. The study also points out that while corporate after-tax profits are at their highest since 1929, labor's share of income is hitting 65-year lows. While in 1980 the average CEO made roughly 42 times more than the average employee, today the ratio is 373 to 1.

4.2 Gaining Influence Through Publicity

Public relations is typically equated with publicity, which is the planned effort to obtain positive news coverage and other favorable exposure to build a favorable image and understanding of a person or organization. A publicist is often an ex-journalist – a skilled writer familiar with William Strunck and E.B. White's *Elements of Style*.[22] Furthermore, he or she is familiar with various readability formulas that match the writing complexity with the audience's level of education. One of the most popular is the Flesch–Kincaid readability test, which measures word length and sentence length.[23]

Publicity is the first of four models of public relations constructed by James E. Grunig and Todd Hunt:

1) Press agentry/publicity: one-way communication whose purpose is propaganda.
2) Public information: also one-way whose purpose is dissemination of information.
3) Two-way asymmetric: communication whose purpose is persuasion, using social science theory and methods.
4) Two-way symmetrical: communication whose purpose is mutual understanding.[24]

Grunig and Hunt view publicity as telling, not listening. Publicists are viewed as believing they needn't tell the whole story nor be entirely truthful. Public relations practitioners are advised not exclusively to identify themselves with publicity or with persuasion lest their credibility becomes damaged. Although Grunig and Hunt acknowledge that the public information model dominates, they advocate the fourth model. Here the sender and receiver exchange messages for mutual benefit, although the sender does not necessarily consider the interests of the public co-equal to those of the organization, as the term *symmetrical* implies. Ideally, public relations identifies the source of its messages and uses honest, straightforward means of conveying information.

Openness is favored by public relations professionals. It is propelled by two forces. One is that the dangers of secrecy are recognized as the public demands greater transparency. The other is the practical fact that it is hard to keep secrets these days, as evidenced by a steady flow of news media and social media reports of corruption and wrongdoing. Furthermore, secrecy can impede the equitable and efficient function of society. It is well known that individuals in positions of power use secrecy to cover up real or imagined mistakes, thus hoping to prevent punishment and demands for restitution. Other dangers of secrecy are that it can be used by holders of privileged information to benefit economically and politically, harm the decision making process, and erode trust within an organization and society.

4.2.1 Applying Perception Management: Putting "a Spin" on a Story

Publicists are associated with "putting a spin" on a story so as to attract media and public attention. Public relations is therefore often accused of manipulating the truth in order to create a favorable impression. Psychologists call this process *perception management* – how a receiver of a message sees a message. Thus, a person's perception is formed by two parts: the stimulus presented by the media and the person's motivations and stored information. As phrased by the philosopher William James, "In human experience the parts are excerpts, built out into wholes by our conceptual additions."[25]

When a person resists a message, communicators sometimes resort to subliminal tactics. For example, in a theater "Drink Coca Cola" might be flashed on the screen but in such low intensity that the viewer is unaware of the message. If sales of Coke are higher in theaters where such subliminal messages are projected, the tactic is deemed effective.

Burson-Marsteller asserts that its business is perception management. Its brochure *Managing the Power of Perceptions*, states the psychological fact that "Perceptions are real. They color what we see . . . how we interpret . . . what we believe . . . how we behavior." In explaining the agency's mission, the brochure says, "In this age of accelerating change and borderless, instantaneous communication, the proactive management of perceptions has never been more important." In recounting the history of Burson-Marsteller, Robert Leaf, the former CEO of the agency, named his "memoirs of a life in PR" *The Art of Perception*.[26]

The term perception management requires careful consideration. It affirms the intention of a communicator to achieve a desired result. But all that can be managed is the coding of a "stimulus situation" consisting of words and other symbols intended to invoke a certain percept by the receiver. The percept moreover is a combination of external symbols contained in the communicator's message along with the stored information and attitudes of the receiver. Such stored information varies among individuals and depends on their past learning. A communicator's effectiveness therefore depends on his or her familiarity with the receiver's background. This familiarity is greatest with people we know. Miscalculations are likely, however, with audiences outside of the sender's "beat," in the journalistic sense. When this beat is in a foreign country with unfamiliar individuals and players, achieving a desired perception becomes more difficult. In a literal sense, therefore, perceptions cannot be managed.

In everyday life, the concept of perception management is closely related to Erving Goffman's thesis of *impression management*.[27] He says that people are concerned about the impression they make because it affects how they are treated. A person in a Mercedes driving into a filling station will be accorded greater attention than someone driving an old Datsun.[28] What essentially happens is that the perception of a person establishes "the terms of trade" between people.

4.2.2 The Challenge Faced by Publicity: Limited Human "Channel Capacity"

Public attention is a scarce resource sought by communicators. Psychologists use the concept of "channel capacity" to indicate that the amount of information a person can receive through a single sense – sight, hearing, taste, smell, and touch are the traditional ones – or the combined senses is limited. The US Air Force faces this problem when it configures how a single pilot can process information about speed, the physical space of the flight, the assigned mission, and possible engine problems. The possibility was explored of providing different kinds of information through other than the usual visual and auditory senses, namely, the olfactory and kinetic senses.[29] Danger, for example, might be indicated by a strong unpleasant odor. Similarly, publicists constantly explore how to use publicity events to reach people through all of their senses.

Journalists have long used photos as a concentrated and powerful means of conveying information and having emotional impact. The saga of Syrian refugees during the summer and fall of 2015 hit home when the photo of a 3-year-old boy named Aylan Kurdi, wearing little Velcro-strap shoes and a red shirt, whose lifeless body had washed up on a Turkish beach, was published worldwide and went viral on social media. Other photos have had similar impact: a 17-year-old civil rights demonstrator attacked by a police dog on May 3, 1963, in Birmingham, Alabama, and Dorothea Lange's photo of a distraught woman and her children during the Great Depression in 1936.

The equivalent of channel capacity in newspapers is the "newshole" – the limited amount of space available daily after advertising has been placed. Competition among public relations practitioners for inclusion in the newshole is fierce. A premium is placed on creativity to devise special events that attract media and public attention. In its early years, Ruder & Finn was known as "a fast growing creative agency, constantly coming up with new ideas." Finn pointed out "how important it was to have a theme in a public relations program in order to achieve a positive effect over a period of time."[30]

4.2.3 Proactive Media Relations Strategy

Because it usually depends on dissemination by the mass media, publicity is typically equated with media relations. "Achieving media coverage" has remained the core activity of public relations, as David Finn said in his *The Way Forward: My First Fifty Years at Ruder-Finn*.[31] David Finn was president of the independent public relations firm of Ruder & Finn (now called Ruder Finn). Like Bernays, Finn gained early experience handling publicity for entertainers.[32] But attracting attention to oneself and one's products and ideas has become a greater challenge than ever as more voices speak with more messages through more media, says Finn. "We were lucky," he says, when "our job was to serve intense press interest. But now most of the time we're competing with other communicators."[33]

4.2.4 Bernays – A Prominent Publicist

Bernays, who was called US's publicist No. 1 by *Time* magazine in 1938,[34] became a leading advocate of public relations and a leader in applying publicity to promote many causes. In his autobiography, *Biography of an Idea*, he stated that he considered ideas more important than words.[35] For example, to promote the sale of books, he used the idea of convincing architects to design book shelves in living rooms walls, which, of course, had to be filled with books. And he helped Ivory Soap sell more soap by conceiving of another use of soap: let kids use it to make sculpture.

Bernays is given credit for popularizing smoking by women, a campaign that illustrates the social science thinking underlying publicity. Mentioning that he was the nephew of Sigmund

Freud also helped his reputation. Among his famous statements are: "I find it easier to change the viewpoint of millions than one man's," and "Age-old customs, I learned, could be broken down by a dramatic appeal, disseminated by the network of media."[36] He analyzed the taboo against smoking by women by consulting psychoanalyst A.A. Brill for an explanation of a woman's desire to smoke. Brill told him: "Smoking is a sublimation of oral eroticism; holding a cigarette in the mouth excites the oral zone. It is perfectly normal for women to want to smoke cigarettes."[37]

Based on his research, Bernays seized upon the idea: Why not a "parade of women on Fifth Avenue lighting cigarettes as symbolic torches of freedom"?[38] They were to do this on Easter Day – a day symbolizing resurrection and transition – that would attract media attention. This custom-breaking behavior of women smoking in public received huge news coverage.

4.2.5 Harold Burson – Thoughts About Public Opinion

Another veteran public relations counselor who studied public opinion is Harold Burson. He was much influenced by Walter Lippmann's 1922 book, *Public Opinion*, and the subsequent book in 1923 by Bernays, *Crystalizing Public Opinion*. He developed ideas about the functioning of public opinion, such as these maxims:

- Truth always prevails.
- Any controversy is best settled as quickly as can be – on the first day and not "dribbled out one fact at a time."
- The American public is extraordinarily forgiving if you tell them the truth, e.g. Burson believed in 2004 that in 10 years Clinton's reputation would be fully restored with Americans, largely because of his tremendous charisma, and he might be remembered as one of the US's best presidents.

4.2.6 Proactive Media Relations

A company is said to engage in proactive media relations when it goes beyond responding to media inquiries and seizes the initiative to convey its message to the public. Instead of reacting to news inquiries, it develops relationships with media outlets and takes the initiative in supplying stories. The goal of this high profile strategy is to seize opportunities to promote information and stories beneficial to one's company.

One of the lessons learned by all organizations and nations that have suffered from negative publicity is that maintaining a low profile is usually unwise. The strategy of not sending out news releases or holding news conferences, and only warily responding to journalists' telephone calls, can be risked only if there is little public interest in an organization. Freeport McMoRan in its New Guinea mining operations was known for shunning the press by following a "No tall trees" policy.[39] Should a crisis occur, however, it would suffer from lack of public goodwill and possible hostility by the media. Perhaps a greater loss is that by maintaining a low profile, an organization loses the opportunity to advance its views on public issues.

Economic pressures on the mass media, which have resulted in reduced staffs, have been making it easier for publicists to get their press releases accepted. In the UK, a study conducted by Cardiff University found that 60% of Britain's leading newspapers and 34% of broadcast stories were wholly derived from wire service copy or public relations material. Moreover, a study by the Australian Centre for Independent Journalism at the University of Technology Sydney concluded that journalists in many instances were not carrying out the traditional practice of checking information provided by public relations professionals. In the US, studies show that public relations provides 50–75% of mass media content.[40] The views of public relations people are, of course typically biased in favor of their employers and clients.

A variety of techniques is used in proactive media relations. "Jump starting" the news has been a major one. Another has been to provide video news releases and conduct public opinion polls so that favorable results can be publicized. Another way has been to use advocacy advertising – also called issue advertising – as an agenda-setting device, a technique associated with Herb Schmerz. When he headed Mobil's communication efforts he initiated broadcast interviews to promote company views on an issue.[41] For those groups that opposed its views and complained that they couldn't afford to do likewise, he offered to finance their opposing advocacy ad. But Mobil still had the advantage of setting the agenda by having chosen the issue.

Agenda setting is a major communication theory that was formally developed by Max McCombs and Donald Shaw.[42] Money plays a larger role in the ability to influence public opinion since the Supreme Court decision on Citizens United, which ruled that corporations and labor unions are accorded the same rights of free speech as individual citizens.

When placing an advocacy ad, the following guidelines should be followed:

- The ad should be part of a larger public affairs campaign and thus supplement activities such as proactive media relations and grassroots lobbying.
- The advertiser should have high credibility, perhaps stemming from past communications.
- The ad is based on facts and persuasive reasoning, not flag-waving, posturing, and preaching.
- The ad creates interest and involvement by talking in terms of the audience's own lives and the things that are important to them.
- The ad presents both sides of an issue.

Some countries have used proactive publicity in power plays to undermine the reputation of others and elevate their own. For example, North Korea's official Korean Central News Agency (KCNA) hailed 2003 as a "proud year of victory" in its atomic standoff with the US, thanks to the wisdom of supreme leader Kim Jong Il and the "might" of the country's armed forces! It called US Defense Secretary Donald Rumsfeld "human scum" and a "political dwarf."[43]

4.3 International Application of Persuasion

The use of persuasion is highly relevant in the international arena because its many players recognize its value in advocating their causes, viewpoints, and missions. These include attempts by the United Nations to seek support for humanitarian efforts in countries like Dafur; the European Union (EU) search for support for a new constitution; and individual nations seeking to build their nation brand and promote tourism by describing their country's unique or major attribute.

The benefit of favorable public opinion is that it enables countries and the organizations within them to work together effectively, recognizing that people who like each other can get along more easily. If they don't like each other, they won't do anything to help one another; even worse, they might want to inflict harm and not stop others from doing so. Most world leaders, therefore, crave favorable public opinion, although a few, such as Joseph Stalin, preferred to be feared and thus able to exert power over his people.[44]

For individual companies and industries, the concern with public opinion is largely about attitudes toward themselves and toward current issues and crises. For example, Google, which faces antitrust actions by the EU and France, wants to know whether influential groups and the general public support those actions. The findings would influence the choice of appropriate public relations and public affairs campaigns. Aside from such issues, companies may seek to make direct investments abroad, merge with other companies, sell goods and services, and obtain favorable treatment by governments.

4.3.1 Public Diplomacy Campaigns

More than a decade ago the US government and business became aware that anti-Americanism was on the rise around the world, largely due to public opposition to the US invasion of Iraq. The Pew Research Center had confirmed the erosion of favorable attitudes in its 2002, 2003, 2006, and 2007 surveys. The US government consequently decided to intensify its public diplomacy efforts to win back favorable world public opinion. Its efforts were led by the United States Information Agency, whose goals were "to understand, inform, and influence foreign publics in promotion of the U.S. national interest, and to broaden the dialogue between Americans, their institutions and their counterparts abroad."[45] It represented an application of soft power as described in the Part II introduction.[46]

Public diplomacy applies the process of changing public opinion of a nation state. As stated by Nancy Snow in "Public Diplomacy and Public Relations: Will the Twain Ever Meet?," the two have indeed merged.[47] Concerned about their standing by people in other countries, a government seeks to garner public support among them for their foreign policies. Public diplomacy is an instrument to attract the publics of other countries, rather than only their governments.

Charlotte Beers, an advertising star, was appointed undersecretary of state for public diplomacy and public affairs. Her advertising campaign, known as "shared values," presented television snippets in Muslim countries that showed successful and satisfied Muslims in the US. The audience perception, however, was that the videos portrayed the US as a "superior" culture attempting to "civilize" an "inferior one."[48] A follow-up campaign by Karen Hughes, a former counselor to President George W. Bush, called a "listening tour." was likewise unsuccessful, for it was seen as a "photo opportunity" and platform for reiterating US policies with "handpicked audiences."

4.3.2 Business Support

Both campaigns were reinforced by business. A coalition was formed of advertising executives and public relations consultants, headed by Keith Reinhard, chairman of DDB Worldwide.[49] Explaining its mission, Reinhard stated that "Companies must develop a series of positive images and behaviors that shows respect and understanding for international cultures and generates respect for us."[50] One of the behaviors was the use of company resources to give tangible support during a natural disaster during the South Asian tsunami in February 2005. When American corporations assisted countries, a poll of 20 000 consumers worldwide found 59% improved their impression of contributing countries.[51] In Indonesia, a poll found that those "with a favorable opinion of the U.S." jumped from a low of 15% in May 2003 following the US-led invasion of Iraq, to more than 44% in January 2006.[52]

As suggested by business involvement, the term *public diplomacy* is no longer restricted to governments. In their book *International Public Relations and Public Diplomacy*, editors Guy J. Golan and Sung-Un Yang explain, "Public diplomacy essentially deals with the *management of communication* among diplomatic actors, including nations and non-state actors, which have specific informational or motivational objectives toward reaching the foreign publics through various channels of communication to promote national interest."[53] Public diplomacy is identified with international public relations, which Gyorgy Szondi, author of *Public Diplomacy and Nation Branding*, defines as a combination of public diplomacy and nation branding, with an aim at relationship-building.[54]

International public relations has similarities with the field of international relations (IR), which is concerned with the relationships among countries, governments, peoples, and organizations all around the world. For this reason, the term corporate diplomacy is gaining currency.[55] Like IR, public relations deals with global issues, such as globalization, economic development, sustainability, and human rights. Both public relations and IR are multidisciplinary in that they draw from politics, history, economics, law, sociology, psychology, philosophy, ethics, and geography. Both deal with foreign cultures, languages, worldviews, and values.

4.3.3 Social Media Support

Further indicating that the US no longer controls the messages is the introduction of digital communications. This was pointed out by James K. Glassman, a former journalist, when he initiated the Public Diplomacy 2.0 program in the US State Department. He focused on using the Web 2.0 phenomena and its interactive digital media possibility to connect "citizen to citizen, person to person."[56] As explained by Matt C. Armstrong, social media has the capacity to break through geographical, cultural and even linguistic barriers, democratizing the access to, and distribution of information.[57]

Nicholas. J. Cull, director of the Master's in public diplomacy program at the Center for Public Diplomacy at the University of South California, explained that this emphasis on people contact was not just rebranding public diplomacy but actually reconceptualizing the role of public affairs within the State Department and the practice of diplomacy as a whole.[58] Public diplomacy was to become an integral part of the policy process. Public diplomacy would not only help understand public opinion and enable this knowledge to be used to advise policy makers but also to advise the global community about the policy decisions. Thus, public policy fulfills an informational and strategic role in the foreign policy context.

The new two-way symmetrical approach conforms to the advanced model of public relations and allows for engagement and the potential for "mutually beneficial communication." E. Comor and H. Bean describe this approach as "participatory persuasion" that allows "many-to-many" communication. Facebook and Twitter are included, and are even used by some top State Department officials such as Ambassador Susan Rice and Secretary of State Hillary Clinton. In 2014, the State Department claimed 2.6 million followers on 301 official Twitter feeds, with 155 million individuals worldwide each day.[59] But for the new approach to be effective, State Department officials had to change their attitude toward listening and engaging; they had to be willing to play an internal advocacy role.

4.4 International Differences and Constraints in Media Relations

Media relations practices must take international differences into account. Newspaper editors in France, for example, are less hospitable to company press releases that tout their products and views, thinking that such material is really advertising and should be paid for. Translators often don't have a word for *publicity*, mistakenly calling it advertising. While some "universal media techniques" apply globally, it is best to consider putting some local touches on them. Carole M. Howard, co-author of *On Deadline: Managing Media Relations*,[60] provides some examples of journalist's attitudes and expectations in various countries:

- Russia: news conferences tend to be longer and reporters look for a historical perspective on a company and products.

- Poland: journalists are skeptical and therefore prefer numerical research from a reputable outside source to support product claims.
- Hong Kong: journalists like to see local VIPs on the stage with presenters.
- Thailand: having lots of keynote speaker at news conference is seen as giving it greater importance.
- France: "reporters want to know how you are sharing the profits of your business, not only with shareholders, but also with employees and society."
- Australia: reporters frown on flashy trappings.[61]

Public relations has been proliferating in China, with more than 100 firms in Beijing alone as early as 1996. Events planning, mainly for the banquets required to do business, is a major public relations activity. Knowing Chinese etiquette is important. A person of equal stature, for example, must respond to a proper toast, which can range from 30 seconds to 15 minutes. Chinese journalists are easy to deal with because they are not competitive among themselves. But because saving face is important, a public relations person must be sensitive; e.g. never demand that a reporter or newspaper correct a mistake.[62]

4.4.1 Use of "Guanxi" and Press Clubs

In China and other Asian countries, the cultural pattern of *guanxi* affects press relations. Publicists know they must establish and nurture personal contacts with journalists rather than depend on the inherent newsworthiness of a story that would make it acceptable for publication. In Japan, press clubs (*kisha kurabu*) mediate between a news source and the media. By the simplest definition, such clubs are reporters' offices in major government, political, business, and consumer organizations that allow those journalists nearly exclusive, early access to news and other information distributed by those organizations. To earn this privileged access to government and corporate information, approximately 160 media organizations pay dues to the Nihon Press Club, the corporation that governs membership to more than 800 press clubs throughout the country.[63]

Almost all press clubs have space allocated inside the buildings of the organizations to which they are attached. Each has two or three *kanji* (chairmen) who arrange members' attendance at press conferences, distribute press releases to members, and are virtually all-powerful during their time. Press clubs seek to create mutual understanding between organizations and media companies. Only Japanese reporters may be members. The system assures that no news outlet gets a "scoop." By reputation, press clubs are known as heavy-handed media gatekeepers. They have earned the label of Japan's "information cartel." Since its first edition in 1988, *Communicating: A Guide to PR in Japan* has been the only English-language publication that explores the way public relations is practiced in Japan.[64]

4.4.2 Unprofessional Practices

Press independence is threatened by unprofessional practices in some countries. For example, upon arriving in Athens, Greece, a public affairs manager of a large American company was asked for a donation (bribe) by the editor of a local newspaper in return for not publishing a damaging story. The manager refused, saying it would be a breach of the company's code of ethics. A negative story appeared the next day. This practice is called black journalism.

Bribes can also be used to have favorable stories published. In Mexico, so-called *chayotes* have been paid to reporters by government officials to have government propaganda printed. It appears that ". . . many of the 30 daily newspapers in this city (Mexico City) exist simply to line the pockets of publishers and columnists . . . . Susceptibility to bribes is high because journalists earn only between $300 and $1200 a month, averaging about $500. In exchange for writing a favorable story, they could receive an envelope stuffed with money. Offers might also include expensive gifts, drugs or prostitutes."[65] A similar practice was reported by the state-run news media in China explaining that journalists who worked for a business news website were under investigation in an underworld scheme to extort Chinese companies to pay in return for producing flattering articles or burying damaging ones.[66]

The British have asked, "What's the role of journalists who cross, and sometimes crisscross, the routes between political public relations and an independent press?" Some journalists who become special advisers to the government "will secretly write a speech for a favored politician and then praise that speech for its perception in the next day's leader columns."[67]

China has another form of corruption of the media: "reporters and editors are quietly selling their columns and broadcast slots to foreign and local merchandisers who are desperate for exposure beyond China's limited advertising opportunities."[68] Space is limited because most newspapers are authorized to print only four pages, about one quarter of which is devoted to advertising. Some reporters bill themselves as freelance publicity agents who can guarantee publication because news items about factory openings and new products are safe compared with lifestyle trends and social problems that might annoy government officials. Providing junkets is a pervasive practice of publicity seekers. Even when money is not outright accepted by journalists in China, they will accept invitations to golf, drinking, or parties; they may also ask for free tickets, invitations for trips, or restaurant certificates.[69]

4.4.3 Constraints on Press Freedom

Many governments restrict press freedom, but China and Russia get the most attention because of their size and power. World Press Freedom Day, introduced by the United Nations General Assembly in December 1993, is an occasion when Reporters Without Borders, which campaigns for media freedom around the world, ranks nations. In 2014, Finland topped the list of the countries with a free media, followed by the Scandinavian countries of Norway and Denmark. Countries with the least degree of press freedom were Eritrea with the worst, followed by North Korea, Turkmenistan, Syria, Iran, and China.

China curtails media freedom in various ways. With television, a simple but direct way is simply to cut off a show. This happened to Peter Ford, The *Christian Science Monitor's* correspondent in China and president of the Foreign Correspondents' Club of China, when he was a guest of CNN's "On China" talk show discussing press freedom in China. After only a few minutes the Chinese censors pulled the plug and the screen went black. Nobody in mainland China could then watch the program.[70]

A major media restriction is that a government and its leaders may not be attacked. For example, some two dozen *New York Times* and *Bloomberg News* reporters in China faced expulsion for reporting on the personal wealth and shady financial ties of top Chinese government officials and their families. Other rules that must be followed are to avoid mention of sensitive subjects, such as reference to Taiwanese or Tibetan independence, the Tiananmen events of 1989, and questions on the legitimacy of one-party rule. Sanctions against US and international journalists include expulsion, denial of visas (especially of newspapers like the *New York Times*), harassment, and detention.[71] Beijing harasses and obstructs its own Chinese reporters. An example is Gao Yu, a 71-year-old who has repeatedly challenged the Communist Party during a decades-long career. She was sentenced to 7 years in prison in 2015 after a court in Beijing found her guilty of leaking state secrets abroad.[72]

In 2014, the Chinese State Administration of Press, Publication, Radio, Film, and Television announced new rules on what the government has called "critical" news articles and barred

Chinese journalists from doing work outside their beats or regions. Reporters must now seek permission from their employers before undertaking "critical reports" and are barred from setting up their own websites.[73]

4.4.4 Singapore's Authoritarianism

Singapore is another example of how, in the extreme, press freedom is attacked or curtailed. At the fifth anniversary celebration of *Today*, a local English-language newspaper, Singapore Senior Minister Goh Chok Tong rebutted the view taken in the West that press freedom is a necessary ingredient of democracy. He said that press freedom does not always lead to a clean and efficient government or contribute to economic freedom and prosperity. He urged Singaporean editors and journalists to practice press freedom in a responsible way to serve national interests, as well as to inform, educate, and unite the people.[74]

The government of Singapore has used public relations to change people's behavior. An early campaign was "Keep Public Toilets Clean." More recent ones are aimed at getting along with others, such as a slogan of how to be a good subway passenger: "Arms-up Stacey and Move-in Martin." Singapore has made remarkable progress in its 50 years of independence from Malaysia, but at a cost, which is authoritarianism. It uses public relations for nation-building and achievement of social harmony, which arguably is needed in a country with a multi-racial/religious make-up.

Not surprisingly, Reporters Without Borders (RSF), which rates countries in its annual press freedom index, ranked Singapore 140th out of 167 countries in its 2005 report. In contrast Denmark, Finland, Iceland, Ireland, the Netherlands, Norway, and Switzerland received the most favorable ratings, while North Korea was at the bottom of the list.[75]

4.4.5 Insult Laws

A major offense to press freedom are so-called insult laws – called *desacato* in Latin America. Journalists are jailed if they "insult" or criticize public officials. The World Press Freedom Committee (WPFC) has been campaigning to eliminate these laws.[76] An example is Angola's case against Rafael Marques. He was charged with defaming the president by referring to the president of Angola as a "dictator" in an article published in the weekly *Agora*. Officers of the National Directorate of Criminal Investigation (DNIC) arrested Marques and detained him for 41 days. He was charged under the Law on Crimes Against State Security and faced a prison sentence of 2–8 years.[77] Thanks to the efforts of the WPFC, some countries are dropping *desacato* laws. In Chile, after more than 4 years of fighting alongside press freedom, the WPFC was able to celebrate the end of *desacato* laws in August 2005.[78]

4.4.6 Concentrated Media Ownership

Press freedom is endangered when media ownership and control is concentrated in either government or private business. In 2014, the Russian government restricted foreign-owned media when Parliament passed a bill restricting such ownership to 20%.[79] In Italy, when media impresario Berlusconi became prime minister of Italy in 2001 (to 2006), he owned or controlled all six of Italy's national television networks, amounting to 90% of the country's airwaves. "This gave him the 'raw might' to 'warp public opinion' by ignoring and distorting the truth or broadcasting outright lies." In 2001, "77.4% of Italians got their information from TV and only 6.4% from newspapers." He knew his audience: millions of voters with little better than a seventh-grade education who "knew little about politics and cared even less."[80]

4.5 Conclusions

Public relations is strongly identified with public opinion and publicity. Companies continue to value their corporate reputations and seek public relations help to shape public perceptions. They want to use public relations not only to influence public opinion toward them but also toward issues of importance to them. The mass media have traditionally been the main instrument to influence public opinion, and account for the importance of the publicity activities of public relations. Social media have diminished the importance of the mass media, but the latter remain a major instrument to reach the general public. Furthermore, as stated by Edward Downes, "they add important 'third party' credibility to a company's claims; and they have survived the tests of time as generally reliable sources of information."[81]

The study of public opinion is rooted in the psychology of perception and attitude change. This foundation applies to a product brand, company brand, and the nation brand. All recognize reputation as a valuable intangible asset.

International differences in media relations must be considered. For example, the hospitality of the mass media in many countries to publicity is not as generous as in the US. The reasons for this resistance vary from country to country, partly because it is seen as free advertising and partly because governments fear possible challenges to their authority. Many unprofessional practices exist in various countries that public relations people must learn about and deal with.

Discussion Questions

4.1. Does persuasion fundamentally describe the meaning of public relations? Discuss.

4.2. How did "muckraking" by newspapers in the turn of the century lead to the rise of public relations?

4.3. How does the public information model of public relations differ from the press agentry model?

4.4. Who are some of the early practitioners of public relations and what principles did they espouse?

4.5. What's the purpose of a public relations audit?

4.6. Why is the use of public opinion surveys essential to public relations? Name some surveys used in public relations?

4.7. What are some difficulties faced by public opinion researchers?

4.8. What are some of the main findings of the Edelman Trust Barometer?

4.9. What was the contribution to public relations of Edward L. Bernays?

4.10. Why is "putting a spin" on a story criticized?

4.11. How is Erving Goffman's thesis of impression management related to public relations?

4.12. What's the danger to a company that espouses a low media relations profile?

4.13. What is an advocacy ad? What is its purpose?

4.14. How do countries apply proactive public relations?

4.15. What are some mistakes made in US public diplomacy campaigns?

4.16. What are some media relations problems faced in the international arena?

4.17. Discuss some differences in how media relations is practiced in different countries.

4.A. Foreign Media Relations Guide

Business for Diplomatic Action, which supported US government public diplomacy, recognized the needs of foreign reporting by publishing a 20-page *Foreign Media Relations Guide*. BDA's founder and president, Keith Reinhard, said, "The way in which American-based multinational companies deal with the foreign media can have a tremendous impact not only on those companies' own images but on the reputation of America as a whole."[82] The guide serves as a useful review of publicity practices.

Michael Morley, a veteran of international public relations who spearheaded the project for BDA, summarizes what the job is: Three-quarters of the job is "Everything you practice on a daily basis with the U.S. media applies to the international media too: clear writing, respect for deadlines, facts not fluff, responsiveness, knowing what the publication and journalist are interested in and routinely cover . . . ." The final quarter is more difficult: "This involves understanding customs, cultures and media conventions in many nations and the ability to adapt your strategies, programs and materials to meet the needs of local media in multiple locations."[83]

The guide reviews some simple rules for interacting with editors and journalists working for the foreign media. The most obvious are remembering time differences, especially when dealing with time-sensitive materials, and being aware of language and cultural nuances. McDonald's applied this rule by allowing its franchisees to keep their strong local identity and allowing them and their vendors, managers, and employees, all of whom are locals, to act as its spokespeople.

Company logos, pictures, designs, and images should be reviewed for the different meanings they may have in foreign cultures. In Thailand, a promotional picture showing cute animals wearing sunglasses would run counter to Thai culture, which considers animals as a base form of life.

Many basics of media relations are contained in the guide's "Ten Golden Rules":

- Remember journalists have a demanding and often difficult job to do. Make their work easier.
- Return calls.
- Be accurate, clear, and concise.
- Brief the press when any major event occurs within your company.
- Listen to journalists and make your best effort to comply with their requests.
- Check announcements for clarity and cultural nuances; be sure to take different time zones into account.
- Make management accessible.
- Arrange regular visits to your offices, and R&D arbitrageurs and manufacturing facilities.

- Get to know the foreign press clubs.
- Build personal relationships with foreign editors and correspondents.

The guide offers this basic advice for corporations:

- The public relations team at a company's headquarters should maintain direct relationships with select media, particularly with (i) foreign correspondents in the US who cover the company's important markets around the world and (ii) editors and industry beat-reporters based in foreign markets.
- Members of these two groups should be invited on familiarization trips to the company's US facilities, receive tailor-made press releases, and be invited to meet the CEO and other senior members of management when the latter travel.
- The names and contact information should be consolidated in a database, which serves as a dynamic tool for managing relationships.

Finally, the guide lists 13 resources, such as the International Public Relations Association (IPRA); three media centers (Overseas Press Club of America, Foreign Press Association, and International Association of Press Clubs); some third parties that can provide help (Foreign Press Centers, US Embassies, Trade Association, and the United Nations); and six services that can measure success (Echo, Carma International, Delahaye, BIZ 360, Cymfony, and news distribution services, such as Bacon's or Medialink).

Endnotes

1 Krishnamurthy Sriramesh and Dejan Vercic, eds., "The Mass Media and Public Relations," in *The Global Public Relations Handbook, Revised and Expanded Edition: Theory, Research, and Practice* (New York: Routledge, 2009), p. 61.
2 My book, *Designs for Persuasive Communication* (Englewood Cliffs, NJ: Prentice-Hall, 1972).
3 Otto Lerbinger, *Designs for Persuasive Communication* (Englewood Cliffs, NJ, Prentice Hall, Inc., 1972), p. 3.
4 Harold Burson, *The Business of Persuasion*. (New York: Rosetta Books, 2017), p. 108.
5 See Loren Baritz, *The Servants Of Power: A History Of The Use Of Social Science In American Industry* (Middletown, CT: Wesleyan University Press, 1960 and 2011).
6 Vance Packard, *The Hidden Persuader* (New York: Pocket Books, 1957).
7 Dennis L.Wilcox, Philllip H. Ault, and Warren K. Agee, Public Relations: Strategies and Tactics, 3rd ed. (London, Harper Collins, 1992), p. 43.
8 James E. Grunig and Todd Hunt, *Managing Public Relations* (New York: Holt, Rinehart and Winston: 1984), p. 30.
9 George Griswald Jr., "How AT&T Public Relations Policies Developed," *Public Relations Quarterly*, Vol. 12, Fall 1967, p. 13.
10 Edward L. Bernays, *Crystallizing Public Opinion* (New York: Boni and Liveright, 1923); Walter Lippmann's 1922 book, *Public Opinion* (New York: Harcourt, Brace and Company, 1922).
11 From a 1961 brochure.
12 Theoretically, an attitude is "an implicit verbal response or 'answer' that an individual gives in response to a particular stimulus situation in which some general 'question' is raised." When the response is a verbal expression, it is called an opinion.
13 Ryan Knutson "Pollsters Forced to Rethink Methods," *WSJ*, October 28, 2016, p. B1.
14 Alexandra Bruell and Suzanne Vrancia, "Advertisers Search for Middle America," *WSJ*, November 21, 2016, p. A1.

15 Josh Zumbrun, "Economists Grapple with Public Disdain," *WSJ*, January 9, 2017, p. A2.
16 Tom Nichols, "How America Lost Faith in Expertise," *Foreign Affairs*, Vol. 96, March/April 2017, p. 61.
17 2015 Edelman Trust Barometer-Annual Global Survey, www.edelman.com/trust2015.
18 "Reputations Won and Lost," *WSJ*, May 10, 2017, p. 10.
19 Richard Edelman, "A Crisis of Trust," in "The World in 2016," *The Economist*, 2016, p. 90.
20 Donald A. Baer, "The West's Bruised Confidence in Capitalism," *WSJ*, September 22, 2014, p. A17.
21 Paul Tudor Jones, "Just Business," in "The World in 2016," *The Economist*, 2016, p. 46. Also see www://justcapital.com/research.
22 William Strunck and E.B. White, *Elements of Style* (Boston, MA: Allyn and Bacon, 1999). See newer editions.
23 See Rudolf Flesch, *How to Write Plain English* (University of Canterbury; archived from the original July 12, 2016; retrieved July 12, 2016).
24 James E. Grunig and Todd Hunt, *Managing Public Relations* (New York: Holt, Rinehart and Winston, 1984), p. 22. See James E. Grunig and Larissa A. Grunig, "Models of Public Relations and Communication," in James E. Grunig, ed. *Excellence in Public Relations and Communication Management* (Hillsdale, NJ: Lawrence Erlbaum Associates, Publishers, 1982), pp. 265–325.
25 William James, *Some Problems of Philosophy* (New York: Longmans, Green and Co., 1911), pp. 98–99.
26 Robert Leaf, *The Art of Perception: Memoirs of a Life in PR* (London: Atlantic Books, 2012).
27 Erving Goffman, *The Presentation of Self in Everyday Life* (New York: Random House, 1959).
28 As reported by my daughter Susan Gesten, who chauffeured a Mercedes for a client.
29 The author conducted research on this problem when working as a psychologist for Boston University's Air Force research center.
30 Finn, op. cit., p. 29.
31 David Finn, *The Way Forward: My First Fifty Years at Ruder–Finn* (New York: Millwood Publishing, 1998).
32 Ibid. p. 16.
33 Ibid., p. 158.
34 "Education: Propaganda Battle," *Time*, January 24, 1938.
35 Edward L. Bernays, *Biography of an Idea: Memoirs of PR Counsel Edward L. Bernays* (New York: Simon and Schuster, 1965).
36 Ibid., p. 387.
37 Ibid., pp. 386–387.
38 Bernays, op. cit., p. 400.
39 See Chapter 11.
40 Jim Macnamara, "The Continuing Convergence of Journalism and PR: New Insights for Ethical Practice from a Three-Country Study of Senior Practitioners," *Journalism and Mass Communication Quarterly*, Vol. 93, No. 1, Spring 2016, pp. 118, 122.
41 Described in Herb Schmertz with William Novak, *Good-Bye to the Low Profile: The Art of Creative Confrontation* (Boston, MA: Little, Brown, 1986).
42 M.E. McCombs and D.L. Shaw, "The Agenda-Setting Function of Mass Media," *Public Opinion Quarterly*, Vol. 36, No. 2. Also see their "The Evolution of Agenda-Setting Research: Twenty Five Years in the Marketplace of Ideas," *Communication Theory*, Vol. 43, No. 2.
43 Gordon Fairclough, "To See North Korea, Keep Your Eyes Peeled on the Official Press," *Wall Street Journal*, February 19, 2004, p. A1.
44 C.E. Osgood, G. Suci, and P. Tannenbaum, *The Measurement of Meaning* (Urbana, IL: University of Illinois Press, 1957). The semantic differential is a potentially valuable research tool internationally because its use of polar adjectives uses a minimum of language. It measures attitudes

toward people, issues, or things along three dimensions: good–bad, strong–weak, and active–passive. For example, surveys showed that Stalin received a low rating on good–bad, but a high rating on strong–weak.

45 R.F. Delaney, "Introduction," in A.S. Hoffman, ed., *International Communication and the New Diplomacy* (Bloomington, IN: Indiana University Press, 1968), p. 3.

46 Joseph Nye, *The Changing Nature of Power* (New York: Public Affairs, Perseus Books Group, 2004), p. 332.

47 Nancy Snow in "Public Diplomacy and Public Relations: Will the Twain Ever Meet?," in Guy J, Golan, Sung-Un Yang and Dennis F. Kinsey, eds. *International Public Relations and Public Diplomacy: Communication and Engagement* (New York: Peter Lang Publishers, 2015), p. 73.

48 Douglas Quenqua, "US Diplomacy Efforts – Can the Private Sector Lead Public Diplomacy Efforts?," *PR Week* (US), November 3, 2003, p. 7.

49 Dan Roberts and Gary Silverman, "Tarnished Image: Is the World Falling Out of Love with US Brands," *The Financial Times*, December 30, 2004, p. 9.

50 Gail Dutton, "Grassroots Diplomacy: How Corporations Can Change the Way People Think About America," *Across the Board*, May/June 2005, p. 29.

51 Ibid., p. 31.

52 Tom McCawley, "US Tsunami Aid Still Reaps Goodwill," *Christian Science Monitor*, February 28, 2006, p. 12.

53 Guy J. Golan and Sung-Un-Yang, "Introduction: The Integrated Public Diplomacy Perspective," in Guy J, Golan, Sung-Un Yang, and Dennis F. Kinsey, eds., op. cit., p. 2.

54 Gyorgy Szondi, "Public Diplomacy and Nation Branding: Conceptual Similarities and Differences," In V. Duthoit and E. Huijgh (eds.) Discussion Paper in Diplomacy, Netherlands Institute of International Relations, October 2008.

55 An excellent example is Witold Henisz, *Corporate Diplomacy: Building Reputations and Relationships with External Stakeholders* (Sheffield: Greenleaf Publishing, 2014).

56 E. Comor and H. Bean, "Americas 'Engagement' Delusion: Critiquing a Public Diplomacy Consensus," *International Communication Gazette*, Vol. 74, No. 3, 2012, pp. 203–220. Professional paper by Molly Meyer, "Public Diplomacy 2.0: Harnessing the Power of the Digital Age." A paper written for CM728, a graduate course in international public relations, at Boston University's College of Communication, May 2014.

57 As paraphrased by Juyan Zhang and Shahira Fahmy, "Live Tweeting at Work: The Use of Social Media in Public Diplomacy," in Golan, Yang, and Kinsey, op. cit., p. 318.

58 Nicholas J. Cull, "The Long Road to Public Diplomacy 2: The Internet in US Public Diplomacy," *International Studies Review*, Vol. 15, No. 1, pp. 123–139.

59 21st Century Statecraft, 2014. Retrieved from www.state.gov/statecraft/overview.

60 Carole M. Howard and Wima K. Matthews, *On Deadline: Managing Media Relations* (Long Grove, IL: Waveland Press, Inc., 2013).

61 Carole M. Howard, "Ten Strategies to Avoid Global Gaffes in Media Relations," *The Strategist*, Vol. 7, Issue 4, Fall 2001, pp. 34–37.

62 Minda Zetlin, "Massaging the Asian Image," *American Management Association*, Vol. 84 August 1995, pp. 20–24.

63 Japanese Newspaper Publishers and Editors Association.

64 Laurie A. Freeman, "Japan's Press Clubs as Information Cartels," Japan Policy Research Institute, Working Paper No. 18, April 1996.

65 Jenalia Moreno, "Change Presses on Newspapers; Corrupt Relationship with Government Likely to Be Reformed," *Houston Chronicle*, November 29, 2000, p. 1.

66 Chris Buckley, "Journalists Describe Extortion Scheme," *International New York Times*, September 12, 2014, p. 15.

67 Peter Preston, "Tainted Journalists: Power; Politics, Money Create Spin Doctors," IPI Report, First Quarter 2000, p. 3.

68 *FIND.

69 Cooper-Chen in Hugh M. Culbertson and Ni Chen, eds., *International PR: A Comparative Analysis* (Mahwah, NJ: Erlbaum, 1996), p. 235.

70 Peter Ford, "Censored in Beijing: A Correspondent Watches Himself Fade to Black," *The Christian Science Monitor*, February 20, 2014.

71 Mark C. Eades, "Protect U.S. Journalists in China; While Chinese Journalists Enjoy Press Freedom in U.S., Beijing Harasses and Obstructs Our Reporters," *USA Today*, December 18, 2013, p. 8A.

72 Chris Buckley, "Longtime Chinese Journalist Given 7-year Sentence," *International New York Times*, April 18, 2015, p. 3.

73 Michael Forsythe, "Chinese Government Tightens Constraints on Press Freedom," *NYT*, June 20, 2014, p. A7.

74 "Press Freedom Not Necessary for Democracy: SM Goh," Xinhua News Agency, October 31, 2005.

75 "Singapore Blasts RSF Press Freedom Ranking," Agence France Presse, October 24, 2005.

76 "Decriminalize Defamation Laws That Jail Journalists," Newsletter of the World Press Freedom Committee, May 28, 2004.

77 "Angola: Defamation Laws Silence Journalists," *Human Rights Watch*, August 12, 2013.

78 Newsletter of the World Press Freedom Committee, December 7, 2005, p. 3.

79 Paul Sonne, "Moscow Moves to Restrict Foreign-Owned Media," *WSJ*, September 27–28, 2014, p. A10.

80 Gail Edmondson, "Barbarian in the Palace," *Business Week*, July 3, 2006, p. 132. "Berlusconi's Improbable Return to Politics: Why Italy Is Giving Him Another Look," *Christian Science Monitor*, December 6, 2017.

81 Edward J. Downes, "Power, New Media and Today's Corporate Public Relations in Rossetta Gambetti and Stephen Quigley, eds., *Managing Corporate Communication: A Cross-Cultural Approach* (Basingstoke: Palgrave Macmillan, 2013). Gambetti Professionals," p. 217.

82 First Edition, Fall 2006, www.businessfordiplomaticaction.org.

83 "Business for Diplomatic Action Launches Foreign Media Relations Guide"; Guide Aims to Help Improve Relationships Between U.S. Corporations and the Foreign Media, Business Wire, November 13, 2006.

5

Public Affairs: Exercising Power in the Socio-Political Environment

The basic function of public affairs is to clarify and strengthen an organization's political power in order effectively to influence public policy and actions. It follows the definition by the Public Affairs Council in Washington, DC that public affairs is simply a concern by an organization for its socio-political environment. As applied to corporations, "the purpose of public affairs is to attain sufficient power to enable an organization to achieve preferred outcomes in the political arena and to forge and maintain a sociopolitical environment favorable to it."[1]

Organizational arrangements in companies reflect the rising importance of public affairs. An early development was that public affairs was no longer an activity assumed to be an unnamed part of public relations and recognized only as another "public" in a company's public relations or communications department. It was often named government relations, alongside investor relations, employee relations, and community relations.

Now public affairs professionals in the business sector typically work in corporate communication departments where they are given responsibility for several activities such as government relations, direct and grassroots lobbying, issues management, and media relations. There they interact with interest groups, media, and government. They also work for professional and trade associations where a growing number report directly to their organization's chief executive officer (CEO). "For many of these organizations," said Doug Pinkham, president of the Foundation for Public Affairs, "public affairs is their primary mission."[2]

Public affairs recognizes that corporations are not only economic but also political institutions. Companies cannot escape politics nor can they consistently pretend to be politically neutral. In the international arena, "geopolitics is back," states John Chipman in a *Harvard Business Review* article, "Companies today take direct control of their international images and reputations."[3] They must deal with national governments the world over, supranational organizations, and civil society organizations of all kinds, especially non-governmental organizations (NGOs) that challenge the policies and actions of corporations.

This chapter begins with the challenges arising from government and advocacy groups. In the US, public affairs started with government relations when regulations grew in number and significance in the 1960s and 1970s. When the civil society sector grew alongside and became active, attention was also directed at what was called the "third sector." Starting with the activity of government relations, negotiations and lobbying inevitably followed.

In Germany, Siemens AG, one of the country's major companies headquartered in Berlin, the public affairs function was recognized when it formed a department of corporate affairs and government affairs headed by Stephan Heimbach. A separate department combines corporate communications and corporate branding, headed by Michael Inacker, whose previous position was as assistant editor-in-chief and head of the Berlin office of the German newspaper *Handelsblatt*. Both Heimbach and Inacker are high-level corporate vice presidents who report to Siemens president and CEO Peter Löscher.[4]

Corporate Communication: An International and Management Perspective, First Edition. Otto Lerbinger.

5.1 Central Role of Government Relations

Government relations in the US was a public relations activity that initially focused on the federal government, especially in highly regulated industries such as utilities, petroleum, and chemical. Attention was gradually also given to the state level because, as noted by Wesley Pedersen of the Public Affairs Council, "the newly powerful decision-makers in our state capitals . . . have assumed many of the political and governmental prerogatives once jealously husbanded by legislators in Washington and by federal regulatory officials."[5] Furthermore, a company's news release originating in several states rather than headquarters could get attention. Internationally, the function of government relations is widely recognized, as the reference to Siemens exemplifies.

5.1.1 Government Relations in China

In China, government affairs has become a critical corporate function. When Harold Burson was asked what Burson-Marseller offices were doing in India and China, he said it was almost exclusively government relations.[6] China's economic and political characteristics account for this role. As described in Yi-Ru Regina Chen's study of how 25 multi-national corporations (MNCs) in China interacted with government, government relations is of top importance because of China's "intriguing environment," which consists of "a socialist market economy, an authoritarian political system, and a complex structure of governing."[7]

Because companies must conform to government laws and regulations, government is often an MNC's most important public. This need is highest for highly regulated industries in China such as energy and oil, express-shipping, aerospace, automotive, and telecommunication. The government determines what markets an MNC may enter and under what rules it must operate. Licensing is a requirement for entry, not only nationally but for each city in which an MNC operates, as well as entry into separate industry sectors such as hi-tech. Not surprisingly, therefore, 16 of the 25 MNCs in Chen's study include government affairs managers in strategic management.

Chen reports that the main objective of government affairs is to obtain "smoother relations," which is especially important in China's "high context" culture and the operation of *guanxi.* When meeting with a government official, a government affairs person must consider the official's "personal situation," meaning the status associated with his office. She states that government officials don't mind being asked why they have a certain policy. In the spirit of Dale Carnegie's *How to Win Friends and Influence People,* Chen said it is a good idea to give credit to officials by occasionally saying, "What a smart idea" – even if the idea was yours.[8] Eighty years after its publication, Carnegie's book remains on Amazon's top 100 best-selling books. As psychologist William James states in the book's early pages, "The deepest principle in human nature is the craving to be appreciated."[9]

Information about government policies has been made more available, thanks to the internet and the government's use of it. Chen states, "Almost every government department or institution has official websites containing important notices, as well as information of the latest issues, policies, or regulations in development."[10]

5.1.2 Cases of Intervention by Governments

Government has become increasingly intrusive in many areas of business. In Europe as a whole, the European Union (EU) has been intensifying antitrust actions and, in specific nation states such as Russia, the government exercises wide control over many of its state-operated enterprises and restricts the activities of the free market system. Three further examples from different parts of the world indicate the rise of government surveillance and regulation of business activities.

5.1.2.1 Novartis in Japan

Japanese regulators sought criminal charges against a unit of Novartis AG, seriously hurting the company's reputation in its second largest market and depressing sales of its best-selling drug.[11] The company is accused of breaking the law by releasing misleading advertising about its blood pressure drug Diovan. Its advertising referred to research findings that the Health Ministry described as altered to support the benefits of the drug. Moreover, research conducted by several Japanese universities was found to contain falsified results and an employee of Novartis was found to have participated in all of those studies without acknowledging his affiliation in published papers. The disclosure also hurt the Japanese medical community. Shinichiro Ueda, professor of clinical pharmacology at the Graduate School of Medicine at University of the Ryuyus in Okinawa, urged the medical community to raise the quality of its clinical research.

Novartis responded to authorities by saying it took the matter "extremely seriously" and would continue to give its full cooperation. It also cut the pay of its top executives for inadequately exercising internal controls. Novartis spokeswoman Yumi Ishi acknowledged, "Since last year, we've been saying in our news conferences that we need to regain any trust we've lost from the issue." But as stated by Iwao Kuwajima, chairman of the Japanese Organization of Clinical Research Evaluation and Review, "It's no easy matter for the company to regain trust."

5.1.2.2 Google's Regulatory Conflicts in Europe

Google is facing increasing tensions with European regulators and publishers. Legislators of the European Parliament are considering a proposal to "unbundle Internet search engines from other commercial services the websites might offer."[12] The importance of accurately assessing the political climate and gauging relationships with regulators is demonstrated by the possibility that Google may have made a strategic error by not arriving at a settlement with the EU's previous more friendly antitrust chief Joaquin Almunias. Google's policy was to avoid antitrust trouble through the mantra: Don't litigate, negotiate.[13] Three settlements were attempted in almost 4 years of negotiations. But the culmination was that in November 2014, the European Parliament passed a resolution calling on the EU's new competition chief Margrethe Vestager to consider a break-up of Google.[14]

Vestager is known to be tougher than her predecessor Joaquin Almunia, who criticized the EU for its "irrational" political response to the investigation. His view coincided with that of the US mission to the EU, which said, "It is important that the process of identifying competitive harms and potential remedies be based on objective and impartial findings and not be politicized."[15] Nevertheless, the efforts by Almunia to arrive at an agreement failed. Now Google faces Vestager, who stated that Google posed "questions about access to markets that are of vital interest to many players, big and small alike, and that have a significant impact on consumers."[16] Google's control over large amounts of data would be investigated, she said. Antoine Auberts, head of the company's public policy team in Brussels, said he was "concerned" about the clause that asks the EU to consider ways to "unbundle" internet search engines from their other commercial services.[17]

Google has also faced conflicts with European newspapers over the search giant's use of headlines and other content on its Google News site. The company has refused to pay publishers for the content and instead opted to forgo linking its contents to stories. Conceding that "we've made some mistakes along the way," Carlo D'Asaro Biondo, Google's president of strategic partnerships in Europe, explained that Google's "relationship with news" was misunderstood.[18]

In April 2015, Google said it would spend $164 million in Europe on grants for digital journalism experimentation. It would also work with European newspapers and journalism organizations to develop products and increase revenue. Biondo said, "Google has always wanted to be a friend and partner to the news industry."[19] Google had already created a €60 million fund in France in 2013, which included creating a new mobile product for the newspaper *Le Monde*. The initiative is bound to assist Google's public affairs efforts.

5.1.2.3 China Curbs Google

China has placed severe restrictions on the showing of Google's search results. Among the topics China deemed objectionable are Tibetan freedom, human rights, Tiananmen Square, Falun Gong (a Chinese spiritual practice), and homosexuality. In 2010, Google effectively pulled its services out of China after refusing to continue self-censoring its search results. Google had discovered a cyberattack from within the country that targeted it and dozens of other companies. It also found that the Gmail accounts of a number of Chinese human rights activists had been hacked. Google did not want to be in a situation in which the Chinese government might lead to their imprisonment.[20] These topics could still be accessed, however, through Google's uncensored search engine in Hong Kong. Had Google accepted China's censorship rules, Google would be complicit in China's conflict with human rights identified in both the United Nations Declaration of Human Rights and in the United Nations international Covenant on Civil and Political Rights.

Yet, says *The Guardian*, Google never really left, for another arm of the company, Google Analytics, the largest web analytics service in the world, has continued actively to operate in China. The service allows website operators to "analyse visitor traffic and paint a complete picture of [the] audience and their needs."[21] Although it is a free service, it gives Google vital knowledge about an individual's interests, allowing it to build digital dossiers on countless Chinese users. It can also be used toward some positive governance changes in China, for it can be used for a "scientific" study of online public opinion.

President Xi Jinping's rationale is to place freedom and order side by side in cyberspace, asserting that freedom is the purpose of order. He said, "We need to fully respect netizens' rights to express themselves, while at the same time, ensure a sound cyberspace in order to better protect the lawful rights and interests of all netizens."[22]

Google recognizes that China is too big a market for it to ignore, noting that Apple Inc., which complies with local laws, made $13.2 billion in the last quarter of 2014 in Greater China, making it its second-biggest market. As a sign of cooperating with China, Apple in April 2016 suspended its iBook and iTunes Movies services in China after talking with regulators who intensified their campaign to bring Web content in line with Beijing's stringent guidelines for traditional media.[23] As for Google, it realizes that it has basically lost all ground in most of its major services, especially search and video streaming, to Chinese players such as Internet giants Baidu, Tencent, Alibaba, and Qihoo 360. All have built their own products and services to replace or even surpass Google's offerings. Xiaomi, dubbed the "Apple of China," has launched its own app store and phones and plans to do so via Google Play, the app store for its Android mobile operating system.[24]

Google's CEO Sundar Pichai has made no secret of the fact that he wants to get back into China. He is seeking approval for a Chinese version of its Google Play app store and also hoping to get support for Android wearable devices. Google is reportedly working on a version of the Google Play app that will comply with Chinese strictures on speech. These include new rules that all US tech companies must uphold if they want to do business in China, including storing their data in China and, ominously, accepting supervision from all parts of society.[25] These new rules require firms to directly pledge their commitment to contentious policies that could require them to turn user data and intellectual property over to the government. American tech companies face the dilemma of wanting to take advantage of business opportunities in China before local rivals sew up the market but being aware of the Chinese government's sensitivities on issues like censorship and security.

Facebook is another company blocked by China's web filters from offering their core services in the country, which is the world's biggest internet market.[26] Mark Zuckerberg, Facebook's founder, is intent on entering China, even if it means abandoning some Western values. At a meeting with China's propaganda chief, Liu Yunshan, he praised China's internet progress and pledged to work with the government to create a better cyberspace. Knowing that Chinese leaders pay a lot of attention to personal relationships, he even asked President Xi Jinping to give his baby (his wife is Chinese) a Chinese name.[27]

Prior to his meeting with President Obama in 2015, President Xi attended a tech conference at the Microsoft campus near Seattle co-hosted by Microsoft. With Apple selling $13.2 billion worth of iPhones in China last quarter, and Alibaba raising nearly twice that on the New York Stock Exchange, it's no wonder Chinese officials wanted to showcase technology as a bright spot of cooperation during President Xi's visit to the US. It was a forum of tech titans from both countries, including Lu Wei, China's internet czar, who oversees China's restrictions on foreign technology companies. The discussion almost certainly will paper over the uncomfortable fact that Chinese government censorship is costing US tech companies billions of dollars in revenue – and the "Great Firewall" isn't likely to come down soon.[28]

At stake is how the global internet will be managed. The US supports a policy whereby the internet is allowed to operate worldwide and users are given free online expression. China, however, believes countries should be allowed to force Web companies to follow local laws, which includes censoring content, monitoring users, and hosting data about Chinese users within China. Furthermore, Chinese policies have emerged in the past 2 years that are meant to wean the country off foreign technology.[29]

5.1.2.4 Taiwan's Beef Imports from the US

A country's food imports are a sensitive matter, mainly because of safety concerns. Such imports had become controversial since 2003 when mad cow disease in Europe and the US raised concerns about the risks of imported beef. Although rules were relaxed in Taiwan in 2006 to allow the imports of US beef from cattle less than 30 months old, a new "hot issue" arose in 2012 over the importation of beef containing the growth additive ractopanine.[30] US beef exporters faced the public affairs challenge of convincing Taiwan's legislators to pass a bill that would lift a ban on US beef imports.

Taiwan farmers and civic groups protested over the food additive. The *Economist* reported that demonstrators marched on America's informal embassy wearing Uncle Sam hats and leering cow masks. Opposition lawmakers chanted slogans and occupied the speaker's podium in Parliament, disrupting the opening session, and delaying the prime minister's inaugural speech. "These are all episodes in a growing row over meat imports into Taiwan that is pitting America, the island's most important ally, against the vast mass of public opinion – and forcing the government of President Ma Ying-jeou to manoeuvre frantically between the two."[31]

In cases such as this, governments and the trading partners must engage in careful public affairs analysis. In Taiwan, researchers examined the variable of trust in government and found that the public based it on its integrity, dependability, and competence. Furthermore, the analysis showed that government officials were perceived more favorably when they served as risk managers rather than technical authorities. Even after providing extensive scientific evidence and proposing such government initiatives as an inspection mechanism and labeling system, the Taiwanese government could not effectively decrease the active public's concern about US beef safety. The source of resistance was apparently more related to people's party identification and personal consumption habits. For example, people who recognized food containing trans fats were most likely to become active communicators.

The Taiwanese president Ma Ying-jeou was caught in the middle. He couldn't afford to offend the majority of the island's citizens, for a poll in mid-February found that 71% supported the ban even if relations with America were harmed. He wanted to get Taiwan into a position to join the Trans-Pacific Partnership (TPP), so it was important to resume trade talks with the US to become a member of the US-led TPP, which has been stalled since 2007. A government statement argued that if the US didn't see Taiwan as a trusted trading partner, it would affect the support for Taiwan to join regional trade groups and hurt its global competitiveness.[32] The president's solution was to propose a panel to solicit technical advice on the health risks and the feasibility of lifting the ban. Public resistance to the government's decision led to a compromise: imports would be resumed but only under certain conditions. Imports were resumed in 2012. Despite these concerns, in 2017 the US withdrew from TPP.

5.2 Government Litigation

In addition to regulation, MNCs must recognize that litigation has become a major way that government has become an active participant in many areas of business. In the US, the government's intention is twofold: to redress harm and to create a disincentive for bad behavior. For example, if a corporate action harms investors because false accounting causes a drop in a company's share price, a government fine might compensate investors and add pressure to improve accounting practices.[33]

Litigation by government has increased to a point where *The Economist* calls it "The Criminalisation of American Business."[34] The US's regulatory system has imposed enormous fines on some large companies, including the following foreign ones:

- In 2014, Bank of America, $17 billion.
- The JP Morgan Chase settlement, $13 billion.
- Goldman Sachs settlement, $1.2 billion.
- BNP Paribas, $9 billion, over breaches of American sanctions against Sudan and Iran.
- BP, $13 billion, over the Deepwater Horizon oil spill.
- Toyota, $1.2 billion settlement, over alleged faults on some cars.

The above actions have resulted in a changed relationship between companies and government, and raise the question of whether the government should play "a direct role in rehabilitating companies by changing the way that corporations are managed."[35] Federal prosecutors essentially help reshape the policies and culture of entire institutions.

Companies in the US are vulnerable to litigation because the Supreme Court in the historic case of New York Central and Hudson River Railroad established three principles: (i) that a company need not have any evil intention to be guilty; (ii) that it is responsible for the actions of its employees; and (iii) that it can be prosecuted as if it were a person – all in the interest of public policy.[36] To avoid long, expensive, and embarrassing trials that would damage their reputations, many companies seek rapid, discreet settlements. Financial companies are especially vulnerable, for an indictment is often lethal. For example, soon after being charged, several banks lost their independence: E.F. Hutton (1987), Drexel Burnham (1990), Riggs National Bank (2005), and Bankers Trust (1999).

The Economist sees three factors that will affect the relationship between business and government: (i) popular anger stemming from the 2007–2008 financial crisis; (ii) growth of the internet and the uncertainties caused by such instant communication systems as Twitter; and

(iii) the continuing impact of globalization.[37] The danger is not only more government interference in company affairs but the uncertainty and unpredictability of the political scene. What business needs most of all is consistency in government regulations and taxes to enable companies to formulate their business plans. Fortunately, leaders on both sides increasingly realize the futility of antagonistic relations. "Governments rely on businesses to drive economic growth, create jobs, and generate the exports to ensure that their countries can pay their way in the world."[38]

5.3 The Term "Corporate Diplomacy" Grows

Because of the prominence of MNCs in the international arena, it was inevitable that the term "corporate diplomacy" would be invented. It appeared in 1995 as the title of a 51-page report called *Corporate Diplomacy Principled Leadership for the Global Community*.[39] The report examines ways in which corporations can play a more proactive role in community building. This includes what role corporations can assume in filling the leadership gap at the local, national, and international levels, given cross-order economic, cultural, technological, and information transactions that have made the task of governing more difficult.

The term "corporate diplomacy" again appeared in Ulrich Steger's 2003 book *Corporate Diplomacy: The Strategy for a Volatile, Fragmented Business Environment*.[40] Using a broad framework, Steger explains what managers can do to manage the business environment when facing such challenging situations as confrontations with activist groups, government regulations, environmental disputes, and human right issues. His solutions include issues management and crisis management, and employ the framework of business and society. These are subjects that have been standard content in the literature of corporate public affairs and business–society relations, and addressed by the Public Affairs Council.

Using numerous cases and empirical studies, Steger describes the non-market forces that receive a growing share of corporate attention. He notes that companies are increasingly intertwined with their surrounding society, even though markets are their dominant concern. In order to "care for the common good" they must deal with interests, institutions, ideas, and rules that lie outside the market domain, which is the role of corporate diplomacy. Accordingly, after quoting the *Oxford English Dictionary* definition of diplomacy as the "art of, skill in dealing with people so that business is done smoothly," he explains corporate diplomacy as "an attempt to manage systematically and professionally the business environment in such a way as to ensure that business is done smoothly." These explanations of corporate diplomacy reinforce its meaning in the application of public affairs, marketing, public relations, and communication with the larger business environment.

The most recent book on the topic is Witold Henisz's *Corporate Diplomacy: Building Reputations and Relationships with External Stakeholders*.[41] The scope is broad, encompassing topics in both public affairs and public relations. He focuses on "stakeholder-facing functions" under which he includes governmental affairs, stakeholder relations, sustainability, enterprise risk management, community relations, and corporate communications. Through such integration, he states, the place where business, politics, and society collide need not be a source of nasty surprises or unexpected expenses. Instead, by elevating corporate diplomacy to the executive level, and applying sophisticated management tools, multi-national firms can create value for shareholders and society. He states that this approach is steeped in an understanding of human behavior and the cultivation of personal relationships. Instead of sparring with each other, players in the international arena learn to deal with one another to arrive at mutually agreeable arrangements.

These descriptions of corporate diplomacy demonstrate that it is derived from the field of international relations (IR). As described in *The Princeton Review*, IR focuses on relationships among countries, governments, peoples, and organizations all around the world.[42] It covers a wide range of global issues, including war, poverty, disease, diplomacy, democracy, trade, economics, and globalization. IR is a multi-disciplinary major that draws from politics, history, economics, law, sociology, psychology, philosophy, ethics, and geography. IR requires dealing with foreign cultures, languages, worldviews, and values. The study of foreign languages is a necessity, as is a sense of empathy, compassion, and goodwill. Many of these aspects of IR are reflected in corporate diplomacy and in this book.[43]

5.4 Tools of Public Affairs

Government relations is the main activity of public affairs. It is supplemented by negotiations among players and lobbying activities aimed at legislative bodies and executive departments.

5.4.1 Negotiations

Negotiations inevitably occur in relationships to settle on the terms of an agreement and to resolve disagreements. Both sides realize that their common interests are greater than their differences and that each needs something that the other has or controls. The purpose of negotiations should never be "to win" but to solve problems. Both sides should focus on their long-term relationship, just as negotiators in labor collective bargaining know that they will have to live together on a daily basis after they sign the agreement. Establishing trust is part of this long-term goal.

These understandings are associated with the Japanese. They see negotiation "not an end in itself to be treated in isolation, but simply one episode in an ongoing relationship."[44] Their cultural emphasis on group orientation reflects Confucian philosophy. In contrast, Americans exhibit the norm of individualism, which makes them task oriented. Finns are even more so, for they begin business right away, without small talk; they use objective facts, rather than subjective feelings.[45] As stated in the widely read book by Roger Fisher and William Ury, *Getting to Yes*, negotiations describe the "back-and-forth communication designed to reach an agreement" efficiently and amicably. It combines the American traits of rationality and pragmatism.[46]

In China, negotiations are quite complex, requiring an understanding of Chinese culture. The Swedish firm Ericsson discovered this in the early and mid-1990s. A key cultural component was Confucianism, which stresses the need to achieve harmony in society through moral conduct in all kinds of relationships. Chinese negotiators are seen as "Confucian gentlemen" who look more for long-term working relationships to solve problems that might occur rather than a one-off legal deal. They assert the superiority of using human wisdom rather than engaging in pitched battles to conquer the opponent. The negotiation process starts with early contacts with the Chinese government authorities and by showing keen interest in getting to know the other party during these initial contacts. Chinese negotiators believe in building trust rather than signing a contract quickly. Patience is therefore the most important qualification for successful negotiators.[47]

When the cultures of the negotiating parties differ widely, semantical problems arise. The meaning of words becomes difficult because with different backgrounds both parties assign a different meaning to whatever subject is discussed. Even the fundamental concept of achieving compromise is questioned in some societies. Persian culture, for example assigns a negative meaning, as reflected in the statement "our integrity was compromised."[48] When cultures vary widely, negotiations have to be carefully prepared for they take longer and include discussions about such details as seating arrangements that recognize the social status of the participants.

5.4.2 Lobbying

In the US the right of people peaceably to assemble and "to petition the Government for a redress of grievances" is guaranteed by the First Amendment of the Constitution. Lobbying refers to contacting lawmakers, but with the growth in regulations, government officials are also targeted. When contact is on a one-on-one basis, lobbying is called direct. It is mostly conducted in an organized fashion by professional lobbyists from law offices, public relations and public affairs consultancies, trade associations, and by corporations and other interests themselves. Another kind of lobbying is indirect or grassroots, which happens when constituents – "the folks back home" – tell a legislator what is on their minds. When grassroots lobbying is organized, it consists of three essential steps: (i) constituency building; (ii) constituency communication; and (iii) constituency activation. Considerable skill is needed to accomplish each step.[49]

5.4.2.1 PAC Contributions by Foreign Companies

Providing candidates and political parties with money is the most important corporate and business electoral activity. Money helps get the "right people" elected and adds clout to lobbying efforts. As Justin Dart, CEO of Dart Industries, said, "With a little money they hear you just a little better."[50] The same applies to lobbying in the US by foreign companies. In the entire 2000 election cycle, foreign-connected political action committees (PACs) raised just over $7 million; in 2008, the total shot up to $15 million. In an early point in the 2012 elections, over $5 million was raised, continuing a trend of increasing contributions from US subsidiaries of foreign interests.

The issue of the legality of such PAC contributions to members of Congress has been debated. These contributions are considered perfectly legal as long as American employees run the PAC and arrange for the contribution of money, and as long as the PAC remains unfinanced by the foreign parent corporation.[51] Thus, the American subsidiaries of UBS, the Swiss financial services company, headquartered in Zurich and Basel, Switzerland, are free to run a PAC to raise money for federal campaigns. Named UBS Americas, it was among Mitt Romney's top 20 donors in the 2012 election cycle, with contributions reaching almost $75 000. Other foreign companies that have raised PAC contributions are Credit Suisse, also headquartered in Zurich, whose US subsidiaries raised over $200 000, and Barclays, headquartered in London, whose US subsidiaries raised over $150 000.[52]

5.4.2.2 Tolerance for Lobbying Varies Among Nations

Countries vary in their tolerance for lobbying by interest groups and the manner in which it is practiced. In the Netherlands, lobbying is highly prevalent because it has thousands of foundations and associations representing a variety of interests. Lobbying is encouraged insofar that groups enjoy a semi-official status because by law the executive branch must consult the big "interest organizations" before drafting legislation. In Norway, lobbying is open and informal. Many companies meet regularly and informally with politicians and civil servants. In Asia, Japan has some powerful pressure groups that can block legislation. Lobbying in China is complex because of the lack of democracy. Lobbyists often don't hear about a law until it has already been enacted, but day-to-day government relations are a partial substitute.[53]

Lobbying in the EU has become a major industry, with participants from a wide variety of interest groups, but with business groups dominating. The EU now surpasses the US in terms of the number of registered organizations lobbying its institutions, says Transparency International.[54] The Corporate Europe Observatory, an NGO, estimates that Brussels has at least 30 000 lobbyists, which is almost the same number as the staff of the European Commission.[55] Their targets are the Parliament, the Commission, which is the executive arm of the EU, and occasionally the Court of First Instance. R.H. Pedler's book, *European Union Lobbying* includes cases that describe the role played by various players and the factors that led to success.[56]

5.4.2.3 Russian Firms and Government Hire Lobbyists

After Russia annexed Crimea in 2014 and lent support to separatists in the Ukraine, the Obama administration retaliated by imposing sanctions on selected Russian firms and leaders with close connections to President Vladimir Putin. The US Senate subsequently considered a bill to broaden the sanctions. This development caused several affected Russian companies to hire US lobbyists to fight the Senate bill. Novatek, Russia's second-biggest natural gas producer, made payments to the Washington lobbying and public relations firm Qorvis MSL Group, which is part of Publicis Groupe SA. Novatek is 23% owned by Russian oligarch Gennady Timchenko, who is closely related to Putin. Two other companies, Gazprombank and Russia Direct Investment Fund, also hired lobbyists.[57]

In 2006, executives from the public relations firm Ketchum, a division of the advertising and marketing giant Omnicom, flew to Moscow to secure an account that has since been worth tens of millions of dollars.[58] President Vladimir V. Putin of Russia had hired Ketchum to provide advice on public relations before the nation hosted the Group of eight meeting in St. Petersburg. It helped Putin be selected as *Time* magazine's "Person of the Year" in 2007. At the time, Putin "cared a great deal about what other leaders, especially presidents, thought about him," said Michael A. McFaul, a former United States ambassador to Russia who now teaches at Stanford. "There has been a sharp turn in how much they care anymore," Mr. McFaul said. "They decided, O.K., we've had enough of these guys, let's not worry so much about our reputation."[59]

Ketchum now finds itself walking an increasingly fine line. It once had three dozen employees in at least six countries working with the Russia account. Now it has cut back to about 10 employees, said Kathy Jeavons, a Ketchum partner in Washington who heads the Russia account, and cited the difficulties of the "global environment." Its deal to represent Russia's giant government-controlled energy company Gazprom recently ended because, she said, Gazprom had decided to focus on Europe.

Ketchum is far from alone in representing foreign governments and their leaders. In 2011, the Washington public relations firm Brown Lloyd James helped arrange a profile in *Vogue* of Asma al-Assad, the wife of Syria's president, Bashar al-Assad. The story, headlined "A Rose in the Desert," was later removed from *Vogue's* website and the magazine's editor, Anna Wintour, issued a statement deploring the actions of the Assad government.

It is well known that American political influence is a commodity for sale to foreign companies. The arsenal of lobbyists primarily includes lawyers and public relations professionals but also political and economic analysts, and management consultants. Their clout and fees increase when they are former congressmen, White House officials, or cabinet members. When they accept a foreign client, these lobbyists must register with the Attorney General to comply with the Foreign Agents Registration Act of 1938.[60]

5.4.2.4 Case: Export–Import Bank

The fight over reauthorization of the Export–Import Bank illustrates the activities of some interest groups. The bank was established by executive order in 1934 to facilitate and finance US international trade.[61] The bank's activities consist of the issuance of long-term capital loans, the offering of guarantees, and the provision of insurance against risk. In 2013, the bank authorized $27 billion to support an estimated $37.4 billion in US export sales.[62]

The 80-year-old agency's charter, which expires September 30, 2014, has pitted business groups against some conservative groups, notably the Heritage Action for America and Club for Growth, which argue that the bank's actions amount to corporate welfare and disrupt the free market. They see it as part of the larger struggle over government's role in helping US business. Benefited the most, says the opposition, are the richest and most politically connected companies. Several groups, such as Generation Opportunity aimed at younger voters, have used the social media to target the bank. It included a cartoon video titled "The Kronies: Laughing All the Way To The Export-Import Bank" that received more than 200 000 views in 3 weeks on YouTube. In response to this threat, supporters of reauthorization have intensified lobbying. The supporters include such corporations as Boeing Co. and General Electric Co., and business groups such as the US Chamber of Commerce and National Association of Manufacturers.

Supporters of the bank illustrate the use of several well-known lobbying techniques. For one, lawmakers are given a personalized index card laying out exactly which companies in their districts benefit from the bank and how many people they employ. Knowing that many lawmakers don't realize that businesses in their district use the bank, they bring in big names such as former House Majority Leader Dick Gephardt, a Democrat, and former Mississippi Governor Haley Barbour, a Republican. Backers of the bill schedule factory tours and one-on-one meetings between business owners who benefit and their elected representatives.

Some businesses encourage their workers to get involved. One company, General Electric (GE) Power and Water, asked workers to consider visiting a website to generate a letter to their representatives in Congress. The parent company GE went a step further by announcing that it planned to begin moving US jobs abroad.[63] It said they are bidding on $11 billion in industrial projects, mostly in developing nations, that require export credit agency sponsorship for customers. Boeing, another lobbyist for the bank's renewal, said a roughly $85 million satellite contract order was in jeopardy.

5.5 Conclusions

Public affairs is a communication practice concerned with an organization's political power relative to government and civil society institutions. MNCs must deal with governments in all the countries and communities where they do business as well as such supranational bodies as the EU. As John Chapman states in an article, "Why Your Company Needs a Foreign Policy," "the most successful MNCs will be those that make experience in international affairs central to their operations."[64] The basic objective of public affairs can be viewed as obtaining and retaining support for a company's license to operate. Although companies generally comply with efforts to protect the environment and abide by other societal goals, they also hope to retain maximum autonomy.

Public affairs consists of government relations, negotiations, and lobbying. Each of these activities is thoroughly discussed in specialized literature, but this chapter introduces the fundamentals of each and how they are affected by differences in a nation's political systems and cultural patterns. Knowledge of political institutions and "politics" is extremely helpful and serves as a reminder that corporate success depends not only on marketplace strength but also political shrewdness. Mixing business with politics is the broad theme of this chapter. A study shows that when this is done, businesses generally receive handsome returns even though there are some risks.[65]

Discussion Questions

5.1. How would you describe the function of public affairs? What forces in society convinced corporations to engage in public affairs?

5.2. Why is government relations of top importance to corporations doing business in China?

5.3. What kinds of regulatory problems have Google and Apple encountered in China? How have they complied?

5.4. What regulatory problems has Google faced in Europe? How has it managed these problems?

5.5. What did the public affairs analysis of Taiwan's restriction on US beef imports show?

5.6. What is the public affairs significance of government litigation of corporations?

5.7. What is the similarity between public affairs and "corporate diplomacy"?

5.8. The purpose of negotiations is to win agreement for your terms? Do you agree? Discuss.

5.9. How do Japanese and Americans differ in their view of negotiations?

5.10. How does Confucianism affect negotiations in China?

5.11. Are foreign companies allowed to make PAC contributions in the US? Discuss.

5.12. What are two kinds of lobbying and how do they differ?

5.13. What are some differences in the tolerance for lobbying in different nations?

5.14. What is the purpose of the Export–Import Bank? If you were advising GE, would you favor its extension? Why or why not?

Endnotes

1 Otto Lerbinger, *Corporate Public Affairs: Interacting With Interest Groups, Media, and Government* (Mahwah, NJ: Lawrence Erlbaum Associates, 2006), p. 5.
2 "Association Compensation Survey: More Public Affairs Professionals Report to CEOs, as Salaries, Benefits and Bonuses Increase," *Impact*, Public Affairs Council, February 2008, pp. 1 and 3.
3 John Chipman, "Why Your Company Needs a Foreign Policy," *Harvard Business Review*, September 2016, Vol 94, No. 9, pp. 36ff.
4 Siemens AG new release, June 27, 2013.
5 Wesley Pederson, ed., *Leveraging State Government Relations: How to Win in Today's Most Critical Public Policy Arenas* (Washington, DC: Public Affairs Council, 1990), p. ix.
6 Personal conversation.
7 Yi-Ru Regina Chen, "The Strategic Management of Governmental Affairs in China: How Multinational Corporations in China Interact with the Chinese Government," *Journal of PR Research*, Vol. 19, No. 3, 2007, p. 284. See her book, *The Business of Corporate Affairs in China: Corporate Competitive Advantage in China's Marketization* (Saarbruecken, Germany: Akademiker Verlag, 2008). Also personal conversation.
8 Dale Carnegie, *How to Win Friends and Influence People* (New York: Simon and Schuster, 1936).

9 Jerry Cliancidlo, "Still Winning Friends and Influencing People," *WSJ*, July 23–24, 2016, p. A13; Carnegie, ibid., p. 31.
10 Chen, op. cit., p. 298.
11 Kana Inagaki and Alexander Martin, "Japan Probe Ratchets Up Pressure on Novartis," *WSJ*, January 10, 2014, p. B4.
12 "EU Says Google Risks Facing Formal Antitrust Charges," *WSJ*, September 14, 2014, p. B4; "Google, the EU and Antitrust," *The Economist*, February 8, 2014, p. 63.
13 Vanessa Mock, Sam Schechner, and Rolfe Winkler, "Aggressively Agreeable Google Cuts Antitrust Deal," *WSJ*, February 6, 2014, p. A1.
14 Tom Fairless and Stephen Fidler, "EU Antitrust Boss Readies Gazprom Other Decisions," *WSJ*, February 19, 2015, p. B4.
15 Foo Yun Chee, "United States says EU's Google case should not be politicized," Reuters. https://www.reuters.com/article/us-google-eu/united-states-says-eus-google-case-should-not-be-politicized-idUSKCN0J91NB20141125.
16 Tom Fairless, "U.S. Cautions EU Over Google Antitrust Probe," *WSJ*, November 26, 2014, p. B4.
17 Ibid.
18 Lisa Fleisher, "Google to Offer Journalism Grants in Europe," *WSJ*, April 28, 2015.
19 Ibid.
20 Issue is discussed by George G. Brenkert, "Google, Human Rights, and Moral Compromise," *Journal of Business Ethics*, Vol. 85, 2009, pp. 453–478.
21 Maria Repnikova and Timothy Libert, "Google is Returning to China? It Never Really Left," *The Guardian*, September 21, 2015.
22 "In Rare Interview, Xi Discusses Ties with the U.S.," WSJ, September 22, 2015, p. A11.
23 Eva Dou and Daisuke Wakabayashi, "China Deals Apple a Rare Setback," *WSJ*, April 23–24, 2016, p. B3.
24 "Google Won't Have Easy Ride Back Into China," *The Express Tribune*, September 10, 2015.
25 Rolfe Winkler, Alister Barr, and Waye Ma, "Google Looks to Get Back Into China," *WSJ*, November 20, 2014.
26 Paul Mozur, Nick Wingfield, and Neil Gough, "China Seeks Compliance Pledges from U.S. Tech Companies," *NYT*, September 18, 2015, p. 1.
27 Emily Parker, "Mark Zuckerberg's Long March in China," *MIT Technology Review*, Vol. 119, November/December 2016, pp. 100–103.
28 Julie Makinen, "Walled Off: China's Censorship Is Shutting Out Many U.S. Tech Giants and Costing Them Billions in Revenue," *Los Angeles Times*, September 22, 2015, p. 1.
29 Paul Mozur and Jane Perlez, "China Flexes Tech Muscles Before State Visit to U.S.; Meeting to Be Attended by Industry Leaders Said to Rankle White House," *International New York Times*, September 10, 2015, p. 16.
30 "Two Communication Scholars Win Best Faculty Paper Award from International Communication Association," *Accomplishments*, Hong Kong Baptist University, School of Communication, May 15, 2014.
31 "Gored: Taiwan, America and Meat Wars," *The Economist*, March 8, 2012.
32 Janet Ong, "Taiwan Farmers Protest Plan on Beef Imports with Ractopamine," *Bloomberg*, March 8, 2012.
33 "A Mammoth Guilt Trip," *The Economist*, August 30, 2014, p. 24.
34 "The Criminalisation of American Business," *The Economist*, August 30, 2014, p. 9.
35 Brandon L. Garrett, *Too Big to Jail: How Prosecutors Compromise with Corporations* (copyright by author, 2014), p. 24.
36 Ibid., p. 22.
37 "A World of Robber Barons," Special Report: Companies and the State, February 22, 2014, p. 15.

38 Ibid., p. 4.
39 According to Sarabdeep K. Kochhar and Juan-Carlos Molleda, the concept of corporate diplomacy was originally suggested in 1966 by Christian A. Herter, the former general manager of the Government Relations Department at Socony Mobil Oil Company. See "The Evolving Links between International Public Relations and Corporate Diplomacy," in Golan, Guy J, Sung-Un Yang, and Dennis F. Kinsey, eds. *International Public Relations and Public Diplomacy: Communication and Engagement* (New York: Peter Lang Publishers, 2015), p. 56.
40 Ulrich Steger, *Corporate Diplomacy: The Strategy for a Volatile, Fragmented Business Environment* (Chichester: John Wiley & Sons, 2003).
41 Witold Henisz, *Corporate Diplomacy: Building Reputations and Relationships with External Stakeholders* (Sheffield: Greenleaf Publishing, 2014).
42 *Princeton Review.*
43 Ibid. p. 54.
44 Frank R. Pfetsch, *Negotiating Political Conflicts* (New York: Palgrave Macmillan, 2007), p. 37.
45 [44] Lynn E. Metcalf, Allan Bird, Mahesh Shankarmahesh, Zeynep Aycanc, Jorma Larimod, and Dídimo Dewar Valdelamar, "Cultural Tendencies in Negotiation: A Comparison of Finland, India, Mexico, Turkey, and the United States," *Journal of World Business*, Vol. 41, 2006, p. 383.
46 Roger Fisher and William Ury, *Getting to Yes* (Boston, MA: Houghton Mifflin, 1981).
47 Pervez Ghauri and Tony Fang, "Negotiating with the Chinese: A Socio-Cultural Analysis," *Journal of World Business*, Vol. 36, No. 3, Fall 2001, pp. 303–325.
48 See Raymond Cohen, *Negotiating across Cultures: International Communication in an Interdependent World*, rev. edition (Washington, DC: United States Institute of Peace Press, 1997), p. 35.
49 See Otto Lerbinger, *Corporate Public Affairs: Interacting With Interest Groups, Media, and Government.* (Mahwah, NJ: Lawrence Erlbaum Associates, Publishers, 2006), 253–269. A major study was Wesley Pedersen, *Winning at the Grassroots* (Washington, DC: Public Affairs Council, 1989).
50 Mentioned in David Cohen, "PAC Power: An Abuse of Power," in *Political Action for Business: The PAC Handbook*, ed. Ken Clair (Washington, DC: Fraser/Associates, 1981), p. 313.
51 Stephen Reader, "Explainer: Can Foreign Companies Make Political Donations?" *WNYC*, Friday, January 20, 2012.
52 "Explainer: Can Foreign Companies Make Political Contributions?" *It's a Free Country*, January 20, 2016. https://www.wnyc.org/story/181667-explainer-can-foreign-companies-make-political-donations.
53 "The Gentle Art of Lobbying in China," *The Economist*, February 17, 2001.
54 Natalia Drozdiak, "Apple Shies Away From Lobbyists in EU Tax Fight," *WSJ*, September 26, 1016, p. B1.
55 "The Rise of the Superstars," *The Economist*, September 17, 2016, p. 14.
56 R.H. Pedler, ed., *European Union Lobbying: Changes in the Arena* (Basingstoke: Palgrave Macmillan, 2002), p. 249.
57 Philip Shishkin, "Russian Firms Hire Lobbyists to Fight Senate Sanctions," *WSJ*, December 1, 2014, p. A4.
58 Ravi Somaiya, "P.R. Firm for Putin's Russia Now Walking a Fine Line," *New York Times*, August 31, 2014,
59 Ibid.
60 The Foreign Agents Registration Act (FARA) is a law passed in 1938 and amended in 1966 requiring that agents representing the interests of foreign powers in a "political or quasi-political capacity" disclose their relationship with the foreign government and information about related activities and finances. http://en.wikipedia.org/w/index.php?

title=Foreign_Agents_Registration_Act&action=edit. The Justice Department reported there were approximately 1700 lobbyists representing more than 100 countries before Congress, the White House, and the federal government as of 2007.

61 Albert H. Hamilton, "The Export-Import Bank," *Financing International Operations*, p. 74.

62 Michael R. Crittenden, "Political Battle Over Export Bank Heats Up," *WSJ*, July 7, 2014, p. A1.

63 Nick Timiraos, "GE Move Rekindles Partisan Bank Fight," *WSJ*, September 16, 2015, p. A1.

64 John Chapman, "Why Your Company Needs a Foreign Policy," *Harvard Business Review*, Vol. 94, No. 9, September 2016, p. 38.

65 Sean Lux, T. Russell Crook, and Terry Leap, "Corporate Political Activity: The Good, the Bad, and the Ugly," *Business Horizons*, Vol. 55, 2012, pp. 307–312.

6

Global Marketing Communication: Facilitating Exchanges

Like public relations, the function of global marketing is to inform and persuade. Its purpose, however, is to facilitate exchanges between buyers and sellers. The foremost communication activity of marketing is advertising, while that of public relations is publicity, for which both employ the mass media and social media. Marketing furthermore employs personal selling and sales promotion, e.g. coupons, contests, samples, and trade shows. The orbit for marketing is the market, a physical place or communication center where exchanges take place between the companies that sell and consumers who buy – or, in the case of business to business (B2B), among companies themselves.

Philip Kotler, author of the best-selling marketing text, *Marketing Management*, says, "the objective of marketing is to attract customers and satisfy their needs and wants at a profit."[1] Providing a more detailed description of marketing activities, the American Marketing Association (AMA) states, "Marketing is the process of planning and executing the conceptions, pricing, promotion and distribution of ideas, goods, services, organizations, and events to create and maintain relationships that satisfy individual and organizational objectives."[2] From an international perspective, Sak Onisit and John Shaw in *International Marketing: Analysis and Strategy* say the same except that they call it an international process.[3]

Markets today are global, the frontier being the entire world. It is the fulfillment of Adam Smith's advocacy of free trade policies that replaced the stifling effect of mercantilism, whereby every country sought to maximize its store of gold through a zero-sum game of achieving trade at the expense of its competitors. Protectionism is the modern version of mercantilism. In contrast, globalization introduces businesses to new markets and consumers in both developing and emerging nations whereby all participants benefit.

In the process of global marketing, public relations can serve as the first wave. As described in Joyce Wouter's book, *International Public Relations*, "Public relations is ideally suited to the diplomatic digging for information that is indispensable to the process of entering a new market successfully and for establishing from the start the most hospitable environment possible."[4] She attributes people skills and an ability to assess the environment to public relations. Much reference has been made to BRIC nations (Brazil, Russia, India, China, and with the recent addition of an "S" representing South America.

6.1 Integrated Marketing Communication (IMC)

The dominance of marketing was boldly stated by Northwestern University's Medill School of Journalism when it established the term "Integrated Marketing Communication" (IMC). It was defined as "a strategic marketing process specifically designed to ensure that all messaging and

Corporate Communication: An International and Management Perspective, First Edition. Otto Lerbinger.

communication strategies are unified across all channels and are centered around the customer."[5] Philip J. Kitchen and Don E. Schultz stated: "IMC is a concept of marketing communications planning that recognizes the added value of a comprehensive plan that evaluates the strategic roles of a variety of communications disciplines . . . and combines these disciplines to provide clarity, consistency, and maximum communications impact."[6] A consistent image or message should result, instead of multiple voices.

Marketing people often claim that public relations is a part of marketing because both depend on promotion, and public relations is simply one promotional tool. In response, public relations managers resent being under the supervision of marketing or advertising because they limit their scope. Furthermore, they argue that the public relations functions of investor relations, employee relations, and community relations are not marketing activities. IBM solved the problem by merging its communications, marketing and corporation, and citizenship units into a single unit. It appointed Jon Iwata, as the senior vice president of marketing, communications, and citizenship.[7]

The first definition of IMC came from the American Association of Advertising Agencies (4As) in 1989. It stated that IMC is "an approach to achieving the objectives of a marketing campaign through a well-coordinated use of different promotional methods that are intended to reinforce each other."[8] This definition recognizes the strategic roles of various communication disciplines – mainly advertising, public relations, sale promotions – and demonstrates that when they reinforce one another in a program they synergetically have greater impact.

IMC is seen not only as communications but as a "business process that strives for greater accountability and pressure to produce business results."[9] This aspect extends IMC into a management function. A newer definition of IMC, therefore, is: "the concept and process of strategically managing audience-focused, channel-centered, and results-driven brand communication programs over time."[10]

Furthermore, IMC suggests that all stakeholder groups must be taken into account, because a company exists within a field of stakeholder interactions among suppliers, distributors, customers, retailers, and even competitors.[11] From a public relations perspective, however, consumers are one stakeholder group among others – investors, employees, and the community. Consumers represent the revenue flow to a company from the sale of products and services that are used to pay the factors of production, namely interest and profits to capital, local taxes and rents for land, land wages and salaries, and labor. Public relations recognizes the managerial business creed which states that the needs of all of these stakeholders should be taken into account in making business decisions.

The need to produce revenue applies not only to sales by companies but also to other organizations. Governments obtain revenue through taxation or borrowing, and individual government departments engage in what is euphemistically called "budget sucking." The nonprofit organizations of civil society engage in fundraising, but also receive government support and income from ancillary business activities. These other forms of raising revenue employ marketing techniques.

The function of marketing is not isolated from other aspects of society. Marketing depends on sound and predictable economic and political systems. It may therefore seek public affairs assistance to assure a healthy environment for marketing.

6.2 The Marketing Mix: The 4 Ps

The marketing mix is a major concept used by marketing managers to recognize the factors involved in making marketing decisions. Known as the *4 Ps*, the factors are product, price, place, and promotion. The public relations role in the marketing mix relates mostly to the fourth P of promotion. But the other Ps may also be relevant. Price becomes an issue when, for example, competition is weak and monopolistic conditions prevail. In international markets, the third factor of place is obviously highly relevant. The product and price factors may also be important when a foreign market requires modifications in a product to suit local conditions.

6.2.1 Product, Price, and Place

Product and price decisions – the first two of the 4 Ps – are especially important. A given product like a shoe may have only one similarity, namely, that it goes on a foot. But it also has other meanings. What is it made of – leather, cotton, linen, plastic, etc.? And is it used for walking, hiking or tennis? Furthermore, a person wearing a Nike shoe will suggest that he or she is possibly an American. And high heels on a woman's shoes confirmed Thorstein Veblin's concept of conspicuous consumption, for a female companion with high heels cannot walk far and needs to be chauffeured.[12] Today, fashion and the desire to be tall make high heels acceptable to many women.

Product variety abounds because what people in different countries want varies. For example, Japanese women don't like shampoos that cut into hair oils. Italian housewives want elevated stoves so they can better clean the floor under them.[13] In Egypt or Malaysia, the color green shouldn't be used because of its association with jungle diseases. Most Malaysians emphasize practicality, not fashion, in buying clothing. Product and price decisions are most important in attracting low-income consumers.[14] An extreme case of product variety is that it not only applies to smart phones but also to smart toilets! Yoshiaki Fujimori of Japan provides a toilet with lids that lift automatically and allow the user to sync with smartphones via Bluetooth so that he or she can program preferences and play favorite music through speakers built into the bowl.[15]

Trade in some products and services is controversial. An illustrative example is the "Wombs for Rent" in India.[16] This is a surrogate birth whereby a woman provides her fertilized egg to an Indian woman who actually carries the baby throughout its typical 9-month span in return for a payment (around $8000). Some fear that the trade would lead to exploitation of women in financial difficulty and lead to problems in surrendering the baby. In European countries that provide maternity leave, administrative questions arise over whether women who become mothers through surrogacy qualify.

Price decisions usually remain in the domain of marketing. However, public relations and public affairs may become involved when price becomes a political problem. For example, hefty price increases by pharmaceutical companies on some drugs have become highly controversial, as discussed in the Part II case study. Neuromarketing has also become relevant because it explores human irrationalities in the marketplace. Such concepts as anchoring (when the initial price of something has undue influence on our future decisions) and relativity (when we infer the value or a product from the prices of similar offerings) have been recognized as important considerations in setting the price of products.[17] Dan Ariely, author of *Predictably Irrational: The Hidden Forces That Shape Our Decisions*, considers price an aspect of a product decision because it signals quality to people.[18]

6.2.1.1 Reaching the Bottom of the Income Pyramid

In the search for new consumers, companies have recognized marketing opportunities among consumers at the bottom of the income pyramid – the more than 4 billion people who individually earn less than $1500 per year.[19] Price is a major consideration in poor countries. Prices must be lowered to attract low-income consumers, which is often accompanied by reducing the size of products.

SC Johnson, the household products company, seriously undertook the long-term strategic potential of selling to the world's poorest people. In Kenya, for example, it created a direct sales model whereby coaches provide hands-on product demonstrations in homes and community gathering places. In their chart showing nine kinds of opportunities in dealing with emerging markets, Erik Simanis and Duncan Duke consider this approach a "new business-model development."[20]

The place factor is again relevant as a distribution problem because of weak infrastructure in roads and household facilities. The latter is illustrated in the famous case of Nestlé's sale of infant formula in developing nations.[21] Households had limited stove facilities, no refrigeration, and low incomes, which encouraged diluting the formula with water that was often unclean. Furthermore, Nestlé deceptively used women dressed as nurses to sell their product. The infant formula issue flared up again in China. Dumex Baby Food Co., a subsidiary of France's Danone SA was named by a China Central Television broadcaster as allegedly paying hospital staff to use its products and influence sales, a charge previously made against Nestlé. China is an important market for infant formula makers, with sales of $12.72 billion in 2012.[22]

When Unilever in 2008 recognized that within just 2 years, emerging markets would account for half of all the world's consumer spending, it shifted its marketing to developing countries. It recognized that more money could be made selling detergents, margarine, soups, and other products there than in developed countries.[23]

6.2.1.2 Place Moves to Space

The third "P" – place – has a meaning beyond a physical location. Theoretically, the concept of a market is not rooted in a place, for it is broadly defined as a process wherein sellers and buyers engage in transactions. In his 1981 classic, *The Principles of Economics*, economist Alfred Marshall defined a market as ". . . the whole of any region in which buyers and sellers are in such free intercourse with one another that the prices of the same goods tend to equality easily and quickly."[24] At the time, the "region" Marshall wrote about was mainly a physical place, as illustrated by the famous New York Stock Exchange, which was initially called "the curb exchange" because buyers and sellers would literally meet on the sidewalk to transact business. Individuals could similarly engage in transactions by meeting personally elsewhere.

Retail stores have been the major marketplace. However, their importance is now diminishing with the growth of digital marketing, which has resulted in place being replaced by space. Sears and Macy's, among others, are closing stores and shopping malls are finding other uses for empty space, such as health clinics. Marshall's definition of a market is appropriate to the global reach of markets and the rising use of the internet in commerce, including seller websites and a profusion of social media.

Even before digital marketing, retail stores faced some competition from direct mail marketing, and some retailers such as Sears Roebuck augmented their store sales with catalogue sales. L.L. Bean went a step further by transacting basing sales not in stores but on the telephone, via mail, or online. Amazon carried this off-store commerce further with the internet, which allows consumers to access its sites to peruse titles of books or product features, place desired items in a "shopping cart," order them, and have them shipped to the customer's home or other destination. Communications does the job through the burgeoning practice of "digital marketing," which is discussed later.

Despite the increasing role of digital marketing and the concept of space, the importance of a physical space must not be overlooked. Attractive locations and features of restaurants are still basic to attracting customers. Starbucks has learned that a store that provides customers with coffee and food "along with feel-good environment where friends meet, students do their homework, and romances come of age does better business."[25] It has also begun to open more

"Roasterys" to showcase its fanciest coffees – and charge higher prices.[26] Physical stores remain important and serve important functions in developing countries. The proverbial "mom and pop" store, for example, provides personal communication and attention, as well as offering advice on product choices and how to use them.

6.2.2 The Promotion Mix

In their book *The Management of Promotion*, Edward Brink and William Kelley define promotion as "the coordination of all seller-initiated efforts to set up channels of information and persuasion to facilitate the sale of a good or service, or the acceptance of an idea."[27] More broadly, the communications function in marketing has five aims: providing information, stimulating desire and raising the level of aspiration, providing assurance, winning customer affection, and inducing the willingness to spend. The last three of these aims are sometimes neglected.

Assurance is provided in several ways. One is to incorporate the use of a product into the cultural patterns of society, as the Pan American Institute did with the "coffee break."[28] Where mom and pop stores exist in countries like India, store keepers can provide assurance, a function now mostly performed by product brands and company brands. Frequent references to the high credibility sources of "science and research" can also reinforce the brands. Customer affection can also be aroused through company philanthropic activities and programs such as cause-related marketing. Willingness to spend – called "propensity to consume" by economists – often depends on people's impression of the health of the economy, which is influenced by news events, particularly during times of a recession, or depression.

6.2.2.1 Advertising

Advertising usually leads in the marketing mix. Advertising consists of non-personal communication by an identified sponsor through a variety of media to inform consumers of new products and product uses, to persuade them to buy the product, and to remind them of the product's existence.[29] To reinforce their brands, many companies use slogans such as Nike's "Just Do It," Burger King's "Have It Your Way," and Target Corporation's "Expect More Pay Less." But sometimes advertising can become too cute.

Toyota showed a beautiful and pricey-looking ad on New Zealand television that was quickly ditched after a backlash on Facebook. One scene showed a forest clearing where a lone stag comes across three hunters and explains how it will be deliberately shot so it could be transported on Toyota's latest Hilux model. In another scene a fish is so enchanted by the Hilux that it asks to be "carried to the local taxidermist," while in the background live anchovies sing about the honor of being transported in the Hilux and crates of lobsters "raise a glass to the legend" while they're eaten for dinner.[30]

At a 2014 international event, technology transformed advertising. Big advertisers used online content to grab the interest of fans instead of the past concentration on big centerpiece TV advertisements. Nike, for example, shifted its investment to online channels such as Facebook, Twitter, and YouTube. It could offer such entertainment as an animated mini-movie and the "Winner Stays" video featuring stars Neymar and Ronaldo. It turned their business storytelling into content marketing so cleverly that viewers hardly realized they were consumer ads.[31]

The five largest advertising agencies, with their estimated worldwide revenues in 2014, were:

1) WPP Group, London $19.0 billion;
2) Omnicom Group, New York City $15.3 billion;
3) Publicis Groupe, Paris $9.6 billion;

4) Interpublic Group, New York City $7.5 billion;
5) Dentsu, Tokyo $6.0 billion.[32]

These firms own several advertising firms.Omnicom's includes BBDO Worldwide, DDB Worldwide, TBWA Worldwide, and CSD&M. Publicis owns Leo Burnett Company Inc., Saatchi & Saatchi, and Publicis Worldwide.

Dentsu, Japan's largest advertising agency, illustrates the global growth of advertising.[33] It controls nearly a third of all traditional advertising in Japan. Its annual revenues in 2011 were over 330 billion yuan ($4.2 billion). It relies on Japan for 84% of its sales. It handles all company marketing activities, not only advertising. Dentsu plans to expand into more dynamic overseas economies to climb from the current 14% to 42% of its business and to provide an avenue for digital marketing.

In 2012 Dentsu agreed to buy the Aegis Group PL, a London-based agency for about $5 billion.[34] For 10 years Dentsu had tried to work with Publicis, but the agencies split in February 2012. *The Economist* reports that Dentsu seems to have cross-cultural problems. It had previously sought to acquire Razerfish, Microsoft's digital ad firm, but it was bought by rival Publicis. Martin Sorrell, chief executive officer (CEO) of WPP, the world's largest advertising firm, said the proposed deal was "driven by ego issues" and a desire to "dislodge WPP."[35]

6.2.2.2 Public Relations

Many big public relations firms also are now consolidated into giant groups. Interpublic owns Golin and Weber Shandwick; Omnicom owns Fleishman-Hillard, Ketchum, and BBDO. David Lubars, chairman and chief creative officer of BBDO, sees an evolution whereby technologically able marketers scale up into full-service agencies mastering new channels and the world with 6 billion individual markets.[36]

The global public relations industry was doing well in 2012 with an 8% increase, the third consecutive year at approximately the same level, with independent public relations firms up 8.6%. The public relations agency industry was worth almost $11 billion and employed more than 75 000 people. Independent firms continued to outperform the large, holding company-owned agencies.[37]

Public relations is increasingly a marketing tool said *The Economist* in 2006 because it is "surprisingly effective" in catching consumers' attention.[38] P&G, with an advertising budget of $4 billion concluded that the return was often better than from traditional forms of advertising. Another benefit of public relations is that its messages have greater credibility than advertising, say Al and Laura Ries in their book *The Fall of Advertising and the Rise of PR*.[39]

A trademark of a good public relations practitioner in the marketing area is that he or she is highly creative in inventing ideas for publicity. David Finn, who headed Ruder–Finn, praised Richard Weiner, one of its vice presidents, for his remarkably fertile mind. He had become "one of the most creative members of the team, especially in regard to consumer product accounts."[40] One of his accomplishments was to design a public relations program to publicize the "Cabbage Patch Kids." He depended heavily on research and the advice of child psychologists and educators, who advised that the dolls' appearance brings out the nurturing instinct in kids.[41]

The dozens of ways to obtain publicity are described in two books by Thomas L. Harris, *The Marketer's Guide to PR in the 21st Century: How Today's Top Companies Are Using the New PR to Gain a Competitive Edge* and *Value-Added PR: The Secret Weapon of Integrated Marketing*.[42] Listed are arts and entertainment sponsorships, awards, birthdays and anniversaries, booklet and brochures, books, B-roll, by-lines stories, cause-related marketing, festivals, grand openings, media tours, parades, plant tours, press kits, product placements, speakers' bureaus, tie-in and trade shows, among others. As suggested by the subtitle of another book, *Marketing PR, The*

Hows That Make It Work, author Rene A. Henry Jr. elaborates on specific media such as print media, radio and television, film and video, and the use of special publications.[43]

In addition to publicity, a second contribution of public relations to marketing is to establish and maintain a favorable corporate reputation that adds value to products and services. Many studies have demonstrated that a significant number of consumers are more likely to buy something from a seller with a good reputation. A recent study of Irish consumers, for example, supports other findings that a company's reputation is considered when making a purchase. Research by Amarach has found that consumers are becoming increasingly conscious of their purchasing decisions, with over 72% of Irish adults stating that they consider a company's reputation before buying a product or service.[44] Reputation is especially important in the international context because of consumer unfamiliarity with many companies. Adding a positive nation brand to a corporate brand can strongly enhance the effect. As previously stated, a country reputation for fashions, good workmanship, and advanced engineering affects consumer behavior.

A major issue in the European Union (EU) is whether country labeling should be required for a wider variety of products. Michele Tronconi, CEO of an Italian textile-finishing company, favors country labeling, saying, "It's all about making it fair for European companies still making their goods in Europe."[45] In 2005 the EU trade commission Peter Mandelson proposed that labels be mandated on 11 categories of goods, including shoes, textiles, and furniture.

Third, public relations can help rebuild public confidence during a recession or other negative event. Confidence was badly jolted by the 9/11 attacks on the World Trade Center and the Pentagon. This drop was recorded by the two major sources of consumer sentiment: The Conference Board (NYC), which recorded a fall by 14.4% in the aftermath, the largest since October 1990, and the University of Michigan, whose index of consumers' expectations about the future fell to 73.5, a plunge of 13.7% from the August reading.

During the 1957–1958 US recession, the first post-war recession, government and business recognized its psychological aspects and launched several advertising and public relations initiatives. When companies began to hire workers they were urged to publicize the fact, and they started "Now is the best time to buy" advertising campaigns. The Advertising Council prepared weekly round-ups of "good news," and companies like Prudential Insurance Company used television broadcasts to confirm "Confidence in a Growing America."[46] The ability of advertising and public relations to influence attitudes and behavior was recognized.

The 2007–2008 recession, which started with the bursting of the housing bubble, led to further discussion about "How to Market in a Downturn." John A. Quelch and Katherine E. Jacz identified the patterns in consumers' behavior and firms' strategies that propelled or undermined performance.[47] They spotted discretionary purchases such as car sales and eating in restaurants as especially vulnerable to the recession. Products were segmented into essentials, treats, postponables, and expendables. Customers were segmented into four types: slam-on-the-brakes (eliminate, postpone, decrease, or substitute purchases), pained but patient (economize in all areas), comfortably well-off (just a little more selective), and live-for-today (extend timetables).

6.2.2.3 Sports Sponsorship

Sports sponsorships, which are used both for marketing, especially advertising, and public relations purposes, are a major promotional tool and have evolved into a specialized field. The main attraction is that they draw huge big audiences. The 2014 World Cup in Brazil was estimated to raise global advertising by 5.4% to reach \$524 billion. The Cup is the world's largest sporting event.[48] Research firm eMarketer estimated that companies would spend \$69 billion on TV advertising and \$56 billion on online media around the Cup; in the 2010 event the split was 80/20.

About 111 million people – 46% of TV households – watched the Green Bay Packers defeat the Pittsburgh Steelers on Fox Broadcasting in February 2015.[49] Such factors as the emotional intensity of a sport have been studied. They show that "highly involved fans may choose to patronize firms that sponsor sporting events and teams in an effort to conform to group norms."[50] Major sports events such as the "Superbowl" provide unique opportunities for companies to reinforce their brands.

Research into sports sponsorships also helps identify suitable "celebrity endorsers."[51] Tiger Woods was once a highly cherished endorser used by the global consulting firm Accenture, whose longstanding slogan has been "High Performance Delivered." Tiger Woods symbolized high performance as portrayed in ads showing him carefully examining the turf from which he must extricate a golf ball. Another company, McDonald's, uses the following criteria to evaluate a sports endorsement:

- Does it enhance McDonald's leadership position?
- Does it deliver national TV presence?
- Can McDonald's own it?
- Does it help McDonald's stand out from the clutter?
- Does it provide local extensions?[52]

Although used mainly to promote a company's products, sports sponsorships form impressions of the ideals and culture associated with a nation brand. Countries use their national teams and athletes as a form of public diplomacy. Keith Dinnie states, "the significance of sport as a determinant of country image perceptions has been massively underestimated in existing country-of-origin research and it is through the emerging field of nation and place branding that sport's role in country image perceptions is beginning to be acknowledged."[53]

Stephen Greyser, a retired Harvard Business School professor and expert on sports sponsorships, discusses the importance of sports in our society. He says it produces lots of "public engagement," as shown by the high weekly attention given to National Football League (NFL) football, which matches weekly church attendance. Superbowl Sunday overcomes the trend of dwindling "mass" events as audiences have increasingly become fragmented, each paying attention to what their "gadgets" provide. A significant benefit of sports sponsorship is that a nation can capture the "energy" of the "emotionally charged environment" inherent in sports. It can also benefit from "balance theory" – that positive attitudes will balance out less favorable ones. The expectation is that highly involved fans may transfer some of their positive attitudes to a nation.[54]

Recognizing the value of sports sponsorship in enhancing its national brand, the US State Department created a division dedicated solely to the advancement of American sport diplomacy. In 2002, it established a branch of the Bureau of Educational and Cultural Affairs (EC), SportsUnited, which has gained thousands of participants in over 140 nations. "Sports Diplomacy" uses the universal passion for sports as a way to transcend linguistic and sociocultural differences and bring people together.

6.3 Accommodating International Differences

6.3.1 "Think Global, Act Local" – Global Brand Architecture

The mantra "Think Global, Act Local" was explored in a global brand survey by Nigel Hollis, author of *The Global Brand*.[55] The survey was designed to contrast a consistent set of global brands with their local competitors in eight countries – the US, Mexico, Brazil, the UK, Germany, Russia, India, and China. He concluded that the mantra does apply but observed that there are few truly global brands and fewer still that manage to create a truly strong connection with consumers. Nigel studied several brands: McDonald's, KFC, Budweiser, Heineken, Toyota, Ford, Pantene Pro-V, Dove, Coca-Cola, and Pepsi. He found that these brands are stronger than local ones, having the advantage of being the first choice or seriously considered for purchase because they are "very easy to recognize," and have "very distinctive identities."[56]

A concept of global brand architecture (GBA) has been developed that "specifically refers to the portfolio of brands a firm controls on a continuum of geographic scope and degree of consistency."[57] One insight is that global brands are likely to perform better in certain markets because they are influenced by national culture. Managers of regional and multi-regional brands, therefore, "may want to consider increasing their global positions, depending on the cultural dimensions of the potential markets for entry."[58]

Hoftsede's cultural concepts are helpful. For example, cultures with a high power distance are likely to view brands positively that reflect increased perceived quality and decreased perceived risk. "Those brands could more strongly symbolize power, prestige, wealth, and status . . . ."[59] Regarding masculinity, people exhibiting it "may demonstrate achievement by having the latest and most prestigious possession, which is essentially a proxy for success and reflects a given level of status." These consumers "tend to buy more expensive watches and real jewelry, fly business class on leisure trips more frequently, and . . . are more likely to favor foreign products and brands over their domestic counterparts." And consumers who rate high on uncertainty avoidance, "will place more emphasis on brands as cues of product quality and process information about them more intensely than consumers from low uncertainty-avoidance cultures".

Local brands typically score higher because they are seen as part of the national culture, but that feature has become less important. Furthermore, some global brands have been "nationalized": Mexicans see Coca-Cola as part of their national culture, which is partly explained by the long time Coke has been on the market. Mexicans also don't necessarily see foreign ownership as a bad thing when, as with Volkswagen, it is locally produced. The British seem no longer to value the cultural origins of the products they buy, e.g. 65% believe Mini is a British product even though BMW manufactures it in Germany. Expressing the same attitude, most Germans believe that Opel is a German brand even though General Motors (GM) produces it.

The survey found that global brands owe their strength to their reliance on the basics of brand-building, whereas local brands draw strength from being made in the country and being part of the national culture. But no hard and fast rules apply: the strategy that produces the best return on investment will vary depending on brand, competition, context, and culture.

6.3.2 Standardization vs Customization

It is convenient to believe, as Theodore Levitt did in 1983, that everyone in the world has the same needs and desire, and that buying habits can therefore be increasingly homogeneous throughout the world.[60] But the assumption that companies could simply sell their standard product abroad was largely untrue. Differences in local tastes, economic systems, and culture had to be considered. These differences become more pronounced as companies enter emerging markets. The answer to the question of whether a company should engage in standardization or customization, was firmly to reject the first option and move toward customization.

6.3.2.1 Unfamiliarity with Products and Sellers

One reason why customization is needed is consumers' unfamiliarity with a seller's products. Furthermore, the ability to learn more about them is handicapped by illiteracy and other language difficulties. How translations are handled can be a source of humor. Mercedes-Benz initially marketed itself in China as "bensi," which in Mandarin means "rush to die."[61] Among translations mentioned in David A. Ricks' *Big Business Blunders: Mistakes in Multinational Marketing* are these:

- An advertisement in a Mexican magazine promotion for an American-brand shirt intended to say "when I used this shirt, I felt good," instead read: "until I used this shirt, I felt good."
- When an American manufacturer in Venezuela advertised its auto battery as "highly rated," it was translated into "highly overrated."
- GM intended to convey to its Belgian market that the car being promoted had a "Body by Fisher," but instead the phrase was interpreted in Flemish as "Corpse by Fisher."
- "software" was translated to "underwear," which led to some interesting reading![62]

Where language is a barrier, companies have reverted to the use of "pedlars," theater, and the use of more visuals. For the business audience, international exhibits, notably those in Frankfurt and Singapore, provide opportunities for personal interaction.

"Innumeracy" is also a problem. Some people have difficulties in making simple calculations such as $2.00 minus a discount of 50 cents equals $1.50. A larger issue is mentioned by behavioral economists; namely, the assumption that everyone is perfectly rational.[63]

6.3.3 Recognizing Cultural Differences

The book, *Global Marketing Strategies*, asks whether consumers the world over are basically the same.[64] Are needs universal or do they vary among countries? The book states that international consumers consider six factors that influence the buying process: (i) needs; (ii) the ability to buy; (iii) a country's GDP; (iv) the family; (v) religion; and (vi) a country's educational system. The first three have already been discussed as important economic variables; the other three also deserve attention.

Cultural and sociological factors affect consumer behavior. In reviewing the factors that influence the consumer buying process, Jean-Pierre Jeannet and Hubert D. Hennessy observe in their book, *Global Marketing Strategies*, that purchase decisions are not always made by individuals alone for other members of a family; a wife or husband, parents, children, and others may have an influence.[65] They note that more joint decisions in families are made in the US than Venezuela because except for groceries and savings husbands make more decisions. In his classic book, *Personal Influence*, Elihu Katz recognized this fact when he describes how daughters influence mothers on what fashions to select. In some societies, the sale of tampons has to overcome the barrier of social embarrassment, so some sellers attempt to form social groups in households to discuss the subject.

The cultural factor of religion is a well-known and conspicuous factor in making certain purchases. Orthodox Jews and Muslims, for example, don't eat pork. Care must also be taken in selling products with religious themes. For example, Amazon was in trouble for selling doormats with images of Hindu gods and goddesses on them. The incident caused outrage among netizens who took to the social media calling for a ban on the U.S. retail giant. Amazon quickly removed these offensive products.[66]

Another factor, a country's educational system, determines literacy, which is required to read advertisements and package labels. Therefore, "products that are complex or need written instructions may need to be modified to meet the educational attainments of members in the channel."[67] Furthermore, advertising slogans may be misunderstood, e.g. "diet" Coke in Japan was interpreted as meaning "medicinal."

The cultural differences among nations are particularly strained in emerging markets. As Erik Simanis and Duncan Duke point out in their "Profits at the Bottom of the Pyramid," a big hurdle is "the reluctance to alter deeply ingrained mind-sets and routines."[68] For example, consumers in sub-Saharan Africa have responded poorly to insecticide-treated bed nets because of misconceptions about how malaria is transmitted. They resist the inconvenience of hanging and taking down nets every day.

Cultural differences affect a variety of other perceptions and behaviors about product use, such as these:

- Beauty preferences vary by cultures. Believers in Confucianism prefer cultivated mannerism and modesty compared to US emphasis on the body and sexuality.[69]
- Women in Brazil are big spenders on beauty products. Door-to-door sales reps account for 50% of all color cosmetics. A shift to selling cosmetics in department stores might therefore be difficult.
- Japanese prefer quiet refrigerators because walls are thin.

Regarding soup, Russia and China were envisioned as large markets because soup is eaten more than five times a week. Chinese consumers serve 320 billion bowls of soup a year in comparison to only 14 billion in the US. Furthermore, as Campbell Soup learned, soup-making is a source of pride for many Russians and Chinese. They're passionate about it and want to talk about it, but they don't want to buy soup. Campbell gave up in China in the 1990s after serving only standard soups, but it introduced a "starter soup" and broths designed to help consumers save time while making soup with their own touches.[70]

With its Dove campaign, Unilever fine-tuned its products for local markets. Knowing that Indian women often oil their hair before washing it, Unilever ditched the conditioner. As one of the largest makers of deodorants, Unilever faced up to these facts: only about half the world and 7 out of every of every 100 Asians use deodorants, and Russians use them only for special occasions, such as weddings, and regularly use lemon juice or talc. It sells deodorant caches with paste that can be applied with fingers. In India and Latin America where mom and pop stores rather than supermarkets predominate, they are important influencers, for "It's the shopkeeper who can recommend or disavow a product."[71]

6.4 Conclusions

Marketing is a communication practice that facilitates exchanges between buyers and sellers. The concept of IMC examines the contribution made by the various communication disciplines to the marketing effort and through their integration produces synergy – the total is greater than the sum of the parts.

The marketing mix explores each of the 4 Ps of product, price, place, and promotion. One application is the goal of reaching poor consumers in developing nations, who have often been unattended by companies. Another application is the Part II case on high drug prices that illustrates how the communication practice of public affairs becomes involved. The appearance of digital marketing and its growth is recognized and shown to have extended the marketplace to include products at the end of "the long tail." This subject serves as a prelude to Chapter 7 on social media and big data.

International marketing faces several challenges, such as making use of a global brand in the face of national and local differences, recognizing consumers' unfamiliarity with many products, and language difficulties in translations. Another challenge is to recognize the effect of cultural differences, such as the influence of family members, the role of religion, and attitudes toward product use.

Discussion Questions

6.1. How does public relations contribute to marketing?

6.2. What is the significance of the IMC concept?

6.3. In your opinion is IMC applicable to stakeholders other than consumers?

6.4. How does the concept of standardization vs. customization relate to a multi-national company's global marketing activities?

6.5. How does the "marketing mix" enlarge a communicator's choice of marketing appeals and media in a communications campaign?

6.6. Should a seller alter product characteristics for consumers in different countries? Why or why not?

6.7. How do sellers appeal to low-income consumers? What special problems are encountered? What are the pluses and minuses of doing so?

6.8. What problems did Nestlé encounter when it sold infant formula to developing nations?

6.9. How is the need for assurance by consumers satisfied?

6.10. How has technology transformed advertising?

6.11. Under what circumstances is the consumer's willingness to spend a critical factor?

6.12. What is the attraction of sports sponsorship to marketers? How is the choice of a particular sport evaluated?

6.13. What did Campbell's learn about soup consumption in China and Russia?

6.14. Give examples of how Hofsted's cultural concepts are used in marketing.

6.15. What social and cultural differences among nations are most important in marketing?

6.16. Do you agree with Theodore Levitt that since everyone in the world has the same needs, there is no need to vary products from country to country?

Endnotes

1 Philip Kotler, *Marketing Management: Analysis Planning Implementation and Control*, 7th ed. (Englewood Cliffs, NJ: Prentice Hall, 1991).

2 D.B. Meinert, S.J. Vitell, and R.F. Reich, "The Domain of Marketing: How Are the Boundaries of the Marketing Discipline Established?" *Journal of Marketing Theory and Practice*, Vol. 2, No. 1, 1994, pp. 1–13.

3 Sak Onisit and John Shaw, *International Marketing: Analysis and Strategy*, 4th ed. (New York: Routledge, 2004).
4 Joyce Wouter, *International Public Relations: How to Establish Your Company's Product, Service, and Image in Foreign Markets* (New York: Amacom, 1991). p. 3. Also see Mary Cowlett, "Using PR to Launch Into New Markets," *Marketing*, February 24, 2000, pp. 35–36.
5 "What is IMC?" *Journal of Integrated Marketing Communication*, Retrieved February 5, 2014.
6 Philip J. Kitchen and Don E. Schultz, "A Multi-Country Comparison of the Drive for IMC," *Journal of Advertising Research*, 1999, pp. 21–38.
7 Donald K. Wright, "The Organization of the Corporate Communication Function," in Rossella Gambetti and Stephen Quigley, eds., *Managing Corporate Communication: A Cross-Cultural Approach* (Basingstoke: Palgrave Macmillan, 2013), pp. 84–85.
8 "Integrated Marketing Communications," https://bangkitw92.wordpress.com.
9 Jerry Kliatchko, "Revisiting the IMC Construct: A Revised Definition and Four Pillars," *International Journal of Advertising*, Vol. 27, No. 1, 2008, p. 140.
10 Ibid.
11 Sandra Moriarty "IMC Needs PR's Stakeholder Focus," *Marketing News*, May 26, 1997, p. 7.
12 Thorstein Veblen, *Theory of the Leisure Class* (New York: Dover Publications, 1994).
13 "Women in Italy Like to Clean but Shun the Quick and Easy," *WSJ*, April 2, 2006, p. A1.
14 G. Tomas, M. Hult, Bruce D. Keillor, and Roscoe Hightower, "Valued Product Attributes in an Emerging Market: A Comparison between French and Malaysian Consumers," *Journal of World Business*, Vol. 3, No. 2, 2000, p. 217.
15 Eric Pfanner and Atsuko Fukase, "Smart Toilets Arrive in U.S.," *WSJ*, May 27, 2014, p. B8.
16 Kevin Voigt, Mallika Kaaur, and Lonzo Cook, "India's Surrogate Mother Boomtown," *CNN*, November 3, 2013.
17 "A Manager's Guide to Human Irrationalities," *M IT Sloan Management Review*, Vol. 50, No. 2, p. 54. Reference is to Dan Ariely's book, *Predictably Irrational: The Hidden Forces That Shape Our Decisions* (London: HarperCollins, 2008).
18 Ariely, ibid.
19 Erik Simanis and Duncan Duke, "Profits at the Bottom of the Pyramid," *Harvard Business Review*, Vol. 92, No. 10, October 2014, p. 88.
20 Ibid., p. 92.
21 "Marketing Infant Formula," in Tom L. Beauchamp, *Case Studies in Business, Society and Ethics*, 4th ed. (Saddle River, NJ: Prentice Hall, 1998), pp. 172–185.
22 Laurie Brukett, "Infant-Formula Issue Flares Anew in China," *WSJ*, September 7, 2013, p. B4.
23 "Unilever and Emerging Markets The Legacy That Got Left on the Shelf," *The Economist*, February 2, 2008, p. 77.
24 Alfred Marshall, *Principles of Economics* (London:, Macmillan and Co., 1947), p. 324. He quotes Cornot.
25 George Anders, "The President of Coffee Nation," *Forbes*, March 21, 2016, p. 41.
26 Ibid., p. 50.
27 Edward L. Brink and William T. Kelley, *The Management of Promotion* (Englewood Cliffs, NJ: Prentice-Hall, Inc., 1963), p. 6.
28 See Gilbert Coburn, "Making the Coffee-break an American Institution," in Allen H. Center, ed., *Public Relations Ideas in Action* (New York: McGraw-Hill Book Co., Inc., 1957), pp. 212–215.
29 Richard L. Sandhusen, *Marketing*, 3rd ed. (Haupauge, NY: Barron's Educational Series), 1993, p. 442.
30 Cas Carter, "Toyota Ad Dump May Be a Sign of the Times," *The Press* (Christchurch, New Zealand), December 31, 2015.

31 Greg Williamson, "World Cup of Marketing," *The Press* (Christchurch, New Zealand), June 17, 2014, p. 8.

32 "Agency Report 2016 Index," "*Advertising Age*," May 2, 2016.

33 "Advertising Agencies: The Lion;s Dentsu," *The Economist*, July 21, 2012, p. 56. Also see Angela Doland, "How Japan's Dentsu Climbed to the Top of the Agency World," *Ad Age*, May 5, 2015.

34 Kenneth Maxwell, Suzanne Vranica, and Hiroyuk Kochi, "Dentsu Looks Beyond Home Market," *WSJ*, July 15, 2012, p. B3.

35 "WPP Chief Celebrates Rivals' Marriage Collapses," *WSJ*, May 10–11, 2014, p. B4.

36 David Lubars's views are explained in Stuart Elliott, "Visa Trims Slogan to Expand Meaning," *New York Times*, January 12, 2014.

37 World PR Report, published by the Holmes Report and the International Communications Consultancy Organization, October 14, 2013.

38 "The PR Industry: Do We Have a Story for You!" *The Economist*, January 21, 2006, pp. 57–58.

39 Al and Laura Ries, *The Fall of Advertising and the Rise of PR* (New York: HarperCollins, 2002).

40 David Finn, *The Way Forward: My First Fifty Years at Ruder–Finn* (New York: Millwood Publishing, 1998), p. 68.

41 Richard Weiner launched the popular Cabbage Patch Kids. See http://plankcenter.eu.edu//resources/leader/legends-in-pr/richardweiner-apr-fellow-prsa

42 Thomas L. Harris, *The Marketer's Guide to PR: How Today's Top Companies Are Using the New PR to Gain a Competitive Edge* (New York: John Wiley & Sons Inc., 1991), p. 135. *Value-Added PR: The Secret Weapon of Integrated Marketing* (Chicago, IL: NTC Business Books, 1998).

43 Rene A. Henry Jr. *Marketing PR, The Hows That Make It Work* (Ames, IA: Iowa State University Press, 1995).

44 "Consumers Base Purchases on Trust; Consumer Trust," *Business World* (Digest), October 8, 2013.

45 John W. Miller, "Country Labeling Sets Off EU Debate," *WSJ*, June 6, 2011, p. B1.

46 Rob Walker, "Confidence Game: Why No One Really Knows How Consumers Feel," *The New Republic*, December 24, 2001, pp. 17–19.

47 John A. Quelch and Katherine E. Jacz, "How to Market in a Downturn," *Harvard Business Review*, 87, No. 4, April 2009, pp. 52–62.

48 Scott Roxborough, "World Cup; to Add $1.5 Billion to Global Ad Spend," (Hollywood, http://reporter.com, June 17, 2014).

49 Sam Schechner, "SuperBowl Sets Viewing Record As ProFootball Defies TV Trend," *WSJ*, February 8, 2015, p. B7.

50 Lara O'Reilly, "Samsung to Boost London 2012 Sponsorship With Corporate Marketing," *Marketing Week Online*, March 28, 2011.

51 A comprehensive article is Jane Summers, Melissa Johnson Morgan, "More Than Just the Media. Considering the Role of PR in the Creation of Sporting Celebrity and the Management of Fan Expectations," *PR Review*, Vol. 34, No. 2, June 2008, p. 176 ff.

52 Harris, op cit., p. 203.

53 Keith Dinnie, "Place Branding: Overview of an Emerging Literature," www.brandhorizons.com

54 Lynn R. Kahle and Angeline G. Close, eds., *Consumer Behavior Knowledge for Effective Sports sand Event Marketing* (New York and London: Routledge, 2011), pp. xiv, 13.

55 Nigel Hollis, "Rethinking Globalization," *Marketing Research*, Vol. 21, No. 1, Spring 2009, pp. 12–18. His book is *The Global Brand* (Basingstoke: Palgrave Macmillan, 2008).

56 Ibid, p. 14.

57 M. Berk Talay, Janell D. Townsend, and Sengun Yeniyurt, "Global Brand Architecture Position and Market-Based Performance: The Moderating Role of Culture," *Journal of International Marketing*, Vol. 23, No. 2, 2015, pp. 55–59.

58 Ibid.

59 M. Berk Talay et al., op. cit.

60 Theodore Levitt, "The Globalization of Markets," *Harvard Business Review*, 61 May–June 1983, pp. 165–167.

61 Mentioned in "Overheard," *WSJ*, November 30, 2017, p. B14.

62 David A. Ricks, *Big Business Blunders: Mistakes in Multinational Marketing* (Homewood, IL: Dow Jones-Irwin, 1983), pp. 76, 83.

63 "Free Exchange; Poor Behaviour," *The Economist*, December 6, 2014, p. 88.

64 Jean-Pierre Jeannet and Hubert D. Hennessey, *Global Marketing Strategies* (Boston, MA: Houghton Mifflin Company, 1992).

65 Elihu Katz and Paul Lazarsfeld, *Personal Influence: The Part Played by People in the Flow of Mass Communication* (New York: Free Press, 1955; new edition 2005).

66 Adrija Bose, "Amazon Removes Doormats with Images of Hindu Gods After Protests Call for Boycotts," *Huffingtonpost*, June 6, 2016.

67 Jeannet and Hennessey, op. cit., p. 194.

68 Erik Simanis and Duncan Duke, "Profits at the Bottom of the Pyramid," *Harvard Business Review*, Vol. 92, October 2014. Also see Erik Simanis, "Reality Check at the Bottom of the Pyramid," *Harvard Business Review*, Vol. 90, June 2012, pp. 120–125.

69 BoRa Yook in a class report, "L'Oreal, Big Beauty Giant's International Business and Communication Strategies and Practices," in an International PR class at Boston University, May 2014.

70 Julie Jargon, "Can M'm, M'Good Translate?" *WSJ*, July 9, 2007, p. 15.

71 Antonio Regaldo, "McCann Offers Peek at Lives of Latin America's Poor," *WSJ*, December 8, 2008, p. 78.

7

Social Media and Big Data: Extending Relationships

Social media are the most prominent "new media" that affect the practice of corporate communications and add a dimension to digital marketing. Social networks allow people to connect with one another and to keep in touch with friends. People can interact with one another in a medium in which they create, share, and exchange information and ideas in virtual communities and networks. Social media allow the creation of user-generated content. Brian Solis, former principal of FutureWorks, and now principal at Altimeter Group, said social media "democratized content publishing and distributing, and more important, they equalized influence." He discussed "how social media affects the role of public relations in the greater landscape of marketing communications."[1]

The power of social media is based on the premise that human relationships and social structures that surround an individual are not passive but exert an influence. A receiver of a message is influenced by the primary groups to which he or she belongs, and both directly and indirectly by the larger social structure. Influentials in particular are the small social groups of three or more people in face-to-face contact. These include the primary group of the family, an informal clique of workers, a problem-solving group in business, or a therapy group. Social media build on such small groups, called "communities," in which 100 or more people are bound together by common backgrounds or interests.[2] A key task is not only to identify them but also to understand them, their language, and what they seek from communications providers. The basic premise "is that everything is more valuable when you have context about what your friends are doing."[3]

7.1 The Internet

Social media are rooted in the internet, which is a kind of network or networks of private, public, academic, business, and government networks worldwide linked by a broad array of technological devices that use the internet protocol suite transmission control protocol/internet protocol (TCP/IP). The world of communications has changed ever since the internet appeared in the early 1990s. It has become a key tool for communicating and sharing ideas and information – not only domestically but internationally. Millions of computers provide access to the websites of all kinds of organizations. The internet is mainly accessed through the World Wide Web (WWW). This is a collection of hyperlinked documents (not computers) using a common protocol that interconnects millions of computers to create an information superhighway.

The seven most popular social media sites are Facebook, Twitter, LinkedIn, Pinterest, Google+, Tumblr, and Instagram. An early social media site was Myspace (formerly MySpace),

Corporate Communication: An International and Management Perspective, First Edition. Otto Lerbinger.

which was launched in 2003 and remained the largest until 2008 when it was overtaken by Facebook. In 2012 Facebook purchased Instagram for the astonishing sum of $1 billion.

The significance of Facebook is described by Sabrina Horn, the founder and former chief executive officer (CEO) of Horn Group, a nationally recognized tech public relations agency recently acquired by the global communications firm Finn Partners.[4] She observes that Facebook has really become a platform for so many other social media sites and applications. The popular app called WhatsApp, recently acquired by Facebook, allows people to text and call each other for free. A lot of the newer apps, continues Horn, leverage the friends you have on Facebook to do other things, like get referrals from friends for dating websites, find local grocery stores or restaurants, or simply just sign in with Facebook to get to other applications.

As well as social media, a large part of the internet is made up of websites by individuals, groups, and organizations that allow viewers to obtain information and interact with them. They allow consumers to connect directly with online merchants to make online purchases. Blogs are a special kind of website, originally maintained by individuals, and now used by groups and businesses to offer commentary and ideas for larger audiences.

Michael Zivina of Precise Value in Australia adds a third component to the internet, The Cloud, which he sees as serving as the network's computer. He states, "The way apps use the cloud creates powerful, two-way data flow in which nuggets of value are moved. Apps themselves provide the enormous depth and breadth of function that software vendors have been chasing for years."[5] While cloud firms create a world of interconnected services, software, and devices, they work only within that universe. If a cloud provider goes bust, a customer may have difficulty retrieving their data. To reduce risk, companies like General Electric keep their most valuable data in their own data centers. Others like Wal-Mart, use several cloud firms that enable them to move data from cloud to cloud.[6]

7.1.1 Overseas Expansion Invites Languages Other than English

Although the US has dominated social media and search firms like Google, several Chinese firms have become prominent and are beginning to expand overseas. Baidu, founded in 2000, is the dominant search company in China. The other two Chinese firms are Alibaba, whose main product is e-commerce, and Tencent, which engages in social networking. The latter's WeChat mobile messaging service has 100 million registered users from outside China.

Languages other than English are becoming more prominent on the internet, with about 246.2 million individuals accessing websites in Asian languages, in contrast to only 25.5 million 3 years ago. Translation is often difficult. Software can go only so far and it might cost upwards of $20 000 to translate a website of 100 pages.[7] Some protocols should be observed. For example, when communicating with the Japanese, sentences written in Japanese should be formal and recipients should not be addressed by their first name. High-context languages are growing more rapidly, so communicators shouldn't start out in the cold business-like manner of cultures like the Dutch or Finns, but rather with the personal approach of the Chinese and Latinos.

Most social media monitoring platforms are good at collecting data about what's being discussed about a product or brand, but they often fail to handle variations in language. However, progress in media monitoring of international platforms has been enhanced by new programs that claim to provide totally seamless solutions for all countries and languages. Socialmetrix, for example, covers English, Spanish, and Portuguese by using semantic analysis and natural language processing. Brandtology is able to monitor conversation and sentiment in 12 languages across most countries.[8]

7.2 Social Media Marketing

Social media marketing is a major application of digital marketing. Tamar Weinberg's book, *The New Community Rules: Marketing on the Social Web*, defines social marketing as: "a process that empowers individuals to promote their websites, products, or services through online social channels and to communicate with and tap into a much larger community that may not have been available via traditional advertising channels."[9] Included in this community may be friends – in excess of 30 for each customer.

It is helpful to see the role of social media marketing in the context of three types of media that constitute communication programs:

1) *Earned media*. Publicity gained through promotional efforts other than paid media advertising, e.g. online word of mouth, good content, and first page rankings on search engines are typically the biggest drivers.
2) *Paid media* such as advertising, billboards, etc.
3) *Owned media*. Website content, blog content, infographics, and video.[10]

Sabrina Horn believes that it is the owned social media that "really brought earned media to life in combination with PR."

7.2.1 Major Types

7.2.1.1 Search Engine Marketing

Search engines, such as Google and Yahoo, provide information about products and services. Search engines contain both unpaid and paid listings. Their placement, based on proprietary algorithms, remains highly controversial, as illustrated by European Union (EU) antitrust suits against Google. This form of internet marketing involves the promotion of websites by increasing their visibility in research engine result pages. In 2012, North American advertisers spent $19.5 billion on it.

Search engines make the marketer's dream come true, says David Meerman Scott, because consumers are actually looking for your product. Search engines are a way to reach buyers directly. The key is to use words and phrases in a site, blog, and other online content in order to give the site the highest ranking possible in the natural search results.

Search engine advertising may be used in the form of small text ads that appear next to the natural search results for a particular search term. Using himself as an example, Scott says that when he wanted to take his family on vacation to Costa Rica, he typed in "Costa Rica Adventure Travel," and not the generic term "travel." Other terms might be "Costa Rica ecotourism," and "Costa Rica rainforest tour."[11]

A further step is to establish a unique identifier for yourself, your product, and your company so it will stand out from the crowd and rise to prominence on search engines. Scott advises that attention be given to the "web landing pages," the place people go after they click on a search hit. They must have "specific content to enlighten and inform the people who just clicked over to your site from the search engine."[12] He also advises users to make sure that key words and phrases are indexed by the search engines.

7.2.1.2 Websites

Websites, another form of social media marketing, enable sellers to engage in email promotion and offer consumers easy access to comparative information. Ebay's website is an outstanding example of website marketing. It is a self-service model. The site "offers filters, mostly in the form of search and a multi-level category structure, to help buyers find what they're looking for."[13]

Ebay offers income possibilities for individuals. In 2005, AC Nielsen reported that more than 724 000 respondents said that eBay was their primary or secondary source of income.

There are four types of websites: (i) company/brand sites, which are directly informational, and indirectly promotional; (ii) information sites, which rely on member loyalty to generate revenue through advertising or subscription rates, e.g. www.WSJ.com; (iii) selling sites, such as Amazon, which are virtual stores that allow customers to buy products, or L.L. Bean, direct catalog marketers; and (iv) service sites such as banks with ATMs that give customers access to account balances, and allow them to pay bills, apply for lines of credit and home equity loans; and Federal Express, which helps customers interactively track packages from initial shipping to destination.

The first type of website is illustrated by Concrete Network, which "provides information about residential concrete products and services and helps buyers and sellers connect with each other."[14] In business to business (B2B) marketing, it links homeowners and builders. The website includes two direct-to-consumer news releases per week and free online catalogs for such categories as pool decks and driveways, and photo galleries.[15]

Urban Outfitters uses its website to provide detailed product information along with the ability to make online purchases. The benefits are (i) improved efficiency and lower costs across supply and demand chains; (ii) improved speed, flexibility, and responsiveness in meeting customer needs; (iii) greater market access, and (iv) enhanced ability to overcome time and distance barriers of global markets.

From a seller's viewpoint, every business has information that can contribute to the education of the marketplace and attract potential customers. It is especially useful in B2B marketing, which comprises more than two-thirds of total internet activity. Internet marketing helps craft marketing mixes of a constant stream of information about current, often changing, wants and needs about products lines and lines of competitors.

Email used in B2B marketing is just one component of a brand strategy. A company might start off with traditional direct mail to drive recipients to a website where they can then "opt in" to receive email newsletters, sales alerts, and other information. These sources have a limited life, however, for people are getting burned out on email promotions. They are seldom successful as a way of attracting new customers, but can be effective as a retention tool. Codes of conduct that are open and honest can help to reduce consumer resistance to email promotions. Furthermore, sites should have a limited life.

7.2.1.3 Blogs

The word "blog" is derived from weblog, which is a frequently updated personal or collaborative website in the form of a diarized journal containing opinions, information, and web links that reflect the interests and personality of the author(s). Scott considers blogs the mainstream vehicles for individuals, groups, and businesses to get their ideas into the marketplace.[16] Smart bloggers regard blogs as one of the few forms of real, authentic communication. Blogs became known as the new influencers and authors of the online world.[17]

For businesses, blogs provide a big opportunity in thought leadership, category creation, and POV (point of view) sharing. They provide an opportunity to promote their brands, market their products and businesses, and to establish themselves as authorities in their niches. Weinberg says blogs can lure customers into a business's brand and then to talk about your business.[18] Unfortunately, blogs share characteristics with native advertising, namely advertorials, and other disguised advertising, including the use of celebrities – and these, believes Sabrina Horn, endanger the authenticity and transparency of the true meaning of blogs.

Scott offers some advice on what needs to be known to get started when blogging. Start with asking, "Whom do I want to reach?" Then find a specific important topic, but don't try to cover too much. He suggests incorporating the standard delivery format of RSS (Really Simple

Syndication) functionality into your blog. It allows bloggers to integrate advertising in their feeds. Also important is to be ethical, for example, by not pretending to be someone you are not. Disclose any conflict of interest, be truthful, and give credit to material obtained from others.[19] Surveys show that the less control a company has over blogs, the more credible its message will be.

7.2.2 Videos – Additional Impact

An advantage of social media is its ability to add videos. This feature is hugely valuable in the "how-to" market for fixing things in the home, cooking, etc. Although non-media companies have been laggards in the video field, some corporate websites are including online videos, which tend to draw more attention to corporate messages. They take advantage of the fast-evolving medium that YouTube has popularized since the late 1990s (it was bought by Google Inc. in 2006 for $1.65 billion[20]). Every minute about 100 hours of content is uploaded onto YouTube.

The benefits of using videos are illustrated by Monsanto Co. To make a case for its controversial bioengineered crops, Tom McDermott, a Monsanto public relations manager, sent camera crews to the Philippines, Australia, and other countries to film testimonials from farmers growing genetically modified corn, soybeans, and other crops using the company's products. Showing a gathering of farmers and their families, the website carried this message:

> A Global Conversation with Growers. In 2005, 8.5 million farmers in 21 countries planted 222 million acres (90 million hectares) of genetically modified (GM) crops. In this global compilation video, you have an opportunity to hear the personal experiences of more than 20 farmers in eight countries who, one-on-one, share their opinions about the benefits of biotech agriculture and perspectives on growing GM crops over the last 10 years.[21]

The Monsanto websites posting these clips attracted 15 000 visitors a month by the end of 2006. Monsanto planned to boost viewership to offset the efforts of environmentalists hostile to the new technology.

Although the videos' impact on public attitudes is uncertain, the likelihood is that a medium that allows "information seeking" is less likely to be perceived as propaganda than one that engages in "information processing," which typifies the mode of users of the mass media. As some would argue, videos' impact on public attitudes can be discreetly measured and quantified over time. But a framework of metrics to wrap around the plethora of digital activities must first be developed. Most organizations are still a way off from this and consequently the communication industry remains undervalued.

Sun Microsystems Inc. is another company that saw a large increase in visitors on its website when videos were introduced. In 2003 it had revamped its press area to resemble that of a broadcast news outline, showing stories, interviews, and live international feeds. Its traffic jumped from 12 000 visitors in August 2003 to 42 000 in December. The worldwide spread of mobile phones, which requires less infrastructure than computers, is expected to speed up access to the internet, says Jonathan Schwartz, CEO of Sun Microsystems. He argues that as information is provided to more people in blogs, the "edges" can participate in providing information on such events as bombings and tsunamis.[22] The widespread use of the internet will have an impact on citizen democracy as well as journalism.

7.2.3 Viral and Buzz Marketing

In the early phase of social media, a new form of marketing known as viral and buzz marketing was introduced: some high-profile viral, buzz, and word-of-mouth marketing campaigns were early entrants to social media. A review of them is instructive because they demonstrate the essence of social media. In 1996 Hotmail email service recruited 12 million subscribers in 18 months with a marketing budget of only $500 000, using the banner: "Get your free email at Hotmail."[23] And in 1999, the Blair Witch project was acclaimed. It cost only $15 000 to produce the Blair Witch Project website, which attracted 75 million visits in the first week of the film's release. It used the appeals of mystery and intrigue to stimulate word-of-mouth mention.

7.2.3.1 Viral Marketing

The term "viral marketing" suggests the similarity of the spread of social media messages to the way a cold is transmitted among people. The Web is ideal for word-of-mouth ad campaigns because of the ease with which messages can be sent. Viral marketing is appropriately defined as "spreading the word with infectious enthusiasm." It aims to sidestep consumer resistance to broadcast advertising by spreading commercial ideas by word of mouth or over the Internet – by "word of mouse."[24] It is based on the premise that people trust their friends more than they trust advertisements.

Email chain letters are one way to spread the contagion. These emails are created in such a way that people are motivated to forward them to friends. They may contain commercial messages. With B2B, the attempt is to broadcast offers to recipients so they go to the company's website or pass the offers to others.

Virgin Net was an example of viral marketing. It created something that is fun, or that contains enough of an incentive for people to want to forward it to their friends. Virgin Net promised people free cinema tickets if they left their email address on the site. Initially 25 people were emailed with the offer; within 3 hours all 20 000 tickets had been taken. In another application, Virgin Wines sent emails inviting people to enter a competition to win a holiday for a group on Richard Branson's Necker Island. The size grew because each entrant had to nominate the group of friends they would take if they won – and those friends then had to enter too.

There are many other examples of viral marketing. One is Ford Motor Company, which found that over 80% of their customers in America had already researched their prospective purchase on the internet before they arrived at a showroom. Another example is Procter & Gamble, which enlisted a stealth army of 600 000 moms to chat up its product.[25]

7.2.3.2 Buzz Marketing

The term "buzz marketing" emphasizes the techniques used in viral marketing. The basic idea is to use a "special 'hook,'" event, or promotion to get consumers and the media talking about a campaign. Its three main techniques are: (i) physical exposure by audience members, which maintains the highest quality of a repeated message; (ii) word-of-mouth, whereby first contacters begin to echo the message of the campaign to two, three, four, and in some cases up to eight or 10 people; and (iii) press coverage and public relations.[26]

The goal of buzz marketers is to reach brand advocates, also called evangelists. These are regular clients, customers, or consumers with no special opinion leading powers, but who like your brand so much they recommend it to others. For example, Unilever Dove's "Share a Secret" advertisement in 1998 invited Dove users to mail in the name and address of a friend with whom they would like to share the Dove secret. The friend would then receive a Dove gift certificate entitling him or her to a free Dove pack of soap and discount vouchers. By supplying their own name and address, participants in the promotion would also themselves receive a Dove certificate.[27]

Mel Gibson's film, " The Passion of the Christ," illustrates buzz marketing. It was shown in advance to churchgoers with the effect of creating "a deafening buzz" around the film that then produced a surprisingly strong debut when it opened on Ash Wednesday. Credit is given to "an unlikely combination of pulpit-to-pulpit grass-roots marketing, star power and controversy."[28]

A promotional gimmick helped create buzz for a client of Fenton Communications that wanted to take sport utility vehicles (SUVs) to task. A religious group used the banner "What would Jesus Drive" in a campaign that challenged auto makers on fuel economy. It accused SUV drivers of supporting terrorism by using high fuel-burning vehicles. Although the ads ran only a few times, they created media buzz and publicity worldwide because of their controversial nature. Jason Vines, former head of Ford Motor Co.'s public relations and now a spokesman for pro-SUV advocacy, said, "This isn't little campaigns that spring up as people come to the same conclusions. It's orchestrated – a track record of creating a crisis out of thin air."[29]

7.3 Social Media Impact on Corporate Communications

Social media have expanded the scope of corporate communication. Sabrina Horn, who was an early pioneer in integrating social media campaigns within an overall public relations program, states, "A great communications campaign today combines digital and visual story telling techniques like videos and web site engagement with earned social media and public relations tactics, as well as paid online and offline advertising." Saying that public relations can no longer operate in a silo, "Companies today need communications programs that have a stronger connection to their brand and utilize more, and different, channels at different times." This means that attention must be given to how new talent is hired and recruited and how clients are served within the agency world. Social media is not 100% of one person's job, says Horn, it should be 20% of everyone's job. And the role of senior public relations counselor really requires knowledge of not just public relations, but general marketing concepts, including promotion, social, and visual story telling.

7.3.1 Changed Power Relations

Since the advent of the internet and social media, public relations professionals no longer exclusively rely on the traditional news release and press conference to disseminate information. An analysis of 120 corporate websites from Denmark, France, Germany, Norway, Singapore, Spain, the UK, and the US shows that 92% have a specific website designed to meet the information needs of the media, including 15 companies with the highest revenue in each of the eight countries in the sample.[30]

A website on the internet can serve as a virtual press room. The main content in these press rooms is made up of press releases (100% of press rooms), backgrounders (59.5%), photo archive (49.5%), financial data (35.1%) biographies (24.3%), history (23.4), press clips (18%), video archive (10.8%), and audio archive (7.2%). The main deficiency of the websites is that corporations neither make use of the full potential of the internet for interactivity nor do they use the interactive features efficiently that the internet today provides. Press room websites ascribe little value to the potential for dialogue as reflected in the fact that up to 70% of the queries made via email or via a request form on the Web go unanswered.[31]

When publicity was conducted through the conventional news media, some public relations persons and firms that employed former journalists or cultivated relationships with editors had a competitive advantage: they could feel that they "controlled" what was considered news. Social media changed that equation; there is no control, no special news market. "Everyone with an internet connection is a publisher and a broadcaster," says Sir Tim Berners-Lee. "Citizen journalists now compete with traditional journalists."[32]

As Steve Quigley of Boston University's College of Communication states, "The social web is shifting the balance of power and control for corporate communicators."[33] "Top-down, command-and-control communication" is giving way to voices from members of the audience. The one-to-many model of communication now competes with the many-to-many model. Social media experts, observes Quigley, urge communicators to give up control, and replace it with interaction. Some research, however, shows that in certain cases the shift in power is under 10%. Traditional media and media relations should not be abandoned.

7.4 Big Data – its Uses and Limitations

Society is awash with information on just about everything, including details about people's characteristics and how they behave. Millions of people create and share data about who they are, what they do, where they're going, how they get there, and, very important to sellers, what they spend their money on. An important aspect of this explosion of sensory data, says Sabrina Horn, is that it is all unstructured and comes in so many different forms, making it more challenging to analyze and measure. Use of the internet for searches and interaction on social media constantly create information that accumulates into big data. Mobile devices are accelerating that growth. With 43 billion mobile devices expected to be activated in the next 7 years, one can start to grasp the amount of data about each one of us that companies have at their disposal and have to make sense of.

In China, 83% of its people use a mobile device of some kind to get online. The sweeping transition from traditional computers to smart phones and other mobile devices has produced an explosion of sensory data such as images, videos, and sound, the kinds of data that stump conventional software.[34] The new measurements of data are no longer in kilobytes, megabytes, and gigabytes, but terabytes and more (petabytes and exabytes). Considering that 100 terabytes of data are equivalent to about 0.5 billion pages of text, the idea of big data becomes real.

Furthermore, the reality about big data is that it comprises different forms of data available from various social media sites, sensors, and satellites. These consist of numbers, text, sound, and images that move quickly – over 10 terabytes per day on Facebook alone. Furthermore, the techniques must be available both to process these data and to use them for descriptive, prescriptive, and predictive analytics.[35]

7.4.1 Analyzing Big Data

With a large accumulation of data, the challenge is to find a way to sort it out. Like the research methodology of content analysis, systems of classification must be designed so that individual content can be assigned to various categories. There are now literally 100s of tools to measure countless new marketing applications, with seemingly a tool for everything, says Sabrina Horn. One is called AirPR.com. This basically gives an executive an online dashboard to see at any given moment in time what one's website traffic is, and the ability to measure the nuances of what people are saying/writing, number of hits, competitors, and so forth.

Andrew Ng, chief scientist at Baidu, hopes to develop software that can in a sense learn on its own. Such software can learn to identify patterns in images, sounds, and other sensory data. It might analyze one's vacation photos and recognize the people shown in each one, identifying what they're doing and recognizing landmarks. For example, the Baidu Translate app can, in seconds, identify an object in a photo and name it in written and spoken English.[36] By processing 10 million images, it learned to recognize cats, human faces, and other objects without any human help.[37]

Companies, such as Ditto Labs Inc., use software to scan images for marketing purposes. For example, they look for someone holding a Coca-Cola can and then identify about 3000 logos to see whether a person is smiling, and whether the background is in a bar or snowy mountain – all of which are clues about where and how customers use their products.[38] Image search technology is being experimented with by Pinterest. It could match what a smart phone user sees, and maybe wants, with some 75 billion images for a visually similar match.[39] This photo recognition shopping could thereby usher in a new kind of consumer shopping behavior. The more specific technology of facial recognition software is finding increasing applications. In the gambling halls of Las Vegas, for example, owners can identify known card sharks before they beat the house.

7.4.1.1 Finding Meaning

The challenge in such data analysis is to find possible solutions to selected problems in all the disparate facts. The scientist's penchant for causality – showing how one set of facts causes certain results – is an ideal, but in dealing with big data simple correlations between bits of information may suffice. But when a correlation exists, it is not necessarily known why. Theoretically, the purpose of analyzing big data is to help decision makers reduce uncertainty. For example, if a new policy is to be launched, uncertainty exists about its eventual impact. Data, when analyzed properly, can help to reduce this uncertainty, and traditional research, such as focus group interviews, can help explain the "why" behind a correlation.

Writing about data analytics, two staffers at the Gallup poll,Sean Williams and Bill Petti, suggest that "starting small is often a winning strategy."[40] They found that clients often hadn't yet identified the problem they were trying to solve. Moreover they had no plans for what they would actually do with the data and insight. They should ask themselves these questions:

- Does your organization effectively use existing data and insights?
- What is the organization doing with the insight it has already produced?
- What specific business problem would the solution solve today?
- Do you know how the analytics people will solve your business problem?
- Who is going to use the new solutions?

They conclude, "Profit increases when talented analysts find business-relevant insights and when energetic data-driven cultures act on those insights to seize opportunities."[41]

New information and insights can better be communicated through another advantage of big data analysis, namely, dramatic means of presentation. One of these is a "word cloud" – a visual representation of commonly used words found in a collection of comments – which quickly summarizes a great deal of information. For example, in a tribute page for Steve Jobs, the words apple, world, thank, and family appear most often; next are great, genius, and technology.[42]

An ad by Accenture Digital in the *Wall Street Journal* presents the promise of the growing field of analytics, described as helping you "see what you can't. So you can see opportunities within." With analytics, it says "We help our clients turn data into insight, insight into action and action into tangible results."[43]

7.4.2 Applications of Big Data Analysis

7.4.2.1 Marketing

The potential value of big data analysis among communicators has been greatest in marketing. It supplements or replaces the familiar techniques of focus group studies, consumer surveys, and motivation research. Big data research further helps understand consumer needs, wants, desires, and concerns. Data from actual purchase behavior are analyzed along with other big data sources. A further objective of market research is to discover bases for audience segmentation. For example, audiences interested in yacht racing and figure skating are quite different from those interested in bowling or auto racing, so different products will be aimed at them.

Brands are wrangling big data, trying to make sense of it and build social media marketing strategies based on its findings. Big data helps identify new customers, realize maximum return customers, increase what they purchase, and avoid organizational behavior that might damage an organization's reputation. As stated by Anna Lawlor:

> Big data can bring producers in closer contact with consumers' wants and needs, perhaps even before the users actually know what they want and need – providing increasingly real-time, unmediated, and holistic views of the consumer. As a lagging indicator, measuring the ROI of a marketing campaign to highlighting dissatisfaction with customer "touch points" that could be addressed internally.[44]

As Andrew Ng states, "One system learns which qualities of an ad make people click on it more often, selects ads to meet those criteria, and runs them at the most opportune moments."[45] Aside from privacy concerns, big data is used to identify new customers when an app notifies a store that someone with appropriate needs and buying habits is approaching. That person is offered a discount or promotion by phone to come to the store and buy things.

A much-cited illustration that demonstrates the predictive power of big data is when the retailer Target became adept at making precise predictions about whether a woman was pregnant and in need of certain products.[46] For example, if in March a 23-year-old woman "bought cocoa-butter lotion, a purse large enough to double as a diaper bag, zinc and magnesium supplements and a bright blue rug, analysts predicted an 87% chance that she was pregnant and that her delivery date would be sometime in late August."[47] Another example of the predictive power of big data is Wal-Mart's correlation of customer data and weather. It knows that before storms people not only buy more flashlights but also more Pop-Tarts, even though there's no causal relationship between weather and toaster pastries.[48]

An example of a practical marketing application of big data is when Kraft learned from BuzzMetrics that over 2.6 million people commented about trans fats and that many comments were associated with Kraft or Oreos. This finding convinced Kraft to eliminate all trans fats from their products.[49]

7.4.2.2 Fundraising, Political Campaigning, and Public Relations

In these applications that make use of marketing, big data may provide non-profits with insights to increase membership and contributions, both financial and volunteering. New "communities" might be discovered that relate to a cause. Similarly, political organizations can more easily identify people who are most like to vote for their candidates and causes and are willing to contribute time and money.

Social media have been associated with public relations since the beginning, states Deirdre K. Breakenridge. In the foreword to her book, *Social Media and Public Relations*, David Armano, executive vice president of Global Innovation & Integration for Edelman Digital, states, "Much of social media is done in public, by the public, and the dynamics that have shaped public relations in the past (media relations, interactions with opinion leaders and influencers, and of course, crisis/reputation management)."[50]

7.4.2.3 Public Opinion Analysis

Many business and political organizations conduct regular public opinion surveys to determine their standing with the public. The data can then be analyzed to determine differences from previous years, draw comparisons with other organizations, and make judgments about ideal situations. Big data from social media is able to refine the analysis of public opinion. A brief for IBM describes how social media channels deliver real-time analysis of public opinion, trends, and usage behavior.[51]

Such analyses can support gap analysis. The typical use of this technique is to determine the gap between a company's desired goals and actual achievement. Public relations goes further by comparing public opinion results with two references: One is whether the results indicate that the public has misunderstood company policies and behavior, in which case corrective communications would be undertaken. A second reference is how a company would ideally like to be perceived, indicating that the company should review its policies and behavior.

Steven Dong, deputy secretary-general of the China Public Relations Association, observes that the work of public opinion analysts is becoming increasingly important in the era of information explosion. The Ministry of Human Resources and Social Security and a news portal run by People's Daily jointly launched a certification public relations program to assist policy makers and reduce malpractice. As stated by He Dan, "Online public opinion analysis provides a new channel for the government to understand public mood quickly although it is not flawless."[52] (But it requires skills to pick up useful information from the mass of junk information.) A potential danger in authoritarian countries is the ease with which "enemies" can be identified. A benefit, however, is that insights from social media analysis will help companies in their political risk analysis of authoritarian countries that curb access to people and information. For example, more will be learned about the corruption of officials, the illegal taking of land, and the basis of many local protests.

7.4.2.4 Detecting Reputational Damage

Social media are particularly effective in spreading news about an organization's wrong-doing. Companies are already routinely examining social media to see whether and how they are mentioned. In some cases, as with Domino's Pizza video prank, quick responses are required.[53] Big data analysis can help by determining how widespread negative news becomes, in what groups, and with what effect. When fast fashion apparel sellers were implicated in the deaths of over 1100 workers in Bangladesh factories (see Chapter 16), the extent of reputational damage had to be assessed. Had there been a strong public reaction (there wasn't), a company might have had to cut that supply chain. It would also have had to decide whether to participate in some reform measures.[54]

7.4.2.5 Issues and Crisis Management

Issues management is a powerful tool used by public affairs professionals to identify and evaluate governmental and societal issues that could significantly impact their organizations (see introduction to Part V). The process starts with monitoring of relevant literature and talks with executives within an organization and their trade associations. An analysis of big data can help identify issues and, once known, to analyze them. For example, if McDonald's and Wal-Mart discover that demands for an increase in minimum wages become a serious disruptive issue, they can determine the likely public support for it. The analysis of other issues could similarly be helped, e.g. equal pay for women. Similarly, insight might be provided on the issue of fracking by showing how many people are worried about it and such specific harms as water contamination.

Twitter is a favorite means of reporting a crisis, as was demonstrated when a Chinese college student was the first to report the devastating earthquake in Sichuan, China, on May 12, 2008.[55] The student's message was followed by microblogging, text messaging, and online videos that resulted in some extremely swift on-the-ground reports, as well, unfortunately, as the viral spreading of rumors. Social media may especially be helpful in detecting so-called smoldering crises. They refer to early signals that are ignored until an event, such as an accident, occurs

Other social media such as Facebook can also be used to determine the most effective responses to a crisis. References to major companies, such as the Fortune 100 or 500, can be analyzed to determine which of the most common responses, such as apologies and two-way communication, were most effective

Risk assessment software helps managers make a wide variety of decisions. Prison authorities, for example, estimate the likelihood that a prisoner will re-offend. Multi-Health Systems, a Canadian firm, used two programs, LSI-R and LS/CMI to reduce parolee recidivism by about 15%.[56]

7.4.2.6 Healthcare

The possibilities for healthcare are enormous.[57] As Serger and Kenneth Clukier, data editors of *The Economist* point out, Google is better than the Centers for Disease Prevention at identifying flu outbreaks. By monitoring billions of search terms, such as "best cough medicine," and location details, it tracks outbreaks. And who would guess that people's credit scores predict who needs reminders to take medicine.

A group of scientists is now developing automated hypothesis generation software that can tally the vast corpus of scientific literature (e.g. at least 50 million scientific papers). John Gordon, one of the leaders of IBM's cognitive computing team, developed a machine called Watson "which is able to digest and analyze large amounts of English text and then draw inferences from it."[58]

During the Ebola crisis of 2014, *The Economist* suggested that mobile phone data could be a promising tool for epidemiologists dealing with the Ebola crisis.[59] A call data record (CDR) is created every time a person makes a mobile phone call. A CDR shows the phone numbers of the caller and receiver, the time of the call, and the tower that handled it (which roughly identifies the device's location). Researchers can thereby obtain insight into mobility patterns. This information could help track population flows from an area where an outbreak had occurred and where it would be most likely to break out next. In the Haiti earthquake and cholera outbreak in 2010, an analysis of over 200 days of the use of CDRs by almost 2 million subscribers showed where people fled. The results were more accurate than those of official estimates.

7.4.2.7 Monitoring Facilities and Energy Consumption

Big data helps keep tabs on bridges, tunnels, and other infrastructure. Sensor-based remote monitoring systems supplement periodic inspections, helping keep continuous track of the loads placed on bridges, even before signs of damage appear. By analyzing the accumulated data, better repair strategies can be formulated.[60]

Josh Marks is the chief executive of one such company, masFlight, which helps airlines use enormous data sets to reduce fuel consumption and improve overall performance. UPS, with 60 000 delivery vans in the US, crunches the data on the 100 miles or so a day covered by each to fine-tune their navigation systems to save as little as 1 mile. Sounds small but it saves $50 million in fuel and other costs per year. The old 80–20 rule that says that 20% of the people account for 80% of improvement is now enhanced by finding out the incremental improvements that the 20% can make.[61]

Smart metering presents the industry with an opportunity to change the way it interacts with customers. Utilities can use smart data to monitor home appliances and proactively intervene on behalf of customers when they see indications of a problem.[62]

7.5 Improving the Reliability of Big Data

7.5.1 Limitations of Big Data

The entire population doesn't use big data and thus it isn't representative of the entire population. Internet users are thus self-selected and cause a bias. Mark Zuckerberg reminds us that only a little more than one-third of the world is connected on the internet – about 2.7 billion people.[63] Pew Research says only 62% of low income households (those earning less than $30 000 a year) use the internet; similarly, usage varies with different age groups and educational levels. As reported by Forrester Research, less than a quarter of adults over the age of 18 in the US and Europe create content such as blogs, online videos or music, or post articles online. Just over one-third of adults engage in more casual social media activities, such as posting updates on social networking sites or contributing online opinions.[64]

Furthermore, the adequacy and reliability of social data to identify a target demographic is limited by what social media users choose to share about themselves and the self-proclaimed titles they select. Some users of social media are simply "lurkers," who look for information but give little. Among other limitations are:

- Social media users sometimes present half truths about themselves. Moreover, Twitter is infested with spam "robot" accounts and other fraudulent messages.
- As the demographics of users joining social networks change, new social networks emerge, user behavior evolves, and it becomes tougher to make full comparisons between social data sets.
- With big data come big noise and, while social data providers are staking their futures on slicing and dicing this information into commercially relevant insights, the algorithms and practices are still at the initial stage.
- The mapping of social conversation is limited. According to Pulsar, a social data intelligence platform, fewer than 5% of social media users make their location publicly available on their profiles.[65]

7.5.2 New Approaches and Research Centers

Today's data sets are so huge and complex to process that they require new ideas, tools, and infrastructures. The EU is funding CEEDs (the collective expansion of empathic data systems) to help our brain deal with big data. It transposes big data into an interactive environment that allows the human mind to generate new ideas more efficiently. Researchers have built what is called an eXperience Induction Machine (XIM), which uses virtual reality to enable a user to "step inside" large data sets. This immersive multi-modal environment, located at Pompeu Fabra University in Barcelona, also contains a panoply of sensors, which allows the system to present the information in the right way to the user, constantly tailored according to their reactions as they examine the data. These reactions – such as gestures, eye movements, or heart rate – are monitored by the system and used to adapt the way in which the data are presented.

Among other facilities being established is Oxford University's £45 million Big Data Institute – thought to be the first of its kind in the world – which will allow researchers to analyze large amounts of data to help improve scientists' understanding of diseases.[66] UK universities are being asked to express their interest in establishing The Alan Turing Institute to further big data research. Another facility is the Maryland-based non-profit Howard Hughes Medical Institute's Janelia Research Campus, which has developed a library of tools, called Thunder. It speeds the analysis of data sets that are so large and complex they would take days or weeks to analyze on a single workstation, if a single workstation could do it at all, said group leaders Jeremy Freeman, Misha Ahrens, and other colleagues. "Being able to apply analyses quickly – one after the other – is important. Speed provides more flexibility to explore and get new ideas," said Freeman.[67]

Business schools are recognizing the importance of big data and its potential to explore and solve business problems. They are responding to the needs of employers. For example, Melissa Lora, president of Yum Brands Inc.'s Taco Bell International, said, "We find it invaluable to have people who can synthesize data" and suggest changes based on those insights.[68] Some B-schools offer specialized, 1-year Master's programs in business analytics. The University of Southern California's Marshall School of Business began its Master of Business Analytics program in fall 2014, which was suggested by its corporate advisory board, which includes General Electric Co., Boeing Co., and Walt Disney Co. The London Business School has used big data to test the' management skills of students in its executive MBA, and the Saïd Business School at the University of Oxford has carried out research into big data and introduced a data module into its MBA course.[69]

A note of caution, however, comes from Clive Holtham, professor of information management at Cass Business School, London. He says: "Big data is a current focus of hype and, for us in MBA teaching, we see a need to emphasize both its potential benefits, as well as the possibility that it is being oversold and may ultimately end up as a fad."[70] Michael Rappa, founding director of the Institute for Advanced Analytics at North Carolina State University believes analytics is best studied in an interdisciplinary context, rather than only through a university's business school.

7.6 The Future of Big Data – The Next Step

7.6.1 Artificial Intelligence (AI)

A major next step will be artificial intelligence (AI). AI is defined as "a fast-moving technology that enables machines to perform tasks that could previously be done only by humans" or, more simply "machine intelligence with the full range of human intelligence."[71] According to the McKinsey Global Institute, AI is "happening 10 times faster and at 300 times the scale, of roughly 3000 times the impact of the Industrial Revolution." Andrew Ng wants to change the world with it. In his new lab, he is developing creation software that can learn on its own. He says, "Just as the Industrial Revolution freed a lot of humanity from physical drudgery, I think AI has the potential to free humanity from a lot of the mental drudgery."[72]

One AI technique is called "deep learning," which allows systems to learn and improve by crunching lots of examples rather than being explicitly programmed. This learning technique can be applied to many different domains, for example to boost the quality of Web search results, understand commands spoken into smart phones, and help translate webpages from one language to another. Applications to various jobs are numerous. One example is that deep learning in medicine can analyze images such as X-rays and CT scans. Another example is that ever smarter machines can perform tasks done by information workers.

Many categories of jobs have become highly vulnerable. A study that examined the probability of computerization for 702 occupations found that 47% of workers in America had jobs at high risk of potential automation. With many jobs at risk, firms promoting AI face public opposition, which makes the process of adaptation to technological change more difficult. To the extent that occupations such as public relations involve empathy and human interaction, they are less likely to be endangered by AI.

7.7 Conclusions

The proliferation of social media and tantalizing possibilities of big data present opportunities in the fields of public relations, public affairs, and marketing. These developments must be explored, but with realistic expectations. What should be done with big data? Does it allow better measurements than the research tools of focus groups, in-depth interviews, and content analysis of the past? Can new insights be found from social media and troves of big data? Is the next frontier about getting the right data and perhaps smaller data that can more quickly produce useful results for business managers?

The possibilities inherent in big data suggest that attention should be given to the creation of new "sensors" – new means of collecting information – as has been done in energy conservation. But even though it might be easier to collect or access data, the principle of economy should still be applied.

Ethical issues and questions of privacy pervade these new areas of exploration. Will some job applicants be rejected because too much was learned about them from Facebook or LinkedIn? Do we learn that a woman is married or pregnant – questions that cannot illegally be asked in job interviews? Are some applicants shown to be pro-union? Will face recognition techniques invite retribution after a protest?

Better analytics are here to stay. Professionals should learn more about them and probably team up with the new breed of analytics experts.

Discussion Questions

7.1. What are social media? Give some examples.

7.2. What's the connection between social media and the internet?

7.3. Why must attention be paid to "The Cloud?" What is it?

7.4. What is a search firm? What are the two prominent ones in China?

7.5. Do social media entirely rely on English? Discuss.

7.6. What are the implications of social media for digital marketing?

7.7. How do search engines work? How can they be used most effectively?

7.8. How are websites and blogs used in marketing?

7.9. What company has effectively used videos in its social media? How?

7.10. How do viral and buzz marketing work? Give examples.

7.11. How have social media affected public relations?

7.12. What's the significance of "big data?" Who uses it? What is it used for?

7.13. What questions should researchers asked themselves before they use big data?

7.14. What are some limitations in the use of big data?

7.15. How has big data been used in the healthcare industry?

7.16. How can big data assist in public opinion analysis?

7.17. How might advances in artificial intelligence affect the use of big data?

Endnotes

1 Brian Solis with Deirdre K. Breakenridge, *Putting the Public Back in Public Relations: How Social Media is Reinventing the Aging Business of PR* (Upper Saddle River, NJ: FT Press, 2009). Solis is also author of *Engage!: The Complete Guide for Brands and Businesses to Build, Cultivate, and Measure Success in the New Web* (Hoboken, NJ: John Wiley, 2010). He is a well-known voice for PR 2.0. See www.briansolis.com.
2 The basic ideas of digital marketing are presented in Tamar Weinberg, *The New Community Rules: Marketing on the Social Web* (Sebastopol, CA: O'Reilly Media, Inc., 2009), pp. 1–2.
3 Brad Stone, "Sell Your Friends," *Bloomberg Businessweek*, September 27–October 3, 2010, pp. 65–72.
4 From personal correspondence.
5 From personal correspondence.
6 "Cloud Computing: The Sky's the Limit," *The Economist*, October 17, 2015, p. 47.
7 Sak Onvisit and John Shaw, *International Marketing: Analysis and Strategy*, 4th ed. (New York and London: Routledge, 2004), p. 392.
8 Marshall Sponder, *Social Media Analytics: Effective Tools for Building, Interpreting, and Using Metrics* (New York: McGraw Hill, 2012), p. 45.
9 Weinberg, op. cit., p. 3.
10 www.titan-seo.com/NewsArticles/trifecta.html
11 Ibid. p. 369.
12 Ibid.
13 "New Study Reveals 724,000 Americans Rely on eBay Sales for Income," eBay, July 21, 2005
14 Scott, op. cit., p. 32. www.concretenetwork.com
15 Ibid., p. 33.
16 Scott, op cit., p. 201; Weinberg, op cit., pp. 76, 85.
17 The year 2004 gave prominence to blogs because of an increasingly visible role in the US electoral race. A scandal surrounded Dan Rather's comment about faked documents concerning George W. Bush's service in the National Guard. It took only minutes by the connected blogging community to find that these documents were not genuine. Kirby, op. cit., p. 245.
18 Ibid. p. 87.
19 Ibid., pp. 202–208.
20 Bobby White, "Firms Take a Cue from YouTube," *Wall Street Journal*, January 2, 2006, p. B3.
21 Ibid.
22 Richard Waters, "The Power of the Internet Hails a New Era of Openness and Collaboration," *Financial Times* (London), September 21, 2005, Business, p. 1.
23 Justin Kirby and Paul Marsden, eds., *Connected Marketing: the Viral, Buzz and Word of Mouth Revolution* (London and New York: Butterworth-Heinemann: Elsevier, 2006), p. xxi.
24 Alex Benady, "Spreading the Word with Infectious Enthusiasm," *Daily Telegraph*, October 12, 2000, p. 22.
25 Robert Berner, "Marketing: I Sold it Through the Grapevine," *BusinessWeek*, May 29, 2006, p. 32.
26 Kirby, op. cit., p. 28.
27 Ibid., p. xxi.
28 See Merissa Marr, "Publicity, PR and 'Passion,'" *WSJ*, February 20, 2004, p. A4.

29 *USA Today*, January 24, 2003, p. 3B.
30 Gonzalez-Herrero Alfonso and Ruiz de Valbuena Miguel, "Trends in Online Media Relations: Web-based Corporate Press Rooms in Leading International Companies," *Public Relations Review*, Vol. 32, No. 3, 2006, pp. 267–275.
31 Ibid.
32 Ibid, p. 415.
33 Steve Quigley, "The Emergence of the Social Web and Its Impact on Corporate Communications Practices," in S. Rossella Gambetti and Stephen Quigley, eds., *Managing Corporate Communication: A Cross-Cultural Approach* (Basingstoke and New York: Palgrave Macmillan, 2012), p. 414.
34 Robert D. Hof, "A Chinese Internet Giant Starts to Dream," *Technology Review*, Vol. 117, No. 5, September–October, 2014, p. 28.
35 Gregory Richards, "Let Us Clarify What We Mean by Big Data; We First Need a Clear Definition," *Ottawa Citizen*, August 2, 2014, p. D9.
36 Hof, op. cit, pp. 25, 27.
37 Robert D. Hof, "A Chinese Internet Giant Starts to Dream," *MIT Technology Review*, August 14, 2014.
38 Douglas MacMillan and Elizabeth Dwoskin, "Smile! Marketers are Mining Selfies," WSJ, October 10, 2014, p. B1.
39 Yoree Koh, "Pininterest Takes a Shot with Image-Search Tools," *WSJ*, July 7, 2016, p. B6.
40 Sean Williams and Bill Petti, "Data Analytics: Starting Small is Often a Winning Strategy," *Gallup, Opinion*, February 24, 2015.
41 Ibid.
42 Wendy W. Moe and David A. Schweidel, *Social Media Intelligence* (New York: Cambridge University Press, 2014), pp. 8–9.
43 *WSJ*, March 31, 2011, p. A11.
44 Anna Lawlor, "Five Inconvenient Truths about Social Data," *The Guardian*, August 4, 2014.
45 Hof, op. cit., p. 27.
46 Charles Duhigg, "How Companies Learn Your Secrets," *New York Times Magazine*, February 16, 2012.
47 Ibid.
48 Constance L. Hays, "What Wal-Mart Knows About Customer Habits," *New York Times*, Business Day, November 14, 2004.
49 Julie Jargon, "Food Makers Move Gingerly on 'Healthier' Fare," *WSJ*, June 24, 2014, p. B1.
50 Foreword by David Armano in Breakenridge, op. cit., p. vii.
51 Ben Taylor and Richard Postance, "The Big Issue," *Utility Week*, June 28, 2013.
52 He Dan, "Public Opinion Analysts Get Exam Recognition," *China Daily European Edition*, October 7, 2013.
53 Described in Otto Lerbinger, *The Crisis Manager: Facing Disasters, Conflicts and Failures*, 2nd ed. (New York: Routledge, 2012), pp. 27–28.
54 See Rebecca Reuber and Eileen Fisher, "Organizations Behaving Badly: When Are Discreditable Actions Likely to Damage Organizational Reputation?" *Journal of Business Ethics*, Spring 2010, Vol. 93, pp. 39–50.
55 Lerbinger, op. cit., p. 95.
56 "Role and Technology: Prison Breakthrough," *The Economist*, April 19, 2014, p. 29.
57 An observation made by Mark Sinyor, "Big Data Meets Big Health Care," *National Post*, July 22, 2014, p. A15.
58 "Automated Hypothesis Generation: Computer Says 'Try This,'" *The Economist*, October 4, 2014, p. 85.
59 "Ebola and Big Data: Call for Help," *The Economist*, October 25, 2014, pp. 17, 81–82.

60 "'Big data' Helps Keep Tabs on Bridges, Tunnels," *The Nikkei Weekly* (Japan), September 23, 2013.
61 "Schumpeter: Little Things That Mean a Lot," *The Economist*, July 19, 2014, p. 60.
62 Michael Fitzgeral and Elizabeth Dwoskin, "Big Data Cuts Energy Use: Buildings Find More Information Leads to Efficiencies," *WSJ*, September 29, 2014, p. R2.
63 Mark Zuckerberg, "Connectivity: A World Where Everyone Will Be Online," *WSJ*, July 8, 2014, p. R3.
64 Wendy W. Moe and David A. Schweidel, *Social Media Intelligence* (New York: Cambridge University Press, 2014), p. 149.
65 "Five Inconvenient Truths about Social Data," Guardian.com, August 4, 2014.
66 "World's first Big Data Institute given go-ahead," *Oxford Mail*, August 8, 2014.
67 "Device to Help Neuroscientists Analyse 'Big Data,'" *Siasat Daily* (India), July 28, 2014.
68 Lindsay Gellman, "Big Data Gets Master Treatment," *WSJ*, November 6, 2014, p. B7.
69 Ibid.
70 Jerry Knight, "More Room for Big Data," *The Times* (London), May 28, 2014, p. 7.
71 Special Report on Artificial Intelligence, *The Economist*, June 25, 2016, p. 3; Ray Kurzweil, "Long Live AI," *Forbes*, August 15, 2005, p. 30.
72 Hof, op. cit., pp. 26, 29.

8

Digital and Social Marketing: Extending Practices and Influencing Behavior

Digital marketing and social marketing extend conventional communication practices and add the objective of changing people's behavior. Digital marketing, through the technology of the internet and social media, has been enabled to vastly expand its offerings and reach – both domestically and internationally. Social marketing extends the purpose of marketing from selling goods and services to also attempting to change the behavior of consumers. The same marketing techniques are used by governments and non-profits to advance a social cause, idea, or behavior.

8.1 Growth of Digital Marketing

Digital marketing has created a state of turmoil, with the traditional marketing campaigns based on mass media advertising that is not working any more, say Justin Kirby and Paul Marsden in their *Connected Marketing: the Viral, Buzz and World of Mouth Revolution*.[1] They point out that the internet and social media play an increasingly larger role in marketing.

8.1.1 Awareness of New Technology by Public Relations and Public Affairs

Even before the appearance of the internet, the public relations industry had become aware of new communication technologies. In the famous Tylenol tampering case, superbly handled by Burson-Marsteller, the technology of the satellite news conference was used. The New York press conference was beamed to 29 other cities so that overall over 500 journalists "attended" the event. Virtually every network and most newspapers in the country carried the story.[2] Firms were proud of their computers. For example, in 1966, Ruder & Finn showcased its computer in a room with a window facing one of the hallways, so that visitors could easily be impressed by it.

The public relations industry was slow in recognizing the emerging technology, even though writers like Shel Holtz reported in 1998 that "The Internet represents one of the most significant tools ever employed in the practice of public relations."[3] The Public Relations Society of America's (PRSA) Information Center did not include the subject of "computers" in its subject listing in May 1966 and waited until 1969 to do so. By 1981, articles began to appear on "the New Communications Technology and Its Impact on Public Relations." Overall, public relations people were laggards. Shel Holtz in his first edition of *PR on the Net* said, "The communications profession lags woefully behind much of the Internet community," and in his second edition lamented, "the profession hasn't progressed much since then."[4]

The PRSA recognized the new landscape when it held a seminar on "How to Conduct Media Relations in Cyberspace" with such topics as how to identify which media prefer to

Corporate Communication: An International and Management Perspective, First Edition. Otto Lerbinger.

communicate electronically and how to reach them effectively. Online services, such as Media Map's Media Manager provided up-to-date listings of editorial contacts, as well as editorial calendars and other information. Email became the way to get information to editorial contacts at media outlets.

Further advances in communications technology occurred with the arrival of the digital revolution. Former dean Brent Baker of Boston University's College of Communication recognized the impact this technology would have on communication practices. He said the digital medium "includes interactive television, computers, interactive and multi-media CD-ROM or on-line products, digital networks, and other digital products that allow people to interact, access, exchange, and manipulate information."[5]

The Foundation for Public Affairs, affiliated with the Public Affairs Council, likewise acknowledged the world of the internet. It published a report on *Public Affairs Strategies in the Internet Age*, with an introduction by the president of the Public Affairs Council, Douglas G. Pinkham, who said: "The Internet has yet to reach its potential as a tool for commerce. But – like the runaway bull on the streets of Pamplona – it has come crashing through the marketplace of *ideas*. It has forever changed the way people 'sell' their opinions, 'buy' into political causes, and build long-term relationships with like-minded individuals."[6]

Gradually, terms such as e-commerce and internet marketing appeared along with digital marketing to represent all the activities of a firm between manufacturers, intermediaries, customers, and other publics that use the internet to help exchange products. Because all transmissions on the internet have gone digital, the term *digital marketing* has gained in currency. However, apart from using many of the techniques and practices contained within the category of internet marketing, digital marketing includes channels that do not require the use of the internet. These include mobile phones and smart phones, display/banner ads, SMS/MMS (Short Message Service/Multimedia Messaging Service), digital outdoor, and many more.

8.1.2 New University Degree Programs and Company Positions

An increasing number of universities have recognized the importance of digital marketing. When Baruch University's Zicklin School of Business developed a digital marketing track, it said: "Over the last thirteen years there has been an explosion of e-commerce and user generated content; acceptance of the digital media by established firms; and new multiple billion dollar digital-only firms. In response to this technological and lifestyle metamorphosis, marketing is going through a similar fundamental change."[7]

Likewise, New York University's Stern School offered a specialization in digital marketing, with this description:

> The Internet and advances in digitization and social networking are transforming how companies and governments interact with customers and partners. Digital commerce is at once a powerful enabler and disruptor of business models. There is growing evidence that a strong digital presence, based on a deep understanding of the complexities and nuances of the digital world, translates into significant business value. This specialization provides students with the strategic and analytical skills to guide organizations navigating in a digital world that is overflowing with data on customers, products, and interactions.[8]

The wide variety of sub-specialization courses illustrates the many aspects of digital marketing, with such names as Digital Strategy; Search and the New Economy; Social and Digital Media Analytics; Design and Development of Web and Mobile Applications; Data

Mining for Business Analytics; Being Digital: Search, Social Media and Crowdsourcing; Networks, Crowds, and Markets; Reasoning about a Highly Connected World; Advertising Management; Digital Media Innovation; Brand Strategy; Social Media for Brand Management; and New Media in Marketing.

As the application of digital marketing grew, new positions were created. At Coca-Cola, for example, Adam Brown became the director of the Office of Digital Communications and Social Media.[9] He described the company's "unprecedented year-long social media program." Another company, Campbell Soup Co., appointed Michael Senackerib as chief marketing officer in October 2012 and used social media to appeal to its younger consumers. Senackerib said, "Campbell Soup is reinventing itself with new products and a focus on the younger generation." Digital marketing is one of his responsibilities. For Campbell's chief executive officer (CEO) Dennis Morrison this meant that the company would "put the consumer in the center of everything we do."[10]

Another example is Procter & Gamble, which in 2011 spent $9.3 billion on advertising. Global marketing chief Marc Pritchard wanted to spend less on traditional advertising and spend more efficiently on lower-cost digital marketing.[11] Restaurants, clothiers, and other small businesses were also using the new technology, especially social media, to generate buzz, aided by startups such as Groupon Inc.[12] Avon Products, Inc., known for its door-to-door selling, was losing traction as time-stressed consumers were increasingly buying cosmetics on the Web. Staff members took online courses to try to learn how to engage customers with social media.[13]

8.1.3 Impact of Digital Marketing

In noting these developments, Tim Armstrong, chairman-CEO of AOL and former president of Google Inc.'s Americas Operations, explains that business is now living in "the lowest-competition and highest-opportunity [environment]" he's seen in 20 years. He compared the current state of the digital sector to the auto industry in the early decades of the twentieth century, saying, "The next 20 years will make the last 20 look small in comparison."[14]

One reason for this rapid development is that merchants benefit by being able to sell items in small demand online because they don't need to be stocked in stores. They can take advantage of the large number of consumers in what Chris Anderson calls "the *long tail*." He says, "Marketers must shift their thinking from the short head of mainstream marketing to the masses to a strategy of targeting vast numbers of underserved audiences via the Web to search for individual items that are not part of the main surge of customers."[15] It holds the promise of immediacy where consumers achieve the ideal market situation: buying something anytime and anyplace.

Digital marketing has been enhanced by QR codes, a new barcode system of "dense grids of black-and-white boxes that can hold 100 times more information than the old bar system." They can be used for inventory tracking, event ticketing, and advertising.[16] The Ethical Bean Coffee Co. stands out in recognizing the greater value of codes and mobile phones. It uses the codes in its train ads, so that when customers scan the little square with their smart phone cameras a coffee menu appears on their screens and they can order a cup of coffee on the train and have it waiting when they arrive at one of Ethical Bean's shops.[17]

8.1.4 Role of Public Affairs and Advocacy Advertising

Social marketing also includes applications to public affairs, mainly through the use of advocacy advertising to promote a view on a controversial issue. An advocacy ad states an organization's views and position on a controversial matter. Because it is a paid ad, the advertiser has complete control over content and placement in chosen newspapers, magazines, and television shows. An organization can decide on the exact wording of a message, its style, timing, frequency of appearance, and, on occasion, its position in a publication.[18]

Advocacy advertising has been used to draw attention to such issues as climate change. For example, Havas Worldwide cooperated with Kofi Annan, the former secretary-general of the United Nations, to campaign for Climate Justice by developing the "tck tck tck" campaign to raise awareness of climate change. And the UK's Department of Energy and Climate Change commissioned two advertisements on the subject. One ad began with "Jack and Jill went up the hill to fetch a pail of water. There was none, as extreme weather due to climate change had caused a drought."[19]

Beyond advocacy advertising, some see the "cutting-edge frontier of social movement advertising and marketing research as a subfield of international management." Like international public relations, it uses a "full range of information and communication technologies" that is "gradually merging toward a form of what might be called cultural movement marketing . . . ." An example is the Occupy Wall Street movement.[20]

Public affairs helps gain government support for company marketing activities. In the US approximately 20 federal government agencies are involved in supporting US exports directly or indirectly. Nine key agencies with programs or activity directly related to export promotion are the US Department of Agriculture (USDA), Department of Commerce, Export–Import Bank (Ex-ImBank), Overseas Private Investment Corporation (OPIC), Small Business Administration (SBA), Department of State, Trade and Development Agency (TDA), Office of the US Trade Representative (USTR), and Department of the Treasury. They perform a wide variety of functions: providing information, counseling, and export assistance services; funding feasibility studies; financing and insuring US trade; conducting government-to-government advocacy; and negotiating new trade agreements and enforcing existing ones – all part of the Obama administration's efforts to double US exports under the National Export Initiative.[21]

The description of the US Department of Commerce's International Trade Administration (ITA) further explains the role of government in trade. It is responsible for assisting new exporters in developing overseas markets for their products. Firms are most aware of local conferences and workshops on "how to get started in exporting," conducting trade shows abroad, and receiving export counseling. Less known are the comparison shopping services, agent/distributor services, and a joint venture/foreign license program.[22]

8.2 Social Marketing – Changing Consumer and Citizen Attitudes and Behavior

Social marketing describes the use of marketing principles and techniques to advance a social cause, idea, or behavior. Expressed more explicitly by Philip Kotler and Eduardo Roberto, "Social marketing is a strategy for changing behavior."[23] Whereas marketing focuses on selling products and services to consumers, social marketing goes further in two ways: (i) by recognizing that attitudinal and behavioral changes may be needed to complete an exchange in the marketplace or to encourage safe use of a product; and (ii) by gaining acceptability of a social idea or practice like self-breast examination for cancer or revising eating habits to prevent obesity.

Generally, social marketing encourages people to do something that will be beneficial to society and not just themselves. Consumers do this when they cooperate with environmental values and the goals of sustainability to preserve nature and its resources. For example, electric utilities may want their customers to reduce energy consumption and water companies to urge users to use this dwindling resource more sparingly. Even when "commercial marketing" is described as "financial," it can still contribute to achievement of the social good. Social marketing is sometimes described as having two parents: a "social parent" and a "marketing parent."[24]

Social marketing began as a formal discipline in 1971 with the publication of "Social Marketing: An Approach to Planned Social Change" by marketing expert Philip Kotler.[25] He defined social marketing as "the design, implementation, and control of programs seeking to increase the acceptability of a social idea or practice in a target group(s)."[26] Together with Eduardo Roberto, he claimed, "It combines the best elements of the traditional approaches to social change in an integrated planning and action framework and utilizes advances in communication technology and marketing skills."[27] Kotler and Roberto broadened the definition of social marketing to "an organizational effort by one group (the change agent) which intends to persuade others (the target adopters) to accept, modify, or abandon certain ideas, attitudes, practices, and behavior."[28]

8.2.1 Application to Public Health

One of the first applications of social marketing was the "designated driver campaign," which the Harvard School of Public Health described as a national media campaign against drunk driving. It was spearheaded by a unique alliance of Harvard, Hollywood, Madison Avenue, and the broadcast networks. "The project's goal was to change American social norms regarding drinking and driving and thereby reduce alcohol-related traffic deaths."[29] Coors joined the cause by placing commercials in the mid-1990s to combat underage drinking with slogans like "We'll wait for your business."[30] The campaign may also want to encourage desirable behaviors, such as using seat belts, wearing helmets when riding a bicycle, and obeying speed limits.

The public health community became one of the major adopters of social marketing.Craig Lefebvre and June A. Flora explained the rationale that healthcare organizations need the cooperation of their patients to follow prescribed medical regimens and healthy practices of exercising, not smoking, and not imbibing excessively in alcoholic drinks.[31] A list prepared by George R. Franke includes interventions to improve sun-protective behaviors in recreational and tourist settings, children's media use, school bullying, adolescent pregnancy prevention, heterosexual adult HIV prevention, condom use in developing countries, and organ donation campaigns.[32]

Some applications of social marketing cross the institutional boundaries of business and government. CVS Caremark shows how a business uses social marketing. As part of its efforts to improve pharmacy healthcare for American consumers, CVS Caremark announced it is expanding its research efforts to include the creation of a Behavior Change Research Partnership. It will help healthcare providers better understand why people choose to follow – or ignore – their prescribed medication regiment, and look for ways to encourage those patients to make effective healthcare decisions. To study the issues through the lens of behavioral economics and social marketing, it is working with academic leaders from Carnegie Mellon University, Dartmouth College's Tuck School of Business, the University of Pennsylvania's Medical School, and Wharton School of Business.[33]

8.2.2 Tackling the Obesity Issue Worldwide

Obesity is increasingly recognized as a major public health problem for which social marketing is being enlisted to change people's behavior. The World Health Organization calls obesity an epidemic. Obesity, once mainly the scourge of the West, is spreading into Asia, threatening health systems and economic growth. A study by the University of Washington's Institute for Health Metrics and Evaluation said 46 million Chinese adults were obese and 300 million were overweight. The author of the study, Eric Finkelstein, one of the world's leading experts in the field, says that while some Asian countries have implemented programs to try and curb the growth in obesity, "the reality is that it is very difficult for governments to combat obesity . . . there are just too few policy levers."[34]

Adult obesity is now more common globally than undernutrition and is the third biggest cause of premature death and disability in the affluent world after smoking and high blood pressure, according to the International Association for the Study of Obesity (IASO). In the US, about one-third of the population is now officially classified as obese, estimated to cause an economic loss of $140 billion a year.[35]

Childhood obesity has received special attention. Heavier children and teens face health threats formerly seen mainly in middle-aged adults. Children also face the risk of asthma, sleep apnea, and fatty liver. Since 1980, child obesity has tripled. Currently, 12.5 million American children and teens ages 2–19 are obese, comprising 17% of the population.[36] Public action is growing. Former First Lady Michelle Obama championed the issue and launched the Let's Move! campaign. As part of this effort, President Obama established the Task Force on Childhood Obesity to develop and implement an interagency plan that details a coordinated strategy, identifies key benchmarks, and outlines an action plan to solve the problem of childhood obesity within a generation.

Faced with soda taxes in several states and cities in the US, France, and elsewhere, Coca-Cola hopes to ward off these taxes not only by lobbying but by turning to social marketing to promote healthy life styles. Since 2005, the soda industry has spent nearly $100 million on lobbying to oppose such taxes.[37] In addition it has placed full-page ads in several newspapers saying: "At Coca-Cola, we believe active lifestyles lead to happier lives. That's why we are committed to creating awareness around choice and movement, to help people make the most informed decisions for themselves and their families."[38] In August 2015, Muhetar Kent, chairman and CEO of Coca-Cola, said in a *Wall Street Journal* article titled "Coca-Cola: We'll Do Better," that it was "Committed to acting with integrity with our customers and our communities, Coca-Cola has always believed that a healthy diet and regular exercise are essential for a healthy lifestyle."[39]

Rival PepsiCo seeks to balance its sales of Fritos, Cheetos, Lay's and Pepsi with some healthy foods such as a fiber-filled nut and fruit bar called Init and sparkling lemonade with real lemon juice called Lemon Lemon. Even with its normal products PepsiCo has set new sugar, sodium, and fat reduction targets for 2025. In 2016, Indra Nooyi, PepsiCo's CEO could point to the rise of its nutritious products to about 25% of revenue from 20% a few years ago. The goal is to provide consumers with a choice: when consumers want to indulge, it has indulgent products; when they want to eat healthy, it offers healthy products.[40]

Business must balance the objectives of commercial marketing activities with those of social marketing. In some areas of public health concern, such as obesity, corporate marketing activities may negate social marketing messages targeting individuals. Traditional social marketing campaigns may be ineffective when commercial marketing activities create an environment that encourages and maintains unhealthy behaviors.[41] The Institute for Social Marketing (ISM), at the University of Stirling, led research showing that many young people took up smoking and drinking earlier in life because they were affected by advertising. "Our research has shown that children must be protected from the commercial marketing of alcohol, tobacco, and junk food, and has enabled national and international policy makers to respond accordingly."[42] ISM has also protected policy makers from legal attacks by multinationals with a vested interest in these markets.

8.2.2.1 Government Health-Focused Programs

Health marketing by government should be thought of as a form of social marketing, say Paul N. Bloom and William D. Novelli.[43] An example is Rwanda's effort to curb HIV/AIDS. It distributed over 23 million condoms in 2010, almost double the 16 million distributed in 2009. The Ministry of Health credited social marketing strategies for the drastic increase in the public's sensitization on condom use. Equally important was the establishment of social mechanisms of setting up free condom dispensing spots in public institutions, including hospitals. The social marketing approach ensured availability of condoms through the commercial sector while the public sector permitted the distribution of free condoms, with health facilities being the traditionally accepted final distribution points.[44]

A European Group, calling itself European Youth Tackling Obesity, involving partners across England, Spain, Portugal, and the Czech Republic, developed peer-led social marketing campaigns to promote healthy eating and physical activity among young people aged 13–16 who are vulnerable to obesity. The campaign transcended cultural barriers to improve motivation among young people to live healthier lifestyles and thereby contribute to a reduction in childhood obesity. Social marketing experts in each country developed campaigns using a range of creative methods matched to the needs, aspirations, cultures, and social norms of their peers. Interventions involved digital and social media elements alongside other activities and events such as roadshows. According to their end of project evaluation, almost 90% of young people who engaged with the campaigns said that the campaigns were effective in encouraging them to eat a healthier diet and be more physically active.[45]

In the UK, the National Health Service (NHS) is increasingly turning to campaigns that try to prevent the public from becoming ill.[46] From drinking and smoking to flu jabs and cervical cancer inoculations, the NHS has ramped up its preventive health campaigns to try to reach the public before they become patients. Primary care trusts (PCTs) will for the first time be judged on their ability to connect with the public, which means changing their role from helping sick people get better to keeping people healthy in the first place.

"Social marketing is the most powerful tool in the NHS communications box," believes Stefi Rucci, communications director at Say Communications.[47] Agreeing with her, Julian Tyndale-Biscoe, managing director of InHealth Communications, says NHS organizations are tailoring campaigns to focus on the highest risk groups: "This means segmenting the population to find a target group, understanding this group's beliefs and how it learns behaviour, then devising a tailored message and delivery chain."[48] He cites the example of Brent PCT, which used teenage peer groups to get safe sex messages across to high-risk teenagers. Another study, however, shows "It can prove challenging to create social marketing materials aimed at a specific subsection of the population, especially when the topic is relatively new and possibly misunderstood." The study "sought to assess adolescent knowledge of and attitudes toward emergency contraception with the goal of creating a locally relevant social marketing campaign and intervention."[49]

Australia applied social marketing to the problem of reducing suicides of people in the prime of life, from adolescence to middle age, noting that it lost 40% more people from suicide each year than died on roads. Yet, because suicide has been such a taboo subject, shrouded in shame and silence, most people have been unaware that it is Australia's greatest preventable public health and social challenge. Mainstream media and social marketing provide huge opportunities to reduce the suicide toll by highlighting the life-long trauma that suicide wreaks on those left behind – families, friends, and workmates. TV advertisements by the Victorian Transport Accident Commission focused on the latter theme.[50]

Public relations agencies have been hired to promote healthcare through social marketing. About $92 million of stimulus money from the American Recovery and Reinvestment Act was awarded to public relations firms, two-thirds of which was for health promotion and social marketing. Ketchum was set to receive nearly $23 million for a campaign to educate consumers and healthcare providers about electronic health records and the Hitech Act. Another $2.2 million would come from the Department of Commerce as a subcontractor to IBM.[51]

8.2.3 Use of Wide Range of Communication Practices

Social marketing uses a wide range of communication practices and media to achieve its objectives. Research is used to select and carefully pinpoint audiences. The need for social mechanisms, such as the availability of health clinics, is recognized to implement social marketing, using techniques from public relations and advertising. The media include personal communications, billboards, newspapers, and broadcasting. Sometimes broadcasters have altered existing practices to accommodate social messages, as illustrated by recent Super Bowl advertising.

8.2.3.1 Super Bowl Advertising Carries Social Message

The Super Bowl is a high viewership event and the biggest day of the year for both sports and advertising. It is therefore appealing for social marketing purposes. Before the 2010 Super Bowl, advertising on issues was limited to spots against smoking cigarettes, abusing drugs, and eating food with high cholesterol. But in 2010, CBS, which broadcast the Super Bowl, sold 30 seconds of commercial time to Focus on the Family, an evangelical organization known for conservative views on subjects like abortion and gay marriage.

The plan was to feature Tim Tebow, the college football star, together with his mother who had decided to give birth to Tom rather than have an abortion. The decision by CBS to sell an advocacy ad during a Super Bowl set off a debate about its use for a controversial issue. CBS, which broadcasts the game every 3 years in rotation with Fox and NBC, changed its policy in 2008 to accept ads that sell opinions rather than products and had since run issue ads on subjects such as healthcare reform and the environment. The monitoring of online conversation by Alterian and Zeta Interactive found that the spot had generated more discussion than any other planned for the game.[52] The Super Bowl incident demonstrates the extension of advocacy advertising to broader issues of social change.

8.3 Conclusions

Social marketing adds the goal of strengthening relationship-building to influencing the behavior of people as consumers and citizens. One of the major beneficiaries of social marketing is public health, which is down to efforts to change people's harmful behavior and to encourage healthy habits. The problems of obesity, HIV, and suicides are among those addressed. Findings of the behavioral sciences that are applied here also provide insights for marketing in general. All the communication practices are rooted in communication theory and the social sciences.

Digital marketing makes use of the internet as well as devices such as smart phones. It also makes inordinate use of "big data." It displaces physical stores but makes product available through the "long tail" that stores often don't carry.

Social marketing adds the goal of strengthening relationship-building to influencing the behavior of people as consumers and citizens. Findings of the behavioral sciences that are applied here also provide insights for marketing in general. All the communication practices are rooted in communication theory and the social sciences.

Discussion Questions

8.1. Why does Shel Holtz consider the internet one of the most significant tools ever employed in public relations? How has it helped?

8.2. What new marketing opportunities has digital marketing created?

8.3. What skills are associated with digital marketing?

8.4. With the advent of digital marketing, does the third P of place still have any significance?

8.5. What is the marketing significance of the "long tail"?

8.6. Why is it sometimes desirable to change people's consumption habits? Give an example.

8.7. Why is social marketing particularly relevant to public health?

8.8. How are Coca-Cola and PepsiCo making use of social marketing?

Case 3 High Drug Prices Become a Public Issue

The extraordinarily high prices of some pharmaceuticals has become a controversial issue that draws public relations and public affairs into marketing. The problem is most pronounced in the US but also affects countries in Europe and Asia that purchase American drugs. The global pharmaceutical industry is concentrated in the US and Europe, where the 10 biggest drug companies are located.[53] In the US, the biggest are Pfizer, Johnson & Johnson, and Merck; the UK has GlaxoSmithKline and Astra Zeneca. Price controls are absent in the US but the majority of European countries have them. For example, the UK's competition regulator fined Pfizer Inc. more than $100 million for excessive prices on an anti-epilepsy drug.[54]

An Epidemic of High Prices

The prices of some new drugs are staggering. Gilead Sciences Inc. launched a new drug for hepatitis C, Sovaldi, in 2013 at a price of $84 000 per person, or $1000 per pill over the 12-week course of treatment. It was the costliest drug to Medicare in 2015, with sales amounting to $1.8 billion.[55] It also introduced Havoni, for which it charged $95 000. That drug earned roughly $9 billion in sales during the first 9 months of 2014. Despite all that pharma companies say about needing high prices to support research into new drugs, Gilead did not invent these drugs: it had acquired both hepatitis C drugs in 2012 with the $11 billion acquisition of Pharmasset Inc.[56] Gilead's sales rose nearly 3.5 times to $32.2 billion in 2015 and stock prices have jumped more than 138% since then.[57]

Marathon Pharmaceuticals exceeded Gilead in charging $89 000 in the US for Emflaza, an old steroidal drug that costs only $1600 a year or less abroad.[58] This price caused a group of US senators to send a letter to Marathon's CEO Jeffrey S. Aronin asking for justification for the drug's price. The company response was evasive, saying "Marathon Pharmaceutical is committed to ensuring that all patients who need this drug have access to it."[59]

Perhaps the greatest attention has been given to Mylan NV, which charged $609 for a two-pen pack of a commonly used allergy drug branded EpiPen, a product children's lives sometimes depended on. EpiPen's list price had climbed nearly 550% from about $94 since 2007. The price in September 2016 had risen 32% from the previous September. Parents voiced their displeasure on Facebook, Twitter, and other social media, which caught the attention of lawmakers who called for an investigation into Mylan's price increases. Mylan responded by selling a generic product for $300 for two injection pens.[60] Nonetheless, in April 2017, Mylan was hit with a lawsuit alleging the company overcharged patients as part of an illegal scheme to secure sales.[61] A related issue is that Mylan's chairman received nearly $100 million in 2016 plus other benefits. The company's CEO Heather Bresch received a pay package of $13.8 million.[62]

Other examples of high drug prices are Ono Pharmaceutical Co. and Bristol-Myers Squibb Co. They put a new class of cancer drugs on the market in Japan in early September 2014 with prices that averaged an annual cost of $143 000.[63] And Vertex Pharmaceuticals charges $250 000 for a drug called Orkambi to treat cystic fibrosis, a deadly lung disorder.[64]

Costs to Governments and Individuals

Governments have been the payers for a large portion of these drug costs. In the US, where healthcare costs represent about 18% of the US's GDP, state Medicaid programs spent $1.33 billion on hepatitis C therapies through the third quarter of 2014, or nearly what states spent in the previous 3 years combined.[65] Individual patients too were burdened with higher drug costs. The number of Americans with annual prescription costs above $50 000 rose by 63% in 2014 to 576 000. Those whose costs were over $100 000 trebled to 139 000.[66]

In the UK limits are placed on spending for life-saving drugs on the basis of analyses by the National Institute for Health and Clinical Excellence. It weighs the health benefits of a new treatment against the costs and advises the government on which treatments to pay for. It generally approves drugs that offer an additional year of good-quality life for less than $30 000–$50 000 (studies in the US, suggest higher amounts – $50 000–$100 000). It recommended against the drug Avastin because it increases life only by an average of roughly 4 months in colon cancer patients.[67]

Drugs prices have risen further because pharmaceutical companies have learned that giving patients combinations of multiple drugs is more effective. When Johnson & Johnson added a third drug, Darzalex, to an older two-drug combination for patients with multiple myeloma, the cancer's growth was slowed significantly. But the combination would cost at least $180 000 for the first full year of treatment for the average patients. By itself, Darzalex costs about $134 550 for the first year and $76 050 each year thereafter. Another company, Bristol-Myers Squibb, combined its Opdivo and Yervoy drugs to treat melanoma, charging $250 000 a patient for the first full year of treatment.[68] A third company, AbbVie, is testing a combination of drugs Imbruvica and Venclexta to treat a form of leukemia. In their currently approved uses, the former costs at least $116 000 a year and the latter $109 500 for the first year of treatment.

Government and Public Outrage Grows

Sellers of high-priced drugs will have to engage not only in careful pricing strategies but also in a public affairs analysis to respond to criticism from doctors, patients, and insurers, as well as possible actions by government officials and legislators. Fortunately for the drug industry, Medicare and other government health programs foot the bill and therefore soften opposition from patients. Pressure is mounting, however, for Congress to reexamine the exemption of pharmaceutical companies from government bargaining for prices. Pharma companies have to weigh the advantage of reaping high profits in the short run against the risk of government intervention.

The pharmaceutical companies argue that high prices are justified because the drugs have high cure rates and can stave off more costly health interventions. "If a surgeon announced they had developed a surgery that would cure 90% of patients and that surgery would cost $200,000 nobody would bat an eye," said Mick Kolassa, a former pharmaceutical industry pricing official. Bristol-Myers said its prices are based on "the value they deliver to patients and society, the scientific innovation they represent and the investment required to support drug research and development."[69] Companies typically argue that it can cost well over $1 billion to bring a new drug to market and that revenue is needed to fund research for new and better drugs. But as noted by Derek Lowe, an organic chemist who previously worked for several major pharma companies and now runs a website monitoring the industry, "There's a big difference between augmenting your own research efforts with outside deals – or trying to – and zeroing out your own research altogether."[70]

Shkreli Blackens Pharma's Image

One occasion often cited as an outrageous price increase is when Martin Shkreli, as chief executive of Turing Pharmaceutical AG, bought the US rights to the drug Daraprim, a decades-old drug used to treat AIDS patients, from Impax Laboratories and immediately raised the price from $13.50 to $750. In his defense, Shkreli said the drug had been underpriced. He lashed out at critics on social media. His credibility suffered, however, when he was arrested in December 2015 by the Federal Bureau of Investigation on a different matter: that he had misled investors in his hedge funds and looted a publicly traded company to cover losses.[71] He was convicted in August 2017 for securities fraud.[72] He seemed to have transferred his Wall Street mentality to the pharmaceutical industry. Shkreli's background was as a hedge fund manager, signifying that the heathcare industry was attracting attention from Wall Street profit seekers.

A year later on February 4, 2016, he was asked to appear before the House Committee on Oversight and Government Reform on the price hike issue. After weeks of negotiation over whether he would attend the hearing, he did, but invoked his Fifth Amendment right not to answer any questions. He asserted, "I intend to follow the advice of my counsel, not yours." Shkreli was combative, saying that he was asked to the hearing merely to help Congress score political points or provide entertaining theater. His behavior was insolent. He appeared to smirk, look away, and otherwise goad lawmakers. After he left the hearing, he tweeted, "Hard to accept that these imbeciles represent the people in our government."[73] His behavior reinforced the impression that the profiteering culture of Wall Street has invaded the pharmaceutical industry.

Canada's Valeant Pharmaceutical Takes Center Stage

However, it was the Canadian company Valeant Pharmaceuticals International that became a poster child for criticism of high drug prices and target of congressional inquiries. Since 2010, Valeant had completed about 100 acquisitions and then raising the price on most of them.[74] Receiving the most attention were the drugs Isuprel and Nitropress, which treat heart problems; their prices were raised by 525% and 212%, respectively.[75]

Its deals helped transform Valeant into Canada's most valuable company, with its shares rising five-fold between 2011 and 2014. But since the stock's high in August 2015, its shares lost more than 85% of their value by April 2016. Its CEO Michael Pearson was called to testify before the Senate Special Committee on Aging. He was accused not only of leveling exorbitant price increases but "shady accounting practices, a weak board, mountains of debt, and absurdly paid managers 'with a mentality of denial.'"[76] Pearson was replaced in May 2016 by Joseph Papa, who immediately assured the Senate, "I understand the concerns our partners in the health care community have had about the pricing of these drugs, and we want to ensure hospitals and partners can get the drugs they need."[77] He doesn't say at what price.

The Drug Marketplace: An Absence of Competition

Patents give the companies the monopoly right for 20 years and possibly longer. Patent protection allows a pharmaceutical company to charge "what the market will bear." The fear of pharma companies is that lower-cost copies of their drugs could be developed and break the monopoly. In February 2016, for example, the Food and Drug Administration (FDA) voted to recommend that the agency approve the sale of a knockoff version of Johnson & Johnson's arthritis drug Remicade, which in 2015 had sales of $4.45 million.[78]

AbbVie and Amgen are attempting to block such "biosimilar" copies by taking out new patents to extend their existing patents into the 2020s and 2030s. AbbVie, which has taken out about 70 patents for its arthritis treatment Humira, is exploring filing additional patents that would keep copycat versions off the US market until at least 2022. AbbVie has also been sued by the Federal Trade Commission for filing baseless patent infringement lawsuits against two generic drug companies to delay competition for its testosterone replacement therapy AndroGel.[79] Keeping the global market in mind, several companies, including Amgen Inc. and Pfizer Inc., had urged US negotiators in trade talks over the controversial Trans-Pacific Partnership trade agreement to grant brand name biologic drugs a period of exclusivity of up to 12 years based on intellectual property rights.[80]

The Force of Government and Countervailing Power

The government is the largest buyer of drugs through Medicare and the Affordable Care Act, but it is not allowed directly to negotiate drug prices. As President Donald Trump bluntly put it: "they're getting away with murder."[81] He said the US would become more aggressive in bidding for drugs and supported allowing Medicare to directly negotiate drug prices. Scott Gottlieb, the new commissioner of the FDA, has set an activist agenda on generic drugs through the Drug Price Competition Act, saying "Simply put, too many patients are priced out of the medicines they need."[82] To facilitate entry of lower-cost alternatives, Gottlieb has asked his agency to intervene in cases in which brand name drug companies are accused of using FDA safety rules to refuse to make drugs available to generic manufacturers, which generic companies need to manufacture equivalent drugs. One application of a rule in the Hatch–Waxman Act of 1984, allowed the drug company Cephalon to protect its sleep disorder drug Provigil by paying four generic manufacturers $300 million each to delay their entry into the market for 6 years.[83]

During her presidential campaign, Hillary Clinton also tweeted about "price gouging," which contributed to a big drop in biotech company share prices. According to a Kaiser Family Foundation poll conducted in the fall of 2016, 80% of Americans favor allowing Medicare to negotiate lower prices for Medicare beneficiaries.[84]

Congress has taken some action, albeit feeble. Three congressional Democrats asked Gilead to justify the cost.[85]

In Ohio a group called the Ohio Taxpayers for Lower Drug Prices placed a ballot measure on November 7, 2018, that would require state government entities, including the Medicaid health insurance program for low-income people, to pay no more for prescription drugs than what is paid by the US Department of Veterans Affairs. The latter is able to buy drugs at a mandatory 24% discount to regular prices. The drug industry spent $49.1 million on TV ads and other efforts to try to defeat the measure.[86]

In July 2014, the US Senate Finance Committee launched an investigation of Gilead's pricing of Sovaldi. On the state level, Philadelphia's transit agency sued Gilead, accusing the company of "price-gouging." Its attorney said the price of Sovaldi is "bleeding health and welfare plans around the country."[87] After it hit the market in December 2013, the drug generated $8.55 billion in sales for the first 9 months of 2014. Another state, Maryland, also enacted a law that authorizes the state attorney general to sue companies to try to roll back certain price increases. Maryland Attorney General Brian Frosh said that the new law "gives Maryland a necessary tool to combat unjustified and extreme price increases for medicines that have long been on the market and that are essential to our health and well-being."[88]

But by spring 2017, government efforts had mostly been ineffective. Prices continued to rise and Congress had not changed the law that prohibits government bargaining. The success of the pharmaceutical industry is attributed to its skill in lobbying and making campaign contributions. Public affairs has certainly become a major activity of the drug industry.

Investor relations is another arena of concern. A group of 300 institutional investors are waging a campaign against drug makers, asking them to justify their price increases. The Interfaith Center on Corporate Responsibility (ICCR) and others have submitted shareholder proposals asking 11 US companies, including Johnson & Johnson, Pfizer, and Merck & Co., to issue reports listing average annual price boosts for their top-selling drugs between 2010 and 2016 and state the rationale for the increases.[89] But several companies are planning to omit the drug price transparency proposal from their proxy ballots by asking the Securities and Exchange Commission to exclude them on the grounds that they would interfere with "ordinary business." Merck bluntly called the proposals "a clear attempt to exert influence on the pricing decisions made by the Merck management team."[90]

Short of government action, when market forces are inadequate, countervailing power supposedly becomes activated, as explained by economist Kenneth Galbraith in his *American Capitalism: The Theory of Countervailing Power*.[91] The power of the drug industry would be offset by opposing power, namely government agencies such as Medicare. One sign of the exercise of this power is the modest effort by companies of hiring middlemen called pharmacy-benefit managers (PBMs) to negotiate discounts and rebates on drug prices from pharmaceutical companies and retail pharmacies. These modest efforts are now being boosted by a US non-profit group called the Health Transformation Alliance. It was formed in 2016 by more than three dozen companies, including American Express, Johnson & Johnson, and Macy's.[92] Their combined negotiating power allows it to win lower prices than any individual company could do alone.

Other efforts to reduce workers health costs are also being planned. One is by Amazon.com Inc., Berkshire Hathaway Inc. and JPMorgan Chase & Co. – companies that have more than a million employees worldwide. Warren Buffet, Berkshire's chairman, said "The ballooning costs of healthcare act as a hungry tapeworm on the American economy." That claim is supported by a 2015 Harvard Business Review article that found that clinical waste, administrative complexity, excessive prices, and "fraud and abuse" accounted for 40% of total healthcare spending in the US. The companies hope the project could save them hundreds of millions of dollars and might serve as a blueprint for others.[93]

Another is by several non-profit hospital systems that are planning to start their own non-profit generic drug company. Intermountain Healthcare, Ascension, SSM Health, and Trinity Health said they will seek Food and Drug Administration approval to manufacture and market generic drugs.[94] So far, however, the forces of countervailing power have not succeeded in substantially lowering the high prices of the drug market.

Drug Industry Response

The drug industry has been facing increasing legislative pressure. In 2017 it faced a Maryland law that barred steep prices increases for generic drugs, and Vermont, Nevada, and California have passed laws requiring companies to disclose information to justify certain price increases. In Ohio a fierce battle was waged over a referendum on high drug prices. The referendum was promoted by Ohio Taxpayers for Lower Drug Prices and Los Angeles-based AIDS Healthcare Foundation. It was opposed by the drug industry in a campaign that spent $49.1 million on TV ads and other efforts to defeat it.[95]

Recognizing growing public pressure, the Pharmaceutical Research and Manufacturers of America (PhRMA) has launched several initiatives. On May9, 2017, its board of directors declared a new membership criterion: companies must spend at least $200 million a year on research and development and R&D must equal at least 10% of global sales. That requirement helps reinforces PhRMA's argument that high prices are needed to support R&D. The directors also ousted 22 members. The *Wall Street Journal* called it "The Drug Lobby's In-House Hygiene."[96]

Another PhRMA effort was its launching of an image advertising campaign, with a 3-year average of at least $100 million, designed to improve its reputation with lawmakers. This has been augmented by institutional advertising by individual companies. Pfizer placed a full-page ad in major newspapers on January 2017 with the headline, "There is one national concern that will always unite us," followed by four statements such as "Of all our national resources none is of more basic value than the health of our people."

A third, more targeted effort was reported by Robert Zirkelbach, senior vice president of communications at PhRMA, who said it is running ads on social media sites, such as Facebook, LinkedIn, and Twitter, aimed at targeting federal and state lawmakers, policy analysts, and other political "influencers." Celgene Corp. Chief Executive Robert Hugin, a PhRMA board member, explained, "We've identified 7,000 Americans who matter. We're focusing on [people] in policy positions, talking to patient groups, to fight structural issues."[97] He added that the industry can't change the minds of more than 300 million Americans. Merck's CEO Kenneth C. Frazier acknowledges that "the entire pharmaceutical industry has a lot of work to do to restore public trust."[98]

These initiatives by the pharmaceutical industry to ward off government intervention and maintain public trust are not new. In 1994, after the then President Bill Clinton characterized the pharmaceutical industry as a bunch of price gougers, the drug companies mounted a sophisticated campaign that included frequent visits to Washington by their top executives, hefty campaign contributions to members of Congress, and a multimillion-dollar advertising blitz.[99]

Gilead, Marathon, Mylan, and other sellers of high-priced drugs will have to engage in careful issues management and public affairs analysis to assess the strength of government actions and countervailing power to limit price increases. So far, the drug industry has been inordinately successful. It has been helped because Medicare and other government health programs at present foot much of the bill and thereby soften opposition from patients. At some time, however, the exemption of pharmaceutical companies from government bargaining for prices may be reexamined by Congress and marketing activities will need continued public relations and public affairs support.

Pharma companies have to weigh the advantage of reaping high profits in the short run against the risk of greater government intervention. As recognized by CEO James Mullen: "If there's price increases that can be taken and delivered to shareholders, we'll go get it, but I do think we got to make sure we take a long enough view and you don't start to put this thing in a box, where you get the backlash."[100]

Discussion Questions

1. Are the pharmaceutical companies justified in charging high prices for their drugs? Why?
2. What arguments does the industry use to justify its prices? Do you agree with them?
3. How are high prices ordinarily tamed in other industries? What exempts drug companies?
4. What are the sources of mounting pressure against the industry? Should the pharmaceutical companies take these pressures seriously? How much power do drug consumers have? Is government likely to invoke its countervailing power?
5. Is Pharma's advertising campaign sound? Do you agree with all of its features? What other steps might the industry undertake?
6. What is your solution to high drug prices?
7. What does all this say about corporate social responsibility?
8. Is it possible for pharmaceutical companies to restore public trust in them?

Case 4 Uber Requires Public Affairs Assistance and Cultural Overhaul

Issues connected with technology and innovation typically require the application of several communication practices. Getting consumers to use new products and services calls for marketing combined with public relations to explain them and gain acceptance. New technologies may also require formidable public affairs efforts because of opposition by vested interests and government authorities. The experience of Uber has demonstrated these features.

The car ride service of Uber is obviously opposed by taxi companies and their drivers and by government officials who find their regulations circumvented. These regulations have had the effect of restricting the number of taxis, which resulted in medallion prices that reached $1.3 million in New York City. The taxi industry in countries and cities throughout the world protested and lobbied to outlaw the new digital competition. In London, taxi drivers conducted a protest in July 2014, and in Brussels a court ruling in April 2015 levied a $12 800 fine for cars taking passengers using the app.[101] As of mid-2015, protests against Uber had been staged in Germany, India, Spain, France, Italy, Brazil, China, and England, among other nations. In Budapest, Hungary, cars will have their license plates removed and won't be allowed on the roads for 6 months if they are detected as being used for illegal taxi services.[102] Opposition in France and China has been particularly strong.

Opposition in France and China

Uber in France

It is France where Uber initially faced the most serious obstacles, even though it chose Paris to launch its European service. A new law forbids non-taxi services like Uber from showing the availability of nearby vehicles in its smart phone maps.[103] It also makes operating a system that puts clients in touch with drivers without commercial licenses punishable by 2 years in prison and a $372 000 fine. In June 2015, taxis filled Paris streets to protest Uber. They blocked access to both of Paris's airports, overturned Uber cars, and burned tires on the city's ring road.

Two top executives of Uber, Pierre-Dimitri Gore-Coty, head of Uber's operations in Europe, the Middle East, and Africa, and Thibaud Simphal, its chief in France, were arrested in Paris on six charges, ranging from deceptive communication practices to illicit storage of personal data.[104] They face a 5-year ban on running a company and fines of £70 000 for Gore-Coty and £50 000 for Simphal. On June 8, 2016, a Paris court did indeed convict Uber and its two executives in France and fined them a total of $1.1 million.[105]

Uber argues that France did not notify the European Union (EU) before passing the law that targets what it strategically calls "information-society services," a category that avoids the association with taxis. Referring to what he calls the "taxi industry cartel," Plouff characterized it as standing in the way of technology and big change. He had the support of Neelie Kroes, former vice president of the European Commission, who said, "The fact is that digital technology is changing many aspects of our lives. We cannot address these challenges by ignoring them, by going on strike or by trying to ban these innovations out of existence."[106]

In May 2017, Uber suffered a blow. The European Court of Justice recommended that the US ride-hailing company be regulated as a transportation company, not an online platform as Uber had argued. The court argued that transport is the company's main service of economic value and that the app is secondary. Moreover, it noted that Uber sets the prices of rides and can exclude drivers from its platform.[107]

In England, the Transport for London authority threatened not to renew Uber's right to operate in London, citing "a lack of corporate responsibility that could undermine public safety and security." [108]

Resistance in China

Uber's CEO Travis Kalanick coveted China, which has the world's largest market of urban commuters, estimated at 750 million. He stated, "The vastness of opportunities really isn't matched in any other market." Kalanick said around 30% of their trips were now in China. Its biggest city, Chengdu, is about 100 times bigger than San Francisco at the same age, he said. That's why he wanted to meet with Chenk Wei, CEO of the dominant ride-hailing company, Didi Kuadi. Wei recalls Kalanick's overture, "His message was they had conquered the whole world and would also conquer China."[109] Proceeding on his own, Kalanick decided to invest $1.2 billion in China in 2015.[110]

Private ride-hailing is technically illegal in most Chinese cities, but Didi Kuaidi hoped to change that by working with taxi companies whose drivers were resisting the competition. As a local player, Didi Kuaidi had an advantage in government relations, but Kalanick countered this advantage by crisscrossing China to hobnob with government officials and businesses. To win their cooperation, Kalanick said in one of his speeches that progress brought by his company had to be "in harmony with stability," words often used by Chinese officials to signal the dangers of social and political unrest.[111] Uber also hired former government employees to key posts, such as placing Jimang Xie, who formerly worked for China's State Administration of Radio, Film, and Television, in charge of its China Communications Lead. Nevertheless, the Chinese government plans to regulate the ride-sharing sector. It plans to require licenses for drives and make pricing more transparent.[112]

Despite almost 3 years of attempting to dominate the market, in August 2016 Uber agreed to sell its China business to rival Didi Chuxing Technology Co. Uber was unable to outmaneuver the homegrown player, which had the advantage of localized features, powerful investors, and favored relations with regulators. Uber's venture in China was a costly one, having lost $2 billion in 2 years, most of which went for subsidies to lure both drivers and passengers. Uber received a 17.7% stake in the merged company and Kalanick was given a place on Didi's board.[113]

Having suffered in China, Uber aims to win other lucrative markets in Southeast Asia. Brooks Entwistle, Uber's chief business officer for Asia, said the area is a "critical" and "growing" market for Uber. But it faces a local competitor, Grab Inc., which has been quicker to meet local preferences and is forging better relations with regulators.[114]

The Independent Contractor Issue

A rising issue with Uber drivers is whether they are truly independent contractors or are employees entitled to health plans and other protections. The issue of defining an "employee" extends beyond Uber to other firms that use "contractors" to clean houses, run errands, and deliver food.[115] Shannon Liss-Riordan, a Boston attorney, argues that Uber has illegally classified drivers as freelancers and not employees.

Uber's lawyers claim that it is a software platform connecting car owners with people seeking rides, not the manager of a fleet of drivers. It insists that its drivers are independent contractors because they set their own schedule, use their own vehicles, and determine which passengers to pick up.[116] Attorney Liss-Riordan, however, questions why Uber and other on-demand firms can't offer drivers flexibility and yet provide them basic labor protections.[117] A new lawsuit holds Kalanick and Garrett Camp, the co-founder of Uber, personally liable for wages owed to California Uber drivers.[118] In England, a British court confirmed a decision that Uber must give its drivers employee rights such as paid vacations.[119]

Seattle has become scene of a unionization drive for app-based drivers by the Teamsters labor union, which challenges Uber's independent contractor model. This model requires drivers to pay for such expenses as fuel, vehicle maintenance, and insurance in exchange for promises of a steady stream of riders and a flexible work schedule. A city ordinance passed in 2015 gives drivers the right to vote to organize and thereby win the right to negotiate fares and benefits. Uber has been fighting back by running podcasts on voting rights and collective bargaining. Fearing the spread of the Seattle model to other cities, Uber threatens to leave Seattle if a union forms.[120] In the UK, Uber faced a setback when the Employment Appeal Tribunal reaffirmed that the company must give its drivers, of which there are 50 000, employee rights such as paid vacations.[121]

Looking to the future, Uber envisions avoiding the employee problem by developing a driverless car. To do so it has entered a strategic partnership with Carnegie Mellon's National Robotics Engineering Center.[122] But Uber faces a huge challenge from rival Alphabet, which alleges it obtained stolen technology.[123]

Uber executives say they are aiming to make Uber explicitly legal everywhere it operates. To this end, David Plouffe, a strategist behind Barack Obama's two presidential wins, has been named as senior vice president of policy and strategy. He will oversee global policy, communications, and branding, and head the approach that Uber CEO Kalanick called "principled confrontation."

Abrasive Management Style and Unethical Practices

Uber must examine its management values and abrasive tactics, which helped it at the beginning but are now damaging its bottom line and reputation. Uber was valued at $68 billion in August 2017.[124] It had gained a reputation for its defiant and aggressive entry into new markets. Kalanick listed "toe-stepping" and "huslin'" as corporate values accounting for Uber's success in entering markets.[125] He was known for his sharp-elbowed management style and speaking harshly to employees; e.g. Kalanick was seen on a video yelling at a driver. He regretted his comments and vowed to "grow up."[126]

Uber is now known for its gross mismanagement and misconduct. A legal feud has erupted with Benchmark Capital, one of its major investors, owning about 13% of the company. It succeeded in ousting Kalanick as CEO and wanted him off the board. Benchmark said that if allowed to continue, "Kalanick's improper actions would cause irreparable harm to Uber by exposing it to reputational, regulatory, and other risks."[127] Uber faced a months-long probe into its culture after a former software engineer alleged rampant sexism and sexual harassment. In addition to Alphabet's lawsuit over stolen trade secrets, it faced a lawsuit in Singapore that accused it of knowingly leasing unsafe cars to drivers.[128]

Defections from management have been numerous. One was Jeff Jones, the company's president, who declared that "the beliefs and approach to leadership that have guided my career are inconsistent with what I saw and experienced at Uber."[129] *The Economist* suggests that Uber's "immaturity and a lack of professional management" will hamper its plan to go public.[130] In August 2017 Uber was left simultaneously seeking a new CEO, heads of finance, marketing and operations, and a new chairman.[131]

Uber has also engaged in unethical practices. It is accused of stealing trade secrets and helping employees dodge regulators' scrutiny. Google-parent Alphabet claims Uber stole driverless car trade secrets from Waymo, one of its units. It is also accused of unearthing trade secrets and competitive intelligence from rivals and using devices to store information outside of Uber's servers. It allegedly trained employees in how to "impede, obstruct or influence" ongoing legal investigations, including the use of disappearing messages.[132]

Uber is slowing examining its work culture and corporate practices. It may also be learning to match aggressiveness with a willingness to seek compromises with government officials in the cities and countries where it operates. It may be learning that plowing into markets and clashing openly with regulators is dysfunctional. The appointment of Dara Khosrowshahi as chief executive and changes in board membership may pave the way for sweeping changes in how the company is run.[133] But will making Uber a kinder company enable it to justify its value of $68 billion, the world's most highly valued privately held company?[134]

Discussion Questions

1 Why is this case one of technology and innovation?

2 What American cultural traits does Travis Kalanick exhibit? How have these traits helped him and how might they create problems for him?

3 How did Uber reduce resistance in the cities where it chose to operate? What can it now do to reduce opposition and hostility?

4 Why is public affairs an essential part of the communication practices needed by Uber?

5 What are the special obstacles Uber faced in China?

6 How well has David Plouffe handled Uber's public affairs problems? What advice would you give him?

7 What problems has Uber's designation of its drivers as independent contractors caused?

8 What changes in Uber's culture should the new CEO, Dara Khosrowshahi, seek? How could he achieve the changes?

Endnotes

1 Justin Kirby and Paul Marsden, eds., *Connected Marketing: the Viral, Buzz and World of Mouth Revolution* (London and New York: Butterworth-Heinemann (Elsevier), 2006), p. 268.
2 I. James Lovejoy, "Villains and Victims of Product Tampering," in Jack A. Gottschalk, *Crisis Response: Inside Stories on Managing Image Under Siege* (Detroit, MI: Visible Ink Press, 1993), p. 175. Also "The Fight to Save Tylenol," *Fortune*, November 19, 1982.
3 Shel Holtz, *PR on the Net* (New York: AMACOM, 1998), p. xi.
4 Ibid, 2002 edition, p. vii.
5 "Changing Technologies: New Challenges and New Opportunities in a Digital World," in William David Sloan, Shirley Stales Carter, William J. Gonzenbach, and James Glen Stovall, *Mass Communication in the Information Age* (Northport, AL: Visin Press, 1996), p. 388.
6 Tom Price, *Public Affairs Strategies in the Internet Age* (Washington, DC: Foundation of Public Affairs), p. 2.
7 Baruch University, Zichlin School of Business, Undergraduate Programs, "Why a Digital Marketing Track?" https://zicklin.baruch.cuny.edu/academic-programs/undergraduate/majors/marketing/digital-marketing-track-faqs
8 New York University, Stern School, Digital Marketing Specialization.
9 He later became executive director of social media for Dell.
10 Julie Jargon, "Campbell to Beef Up Its Marketing Efforts," *WSJ*, October 31, 2012, p. B8. Also see Campbell's news release.
11 Emily Glazer, "P&Gs Marketing Chief Looks to Go Digital," *WSJ*, March 14, 2012, p. B7.

12 Sarah E. Needleman, "Services Combine Social Media, Marketing," *WSJ*, February 23, 2010, p. B7.
13 Emily Glazer, "Avon Is Late to Social Media's Party," *WSJ*, April 25 2012, p. B1.
14 John Obrecht, "B to B: Executives See Golden Age for Digital Advertising," Vol. 98, Issue 1, March 4, 2013, p. 0003.
15 Chris Anderson, *The Long Tail: Why the Future of Business is Selling Less of More* (New York: Hyperion 2006), p. 19. Later published by Hachette Books.
16 "Technology," *Bloomberg Businessweek*, July 2–July 8, 2012, p. 28.
17 Emily Glazer "Target: Customers on the Go," *WSJ*, May 16, 2011, p. R3.
18 See chapter 6, "Gaining Complete Control Over the Media: Advocacy Advertising," in Otto Lerbinger, *Corporate Public Affairs: Interacting With Interest Groups, Media, and Government* (Mahwah, NJ: Lawrence Erlbaum Associates, Publishers, 2006), pp. 151 ff.
19 Matthew Moore, "Global Warming Ads Overstated the Risk," *The Daily Telegraph* (London), March 15, 2010, p. 8. Matine Mittelstaedt, "Skeptical Ads Anger Green Groups," *The Globe and Mail* (Canada), November 18, 2009, p. A12.
20 Anshu Saxena Arora and Sabine Bacouel-Jentjens, eds. *Advertising Confluence: Transitioning Marketing Communications into Social Movements* (New York: Palgrave Macmillan, 2015), pp. x–xi.
21 Shayerah Ilias, Charles E. Hanrahan, and M. Angeles Villarreal, "U.S. Government Agencies Involved in Export Promotion: Overview and Issues for Congress," *Journal of International Business Studies*, Vol. 23, No. 4, 1992.
22 Henry Vanderleest, "What New Exporters Think About US Government Sponsored Export Promotions and Services," *Multinational Business Review*, Vol. 4, Fall 1996, pp. 21ff.
23 Philip Kotler and Eduardo L. Roberto, *Social Marketing: Strategies for Changing Public Behavior* (New York: The Free Press, 1989), p. 24. Also "Social Marketing: An Approach to Planned Social Change," *Journal of Marketing*, Vol. 35, 1971, pp. 3–12.
24 Jeff French, ed., *Social Marketing and Public Health: Theory and Practice* (New York: Oxford University Press, 2017), p. 20.
25 Philip Kotler, *Journal of Marketing*, Vol. 35 July, 1971, pp. 3–12.
26 Philip Kotler, *Marketing for Nonprofit Organizations* (Englewood Cliffs, NJ: Prentice Hall, 1975), p. 490. A fuller definition by Kotler and Roberto, ibid., is "the design, implementation and control of programs calculated to influence the acceptability of social ideas and involving consideration of product planning, pricing, communication, distribution, and marketing rese."
27 Philip Kotler and Eduardo L. Roberto, op. cit., p. 24.
28 Ibid., p. 6.
29 Ibid., p. 24.
30 See Michael L. Rothschild, "Marketing Communications in Nonbusiness Situations or Why It's So Hard to Sell Brotherhood Like Soap," *Journal of Marketing*, Vol 43, No. 2, Spring 1979, pp. 11–20. Gerhard Wiebe, later to become dean of the School of Public Relations and Communication at Boston University, is sometimes credited with inventing social marketing when he wrote an article in the *Public Opinion Quarterly* in 1952, p. 679, which asked, "why can't we sell brotherhood like we sell soap?"
31 "Marketing Social Change: Changing Behavior to Promote Health, Social Development, and the Environment," *Jossey-Bass and Health Education Quarterly*, Vol. 15, No. 3, pp. 300–301. Alan R. Andreasen, *Marketing Social Change; Changing Behavior to Promote Health, Social Development, and the Environment* (Hoboken, NJ: Jossey-Bass, 1995).
32 George R. Franke, "Empirical Generalizations for Social Marketing," in David W. Stewart, ed. *The Handbook of Persuasion and Social Marketing: Historical and Social Foundations* (Santa Barbara, CA: Praeger, 2015), pp. 208–211.

33 "CVS Carema Launches the Behavior Change Research Partnership to Develop Ways to Encourage Adherent, Healthy Behaviors While Saving Patients Money," *Drug Week*, March 19, 2010, p. 4390.
34 Karl Wilson, "Processed Food a Big, Fat Problem," *China Daily*, August 4, 2014.
35 Joe Mullich, "Obesity Comes with an Unexpected Price Tag, *WSJ*, May 18, 2010, p. D6.
36 Lisa Collier Col, "Nationwide Efforts Underway to Save a Generation at Risk," *WSJ*, May 18, 2010, p. D4.
37 Mike Esterl and Paul Zioo, "Coke's Low-Calorie Push," *WSJ*, May 9, 2013, p. B1.
38 Ibid., pp. A7, B1, B2.
39 Muhtar Kent, "Coca-Cola: We'll Do Better," *WSJ*, August 20, 2015, p. A11.
40 Mike Esterl, "Pepsi Learns Consumers Mostly Want Chips," *WSJ*, December 12, 2016, p. A1.
41 *Walter Wymer*, "Rethinking the Boundaries of Social Marketing: Activism or Advertising," *Journal of Business Research*, Vol. 63, No. 2 February, 2010, p. 99.
42 Jenny Knight, "An Appetite for Battling Junk Food and Drink," *The Times* (London), February 27, 2014.
43 Paul N. Bloom and William D. Novelli, "Problems Applying Conventional Wisdom to Social Marketing Programs," in M.P. Mokwa and S.E. Permut, *Government Marketing Theory and Practice* (New York: Praeger, 1981), pp. 69ff.
44 "Rwanda; 23 Million Condoms Distributed in 2010," *Africa News*, February 23, 2011.
45 "European Youth Tackling Obesity (EYTO)," TendersInfo – Project Notices, November 6, 2014. See also https://www.ncb.org.uk/sites/default/files/uploads/Images_misc/EYTO%20final%20evaluation%20report%202015.pdf
46 Gemma O'Reilly. *PR Week*. (London ed.), October 24, 2008, p. 25ff.
47 "Stefi Rucci, Say Communications: The True Agents of Change," *PR Week*, February 24, 2011.
48 Gemma O'Reilly, "Prevention is Better Than Cure," *PR Week*, October 27, 2008.
49 "Contraception: Reports Outline Contraception Research from Columbia University," *Biotech Business Week*, March 15, 2010, p. 1317.
50 Patrick McGorry, "The Next Government Must Take Real Action to Reduce Suicide," *Sunday Mail* (South Australia), August 29, 2010, p. 26.
51 Jaimy Lee, "The Recovery Act Stimulates New Business for PR Agencies," *PR Week* (US), January 1, 2011, p. 1.
52 Stuart Elliott, "An Advocacy Ad Stirs a National Debate," *New York Times*, February 2, 2010, p. B4.
53 For background of the industry, see article by Larry Davidson and Gennadiy Greblov, "The Pharmaceutical Industry in the Global Economy," Bloomington, Indiana: Indiana University Kelley School of Business, Summer 2005.
54 Jonathan D. Rockoff, "Drug Prices Draw New Fire," *WSJ*, December 20, 2016, p. A13.
55 Joseph Walker, "Drug Costs Hit Medicare," *WSJ*, November 15, 2016, p. B7.
56 Jonathan D. Rockoff, "$1,000-a-Day Hepatitis C Drug is Rapid Blockbuster," *WSJ*, April 1, 2014, p. B1.
57 Jonathan D. Rockoff, "Pricey Drugs Are Hurdle for New Biotech CEO," *WSJ*, June 7, 2016, p. B1.
58 Jonathan D. Rockoff and Peeter Loftus, "Drug Companies Keep Lid on Price Increases," *WSJ*, February 27, 2017, p. A1.
59 Joseph Walker, "Marathon under Fire Over Price for Drugs," *WSJ*, March 6, 2017, p. B3.
60 Joseph Walker, Ro Winslow, and Anne Steele, "Mylan to Offer Generic EpiPen," *WSJ*, August 30, 2016, pp. A1–A2. "Drugs in America: Seizure-inducing," *The Economist*, September 3, 2016, p. 56.
61 Jonathan D. Rockoff, "Suit Claims Overcharge by Mylan on EpiPen," *WSJ*, April 4, 2017, p. B3.
62 Mark Maremont and Theo Francis, "Big PayDay for Mylan Chairman," *WSJ*, May 3, 2017, p. B3.
63 Peter Loftus, "Powerful New Cancer Drugs Offer Hope – at Steep Cost," *WSJ*, September 4, 2014, p. A1.

64 "Drugs in American: Seizure-Inducing," op. cit.
65 Joseph Walker, "$1,000 Hepatitis C Pill Is Hard for States to Swallow," *WSJ*, April 9, 2015, p. B1.
66 Item in Business section of *The Economist*, May 16, 2015, p. 7.
67 Amanda Schaffer, "The Cost of Life," *Technology Review*, Vol. 114, No. 3, May–June, 2011, pp. 82–83.
68 Peter Loftus, "Combining Medicines for Cancer Gets Costly," *WSJ*, June 6, 2016, p. B1.
69 "Gilead Gets U.S. Approval to Sell New Hepatitis Drug," *WSJ*, October 10, 2014.
70 Omar El Akkad, "Pharmaceutical; Valeant Sinks as Confidence Sags," *The Globe and Mail* (Canada), November 6, 2015, p. B1.
71 Christopher M. Matthews, Rob Copeland, and Rebecca Davis O'Brien, "Fraud Arrest for Drug CEO," *WSJ*, December 18, 2015, p. A1.
72 Rebecca Davis O'Brien, "Ex-Drug Executive Shkreli Convicted of Fraud," *WSJ*, August 5, 6, 2017, p. A1.
73 Stephanie Armour and Jonathan D. Rockoff, "Shkreli Takes Fifth Before Congress," *WSJ*, February 5, 2016, p. B1.
74 Jonathan D. Rockoff, "Valeant's CEO to Testify," *WSJ*, January 21, 2016, p. B8.
75 Stephanie Armour and Jonathan D. Rockoff, "Shkreli Takes Fifth Before Congress," *WSJ*, February 5, 2016, p. B1.
76 "Issue of the Week: A Drug Company Goes Septic," *This Week*, April 1, 2016, p. 34.
77 Amy Steele, "Valeant to Expand Drug Discounts," *WSJ*, May 17, 2016, p. B3.
78 Peter Loftus, "FDA Panel Approves Knockoff of Pricey J&J Drug," *WSJ*, February 10, 2016, p. B1.
79 Peter Loftus, "FTC Clout Tested in Suit Versus Drugmaker," *WFJ*, February 21, 2018, p. B3.
80 William Mauldin, "Rift Over Drugs Clouds Trade Talks," *WSJ*, October 2, 2015, p. A6.
81 Joseph Walker, "Trump Assails Drug Industry, Prices," *WSJ*, January 12, 2017, p. A6.
82 Thoas M. Burton, "FDA Chief Aims to Curb High Drug Prices," *WSJ*, May 26, 2017, p. A2.
83 Michael A. Carrier, "How Big Pharma Sandbags Generic Competition," *WSJ*, November 15, 2017, p. A19.
84 Charley Grant, "Health-Care Reform's Wild Card," *WSJ*, March 10, 2017, p. B11.
85 Jonathan D. Rockoff, "Once-a-Day Hepatitis Pill Approved," *WSJ*, October 11, 2014, p. B1.
86 Peter Loftus, "In Ohio, Drugmakers Fight Price Cap," *WSJ*, November 2, 2017, p. A3.
87 Peter Loftus, "Gilead Accused of Gouging on Drug," *WSJ*, December 11, 2014, p. B3.
88 Peter Loftus, "Maryland Law Goes After High Drug Prices," *WSJ*, May 27–28, 2017, p. A3.
89 Peter Loftus, "Faith-Based Group Wants Drug Firms To Explain Pricing," *WSJ*, October 25, 2016, p. B5.
90 Peter Loftus, "Drugmakers Resist Investor Campaign," *WSJ*, March 2, 2017, p. B3.
91 Kenneth Galbraith, *American Capitalism: The Theory of Countervailing Power* (Boston, MA: Houghton Hifflin, 1952).
92 Joseph Walker, "Health Costs Get a Rethink," *WSJ*, March 8, 2017, p. B8.
93 Melanie Evans, "Hospitals to Make, Sell Generic Drugs," *WSJ*, January 19, 2018, p. B6.
94 Anna Wilde Mathews, Emily Glazer and Laura Stevens, "Health Venture Rattles Insurers," *WSJ*, January 31, 2018, p. A1; and Charley Grant, "New Threat for Health-Care Firms," *WSJ*, January 31, 2018, p. B18.
95 Peter Loftus, "In Ohio, Drugmakers Fight Price Cap," *WSJ*, November 2, 2017, p. A3.
96 "The Drug Lobby's In-House Hygiene," editorial in *WSJ*, May 11, 2017, p. A16.
97 Joseph Walker, "Drugmakers Bid to Burnish Image," *WSJ*, February 8, 2016, p. B1.
98 Loftus, op. cit.
99 Neil A. Lewis with Robert Pear, "U.S. Drug Industry is Battling Image for Price Gouging," *WSJ*, March 7, 1994, p. A1.
100 Joseph Walker, "Price Increases Drive Drug Firms' Revenue," *WSJ*, October 6, 2015, p. A1.

101 Frances Robinson, "Uber Willing to Discuss Regulation," *WSJ*, September 25, 2014, p. B12.

102 Margit Fisher, "Uber Faces New Europe Challenge," *WSJ*, June 14, 2016, p. B4.

103 Sam Schechner and Matthew Dalton, "Uber Seeks EU's Help To Fight a French Ban," *WSJ*, December 18 2014, pp. B1, B4.

104 Sam Schechner, "Uber Wins Delay in Key Court Case," *WSJ*, October 1, 2015, p. B1; "Prosecutors Seek Fines in Uber Case," *WSJ*, February 13–14, 2016, p. 13.

105 Sam Schechner, Douglas MacMillan, and Nick Kostov, op. cit.

106 Douglas MacMillan, Reid J. Epstein, and Peter Nicholas, "Uber Hires a Campaign Chief," *WSJ*, August 20, 2014, p. B5.

107 Natalia Drozdiak, "Uber Takes Hit in Europe," *WSJ*, May 12, 2017, p. B4.

108 Sam Schechner and Wiktor Szary, "Uber Loses License to Operate in London," *WSJ*, September 23–24, 2017, p. A1.

109 Eva Dou and Rick Carew, "In Big, New Market, Uber Hits a Great Wall," *WSJ*, September 3, 2015, pp. 1, A10.

110 Lynsey Barber, "Uber China Raises $1.2bn Helped by Baidu as Rival Didi Kuaidi Bags $3bn," *City A.M.*, September 8, 2015, p. 16.

111 Ibid.

112 Juro Osawa and Eva Dou, "Uber Takes on China Rival," *WSJ*, June 4–5, 2016, p. B4.

113 Eva Dou, "Uber's Retreat Shows Limits U.S. Companies Face in China," *WSJ*, August 2, 2016, p. A1. "Ride-Hailing in China: Uber Gives App," *The Economist*, August 6, 2016, pp. 49–50.

114 Newley Purnell, "Uber Hits Bumps in Southeast Asia," *WSJ*, November 29, 2017, p. 2.

115 Greg Bensinger, "Startups Scramble to Define 'Employee,'" *WSJ*, July 3, 2015, p. B1.

116 Douglas MacMillan, "Uber Settles Suits Alleging False Advertising," *WSJ*, February 12, 2016, p. B3.

117 Lauren Weber and Rachel Emma Silverman, "Meet the Lawyer Who's Putting Uber on Trial," *WSJ*, November 4, 2015, p. B1.

118 "News about Liss Riordan Uber Trial," bing.com/newss, June 22, 2017.

119 Sam Schechner, "Uber Drivers Score U.K. Win," November 11–12, 2017, p. B3.

120 Greg Bensinger, "Uber Fights Unionization," *WSJ*, March 13, 2017, p. B2.

121 Sam Schechner, "Uber Drivers Score U.K. Win," *WSJ*, November 11–12, 2017, p. B3.

122 Mike Ramsey and Douglas MacMillan, "Uber Lures Robot Gurus from Carnegie Mellon," *WSJ*, June 1, 2015, p. A1.

123 Greg Bensinger, "Latest Exit at Uber Adds to List of Woes," *WSJ*, March 20, 2017, p. A1.

124 Greg Bensinger, "Investor Sues Uber Ex-CEO Kalanick," *WSJ*, August 11, 2017, p. A2.

125 Greg Bensinger, "Uber Seeks Deputy to Help Its Chief," *WSJ*, March 8, 2017, p. B1.

126 Resty WoroYunia, "Uber Executive Flags Workplace Problems," *WSJ*, March 3, 2017, p. B4.

127 Greg Bensinger, "Investor Sues Uber Ex-CEO Kalanick," op. cit.

128 Douglas MacMillan and Newley Purnell, "Uber Knowingly Leased Unsafe Cars to Drivers," *WSJ*, August 4, 2017, A1.

129 "Uber's Future: Hard Driving," *The Economist*, March 25, 2017, p. 55.

130 Ibid.

131 Greg Bensinger and Douglas MacMillan, "Uber Shareholders Battle Over Former CEO," *WSJ*, August 12–13, 2017, pp. A1–2.

132 Greg Bensinger, "Uber-Formed Covert Unit to Steal Trade Secrets, Ex-Employee Says," *WSJ*, November 29, 2017, p. A1.

133 Greg Bensinger, "Uber Hires CEO from Expedia," *WSJ*, August 28, 2017, p. A1.

134 "Tech's Toughest job: From Uber to Kinder," *The Economist*, October 7, 2017, pp. 6–66.

Part III

International Perspective

The opening chapter on the force of globalization sets the stage for the international perspective of corporate communication. Chief communication officers (CCOs) increasingly work for multinational corporations (MNCs) and must therefore extend their knowledge beyond their home countries. First, they must understand the process of globalization itself – the drivers and obstacles with which they must contend. They must then familiarize themselves with new players and issues and understand the variety of political, economic, social, and cultural patterns of different countries and regions.

Corporate communication became international as MNCs began spreading throughout the world. This occurred in three waves as represented by major books. The first wave consisted of books such as John Fayerweather's *Management of International Operations: Text and* Cases[1] and Raymond Vernon's *Sovereignty at Bay: The Multinational Spread of U.S. Enterprises.*[2] The presence of MNCs became a reality and they challenged nation states that were torn between welcoming their capital and technology and, on the other hand, fearing their power.

The second wave focused on business–government relations, as illustrated by Robert Grosse's *International Business and Government Relations in the 21st Century.*[3] The focus was on the growth of civil society, which began to parallel that of government. The degree of activism in a country became a major consideration. Business realized that it must relate to non-governmental organizations (NGOs) and other groups that increasingly put pressure on it to change its policies and behavior.

The third wave enlarged business's perspective from government and civil society to society at large. Van der Zwart and van Tulder's book, *International Business-Society Management,*[4] reflects this recognition of civil society. These authors recognized that an MNC's reputation makes it a vulnerable target for confrontations with NGOs and government. Activism in society thus became a major variable. They also recognize that dialogue and bargaining between an MNC and its stakeholders is the most important way to alleviate tension and, more importantly, to find ways of working together for the common good.

Public relations responded to the spread of MNCs throughout the world by responding to the new international variables. This was most notably done by Krishnamurthy Sriramesh and Dejan Vercic in their encyclopedic *The Global Public Relations Handbook.*[5] They examined the new global environment that public relations would have to take into account. They initially listed five variables: political ideology, economic system (including the level of economic development), degree of activism, culture, and media system.[6] They then condensed them into three factors: a country's infrastructure, media environment, and societal culture. Their purpose was to analyze these factors to "predict which strategies and techniques are better suited to a particular organizational environment."[7] Their book contains 23 country profiles that apply these factors.

Corporate Communication: An International and Management Perspective, First Edition. Otto Lerbinger.

Part III of this book discusses the above variables in three chapters: (i) a country's political and economic system; (ii) its societal and cultural system; and (iii) its nation brand and nation-building efforts. The emphasis is on the scope of corporate communication and how it is practiced. A review of these variables shows that corporate communication thrives in the democracies and free market systems of the US and UK, and falters in Russia and China where authoritarian governments rule and economic systems are a hybrid of the free market and state enterprises. Authoritarian governments operating socialist economies leave little or no scope for public relations, while democratic and free market economies allow the maximum.

Whereas a country's political and economic systems determine the extent to which corporate communication can operate, differences in social systems and national cultures affect *how* corporate communication is practiced. For example, whether news releases are judged on their merit or on the relationship with a journalist or editor is determine by national cultures.

Sriramesh and Vercic also sought to determine the prominence of public relations in a country. Their measures were: (i) the number of public relations and communication practitioners employed; (ii) their status in society; and (iii) rank achieved in the organizations where they are employed. For example, in his chapter on Canada, Fraser Likely reports that in 2004 public relations had 36 800 practitioners, that public relations is not recognized as a profession, and that most belong to a middle managerial class both in terms of earnings and in terms of power and prestige.[8] He concluded that with such a standing, public relations cannot be expected to exert much influence in an organization.

The need to know more about other countries has heightened the desirability of experience in living and working abroad. MBA programs consider international knowledge and experience important. About three-quarters of executive programs offer international trips and some make them mandatory. In one of them, before leaving classes, students spend time studying and writing papers about each country's social, political, and economic history. They learn basic facts: what motivates people in different cultures; what countries are optimal for company investments, and an analysis of the role of government in economic affairs is relevant.

Some universities have started 1-year Master's programs that include course work in other countries. The Graduate Management Admission Council found that about 25% of prospective students were considering 1-year degrees, up from 15% in 2009. About 3% were interested in pursuing a career abroad. The University of Virginia's Darden School of Business covers three continents: the US; Lingnan University in Guangzhou, China; and Ramon Llull University's ESADE Business and Law School in Barcelona. "There is a great demand and need for people in existing businesses to understand an international environment," said Paul Almeida, a professor at Georgetown University's McDonough School of Business.[9] Another development is that some business schools have launched business schools overseas, as Harvard's Business School has done in China, India, and Europe.[10]

Part III's Chapter 11 discusses political and economic features affecting corporate communication and Chapter 12 discusses the social and cultural features affecting corporate affairs practice. Chapter 13 looks at the attention given by countries to their nation brands. The concept of the nation brand is rooted in the marketing concept of the product brand and company brand, which public relations people usually call a company's reputation. The three levels of brands – product, company, and nation – share common roots in the psychology of perception and attitudes.

Endnotes

1 John Fayerweather, *Management of International Operations: Text and Cases* (New York: McGraw-Hill, 1960).

2 Raymond Vernon, *Sovereignty at Bay: The Multinational Spread of U.S. Enterprise* (New York: Basic Books, 1971).

3 Robert Grosse (ed.) *International Business and Government Relations in the 21st Century* (Cambridge: Cambridge University Press, 2005).

4 Rob van Tulder and Alex van der Zwart, *International Business-Society Management* (New York: Routledge, 2005).

5 Krishnamurthy Sriramesh and Dejan Verčič, eds., *The Global Public Relations Handbook, Revised and Expanded Edition: Theory, Research, and Practice*, 2nd ed. (New York: Routledge, 2009).

6 Ibid., p. 40.

7 Ibid., p. 3.

8 Fraser Likely, "A Different Country, A Different Public Relations: Canadian PR in the North American Context," in Sriramesh and Vercic, ibid., pp. 654–675.

9 Dahlia Bazzaz, "Taking a Fast Track to Global Business," *WSJ*, September 2, 2016, p. B6.

10 Diana Middleton, "Foreign Policies: International Trips for E.M.B. Students Are More Valuable Than Ever," *WSJ*, September 30, 2010, p. A7, and Joe Light, "Harvard Works at China, India," *WSJ*, November 4, 2010, p. B10.

2 [illegible] Basic Books, 1983.

3 [illegible] Cambridge University Press, [illegible]

4 [illegible] Routledge, 2001.

5 [illegible]

6 Ibid., [illegible]

7 Ibid.

8 [illegible]

9 [illegible]

10 [illegible]

9

The Force of Globalization

Globalization has been the major force behind the growth of global corporate communications. Under the banner of the free market system, corporations expanded sales and business activities beyond their home countries, thereby becoming multi-national corporations (MNCs). This process involved the exchange of goods and services, capital, and technology. Public relations, public affairs, and marketing professionals accompanied this expansion and helped companies adapt to the characteristics of different nations and regions and to build new relationships.

In his influential book *The World is Flat*, Thomas I. Friedman, a *New York Times* columnist, names the 10 forces that created globalization and the "multiple new forms and tools for collaboration that this flattening has created."[1] These forces explain how a shift in ideologies, technological advances, and management innovations penetrated existing barriers and led to greater international trade. He describes how the fall of the Berlin wall in 1989, "tipped the balance of power across the world toward those advocating democratic, consensual and free-market-oriented governance, and away from those advocating authoritarian rule with centrally planned economics."[2] He goes on to explain how the diffusion of personal computers, fax machines, Microsoft's Windows, and dial-up modems connected to a global telephone network all came together in the late 1980s and early 1990s.

Although globalization remains the dominant force in world economies, it faces a serious backlash from a growing number of disgruntled people who have lost jobs or feel their incomes have grossly fallen behind owing to globalization in comparison with the small percentage that have largely benefited. This disparity has led to a strain in social cohesion, which can be seen in the growth of populist political movements, such as Donald Trump's success in becoming America's president, and in the Brexit referendum decision in Britain, where a majority (52%) of British voters decided to leave the European Union (EU). Issues revolving around globalization have been central to these movements – whether to support trade agreements and even to abandon existing ones (such as the North American Free Trade Act (NAFTA)), and whether to restrict immigration. Growing protectionist sentiment is a serious threat to globalization and there is serious concern that globalization may give way to nationalism and protectionism.[3]

The forces affecting globalization are summarized in the sections below dealing with both drivers and obstacles. It is clear that the strength of drivers is dropping while obstacles are growing. Public opinion reflects these forces and creates a challenge to MNCs that favor globalization. Corporate leaders, world leaders, and economists must pay urgent attention to the problems globalization has created.

Corporate Communication: An International and Management Perspective, First Edition. Otto Lerbinger.

9.1 Conditions That Facilitate Globalization

9.1.1 Enabling Effect of Communication and Other Technologies

Throughout history, technology has accelerated globalization. A major advance was when full-masted ships were constructed in the fifteenth century. Now, container-laden cargo ships enable countries, notably China, to send products all over the world. Refrigerated cargo ships and cargo aircraft allow import of fruit in winter from Chile to the US and other temperate zone countries.

A more important impetus to current globalization has been the impact of communication technology. As Thomas Friedman pointed out, the installation of fiber-optics worldwide enabled the spread of the internet. Data and digitized voices could now be transmitted farther and faster in large quantities. Eric Schmidt, executive chairman of Google, and Jared Cohen, director of Google Ideas, stated, "Through the power of technology, age-old obstacles to human interaction, like geography, language and limited information, are falling and a new wave of human creativity and potential is rising." They also stated, "Being able to do more in the virtual world will make the mechanics of our physical world more efficient. As digital connectivity reaches the far corners of the globe, new users will employ it to improve a wide range of inefficient markets, systems and behaviors, in both the most and least advanced societies."[4]

Siemens and General Electric are working on digitizing their manufacturing processes and developing software platforms and automation tools to sell to other industrial players. Both are leaders in the Industrial Internet, which is a global effort to combine heavy industry with the "Internet of Things." In Germany, the endeavor is driven by a joint effort of private and public sectors, known as Industrial 4.0. In accordance with this goal, Siemens acquired the Oregon-based automation and industrial software provider Mentor Graphics Corp in 2017.[5] In a reverse process, China has been raiding Germany to catch up on high-tech industries. German companies under Chinese control rose to 270 in 2014. In 2016, Chinese firms, often backed by government funds, bought German firms at the rate of one a week. To protect its technology from China, Germany in July 2017 adopted new rules to protect its defense sector and developers of critical software that power financial and telecommunications services.[6]

Gordon M. Goldstein, author of the article "The End of the Internet?" observed that the World Wide Web in 2014 celebrated its 35th birthday, with the global network serving almost 3 billion people.[7] The McKinsey Global Institute estimated that transborder online traffic grew 18-fold between 2005 and 2012. At the same time, the global flow of goods, services, and investments, which reached $26 trillion in 2012, could more than triple by 2025.[8] As Marshall McLuhan, author of *The Global Village*, foresaw, the world was becoming a global village.[9]

The single most transformative technology for development has been the basic mobile cell phone, states Jeffrey Sachs, director of the Earth Institute at Columbia University and an outspoken proponent of globalization. It saves wasted trips, provides information about crop prices, summons medical help, and even serves as a conduit to banking services.[10] The expected economic effect in developing countries is that every 10 extra mobile phones per 100 people increases the rate of growth of gross domestic product (GDP) per person by more than one percentage point. Furthermore, since the introduction of the smart phone by Apple's chief executive officer (CEO) Steve Jobs in 2007, it has become the "defining technology of the age."[11] *The Economist* states, it "generates the most profits, it attracts the most capital and the brightest brains."[12] By February 2015 about half of the adult population owned a smart phone and by 2020 80% are expected to.

Africa's economic development has one of the greatest growth rates in the world. Of the world's 10 fastest growing economies, 6 are in Africa, as stated at a gathering of political and business leaders in May 2014.[13] At a subsequent 3-day US–Africa Leaders Summit, which was convened on August 4, 2014, by President Obama, it was said that the US private sector should recognize the new Africa. "No longer exclusively a natural-resource play, the content holds great potential for a wide range of sectors, from manufacturing, retail and agri-business to hospitality and financial services." Africa is most interested in capital, ideas, and innovations. General Electric is investing in railway manufacturing, Wal-Mart is expanding in South Africa through Massmart (Africa has 1 billion consumers), and IBM selected Nairobi as its hub for an aggressive African expansion strategy.

9.1.2 Rise of Scientific Thinking

Scientific thinking, which underlies technology, has created a language and way of thinking that is universal and has promoted globalization. As Walt Rostow observed in his *The Stages of Economic Growth,* in the late seventeenth and early eighteenth centuries modern science began to be translated into new methods of agriculture and manufacturing.[14] Major examples are Monsanto and DuPont, among others, who have created genetically modified seeds that produce better and more crops. Efforts to conserve more than 1000 wild relatives of the world's most important crops are also continuing to solve such problems as allowing plants to withstand heat. New varieties of crops produced by crossing crops with wild relatives are cheaper and less controversial than genetic modification.[15] Inventions across virtually all industries have improved products and lowered costs.

The transfer of intellectual property (IP) across nations is commonplace. Sometimes it is done internally when a company opens operations abroad; other times the acquisition of IP is negotiated; and sometimes IP is simply stolen. Knowledge of science and technology is largely available through the internet and educational institutions. Students who attend the Massachusetts Institute of Technology (MIT), for example, come from all parts of the world.

The dissemination of technology is further enhanced as an increasing number of MNCs, including China's, are decentralizing their research and development (R&D) activities to laboratories in other locations.[16] Pharmaceutical companies have particularly benefited from such decentralization, as illustrated by the British drug firm AstraZeneca, which has research centers in Britain, Sweden, and the US. It also has formed partnerships to discover and test new drugs. Through mergers or licensing agreements, the company has obtained promising new drugs. It uses the US clinical research organization Quintiles Transnational, which works in 100 countries, to conduct its testing.[17]

With every extension of economic activity abroad, public relations has followed. It now operates throughout the world with a new mix of players and accompanying issues. Public relations has extended to scientific settings (see Chapter 15), which help to report on technological advances. Science communicators in both the industrialized and emerging nations, who form an ever-wider circle of contacts, now share many common goals and activities.

9.2 Drivers of Globalization

The process of globalization was accelerated as companies searched for new markets and recognized the benefits of offshoring production and services to countries with low labor costs. Furthermore, some companies also took advantage of weak regulatory structures in host countries, leading to charges of human rights violations and environmental degradation.

9.2.1 Search for New Markets

The search for new markets is reflected in Joyce Wouters' *International Public Relations: How to Establish Your Company's Product, Service, and Image in Foreign Markets.*[18] She spent 25 years as a senior public relations executive in Asia and Europe helping with such objectives as introducing Isuzu cars to the US and maintaining Coca-Cola's attractiveness in Japan. She spelled out how to establish credibility in an unknown market; how to approach local businesses, government officials, and influential individuals; and how to tailor projects to take advantage of a country's business and cultural climates. These concerns became part of international public relations.

As Wouters' book mentions, public relations consulting firms such as Eric White Associates in Australia in 1947 and Hill & Knowlton (H&K) in Europe in the mid-1950s followed corporations abroad and led the way for international public relations. H&K established a closely coordinated network of eight wholly owned offices and developed close relationships with leading practitioners covering all of Western Europe and the UK.[19]

Individual companies also recognized that an international presence was necessary "to help create, maintain, and improve public attitudes that are favorable to the company's long-term growth in sales and earnings."[20] Upjohn (now Pfizer) in 1972 hired the best in-country foreign-based agencies in England, France, Belgium, and Italy. And in 1978, it established a regional office in Brussels because supranational European organizations – such as the World Health Organization (WHO), the European Economic Community (EEC), and the Organisation for Economic Co-operation and Development (OECD) – were affecting the company's main business operations in Europe and its policy decisions at company headquarters.[21] Advertising agencies also went global in a big way and continued their growth. WPP headed by the well-known Martin Sorrell, became the world's biggest advertising firm.[22] It comprised more than 400 companies and 200 000 employees in more than 100 countries.[23]

9.2.2 Seeking Low Labor Costs

The process of globalization was accelerated when companies recognized the benefits of outsourcing production to countries with low labor costs. The textile and shoe industries were among the first to take advantage of wage differentials, followed by a variety of manufacturing industries in telecommunications, automotive, and machinery. Chinese labor costs were just 60 cents an hour as late as 2002.[24] And in India, Tom Friedman explains why so many American and Western companies outsourced customer telephone calls to Bangalore because wage and rents were less than one-fifth of those in Western capitals. He reported, "There are currently [2005] about 245 000 Indians answering phones from all over the world or dialing out to solicit people for credit cards or cell phone bargains or overdue bills."[25]

Outsourcing companies have also used the advertising agencies to obtain visas for employees to do work in the US on the grounds that they can't find Americans for the jobs. In 2016 the US provided 85 000 visas, of which 20 000 were reserved for people with advanced degrees, to controversial outsourcing companies. Over 236 000 had applied. President Trump has targeted the H-1B program saying, "These are temporary foreign workers, imported from abroad, for the explicit purpose of substituting for American workers at lower pay."[26]

US labor and unions consequently suffered from globalization through loss of jobs and declining wages. In manufacturing, jobs declined every year from 1998 to 2009; about 8 million jobs have been lost since the late 1970s.[27] A study by Gordon Hanson of the University of California, San Diego, estimates that the US lost 2–2.4 million jobs due to Chinese import competition in the 2000s, after China's entry to the World Trade Organization (WTO) in 2001.[28]

In manufacturing alone, imports from China displaced as many as 982 000 workers from 2000 to 2007, according to economists David Autor, David Dorn, and Gordon Hanson.[29]

But trade is not the main culprit for job loss and low wages: it is technology. As Douglas A. Irwin of Dartmouth College's Economics Department has argued, many blue-collar jobs have become obsolete as automation and other technologies have enabled vast productivity and efficiency improvements. He cites a study by the Center for Business and Economic Research at Ball State University that found that productivity growth accounted for more than 85% of job losses in manufacturing between 2000 and 2010, a period when employment in that sector fell by 5.6 million.[30]

9.2.2.1 NAFTA

In the 30 years of existence of NAFTA, Mexico and the US have traded half a trillion dollars worth of goods and services each year.[31] According to Irwin, it has been a huge economic and foreign policy success, citing booming trade between the US and Mexico. He notes that about 40% of the value of imports from Mexico consists of content originally made in the US.[32] US exporters argue that they would be at a disadvantage with their foreign competitors were it not for transferring some manufacturing to Mexico. He cites the example of the German car manufacturer Audi choosing southeastern Mexico over Tennessee for the site of a new plant because it could save thousands of dollars per car exported, thanks in part to Mexico's many more free-trade agreements, including one with the EU.

President Trump and United Auto Workers President Dennis Williams, however, have attacked NAFTA for unfairly taking away jobs from American workers. Production of cars and light trucks in Mexico rose from about 1.1 million in 1994, the year NAFTA was enacted, to 3.4 million vehicles in 2015. Mexico's automotive manufacturing is its second biggest manufacturing industry, behind food processing. Its 10 foreign-owned auto-makers employ 730 000 people directly.[33] Labor rates in Mexico are about one-fifth of those paid to union workers in the US.

In response to Trump's attacks, Ford Motor Co., which in April 2016 planned to spend $1.6 billion to build a new factory in Mexico, consequently decided to reinvest in its existing factories, including the upgrade of its Detroit-area plant.[34] Ford's CEO Mark Fields warned, however, that high tariffs on automobiles and other products coming into the US would be a blow to the auto industry and broader US economy.[35]

Trump's criticism was also extended to Toyota Motor Corp's plan to build a new Mexican plant. He threatened to impose a tariff on imported Corolla cars. Toyota's ambiguous response was to deny that US production and employment levels would be reduced as a result of the new plant in Mexico, stating, "Toyota looks forward to collaborating with the Trump Administration to serve the best interests of consumers and the automotive industry."[36]

Caution is needed in evaluating the effects of NAFTA, for saying that a car has been manufactured in Mexico usually only means that it is assembled there. The tens of thousands of parts that make up any vehicle may come from multiple producers in different countries and travel back and forth across borders several times. "The free flow of components is integral to the supply chain in auto manufacturing," said Steve Arthur, an automotive analyst.[37] Where a product is assembled increasingly has little bearing on where its component parts are made.

9.2.2.2 Outsourcing Reconsidered

Aside from trade pacts, there's been a slowdown in outsourcing and some reversals – called "reshoring." Headlines exclaim "Why US Manufacturing is Poised for a Comeback."[38] The wage differential with China is narrowing. In 2015, wages on China's highly industrialized coast were

$14.60 an hour vs. $22.60 in the US. China is now a more expensive place to manufacture than Indonesia, Thailand, Mexico, and India, says the Boston Consulting Group.[39]

Companies are looking more closely at shipping costs, the months-long wait for supplies to arrive and clear customs, and the cost of inventories. They also recognize the advantage of a US location in being able to react more quickly to changes in demand. Levi's, whose history traces the course of globalization, has been localizing production. As stated by Liz O'Neill, senior vice president of product development at Levi's, "The real money is having the right product in front of the customer at the right time."[40] Localized production is also less vulnerable to disruptions in the supply chain caused by natural disasters, such as Japan's Fukushima 2011 earthquake, or technological breakdowns.

However, companies wanting to shift more production back to the US often find it difficult because many suppliers have contracted or gone out of business. American companies often lack skilled workers and up-to-date machinery. For example, Euro-Pro Operating LLC, based in Newton, Massachusetts, which designs its Shark vacuum cleaners and Ninja blenders in the US, makes them in China because of its abundant ecosystem of suppliers for all sorts of parts like small motors and electronic parts. Chinese companies are also praised for their agility and flexibility in designing a product and accommodating requests for frequent changes in them.

Chinese and Taiwanese companies are looking beyond being a manufacturer for brand products to fashioning their own brands. One of these companies is Hon Hai Precision Industry Co., a Taiwanese firm better known as Foxconn, which assembles most of Apple's iPhones and iPads and is the employer of more than 1 million workers with factories spanning from Shenzhenin in southern to Zhengzhou in northern China. Terry Gou, the founder and head of this $130 billion-a-year company, said at a shareholder meeting that he wanted to "test a new business model that integrates software, hardware, and wireless network in Taiwan and then expand the business globally."[41] He is said to be investing in biometric sensors for wearable devices and had filed 300 patent applications for face-recognition technologies. As a further sign that Foxconn intends to transform itself from a contract manufacturer to a technology powerhouse, it acquired Japan's Sharp Corporation in 2016.[42]

9.2.3 Seeking National and Company Growth

The desire by nations for economic growth to raise living standards and reduce poverty is another impetus to globalization. Developing nations want to become developed ones. Although ongoing international trade and foreign direct investments (FDIs) account for most economic development, aspiring nation states also engage in planned efforts to achieve economic development. They employ public relations and marketing to publicize the benefits of doing business in their countries. They display the comparative advantage of doing business in their countries placing full or multi-page advertisements, distributing brochures, and holding conferences and expos.

Economic development often starts with tourism. In Malaysia it was the second highest foreign exchange earner, aided by the multiplier effect. This economic concept states that the infusion of new money, such as through tourism, stimulates the economy as the new money is spent on purchases such as transportation, retail trade, and recreational and leisure facilities.[43]

9.2.3.1 China's Expansion Abroad

Motivated by the search for new markets, raw materials, and acquisitions, China joined countries such as England and France that have historically explored opportunities for further growth in developing nations. Notable acquisitions are US's Smithfield Foods Inc. in 2013 by meat processor Shuanghui International Holdings Ltd., and General Electric's appliance business by China's Haier Group.[44] The Chinese Anbang Insurance Group made an unsuccessful bid $14 billion for Starwood Hotels and Resorts Worldwide. Starwood owns the Westin, W Hotels, and other well-known brands.[45] Chinese companies were expected to invest $20–30 billion in the US in 2016 through mergers and acquisitions, which represents only one-eighth of China's $120 billion in outward investment in 2015.[46]

Africa has been a major target, as explained by Howard French's *China's Second Continent: How a Million Migrants Are Building a New Empire in Africa*.[47] French states that China's Export–Import Bank extended $627 billion in loans to African countries between 2001 and 2010, more than the $12.5 billion supplied by the World Bank. In December 2013, China inaugurated the largest single project with a $13.8 billion standard gauge rail line in East Africa to link five East African countries. The massive rail networks, almost all of them leading to the sea, will doubtless reinforce the image of a resource-hungry China eager to extract as much as possible from the continent.[48]

But Chinese companies operating in Africa have not created many new jobs for they brought Chinese workers there rather than hire local ones, saying that "90% of Africans are thieves." From an African viewpoint, the Chinese are seen as "despoiling the environment, dispossessing powerless landholders, and, most of all, empowering awful governments."[49] They are accused of dumping cheap and shoddy goods and maintaining poor safety standards at work. But some African leaders like the way Chinese companies ignore human rights and transparency or give them low priority.

9.2.3.2 Company Growth: Sanofi SA

Globalization not only helps nations grow but also individual companies, many of which do so by acquiring foreign companies. The French pharmaceutical giant Sanofi SA, one of the world's largest drug and vaccine makers with sales of $42 billion in sales in 2013, did this by purchasing the consumer healthcare group Chattem for $1.9 billion in 2009 and US biotech Genzyme for more than $20 billion in 2011. These acquisitions helped refashion the once-French-focused company into an international corporation.[50]

The complications of how such deals are engineered and the factors that are considered are a revealing aspect of international public relations. At Sanofi the company's chief executive, Christopher Viehbacher, initiated the deal. Viehbacher is not French but has dual citizenship in Canada and Germany, illustrating how companies recruit managers from more than their home countries. Viehbacher had built close relations with outside research partners and was considering a partnership with Regeneron Pharmaceuticals Inc., a Tarrytown, New York-based biotechnology company. But, despite receiving praise for transforming the company, Viehbacher was abruptly fired on October 29, 2014, supposedly for his uncommunicative management style. Furthermore, the chairman of the board, Serge Weinberg, told reporters, "There was a lack of trust; the relationship wasn't close enough." Perhaps more accurately, he displeased the board of directors when he planned to move its headquarters from Paris to Boston. That fueled government concern that France was losing its grip over a national champion and indicated that nationalistic concerns still linger despite globalization.

9.2.4 The Newest Driver: Inversion Deals

Some companies have long sought to reduce or eliminate the payment of corporate taxes; for example, by incorporating in the British Overseas Territories of Bermuda, the Cayman Islands, or accommodating countries like Ireland. This tax incentive has received more attention lately as some major companies openly speak about avoiding the US corporate tax rate of 35%, the highest among the 34 mostly rich-country members of the OECD.[51] The OECD points out, however, that the US tax raises less revenue than other OECD nations because of its many loopholes and tax breaks, which amount to $150 billion annually in forgone revenue. Inversion deals enable a corporation to relocate its headquarters to a different country with a lower tax rate, while retaining its operations in its country of origin. US corporations were especially attracted to these deals because the US corporate tax rate, until the 2017 tax reform, was 35%, the highest among the 34 mostly rich-country members of the OECD.[52] Between 2004 and 2016 36 companies engaged in inversion deals, which allow them to keep profits overseas. The result has been that American companies have stored some $2 trillion in their foreign units' balance sheets.

9.2.4.1 Pharmaceutical Companies

Pharmaceutical companies have been particularly active with inversion deals. In late November 2015, Pfizer Inc. and Allergen PLC agreed on a historic merger of more than $150 billion. The takeover would be the largest inversion ever, with the smaller Dublin-based Allergan buying New York-based Pfizer.[53] In this type of inversion deal, a US company buys a foreign company and adopts its home country's domicile and lower tax rate, or establishes a holding company in a country with a low tax rate. In the previous year, Pfizer bid $120 billion for the UK's AstraZeneca Plc, but the British rival rejected the deal.[54] The Allergen deal was also dropped because the US Treasury Department imposed tough new curbs on inversions. As Robert Willens, a New York-based tax analyst stated, "They've addressed literally every benefit that one attempted to gain from an inversion and shut them all down systematically."[55]

Two other drug firms illustrate inversion moves: Illinois-based AbbVie Inc. aimed to take over Dublin-based Shire Plc for nearly $54 billion (a deal that later fell through), and Pennsylvania-based Mylan Inc. agreed to pay $5.3 billion for Abbott Laboratories' overseas generic drug business.[56] Although its legal home was moved to the Netherlands, Mylan's senior management remains based in Pennsylvania.[57] Walgreen is another company at one point considered an inversion deal. It bought additional shares of the European pharmacy Alliance Boots GmbH. A year later, Walgreen said that it never intended an inversion deal and that headquarters wouldn't leave the US.

Some companies fretted over political criticism and the ensuing bad publicity of such deals, but US politicians have not agreed on how to solve the problem. Some want to impose a higher threshold of foreign ownership, but the US still seeks to tax their firms on their global earnings rather than only domestic earnings.[58] Even after Pfizer's merger with Allergan PLC, the largest inversion deal ever, US lawmakers were still talking more than acting. Responding to political criticism, the chairman and CEO of Merck & Co., Kenneth C. Frazier, wrote a letter published on the op ed page of the *Wall Street Journal* explaining how the high corporate tax rate encouraged companies to engage in inversion deals. He also referred to the handicap that American companies are obligated to pay US taxes on worldwide income.[59]

9.2.4.2 The New Tax Bill

Congress finally acted when it passed the December 2017 tax bill that removes the need for inversion deals. The corporate tax rate was reduced to 20%, which encourages corporations to send foreign-held earnings to the US.[60] Apple Inc. responded by announcing it would pay a one-time tax of $38 billion on its overseas cash holdings and ramp up spending in the US.[61]

9.3 Obstacles to Globalization

As noted by Henry Kissinger, "The economic system has become global, while the political structure of the world remains based on the nation-state." The international order therefore faces a paradox: "Its prosperity is dependent on the success of globalization, but the process produces a political reaction that often works counter to its aspirations."[62] Kissinger's observation relates to the impediments to globalization, such as resurgent nationalism and national security concerns.

9.3.1 Resurgent Nationalism

By announcing his "American First" campaign, President Donald Trump exemplified nationalism. Trade agreements, such as Nafta, would be reviewed and renegotiated and tariffs threatened on major imports – 25% on steel and 10% on aluminum. In this economic sphere, nationalism promotes protectionism, which is anathema to globalization.

Previously, nationalism was invoked more sparingly. When countries become aware of the strategic importance of their resources, they are motivated to restrict exports. China did this with a substance called rare earth by limiting exports to Japan and other countries. Indonesia, which is the world's No. 2 exporter of nickel ore and has rich resources of tin and bauxite (the feedstock of aluminum), decided to tighten control of exports, which amounts to protectionism.[63]

9.3.1.1 The Island Dispute Between China and Japan Harms Trade

Nationalism harmed Japanese retail businesses in China in a political dispute between China and Japan over sovereignty of several small, uninhabited islands in the East China Sea near Taiwan island. This confrontation led to violent protests in several Chinese cities where Japanese products were boycotted and stores vandalized. Because of their physical vulnerability on streets, Japanese vehicles became targets and were fiercely damaged, with people cheering. Japanese stores were shuttered and in other stores Japanese goods were taken off the shelves. Products became proxies for the Japanese government.[64]

The protests in China were fueled by past conflicts with Japan and its unwillingness to acknowledge its past military action in China. Past hatreds are kept alive by annual visits by Japanese officials to the Yasukuni Shrine, a temple that consecrates Japanese heroes, but also some Class A war criminals. Crisis managers are reminded that they must always keep antecedent events in mind when analyzing a particular situation and remember that certain anniversary events can serve as triggers for nasty actions. For example, approximately 60 000 Beijing citizens participated in a demonstration on September18, 2012, the anniversary of the Manchurian Incident in the Second Sino-Japanese War, a date considered as the National Humiliation Day.

Also important in understanding the protests is the involvement of social media platforms as channels of discussion and information circulation. Weibo, the Chinese equivalent of Twitter, played a major role in spreading the word and organizing the events. Other platforms such as Renren, the Chinese equivalent of Facebook; QQ, the most popular online chat room software; and forums were also used to disseminate information. Internet users spontaneously took up responsibilities as organizers. They brainstormed with each other on slogan ideas. Non-governmental organizations (NGOs), civil groups, companies, and other entities also reached out to their members, inviting them to gather together at one place and march to the designated gathering location together.[65]

9.3.1.2 Sanctions

Globalization is deliberately interrupted when a country or group of countries impose sanctions on a country. A notable historic example is when the US and other nations imposed sanctions against the apartheid government of South Africa and were broadly credited for helping end that apartheid system. Even though the sanctions may not have been decisive, they contributed to the psychological impact on the governing party.

After Russia annexed Crimea in 2014, President Obama imposed sanctions to punish Russia and to dissuade Putin from the temptation to do the same in the Ukraine. Further sanctions were imposed when Russia was seen as helping pro-Russian Ukrainians seize parts of eastern Ukraine. European countries like the UK and Germany were asked to join the US effort and EU foreign ministers adopted new measures against 19 individuals and 9 entities.[66]

The *Wall Street Journal* columnist David Wessel, in a review of sanctions, gives this one a fair chance of having an impact because the sanctions were not unilateral and the objective was "fairly modest and well-devised." Furthermore, he states, "Today's sanctions, particularly the increasingly sophisticated ability of the US to unplug a target from the global financial system, are more likely to actually work."[67]

Globalization and economic growth have been hurt by these sanctions, as illustrated by a drop in Germany's GDP. Matters became worse after Putin declared counter-sanctions against Western foods. Norwegian fisherman have seen their catch rot and Polish farmers have seen their fruits spoil. 25 metric tons of tomatoes, 5 metric tons of apples, and 9 metric tons of carrots – all of allegedly forbidden Polish origin – were seized in a warehouse and taken to a dump. Footage aired on national television shows a bulldozer destroying piles of yellow blocks of cheese before they were dumped into a landfill. In Russia's top-down system, Putin's "culinary nationalism" was carried out and officials vied to destroy and burn as much as possible to impress superiors.[68]

9.3.2 National Security Concerns

In 2006 when Dubai Ports World (DP World) agreed to buy Peninsular & Oriental Steam Navigation Co. of London (P&O), the US government became concerned because DP World owned and operated the Port of New York and other US facilities. DP World is a state-owned company of the Emirate of Dubai, one of seven sheikdoms of the United Arab Emirates (UAE). The investment needed approval by the US Committee on Foreign Investment (CFIUS), a 12-member interagency panel headed by the Treasury. The investment was initially rejected by CFIUS. At issue was the sale of the port management business in six major US seaports to a company based in the UAE, raising the question of whether such a sale would compromise port security at a time when actions by terrorists were feared. The deliberations of CFIUS are secret, but administration officials provide periodic briefings and written summaries of all actions taken. DP World eventually sold P&O's American operations to American International Group's asset management division, Global Investment Group, for an undisclosed sum.

National security concerns were also expressed over other Chinese takeover plans. One was the planned $43 billion takeover of seed giant Syngenta AG by the China National Chemical Corp. Some senators objected. Senator Charles Grassley said, "We need to consider the long-term implications of letting foreign entities control significant market share in U.S. agriculture, especially in consolidated markets, like the seed market has become."[69] Another factor is that Syngenta's US chemical plants are potential terror targets, including some near military bases. Nevertheless, CFIUS approved the planned takeover. Erik Fyrwald, Syngenta's chief executive, said the deal would benefit farmers and crop production globally by placing Syngenta under ownership of a deep-pocketed company that will support long-term investments in research.[70] The EU antitrust authorities are also reviewing such megamergers.[71]

Senators also objected to Zhongwang USA LLC's plan to buy Cleveland-based Aleris Corp., a global leader in the manufacture and sales of aluminum products They feared that the deal "creates potential for military know-how and sensitive technology to be transferred to China's government," noting that Aleris has supplied aluminum plate used by the US military, including for armored vehicles.[72] Unresolved national security concerns were also cited by CFIUS as reasons for its objection to the Chinese takeover of the European chip-equipment manufacturer Aixtron SE of Germany because of involved certain technologies.[73] Germany's economics ministry also halted China's takeover.[74] China has also expressed concern about foreign ownership. The Chinese banking regulator excluded foreign investors from buying into a Chinese internet bank backed by the social network giant Tencent out of concern about foreign ownership.[75]

Concern about China was also expressed in Australia where Chinese investors intended to buy the Kidman property, the country's largest cattle ranch empire, which contains a herd of 200 000 cattle across 11 ranches and covers 9142 square miles, almost the size of the state of Vermont and larger than Ireland.[76] The deal would place 80% of the century-old S. Kidman empire in Chinese hands. Treasurer Scott Morrison said that "Australia welcomes foreign investment . . . . However, we must be confident that this investment is not contrary to the national interest."[77]

9.3.2.1 US Turns Down China's CNOOC and Huawei

When the Chinese state-owned oil giant China National Offshore Oil Corporation (CNOOC) made a hostile $18 billion bid for Unocal, an American gas company, the deal was turned down by American lawmakers as a threat to national security. However, CNOOC succeeding in July 2012 in reaching a $15 billion deal to buy Nexen, a Canadian energy firm with large holdings in tar sands and expertise in drilling for shale gas. This expertise was a major motivation for this acquisition as China's thirst for knowledge grows.[78]

Increasingly concerned about foreign intrusion into US telecommunications networks, the US government is determined to limit access by Chinese equipment suppliers like Huawei Technologies Co. to the American market.[79] The US fears that the company is little better than a front for the Chinese state, considering that its CEO Ren Zhengfei was an engineer in the People's Liberation Army before he founded Huawei in 1987.[80] The deal was reviewed by representatives from the departments of Justice, Defense and Homeland Security, the Federal Bureau of Investigation, and CFIUS.

CFIUS looked into the proposed purchase by Tsinghua Unigroup Ltd., a Chinese state-owned company and China's largest chip design company, of chip giant Micron Technology Inc. If it had gone ahead it would have been the biggest US takeover yet. It shows China's determination to be a major player in owning the key components that power electronics such as smart phones and computers and not just assembling them. Micron is the last remaining US supplier of a widely used variety of dynamic random access memory (DRAM). If China were to acquire Micron, it would automatically get onto the leading edge of technology, for the chip maker holds many memory-technology patents and maintains advanced factories in the US, Taiwan, Japan, and Singapore. China would again be revealing its "growing ambition to push beyond gadgets and become a broad technology superpower."[81] It now spends more than $200 billion a year on public and private R&D, more than the EU.[82]

The US also fears China's strategic efforts to dominate the semiconductor market as shown by the finalizing of a study by the Obama administration that could lead to restrictions on Chinese investment in that sector. John Holdren, the president's chief science adviser at the time, said, "A loss of leadership in semi-conductor innovation and manufacturing could have significant adverse impacts on the US economy and even on national security."[83] Determined to become a major player in the global chip market, China was spending $24 billion to build the country's first advanced memory chip factory.[84] The semiconductor sector makes computer chips for everything from smart phones to missiles, satellites to energy grids. Accordingly, in December 2016, CFIUS rejected the proposed sale of Aixtron SE of Germany, which has a US subsidiary, to Grand Chip Investment GmbH, the German unit of China's Fujian Grand Chip Investment Fund.

The treatment by the US of Japan's SoftBank was different. In July 2013, the Federal Communications Commission (FCC) approved the bank's acquisition of 78% ownership in

Sprint Nextel Corp., despite the US's concern about foreign intrusion into US telecommunications. SoftBank is a major telecommunication and internet company. To win approval and avoid the problems faced by Huawei, SoftBank made the concession of giving the federal government the right to approve one of its directors who would be responsible for overseeing national security issues.[85]

ZTE Corp. is the latest US and British target of national security concern. ZTE is the world's No. 4 telecom gear maker. In April 2018 the US Commerce Department banned American companies from selling products to ZTE because it illegally violated sanctions involving sales to North Korea and Iran. The Federal Communications Commission also proposed rules to make it harder for Chinese firms like ZTE and Huawei to sell equipment to a few small, rural US phone providers that use it.[86]

9.3.2.2 Canada's Strategic Potash Corp. Decision

Canada has a review board, the Foreign Investment Review Agency (FIRA), which in 2010, rejected Australia-based BHP Billiton Ltd.'s $39 billion attempt to buy Potash Corp. of Saskatchewan Inc. It said the deal wouldn't bring enough economic benefit to Canada. Furthermore, Potash Corp. holds a significant chunk of the world's reserves of potash, a critical raw material in fertilizer which Canada thought should be viewed as a strategic asset that should remain in Canadian hands.[87] Changing its role, however, Potash in 2015 sought to take over the German salt and fertilizer company K+S AG valued at $8.57 billion. Both companies mine potash and a tie-up would create a giant that could control as much as 30% of the global market. K+S said its Saskatchewan Canadian mine was developing a project known as Legacy, which would make it the only potash producer with its own large production facilities on two continents. It claimed that Potash, while valuing this facility, had not reflected this in the offer price.[88]

A consequent development is that the Canadian fertilizer company Agrium Inc. and Potash Corp., the two top fertilizer giants, plan to merge in a deal that would create a crop nutrient giant valued at about $27 billion. Together they would control 60% or more of North American capacity and 23% of global production. Although cost reductions are cited as the main motivation for the merger, the reduction in competition raises concerns about price increases.

Other pending global farming sector deals are between Dow Chemical Co. and DuPont Co., and the planned takeover by China National Chemical Corp. of Swiss pesticide and seed company Syngenta AG.[89] In March 2017 these deals were approved by the EU's European Commission.[90]

Monopolistic competition on a global level is a rising danger. Since 2008 there have been an average of 30 000 merger and acquisition deals a year worldwide, worth 3% of GDP.[91] Each year announcements of planned or actual mergers and acquisitions are made. In November 2016, for example, Praxair Inc., based in Danbury, Connecticut, restarted negotiations with Germany's Linde AG that would create a $60 billion industrial gas giant. The merger would create the world's largest producer of industrial gases, which are used in manufacturing food production, healthcare and the like. Air Liquide SA claimed the No. 1 spot earlier in the year when it acquired rival Airgas Inc.[92]

Another example is the planned merger of Luxottica Group SpA, maker of Ray-Ban eyewear, with French optical lens-maker Essilor International SA. The combined companies would have about 27% of the eyewear market, far ahead of other competitors such as Johnson & Johnson.[93]

9.3.3 Weak Infrastructures

A major impediment to globalization is the lack of adequate roads, water supply, electric utilities, and communications facilities. This deficit in infrastructure applies particularly to developing nations in Africa and India.

9.3.3.1 Nigeria

Doing business in Africa faces many obstacles, as consumer goods firms in Nigeria, Africa's biggest market, demonstrate. Its population is projected to exceed the US's by 2045.[94] Nigeria's infrastructure is terribly weak, with a shortage of electricity among the worst problems. Its power stations generate only about a tenth of the capacity of South Africa, the continent's second largest economy. Roads are so poor and congested that accidents pose one of the biggest problems. International trade is hindered by the absence of deep water ports and a cumbersome customs system for the two ports close to Lagos.

Dispersed customers and inefficient supply chains are further complications. Added to these problem is the variety of languages spoken in Nigeria, which makes it difficult to reach customers. To get around this obstacle, Unilever employs women who understand the areas' languages as local agents, a system that worked well in India.

9.3.4 Widening Income Disparities

A final obstacle to globalization – and one currently emphasized in the US – is its association with wage stagnation and growing income inequality. Robert Rubin, former treasury secretary who became executive co-chair of Citigroup, blames globalization for income disparities, saying they are a deeply troubling fact of American economic life that threatens the trading system, even the stability of "capitalist, democratic society."[95] Although critics of free trade had been saying it for years, Rubin makes news when he acknowledges globalization's role in generating a 30-year stagnation of US wages, squeezing middle-class families and below, while directing income growth mainly to the upper brackets. In a strategy paper he co-wrote for the Hamilton Project – a policy group of like-minded economists and financiers who are developing ameliorative measures to the threatened workforce – Rubin concludes, "Prosperity has neither trickled down nor rippled outward. Between 1973 and 2003, real GDP per capital in the United States increased 73%, while real median hourly compensation rose only 13%."[96]

9.3.4.1 Piketty's Capital in the Twenty-First Century

The explanation of income and wealth disparities is more complicated, however, than the spread of globalization. Based on 15 years of research, the French economist Thomas Piketty presented detailed evidence of the dynamics of the distribution of wealth and income since the eighteenth century.[97] He describes two forces: one toward "convergence" (of incomes and wealth) associated with the diffusion of knowledge and skills; the other toward "divergence" (or inequality of incomes and wealth). He considers the latter as "potentially threatening to democratic societies and to the value of social justice on which they are based."[98]

He explains inequality by the formula $r > g$, where r is the rate of return on capital and g is the rate of growth of income and output. In other words, when the GDP is lower than money made from capital (i.e. wealth), the outcome is inequality. In carefully crafted charts he shows that since the beginning of the twentieth century, inequality of incomes and wealth peaked just before World War I, then declined and peaked again in 1929, the year of the stock market crash. Inequality remained low until the late 1970s.

Income inequality sharply started to grow around 1977 and continues to grow, reaching the levels of 1928. The median income in 2010 was an inflation-adjusted $49 445.[99] Between 1977 and 2007, the richest 10% "appropriated" three-fourths of the growth in income, and the richest 1% received 60% of income growth. Almost all (95%) of the income growth in the economy between 2010 and 2012 accrued to the top 1%.[100]

During and after the 2008 recession, the gap between the richest and poorest Americans further widened. The top 1% of households in 2012 took 22.5% of total income, the highest figure since 1928.[101] While the pretax income for the wealthiest 10% of US families rose 10% in 2013 from 2010, that of families in the bottom 40% saw their average inflation-adjusted income decline.[102] The Census Bureau reports that from 2000 to 2010, median income in the US declined 7% after adjusting for inflation.[103]

The result is that since 1980, "inequality has exploded in the US": The upper 10%'s share rose from 30–35% of national income in the 1970s to 45–50% in the 2000s. If change continues at this pace, says Piketty, the upper decile will be taking in 60% of national income by 2030. Piketty concludes that the level of inequality in the US is "probably higher than in any other society at any time in the past, anywhere in the world."[104]

Looking at the top 1% of the income hierarchy, it is estimated that 60–70% consists of top managers.[105] Piketty calls them "supermanagers," and says they are the primary reason for rising income inequality in both the financial and non-financial sectors in recent decades. Paul Tudor Jones of Just Capital, writes: "In 1980 the average CEO made roughly 42 times more than the average employee. Today the that ratio is 373 to 1."[106] The managers have amassed enormous power, abetted by compliant boards of directors, who themselves are richly rewarded, and supporting executive search firms, such as Korn Ferry International, that portray these managers as exceptionally talented and scarce in numbers.

The poverty rate is another indicator of pressure on the lower and middle classes. It has remained essentially unchanged at 12.6%, about $20 000 for a family of four, well above its recent low of 11.3%. Adding to this pressure, healthcare costs are not only rising, they increasingly are being paid by consumers, not by employers or the government. Pensions are disappearing as is the job security feature.[107]

Beyond the US, the main criticism of globalization is that globalization is not helping many poor countries. Inequality of income around the world – the antithesis of justice and fairness – is growing, with the result that poverty remains entrenched in the developing world. The promised "convergence" – reducing the disparity in incomes and wealth between rich and poor countries – has not been achieved, asserts Joseph E. Stiglitz in his *Globalization and its Discontents*.[108] Stiglitz, winner of the Nobel Prize in Economics in 2001, acknowledges that although globalization has brought enormous benefits to some countries, notably China, in other cases convergence was not achieved. For example, he concludes that NAFTA has not reduced the disparity in income and wealth between Mexico and the US; too often wealth goes to a few people at the top who don't compensate the losers.

9.4 Saving Globalization

Globalization is facing resistance as seen in the expected revisions in NAFTA and, more recently, when President Trump abandoned the Trans-Pacific Partnership (TPP), saying it would result in a loss of US jobs.[109] The TPP was a decade in the making and would have been the largest regional trade deal in history, encompassing 12 Pacific countries, including the US, Japan, and Canada, but excluding China. It would have included strong safeguards for the environment, labor rights, and intellectual property. Its collapse was seen as a "body blow" to American economic policy in Asia, said Matthew Goodman of the Centre for Strategic and International Studies.[110] It also put the world on notice that "all of America's traditional economic and political alliances are now open to reassessment, renegotiation and possibly even reversal," said Eswar Prasad, a Cornell University economist and former top China official at the International Monetary Fund.[111] Assuming

Trump sticks to his decision, the remaining 11 countries will sign a renegotiated version of TPP expected to be called the Comprehensive and Progressive Agreement or Trans-Pacific Partnership, or TPP-11.[112]

In what is now known as the "Battle of Seattle" of 1999, the very idea of globalization was attacked. The International Monetary Fund and the World Bank, both associated with globalization, were holding their meeting when the streets were filled with students, trade unions, and several civil society organizations protesting against them and what they considered the excesses of foreign trade. Some 60 000 demonstrators gathered to oppose further trade liberalization.[113] The shadow of protectionism lurked over Seattle.

As a further sign of protectionist sentiment, newspaper headlines appeared, such as "Wake Up, America! America Companies Are Being Sold to Foreign Interests" and "The Most Famous American Brands in Foreign Hands."[114] Not only globalization but the ideology of the free market system was on trial.

Globalization has become a highly controversial issue and debate over it is expected to escalate. Some see Brexit, Britain's withdrawal from the EU, as the start of an unraveling of globalization, for "When people feel they do not control their lives or share in the fruits of globalization, they strike out."[115] British business itself was divided over whether Britain should remain in the EU. Just before the referendum vote on June 6, 2016, the Remain camp sent a letter to the *Times* signed by 500 business leaders warning that Brexit would cost jobs, lead to lower levels of investment, and reduce living standards.[116] On the other hand, John Longworth, director general of the British Chambers of Commerce (BCC) publicly said that Britain had a brighter future outside the EU. He was suspended and later resigned.[117] Prime Minister David Cameron's efforts to persuade business and the public to remain in the EU failed.

9.5 Conclusions

Public relations and marketing have accompanied companies when they went abroad. They, together with public affairs, have also paved the way by influencing public opinion to support globalization efforts. The dynamics of trade, however, has changed as wages rise in developing nations and concerns about environmental degradation and abuse of worker rights and human rights grow. And while globalization has reduced poverty in the world, it has also resulted in rising inequality of income and wealth in nations.

Deglobalization forces are now on the rise and corporate communication must influence policies and develop strategic communications programs to address the issues raised. Until recently, the belief (including this author's) was that globalization was an unstoppable force. But now it is no longer seen as inevitable and irreversible.[118]

What eventually happens depends on whether people are, as Tom Friedman in his *The Lexus and the Olive Tree* calls them, "Social-Safety-Netters" or "Let-Them-Eat-Cakers." The former believe that globalization is sustainable if it is democratized both economically and politically so as to cushion the fall of the left-behinds and help them acquire the tools and resources to compete. The other group are "people who believe that globalization is essentially winner take all, loser take care of yourself."[119]

Recognizing that recent attacks on globalization reveal that nations no longer have "shared values," Klaus Schwab, the head of the World Economic Forum, acknowledges that globalization needs a reevaluation to make it more inclusive and spread the benefits more widely. "I think we have to find a new balance. I would call it equitable globalization."[120]

Discussion Questions

9.1. What are some indicators of the spread of globalization? What factors drive globalization?

9.2. A manufacturer of women's apparel in South Carolina is considering outsourcing production to China. What factors should it consider?

9.3. What are some signs that globalization faces resistance? What are the reasons for this resistance?

9.4. How have labor unions been affected by globalization? How can cooperation from labor unions be obtained?

9.5. What role has public relations played in globalization?

9.6. What is an "inversion deal"? What companies have been attracted to it?

9.7. What are some national security concerns of globalization? Name some countries and their specific concerns.

9.8. What is CFIUS? How does it work?

9.9. Do you agree with Australia's opposition to the purchase of a large cattle farm to Chinese interests?

9.10. Do you agree with Canada's rejection of an Australian company's bid to buy its Potash Corp.? Why or why not?

9.11. Should income disparities within and between nations influence attitudes toward globalization?

9.12. What problems has Brexit created for globalization?

9.13. What role can public relations play in determining the future of globalization?

Endnotes

1 Friedman, Thomas L., *The World is Flat: A Brief History of the Twenty-First Century* (New York: Farrar, Straus and Girous, 2005), p. 48.
2 Ibid., p. 49.
3 Greg Ip, "Globalization Gives Way to Nationalism in U.S.," *WSJ*, January 28–29, 2017, p. A1.
4 Eric Schmidt and Jared Cohen, *The New Digital Age* (New York: Vintage Books, 2013), p. 4.
5 Christopher Alessi and Natascha Divac, "Siemens Deepens Push to Digitize," *WSJ*, November 15, 2016, p. B4.
6 Andrea Thomas, "Germany Raises Hurdles to Bids By Foreign Firms," *WSJ*, July 13, 2017, p. A7.
7 Gordon M. Goldstein, "The End of the Internet? How Regional Networks May Replace the World Wide Web," *The Atlantic*, July/August, 2014.

8 Ibid., p. 24.
9 Marshall McLuhan, *Understanding Media* (New York: McGraw-Hill, 1964).
10 Jack Ewing, "Upwardly Mobile In Africa," *BusinessWeek*, September 24, 2007, pp. 64–65.
11 "Planet of the Phones," *The Economist*, February 28, 2015, p. 9.
12 "The Truly Personal Computer," *The Economist*, February 28, 2015, pp. 19–20.
13 Drew Hinshaw, et al., "Troubles Cloud Africa's Outlook," May 8, 2014, p. 20.
14 Walt Rostow, *The Stages of Economic Growth: A Non-Communist Manifesto* (Cambridge: Cambridge University Press, 1960), p. 6.
15 "Agricultural Biodiversity: Banks for Bean Counters," *The Economist*, September 12, 2015, pp. 54–55.
16 See Jack N. Behman and William A. Fischer, "Overseas R&D Activities of Transnational Companies," *Thunderbird International Business Review*, Vol. 22, Issue 3, pp. 15–17, Fall 1980.
17 "Decentralising Drug Research: Pharmed Out," *The Economist*, May 24, 2014, p. 60
18 Joyce Wouters, *International Public Relations: How to Establish Your Company's Product, Service, and Image in Foreign Markets* (New York: Amacom, 1991).
19 Executives and Associates of Hill and Knowlton International, *Handbook on International Public Relations*, Vol. 2 (New York: Frederick A. Praeger, Publishers, 1968), p. v.
20 Charles Mangee, "Building an International Public Relations Network," in Bill Cantor, edited by Chester Burger, *Experts in Action: Inside Public Relations*, 2nd ed. (New York: Longman, 1989), pp. 434–443.
21 Ibid, p. 44.
22 Ruth Bender, Natalie Tadena, and Suzanne Vranica, "Failed Merger Leaves Holes for Ad Giants," *WSJ*, May 10–11, 2014, p. B1.
23 "WPP: Ads and Subtracting," *The Economist*, April 21, 2018, p. 55.
24 Kathy Chu and Bob Davis, "A Nation of 1.4 Billion Faces a Labor Shortage," *WSJ*, November 24, 2015, p. A10.
25 Friedman, op. cit., p. 18.
26 Laura Meckler, "U.S. Puts a Curb on Visa Program," *WSJ*, April 4, 2017, p. A6.
27 Josh Zumbrun, "Forces That Opened Up Borders Show Signs of Sputtering," *WSJ*, April 4, 2016, p. A2.
28 Ibid.
29 Douglas A. Irwin, "The Truth About Trade: What Critics Get Wrong About the Global Economy," *Foreign Affairs*, Vol. 95, No. 4, July–August 2016, p. 89.
30 Ibid., p. 88.
31 David Luhnow and Jacob M. Schlesingerf, "Mexico Reconsiders Its U.S.·Friendship," *WSJ*, February 6, 2017, p. A1.
32 Ibid., p. 92.
33 Dudley Althaus, "Attacks on Car Exports Put Mexico at Risk," *WSJ*, January 20, 2017, p. A5.
34 Christina Rogers and In-Soo Nam, "Ford Plans New Factory in Mexico for Small Cars," *WSJ*, April 6, 2016, p. B2. Mike Colias, Christina Rogers, and Joann S.·Lublin, "Auto Makers in the Crosshairs," *WSJ*, January 24, 2017, p. A8.
35 Tim Higgins, "Ford CEO Wary of Trump Tariffs," *WSJ*, November 16, 2016, p. B3.
36 Adrienne Roberts and Chester Dawson, "Toyota Draws Trump's Outrage," *WSJ*, January 6, 2017, p. B1.
37 Dudley Althaus and Christina Rogers, "Global Car Industry Runs on NAFTA," *WSJ*, November 11, 2016, pp. A1, A12.
38 James R. Hagerty, *WSJ*, June 2, 2014, p. R1; and James R. Hagerty and Mark Magnier, "Companies Tiptoe Back Toward 'Made in the USA,'" *WSJ*, January 14, 2014, p. A1.
39 Chu and Davis, op. cit.

40 Ibid.
41 Lorraine Luk "Foxconn Recrafts Its Future," *WSJ*, June 28–29, 2014, p. B3.
42 Eva Dou, "Foxconn Sees Future Path Beyond Apple," *WSJ*, April 1, 2017, p. B5.
43 "Tourism Sector Continues to Drive Growth," *South China Morning Post*, August 31, 2014, p. 4.
44 Eva Dou and Don Clark, "Chinese Firms Bids $23 Billion for Micron," *WSJ*, July 14, 2015, p. B1; Joann S. Lublin, Dana Mattioli, and Ted Mann, "GE Nears Deal to Sell Unit to China's Haier," *WSJ*, January 15, 2016, p. B1.
45 Craig Karmin and Joshu Jamerson, "Starwood Battle Intensifies as Chinese Group Boosts Bid," *WSJ*, March 29, 2016, p. B1.
46 William Mauldin, "Rising Chinese Investments Draw Scrutiny," *WSJ*, April 13, 2016, p. A2.
47 Howard French's *China's Second Continent: How a Million Migrants Are Building a New Empire in Africa* (New York: Alfred A. Knopf, 2014).
48 Murithi Mutiga, "Africa and the Chinese Way," *The International New York Times*, December 16, 2013, OpEd section.
49 "China in Africa: Empire of the Sums," *The Economist*, August 23, 2014, p. 76.
50 Noemie Bisserbe, Jeanne Whalen, and Hester Plumridge, "Sanofi Fires CEO as Tensions Boil Over," *WSJ*, October 30, 2014, p. B1.
51 "Corporate Tax in America; How to Stop the Inversion Perversion?" *The Economist*, July 26, 2014, pp. 12, 14.
52 "Corporate Tax in America; How to Stop the Inversion Perversion?," *The Economist*, July 26, 2014, pp. 12, 14.
53 Jonathan D. Rockoff and Dana Mattioli, "Pfizer, Allergan Agree to Merge," *WSJ*, November 23, 2015, p. A1.
54 Dana Mattioli, "Acquirers Plot Escape from a Turn on Taxes," *WSJ*, July 7, 2014, p. C1.
55 Richard Rubin and Liz Hoffman, "U.S. Sets Tougher Rules on Tax Deals," *WSJ*, April 5, 2016, p. A1.
56 Liz Hoffman and Hester Plumridge, "Race to Cut Taxes Fuels Urge to Merge," *WSJ*, July 15, 2014.
57 Shayndi Raice and Liz Hoffman, "Dutch Law Sinks Drug Tie-Up," *WSJ*, July 28, 2015, p. A1.
58 John D. McKinnon, "Congress at Odds Over How to Curb Tax-Inversion Trend," *WSJ*, July 17, 2014; "To Deter 'Inversions,' Overhaul Corporate Taxes," *USA Today*, August, 2025, p. 8A.
59 Kenneth C. Frazier, "The Senate Tax Bill Has a Cure for Corporate Inversion," *WSJ*, November 28, 2017.
60 Thomas Kaplan and Alan Rappeport, "Republican Tax Bill Passes Senate in 51–49 Vote," *New York Times*, December 19, 2017.
61 Tripp Mickle, "Apple Set to Pay Big Tax Bill, Touts U.S. Spending," *WSJ*, January 18, 2018, p. 1.
62 Henry Kissinger, "The Assembly of A New Global Order," *WSJ*, August 30–31, 2014, p. C3.
63 Francesca Freeman, "Tin Market Rattled by Indonesia Ban," *WSJ*, December 7–8, 2013, p. B5.
64 Juro Osawa, "Wary of Protests, Japan Firms Lie Low," *WSJ*, September 18, 2012, p. A8. Chester Deawson, "Japan Firms See Backlash," *WSJ*, September 19, 2012, p. A11.
65 Reported in a final paper by Ruyu Wang in a graduate International Public Relations course at Boston University's College of Communication.
66 "Sanctions Against Russia: Fancy Footwork," *The Economist*, February 14, 2014, p. 59.
67 David Wessel, "The Art and Science of Sanctions," *WSJ*, December 12, 2013, p. A2.
68 Thomas Grove "Russia Destroys Tons of Banned Foods from West," *WSJ*, August 7, 2015, p. A12.
69 Jacob Bunge, "Opposition Rises Over Chinese Bid for Syngenta," *WSJ*, March 24, 2016, p. B1.
70 Jacob Bunge, Brian Spegele, and William Mauldin, "U.S. Panel Approves Chinese Takeover," *WSJ*, August 23, 2016, p. A1.
71 Natalia Drozdiak and Brian Blackstone, "Mergers Face Delays from EU Scrutiny," *WSJ*, October 27, 2016, p. B7.

72 Scott Patterson, "Senators Petition to Block China Metals Deal," *WSJ*, November 3, 2016, p. B3.
73 Eyk Hening, "U.S. Panel Resists Chinese Takeover of German Firm," *WSJ*, November 21, 2016, p. B3.
74 William Wilkes, "Germany Halts China Takeover," October 25, 2016, p. B5.
75 Rick Carew and Juro Osawa, "Beijing Blocks Foreign Investors in WeBank Deal," *WSJ*, June 7, 2016, p. C3.
76 Rob Taylor, "Australia To Reject Deal for Ranch," WSJ, April 30–May 1, 2016, p. B3.
77 Ibid.
78 "A Chinese Oil firm in Canada: Canucks, Meet CNOOC," *The Economist*, July 28, 2012, p. 56.
79 Anton Troianovski, Danny Yadron, and Spencer E. Ante, "U.S. Steps Into Sprint's Board," *WSJ*, May 23, 2013, p. B1.
80 "Huawei: Seeking its Own Path," *The Economist*, May 10, 2014, p. 64.
81 Eva Dou and Don Clark, "Bid for Chip Giant Signals Lofty Ambitions," *WSJ*, July 15, 2015, p. A1; also "Chinese Firm Bids $23 Billion for Micron," July 14, 2015, p. B1.
82 "Schumpeter; Calibrating Chinese Creativity," *The Economist*, July 11, 2015, p. 60.
83 Ian Talley, "U.S. Gears Up to Restrict Chinese in Chip Industry," *WSJ*, January 3, 2017, p. B5.
84 Bob Davis and Eva Dou, "China's Next Target: U.S. Microchip Hegemony," *WSJ*, July 27, 2017.
85 Anton Troianovski, Danny Yadron, and Spencer E. Ante, "U.S. Steps Into Sprint's Board," *WSJ*, May 23, 2013, p. B1.
86 Jason Douglas and Robert Wall, "U.S., Britain Tighten Vice on Chinese Firms," *WSJ*, April 17, 2018, p. A1.
87 Edward Welsch, "China Deepens Push in Canadian Oil," *WSJ*, October 10, 2011, p. B1; "Fertilizer Prices: Rich in Potassium," *The Economist*, August 3, 2013, p. 62.
88 Sarah Sloat, "Germany's K&S Says No to Bid from Potash," *WSJ*, July 3, 2015, p. B6.
89 Jacquie McNish and Judy McKinnon, "Merger to Create Global Fertilizer Giant," *WSJ*, September 13, 2016, p. B1.
90 Natalia Drozdiak, "DuPont, Dow Get EU Approval for Mergers," *WSJ*, March 28, 2017, p. B3.
91 "Schumpeter: Out With the Old," *The Economist*, December 17, 2016, p. 61.
92 Dana Mattoli and Eyk Henning, "Praxsair Courts Rival Again," *WSJ*, November 30, 2016, p. B1.
93 Inti Landauro and Manuela Mesco, "Merger to Create Eyewear Giant," *WSJ*, January 17, 2017, p. B1.
94 "Business in Nigeria: Africa's Testing Ground," *The Economist*, August 23, 2014, pp. 59–62.
95 William Greider, "Born-Again Rubinomics," *The Nation*, July 31–August 7, 2006, p. 20.
96 Ibid., p. 21.
97 Thomas Piketty, *Capital in the Twenty-First Century* (Cambridge, MA: Belknap Press, 2013) p. vii.
98 Ibid., p. 571.
99 Conor Dougherty, "Income Slides to 1996 Levels," *Wall Street Journal*, September 14, 2011, p. A1.
100 Alan S. Blinder, "The Supply-Side Case for Government Redistribution," *WSJ*, August 15, 2014, p. A13.
101 John Cassidy, "Piketty's Inequality Story in Six Charts," *New Yorker*, March 26, 2014, p. 70.
102 Ben Leubsdorf, "Rich-Poor Gap Widened Amid Recovery, Fed Finds," *WSJ*, September 5, 2014, p. A2.
103 Phil Izzo, "Bleak News or Americans' Income," *Wall Street Journal*, October 14, 2011, p. A6.
104 Piketty, op. cit., p. 294.
105 A book by Brooke Harrington, *Capital without Borders: Wealth Managers and the One Percent* (Boston, MA: Harvard College, 2016) discloses how assets are hidden and taxes dodged in an offshore world as the "Panama Papers" leak revealed.

106 Paul Tudor Jones, "Just business, The World in 1016," *The Economist*, p. 46; https://justcapital.com/research
107 Robert J. Samuelson, "Trickle-Up Economics," *Newsweek*, October 2, 2006, p. 40.
108 Joseph E. Stiglitz in his *Globalization and its Discontents*. (New York: W.W. Norton, 2002).
109 Carol E. Lee and Damian Paletta, "Trump Pulls U.S. Out of Trade Pact," *WSJ*, January 24, 2017, p. A1.
110 "The Collapse of TPP: Trading Down," *The Economist*, November 19, 2016, p. 31.
111 Lee and Paletta, op. cit., p. A4.
112 Ed Gerwin, "In America's Absence, the TPP Goes On," *WSJ*, March 8, 2018, p. A17.
113 "The New Trade Law," *The Economist*, December 4, 1999, p. 25.
114 Michael B. Sauter, Charles B. Stockdal, Douglas A. McIntyre, "The Most Famous American Brands in Foreign Hands," HuffPost, May 25, 2011.
115 "The Politics of Anger," *The Economist*, July 2, 2016.
116 Larry Elliott, "Business has a powerful voice in the Brexit debate," *The Observer*, February 6, 2016.
117 Denis Staunton, "Pro-Brexit Side Accused of 'Bizarre' Theories as Business Leader Resigns," *The Irish Times*, arch 8, 2016, p. 11.
118 This is the view voiced in "Schumpeter: Out with the Old," *The Economist*, December 17, 2016, p. 61.
119 Thomas L. Friedman, *The Lexus and the Olive Tree: Understanding Glohalization* (New York: Picador, 2000), pp. 437–438.
120 Gerard Baker, "Head of Davos Forum Sees Signs of Progress in Trump's First Year," *WSJ*, January 10, 2018, p. A6.

10

Interacting with International Players

There are many more players in the international arena than the domestic one. Surrounding the modern multi-national corporation (MNC), which is the focus of this book, are other types of players, sometimes called "actors." They include: (i) nation states, (ii) supranational organizations like the United Nations (UN) and European Union (EU), and (iii) civil society entities, especially non-governmental organization (NGOs) that advocate such causes such as human rights and climate change reforms.

Chief operating officers (COOs) in domestic situations are accustomed to dealing with their own governments and social action groups. Many of the strategies and tactics they use are also applicable internationally, but the presence of new players requires a fresh look. As Microsoft learned in its dealings with the EU, the victories in dealing with antitrust and other issues in the US are not necessarily repeated in a tougher European political environment. The views and attitudes of new players must be assessed carefully and changes in the game recognized.

10.1 Powerful MNCs

Modern MNCs – also called transnational corporations, global corporations, or multi-enterprise corporations – are the most powerful members of the private sector. Although government is the dominant political power in society, MNCs excel in economic power. The Fortune 500 companies, which represent the bulk and breadth of American and global business, had total revenues that equaled two-thirds of US gross domestic product (GDP).[1] The biggest Fortune 100's share of nominal GDP rose from about 33% of GDP in 1994 to 46% in 2013. And the McKinsey Global Institute calculates that 10% of the world's public companies generate 80% of all profits. No wonder *The Economist* speaks of "The Rise of the Superstars."[2]

An oft-quoted fact is that of the top economies in the world in 2011, 51 were MNCs and the other 49 were countries, based on sales and national GDPs. The sales of MNCs equal 23.7% of world economic activity and the sales of the top 200 are the equivalent of 27.5% of world economic activity, even though they employ only 0.78% of the world's workforce. Exxon's annual revenues of more than $400 billion were about the same as the GDP of Norway.[3] Digital companies dominated in 2014. The top three companies in Silicon Valley – Apple, Alphabet, and Microsoft – had revenues of $247 billion and a market capitalization of over $1 trillion, but just 137 000 employees.[4]

The orientation of an MNC can be discerned by whether it describes itself as ethnocentric, polycentric, or geocentric. Believing in the superiority of its own ethnic group, the headquarters of an ethnocentric company would send advice, counsel, and directives to its subsidiaries. A polycentric company has many centers of authority and control that would allow a subsidiary to be managed locally. The trend is toward the geocentric model, which takes a world view where headquarters consist of managers representing multiple nationalities. As Howard J. Perlmutter states, "The payoffs are more powerful total company throughout, a better quality of products and services, worldwide utilization of best resources, improvement of local company management, a greater sense of commitment to worldwide objectives, and last but not least, more profit."[5]

10.1.1 Illustrative Company Profiles

The giant American conglomerate General Electric (GE) is illustrative of the modern MNC (see Case 1). It holds more assets abroad than any other non-financial firm in the world – over $500 billion worth. Its foreign assets comprise over 70% of its total. Of the 100 companies with the most foreign assets, 17 hold over 90% of their assets abroad, including ArcelorMittal – the world's leading integrated steel and mining company – Nestlé, Anheuser-Busch InBev, and Vodafone. Their share of foreign sales is substantially larger than GE's. In terms of employees, more than half of GE's 300 000-strong workforce is based outside the US. Toyota, which has slightly more employees, has 38% of its 326 000 workers abroad.

Toyota and Honda are the only two Asian firms to make it into the top 20 transnational companies by assets. Three of the top five firms are oil companies. ExxonMobil had the largest foreign sales in 2011 at $317 billion, 73% of its total. MNCs benefited from the more favorable economic climates in emerging markets, and some developed markets such as the US. According to the latest World Investment Report from the UN Conference on Trade and Development (UNCTAD), production by foreign affiliates increased in 2011; sales rose by 9% to $28 trillion; employment rose by 8% to 69 million; and total assets rose from around $75 trillion in the previous 2 years to $82 trillion. Thanks mainly to economic uncertainty, UNCTAD reckons transnational companies are hoarding some $5 trillion in cash. This could lead to a surge in foreign direct investment, although firms might instead opt for liquidity, or to pay off debts or pay out dividends to maintain share prices.[6]

The economic power of MNCs is further demonstrated by these additional facts: Wal-Mart employed 2.2 million "associates" worldwide in 2014, making it the world's largest private employer.[7] The percentages of foreign sales accounted for by the five companies with the largest assets are:

BP	79.8%
ExxonMobil	73.0%
Toyota	60.8%
Royal Dutch Shell	60.1%
GE	52.6%)

Corporations can use their economic power to influence, and some cases to "dominate," public thought and discourse. In the US, the Supreme Court declared in 1886 that the Constitution asserts the same rights and protection to a corporation as to a natural person, including the right to free speech. This right was further strengthened in 2010 by the Supreme Court's five-to-four decision in the "Citizens United" ruling that gave corporations and unions the right to spend unlimited money on ads and other political tools that call for the election or defeat of individual candidates.[9]

Today, global corporations are identified with a wide range of nations. In addition to those owned by developed nations, emerging countries have acquired several Western icons. Among them are India's Mittal, which bought France's Arcelor; Tata Motors, which bought Jaguar Land

Rover; and Brazil's AmBev which was acquired by Anheuser-Busch InBev, owned by Belgium.[10] Among the world's 500 largest companies, nearly 100 are Chinese, ranked by revenue.

10.2 Nation States

A growing number of nation states are increasingly regulating the behavior of MNCs. More than 100 international jurisdictions – including China, Brazil, and the Ukraine – now claim antitrust authority to examine acquisitions and mergers (A&M), using different approaches for judging whether an A&M might harm consumers or national interests. In Africa, the competition section of the Common Market for Eastern and Southern Africa (COMESA) – a regional commission representing 19 states in eastern and southern Africa, including Egypt Ethiopia and Sudan – can charge companies fees as high as $500 000 to submit deals for approval and demand concessions. An expanding roster of countries is exerting power over merger deals.[11]

10.2.1 China's Antitrust and Bribery Actions

In recent years, China has increased its antitrust surveillance and actions. Foreign companies in China are being disproportionately targeted, asserts the EU Chamber of Commerce in China.[12] Antitrust actions have grown since 2008 when China's anti-monopoly law came into force. Although domestic firms are also targeted, foreign firms, especially car makers, have faced the brunt. China is focusing on foreign technology and auto companies, which experts says is designed to give Chinese companies greater bargaining power in dealing with foreign firms. For example, 10 Japanese car-parts firms were fined a total of $200 million and the German car maker Daimler was found guilty of illegally using its market power to inflate the price of its spare parts.[13] To appease Chinese authorities, Microsoft in May 2016 decided to shut down its Chinese web portal, which provided online content, and instead focus on offering Windows software and cloud-computing services.[14]

Three agencies are responsible for enforcing the laws. The National Development and Reform Commission (NDRC) is the largest, with the mandate to control prices. For example, Audi AG and Fiat Chrysler Automobiles were accused of pursuing monopolistic practices in Hubei province and Shanghai, respectively. They were said to push Chinese auto dealers to take more cars than they wanted and stipulated that dealers must buy auto parts from the car maker.

A second agency is the State Administration for Industry and Commerce (SAIC), which oversees non-pricing antitrust issues. Of interest is its investigation of Microsoft in regard to suspected monopolistic practices. The agency had been concerned about the company's efforts to switch users to its Windows 8 operating system. Officials were also probing issues around the distribution of its media iPlayer and browser software. There was anger at the dropping of support for Windows XP. Microsoft responded by saying, "We're serious about complying with China's laws and committed to addressing SAIC's questions and concerns."[15]

In other cases, China was able to gain the concession from Microsoft Corp to license certain patents to Chinese smart phone manufacturers in order to win its approval to buy Nokia Corp.'s handset business. Chinese antitrust authorities extracted a $975 million fine from Qualcomm Inc., one of the world's biggest chip makers, and secured several changes in the company's practices in licensing patents for mobile phone sold in China.[16] A third agency, China's Ministry of Commerce, oversees mergers.[17]

Fearing that it might discourage foreign investments, China took out a three-quarter-page advertisement with the headline "Foreign Firms Not Targeted."[18] At the same time, governments introduced strict new regulations and are seeking to crack down on the use of offshore tax havens.

This tension has fueled the lobbying industry and many people now suspect that the key to success in business may largely hinge on who is best connected.

On bribery, Chinese authorities warned GlaxoSmithKline (GSK) plc's Chinese arm against fostering a culture of bribery. Glaxo's former China chief, UK national Mark Reilly, was accused of ordering his subordinates, his sales team, and other employees to bribe hospital doctors, healthcare organizations, and other parties on "a large scale" to boost the company's drug sales in China. Several Glaxo offices in China were raided by law enforcement officials, who seized documents and retained some employees. Reilly met with Chinese officials regularly to help with their investigations. Nevertheless, he was accused by Chinese officials of orchestrating whole departments of Glaxo staff to bribe doctors and healthcare organizations.[19] Glaxo responded with the standard statement that it takes the allegations seriously and the allegations "are deeply concerning to us and contrary to the values of GSK."[20]

10.2.2 France Confronts Google Over Its Tax Deal

Many MNCs take advantage of tax deals in European countries by channeling profits from countries with high tax rates to those with low tax rates, such as Ireland. Google's approach to taxes is to have ads sold in France, Germany, the Netherlands, and the UK to appear as sales by Google Ireland Ltd. The latter then pays royalties for intellectual property to Google Netherlands Holdings, a company that is Irish-registered but controlled via Bermuda, where there is no corporate income tax. Furthermore, Google claims it makes no income in France because it doesn't have a "permanent establishment" there. It states that its around 500 people in France work as engineers or as marketers performing such services as search and business software. Google claims that it complies with laws everywhere it operates and that its "effective global tax rate" was about 20% in the 2014 first half.[21]

France is tackling this issue head on with Google, whose chief executive Larry Page exercised corporate diplomacy by meeting with France's Prime Minister Manuel Valls in September 2014 to discuss the issue. To offset the tax issue, Page said that Google has invested heavily in France and is willing to do more. He cited having expanded its Paris operation in recent years and setting up a fund for French newspapers. He added that Google was "totally prepared to continue investing in France."[22] But these efforts did not dissuade prosecutors from raiding Google's Paris headquarters in May, 2016. French authorities are seeking more than $1.12 billion from the search company.[23]

Compliance with the regulations of nation states in China, Europe, and elsewhere adds to the issues facing MNCs. As in the US, corporate public affairs must be applied to analyze and respond to the actions by various nation states.

10.3 Supranational Organizations

At a higher level than nation states, a new type of player is the supranational organization. Among the more prominent ones are the UN, several important international organizations such as the International Monetary Fund (IMF), the EU, and a variety of civil society organizations, notably NGOs. Not only nation states but MNCs are subject to their authority.

In supranational organizations, English has become the new lingua franca. The English language had already become the most commonly spoken language in the world at the turn of the century. In 2001 some 380 million people spoke English as their first language and perhaps two-thirds as many again as their second.[24] After the US, the highest populations of English-speakers were in the UK, Nigeria, and India. It was not, however, the most-spoken language in the world. Because of China's large population, about 1.113 million people spoke Chinese (Mandarin) as their mother tongue, whereas about 372 million spoke English.[25]

English has official status in 87 countries and territories. Of the world's roughly 12 500 international organizations, 85% make use of English, with one-third using English exclusively.[26] English is also the official language in several spheres: (i) the European Central Bank (which is located in Frankfurt); (ii) ships' pilots around the world use "Seaspeak" or the new "Standard Marine Communication s Phrases" (SMCP); and (iii) "Airspeak" is used by airplane pilots and air-traffic controllers.[27] English is also the de facto working language of 98% of German research physicists and 83% of German research chemists.[28] Specialized fields must consider the language used in various professional communities.

Although English has become the EU's dominant working language, French is spoken in the EU's corridors and meeting rooms because EU institutions are located in the francophone cities of Brussels, Luxembourg, and Strasbourg. Considering the implications of the Whorfian hypothesis – that the language and words we use shape our thoughts – the French worry about whether "it is possible to speak English without thinking American."[29] They feel that France's own distinct intellectual tradition in economics, philosophy, and law has been eclipsed. Humorously, however, the French subdue the trauma with the thought, "Our only revenge is that the English language is being killed by all these foreigners speaking it so badly."[30]

Even though 80% of what is available on the internet is in English, communicators should not fixate on English for all uses. As a study by Euro Marketing Associates estimates, nearly 44% members of the world's online population now speak a language other than English at home. Even though satellites can deliver programming and advertising instantaneously and simultaneously across the more than two dozen language spoken in Western Europe, viewers want their television delivered in local tongues.[31] Diplomats with a knowledge of local languages of the people with whom they deal have a distinct advantage.

10.3.1 United Nations

The UN is known for having lots of targets, goals, and declarations but little power to enforce them. Nevertheless, MNCs must be familiar with their declarations because they are often asked to observe them. This sometimes occurs through "complicity" – by simply operating in a country that violates human rights. Three major declarations are the Universal Declaration of Human Rights, the Millennium Development Goals, and the Global Compact.

10.3.1.1 Universal Declaration of Human Rights

The primary mission of the UN is to preserve world peace, so its dealings are mainly with nation states. The UN also seeks to protect and advance human rights as announced in the much heralded 1948 Universal Declaration of Human Rights. The Commission on Human Rights, which drafted the statement, was made up of 18 members from various political, cultural, and religious backgrounds. Eleanor Roosevelt, widow of American President Franklin D. Roosevelt, chaired the commission.

The UN General Assembly proclaimed the declaration as a common standard of achievement for all peoples and all nations. To this end, every individual and organ of society is asked to promote respect for these rights and freedoms through teaching and education. . MNCs are expected to uphold the declaration. Moreover, by progressive measures, both national and international, they should aim to secure their universal and effective recognition and observance, both among the peoples of Member States themselves and among the peoples of territories under their jurisdiction.

MNCs have learned to be aware of possible human rights violations. When Calgary-based Talisman Energy acquired outstanding shares of Arakis Energy, an independent Canadian company, it became the partial holder of shares in the Sudan's Greater Nile Petroleum Operating Company Limited (GNPOC).[32] Although Talisman was aware of the high risk involved in becoming associated with Sudan's human rights violations, it reckoned that the risk was offset by the investment that it categorized as "high return."

Even though Talisman itself committed no human rights violations, it learned the meaning of complicity. It was complicit because its business operations depended upon, or benefited from its presence in Sudan. It proceeded with the investment despite opposition by the Canadian Minister of Foreign Affairs and Canadian NGOs. The US joined Canada in opposition and filed a suit under the 1789 Alien Torts Claims Act (ATCA), which grants jurisdiction to US Federal Courts over "any civil action by an alien for a tort only, committed in violation of the law of nations or a treaty of the United States." But it was not Canadian and US government opposition that convinced Talisman to withdraw from the Sudan: it was opposition by institutional investors such as the California Public Employees' Retirement System (CalPERS) and Teachers Insurance and Annuity Association – College Retirement Equities Fund (TIAA-CREF), which resulted in the market decline of its shares.

10.3.1.2 Millennium Development Goals

The Millennium Summit of the UN in 2000 was extraordinary as 100 heads of state and 47 heads of government participated and adopted the Millennium Development Goals.[33] All 189 UN member states at the time (there are currently 193) and at least 23 international organizations committed to help achieve eight goals by 2015:

1) To halve the number of undernourished people.
2) To achieve universal primary education.
3) To promote gender equality and empower women.
4) To reduce child mortality.
5) To improve maternal health.
6) To combat HIV/AIDS, malaria, and other diseases.
7) To ensure environmental sustainability.
8) To develop a global partnership for development.

Much has improved as governments, international institutions, and private foundations have backed the goals with billions of dollars. Between 1990 and 2012, starvation has been reduced from about 24% of those living in the developing world to roughly 15%. Maternal, child, and infant mortality rates in the developing world have dropped 50% since 1990. Business's responsibility to safeguard human rights was further buttressed by the Global Compact of 2000 (see Chapter 16), which embellished the Millennium Development Goals and asked business to sign on.

To prepare for the next step beyond 2015, high-level panels, working groups, and researchers are pumping out a dizzying number of proposed targets, which some estimate at 1400. Bjorn Lomborg, director of the Copenhagen Consensus Center, argues that this international wish list must be reduced and subjected to economic analysis. A group of 32 economists chosen by him prepared "A Report Card for Development Goals" that ranks the goals according to "Phenomenal, Good, Fair, and Poor." Fighting malaria is evaluated as phenomenal because its costs are small, amounting to only $1000 a person, whereas preventing a single HIV fatality totals roughly $10 000. The goals of sustainable tourism and providing affordable housing for all are ranked as poor and seen by Lomborg as peripheral. He notes that the problem of indoor air pollution gets no mention even though almost 3 billion people cook and keep warm by burning twigs and dung, creating fumes that account for one of every 13 deaths globally.

10.3.2 World Economic Institutions

Three world economic institutions play important roles in the international arena: the World Bank, the IMF, and the World Trade Organization (WTO). The World Bank is a vital source of financial and technical assistance to developing countries. Headquartered in Washington, DC, it has offices in 100 countries around the world. The bank's mission is global poverty reduction and the improvement of living standards. It provides low-interest loans, interest-free credit, and grants to developing countries for education, health, infrastructure, communications, and many other purposes. The World Bank has also helped MNCs, as it did when it helped finance the ExxonMobil Chad–Cameroon pipeline development project in Africa.

The IMF is the central institution of the international monetary system, providing international payments and exchange rates among national currencies that enables business to take place between countries. The IMF encourages countries to adopt sound economic policies, which is evidenced in its demands for tough and sometimes harsh market-minded reforms in exchange for providing temporary financing for members running low on hard currency. The IMF believes that reforms will eventually lower poverty.

The WTO deals with the rules of trade between nations with the goal of helping producers of goods and services, exporters, and importers to conduct their business. It is mainly known for acting as a referee for many trade disputes. A recent example is its decision to call discriminatory the US Department of Agriculture's rule requiring disclosure of the national origin of beef, pork, and other meats sold in the US When the Obama administration moved to have the WHO's decision appealed, Canadian officials objected.[34]

10.4 European Union

The EU is the major regional organization in the world that operates as a single market.[35, 36] Within the Schengen area, passport controls have been abolished, allowing for the free movement of people, goods, services, and capital within the EU. Its institutions employ over 40 000 men and women, excluding the UK and Norway.[37] The EU has been most active primarily with the issues of antitrust, privacy, and genetically modified (GM) foods. Its 28 nations have shrunk to 27 since March 29, 2017 when the UK officially invoked Article 50 of the Lisbon treaty and started the process of leaving the EU. The British seek to "take back control" by ending the free movement of EU citizens to Britain and the jurisdiction of the European Court of Justice.[38] A major issue will be the rights of 3 million EU citizens to stay in Britain and 1 million Britons to stay in the EU.[39]

There are several other regional organizations. In Europe there is the Eurasian Economic Union established in 2014 by leaders of Belarus, Kazakhstan, and Russia to counteract the EU. It has an integrated single market of 183 million people. In Asia there is ASEAN, a trading bloc[40] formed in 1967 by Indonesia, Malaysia, the Philippines, Singapore, and Thailand, and later joined by Brunei, Cambodia, Laos, and Myanmar with a combined population of 625 million, bigger than the EU. It is feared that China's claims in the South China Sea and growing rivalry with the US may threaten ASEAN.[41]

10.4.1.1. Google Faces Antitrust Action

The most troublesome and frequent issue facing US companies in their dealings with the EU has been antitrust. One of the earliest actions occurred in 2001 when the EU refused to allow GE to acquire Honeywell International, even though the US had approved it. The big issue was the accusation in 2000 by the European Commission (EC), the executive body of the EU, that

Microsoft was behaving in a monopolistic manner that was detrimental to competition. While US antitrust laws protect consumers, the EU's laws protect competitors as well. Microsoft ultimately paid $2.3 billion in fines and changed its company culture, "making it less brash and more cautious."[42]

The largest current antitrust case by the EU is against Google for its "search bias."[43] On June 27, 2017, Margrethe Vestager, the EU's antitrust chief, fined Google a record €2.42 billion ($2.71 billion) for favoring its own comparison shopping service.[44] It is charged with skewing results in its search engine by highlighting its own shopping services in response to search queries ahead of links to similar services run by rivals.

Regulators believe Google has outsized control over internet traffic. According to research firm StatCounter, it handles about 92% of global internet searches. With this high share of online searches in Europe, Google can squeeze competitors in related markets where it also competes, such as travel, mapping, and local guides. Margrethe Vestager said she was also continuing to examine these other domains.[45]

A similar charge was made in August 27, 2015, following 5 years of attempted settlement. At the time, the EU's Parliament – the Parliament is the legislative body of the EU – passed a supportive resolution. It was led by a member of German Chancellor Angela Merkel's Christian Democratic Union (CDU) party and backed by legislators from countries including France, Poland, and Spain. A critic of Google is the European consumer organization Bureau Européen des Unions de Consommateurs (BEUC), whose spokesman John Phelan said, "Parliamentary pressure on the new commission is timely and welcome."[46]

Google publicly responded to Vestager's 2015 charges by arguing that the EU erred in its analysis of the fast-changing online shopping business and specifically that it failed to account for the fast growth of companies such Amazon.com Inc. and eBay Inc.[47] It said that these firms posed a competitive threat. Google general counsel Kent Walker said, "We believe that the SO's (Statement of Objections) preliminary conclusions are wrong as a matter of fact, law and economics."[48] In response to the 2017 fine, Google repeats the same arguments, but EU regulators may require Google to retool the system so that competing comparison shopping sites are mixed in and are as easy to click through to as Google-hosted ads.[49]

In 2016, a charge was leveled against Google over the dominance of its Android mobile-operating system, which potentially threatens Google's position in the fast-growing mobile-advertising market – a market that generated more than $67 billion in revenue in 2015. Google's strategy has allegedly been to create an ecosystem that encourages handset makers and phone carriers to install Google apps, so that users continue to see the ads that Google sells. In Europe, Android accounts for 71% of the operating systems used on smart phones.[50]

The larger question is whether digital monopolies like Google should be broken up as they have a huge advantage in knowing what people want to buy, which helps in selling advertising. Google has been highly profitable because it amasses huge amounts of data and has data scientists to mine the information to make it more relevant. Its profit margin is nearly 20% and net income is $13 billion, mostly from advertising. Google argues that its customers are simply paying for an efficient way to reach global audiences.[51]

Some fear that Google might leverage its advantage in one area to enter new areas and take control of other industries. *The Economist* believes that the European Parliament's "Google-phobia" is largely motivated by the desire to protect European companies, such as the two German media giants Axel Springer and Hubert Burda Media: "European leaders should ask themselves why their continent has not produced a Google or a Facebook." *The Economist* believes that "Opening up the EU's digital services market would do more to create one than protecting local incumbents." It is also sanguine that Google will be disrupted one day, just as IBM was forced by Microsoft to end its mainframe monopoly.[52]

Other companies are also facing antitrust action. Among them is Qualcomm Inc., which was fined $1.23 billion by the EU's antitrust chief. Margrethe Vestager accused Qualcom of having abused its dominant position by paying billions of dollars to Apple from 2011 to 2016 on condition it wouldn't buy from rivals.[53]

10.4.1.2. Privacy Issues – The Right to Be Forgotten

Facebook, Apple, and over 3000 US companies were challenged by the EU on the right to bring home European personal data, a right previously granted by the so-called Safe Harbor agreement. Jan Philipp Albrecht, a Green Party member of the European Parliament and privacy advocate said, "Every collection of a piece of data is a violation of a fundamental right, and must be justified."[54] The danger is that data flows in and out of Europe could be restricted, for example, by negotiating Europe's demand to tighten the Safe Harbor measures. In February 2005 the EU put the finishing touches on a tough data privacy regime with the aim of establishing a de facto standard that companies would have to embed to sell products in the giant European market.[55]

A special issue arose when social media users became concerned about exposure of personal data on their sites – they asked for the right to have some sensitive data removed from their sites. In May 2014, the European Court of Justice, the EU's highest court, reinforced the right of Google users to have some personal information removed from their sites – which is commonly known as the "right to be forgotten." Google, which handles more than 90% of all online searches in the EU, worries that having to balance privacy against freedom of information and the public's right to know would create a huge burden.[56] Google, however, has softened its opposition and decided how to handle the incoming takedown requests. It has set up a web page that allows people to request that links be removed from articles about them that they consider to be outdated or an invasion of privacy. In its first 4 days, 41 000 people made such requests.[57]

But when on July 30, 2015, France publicly ordered Google to apply the rules globally, namely to all domain names, including google.com, Google firmly rejected the French regulator's demand. It fears that complying with the EU rules globally would result in an unprecedented censorship of internet content worldwide. It would also lead to a dangerous expansion of foreign regulators' control over what Americans can see on the Web.[58]

Litigation is expected to go on for some time, especially since the data protection regulator rejected Google's appeal in September 2015.[59] The legal battle intensified when France's Commission Nationale de l'Informatique et des Libertes (CNIL) fined Google $112 000 for not following the order. Dave Price, a Google lawyer, said "This isn't about just France. This is about a risk to the way the Internet is governed globally."[60] CNIL retorts that it wants only to fully apply EU law to individuals in Europe.

On the larger issue of the EU's privacy laws, EU officials agreed on a new digital privacy regime that would replace the patchwork of 28 national laws. US companies, ranging from advertising to healthcare, would be affected. Until now they have been able to analyze vast amounts of data collected from apps, sensors, and other sources. Such data mining and user profiling would change. One provision would challenge "secondary" uses of social data. The new EU-wide data protection law might require specific consent for each use. The law poses a big threat because of its uncertainty and massive fines of up to 4% of a company's global revenues. The European Parliament and EU governments must approve the law before it goes into effect in.[61]

10.4.1.3. Tax Avoidance

The EU is seeking to curb tax avoidance by foreign MNCs.[62] Apple, along with Google, Fiat, Starbucks, and others, is being investigated for alleged sweetheart tax deals.[63] On August 30, 2016, Margrethe Vestager ruled that Apple would be required to pay back up to $19 billion to Ireland, an amount later reduced to $13.5 billion. The EU contends that two Apple units registered in Ireland brought in $130 billion in profit over an 11-year period, which should have been taxed at Ireland's 12.5% corporate tax rate.[64] The company was accused of having struck tax arrangements with Ireland in 1991 and 2007 whereby it paid only around 1% to almost zero taxes on its European profits between 2003 and 2014. This was accomplished by giving two Irish-registered subsidiaries the right to use Apple's intellectual property to make and sell its products outside the Americas. The profit allocation deal allowed most of their profits to be transferred to a "head office" that existed only on paper and was tax resident in no country.[65] However, its profits actually accrued from the sale of its products, especially the smart phone, in retail operations in countries such as Germany.[66]

Through such stratagems, Apple held $215 billion in cash and other liquid investments outside the US. Ireland benefited by attracting more jobs into the country. But Vestager argued that the deals amounted to state aid, which is prohibited by the EU. Her wider strategy is to close down tax havens and loopholes in the bloc. Apple in turn is using corporate diplomacy instead of using an army of lobbyists and public relations campaigners in its fight with the EU. Apple's Tim Cook and Google CEO Sundar Pichai, whose company faces the same tax fight, have made treks to Brussels to explain their positions directly to Vestager.[67] The US Treasury Department also defended Apple, saying that the EU's decision is "retroactively applying a sweeping new State aid theory that is contrary to well-established legal principles" and threatens to undermine the overall business climate in Europe.[68]

US companies try to keep profits offshore because until recently in the US they faced a 35% corporate tax. Together, US companies hold some $2 trillion in cash offshore. Tim Cook said he wouldn't bring company money back to the US "until there's a fair rate."[69] In the meantime, Vestager's charge opened the door to further scrutiny of Apple finances, legal structure, and payments by national governments across the continent.

Other companies are facing similar problems. The EU is investigating Amazon.com in Luxembourg for tax avoidance, estimating that tax avoidance by MNCs costs the bloc up to $82.5 billion annually in lost revenue.[70] In 2014, Starbucks planned to move its headquarters to London from Amsterdam, partly in response to criticism of tax avoidance in the UK, which hurt sales. It paid $14.4 million in UK corporate tax between 1998 and 2012.[71] Other targets of the investigation are Apple Inc. and Fiat SpA.[72] In the aftermath of the "Panama Papers," the EU will require MNCs to publish details of profits and tax bills generated in countries considered to be tax havens.[73] The Organisation for Economic Co-operation and Development (OECD) is also seeking to better coordinate its members' national tax laws.[74]

The EU's executive arm, the European Commission, has started a corporate tax overhaul. In late October 2016 it published a proposal known as the Common Consolidated Corporate-Tax Base (CCCTB), which would require multi-national companies to pay taxes based on where their assets and employees are located and where their sales take place. The EU estimates that the CCCTB would eliminate 70% of profit-shifting by companies.[75]

But as political scientist Mancur Olson observed in his 1982 book, *The Rise and Decline of Nations*, producers "have a strong incentive to band together to protect existing tax breaks and subsidies."[76] Among Fortune 100 companies, the 10 that lobbied most in 2010 paid an average effective tax rate of 17%; the 80 that lobbied least paid an average of 26%, suggesting that lobbying pays off. Companies rely on lobbyists to find out what is going on in government and to respond to unwanted regulations. In Brussels, lobbyists have created an equivalent to DC's K Street, the Rue Belliard. Roughly 30 000 lobbyists are registered in Brussels.[77]

10.4.1.4. National Sentiments Endanger the EU

Euroskeptics in the UK, France, Greece, and other countries, motivated by nationalistic sentiments, are threatening to withdraw from the EU, as the UK is doing. They are worried about threats to their independence and losing jobs to "outsiders."[78] In recent years migrants, not only from Eastern European countries but also from the Middle East have been creating an enormous burden on the EU. More than a million asylum-seekers arriving from Syria and other parts of the Middle East in 2015, most of whom hoped to reach Germany and other northern countries such as Sweden. Once they reach Greece and other entry countries, they are allowed by the EU's Schengen agreement to travel anywhere in Europe.

Germany welcomed migrants as a source of new labor, because it has a low unemployment rate of 4.6%. Because of the labor shortage, business software giant SAP SE and industrial group TyssonKrupp AG are hiring Syrians. SAP plans to offer 100 internships and at least 10 additional apprenticeships to refugees. Chief human resources officer Stefan Riest says that its past hires of migrants "have exceeded our expectations."[79]

Resentment among EU countries grew when the president of the European Commission unveiled a plan to relocate refugees over a 2-year period to other EU countries, giving them little choice.[80] But countries along the entry route, such as Hungary and Austria, erected barriers, and Denmark and Sweden have limited the number of entering migrants. An irritant is the ease with which immigrants can claim benefits, which places an enormous burden on Europe.[81] Some EU Member States want to cut the EU's powers, but weakening of the Schengen agreement puts at risk the EU's "four freedoms" of movement of goods, services, capital, and labor, which underpin Europe's single market.

The big threat to the EU came on June 23, 2016, when Britain voted in a referendum to leave it. The so-called Brexit vote won with a narrow 52% majority, which pollsters failed to predict. Politicians on both sides of the issue campaigned furiously, aware of the consequences of the decision. Business leaders overwhelmingly called for Britain to remain in the EU. More than 1000 chief executives signed a letter backing a remain vote just days before the referendum. Some of the world's largest companies warned they could relocate their British-based operations. The investment bank JP Morgan, airplane maker Airbus, and car manufacturers Toyota and Ford all said they will review their investments in the UK. The Brexit decision may affect Tata Steel's decision to keep its UK business; the company employs 11 000 people. Several UK companies, including Aviva and easyJet, issued stock market statements stating that there would not be a material impact to their finances as a result of the vote.[82]

It may take up to 2 years for the completion of the exit process. The further danger to the EU is that other nations, notably France, may decide to follow England.

10.4.1.5. GMO

Europe has long been resistant to GM crops and foods. Monsanto, DuPont, and Novartis have faced continuing EU opposition to GM crops and foods. It imposed an EU-wide ban, with some exceptions; for example, Spain has over 130 000 ha of one variety of GM maize. But from January 13, 2015, the EU has allowed national governments to impose their own restrictions. This makes little difference, however, because most European governments have opposed GMOs. Previously the EU was supposed to consider scientific evidence but now governments are free to impose national bans for almost any reason.[83]

10.5 Civil Society

In the triangle of the major institutions in society, civil society is "the third sector." It comprises the community organizations of religion, recreation, fraternal organizations, and a host of charitable organizations. A vigorous civil society is needed for countries to transition from a traditional society to a developed one. Walt Rostow includes the existence of civil society as one of the "preconditions for take-off," saying that it prepares the soil upon which a nation state is built.[84, 85] By developing relationships with civil society groups, a company builds its social capital, which facilitates collective action.

Some writers use the term *non-profits* synonymously with civil society, simply saying that these organizations are in contrast to the government and business sectors.[86] Civil society constitutes a large part of the world's economies. If the operating expenditures of non-profits across the 40 countries studied by the Johns Hopkins Comparative Nonprofit Sector Project were aggregated, they would rank as the world's seventh largest economy, only slightly smaller than France.[87] Civil society organizations are supported by the sale of goods and services (about 50% of income), governments (36%), and philanthropy (14%). They are almost universally exempt from income, property, value-added, and inheritance taxes, but at the expense of being generally limited in political and business activity. Advocacy groups are generally treated more severely than social service organizations. The cross-border flow of philanthropic capital and non-profit activity has increased, but inflows of foreign funding are increasingly restricted.[88]

10.6 NGOs as Advocacy Groups

Organizations known as advocacy groups or social action groups play an important role as countervailing powers to business and government. In describing a country's civil society, Krishnamurthy Sriramesh and Dejan Verčič in their *The Global Public Relations Handbook* pay special attention to the role of advocacy groups, saying they are best known for pressuring businesses and governments to maintain ethical standards and uphold some of the goals of international declarations.[89] They represent a wide range of causes, such as protecting the environment, human rights, women's rights, and economic development. Environmental groups, for example, have stopped or slowed the clear cutting of forests in countries such as Indonesia and the dumping of waste materials in Africa. They attract attention to their causes and often confront corporations, seeking to changes their policies and behavior. However, advocacy groups can also be strategic allies in lobbying activities.

This swiftly growing universe, wrote Jessica T. Mathews in her article "The Rise of Global Civil Society," includes "neighborhood, professional, service, and advocacy groups, both secular and church-based, promoting every conceivable cause and funded by donations, fees, foundations, governments, international organizations, or the sale of products and services."[90] They easily number several million when local ones are included. The larger international ones, such as Greenpeace and Amnesty International, serve as powerful engines of change.

In countries where governments are weak, civil society groups often set standards of behavior and serve as a substitute for regulatory constraints on business. They also compensate for a country that is relatively disengaged from meeting basic human needs.[91] For example, a placement ad in *The Economist* by the Children's Investment Fund announced the position of director of communications in London, and states that the foundation's goal is "to demonstrably improve the lives of children in developing countries by achieving large-scale, sustainable impact."[92]

Recognizing the power of NGOs, some countries are seeking to control them. In the latest of a series of Kremlin statements assailing Western-funded NGOs, President Vladimir Putin said Russia wouldn't allow foreign organizations to finance political activities in the country.[93] China is similarly cracking down on foreign non-profits, considering them security risks. It views outsiders as potential purveyors of subversion. On July 1, 2015, China passed a national security law to protect the country from hostile elements, followed by a law for regulating NGOs. No funding from abroad is allowed.[94] This is unfortunate in that the expanding Chinese economy has created new needs and opportunities for the Chinese to become involved in health, the environment, and other issues that were once the preserve of the government. Foreigners joined them, providing expertise and funding.

The legislation allows the Ministry of Public Security and the nation's police to monitor their activities. Foreign groups have to find a sponsoring government agency, which is difficult for groups working on human rights, legal reform, and other political issues.[95] The draft law was so broad and vague that even foreign trade associations, such as the American Chamber of Commerce in China, were alarmed.

10.7 Collaboration is Growing

Although confrontation has been the traditional tactic of advocacy groups, they are amenable to collaboration. When corporations partner with NGOs, they benefit from their high credibility and their often detailed knowledge of other actors in civil society. Some have developed various certification programs that assist companies with their sustainability program.

Such collaboration should be differentiated from the practice of some companies that consult communities, shareholders, employees, and organizations, "and then go off and do what they wanted." Instead, says Ann Svendsen, management consultant and adjunct professor at Simon Fraser University in Vancouver, Canada, they should adopt the "co-creative" stakeholder engagement model that even includes working with competitors.[96]

10.7.1.1. How Starbucks Works with NGOs

In his article on "Collaborating with Activists," Paul A. Argenti, professor of corporate communications at Dartmouth University's Tuck School of Business, describes how Global Exchange, an NGO, was able to convince Starbucks to sell fair trade-certified coffee.[97] The issue was important because the coffee market was highly fragmented between the coffee bean producers and the end consumers, to the detriment of farmers. This focus on fair trade-certified coffee gave Global Exchange the opportunity to become a "category killer": having a single-minded focus on a single specific issue at a time. This feature gives an NGO the power to damage an opposing corporation's reputation.

To get Starbucks' attention, Global Exchange engaged in a protest in front of one of Starbucks' downtown San Francisco restaurants. This was a smart move because its location attracted media attention. As recommended for all companies confronted by an NGO, Starbucks assessed the power of this advocacy group and found it credible. The assessment includes an NGO's ability to use public relations to raise funds, engage in effective publicity and other communication, and employ standard lobbying techniques for the purpose of influencing political and social outcomes. Global Exchange's use of effective tactics was further proven when it attended Starbucks' stockholder meeting and raised the question of why it didn't use fair trade coffee. Starbucks was vulnerable to the issue because it portrays itself as "People first and profits last."

After some compromises and the involvement of additional NGOs (Transfer USA, Conservative International, Co-op America, and Organic Consumers Association), Starbucks gradually developed a collaborative arrangement with Global Exchange. Argenti defines the advantage of collaboration as one in which "each party can move beyond their respective organizational constraints to achieve results that exceed what each can accomplish individually."[98] Learning the importance of relations with NGOs has been a major part of Starbucks' management accomplishments.

10.8 Conclusions

International players are the main new consideration in Zone 3, which surrounds the extended enterprise of the corporation. These players must be identified and their functions explained. Dealing with a variety of nation states is further complicated by the presence of supranational organizations that impose a variety of expectations on MNCs. The EU presents the greatest challenges to US companies. But even the expectations of the UN become real when an MNC, like Talisman, is trapped by the concept of complicity. Civil society groups, mainly NGOs, often confront MNCs and endanger their reputations.

The issues created by these international players must carefully be analyzed. The antitrust and tax issues have been the most troublesome, involving countries like France and China and the regional organization of the EU. The huge fine laid on Google by Vestager presents a huge legal challenge to Google as well as to its public relations and public affairs professionals.

The need to develop relationships with the many players and to understand the many complex issues that arise challenges those in global corporate communication. It is clear that the art of developing relationships is no longer monopolized by government diplomats but shared with private sector diplomats.

Discussion Questions

10.1. What measures are used to indicate the power of the modern MNC?

10.2. What issue of nation states has been the most troublesome for MNCs? What actions has China taken? What are its criticisms of the behavior of MNCs?

10.3. What objections did France have to Google's tax payments? Do you agree with France?

10.4. What is the meaning of complicity from the viewpoint of a company? How was Talisman Energy affected?

10.5. What's the relevance of the WTO to business?

10.6. What was at issue in the EU's actions against Google? How is Google attempting to justify its behavior?

10.7. What is the "right to be forgotten"? Why is it important?

10.8. Why is the problem of tax avoidance such a contentious issue in the EU?

10.9. What are the current problems facing the future of the EU? Discuss.

10.10. What problem did Starbucks face with NGOs? How was the conflict resolved?

Endnotes

1 Alan Murray, "Lessons From the *Fortune* 500," *Fortune.COM*, June 15, 2016, p. 14.
2 "The Rise of the Superstars," Special Report, *The Economist*, September 17, 2016, p. 4.

3 Sarah Anderson and John Cavanagh, "Top 200: The Rise of Corporate Global Power," Institute for Policy Studies, December 4, 2000.
4 "The Rise of the Superstars," op. cit., p. 5.
5 Howard V. Perlmutter, "The Tortuous Evolution of the Multinational Corporation," *Columbia Journal of World Business*, January–February 1969.
6 *The Economist*, online, July 10, 2012.
7 www.news.Walmart.com/walmart-facts
8 "Biggest Transnational Companies," *The Economist*, July 10, 2012.
9 The Center for Public Integrity, "The 'Citizens Limited' Decision and Why It Matters." https://www.publicintegrity.org/2012/10/18/11527/citizens-united-decision-and-why-it-matters
10 Rosabeth Moss Kanter, "Why Global Companies Will Behave More and More Alike," *WSJ*, July 8, 2014, p. R8.
11 Brent Kendall, "From Africa, to Ukraine, Deal Police Proliferate," *WSJ*, September 30, 2014, p. B1.
12 "Trust-Busting in China: Unequal Before the Law," *The Economist*, August 23, 2014, p. 62.
13 Ibid.
14 Jay Greene, "Microsoft to Shut China Web Portal as Focus Shifts," *WSJ*, May 20, 2016, p. B4.
15 "China regulator queries Microsoft on findings in anti-trust probe," Reuters, January 5, 2016, https://www.reuters.com/article/us-china-microsoft-idUSKBN0UJ0TR20160105
16 Don Clark, "Qualcomm to Pay $975 Million Fine in China," *WSJ*, February 10, 2015, p. B1.
17 Colum Murphy and Eva Cou, "China Steps up Antitrust Duel with West," WSJ, August 7, 2014, p. B1.
18 *WSJ*, September 29, 2014, p. A4.
19 Hester Plumridge, Christopher M. Mathews, and Laurie Burkitt, "Glaxo Expat Who Helped Investigation Now Accused," *WSJ*, March 14, 2014.
20 Laurie Burkitt, "Beijing Warns Sternly on Glaxo," *WSJ*, May 15, 2014.
21 Sam Schechner, "Google Faces a Fight in France Over Its Tax Bill," *WSJ*, October 9, 2014, p. A1.
22 Ibid.
23 Sam Schechner, "France Raids Google in Tax Probe," *WSJ*, May 25, 2016, p. B4.
24 "A World Empire by Other Means," *The Economist*, December 22, 2001, p. 63.
25 Barbara Wallraff, "What Global Language," *Atlantic Monthly*, November 2000, pp. 55–56.
26 Howard Richler, "The Language of Globalization is English," *The Gazette (Montreal)*, December 12, 2000, p. H2.
27 Ibid., p. 58.
28 Ibid., p. 52.
29 "Charlemane: The Galling Rise of English," *The Economist*, March 1, 2003, p. 50.
30 Ibid.
31 Ibid., p. 61.
32 See discussion of case in Otto Lerbinger, *The Global Manager: Contemporary Issues and Corporate Responses* (London: Palgrave Macmillan, 2014), pp. 138–139.
33 Bjorn Lomborg, "Promises to Keep: Crafting Better Development Goals," *Foreign Affairs*, Vol. 93 November/December 2014, p. 130.
34 Damian Paletta and Paul Vieira, "U.S. Meat-Labeling Move Angers Canada," *WSJ*, November 29–30, 2014, p. A4.
35 See D. Leonard, "Guide to the European Union," *The Economist*, 10th ed., 2010. Also Rohan Bolton and Joanne Eastwood, Guide to the EU Institutions (Federal Trust for Education and Research, 2003).
36 Another regional organization is the 20-country Association of South-East Asian Nations (ASEAN).

37 The European Personnel Selection Office (EPSO) organizes 'open competitions' to select personnel for permanent and non-permanent positions. Besides permanent staff, the EU also employs contractual agents and temporary staff, offers traineeships, and maintains databases of area experts. The EPSO is the first port of call for anyone wanting to work for the EU. Its website explains the selection process and gives advice on preparing for competitions.

38 "Britain and the European Union: The Negotiator," *The Economist*, April 1, 2017, p. 10.

39 "Britain and the European Union: A Race Against Time," *The Economist*, April 1, 2017, p. 47.

40 "The Eurasian Union: The Other EU," *The Economist*, August 23, 2014, p. 50.

41 "The ASEAN Way," in "The World in 2017," *The Economist*, p. 51.

42 Tom Fairless, Rolfe Winkler, and Alistair Barr, "Europe Charges Google Over Searches," *WSJ*, April 16, 2015, p. A1.

43 "EU Says Google Risks Facing Formal Antitrust Charges," *WSJ*, September 14, 2014, p. B4. "Google, the EU and Antitrust," *The Economist*, February 8, 2014, p. 63.

44 Natalia Drozdiak and Sam Schechner, "EU Slaps Google with Record Fine," *WSJ*, June 28, 2017, pp. 1, 2.

45 Fairless, op. cit. Also see Alistair Barr, "'Search Bias' is at the Heart of Case," *WSJ*, April 16, 2015, p. A10.

46 Tom Fairless, "U.S. Expresses Concern over EU Antitrust Debate on Google," *WSJ*, November 25, 2014.

47 Natalia Drozdiak, "Google Faces New Charges," *WSJ*, July 11, 2016, p. B7.

48 Ibid.

49 Drozdiak and Schecher, op. cit., p. 2.

50 Natalia Drozdiak and Sam Schechner, "EU Set to Formally Charge Google," *WSJ*, April 20, 2016, p. B4.

51 "Should Digital Monopolies Be Broken Up?," *The Economist*, November 29, 2014, pp. 11, 21.

52 Ibid.

53 Natalia Drozdiak and Ted Greenwald, "Qualcomm Takes Hit in EU," *WSJ*, January 25, 2018, p. B3.

54 Sam Schechner, "Oceans Apart Over Privacy," *WSJ*, January 9, 2014, p. B7.

55 Tom Fairless and Stephen Fidler, "Europe Aims to Impose Data Rules," *WSJ*, February 24, 2005, p. B1.

56 Sam Schechner, "Google Pivots on Privacy," *WSJ*, May 31–June 1, 2014, p. B1. "Google and Online Privacy: Cut That Link," *The Economist*, May 27, 2014, p. 60ff.

57 "Business," The Economist, June 7, 2014, p. 9.

58 James L. Gattuso, "Europe's Latest Export: Internet Censorship," *WSJ*, August 12, 2015, p. A9.

59 Sam Schechner, "French Regulator Rejects Google Appeal in 'Forgotten' Battle," *WSJ*, September 22, 2015, p. B3.

60 Sam Schechner, "Google Appeals French Order," *WSJ*, May 20, 2016, p. B4.

61 Sam Schechner, "Deal Set on EU Privacy Law," *WSJ*, December 16, 2015, p. B3. Elizabeth Dwoskin, "EU Privacy Law Raises Daunting Prospects for Firms," *WSJ*, October 17, 2015, p. B1.

62 "Corporate Taxation: The E13 Billion Bite," *The Economist*, September 3, 2016, pp. 55–56.

63 Tom Fairless, "EU Official Decries Google Pressure," *WSJ*, October 16, 2014, p. B1.

64 Sam Schechner, "Apple EU Trade Jabs in Tax Case," *WSJ*, December 20, 2016, p. B1.

65 "Corporate Taxation: The L13 Billion Bite," *The Economist*, September 3, 2016, p. 55; Greg Ip, "Apple Exposes Tax-Law Gap," *WSJ*, September 8, 2016, p. A2.

66 Natalia Drozdiak, Viktoria Dendriou, and Sam Schechner, "EU Set to Disrupt Apple's Irish Tax Deal," *WSJ*, August 30, 2016, p. B1.

67 Natalia Drozdiak, "Apple Shies Away from Lobbyists in EU Tax Fight," *WSJ*, September 26, 2016, p. B1.

68 Schechner, ibid.

69 Paul Hannon and Sam Schechner, "Apple May Send Cash to the U.S.," *WSJ*, September 2, 2016, p. B2.
70 Tom Fairless, "EU Presses Amazon on Taxes," WSJ, January 7–18, 2015, p. B3.
71 Peter Evans, "To Move Europe Base to U.K.," *WSJ*, April 17, 2014, p. B6. "Corporate Taxation: Wake Up and Smell the Coffee," *The Economist*, December 15, 2012.
72 Tom Fairless, "EU to Air Amazon Tax Case," *WSJ* January 16, 2015, p. B3.
73 Natalia Drozdiak, "EU Wants Firms to Publish Profits," *WSJ*, April 13, 2016, p. A10.
74 Tom Fairless, "EU Attacks Corporate Tax Loophole," *WSJ*, November 26, 2013, p. B2.
75 Nina Trentmann, "EU Starts Corporate-Tax Overhaul," *WSJ*, November 1, 2016, p. B5.
76 Mancur Olson, *The Rise and Decline of Nations: Economic Growth, Stagflation, and Social Rigidities* ((New Haven, CT: Yale University, 1982), p. 14.
77 Ibid.
78 "Europe's Angry Voters: Bucked Off," *The Economist*, May 31, 2014, p. 12.
79 Friedrich Geiger, "Germany's Next Test: Jobs for Migrants," *WSJ*, September 16, 2015, p. A8.
80 "Charlemagne: Leading from the Front," *The Economist*, September 12, 2015, p. 50.
81 "Forming an Orderly Queue," *The Economist*, February 6, 2016, pp. 19–22.
82 Graham Ruddick, "Multinationals Warn of Job Cuts and Lower Profits after Brexit Vote," *The Guardian*, June 24, 2016.
83 "Europe and GMOs Gently Modified," *The Economist*, January 17, 2015, p. 52.
84 For an overview, see Mark Lehrer and Christian Delaunay, "Multinational Enterprise and the Promotion of Civil Society: The Challenge for 21st Century Capitalism," *California Management Review*, Vol. 51, No. 4, Summer 2009.
85 Walt Rostow, *The Stages of Economic Growth: A Non-Communist Manifesto*. (Cambridge: CambridgeUniversity Press, 1960), p. 6ff.
86 Elizabeth T. Boris, Brice McKeever, and Beatrice Leydier, "Introduction: Roles and Responsibilities of Nonprofit Organizations in a Democracy," in Elizabeth T Boris and C. Eugene Steuerele, eds. *No profits and Government: Collaboration and Conflict*, 3rd edition (Lanham, MD: 2017), p. 1.
87 Susan D. Phillips and Mark Blumberg, "International Trends in Government-Nonprofit Relations," Ibid., p. 314.
88 Ibid., pp. 315, 326, 332.
89 Krishnamurthy Sriramesh and Dejan Verčič, eds. *The Global Public Relations Handbook: Theory Research, and Practice* (Mahwah, NJ: Lawrence Erlbaum Associates, 2003), pp. 8–9. Also see Jeong-Nam Kim and Krishnamurthy Sriramesh, chapter 5, "Activism and Public Relations," pp. 79–97.
90 Jessica T. Mathews, "Power Shift: The Age of Non-State Actors," *Foreign Affairs*, January/February 1997. Included in Dale Reef, G. Anthony Siesfeld, and Jacquelyn Cefola, eds. *The Economic Impact of Knowledge* (Boston, MA: Butterworth Heinemann, 1998), pp. 93–106.
91 Christopher Gunn, *Third Sector Development: Making Up for the Market* (Cornell University Press, NY: 2004).
92 Ad appeared on February 22, 2014, p. 16.
93 Alan Cullison "Russia Slams U.S. Agency for 'Political' Aid Agenda," *WSJ*, September 19, 2012.
94 "Non-Governmental Organisations: Uncivil Society," *The Economist*, August 22, 2015, p. 37.
95 Josh Chin, "China Cracks Down on Foreign Nonprofits," WSJ, March 7–8, 2015 p. A5.
96 Leon Gettler, "Consultants Have to Adapt to a Brave New World," *The Age* (Melbourne, Australia), October 26, 2006, p. 2.
97 Paul Argenti, "Collaborating with Activists: How Works with NGOs," *California Management Review*, Vol. 47, No. 1, Fall 2006. He is author of *Corporate Communication* (New York: McGraw-Hill; several editions).
98 Ibid., p. 107.

11

Political and Economic Features of Nation States

Differences among nation states are largely defined by their political and economic features. This was especially pronounced when communist nations such as the Soviet Union existed. But as the advantages of the free market system were recognized, even the Soviet Union accepted the price system and other features in its economic system. Changes in political systems have been more stubborn, as authoritarian governments in Russia and China cling to their power.

This chapter provides an overview of major political and economic systems. Although details of these systems must be augmented to meet situational needs, the overview is sufficient to indicate the hospitality of countries to the practice of corporate communication.

11.1 Major Political Systems and Ideologies

Corporate communication is more likely to flourish in a democratic, pluralistic political system and supporting legal system that allows people to voice opinions and influence outcomes. The political science and international relations literature refers to various types of government: parliamentary, authoritarian, socialist, communist, and dictatorship. The presence of three branches of government – executive, legislative, and judiciary – is also critical.

In a democratic system, the function of public affairs is important, for it "focuses on gaining support from officials – on power relationships with clients and the public at large."[1] The choice of strategies and tactics depends on what interest group activities are acceptable. The choices are primarily direct and grassroots lobbying, advocacy advertising, and financial contributions by political action committees (PACs).

11.1.1 Authoritarian Systems

Authoritarian systems are exemplified by Russia, a country whose government doesn't feel obliged to consider the views of citizens in its decision making. Public opinion is mostly ignored, unless it becomes extreme and threatens government. Furthermore, governments such as Russia, China, and Turkey engage in censorship, both of the mass media and social media.

In China, Google and Facebook have been told that acceptance of government censorship is a prerequisite to being allowed to operate there. Google has flatly refused and offered its Hong Kong site as a port or entry. Facebook, however, is willing to comply with China's request to respect its laws and regulations. It recognizes, however, that such acceptance could create a backlash among the site's 1.8 billion active users. Chief executive officer (CEO) Mark Zuckerberg

Corporate Communication: An International and Management Perspective, First Edition. Otto Lerbinger.

has wooed China through such tactics as securing a high-profile board seat at one of China's top universities, learning Mandarin, and jogging in Tiananmen Square on a smoggy day without a pollution mask.[2] In the meanwhile China's social media giants Weibo, and Tencent Holdings Ltd.'s WeChat and QQ are now dominant in China. Although Zuckerberg considers the huge country and its 700 million internet users crucial to Facebook's future, his efforts may have come too late.

Civil society organizations are few in authoritarian systems and are discouraged or prohibited from engaging in overt lobbying. Business organizations therefore use public relations sparingly and mainly for publicity activities, which makes media relations the focus of public relations activity.[3]

The scope of public relations is therefore exceedingly limited because government is the main user of public communications, and public relations propaganda is the favorite way of influencing public opinion. Information in a totalitarian state is manipulated to advance the goals of a single dominating party. As stated by the former German Public Relations Propaganda Minister Joseph Goebbels, propaganda must be planned and executed by only one authority.[4]

11.1.1.1 Russia's "Black Public relations"

In Russia, the term "black public relations" stands for propaganda and the absence of ethics, in contrast to "white public relations," which is associated with Western scholarship, ideas, public relations practices, and mindset.[5] One of the public relations practices is *zakazukha*, which is the publication of material favorable to an organization in return for payment by it. Public relations is associated with advertising when products are promoted through publicity. The distinction between black and white public relations also applies to other countries, such as South Africa.

Russia, however, should not be viewed as one country but as five megaregions that are geographically, politically, and economically different and culturally diverse.[6] Most references to Russia refer to the Moscow/St. Petersburg region where economic development is most advanced. The other four regions are the Ural metaregion, the ZaBaikal metaregion, and the Far East metaregion, where public relations is less developed.

11.1.1.2 Singapore

An authoritarian government is a major feature of the country of Singapore. It uses public relations for nation-building and the achievement of social harmony. Its Prime Minister Lee Kuan Yew, who died on April 27, 2015, was a remarkable leader whose core principles focused on clean and efficient government, business friendly economic policies, and social order.[7] Yew justified his tough policies by saying they were needed because of the country's multi-racial/religious make-up. A cultural feature affecting economic behavior is *kiasuism*, which means taking extreme measures to avoid risk. Its root word *kiasu*, which is derived from vernacular Chinese, means "fear of losing" and is often used to refer to anxious, selfish behavior characterized by fear of losing out.[8]

An advantage of authoritarianism was Singapore's exemplary response to the severe acute respiratory syndrome (SARS) outbreak crisis of 2003. Unlike China, it promptly reported the outbreak and engaged in open reporting. It carried out thermal imaging of all air passengers to detect anyone who had a high temperature, and quarantined those with symptoms, drafting the army to enforce containment.[9]

Public relations is practiced in Singapore businesses and public relations agencies and has been adopted by Singapore's civil society. As is typical of authoritarian organizations, public relations is seen as tactical rather than strategic activity, indicating that public relations practitioners are usually not consulted by higher management when decisions are made.

11.1.2 Democratic Systems

The purest meaning of a democracy is a system of government by the whole population or citizens of a state who rule either directly or through freely elected representatives. The US is one model, having three branches of government: Congress, the executive branch, and the judicial branch. The parliamentary democracy is another form in which the party, or a coalition of several with the greatest representation in the parliament, forms the government. It is exemplified by the UK. The basic idea of a democratic system is that the opinions of people count.

11.1.2.1 Norway's Parliamentary System

A variation of a democratic parliamentary system is Norway's. It has a parliamentarian political system combined with strong social corporatism, defined as the sociopolitical organization of a society by major interest groups. It allows for an understanding of, and appreciation for, collectivist concerns. Combined, these features characterize a pluralistic political system in which lobbying is fully accepted and characterized by bargaining and compromising.[10]

Civil society organizations flourish in Norway, as illustrated by the admission of environmental groups into the decision making arenas and their close ties to the authorities.[11] Norwegian ministries and their directorates normally circulate legislative proposals to affected public or private organizations to solicit their comments. Labor unions are included.

Public relations therefore thrives in Norway, including both in-house practitioners and outside agencies. They have moved into the boardroom and provide strategic advice on financial transactions, investor relations activities, and public affairs when companies experience regulatory challenges. Companies turn to public relations firms when they "need access to the networks that the agencies or the individual practitioner have in the media, the Parliament, the Government, or the bureaucracy."[12] These arrangements illustrate Norway's low rating on Hoftede's power distance measure (described in Chapter 12), which characterizes Norway's egalitarian society. Helping with the recognition of corporate communication is the importance accorded to reputation by Norwegian businesses and organizations in general.

Public relations managers play a crucial lobbying role, although usually on the deputy minister level, whereas the CEOs deal with the deputy minister. One study found that 14 of 24 companies met regularly and informally with politicians or civil servants, "usually in the form of more or less regular dinner parties."[13]

11.2 Major Economic Systems

The purest economic system is the free market system in which the forces of supply and demand determine what is produced and sold at a price determined by the interplay of these forces. Government plays a minimum role, especially in the extreme version of a laissez-faire system. At the other end of the spectrum are communism and socialism in which the means of production are owned and managed by government. To varying degrees, both forms may tolerate the operation of the price system that allows the market to determine the price of goods and services.

11.2.1 Free Market System

A free market system provides the widest scope for the exercise of corporate communication because its potential employers are competitive buyers and sellers of goods and services who can benefit from marketing and public relations. Product publicity and company reputations are important in such a competitive system. Public affairs plays a large role in a free market because of government regulations and demands from advocacy groups.

Corporate communication helps a company build and preserve favorable public opinion toward the free market system. Post-World War II, for example, many companies launched major economic education public relations programs to dissuade employees from embracing socialistic and communist ideas that were rampant in Europe. A major program, HOBSO – How Our Business System Operates – emphasized the role of capital and the importance of profits. In addition to defending the free market system, public relations has also been used to enlarge the scope of the free market system by promoting the concept of privatization.

11.2.1.1 Privatization

The privatization movement is a wholesale change that restructures the relative strength of the public and private sectors of society by selling government assets. After Margaret Thatcher became prime minister in 1979, her Conservative government publicized the sale of British Telecom and urged the general public to buy shares. Thatcher's motivation was largely to curb the power of trade unions, but she later used it to dismantle command economies, such as mining and steel. Showing the spread of privatization, in 1987 the British Airports Authority (BAA) acquired London's Heathrow airport and, in December 2005, BAA acquired Budapest Airport for £1.26 billion, the largest overseas deal in its history.[14] Carrying ownership another step, BAA was bought in 2006 by a consortium led by Ferrovial, a Spanish firm specializing in the design, construction, financing, operation, and maintenance of transport, urban, and services infrastructure.

Privatization of infrastructure facilities such as water works, highways, and bridges has been particularly rampant because it allows governments to reduce their public debt and for private companies to acquire a stream of income. Notable was the leasing in 2005 of the 8-mile Chicago Skyway for 99 years to an international consortium. Indiana also recently turned over its 157-mile turnpike to the same group for 75 years.[15] Although helpful to government bodies, the privatization of these public facilities led to resentment by citizens when tolls and fees rose.

Privatization gathered pace after 1991 when Eastern Europe sold many state-owned enterprises. Governments were motivated by the opportunity to reduce debt, finance infrastructure, and boost economic efficiency. Many countries have turned to privatization. In 2012, the Chinese state-run Investment Corporation swooped up 8.7% of the holding company that owns England's Thames Water.[16] Also in 2012, according to the Privatization Administration of Turkey, three consortiums offered bids for the privatization of highways and bridges, including their facilities.[17] In 2014, the operators of Tournament Parking offered $75 million to buy the downtown car park from Auckland Council.[18] Developing countries are also benefiting. Between 1988 and 1992, developing country governments earned almost $62 billion in revenues from the sale of state-owned assets. About a third of those revenues came from foreign sources.[19] In 2014, *The Economist* recommended that governments launch a new wave of privatization.[20]

Public relations firms are among the beneficiaries of privatization. Plans to privatize England's Royal Mail were a bonanza for bankers, lawyers, accountants, and public relations firms, which will collect millions of pounds of government cash for advising on the Royal Mail flotation, with investment banks alone earning about £15 m. One of the biggest beneficiaries will be Mark Sorrell, the son of Sir Martin Sorrell, who formerly headed WPP.[21] Image-building ahead of its planned privatization was seen as a necessity by Pakistan International Airlines (PIA) when in November 2014 it announced bids to hire a public relations and media management firm.[22] And in another privatization bid, Newgate Communications was set to earn $1.3 million for providing "strategic communications and issues management support and communications advice."[23]

11.2.1.2 South Korea

Officially called the Republic of Korea, the country conforms to the free market system except for the market power of combinations of businesses known as *chaebols*. On the whole, Korea has political and economic conditions that are favorable to the growth of public relations. Government uses public relations for nation-building; business for stakeholder relations and marketing; and non-profits, especially labor unions, to promote their special interests. The political evolution from authoritarian to a democratic government has helped, along with the prevalence of the free market system. All three sectors – government, business, and civil society – play a role in society and recognize public relations.

Korea has many public relations consulting firms, including some prominent international ones such as Edelman and Ketchum. Ironically, even the anomaly of *chaebols* has created a demand for public relations skills in crisis management. Pointing out that the South Korean public no longer tolerates corporate wrongdoing and government intervention, Kim Yungwook, in her chapter on the evolution of public relations in South Korea, explains how some companies elevated their head of the public relations department, who was seen as a speechwriter and organizational journalist, to a vice presidency.[24]

11.2.2 Command and Control Economies

On the other extreme of economic systems are "command and control" economies, such as state-owned enterprises (SOEs) in Russia and a large portion of the Chinese economy. These provide little or no opportunity for the practice of corporate communication. The United Nations Conference on Trade and Development defines a SOE "as one in which the state owns more than 10% of the shares."[25] In China the state sector accounts for about a quarter of industrial output. SOEs have little or no need for investor relations to help raise capital or marketing and product publicity to sell their products. However, in a modest move toward greater private sector involvement, China is considering letting private investors take larger stakes – up to 15% – in them.[26] In 2015, this policy was approved, but China's brand of state capitalism would still make SOEs bigger. Chinese President Xi Jinping continues to want the state sector to play a dominant role in the Chinese economy.[27]

Besides the large SOE sectors in Russia and China, other countries with predominantly free market economies also hold large shares of industry. France owns 100% of several organizations, such as SNCF (Société nationale des chemins de fer français; its rail services), SNCF Réseau (its rail infrastructure), LaPoste (its mail service), and Nexter (its defense equipment manufacturer). It also owns over 80% of Arva (nuclear reactors), and Électricité de France (EDF) (electricity).[28]

11.2.2.1 China's Hybrid Socialist–Market Economy

China is both a communist state and has a hybrid socialist–market economy. The economic system follows the model of "command and control" economies in its SOEs, the state sector that accounts for about a quarter of industrial output. These economies have advantages and disadvantages. During the 2008 economic crisis, SOEs in China were credited with maintaining stability because the government could control the economy. But more recently, the sprawling state sector has been seen as a major drag on growth. State firms generated an average 4.6% return on assets in 2012 compared with 12.4% in the private sector. Some firms made wasteful investments. An example is China Cosco Holdings Co. Ltd., a massive state-owned shipping firm, which ramped up shipping capacity by more than 50% from the end of 2008, contributing to overcapacity on a global scale.[29]

The "command–control" model provides little or no opportunity for the practice of public relations. SOEs don't need investor relations because they receive cheap government financing and pay low prices for land, energy, and water. In top level talks with the US in July 2013, China pledged to make state firms pay market prices, to help raise capital, and employ marketing and customer relations to sell products. However, in a modest move toward greater private sector involvement, China is considering letting private investors take larger stakes – up to 15% – in them.[30]

As the share of state-owned enterprises shrinks in the economy and the free market grows, the scope of corporate communication will expand. More attention will be given to product branding and company reputation. Beyond these strategic concerns, it is doubtful that corporate communication will play a policy role in Chinese managements because of China's cultural pattern of high power distance.

11.2.3 Mixed Systems: Social Corporativism and Social Capitalism

Mixed systems, also called social corporativism, call for a coalition of all the interests in society – government, firms, and civil society – to protect common interests. Sandra C. Duhe and Krishnamurthy Sriramesh characterize Austria, Sweden, and Germany as "highly centralized, interventionist and collective" compared to the individualist nature of classical political economy.[31] Variations depend on how it is done and whether government or business dominates.

11.2.3.1 Slovenia's Corporativism

Verčič describes Slovenia's corporativism with reference to its almost 15 000 non-governmental organizations (NGOs), with 10 000 of them active.[32] Many NGOs have "been acknowledged as vital and important to the state" and "elevated to a special status and institutionalized in the National Council," which is the second chamber of the parliament.[33] The interests of society are therefore institutionalized in a corporativism system and don't require the kinds of lobbying associated with public relations. Verčič concludes, "A study on the consequences of corporativism on public relations development remains a project for the future."[34]

In sum, the extent of regulation of the economy determines how much freedom of action managers of enterprises and consumers have. When price controls are imposed, the market ceases to perform its function of establishing an equilibrium between supply and demand. The resulting shortages then require government intervention. Lobbying efforts are thereby encouraged to modify and reduce regulations, provided that the system of government allows interest groups to exist and operate. When economies are highly regulated, civil society organizations play a smaller role because it is assumed that government assumes most of the responsibility for social welfare. Public relations jobs in non-profit organizations, e.g. fundraising, therefore tend to be fewer.

11.3 Political Risk Assessment

The examination and appraisal of a country's political and economic systems has become a major part of a specialized activity known as political risk assessment. First applied to investment decisions, this activity consists of both information gathering and the forecasting of social, political, religious, and cultural events and developments that affect the investment climate of a foreign country or region. Political risk analysis provides needed information in choosing optimal countries in which to invest. An early book by the American Management Association on *Financing International Operations*, which refers to political risk assessment, suggests that potential overseas investors consider six factors: "the attitude of the government, the political structure of the country, the social structure, the long-range economic possibilities, the labor market, and the availability of investment guarantees."[35]

Analysts differ on the variables they consider important, but they typically examine political instability and restrictions on business. Some of the key questions are:

- How stable is the host country's political system?
- How strong is the government's commitment to specific rules of the game, such as ownership of contractual rights, given its ideology and power position?
- How long is the government likely to remain in power?
- If the present government is succeeded, how would the specific rules of the game change?
- What would be the effects of any expected changes in the specific rules of the game? In light of those effects, what decisions and actions should be taken now?

Additional variables are outright expropriations, restrictions on repatriation of profits, tax environment, turmoil in the streets, upcoming elections, repatriation risks, attitudes toward the private sector, size and the influence of the middle class, and miscellaneous government policies and regulations.

Political risk assessment is similar to a SWOT analysis, which is a structured planning method used to evaluate the strengths, weaknesses, opportunities, and threats involved in a public project or a business venture. Because the strengths and opportunities are already recognized in an investment decision, some analysts emphasize the weaknesses and threats, e.g. "governmental or societal actions and policies, originating either within or outside the host country, and negatively affecting either a select group of, or the majority of, foreign business operations and investments."[36]

Another more detailed approach to political risk analysis is Witold J. Henisz's "Political Constraint Index Dataset (POLCON)." He describes it as an endeavor to measure political constraint by identifying underlying political structures and measuring their ability to support credible policy commitments. The dataset contains 90 variables (including country identifiers) that measure various features of the legislative, executive, and judicial branches of government. The central variables are indices that seek to estimate the degree of political constraints. The dataset covers 226 present and historical countries.[37]

11.3.1 Due Diligence in AES's Acquisition of Telsi in the Republic of Georgia

Henisz comprehensively describes a major case that demonstrates the importance of carefully assessing the political and economic aspects of an acquisition decision in the Republic of Georgia about 10 years after the end of the Cold War. In December 1998, AES Corporation, based in Arlington, Virginia, acquired Telsi in the Republic of Georgia. It had the support of President Eduard Shevardnadze, who was friendly toward the West. The acquisition opportunity was spotted and recommended by one of AES's managers, Michael Scholey. With previous work experience in geology and accounting, his background seemingly qualified him to make the decision.[38]

Scholey faced three major problems: securing reliable sources of electricity, getting customers to pay for it, and reducing costs. The second problem was particularly difficult.

Scholey discovered that only about one in 10 customers paid their bills and even some of these obtained additional electricity by illegally tapping the power lines. What Scholey learned was that most people felt electricity should be free, a hangover from the Soviet Union and communism, which decreed that people should receive according to their needs and give according to their ability. He took the needed step of installing reliable meters, which were placed outside of buildings in metal boxes after learning that placing them in basements invited tampering. Telsi became a losing proposition and Scholey was dismissed.

His replacement was Ignacio Iribarren. AES management reasoned that one of his strong qualifications was his familiarity with "emerging markets," having worked in Venezuela and El Salvador. The differences in the culture of Russia's emerging market were not recognized. He antagonized regulatory and political bodies. As might be expected, relations with the government and the Georgian people soured. The Minority Party referred to AES as "an American occupier" and sued to annul the privatization deal. Russia, its neighbor, never liked US involvement in the Georgian energy sector. Seemingly, the Cold War was not yet over.

In escalating events, the government seized AES's bank account for non-payment of taxes, and the chief financial officer (CFO) of AES-Telas was found murdered in his apartment and a police officer threatened to kill others. Two employees were beaten by the police and the new CFO was charged with fraud. On the labor front, workers went on strike. Iribarren was a disaster. AES paid $34 million to leave the country.

Henisz states that AES was doomed by lack of due diligence: "What they did not appear to factor into their plans were the Georgians themselves – their history, their habits and their expectations."

11.4 Conclusions

People who work in global corporate communication must have a background in economics and political science. Students who major in public relations have likely, but not necessarily, taken courses in these subjects, but their coverage may not extend to "comparative" studies that familiarize them with international differences. This chapter seeks to provide the necessary background to recognize how public relations practice is affected by such differences and what adjustments must be made.

Public relations and public affairs professionals are familiar with government and political processes, such as lobbying, many of which are applicable internationally. But they must know what countries are most similar to their own and where differences substantially inhibit or alter public affairs and public relations practices.

Most introductory public relations texts say little about economics and politics except with reference to the legal context of public relations practice, e.g. libel law, security and exchange regulations affecting investor relations, and First Amendment rights allowing lobbying activities. The overview of variations in political and economic systems enlarges this knowledge and helps those with overseas assignments know what further information is needed.

Discussion Questions

11.1. Choose a country where corporate communication is likely to flourish and one in which it would not. What are the main characteristics of each?

11.2. Describe the scope of public relations in Norway.

11.3. What are the features of a free market system?

11.4. Why is privatization so attractive to many governments?

11.5. What is an SOE? What use does it make of public relations?

11.6. What is corporativism? Describe how it is applied in one country.

11.7. Describe political risk analysis and its significance to public relations.

11.8. Was AES right in getting tough with the Georgian government?

Endnotes

1 "A Theoretical Framework for Global PR Research and Practice," in Krishnamurthy Sriramesh and Dejan Verčič, eds., *The Global PR Handbook, Revised and Expanded Edition: Theory, Research, and Practice* (New York: Routledge, 2009), p. 4.

2 Alyssa Abkowit Deepaa Seetharaman and Eva Dou, "Facebook's Big China Comeback is Stalling," *WSJ*, January 31, 2017, p. A1.

3 Katerina Tsetsura, "The Development of PR in Russia: A Geopolitical Approach," in Krishnamurthy Sriramesh and Dejan Verčič, ibid., p. 608.

4 Daniel Katz, Dorwin Cartwright, Samuel Eldersveld, and Alfred McClung Lee, *Public Opinion and Public relations Propaganda* (New York: Dryden Press, 1954), p. 510.

5 Ibid., p. 605.

6 Tsetsura, op. cit., p. 601. Also a graduate paper from the International Public Relations course at Boston University by Molly Meyer, April 2013.

7 Chu Han Wong and P.R. Venkat, "Lee Kuan Yew, Singapore's Founding Father, Dies at 91," *WSJ*, March 22, 2015.

8 Constance Chay-Nemeth, "Becoming Public Relations Professionals: A Portrait of Public relations in Singapore," in Krishnamurthy Sriramesh and Dejan Verčič, eds., *The Global Public relations Handbook: Theory Research, and Public relations Practice* (Mahwah, NJ: Lawrence Erlbaum Associates, 2003), p. 99.

9 Alan Fung, "SARS: How Singapore Outmanaged the Others," *Asia Times* (Hong Kong), April9, 2003. The Peter Sandman Risk Communication website is helpful: www.psandman.com

10 Magne Haug and Haavard Koppang, "Lobbying and Public relations in a European Context," *Public Relations Review*, Vol 23, No. 3, 1997, p. 443ff.

11 Oyvind Ihlen and Kjell Rakkenes, "Public Relations in Norway: Communication in a Small Welfare State," Sriramesh and Verčič, op. cit., 2009 edition, p. 440.

12 Haug and Koppang, op. cit.

13 Ibid., p. 233.

14 "BAA Wins Control at Budapest," *Western Daily Press*, December 19, 2005. BAA was renamed Heathrow Airport Holdings in 2012.

15 "Privatizing the Turnpike?," *New York Times*, October 22, 2006, p. 33.

16 "Mark Reynolds, China Buys a Stake in Thames Water . . . Now Will Floodgates Open?" *The Express*, January 21, 2012, p. 2.

17 "Parking Company Makes Surprise Bid for Prime CBD Spot," *The New Zealand Herald*, June 6, 2014.

18 Anadolu Agency, "3 Consortiums Offer Bids for Privatization of Highways, Bridges and Facilities on Them," October 31, 2012.

19 Frank Sader, "Privatization and Foreign Investment in the Developing World," 1988–1992, Policy Research Working Papers, WPS 1202 (Washington, DC: World Bank, 1993), p. 9.

20 "The $9 Trillion Sale," *The Economist*, January 11, 2014, p. 18.
21 Rupert Neate, "Royal Mail Privatisation: Advisers' Fees: Banks, Lawyers and Public Relations Firms All in Line for Bonanza," *The Guardian*, September 13, 2013, p. 5.
22 "Pakistan: PIA Invites Bids from Public Relations Firms to Improve Image," *Right Vision News*, November 1, 2014.
23 Will Glasgow, "Advisors Share Power Spoils," *Australian Financial Review*, May 29, 2015, p. 3.
24 Yungwook Kim, "Professionalism and Diversification: The Evolution of Public Relations in South Korea," in Krishnamurthy Sriramesh and Dejan Verčič, eds., ibid., 2009 edition, pp. 152–153.
25 "Special Report: State Capitalism – the Visible Hand," *The Economist*, January 21, 2012, p. 6.
26 Llyan Qi, "Beijing Weighs Bigger Private Role in State Firms," *WSJ*, November 12, 2013, p. A11.
27 Lingling Wei, "China to Overhaul State Sector," *WSJ*, September 14, 2015, p. A1.
28 "The State as Shareholder: Raison d'Etat," *The Economist*, June 28, 2014, p. 55.
29 Tom Orlik, Yajun Zhang, and Richard Silk, "State Firms Cloud Chinese Growth Hopes," *WSJ*, August 10–11, 2013, p. A7.
30 Llyan Qi, op. cit.
31 Sandra C. Duhe and Krishnamurthy Sriramesh, "Political Economy and Public Relations," in Sriramesh and Verčič, op. cit., 2009 edition, p. 33.
32 Dejan Verčič, "Public Relations in a Corporativist Country: The Case of Slovenia," in Sriramesh and Verčič, ibid., p. 538.
33 Ibid., pp. 535, 538.
34 Ibid., p. 544.
35 B.H. Witham, Jr., "Some Basic Questions," in *Financing International Operations: A Guide to Sources and Methods* (New York: AMA, 1965).
36 Matthew C. Mitchell, Ilan Alon, and Theodore T. Herbert, "Assessing and Managing Political Risk," in Bruce D.E. Keillor, ed., *International Business in the 21st Century* (Santa Barbara, CA: Praeger, 2011), p. 110.
37 Witold Henisz, *Corporate Diplomacy: Building Reputations and Relationships with External Stakeholders* (Sheffield: Greenleaf Publishing, 2014), p. 8. See www.nsd.uib.no/macrodataguide/set.html?id=29&sub=1
38 Ibid., pp. 1–19.

12

Social and Cultural Features of Nation States

A country's social and cultural features shape the manner in which corporate communication is conducted. The two basic frameworks are a society's social system and culture. In his *The Social System*, Talcott Parsons defines the social system as "the patterned interrelationships among individuals, groups, and institutions that form a coherent whole."[1] The local community comprises such a social system, and in nation states the sum of individual relationships among their people constitutes a social system. The second societal framework is culture. Broadly stated, it's the way society thinks and acts about things and explains how things ought to be done. Culture applies to individual organizations as well as to society as a whole.

Corporate communication operates in the context of a society's social system. This interaction is clearly seen in stakeholder relations with employees and the community. Employees are recruited from a community's social system, involving both families that nurture them and the schools that educate them. Community relations constitutes contact with civic organizations, community leaders, and various individuals. When a public relations plan requires reference to specific audiences, these contacts and the community institutions listed below are relevant.

The second framework of society, culture, affects how corporate communication is conducted. Companies have learned to observe a country's cultural practices. Walmart learned this when it entered the European market in 1997 by targeting Germany, Europe's largest and strongest economy. Its entry strategy was to acquire the local chains of Wertkauf and Interspar, which stocked the same variety of goods as US stores, with about 75 000 items on the shelves. But the cultures were different as Walmart discovered when it sought to apply its standard employee policies and practices. Among them were:

- Aggressive Hospitality: a "greeter" stands and welcomes the customer to a Walmart store.
- Ten Foot Rule: Whenever a customer comes within 10 ft of an employee in a Walmart store, the "associate" should look him or her in the eye, give a greeting, and ask if help is needed.
- Walmart Cheer: led by a manager, the staff all come together and spell out Walmart in the style of cheerleaders cheering at a sports event, the cheer ends with the lines "Who's number one? The customer! Always!"
- Sundown Rule: any question a customer has must be answered by sundown on the same day.[2]

Walmart learned the hard way that the culture of friendliness is not part of the shopping experience in Germany, especially in supermarkets and large general merchandise stores. Such friendliness by sales people is construed as insincere and inconsistent with a serious culture focused on efficiency. For the same reason, employees resisted the Walmart cheer because work is taken seriously and yelling out cheers is not seen as appropriate in the workplace. Social norms regarding privacy are strictly observed in Germany so any attention by sales people not initiated by the customer is regarded as an unwanted invasion of privacy. As stated by an employee who handled publicity for Walmart in Germany, "As a German, I

Corporate Communication: An International and Management Perspective, First Edition. Otto Lerbinger.

find the idea of being greeted at the door uncomfortable. I would feel astonished if someone I didn't know started talking to me."[3]

Public relations contributes to the shaping of local and national cultures. A notable example is Edward L. Bernay's campaign to change public and women's attitudes toward smoking in public (described in Chapter 4). Another example from Bernays was getting people to eat bacon with their eggs, a culinary change that is part of a country's culture.[4]

12.1 Major Aspects of a Country's Social System

Corporate communicators deal with many players in the countries and communities where their employers, clients, or customers are located. It helps to know how these social systems are organized and how their populations can be categorized in a meaningful fashion. A practice of public relations and marketing has been to examine the general public more closely and break it down to what public relations people call publics and marketing people call market or demographic segments.

12.1.1 Community Institutions

The social system of a country is reflected in its local communities. When corporate communication professionals are located in a community in a foreign country, they must use their knowledge of social systems to study their characteristics. Such information provides them with a useful directory of the groups, institutions, and people with which they must deal. An early book on this subject is Irwin Sanders' *The Community* in which he describes the social traits of a community, its major systems, and forms of community action.[5] A community is a place with a distinct shape, size, and communication and transportation routes. It has a demographic structure, culture, and the following institutions:

- local government;
- the economy;
- family, religion, and morality;
- education;
- health and social welfare;
- recreation.[6]

Of the above institutions, family, education, and religion have received special attention.

12.1.1.1 Family

A society's family structure is of interest to marketers who know that purchase decisions are not always made by individuals but also by other members of a family or in consultation with them. Furthermore, advertising styles in different countries are influenced by the importance of family in their cultures. In Spain, which has a collectivistic culture, people in advertisements are often shown in groups, particularly the family. It gives the individual a sense of identity and stability.[7]

Family structures also affect the way family businesses are run. Sometimes public relations practitioners may have them as clients or must deal with them. The structure and management of a family business duplicates family structure. Where Confucian values prevail, as in China, sons appear in the family hierarchy after the father and may predominate over professionally trained employees. Even in large companies, when nepotism reigns a member of a family may cause serious problems when he or she is less qualified than an outsider or is given inordinate authority.

A notorious example is when Heather Cho, head of Korean Air's in-flight service, and the daughter of the airline's chairman Cho Yang-ho ordered the plane she was on to return to the gate because she wanted to fire a flight attendant who served her macadamia nuts in a bag instead of on a plate.[8]

12.1.1.2 Education

The educational level of people in a region or country is of special importance to communicators, mainly because it is closely related to literacy. As noted by Jean-Pierre Jeannet and Hubert D. Hennessey, illiterate people can't read advertising messages and package labels. Therefore, "products that are complex or need written instructions may need to be modified to meet the educational attainments of members in the channel."[9] Similarly, innumeracy and difficulty in abstract thinking are deterrents. Sales clerks may have difficulty figuring out the purchase price of a product listed at $2.00 minus a discount of 50 cents. Furthermore, as customers, less educated people are more anchored in the "here and now" and favor a product because it looks attractive, based on factors such as packaging colors or label illustrations, without regard to whether they even need a product.[10]

12.1.1.3 Religion

Religion is a core cultural factor. Nearly 75% of the world population follows only five religions: Christianity, Islam, Hinduism, Buddhism, and Judaism. The importance and influence of religion in human affairs varies with different religions and with the secularization of society. In Islamic countries, religion is not separated from the rest of life, as followers know when they must pray five times a day when the call is made from minarets. China and some East Asian countries sometimes consider Confucianism a religion. It emphasizes personal relationships, honesty, high moral standards, and loyalty to one's group.

Business tends to keep religion in the background. Historically, however, the Christian religion has buttressed capitalism. Max Weber described its influence in his *The Protestant Ethic and the Spirit of Capitalism*, as did R.H.·Tawney in his *Religion and the Rise of Capitalism*.[11] Weber found support for profit-making in Calvinism, saying that profits were a sign that a business person was favorably recognized by God. Tawney found that religion and capitalism were concurrent developments.

One way Christianity affected business in the past was by asserting that charging interest for loans was incompatible with religion. Interest was perceived as a payment for time, but "time belongs to God," so interest could not be charged. Jews in the Middle Ages became the money lenders. The Islamic faith adheres to the same Christian prohibition against charging interest, but Muslims have found a way around the restriction by lending money in exchange for a share of profits.[12] Experts on Sharia law dictate whether a bond offering, for example, is acceptable. Dubai is a key location of such experts. The field of investor relations must give consideration to this religious view.

Consumption of certain products by adherents to certain religions are dictated by religion. Jews and some Muslims are forbidden to eat pork; Muslims may not drink alcoholic beverages. A foreign visitor to Pakistan who wants a drink of scotch would be exempt by declaring himself to be an alcoholic! On the side of sellers, some small business owners refuse to serve customers with objectionable religious views. An example is a small bakery that refused to make wedding cakes for gays.[13]

Employment has been influenced by religion. In the past, Jews in the US were discriminated against by some law offices and corporate executive suites. When race rather than religion became an employment issue in the US, business executives had to decide how vigorously to demand "equal employment" and only a few initially announced that such a policy would be enforced. In France, only a few employers have responded to the problem of high unemployment among Muslims who live mainly in the *banlieues* of Paris and other major cities.

12.1.1.4 Islam

In recent years, the US and Europe have been especially disturbed by the actions of extremist Islamists who are intolerant of all religions except their own interpretation of the Quran, the sacred book of Islam. Islam began in Arabia and was revealed to humanity by the Prophet Muhammad. Those who follow Islam are called Muslims. They believe that there is only one God, whom the Arabic world calls *Allah*. The word *Islam* means "submission to the will of God." Islam is the second largest religion in the world, after Christianity, with over 1 billion followers. Estimates are that Britain has 4.5% Muslims, Germany 5%, and the US around 1%. The source of the Muslim population in each country varies. In France it's Algeria, in the Netherlands it's Morocco and Turkey, and in the US it's from 77 countries, making them "the Episcopalians of the Islamic world."[14]

The clothing worn by Muslims has sometimes become controversial. When France banned the wearing of body garments with full-face veils (variously known as niqab or burqa) in public, the European Court of Human Rights upheld it. The French government argued that the ban helped to protect public safety as well as advancing women's rights and improving social cohesion.[15] Requiring people to show their faces is usually considered a fair infringement of religious freedom for passport control or where it is necessary for legitimate work reasons, e.g. if they work as social workers or teachers.[16] In the case of a dress code that applies to all staff members, no matter what religion they are, an employer should still be aware of indirect discrimination if an employee's request is not fairly considered.[17]

The religion of Islam has created several major crises in the past decade. One is the so-called Danish cartoon crisis, which started when in 2005, Flemming Rose, the cultural editor of the Danish newspaper *Jyllands-Posten*, published a series of 12 cartoons satirizing the Prophet Muhammad. One cartoon depicted him wearing a turban shaped like a bomb, another showed a turbaned figure in heaven telling an ascending suicide bomber to stop because "we've run out of virgins," which is the supposed reward awaiting male Islamic martyrs.

Local Muslims strongly objected and sought an apology from the newspaper editor and the Danish prime minister. But the editor defended his action by pointing to Denmark's strong free speech tradition. After neither the prime minister nor the editor apologized, and the prime minister even declined to see a representative, Muslim leaders in Denmark subsequently took their grievance to the Middle East and organized a boycott against Arla, the big Danish seller of diary goods, which was a vulnerable target. The crisis was eventually resolved after both the prime minister and the newspaper editor apologized on Danish television and Arla representatives met with Middle East leaders.

A decade later, in early January 2015, after the French magazine *Charlie Hebdo* published satirical images of Muhammad, two radical Islamists shot and killed eight of its staff in revenge for the blasphemy.[18] The French public rallied behind the magazine with signs saying "Je Suis Charlie." The first subsequent issue of *Charlie Hebdo* was expected to sell as many as 5 million copies, indicating public support for the publication and for free speech.[19] For a country that celebrates the philosopher Voltaire, who famously said, "I do not agree with what you have to say, but I'll defend to the death your right to say it," the event fortified the Western value of freedom of speech.

Considering that 84% of people around the world identify with a religious group, religion is considered a powerful force in global politics and civil society. Recognizing this, the US Department of State announced: "Religion has a significant impact on a range of US foreign policy priorities, making it critical that we continue and strengthen our efforts to assess religious dynamics and engage religious actors while pursuing our diplomacy and development objectives."[20] Business must similarly consider the importance of religion.

12.1.2 Demographics and Other Forms of Audience Segmentation

Demographic analysis is the marketer's main approach to market segmentation and public relations' approach to audience segmentation. In addition, Philip Kotler includes geographic, psychographic, and behavioral segmentation.[21] The geographic basis is particularly relevant in the international arena because the public and markets are divided into geographical units such as nations, states, regions, counties, cities, or neighborhoods. The psychographic designation refers to social class, lifestyle, and personality. The behavioral includes use occasion, benefits sought, user status, usage rate, loyalty status, readiness stage, and attitude toward product. Most of these relate more to marketing than public relations.

The more widely used demographic segmentation includes such variables as age, sex, family size, family life cycle, income, occupation, education, religion, race, and nationality. These are typical categories used in public opinion surveys and by marketers in selecting the appropriate audiences for advertising and sales purposes. Each of these variables can be analyzed separately and in combination; for example, marketers explore the connection between age and life cycle stages when certain products, such as toys for babies and children, and services are most in demand.

Marketers are interested in consumers' income levels and place of residence, for they indicate the ability to spend. Retailers in China have recognized the population's rising middle class and demand for luxury goods. In India, the middle class is also growing, with more than 1 million households earning more than $100 000 each. About 300–400 million are routinely included in the ranks of the global middle class, even though they has little money to spend. Nevertheless, Unilever's CEO Paul Polman describes India as potentially the company's biggest market.[22] In Brazil, where low-income groups make up 87% of the population and account for about 53% of income or about $240 billion, the well-off groups account for about $454 billion of the income. In countries and regions where poverty exists, companies have offered smaller sizes of products at lower prices. Not only marketers but public relations professionals watch public opinion polls and extract more significance from them by analyzing findings according to such demographic categories as geographical sections of a country, sex, marital status, occupation, and age.

In psychographic analysis, social class reflects the social stratification in a country – the ranking of people in a hierarchy. It is a feature of most societies but is particularly rigid in India's caste system with Brahmins as the highest caste and "untouchables" the lowest. Caste determines who can legitimately communicate with certain people and influences society's division of labor and distribution of income. As applied to marketing applications, Audrey Driscoll reports that Mercedes Benz was able to sell more cars in India when Brahmins were employed in the sales department, because other Brahmins were more willing to purchase cars from their own caste.

Lifestyle influences much human behavior. For example, people who subscribe to a "simplistic" lifestyle curb their consumption habits and are more likely to embrace environmental goals. Personality types may also be relevant. Motorists who have authoritarian personalities were said to be attracted to the Esso gasoline brand because one of Esso's attributes was thought to be its authoritarian culture. In the US participation in protest movements may be influenced as more people self-demote themselves from upper middle and middle class to lower middle class because of their falling sense of well-being.

12.2 Features of Cultural Systems

Countries are commonly distinguished from one another by their culture. People in one country are seen as different and acting differently from those in other countries. There are many formal definitions of culture. Geert Hofstede, whose research on cultural patterns is widely known, defines culture as "the collective programming of the mind which distinguishes the members of one category of people from another."[23] Larry A. Samovar and Richard E. Porter's fuller definition lists some of the elements that comprise a culture: "the deposit of knowledge, experience, beliefs, values, attitudes, meanings, hierarchies, religion, notions of time, roles, spatial relations, concepts of the universe, and material objects and possessions acquired by a group of people in the course of generations through individual and group striving."[24] Their book, *Intercultural Communication: A Reader*, is one of the first efforts to apply the subject of culture to communications.[25]

Culture also applies to organizations. As defined by Richard L. Daft in *Organization Theory and Design*, "Culture is the set of key values, guiding beliefs, and understandings that are shared by members of an organization. It defines basic organization values, and communicates to new members the correct way to think and act, and how things ought to be done."[26] In describing the cultural elements in an organization or group, Edgar Schein, the well-known authority on organizational culture, lists 12 variables, such as observed behavioral regularities when people interact and rules of the game.[27]

In his assessment of Apple Computer's culture as part of a long-range planning process, Edgar Schein lists the following four "governing assumptions":

1) We are not in the business for the business alone but for some higher purpose – to change society and the world, create something lasting, solve important problems, and have fun.
2) Task accomplishment is more important than the process used or the relationships formed. For example, seniority, loyalty, and past experience don't count relative to present task achievements.
3) The individual has the right and obligation to be a total person. For example, Apple neither expects company loyalty from individuals nor does it expect to guarantee employment security to individuals.
4) Only the present counts. For example, Apple is not a lifetime employer.[28]

Countries vary in their organizational cultures, and some may provide competitive advantage. In a study of German and Japanese companies in Alabama and Austria, German companies were characterized as "expert culture" and Japan as a "lean production culture." In Germany's *Meister* system the expert knows his boundaries and does not take risks beyond what is reasonable; he is concerned with proper order. Japan favors functional relationships whereby employees collaboratively seek solutions that improve the output.[29]

The study of different national cultures has been popular among global managers who seek a quick way to understand what works and doesn't work abroad. In *Managing Cultural Differences*, Philip R. Harris and Robert T. Moran sought to make global managers aware of the "pervasive influence of culture upon employee behavior, customer relations, work, and productivity."[30] A major part of their book examined cultural specifics in regions and countries in North America, Latin America, Asia, Europe, the Middle East, and Africa.

Corporate communicators have also realized the need to understand the cultures of the individual countries in which they operate. Hugh M. Culbertson and Ni Chen's *International Public Relations* serves this purpose in examining public relations in specific countries and regions.[31] A more recent book is by Nilanjana Bardhan and C. Kay Weaver, eds., *Public Relations in Global Cultural Contexts: Multi-Paradigmatic Perspectives*.[32] The most complete and notable book is Krishnamurthy Sriramesh and Dejan Verčič's *The Global Public Research Handbook.* It extends this purpose by containing a section on the connection between culture and public relations in each of the 31 country chapters. Each describes the cultural variables, with special reference to the ratings by Geert Hofstede.

Hofstede established the most-mentioned system of studying cultural variables, using the following variables and rating them – from 0 to 100 – for each country. His variables include the following.

12.2.1 Individualism vs. Collectivism

The degree of interdependence a society maintains among its members is defined by the pattern of individualism vs. collectivism, which is reflected in whether people's self-image is defined in terms of "I" or "We." People in individualist societies are supposed to look only after themselves and their direct family. Individualism represents the core of American culture, as symbolized by the Marlboro Man advertisement. He represented the ultimate American cowboy and masculine trademark, which helped establish Marlboro as the best-selling cigarette in the world. Individualism is congruent with the free market system and its profit maximizing ethic.

In contrast, collective cultures are characterized by interdependence and reciprocal obligation.[33] In collectivist societies, people belong to "in-groups" that take care of one another in exchange for loyalty. They de-emphasize their individuality, saying that like a nail, an individual who stands out will be hammered down.

The choice of advertising themes reflects this pattern. An ad shows a young German woman jealously guarding her Magnum ice cream as she savors it and says "I share much, but not everything."[34] This selfish attitude is acceptable in an individualist nation like Germany but not in a collective one like China or Spain.

12.2.1.1 Saudi Arabia and China

With a low score of 22 out of 100 on individualism, Saudi Arabia is an extreme case of a collectivistic society. This is manifested in a close long-term commitment to the member "group," be that a family, extended family, or extended relationships. Loyalty in a collectivist culture is paramount, and overrides most other societal rules and regulations. In collectivist societies offense leads to such consequences as shame and loss of face. Its society fosters strong relationships where everyone takes responsibility for fellow members of their group. Employer–employee relationships are perceived in moral terms and an employee's in-group is considered in making hiring and promotion decisions.

Collectivism is reflected in the prevalence of *guanxi* in Chinese culture, which refers to a network of connections and friendships. Its positive side is that it serves as a lubricant in building interpersonal relationships and networks. But it has a "backdoor" side, where the professional merits of a news release, for example, are subordinated to the relationship between the publicist and the journalist.

Like its neighbors in Southeast Asia, South Korea, and Japan, China follows the collectivism cultural pattern rather than an individualistic one. This pattern was evident recently when the Chinese tennis champion Li Na took individual credit for her success even though Chinese authorities wanted her to acknowledge the support she received from them.[35]

12.2.1.2 Japan's Consensus Decision Making

Consensus decision making in Japan reflects the collectivist pattern. In line with its *oyabun–kobun* relationship, nothing is done without considering how the outcome affects all. In this way conflict is avoided. Ideas and plans are therefore circulated up and down the company hierarchy until everyone has had a chance to react. By having their sentiments and interests considered, all members may be assured that what is good for the company will ultimately be good for them. Insofar as the Japanese avoid verbalizing objections or doubts in order to preserve group harmony, this system violates the principle of open communication.[36] It's a time-consuming process that if applied to a crisis situation would deter the need for quick action.

12.2.2 Power Distance

This pattern defines the extent to which the less powerful members of institutions and organizations within a country expect and accept that power is distributed unequally A high rating shows that inequalities between people are accepted and desired, that there is deference to authority, and subordinates expect to be told what to do. This pattern follows the Confucian philosophy that advocates a stratified society. On a family level, the father is the supreme leader, followed by the mother, the son, and daughter. On a societal level, local and provincial leaders are revered. This arrangement leads to harmony and stability, which is desired by the Chinese government. Harmony is also one of the goals of corporate public relations, attained by developing sound relationships between government and the public or an organization and its stakeholders.

Power distance is particularly important within organizations. It affects employee relations and the role of managers. A high power distance does not accommodate public relations as a member of top management, the so-called dominant coalition. In such situations the primary function of public relations is likely to be in making "protocol and ceremonial" arrangements.

12.2.2.1 Japan

Compared to other countries, Japan scores highest on power distance. One expression is the bow, the traditional Japanese greeting, as opposed to the American handshake. It is important to take note of how low the person greeting you has bowed, and return it with a bow as low as the one you have received, as this gesture indicates the relationship status between the two. It is also essential to keep the eyes low and the palms laid flat against the legs during the bow. Another expression of high power distance is the protocol that "meetings in general are highly scripted affairs with a seating chart and a specific order (according to seniority) for making speeches."[37]

A consequence of high power distance is that public relations advice, if given at all, doesn't reach top management or is rejected outright. Accordingly, the organizational status of public relations is diminished; vice presidents of public relations and chief communication officers (CCOs) are rare. This hierarchical arrangement provides stability, but it carries the danger that if something goes wrong, the leader is blamed. This happened at Toshiba, where chief executive officer (CEO) Hisao Tanaka resigned because he and previous CEOs set the tone for $1 billion in accounting irregularities. The CEOs set unrealistic profit targets and demanded that subordinates meet them. "There was a corporate culture under which it was impossible to go against the intentions of superiors."[38] The company had a system under which the CEO would set a "challenge" for subordinates to meet. That left managers with little choice but to fudge their numbers.[39]

Saving face is an important societal concept in Japan, related to its high power distance. In general, the people of Japan believe that denying a person's request will cause them embarrassment and a "loss of face." They refrain from doing things that will cause this and do not openly insult, criticize, or put anyone on the spot in a social setting. Rather than saying "no" to a person's request, an individual may instead say they are "taking it into consideration." Saving face is a mark of one's dignity and status in Japanese culture.

12.2.2.2 Other Countries

Saudi Arabia also scores high on power distance as demonstrated by the acceptance of the hierarchical order in which everybody has a place and needs no further justification. Subordinates expect to be told what to do by a benevolent autocrat. In India, with its strong elitist nature, deference to authority is strong, sometimes arising out of social or class status, age, or seniority in organizations. This leads to an authoritarian style of management, which makes it difficult for subordinates, such as public relations professionals, to give advice to superiors.[40]

12.2.3 Uncertainty Avoidance

Managers who score high on this criterion try to minimize the occurrence of unknown, ambiguous, or unusual situations. They try to proceed with careful changes in step-by-step planning, implemented by rules, laws, and regulations. In Arab cultures it is believed that the future can never be known, so that rather than attempt to control the future it should just be allowed to happen.

Countries exhibiting high uncertainty avoidance maintain rigid codes of belief and behavior and are intolerant of unorthodox behavior and ideas. In Brazil, where 80% are strong adherents to Roman Catholicism, tolerance of other religions is low. To escape the high level of anxiety in society, Brazilians display a great passion for life and optimism.[41] In China, the concern is about social harmony and stability. It partly accounts for its fear of social media, because it threatens government's monopoly over the mass media and, therefore, its control over society.

Language use is influenced by a high uncertainty pattern. As shown in its advertising style, the German need for structure and explicit language leads to an avoidance of ambiguity. German advertisements are informational, direct, and factual. They downplay imagination and favor orderly logical presentations. Their style is rational, straightforward, and serious. Endorsements are made by experts, scientists with academic titles, researchers, or by company CEOs.[42]

Innovation may be a casualty of uncertainty avoidance, which reduces creativity in advertising and ideas for public relations events. People have an inner urge to be busy and work hard following the norms of precision and punctuality. Security is an important element in individual motivation. In contrast, low uncertainty avoidance cultures accept and feel comfortable in unstructured situations and changeable environments. They try to have as few fixed rules as possible, preferring policy guidelines. People in these cultures tend to be more pragmatic and more tolerant of change.

Uncertainty avoidance is a strong Japanese characteristic and may explain the avoidance of unsettling news, especially about crises. An indirect communication style is preferred as reflected in TV commercials that avoid stating a point of view because it makes people uncomfortable. A direct approach might be perceived as an "insult" to the consumer's intelligence.[43]

12.2.3.1 Japan's Toshiba Soviet Union Case

A prominent example of uncertainty avoidance, which amounted to risk avoidance, is the Toshiba Soviet Union case. One of Toshiba's subsidiaries sold military-sensitive machine tools to the former Soviet Union. It thereby violated the Coordinating Committee for Multilateral Export Controls (COCOM) agreement among North Atlantic Treaty Organization (NATO) countries (excluding Iceland) and Japan.[44] Toshiba's top management ignored early warnings of an imminent crisis. Even after the *Washington Times* reported the violation and 2 days later a leading Japanese newspaper *Asahi Shibun* covered the story, top management did nothing. Even over 2 months later, Toshiba's president said he was still optimistic about the outcome of the whole affair. It took a 92–95 Senate vote a month later on a provision that would place a 2–5-year ban on Toshiba imports, to convince Toshiba that it faced a crisis of major proportions. Besides avoidance behavior, fear of embarrassment, i.e. admitting to a mistake, contributed to Toshiba's obliteration of the situation. As stated earlier, saving face may be a related aspect of the Toshiba incident.

12.2.4 Masculinity–Femininity

Masculinity is behavior that is competitive, assertive, materialistic, ambitious, and power seeking. Femininity is defined as being nurturing and compassionate and placing more value on relationships, caring for others, and quality of life. The fundamental issue is what motivates a person: wanting to be the best (masculine) or liking what you do (feminine). A society with high masculinity will be driven by competition, achievement, and success, with success being defined as being the winner or best in a field. It is a value system that starts in school and continues throughout organizational behavior.

Masculinity is associated with the free market system where people in workplaces "live in order to work." Managers are expected to be decisive and assertive. The emphasis is on equity, competition, and performance; conflicts are resolved by fighting them out. In contrast, femininity is associated with the values of non-profits.

12.2.5 High vs. Low Context

In high-context societies, such as China, Japan, other Asian societies, and South America, personal relationships embody norms and other information that serve as background for mutual understanding. In conversation, the other person needs little additional information to know what you're talking about. Foreign managers and public relations professionals dealing with these high-context cultures will have great difficulty because they lack the background to follow people's train of thought. Misunderstandings can therefore easily occur. Getting the services of "cultural interpreters" as well as translators would be advisable in order to know what is missed in high-context communications.

The concept of high- and low-context cultures was popularized by Edward T. Hall. In a high-context culture, people interpret a message through the lens of the shared culture, which can be either in the physical context or in the behavior of a person through non-verbal communication or body language, in silences and pauses, in relationships and empathy.[45] Eye contact has received much attention. The Japanese tend to favor indirect eye contact when speaking with their superiors as a sign of respect and deference. In Saudi Arabia, however, where members have a strong sense of loyalty to their group, eye contact should be frequent, almost to the point of staring. When Hall was asked how Arabs were different from North Americans, he explained that the basic difference is that Arabs are highly "contexted," meaning that Arabs examine the entire circumstance in which events are happening in order to understand them.

Attitudes toward the personal space surrounding a person are another cultural factor. Intimate space, reserved for lovers, children, and close family members, is for touching and whispering; the distance is less than 6–18 inches. Personal distance is used for conversations with friends, to chat with associates, and in group discussions; distances vary between 4 and 12 ft. Public distance is for public speaking and is between 12 and 25 feet.

Hall gives the example of banking in the Middle East. Reflecting a low-context approach, an American banker is required to send a financial statement to the local bank's New York office to obtain approval for a loan above a certain amount. But a Middle East banker could simply agree on a loan on the strength of a personal recommendation by a mutual friend. As Hall states, "If you know the man and you know his business and he knows you and you're part of the same social group, he cannot afford not to pay back that loan."[46] High-context societies require much less legal paperwork than in the US for a person's word is his or her bond and you need not spell out the details to make him behave.

An expression of high-context behavior is the formality of socializing with a visitor before doing business. This contact provides an opportunity to learn more about the other's "field of experience," therefore reducing uncertainty. The opportunity to create mutual understanding, and perhaps also trust, is enhanced. To some extent, the same result is expected when employees and guests are invited to participate in *enkai*, formal after-hours drinking parties, where everyone is equal and any transgression can be blamed on alcohol.

12.2.6 Other Cultural Variables

Talcott Parsons, Fons Trompenaars, and Charles Hampden-Turner have presented additional cultural variables.[47] Among the more prominent are:

- *Particularism vs. Universalism.* In particularistic societies, such as Italy or South America, the unique features or rights of an individual and his or her circumstances govern. In universalistic societies the same standards and rules are applied to everyone. Universalism is associated with Germans and the Swiss.
- *Ascription vs. Achievement.* Ascription means that primacy is given to an actor's "attributes or qualities, independently of specific expected performances." Achievement emphasizes performance, either in process, or expected in the future.
- *Pragmatism.* Describes how people respond to the fact that so much that happens around us cannot be explained. In societies with a normative orientation, most people have a strong desire to explain as much as possible. In societies with a pragmatic orientation most people don't have a need to explain everything, as they believe that it is impossible to understand fully the complexity of life. The challenge is not to know the truth but to live a virtuous life.

  The normative nature of Saudi Arabian society can be seen in its low score of 36 out of 100 on this dimension. People in such societies have a strong concern with establishing the absolute truth; they are normative in their thinking. They exhibit great respect for traditions, a relatively small propensity to save for the future, and a focus on achieving quick results.
- *Indulgence.* Defined as the extent to which people try to control their desires and impulses, based on the way they were raised. Relatively weak control is called "indulgence" and relatively strong control is called "restraint." Cultures can, therefore, be described as indulgent or restrained.
- *Time Orientation.* Attitudes to time may differ significantly between different cultures. In most Mediterranean and Arab countries, for example, being late for an appointment, or taking a long time to get down to business, is the accepted norm. Such behavior, though, would be anathema in punctuality-conscious Japan, the UK, the USA, Germany, and Switzerland.

Public relations is closely associated with publicity gained through its relationship with the mass media. Their availability in different countries therefore affects how public relations is facilitated or hindered. The assumption is that the mass media have the power to influence public opinion and shape public discourse. Product publicity and marketing help in promoting goods and services, and advertising and social marketing help governments and non-profits to influence such behavior as stopping to smoke, driving safely, and other socially desirable behavior.

12.3 Media Systems

The subject of media systems as they apply to different regions and countries is too detailed to discuss in detail. But some general approaches to them can serve as guidelines. A general approach is to classify differences in media systems according to three theories:

- Authoritarian: government controls the press and mass media for the sole intent of maintaining social and political control over the population.
- Libertarian: many media avenues representing all views within society are available.
- Social responsibility: when a wide degree of media competition does not exist, a conscious effort must be made by the existing media to capture, represent, and print opposing points of view.[48]

The aspects of media systems of concern to public relations are the prevalence and variety of media and such specifics as: analyzing who controls the media (and, therefore, the editorial content), how much access various segments of the populations have to the media, and the extent of media outreach.[49] Media professionalism and ethics influence the effectiveness of the media, and people's illiteracy and poverty are recognized as barriers. Attention is given to the agenda-setting role of the media – suggesting what people should be thinking about – and, increasingly the rise of alternative social media.

12.3.1 Al Jazeera

The relative void in coverage of the Middle East was filled by the establishment of *Al Jazeera* in 1966 and the launching of the English sister channel in November 2006. Both are based in Qatar. Research shows that 80% of those who tune in to the English channel, out of a potential audience of 88 million outside North America, speak English as a second language.[50] *Al Jazeera* has become the preferred station for close to 40% of all Arab TV viewers. The news channels are an important source of information and link with the Middle East.

12.4 Conclusions

On a day-to-day basis, company personnel abroad are most likely become aware of a country's many social and cultural features in their daily interactions. When executives are assigned abroad, they are often provided with "Berlitz" type advice to "connect with new people" and avoid blunders. Such details as how to present one's business card and whether to shake hands with someone of the opposite sex are explained.

Instead of providing specific information about social and cultural differences in varying countries, social scientists have summarized the key features of cultural systems across societies. Countries that have been most visited by professionals from corporate communication are mentioned more frequently. A person then knows what to look for and to study a society more closely. Examples in different countries, however, have been provided to illustrate variations, especially as they pertain to corporate communication applications.

Discussion Questions

12.1. Friendliness is considered a desirable trait. What did Walmart learn about the behavior of Germany customers when it opened stores in Germany?

12.2. When should marketers consider a customer's family and not only him or her as an individual?

12.3. How have marketers adjusted to the importance of religion in society?

12.4. Why must there be special sensitivity to Islam as a religion?

12.5. In what different ways do marketers classify customers?

12.6. Choose a feature of a cultural system and explain how it affects decisions within a company?

12.7. What cultural feature makes it difficult for public relations people to be members of a company's "dominant coalition?"

12.8. How can an executive overcome the barriers of a high-context culture?

Endnotes

1 Talcott Parsons, *The Social System* (Glencoe, IL: The Free Press, 1951), pp. 3–22. Also see Talcott Parsons and Edward A. Shils, *Toward a General Theory of Action* (Cambridge, MA: Harvard University Press, 1954).

2 Thomas A. Hemphill, "Rejuvenating Wal-Mart's Reputation," *Business Horizons*, Vol. 48, January–February 2005, pp. 11–21.

3 Ibid. Also see "Wal-Mart: Struggling in Germany," *Bloomberg Business Week*, April 10, 2005, and Anita Chan, ed. *Walmart in China* (Ithaca, NY: Cornell University Press/ILR Press, 2011). The latter is primarily a book about Walmart and labor in China.

4 For these and other examples, see Edward L. Bernays, *Biography of an Idea: Memoirs of PR Counsel Edward L. Bernays* (New York: Simon and Schuster, 1965).

5 Irwin T. Sanders, *The Community: An Introduction to a Social System* (New York: Ronald Press Company, 1958), pp. 4–8.

6 See E.M. Burke, "Defining the Community for Community Relations Planning," Institute on Corporate Community Relations, 1995, pp. 1–3, 8.

7 Marieke De Mooij, *Global Marketing and Advertising: Understanding Cultural Paradoxes* (Thousand Oaks, CA: Sage Publications, 1998), p. 276.

8 "South Korean Heiress Apologizes to Flight Attendants for 'Nut Rage,'" *Legal Monitor Worldwide*, December 15, 2014. Denver Nicks, "Koran Air Exec Sorry in Macadamia Nut Controversy," *Time*, December 12, 2014.

9 Jean-Pierre Jeannet and Hubert D. Hennessey, *Global Marketing Strategies*, 2nd ed. (Boston, MA: Houghton Mifflin Company, 1992), p. 194.

10 G. Gomas, M. Hult, Bruce D. Keillor, and Roscoe Hightower, "Valued Product Attributes in an Emerging Market: A Comparison between French and Malaysian Consumers," *Journal of World Business*, Vol. 35, No. 2, 2000, p. 217.

11 Max Weber, *The Protestant Ethic and the Spirit of Capitalism* (New York: C. Scribner & Sons, 1930). R.H.·Tawney, *Religion and the Rise of Capitalism* (New York: Harcourt, Brace and Company, 1947).

12 David Henry, "Islamic Law; Returns Muslims Can Live With," *Business Week*, July 17, 2006, p. 9. "Islam: The Choice Facing Muslims," *The Economist*, April 18, 2009, p. 89.

13 Richard Wolf, "Baked in the Cake: Legal Battles Follow Gay-Marriage Ruling," *USA Today*, July 23, 2015, p. 8A. Nathan Koppel and Ashby Jones, "Firms Balk at Gay Weddings," *WSJ*, October 2, 2013, p. A3.
14 "Muslim America; Islam, Yet Integrated," *The Economist*, September 6, 2014, p. 31.
15 Gabriele Steinhauser and Inti Landauro, "Court Upholds French Ban on Full-Face Veils in Public," *WSJ*, July 2, 2014, p. A9.
16 "Burqa Bans: The Freedom to Dress Modestly," *The Economist*, December 10, 2015, p. 18.
17 Amanda Trewhella, "Burqas, Niqabs and Work: What Should Employers Do About Staff Wanting to Wear Veils?" *International Business Times*, October 7, 2013.
18 "Terror in Paris: A Blow Against Freedom," *The Economist*, January 10, 2015, pp. 45–46.
19 Sam Schechner, "Crowds Rush to Buy Latest Charlie Hebdo," *WSJ*, January 15, 2015, p. A8.
20 "Washington: Religion and Global Affairs," *US Official News*, March 4, 2015.
21 Philip Kotler, *Marketing Management: Analysis Planning Implementation and Control*, 7th ed. (Englewood, NJ: Prentice Hill, 1991), pp. 255–263.
22 "Briefing India's Middle Class, The Elephant in the Room," *The Economist*, January 13 2018, p. 20.
23 Geert Hofstede, "Business Cultures," *UNESCO Courier*, Vol. 47, Issue 4, April 1994, p. 12.
24 Larry A. Samovar and Richard E. Porter, *Intercultural Communication: A Reader*, 7th ed. (Belmont, CA: Wadsworth Publishing Company, 1994), p. 11.
25 Ibid.
26 Richard L. Daft, *Organization Theory and Design* (New York: West Publishing Company, 1989, p. 503. A useful reference is John Childress, *Leverage: The CEO's Guide to Corporate Culture* (London: Principia Associates, 2013). A classic is Edgar Schein, *Organizational Culture and Leadership*, 4th ed. (Hoboken, NJ: John Wiley & Sons, 2010).
27 Edgar H. Schein with Peter Schein, *Organizational Culture and Leadership*, 5th ed. (Hoboken, NJ: John Wiley & Sons, 2017), pp. 4–5. pp. 308–309.
28 Ibid., pp. 308–309.
29 Gerhard Apfelthaler, Helen J. Muller, and Robert R. Reher, "Corporate Global Culture as Competitive Advantage: Learning from Germany and Japan in Alabama and Austria," *Journal of World Business*, Vol. 37, Summer 2002, pp. 108–118.
30 Philip R. Harris and Robert T. Moran, *Managing Cultural Differences*, 2nd ed. (Houston, TX: Gulf Publishing Company, 1981), p. xii.
31 Hugh M. Culbertson and Ni Chen, *International Public Relations: A Comparative Analysis* (Mahwah, NJ: Erlbaum, 1996).
32 Nilanjana Bardhan and C. Kay Weaver, eds., *Public Relations in Global Cultural Contexts: Multi-Paradigmatic Perspectives* (New York and London: Routledge, 2011).
33 Dejan Verčič, Larissa A. Grunig, and James E. Grunig, "Global and Specific Principles of PR: Evidence from Slovenia," in Hugh M. Culbertson and Ni Chen, eds., *International PR: A Comparative Analysis* (Mahwah, NJ: Erlbaum, 1996), p. 48.
34 De Mooij, op. cit.
35 Simon Barnes, "Li's Freedom of Expression Requires No Interpretation," *The Times* (London), June 26, 2014, pp. 68, 69.
36 Georgiana Surou, "How Japanese Run Their Businesses," *Romanian Economic and Business Review*, Vol. 2, No. 2, 2007, pp. 77–82.
37 www.japanesebusinessresource.com
38 Takashi Mochizuki, "Blame is Laid on Chiefs at Toshiba," *WSJ*, July 21, 2015, p. B3.
39 Ibid.
40 Deference to authority is discussed by K. Sriramesh, "Power Distance and Public Relations: An Ethnographic Study of Southern Indian Organizations," in Hugh M. Culbertson and Ni Chen, eds.,

International Public Relations: A Comparative Analysis (Mahwah, NJ: Erlbaum, 1996), pp. 181–182.

41 For a discussion about Brazil, see Melvin L. Sharpe and Roberto P. Simoes, "Public Relations Performance in South and Central America," in Hugh M. Culbertson and Ni Chen, ibid., pp. 273–297.

42 De Mooij, op. cit., p. 274.

43 Ibid., p. 281.

44 Otto Lerbinger, *The Crisis Manager: Facing Risk and Responsibility* (Mahwah, NJ: Lawrence Erlbaum Associates, 1997), p. 8.

45 Described in Phillip R. Harris and Robert T. Moran, *Managing Cultural Differences*, 2nd ed. (Houston, TX: Gulf Publishing, 1977), p. 36.

46 Edward T. Hall and Elizabeth Hall, "How Cultures Collide," in Gary R. Weaver, ed., *Culture, Communication, and Conflict: Readings in Intercultural Relations*, 2nd ed. (New York: Simon & Schuster, 1998), p. 18.

47 Talcott Parsons, op cit., p. 109; Fons Trompenaars and Charles Hampden-Turner, *Riding the Waves of Cultures; Understanding Cultural Diversity in Global Business*, 2nd ed. (New York and London: McGraw-Hill, 1998).

48 Adapted from Frederick S. Siebert, Theodore Peterson, and Wilbur Schramm, *Four Theories of the Press* (Champaign, IL: University of Illinois Press, 1963). The fourth, Soviet Communist Theory is excluded.

49 Krishnamurthy Sriramesh and Dejan Verčič, eds., *The Global Public Relations Handbook, Revised and Expanded Edition: Theory, Research, and Practice* (New York: Routledge, 2009), p. 75.

50 David Marash, "Al Jazeera English: News with a New Perspective," *Global Journalist*, Vol 12, December 2006, pp. 17–19.

13

The Nation Brand: Comparison with Product and Company Brand

All countries aspire to develop strong, attractive nation brands. A nation brand is how people perceive a country – what qualities they associate with it, and what attitudes they have toward it, its people, and its products. A visitor might like the terrain and mountains of Switzerland, find its people friendly, and admire the high quality of its watches and instruments. "Italian designs," "French fashion," "German engineering," and "Apple of America" are successful models of the value-added strategy of nation branding.

Peter Hanlon, chief executive officer (CEO) and founder of Thinktopia – a global brand transformation and innovation firm – wrote in his column for *Forbes* magazine that "Having a national brand matters, because it makes products emerging from that nation more meaningful. It gives them a context, and makes them part of a continuing legacy of quality, design, smarts, whatever."[1]

A product's nation brand – also called country-of-origin – helps differentiate it from competitors in the globalized and highly competitive world market. As stated by Natalie Domeisen, "A positive national image is an essential ingredient for export promotion."[2] She points out that countries must be sure they understand how they are perceived abroad and that national characteristics selected for promotion have a basis in business reality. Research shows that the importance of the country of origin has grown along with globalization. With cosmetic products, say French cosmetics professionals, the "Made in France" designation adds value to a product. It is "part of the brand's capital, proving products with a veritable added value."[3]

The nation brand builds on the idea of a product brand and company brand. On the level of a product, a brand differentiates a company's products from those of its competitors and associates them with positive attributes, a process marketers call product differentiation. Many meanings are associated with a product brand. Richard Weiner in his *Webster's New World Dictionary of Media and Communications* defined a brand as "the distinctive name of a product, the word part of a trademark; sometimes the name of the manufacturer."[4] Laurence Urdang in the *Dictionary of Advertising Terms*, defines a brand as a graphic symbol, a word or words, or combination of both that distinguishes a product or service of one seller from those of others.[5] The public relations firm of Hill & Knowlton defines a brand as "the sum of perceptions, held primarily by a company's current and potential customers or clients, about a company's specific product, service, or line of products or services."[6]

Wally Olins, who died in 2014, was known as the high priest of branding. He thought companies spend as much time thinking about their brands as their products. He told his clients "they needed to think more seriously about the collective identity of their organizations."[7] This refers to the second level of a brand, namely, the company brand, or what public relations professionals prefer to call the company reputation. Millward Brown, a consulting firm, states that the top 100 brands worldwide were worth $3.3 trillion in 2015.[8]

Corporate Communication: An International and Management Perspective, First Edition. Otto Lerbinger.

On the level of a company, a company brand is an umbrella covering all of its product brands. Like a company's reputation, it tells how well known and liked a company is and what attributes are associated with it. Attributes like "progressive," and "innovative" enlarge the perception of a product brand. Other attributes, such as being socially responsible, pertain to a company's customer relations and assist in such campaigns as cause-related marketing. The attribute of being friendly is especially helpful in marketing because it adds a positive dimension to other attributes.

13.1 Differences between Brand and Reputation

Although the terms company reputation and company brand are often used synonymously, a *Sloan Management Review* article advises, "Don't Confuse Reputation with Brand." The distinction is that a brand is a "'customer centric' concept that focuses on what a product, service or company has promised to its customers and what that commitment means to them."[9] In contrast, reputation is a "'company-centric' concept that focuses on the credibility and respect that an organization has among a broad set of constituencies, including employees, investors, regulators, journalists, and local communities – as well as customers." "Ibid."

Despite their differences, a brand and reputation share the characteristics that both are intangible assets and both rely on strategic communications to shape people's perceptions. But reputation is affected by more factors and publics than a brand, including management strength, financial performance, innovation, treatment of employees, and handling of other issues. As with a person, a company's reputation reflects its moral standing. Its importance was noted by Warren Buffet, the well-known US investor and head of Berkshire Hathaway, who in one of his memos to his staff famously said, "Our reputation is our only asset. Without it, we are worthless."[10]

Faith in product and company brands, however, may be dropping. According to a poll by Havas, North American consumers say they trust only about a fifth of brands, and in Europe it's about a third. Big brands are more vulnerable, with about 36% saying they trust them versus about a half who trust small companies. In brand-conscious China, foreign brands were losing market share in 18 out of 26 categories of consumer goods, according to a study by Bain, a consulting firm. The ability of consumers to consult the social media to determine a product's underlying merits and demerits has weakened the power of brands. To offset this trend, companies are striving to bestow "authenticity" on their brands, says Schumpeter in *The Economist*. It's easier to do, he says, when a product has some "real-world qualities that its competitors lack." Interbrand, a consultant on branding, describes "authenticity as an internal truth and capability," a "defined heritage" and a "well-grounded value set."[11]

13.1.1 Anholt-GfK Roper Nation Brands Index

The Anholt-GfK Roper Nation Brands Index (NBI) uses a panel of over 20 000 ordinary people in 20 different countries to find out how they really think about other countries – their people, the products, the governments, the culture, the education, the tourist attractions, and the lifestyle.[12] For example, the NBI 2013 found that the US was voted the top country for attracting talent and investment (but with a reducing lead); Canada, Germany, the UK, and Switzerland are listed as the top five brands with positive perceptions. In 2014, Germany replaced the US for the top position as the world's most admired country.[13]

Simon Anholt is an independent policy advisor who helps national, regional, and city governments develop and implement strategies for enhanced economic, political, and cultural engagement with other countries. He states that reputation management is essential: "the reputations of countries function like the brand images of companies and that they are equally critical to the progress and prosperity of those countries."[14] And just as reputation management for organizations is about how you treat every stakeholder in the business and meet the expectations of those people in whose lives you play a part, the same is true of how nations handle relationships.[15]

13.2 Building and Strengthening a Nation State

A country's government rather than its companies has the chief responsibility to build and strengthen a nation state. Two processes are involved: nation-building and economic development. The private sector is particularly involved with the second of these.

13.2.1 Nation-Building

Nation-building has been an emerging opportunity in developing nations. One way public relations contributes to nation-building is by promoting government campaigns that will rally citizens together to support a policy or a cause that will lead to the betterment of society and the nation. Such a nation would be cohesive, united, harmonious, happy, progressive, and growing in tandem with the world.

As stated by Abdulrahman H. Al-Anad, a Saudi Arabian professor educated in the US, public relations in a developing nation works as an information office in ministries and governmental agencies. Its goals are typically those of government: to gain support and compliance with government programs. Examples are to encourage parents to send their children to school, cooperate with immunization efforts, and generally to publicize achievements of the government and the society as a whole, i.e. to "make the public feel satisfied."[16]

13.2.1.1 Country Examples: Singapore, Malaysia, and Nigeria

Singapore engaged in nation-building in a serious way after becoming its own republic in 1965. The government sought social cohesion at any cost by creating shared values, a common will and a single national identity among the Chinese, Malaysian and Indian peoples. It also conducted several campaigns on "anti-litter," "lungs for Singapore," and "Speak Mandarin."[17]

In Malaysia, the government is the major employer of public relations and uses it for nation-building. It seeks to establish cultural acceptance among its various ethnic groups. Its strategy has been to enhance interactive, ethical, and sustainable communication to win the understanding and support of various publics. Media relations is the government's main activity, which is aided by being a major owner of newspapers as well as using other print, audio, and visual media. Internet usage has also risen.

Nation-building in Nigeria involved an attempt by one of its regions, Biafra, to gain independence.

13.2.1.2 Biafra's Attempt to Gain Independence from Nigeria

Although Nigeria gained its independence from Britain in 1960, it faced the challenges of military coups and a civil war to become a nation. To do so, the Nigerian government continued the public relations activities of the British colonial administration by creating the Federal Ministry of Information. Its public relations tasks were formidable, for it had to remove Nigeria's negative image, fight rampant corruption, encourage foreign companies to invest in Nigeria, and eradicate poverty and several communicable diseases, including HIV/AIDS. Public relations was employed not only by government but also by several human rights organizations and organized labor. Corporations embarked on public relations by starting in-house services in speechwriting, public speaking, and media training.[18]

Nation-building was difficult, for Nigeria consists of about 250 ethnic groups, with three major tribes accounting for over 40% of the population. A major challenge to the government was when one group, the Ibos in the Eastern region, announced their independence in May 1967 and called itself the Republic of Biafra.[19] Two months later Nigeria declared war on Biafra.

A special application of international public relations was when Biafra engaged in a public relations campaign to gain international recognition and enlisted the help of a New York public relations firm, Ruder & Finn (R&F). The plan was "to conduct a program of general public and government relations" by calling a conference of "leaders in business and public life whose judgments have extraordinary influence on mainstream of American thought," and to seek support from friendly congressmen. The plan was for a Biafran representative in New York and an R&F staff member to visit selected congressmen and senators. This involvement required R&F to comply with the Foreign Agents Registration Act, which requires counselors who serve foreign governments to register with the US attorney general and provide the names of the foreigners for whom they work, the activities they carry out, and where they get and spend their money.[20]

Biafra hoped to influence public opinion, having faith that if Biafra's story were known, goodwill would result. The belief was, "Given the facts, people will change." It wanted to take their case "directly to the American people" and help them understand the plight in which eastern Nigeria found itself, the causes of the situation, and the enormity of the refugee problem. It asked R&F to "help us tell our story."

The Biafra representative requested that an ad be placed with the *New York Times* and *Washington Post.* But when R&F examined the full-page ad authored by them, it did not agree with some of the ad's contents and ultimately the ad was not published. It said that after careful consideration it came to the conclusion that the appearance of an ad would be interpreted as a disruptive event, no matter how factual and justified, and harm the interests of eastern Nigeria. Biafra assumed that the public was knowledgeable, interested, and caring. But it was unlikely that Americans would be interested in the ad, for they know little of Nigeria and had never heard of Biafra. R&F recommended an "artillery approach" of allowing newspaper reporters and magazine writers to visit eastern Nigeria. However, R&F's relationship did not last.

13.2.2 Economic Development

A major application of the nation brand is in a country's economic development efforts. Countries want to increase their gross domestic product (GDP) to create more jobs and improve standards of living, and, in developing countries, to reduce poverty. The eradication of extreme poverty and hunger is one of the United Nations' eight Millennium Development Goals. To achieve their goal, many countries place multi-page advertisements in newspapers and magazines extolling their benefits and building nation brands.[21]

The stage of a country's economic development affects the practice of corporate communication. Developing nations are more aware of using public relations and marketing to stimulate growth through tourism and attracting industry. They know that they need more economic activity, along with better infrastructure, both physical and social. In contrast, developed economies are populated with more businesses, government assistance, and civil society organizations. Although the role of corporate communication in foreign investment decisions is limited, its involvement becomes essential after business operations are established. Its overall role is to help a multi-national corporation (MNC) keep risk and uncertainty to a minimum and to create favorable conditions for sales and operations.

Economic development involves both government and civil society. Governments may facilitate trade and investment by removing or reducing restrictions such as tariffs and import quotas and providing positive incentives such as tax breaks and creating free trade zones. These are geographic areas where goods can be landed, handled, manufactured, and reconfigured without the intervention of custom authorities. Civil society institutions can help by strengthening the educational system and helping solve social problems that impede progress.

13.2.2.1 Tourism

Tourism is often considered the world's largest industry, although it is actually a collection of industries.[22] Either way, it is not surprising that developing nations give tourism a high priority as a means of stimulating economic development. Tourism is a major application of public relations and marketing. It illustrates the value of a distinctive nation brand. When a country seeks to become a tourist "destination," it examines its special and perhaps unique natural and cultural resources and searches for locations of potential tourists who would most be attracted to them.

A useful approach to tourism is to apply a SWOT analysis that lists a destination's strengths, weaknesses, opportunities, and threats. Turkey, for example, boasts of its diversity of tourist attractions such as the recreational activities of yachting, cruising, hunting, golf, mountaineering, spelunking, rafting, and diving. It also mentions its historic sites, such as "the exotic allure of Istanbul at the monumental Blue Mosque and Topkapi Palace . . . and some of the oldest – and best preserved – ruins of ancient empires."[23] Mexico lists its historic Inca sites and ocean beaches, but it would also have to recognize the threats of criminal activity. Similarly Jamaica must contend with the threat of drug-smuggling and rising crime.

New forms of tourism have appeared, such as ecotourism and medical tourism.Ecotourism has been one of the fastest-growing sectors of travel, as recognized by the Madrid-based World Tourism Organization and the United Nations Environment Programme (UNEP).[24] The scope of medical tourism includes cosmetic surgery in countries like Brazil and South Korea and dental care in Budapest, Hungary. The Medical Tourist Association estimated 1.3 million medical tourists a year visit Asia alone. In India, some spas are applying the country's 50 000-year-old massage tradition. One customer, a Chicago lawyer, was slathered for about an hour with oil containing pungent herbs along the length of her body. A trendy treatment is *ayurveda*, which involves a massage and, sometimes, dietary advice and yoga.[25]

A tourism plan applies the model of a communications campaign[26] or marketing communications (MARCOM) campaign (discussed in Part II). Special attention is paid to demographics to identify categories of people, such as northern Europeans who relish warm climates in winter, or those with the greatest amount of leisure time, such as the elderly .Michael Hayman, the author of *The Power of Destinations Why It Matters to Be Different*, sees public relations as playing a large role.[27] He states: "Public relations is set to be at the frontline in helping locations around the world become destinations. This is because good public relations is central to harnessing and communicating the authentic 'legends and stories' that make people want to visit, and work in, these places."[28] Some of the typical communication tools used are print or TV advertising, exhibitions, and window displays at travel agencies, and visits by travel editors.

13.2.3 Attracting Industry: Approaches by Countries and Cities

Economic development is stimulated by attracting foreign investments. The strengths of a nation state are displayed. A country can reach a wide business audience by advertising its profile and opportunities in major newspapers such as the *New York Times* or journals such as *Foreign Affairs*. Cities and states may do similarly. Several examples are ads by Poland, Kenya, and Dubai, and a campaign by Charleston, South Carolina.

13.2.3.1 Poland, Kenya, and Dubai

A one-page advertisement in *The Economist* features an article, "Poland continues to draw investors," by Poland's Minister of Economy.[29] Typical of such ads, it lists the advantages of investing in Poland:

- In its large economy, exports account for about 40% of GDP.
- Polish entrepreneurs show a flair for business; they exhibit "entrepreneurial dynamism."
- Low unit labor costs and in one of Organisation for Economic Co-operation and Developments (OECD) hardest working nations.
- Well-educated, competitive, and smart workforce.
- Stable government.
- Debt is under control; fiscal conservatism is exercised.
- "The story of Poland as a smart, fast-growing, politically stable and culturally vibrant country."

Kenya sought to stimulate its economic development with an eight-page insert in the May–June 2014 issue of the *Foreign Affairs* journal. Its headline was "Ready to Accelerate – East African Powerhouse Lays Foundations for Future Growth." In saying, "The Kenyan economy is on a runway and wants to take off," it builds on the reputation of its world-renowned marathon runners. It refers to the incentive of improved government by slashing bureaucracy and introducing "devolved" government that grants greater autonomy to the 47 counties, three of which advertised in the insert. Four banks also placed ads. One of them, CfC Stanbic Bank, had a full-page ad headlined "Kenya is a shining investment opportunity." It claims to understand the development needs of the country and states, "Over the years, we have helped structure finance and support growth in infrastructure, agriculture, energy and power."

Dubai, the second largest emirate of the Gulf region, placed an eight-page advertising insert in *Forbes* to fortify its position as the "undisputed hub for business trade, financial services tourism, leisure and shopping" for business, trade, and finance in the Middle East, North Africa, and South Asia region.[30] Its major promotion agency is the Dubai Chamber of Commerce and Industry, established in 1965. It now has three overseas branch offices and plans to increase the number to 20 in 5 years. It actively pursues business opportunities abroad and to do so it attended 41 trade events across 25 countries in the first 6 months of 2014 alone and hosted 102 visiting international trade delegations.

According to Steen Jakobsen, director of Dubai business events, Dubai has made the "meetings, incentives conventions and exhibitions industry a priority area within its bigger economic development approach" and is the leading city for Middle Eastern business events. Dubai launched the Dubai International Financial Centre in 2004 to "serve as a gateway for capital and financial services between East and West." It aims to become the global hub of the Islamic economy, estimated to be worth $2.47 billion by 2018. It also looks to become a major participant in "the production, supply, certification and standards for food products compliant with Islamic law."

13.2.3.2 Charleston and Beaufort County, South Carolina

Chambers of commerce play a major role in economic development of cities, states, and regions. Charleston, South Carolina, gave it a high priority and hired R&F to explore the possibilities of attracting industry to the city. It recognized the obstacle that leaders in its well-known historical district did not want to blight its attractiveness. Based on interviews with business and community leaders, the Chamber supported further economic development but recommended that only "clean" industries be sought.

The nearby resort of Hilton Head Island was also concerned about the environmental problems of industrialization in and around Charleston. It had previously battled with the

German chemical manufacturer BASF and the state of South Carolina. In 1969, BASF announced a plan to build a petrochemical plant in an area of Beaufort County. The company used the classical marketplace approach of viewing its decision in terms of efficiency and profitability. It ignored the business ecology model, which examines the broader relationships between business with various interests and concerns in a community and society. For example, it did not consider the environmental impact of drawing some 2.5 million gallons of water a day from the adjacent Colleton River and then dumping polluted water back. Furthermore, the reshaping of the river bottom would ruin shrimp and oyster beds, creating an economic disaster for the local fishing industry.

BASF committed many blunders. One was that it never revealed to the public exactly what kind of plant it planned to build, nor outlined its specific plans to prevent pollution. Nor did it conduct community research to determine who its allies or opposition might be. It did not hold meetings with business, environmental, church, and other citizen groups. BASF eventually withdrew from Beaufort and sold the land back to the state. The case illustrates that companies and governments that seek economic development must be aware of the environmental standards that communities demand. Often, however, communities in developing nations and communities don't have the power to overcome the pressures from companies seeking new locations and governments eager for more economic development.

13.3 Strategy to Attract Foreign Investment

Even a developed country may seek investments in selected industries. One country's investment authorities (not mentioned for reasons of confidentiality) sought to attract companies in five industries from the US. It hired a public relations firm to develop a plan. The following major steps were outlined:

- Examine the literature to learn how companies make investment decisions: what departments are involved, what factors are considered, and who makes the decisions.
- Prepare a document showing the economic strengths of the client country, its standing on political risk factors, and the advantages of its geographical location.
- Send letters and promotional material to designated executives.
- Decide on an advertising campaign in selected media, which included the *New York Times*, *BusinessWeek* and trade magazines of the five industries, e.g. *Chemical World*. Also advertise in banking publications to reach bankers that prospective investors might consult.
- Prepare advertising copy to announce the investment opportunity, present fundamental information, and state where more information might be obtained.
- Arrange meetings in cities for executives that have expressed interest. Announce these meetings in local media so that others might attend. Government officials from the client's country would attend, and, importantly, representatives of businesses that had facilities there.
- Invite executives from companies that expressed serious interest to visit the country and meet with government officials and executives from companies that had invested in the country.

These steps incorporate ideas from the diffusion of innovation (see Chapter 15). It was deemed important that personal contacts with both knowledgeable people and those who were familiar with the risk were included in the plan.

13.4 How Nation Brands Are Tarnished

What people read and hear in the media and their personal experiences with a country influence their perceptions and attitudes of it. Other impressions of a country may come from personal visits, reports from friends and relatives, and, most frequently, from experience with its products and services. Negative events get much media attention, such as the kidnaping in Nigeria of 200-plus girls from a school on April 14, 2014, by the terrorist group Boko Haram. The leader of this group, who has made bloodcurdling threats to kill all Christians, said, "I took the girls. By Allah I will sell them in the marketplace. I will marry off a woman at the age of 12. I may sell off a girl at the age of nine."[31] The most damaging aspect has been the report that the Nigerian government was negligent in handling the abduction and seemingly indifference to the plight of the girls' families.

13.4.1 Reputational Risks and Crises

A nation brand is damaged when the products a company sells are deficient or when a country's statements and actions are deemed undesirable. In the aftermath of the vanishing Malaysian Airline flight from Malaysia to Beijing, both the airline and the Malaysian government damaged their brands by their ineptness in crisis communication. It took 5 hours for the airline to admit that it had lost contact with the aircraft, keeping anxious relatives in Beijing bundled into a hotel room waiting for information. Subsequent information was patchy and often wrong. Malaysia Airlines' CEO Ahmad Jauhari Yahya did address the crisis via press briefings, but the search area was initially given as being off the Vietnamese coast and the flight time given as 1 hour before contact was lost, and not the 5 hours that was later disclosed. The situation was, however, later helped by the airline's digital response. Lack of international experience by Malaysia Airlines public relations was named as a problem, as was government inexperience.[32]

The auto industry worldwide has experienced several crises. In the highly publicized Toyota recall in 2010 of 2.3 million cars, not only was the company's reputation damaged, but so was Japan's reputation as a reliable producer.[33] Honda Motor Co. faced $70 million in fines for not submitting early warning reports detailing 1729 death and injury claims for 11 years up to 2014. Honda acknowledged that its reporting systems contained "systemic failure" that led to the reporting failures. The company had also been dealing with defective Takata Corp. air bags prone to explosions, which were linked to five deaths worldwide.[34]

The biggest fines have been imposed on General Motors (GM) for failing to alert regulators to a deadly ignition-switch problem, for which it will pay a $900 million penalty. The defect led to a recall of roughly 2.6 million vehicles and was linked to 124 deaths. GM launched an internal investigation, dismissed employees over their handling of the switch defect, and established a compensation fund for victims. No executives were charged for the problem.[35] The latest event is the admission by Volkswagen in September 2015 that it falsified its diesel engine emissions (which is discussed in Case 8).

13.4.1.1 China's Sanlu Milk and Mattel Toys

When the milk industry in China was found to cause the death of six infants and injury to 50 000 others, China's nation brand was severely damaged. The crisis focused on China's largest milk producer, the Shijazhuang Sanlu Group. The company at first denied that it had a problem and, after confirming that it had one, it delayed making a public announcement, partly because it did not want to disturb the nation-building efforts of the 2008 Beijing Olympics. When a country does not give top priority to the protection of public health and safety, its nation brand suffers.

The Chinese nation brand also suffered earlier when Mattel, the US's largest seller of toys, withdrew nearly 1 million lead-tainted toys made in China from the market. The damage to the

Chinese nation brand was worsened when Mattel's chairman and CEO Bob Eckhart immediately blamed the media, saying "the character of Mattel has been maligned." Furthermore, at a Senate subcommittee hearing, Eckhart directly blamed China for the product recall, saying that certain Chinese vendors or their subcontractors violated its "well-established rules."[36] However, in an about-face, Mattel's executive vice president for worldwide operations, Thomas A. Debrowski, later apologized to China, saying that the vast majority of the recalled products were "the result of a design flaw in Mattel's design, not through a manufacturing flaw in Chinese manufacturers."[37] But the damage had been done.

Juan Carlos Molleda, former chairman of the public relations department at Florida University, summarized some lessons learned from such crises:

- Transnational businesses and national governments involved in a cross-national conflict should analyze and project the highest picks of news coverage to proactively respond and follow up other actors' responses through mediated, interpersonal, and controlled communications.
- Knowing the world locations from where the news stories are filed by news agencies and global or large media outlets would allow for better coordination and control of the crisis response strategies. The availability of culturally appropriate spokespeople and the timely provision of information subsidies according to time zones would result in a coordinated and consistent strategic communication function.
- A close look at the series and chronologically published headlines and lead paragraphs facilitates the identification of key terms that define a transnational crisis and its main actors. In this study, the most cited terms were "tainted," "safety concerns," and "poor quality." The study also found significant associations between these key terms and the transnational businesses and national governments involved. The symbolic associations and the issues raised by the key terms should be a component of key messages and response actions of a strategic communication plan during the crisis. These terms may change during the chronological cycle of the cross-national conflict shift.

  What is important to reiterate is that government and transnational business representatives are the most cited and quoted sources in global and national news coverage. Thus, an efficient coordination and control of responses and actions, as well as location of information subsidies provision would increase the likelihood of a successful crisis control program.
- Finally, international news agencies appear to have different professional standards and policies regarding the use of news sources. In this study, Agence France-Presse (AFP) and Xinhua cited and quoted Chinese sources more often, and Associated Press (AP) cited and quoted a variety of other sources, including activist and consumer groups. This may indicate that some news sources may have various levels of access to the media to share their positions. Understanding the reporting practices of influential media outlets and agencies would refine the development and provision of information subsidies with key messages, actions, and other responses of the actors involved in a transnational crisis. This may allow for a better coordination and control of strategic communication responses globally.[38]

13.5 Strengthening a Nation Brand

Even in countries that have not experienced a major reputational crisis, efforts are undertaken to strengthen their nation brands. For example, an American branding expert suggested that South Korea needs to build up a stronger nation brand to give momentum to business powerhouses and let products of other Korean companies benefit from the brand power.

According to Samsung Economic Research Institute, the nation brand of Korea ranked 13th in 2012, up two spots from the previous year.[39] The Lee Myung-bak administration has repeatedly stressed its desire to improve the Korea brand. It became the first country to establish a presidential council on the issue to coordinate and support efforts to bolster the nation's image. But the council admits it isn't even aware of all nation branding projects, and its chairman's primary aim of replacing the "Dynamic Korea" slogan remains undone.[40] As well as people's contact with executives, products, and services, or with employees of a country's foreign subsidiaries, efforts to improve a nation's brand can be stimulated by some special strategies. Among these are sponsorship or participation in Olympics events.

13.5.1 Olympics

The Olympics are known as the foremost way for a country to attract world attention to its nation brand. China hosted the Summer Olympic Games on August 8–24, 2008, at a cost of $42 billion to put the country on the world stage. It was the most watched in history, attracting 4.7 million viewers worldwide. Viewers could see some spectacular infrastructure, which demonstrated China's technological progress. But they could also see the downside of dense smog in the Beijing Olympic site, even though many surrounding smoke-producing factories were shuttered during the games. Along with international brands, such as Coca-Cola, McDonald's, Visa, and Samsung, Chinese brands such as Lenovo and Haier got a big boost.[41]

London's 2012 "Brand Britain" Olympics is also considered hugely successful. It enabled Britain to overtake Japan as the fourth most valuable nation brand, according to the Anholt-GfK Roper NBI.[42] The event improved Britain's sporting credentials said *Brand Republic.*[43] The Olympics are also worldwide opportunities for a country's companies, as recognized by Samsung's sponsorship of the London 2012 Olympic Games. The value of success is more important than ever, according to leading York accountants Garbutt & Elliott. Boosted by the Olympics and Diamond Jubilee, "Brand Britain" was now worth £1.4 billion and had become the world's fourth most valuable nation brand.[44]

The Winter Olympics held in Sochi, Russia, in February 2014, was intended to bolster Russia's nation brand and to introduce people to the recreational facilities in and around Sochi. It was the most expensive Olympics ever, costing $51 billion. The Olympics followed the sports supremacy policy of the Soviet Union era, which sought to enhance the status of the USSR and Soviet communism abroad – to show the masses the advantages of socialism over capitalism.[45] In Sochi, however, its benefits were soon overshadowed when President Putin seized Crimea, which was part of the Ukraine. The US and Europe were outraged by the action and whatever goodwill the Olympics created was largely destroyed. The Olympics cannot triumph over political deficits.

Besides the Olympics, other events such as the 2014 Fédération Internationale de Football Association (FIFA) World Cup held in 12 cities across Brazil can also affect a country's nation brand. When Brazil lost the soccer game to Germany in home territory, its nation brand suffered, at least temporarily, and Germans were joyous because "A positive attitude would really do Germany good."[46]

13.6 World Economic Forum

The World Economic Forum brings together some 2500 top business leaders, international political leaders, selected intellectuals, and journalists, for a meeting to discuss the most pressing issues facing the world, including health and the environment. Participation in it can produce valuable positive publicity for a nation.

The World Economic Forum is a Swiss non-profit foundation, based in Cologny, Geneva, and headed by Klaus Schwab, its executive chair. It describes itself as an independent international organization committed to improving the state of the world by engaging business, political, academic, and other leaders of society to shape global, regional, and industry agendas. The forum is best known for its annual winter meeting in Davos, a mountain resort in Graubünden, in the eastern Alps region of Switzerland. Often reference to this location alone is used to identify meetings, participation, and participants with such phrases as, "a Davos panel" and "a Davos Man."

The Annual Meeting of the World Economic Forum at the beginning of the year provides an unparalleled platform for leaders to map the complexity and interconnectivity of the changing world. The aim is to develop the insights, initiatives, and actions necessary to respond to current and emerging challenges. It achieves this by convening global leaders from across business, government, international organizations, academia, and civil society in a series of strategic dialogues that map the key transformations reshaping the world. The meetings serve another purpose: polishing corporate and national images.[47]

Taking a 10-year outlook, the World Economic Forum's report assesses 31 risks that are global in nature and have the potential to cause significant negative impact across entire countries and industries if they take place. The risks are grouped under five categories – economic, environmental, geopolitical, societal, and technological – and measured in terms of their likelihood and potential impact.

13.7 Conclusions

The nation brand connects the public relations concept of reputation and the marketing concept of brand to a nation. Although government rather than corporations are responsible for a nation brand, corporations are affected by a nation brand because it is added to its product brands and company brand (i.e. reputation). Countries may also design specific programs that show that they are safe and reliable for conducting business as well as specific advantages of investing in them. Public relations firms have helped in designing some programs to attract foreign investment.

As with companies, nations are afflicted with reputational crises. Often, as with the Toyota, Sanlu, and Mattel crises, damage to a company also damages a nation brand. The reverse also holds: Samsung's innovative products and reputation have helped South Korea fortify its national brand. A nation brand is also strengthened when nations and companies participate in such special occasions and events as the World Economic Forum, and such sports events as the World Cup.

Discussion Questions

13.1. Why is a nation's brand important for a company?

13.2. In what ways is a company's reputation different from a nation brand?

13.3. Why should a developing nation pay attention to its nation brand? Give an example.

13.4. What was Biafra's strategy in seeking recognition as an independent state? Was it a sound strategy?

13.5. Why is tourism a particularly important industry for a developing country?

13.6. What mistakes did BASF make when it tried to expand to the Charleston area of South Carolina?

13.7. What sorts of company characteristics are included in the Anholt-GfK Roper NBI?

13.8. What advice would you give a country that wants to attract companies in another country to build factories in it?

13.9. How are nation brands tarnished? Discuss a specific situation?

13.10. What are some ways a country can bolster its nation brand?

Case 5 Can Public Relations Promote Globalization?

If public relations, one of the communication practices of corporate communication, is the art and science of influencing public opinion, can it help promote globalization and stave off opposition to it? In the US, could public relations help stave off protectionist sentiments by some Americans? In the UK, could public relations have stopped Brexit? The majority of companies in the UK were in favor of "Remain," which favored globalization, but the voice of these companies was mute. Their single big effort seemingly was to place a newspaper ad against Brexit signed by 500 company executives.

Unfortunately, one of the requirements for influencing public opinion is the credibility of the sender. Fewer and fewer people look up to business leaders, and opinion surveys show that employees are uncertain whether their bosses are on their side. CEOs are seen as benefiting themselves when they hear that their board of directors grant them ever higher salaries and bonuses. This perception is reinforced by such headlines as "Expedia CEO's Pay Nears $95 Million,"[48] "At Yahoo, CEO Pay Exceeds $27 Million,"[49] and articles stating that "Google Chief Executive Sundar Pichai's pay package doubled to $200 million last year [2016], making him the highest paid executive at parent company Alphabet Inc."[50] The average ratio of executive salaries of major companies is over 300 to 1. Most businesses were operating on the classical business creed that the sole purpose of a business was to maximize profits for a company's owners. And for some CEOs the goal seemed to be personal benefit.

Opposing views

Populism is on the march in the Western world, concludes Fareed Zakaria, a journalist and host on CNN's "Fareed." He says that a common meaning of populism is "a suspicion of and hostility toward elites mainstream politics, and established institutions."[51] He cites a research paper for Harvard's Kennedy School of Government by Ronald Inglehart and Pippa Norris, which estimates that since the 1960s populist parties of the left have seen more than a five-fold increase in their share of the vote in European countries, and populists of the right have doubled theirs. This trend was shaped by the basic twentieth-century left–right divide. Left-wing parties stand for increased government spending, a larger welfare state, and regulation of business. Right-wing ones seek limited government, fewer safety nets, and more laissez-faire politics.[52] But economics, say Inglehart and Norris, is now no longer the pivot of politics. In the US, views on such social issues as same-sex marriage, gender, and race dominate voting preferences. They conclude the broader explanation is that cultural values predominate.

Business Should Address Issues in Employee Relations Programs

In the UK's Brexit vote, sentiments against immigration, particularly by workers, dominated. Zakaria states that immigration is the final frontier of globalization. It accelerates the pace of change in a society, which, he says, can be too fast for society to digest. Western countries, he says, must devote more resources to integration and assimilation. They also need stronger retraining programs for displaced workers easily available to all – and with the government, the private sector, and educational institutions all participating.[53]

The implication for corporate communication is that stakeholder relations with employees and local communities should take on the task of helping in the assimilation process by their employers. A precedent is that when race was a major employee issue in the US, many employee communication programs openly discussed the issue and some CEOs unequivocally demanded that employees accommodate the new employees. In France too, some employers such as PSA Peugeot Citroen SA and L'Oreal, hired Muslim youths.[54]

The Precedent: Employee Economic Programs in the US

Addressing the broader issue of the free market system, which supports globalization, many American companies after World War II inaugurated economic education programs for their employees. They sought to stem communist and socialist ideologies that were taking hold in Europe.

A particularly favored program was "How Our Business System Operates," which was developed by the right-wing Heritage Foundation. Employees were generally given time off from work to participate in several sessions, which reviewed such topics as the function of capital in supporting jobs. They also learned that profits were important not only as an incentive for conducting a business but also as a source of further investment. The question now is whether such a program on the subject of globalization might win advocates for it.

The conclusion from several studies of economic education programs, however, is that while they helped employees better understand the economic system, they did not gain support by themselves for the free enterprise system. What counted is employee satisfaction with their jobs and a feeling that they were getting ahead.

The same might apply to globalization. Opposition has grown over recent decades because of dissatisfaction with the economic system. Too many jobs in the US were seen as lost when companies outsourced production to low-wage countries. Overlooked were other explanations for job loss, such as the impact of new technologies, which made many unskilled and semi-skilled jobs obsolete.

The Economist recently displayed Canada on its cover page, showing it as an "example to the world."[55] It admitted 321 000 immigrants in the year to June 2016, nearly 1% of its population. It encourages immigrants to keep their cultures and continues its habit of accommodation. Canada has a generous safety net with unemployment benefits replacing a much larger share of lost income than in America, and its universal healthcare makes a huge difference in creating a high level of public security. Furthermore, the new prime minister, Justin Trudeau, has raised taxes on the top 1% of incomes to help pay for a middle-class tax cut.

The lesson to be learned is two-fold: First, when globalization helped employers retain or grow the number of jobs, employee communications should include those stories. Had British companies that benefited from trade done this, the Brexit referendum might likely have had a different outcome. Why didn't the nearly 500 MNCs that have their European or global headquarters in the UK voice an opinion?[56] Second, if globalization has reduced employment, companies should do more in the public affairs by advocating government programs that help worker to adjust to the realities of globalization.

Discussion Questions

1. Are business leaders in a position to influence their employees' attitudes toward globalization? Explain.

2. What is populism? How does it affect attitudes toward globalization?

3. What role, if any, can employee communications play in influencing worker attitudes toward globalization?

4. What can be learned from previous programs of employee economic education?

Case 6 Building China's Nation Brand

China realizes that its nation brand is one of its most important assets, adding value to sales and attracting investments. It is worrisome, therefore, that Joshua Cooper Ramo in his Brand China states that "China's greatest strategic threat today is its national image."[57] The future of Chinese development and reform, he says, lies with "How China is perceived by other nations – and the underlying reality that perception reflects."[58] Now that China has become the second largest world economy and its dream of becoming a world power has been achieved, it must fortify its nation brand and improve its relationship with other nations and businesses.[59]

Global opinion polls show that China enjoys a decidedly mixed international image. To improve its image it has mounted a major public relations offensive in recent years to increase its "soft power." Its main instrument is money, spending $50 billion for the Asian Infrastructure Investment Bank, $41 billion for the New Development Bank, $40 billion for the Silk Road Economic Belt, and $25 billion for the Maritime Silk Road.[60] The latter two investments support President Xi Jinping's initiative known as "One Belt, One Road." Furthermore, as an emblem of its inroads into the Middle East, China has recently completed a rail service to Tehran that delivers goods via Kazakhstan and Turkmenistan.[61]

China wants its policies to be understood and its culture to be embraced, said Ingrid d'Hooghe, senior research associate of Clingendael, Netherlands Institute of International Relations. But China's image in the Western world is often portrayed differently, she states, and the Chinese government is very much aware of this image and feels misjudged. It has undertaken efforts to promote global public diplomacy, a subject that was discussed at a seminar organized by the Carnegie-Tsinghua Center for Global Policy.[62]

Public Diplomacy

China shows great interest in public diplomacy and has clearly set its sights on learning how to promote Chinese soft power and express itself positively to the world, states Yiwei Wang.[63] He says that in recent years China has sought to supplement its traditional use of hard power with soft power, but the concept of public diplomacy is a foreign concept in China. The government usually uses the term *dui wai xuan chuan* or *wai xuan* (external propaganda) and emphasizes advertising Chinese achievements and boosting the country's image overseas. Propaganda has a positive connotation associated with such essentially benign activities as the release of news, general shaping of ideology, or advertising.

China has an official propaganda department run by the Central Committee of the Communist Party. The nerve center of these operations is the State Council Information Office (SCIO).[64] Its main role is to oversee the media and coordinate all of China's external communications. It supervises 3300-odd television stations, almost 2000 newspapers, and nearly 10 000 periodicals. Its official state news service, Xinhua News Agency, employs approximately 3000 journalists, 400 of whom are posted abroad in its 170 bureaus.

Its premier state television channel, CCTV (China Central Television), launched its first 24-hour English channel, CCTV International, in 2000 and now broadcasts in six languages around the world.

China's communist system has always thought that information must be managed and that people must be indoctrinated. Propaganda is thus not a derogatory term. But it recognizes that the term has negative connotations, so in English it calls itself the publicity department. The department deals only with party officials. Chinese President Xi Jinping seeks to use it to increase his control over the party. The department decides which speeches to print and how much to push a new campaign.[65]

An advertising campaign in 2009 by China's Ministry of Commerce focused on bringing forth some favorable changes to the perception of its exports. Entitled Made in China, Made with the World, the 30-second ad showcased five Chinese products with "American sports technology" (footwear); "European styling" (refrigerator); "software from Silicon Valley" (MP3 players); "French designers" (dress); and "engineers from all over the world" (airplane).[66] The campaign was considered successful because "the open, suggestive message strategy invites viewers to reconsider Chinese-made products." It was a factual approach, not a hard sell nor an overly optimistic message strategy.[67]

Thanks to its strong economic growth and the highly regarded 2008 Olympic Games, the national image of China has improved in recent years, according to a latest report on nation brands by the 2011 Anholt-GfK Roper NBI.[68]

Perception Gap

China's nation brand is said to suffer from a "perception gap" between its self-image and how some Western countries view it and its relationship to the world. In such situations, public relations employs gap analysis to decide how to respond to given survey results: should a communications campaign be launched to change public opinion, or does the fault lie with China, which should be prepared to consider a change in policies and behavior as it rises in global influence? Liu Kang, director of Duke China Research Center, believes in the latter, but China's suppression of opposing voices suggests that its willingness to change is limited.[69] Such suppression is becoming more difficult. China has over 2 million non-governmental organizations (NGOs), of which about 7000 are foreign. Tsinghua University reports there were 180 000 protests in 2010, which are likely to grow with the rise of the middle class.[70]

One way China's President Xi Jinpin seeks to reinforce his nation as a great world power is to forge a new nationalist ideology and gain a source of legitimacy by linking China with Confucian beliefs. He thereby seeks to inoculate Chinese people against the spread of Western political ideas of individual freedom and democracy. Confucius, who lived in the sixth and fifth centuries BCE, emphasized respect for elders, social ritual, and personal moral virtue. These values would justify China's authoritarian government as an extension of an ancient political tradition.[71]

Reference to China's culture gets both positive and negative reactions. On the one hand, the 2011 Anholt-Gfk Roper NBI, which annually measures the image of 50 nations, ranked China an impressive third for its "culture/heritage" brand. Countries with long histories and rich cultural resources tend to do well in this branding attribute, with France and Italy perennially topping the rankings. On the other hand, Joseph Nye has commented that the Chinese government just "doesn't get" soft power.[72] He quotes Pang Zhongying of Renmin University as describing Beijing's focus on promoting ancient cultural icons in terms of a "poverty of thought" among Chinese leaders. Ramo suggests infusing old cultural symbols with ideas of newness and innovation.[73] And in late 2006, Wu Youfu, vice president of the Shanghai Public Relations Association and chancellor of Shanghai Foreign Language University, suggested that China should use the panda rather than the dragon as its national symbol.

Another way for China to build its nation brand is for its private corporations and state-owned enterprises (SOEs) to lead the way and adopt "business diplomacy" initiatives. China's corporations are now among the largest and most internationalized companies in the world, playing an increasingly important role in the global economy. With their prominence and economic success come responsibilities and challenges that go beyond the commercial, say Jan Melissen and Paul Sharp, senior research fellows at the Netherlands Institute of International Relations in The Hague and co-editors of The Hague Journal of Diplomacy. China's large corporations have an impact on the country's reputation, for good or bad.[74]

Similar to corporate diplomacy, the concept of business diplomacy helps corporations identify and manage political and other non-commercial risks to their international operations. Calling it the GPS of the twenty-first century, the core purpose of business diplomacy is "to identify the political and other non-commercial risks to a corporation's international operations, identify those stakeholders who can influence or control those risks and develop strategies for the cultivation of key stakeholders and thus the more effective management of the risks."[75]

Events affect a nation brand. China's nation brand suffered when its toy industry was found to use dangerous lead paint and when its milk industry knowingly and secretly contaminated their baby formula with the toxic chemical melamine.[76] But when China sponsored the 2010 Olympics in Beijing, it gained worldwide attention and praise for its architectural and infrastructure accomplishments.

The risks must be analyzed in all international markets concurrently because measures taken in one country can adversely affect a corporation's operations in another or its reputation at home. For example, when Chinese companies first entered Africa, they were thought to be more enlightened than many Western corporations chiefly those in oil and mining, which were seen as sacrificing the environment and local communities. But now almost half of Africans have a negative impression of Chinese employment practices and sometimes perceive China as the continent's "new colonialist."[77]

Nonetheless, there are now more than 10 000 Chinese firms operating in Africa, according to a McKinsey & Co research project.[78] These firms have invested $34 billion in Africa over the past decade and employ millions of Africans. About one-third are in manufacturing. All 52 African countries with diplomatic relations with China have received investments.

Chinese companies in the past have failed to take into account the political and social aspects of their operations. A recent example is when Chinese solar panel manufacturers sought to sell their products more cheaply than their competitors in Europe, but were forced to limit their exports to avoid tough sanctions. The authors stated that had they applied business diplomacy they would have known to cultivate the powerful environmental lobby. "If they had convinced this lobby that they offered a cheap and effective way to reduce Europe's carbon emissions, they would have become untouchable by competitors."[79]

Public relations efforts to strengthen its nation brand may be helped by the rising number of national public relations firms. They are taking on foreign rivals, such as Burson-Marsteller and Hill & Knowlton Strategies, which came to China in the mid-1980s. Some communication agencies are listed on the Shenzhen Stock Exchange. The first in 2010 was BlueFocus Communications Group LLC, one of China's biggest marketing service companies. It earned $358 million in 2012 and grew almost 100% for the 3 years preceding 2015. Showing great confidence, its CEO Oscar Zhao believes his company has everything it takes to thrive on the global stage.

Continuing Economic Progress

China is no longer a country chiefly known for low labor costs and profitable destinations for direct investments. Instead of using only manufacturing parts used by Apple's iPhone 6 and iPhone 6 Plus, China's Huawei, already the world's third largest smart phone maker, is now challenging Apple, as well as the other global leader, Samsung Electronics Co. Huawei, and other Chinese technology giants such as ZTE Corporation and Lenovo Group Ltd. are doing this by acquiring patents through licensing deals, acquisitions, and major spending on research and development.

High-speed rail exemplifies the Chinese government's prowess at identifying priority industries and investing in them. It has the world's fastest long-distance bullet train, which speeds at 350 kph between Beijing and Shanghai. In total, it has 20 000 km of high-speed track, more than the rest of the world combined. Some of its new industrial targets are alternative energy and biotechnology, which are part of its "Made in China 2025" scheme announced in 2015.[80]

In 2015, Huawei was the largest filer of international patent applications under the Patent Cooperation Treaty Corporation, which makes it easier for companies to file patents in multiple countries. Huawei has increased its number of patents through its extensive R&D investments, which totaled nearly $30 billion in 2015.[81] Fearing other challenges in China – such as shutting down Apple's iBooks and iTunes Movies services – Apple's CEO Tim Cook has made diplomatic efforts to win goodwill. He has traveled to China more than any other country in the past 3 years and is on the advisory board of Tsinghua University's School of Economics and Management.

The digital giant Alibaba is listed on the New York Stock Exchange, and the smart phone company Xiaomi is going global. Lenova produces more computers than any company in the world. Tencent, China's largest internet company, is now the fastest growing brand in the world. As for nation brands, China is in second place in the Brand Finance Nation Brands report, valued at $6.4 trillion. It follows the US, which continues its domination with brand value of $19.3 trillion.

China has intensified its foreign investments. In 2013, China's Shuanghui purchase of the American meat giant Smithfield for $4.7 billion was the largest Chinese takeover of a US company. Since then China's Haier Group has negotiated with General Electric to buy its appliance business for more than $4 billion.[82] Its newest acquisitions target small and medium-size German engineering companies, such as the robot maker Kuka AG, which is a leader in factory automation. China seeks to become a manufacturing superpower by rebuilding its economy around services and "smart manufacturing" that connects machines digitally to logistics networks and customers.[83] Its outbound direct investment is for the first time set to exceed investment in the country, with many Chinese companies going global. In 2014,Chinese foreign direct investment (FDI) globally reached $101 billion, with $12 billion going to the US.[84]

China has a hybrid socialist market economy consisting in part of SOEs and businesses in the free market system. Its government highly regulates the economy through barriers of free entry, antitrust actions, and other interventions, showing that while it professes to move closer to a free market system, it still intervenes to achieve its economic goals. An example is that when its financial markets plunged in August 2015, the government almost immediately intervened by forbidding SOEs to sell shares, buying hundreds of billions of dollars' worth of stocks, and lowering interest relates to stimulate stock purchases.[85]

China had succeeded in establishing two new stock markets: Shanghai, where 831 companies are listed, and Shenzhen with some 1700 companies. Reflecting the volatility of these markets, by June 2015 the Shenzhen market had risen 135% and Shanghai about 150%. Their combined market capitalization was more than $9.5 trillion.[86] The obedience of these markets to government wishes is limited, however, as the issues of economics and politics and those of psychology and authority became intertwined. In the future, states Orville Schell, the government's reputation would rise or fall with those of the market. That's the inevitable consequence of party leadership and a central government that purports to control so many aspects of Chinese life.

Conclusions

Zi Jinping is now venturing on having China "guide international society" toward a "more just and rational new world order." He also asserted that the Chinese people were "fully confident that they can provide a China solution to humanity's search for better social institutions." In the light of President Trump's retreat from globalization, China may see itself as "guiding globalization" but not challenging the existing global order. In 2015 it secured the adoption of the yuan as one of the International Monetary Fund's five reserve currencies and, modeled after the World Bank, set up two financial institutions: the Asian Infrastructure Investment Bank and the New Development Bank. It is the third-largest donor to the UN's budget, after the US and Japan. As chairman of the G20 in 2016, Xi championed the fight against climate change along with the US now that the US has withdrawn from its commitment, Xi is prepared to go it alone.[87]

Discussion Questions

1 What is your view of China's national image?

2 How does China seek to benefit from exercising public diplomacy?

3 How did China use advertising to improve its nation brand? What "tone" must advertising use to be successful?

4 What is meant when China is described as suffering from a "perception gap"?

5 Was it a good idea for China's President Xi Jinpin to link China's brand with Confucianism?

6 How does "business diplomacy" differ from public diplomacy?

7 What events influenced public perception of the China brand?

8 How is China attempting to grow its product brands into national ones?

9 Does China's success with industrial policy suggest that it should be tried more in the US? What is industrial policy?

Endnotes

1 Peter Hanlon, CEO and founder of Thinktopia wrote in his column for *Forbes* magazine.
2 Natalie Domeisen, "Is There a Case for National Branding?," *International Trade Forum*, Issue 1, 2003, p. 14.
3 Manon Rebufet, Leila Loussaief, and Sabine Bacouel-Jntjens, "Does the Country of Origin Matter for Cosmetics, the 'Made in France' Argument," in Anshu Saxena Arora and Sabine Bacouël-Jentjens, eds., *Advertising Confluence: Transitioning Marketing Communications into Social Movements* (New York: Palgrave Macmillan, 2015), p. 58.
4 Richard Wiener, *Webster's New World Dictionary of Media and Communications* (New York: Simon and Shuster, 1990).
5 Laurence Urdang, *Dictionary of Advertising Terms* (Chicago, IL: Tatham-Laird & Kudner, 1977), p. 19.
6 Peter Zandan, "An Executive View of the Difference between Brand and Reputation," A White Paper, May 27, 2016.
7 "Schumpeter: The Ascent of Brand Man," *The Economist*, April 26, 2014, p. 66.
8 www.millwardbrown.com/brandz/top-global-brands/2015#sthash.tsW4tWhz.dpuf

9 "Don't Confuse Reputation with Brand," *Sloan Management Review*, Vol. 49, No. 2, Winter 2008, p. 19.

10 Quoted in Judy Larkin, *Strategic Reputation – Risk Management* (New York: Palgrave Macmillan, 2003, pp. 8–9.

11 "Schumpeter: It's the Real Thing," *The Economist*, November 14, 2015, p. 69.

12 S. Anholt, *Nation Brands Index*. Retrieved June 11, 2012, from www.simonanholt.com/Research/research-introduction.aspx

13 GFK Press Releases, "Germany Knocks USA Off Best Nation Top Spot after Five Years," November 12, 2014.

14 Keith Dinnie, *Nation Branding: Concepts, Issues, Practices* (New York: Routledge, 2010), p. 22.

15 Paul Goldsmith, "PR is Not the Key to Reputations," *Financial Times*, February 1, 2005, p. 18.

16 James K. Van Leuven and Cornelius B. Pratt, "Public Relations' Role: Realities in Asia and in Africa South of the Sahara," in Hugh M. Culbertson and Ni Chen, *International Public Relations: A Comparative Analysis* (Mahwah, NJ: Erlbaum, 1996), p. 97. Also see "Public Relations' Role in Developing Countries," *Public Relations Quarterly*, Vol. 35, Spring 1990, pp. 24–26.

17 Van Leuven, ibid.

18 Eric Koper, Taye Babaleye, and Julia Jahnsoozi, "Public Relations Practice in Nigeria," in Krishnamurthy Sriramesh and Dejan Verčič, eds., *The Global Public Relations Handbook, Revised and Expanded Edition: Theory, Research, and Practice* (New York: Routledge, 2009), pp. 289–305.

19 Ibid., p. 291.

20 See Scott M. Cutlip, Allen H. Center, and Glen M. Broom, *Effective Public Relations*, 6th ed. (Englewood Cliffs, NJ: Prentice-Hall, 1985), p. 129. Also Morton J. Simon, *Public Relations Law* (New York: Appleton-Century-Crofts, Educational Division, Meredith Corporation, 1969), Chapter 24, "Activities and Control of Foreign Agents," pp. 825–842.

21 Jeffrey D. Sachs, *End of Poverty: Economic Possibilities for Our Time* (New York: Penguin Press, 2005).

22 Tourism programs have been ranked by Denver E. Severt, Dana V. Tesone, Timothy J. Bottorff, and Monica L. Carpenter, "A World Ranking of the Top 100 Hospitality and Tourism Programs," *Journal of Hospitality and Tourism Research*, Vol. 38, No. 4, November 2009, pp. 451ff.

23 See tourist attractions in Turkey.

24 Susan Litherland, "Tourism-Environment: Green 'Goals' Trampled by Commercial Concerns," Inter Press Service, February 11, 1995.

25 Karen Mazurewich, "India's New Export: Massages," *WSJ*, November 5 and 6, 2005, p. 7.

26 A communication campaign system model is outlined in Robert E. Simmons, *Communication Campaign Management: A Systems Approach* (New York: Longman, 1990), p. 6.

27 Michael Hayman, a report by The Communications Group, "The Power of Destinations: Why It Matters to Be Different," www.traveltoukraine.org/kyiv_winningdestination.php

28 Michael Hyman, "Create a Special Sense of Place," *PR Week*, June 22, 2007, p. 17.

29 *The Economist*, December 17, 2011, p. 112.

30 Ad appeared in November 24, 2014, edition, pp. 77–84.

31 "Kidnappings in Nigeria: A Clueless Government," *The Economist*, May 19, 2014.

32 Harriet Alexander, "Officials Out of Their Depth in Crisis Management," *The Daily Telegraph* (London), March 18, 2014, p. 8.

33 "Toyota Recall: 2.3 cars," CNN Money, January 22, 2010.

34 Mike Spector, "Honda Hit with $70 Million in Fines," *WSJ*, January 9, 2015, p. B3.

35 Mike Spector, "Honda Hit with $70 Million in Fines," *WSJ*, January 9, 2015, p. B3.

36 Jane Spencer and Nicholas Casey, "Toy Recall Shows Challenge China Posses to Partners," *WSJ*, August 3, 2007, p. A1.

37 Nicholas Casey, Nicholas Zamiska, and Andy Pasztor, "Mattel Seeks to Placate China with Apology," *WSJ*, September 22–23, 2007, p. A1.
38 Institute for PR Research: Global PR; posted on January 10, 2011 by Juan-Carlos Molleda.
39 "Korea Needs Stronger Nation Branding Expert," *The Korea Herald*, January 14, 2013.
40 "Nation Branding Led by Government?," *The Korea Herald*, August 30, 2011.
41 John Quelch, "How Olympics Branding is Shaping China," *Harvard Business Review*, August 11, 2008. https://hbr.org/2008/08/how-olympics-branding-is-shapi
42 Jessica Winch, "Olympics Help 'Boost Brand Britain'," *The Telegraph*, December 2, 2013.
43 Alex Brownsell, "London 2012 Delivered Brand Britain a Boost," *Campaign*, January 17, 2013.
44 "British Brand 'More Valuable Than Ever'," *York Press*, December 28, 2013.
45 Bruce Orwall and Lukas I Alpert, "Sochi Gambles on Future Gold," *WSJ*, February 11, 2014, p. D4. James Riordan, "Soviet Sport and Soviet Foreign Policy," *Soviet Studies*, Vol. 26, No. 3, pp. 322, 331.
46 Anto Troianovski and Harriet Torry, "Germans Are Joyous, Not Smug After Their World Cup Victory," *WSJ*, July 15, 2014, p. A8.
47 Drew Fitzgerald and Theo Francis, "Expedia CEO's Pay Nears $95 Million," *WSJ*, May 2, 2016, p. B3.
48 Drew Fitzgerald and Theo Francis, "Expedia CEO's Pay Nears $95 Million," *WSJ*, May 2, 2016, p. B3.
49 "At Yahoo, CEO Pay Exceeds $27 Million," *WSJ*, May 1, 2017, p. B4.
50 "Google Chief's Compensation Doubled Last Year," *WSJ*, May 1, 2018, p. B4.
51 Fareed Zakaria, "Populism on the March: Why the West is in Trouble," *Foreign Affairs*, Vol. 95, No. 6, November/December 2016, pp. 9–15.
52 Ibid., p. 10.
53 Ibid., p. 15.
54 Marie Valla, "France Seeks Path for Workplace Diversity," *Wall Street Journal*, January 3, 2007, p. A2.
55 *The Economist*, October 29–November 4, 2016. See "The Last Liberals," pp. 9–10.
56 Will Hutton, "Leaving EU Will Cause Pain," *The Guardian Weekly*, February 9, 2016, p. 2116.
57 Joshua Cooper Ramo, *Brand China*, Foreign Policy Center, February 2007.
58 "The World's Most Valuable Nation Brands," MediAvataarME.com, December 29, 2014. Brand Finance is the leading brand valuation and strategy consultancy, using a method more usually applied to companies. It provides a comprehensive report on the world's leading nation brands and the impact that a country's reputation and image has on governments, investors, students, and consumers.
59 The subject of branding is reviewed by T. Loo and G. Davies, "Branding China: The Ultimate Challenge in Reputation Management," *Corporate Reputation Review*, Vol. 9, No. 3, 2006, pp. 198–210.
60 David Shambaugh, "China's Soft-Power Push," *Foreign Affairs*, Vol. 94, No. 4, July/August 2015, pp. 99.
61 Tom Miller, *China's Asian Dream* (London: Zed Books, 2017). From book review by Benjamin Shull, *WSJ*, February 27, 2017, p. A17.
62 "Reform and Innovation Needed to Promote Global Public Diplomacy," *Global Times* (China), October 23, 2014.
63 Yiwei Wang, "China Shows Great Interest in Public Diplomacy and Has Clearly Set Its Sights on Learning How to Promote Chinese Soft Power and Express Itself Positively to the World," *The American Academy of Political and Social Science*, March 2008.
64 Shambaugh, op. cit., pp. 101–103.
65 "Propaganda: Who Draws the Party Line?," *The Economist*, June 25, 2016, pp. 36–37.

66 Kineta Hung, "Repairing the 'Made-in-China' Image in the U.S. and U.K.: Effects of Government-Supported Advertising," in Guy J. Golan, Sung-Un Yang, and Dennis F. Kinsey, eds., *International Public Relations and Public Diplomacy: Communication and Engagement* (New York: Peter Lang Publishers, 2015), p. 212.

67 Ibid.

68 Tan Yingzi, "China's Brand Image Improves: Report," *China Daily*, October 13, 2011. Jing Wang, *Brand New China: Advertising, Media, and Commercial Culture* (Cambridge, MA: Harvard University Press, 2008).

69 Chen Bei, "China Should Face Perception Gap, Says Scholar," *China Daily – Africa Weekly*, September 9, 2014.

70 "China's Middle-Class: 225m Reasons for China's Leaders to Worry," and "Daring to Think, Daring to Act," *The Economist*, July 9, 2016, pp. 10, 12.

71 Jeremy Page, "In China Confucius Makes a Comeback," *WSJ*, September 21, 2015, p. A1, A10.

72 Nicholas Dynon, "Beijing's 'All-culture' Focus Is Delivering a Poor Return on Its Soft Power Investment," *The Diplomat Magazine*, January 13, 2014.

73 Ramo, op. cit., p. 12.

74 Shaun Riordan, Jan Melissen, and Paul Sharp, "Chinese Firms Need Business Diplomacy," *Global Times* (China), November 21, 2013.

75 Ibid.

76 Gordon Fairlough, "Tainting of Milk is Open Secret in China," *WSJ*, November 3, 2008, p. A1; Gordon Fairclough and Loreta Chao, "Chinese Formula Maker Hid Toxic Danger for Weeks," *WSJ*, September 18, 2008, p. A1.

77 Shaun Riordan, Jan Melissen, and Paul Sharp, op. cit.

78 Irene Yuan Sun, "Africa's Factories, Made in China," *WSJ*, November 11–12, 2017, p. C3.

79 Ibid.

80 "China's Economy: Biting the Bullet," *The Economist*, September 23, 2017, p. 65.

81 Juro Osawa, "Patents Drive Chinese Phone Push," *WSJ*, June 21, 2016, p. B1.

82 Joann S. Lublin, Dana Mattioli, and Ted Mann, "GE Nears Deal to Sell Unit to China's Haier," *WSJ*, January 15, 2016, p. B1.

83 Andrew Browne, "Protectionist Backlash against China Builds," *WSJ*, June 22, 2016, p. A14.

84 "Florida: C-H-I-N-A: Five Strategic Considerations for Chinese Companies Going Global," *U.S. Official News*, July 30, 2015.

85 Orville Schell, "China's Reckoning," *WSJ*, August 29–30, 2015, p. C1.

86 Ibid., p. C1.

87 "China and American, Tortoise v Hare," *The Economist*, April 1, 2017, pp. 35, 36.

Part IV

Pivotal Issues Facing Management

Management must attend to issues that arise in interaction with its company's players and its economic, socio-political, cultural, and physical environment. Part IV concentrates on two pivotal issues that increasingly affect company operations: sustainability and technology. Sustainability examines whether current production and consumption patterns can be maintained. Are we destroying and depleting nature so fast that necessary natural resources will be in short supply for future generations. What is happening to livability on Planet Earth as its atmosphere is degraded? Technology recognizes that science is producing new products and methodologies so rapidly that better communications and more innovative management solutions are required to maintain equilibrium of our economic system.

Issues Management

In dealing with both issues, corporate communication has an opportunity to exercise leadership in issues management. Public relations counselor Howard Chase is given credit for inventing this field, and public relations professionals, along with those in public affairs, are major leaders in issues management.[1] They now compete with other entrants to the field, including management consulting firms and law departments.

The questions raised by technology and sustainability are whether the issues management process sufficiently reports on significant and relevant changes? Are managers kept informed? Are the dangers of Schumpeter's "destructive capitalism" recognized? Are necessary adjustments made in marketing? The need to explain changes to consumers, employees, and the public is growing. There must be a readiness to respond to opposition by government and advocacy groups. Efforts must also be undertaken to gain public acceptance for constructive technological change.

Issues management is a fivefold process that discovers what issues and trends affect an organization:

1) Issue identification starts the process, which requires monitoring the media, examining public opinion surveys, reading relevant literature, and talking with people in one's industry and others in the know. The global scope of corporate communications expands the monitoring process to include supranational and international organizations as well as non-governmental and other civil society organizations. Because of regional and national differences, the number and variety of issues are magnified.
2) Issue prioritization considers three major factors: the imminence of action, impact on the company in question, and actionability, i.e. something you can do something about.

Corporate Communication: An International and Management Perspective, First Edition. Otto Lerbinger.

3) Issue analysis of the key selected issues based on such factors as: the nature of an issue; its life cycle stage; identification of public and political participants; importance of public opinion; amount and kind of media coverage; and its legal, regulatory, and constitutional context.
4) Strategy formulation follows when a company decides on the position it will take on specified issues and ways of responding to them.
5) Implementation of the strategic plan.[2]

The larger context of issues management is the study of public policy, one of the recognized fields of political science. Public policy considers such additional factors as:

- Identifying the participants in the public policy process.
- Considering the constraints affecting their actions and choices, such the physical, legal, organizational, political, distributional, and budgetary.
- Referring to the central institutional features of government, such as federalism, separation of powers, and the role of interest and pressure groups.
- Being aware of many sources of potential disagreement among participants based on: (i) factual uncertainties; (ii) disagreement over likely consequences of particular policy alternatives; (iii) different professional backgrounds, e.g. lawyers vs. economists; (iv) different perceived self or organization interests' and (v) different values structures and ideological orientations.[3]
- The process of issues management is enhanced when its participants can draw on a strong background in political science, again showing the value of the social sciences to corporate communications.

Endnotes

1 His presentation is explained in W. Howard Chase, *Issue Management: Origins of the Future* (Stamford, CT: Issue Action Publications, 1984).

2 For more details, see Otto Lerbinger, *Corporate Public Affairs: Interacting with Interest Groups, Media, and Government.* (Mahwah, NJ: Lawrence Erlbaum Associates, Publishers, 2006), pp. 19–22.

3 Robert C. Sahr, "Teaching Public Policy in the Introductory American Government Course," *Policy Studies Journal*, Vol. 11 September 1982, pp. 8–24.

14

Sustainability and Climate Change

No issues are more international and global than sustainability and climate change. Like the globalization movement, they involve all nations and require their cooperation. The supply chains extend to every corner of the world. The issues begin with the long-existing concern of preserving the environment, which was inspired by Rachel Carson's *Silent Spring* (1962), Paul Ehrlich's *The Population Bomb* (1968), and Barry Commoner's *The Closing Circle* (1971).[1] The environmental issue was gradually enlarged to the issue of sustainability, which raised questions about the continuing availability of natural resources. Traditional concepts of a firm's boundaries did not give adequate consideration to adequacies of the supply chain. On a large scale, growing evidence of climate change – although stubbornly resisted by some – further extended the boundaries business needed to consider.

14.1 Sustainability Begins with the Environment

The issue of sustainability is an extension of the environmental movement, which gained public notice on Earth Day 1970. It focused on air and water pollution, degradation of the environment from clear cutting of forests, and the side effects of mining and oil production. Not only business but consumers have been held responsible for auto exhausts, excessive use of water and electricity, and, in general, for overconsumption. The issue of sustainability has become so important that, as of 2005, nearly all of the world's 150 largest companies had a sustainability officer with the rank of vice president or higher.[2]

The main task of corporate communication has been to make company management, its stakeholders, and the general public aware of the environmental issue and gain their cooperation for measures needed to address it. From the beginning, public relations people became active on both sides of the environmental issue. The environmentalists, consisting of interest groups, lobbyists, litigators, and impact assessors, sought to create public awareness and to hasten environmental reforms and regulations. On the other side, companies and industries defend themselves against hasty or misguided efforts to change productive and profitable practices. Public relations has come a long way from early responses to environmental criticisms when, for example, the dumping of bottles was justified on grounds that glass provides "ballast" in a dump.

The two sides have been coming closer together as they become more amenable to collaborative solutions. The assumption is that "group decisions" are generally superior to individual ones and are more likely to be accepted. The goal of such participation is to produce the highest quality decision possible. Stated another way, all parties should avoid the goal of "winning" and replace it with a win–win solution.[3]

Corporate Communication: An International and Management Perspective, First Edition. Otto Lerbinger.

14.1.1 Social Costs and Social Reports

From an economics viewpoint, environmental costs are considered social costs: the burden that a business does not include in its internal accounting of costs and instead falls on society. Economists and accountants acknowledge this distinction when they speak of internal and external costs. A company assumes the internal costs of materials and labor costs, which are accepted as the cost of production in its accounting system. External costs, which include wastes from manufacturing and damage to the environment, are treated as external costs that are passed on to society. Environmentalists, through direct confrontations with business and lobbying for government regulations, have aimed at curbing harmful practices and forcing companies to internalize social costs, namely by reducing and paying for them.

In recognition of its new responsibilities, companies now speak of a double or triple bottom line: one for financial performance, a second for protecting the environment, and a third for corporate social responsibility. The traditional corporate financial annual report might include a section on the environment, employee satisfaction program, corporate philanthropy, and other social responsibility matters.

Now most companies go beyond publishing annual financial reports by adding separate reports – variously called environmental, social, or sustainability reports. Esso Corporation was the first to issue a social report. It had received so many requests for information about its social behavior that it decided to consolidate its answers in a single report. Corporate communicators author many social reports because their regular activities require them to know what's going on in their companies and communities and how its various stakeholders are affected by their companies' activities. They are also aware of company measures to reduce harmful impacts and to provide social benefits. For example, General Electric's 2014 Sustainability Report states that it had reduced freshwater use by 45% based on a 2006 baseline, and greenhouse gases (GHGs) by 32% since 2004.[4]

14.1.2 Environmental Programs

Companies have engaged in both consumer-oriented and production-oriented programs to address environmental issues. An example of the former is green marketing and an example of the latter is Chevron's environmentally sound way of opening up a new oil field.

14.1.2.1 Green Marketing

The green marketing approach has been adopted by many marketers. The assumption is that consumers are influenced by "earth-friendly" products and some are willing to pay more for them. When consumers are categorized into five categories – "True-Blue Greens," "Greenback Greens," "Sprouts," "Grousers," and "Basic Browns" – the first two categories are on the whole willing to pay more for green products. Members of the third category, the largest, have some environmental awareness but take only small steps, including being willing to pay a bit more; the last category is not environmental at all.[5]

In her *The New Rules of Green Marketing*, Jacquelyn A. Ottman asserts that "green has become mainstream and the rules of the game for marketers are rapidly changing."[6] She adopts the categories of the Natural Marketing Institute (NMI):Lohas (Lifestyles of Health and Sustainability), Naturalites, Drifters, Conventionals, and Unconcerneds, with 83% of the US population falling into some shade of green. Lohas, representing 19% of all US adults, are the most environmentally conscious, holistically oriented, and active of all consumers.

Business strategies are gradually embracing the values of sustainability, led by such company brands as Seventh Generation, Timberland, Starbucks, Nike, and Stonyfield Farm. As stated earlier, Starbucks has embraced the concept of fair trade-certified coffee. This is one reason why Ottman refers to Starbucks as a company that "has been able to turn sustainability and social initiatives into quantifiable returns on investment . . . ."[7]

There are further signs of green marketing and sustainability efforts. Logos, trademarks, and symbols for greener product labels and certifications have spread on product packaging and advertising communications, as well as on websites and at trade shows. In Germany the official eco-label is Blue Angel, covering 10 000 products and services. Some retailers have focused on health concerns, pesticide-free foods, and organically grown cotton, and some have created their own lines of eco-branded products. Among the leaders are IKEA, Trader Joe's, Wal-Mart, and Whole Foods Market.

14.1.2.2 Chevron in New Guinea Reduces Environmental Damage

Jared Diamond, author of *Collapse: How Societies Choose to Fail or Succeed*, gives an example of how environmental practices are gaining acceptance. Chevron Corporation, which had a bad environmental reputation in Equador, responsibly developed the Kutubu oil field in the Kikori River watershed of Papua New Guinea. It engaged the World Wildlife Fund (WWF) to prepare a large-scale integrated conservation and development project for the whole watershed.

The results were impressive: "Chevron's expectation was that WWF would be effective at minimizing environmental damage, lobbying the Papua New Guinea government for environmental protection, serving as a credible partner in the eyes of environmental activist groups, benefiting local communities economically, and attracting World Bank funding for local community projects."[8] By engaging in environmentally clean practices, it gained a reputation that gave it a competitive advantage in obtaining contracts, e.g. with Norway for development of an oil/gas field in the North Sea.[9]

14.2 Focus on Availability of Natural Resources

The broad concept of sustainability extends concerns about the environment by asking the fundamental question of whether a practice of the production and consumption of an existing product can indefinitely be continued into the future. The futuristic *Limits to Growth* book published in 1972 by the Club of Rome predicted that current patterns of consumption and production were not sustainable.[10] Although questioned, this conclusion is reinforced by the population growth from 7.2 billion people on the planet in 2014 to an estimated 8 billion in 2020. And the long run should be defined not in terms of the next 20, 50, or 100 years but, as the subtitle of Curt Stager's book, *Deep Future*, proposes, *The Next 100 000 Years of Life on Earth*.[11]

Stager and Jeffrey Sachs have applied the term *Anthropocene* to remind us that "The Anthropocene is our current, unprecedented epoch of the Earth in which the Earth's physical change – climate, biodiversity, chemistry – is mainly driven by human activity."[12] To keep a perspective on time, they remind us that the Age of Dinosaurs dates back 65 million years. The basic question of sustainability is that mankind cannot maintain its current rate of population growth and consumption of resources. As stated in *Natural Capitalism*, "Humankind has inherited a 3.8-billion-year store of natural capital. At present rates of use and degradation, the authors warn there will be little left by the end of the next century."[13] More attention urgently must be given to the issue of sustainability over time.

A formal and widely accepted definition of sustainability is that of former Norwegian prime minister Gro Harlem Brundtland, who called it "meeting the needs of the present without compromising the ability of future generations to meet their own needs."[14] In ecology, the meaning of sustainability is how biological systems endure and remain diverse and productive.

Paul Hawken states, "Sustainability is the careful and efficient stewardship of resources by business, communities and citizens. It is the practice of meeting our needs in ways that are respectful of future generations and restorative of natural, cultural and financial assets."[15] The book states that sustainable management is a whole-systems approach to achieving superior performance and delivering desired outcomes to all stakeholders by business, government, and civil society.

14.2.1 The Price System and Recycling

The marketplace's price system is the traditional solution to shortages, for when demand for a product exceeds its supply, its price rises and thereby reduces demand, as well as providing the incentive to find substitute materials. When China learned to use nickel pig iron in the production of stainless steel, the price of nickel soared to $50 000 per metric ton in 2007 from less than $41 000 just few years earlier and led to a search for substitute materials.[16] In communications, optic fibers replaced copper wires, and in energy production, solar power and wind power have become more competitive with fossil fuels as the latter's prices rise. Large US utilities, such as Duke Energy Corp. and Southern Co., are investing more in solar and wind farms in anticipation of tougher new regulations on carbon emissions.[17] Environmental regulations, however, remain a major public policy battleground with robust public affairs activity.

The price system will also play a larger role in addressing the issue of global water scarcity. By the middle of the century more than half of the world's population will live in water-stressed areas, say researchers at Massachusetts Institute of Technology (MIT).[18] Rainfall is too sparse and stored water in aquifers is being pumped out in unsustainable amounts. Agriculture, which uses 70% of global fresh water, and water-intensive industries such as coal mining, textiles, and chemical, are huge users of water. Recycling waste water, building desalination plants (in which Israel is the world leader), and repairing old (and sometimes wooden) pipes are all part of the solution. Even with new technologies, ways must be found to control water usage. What is urgently needed are clearer ownership of water, cooperation, and clever pricing.[19]

Public relations will be needed to explain the urgency of water scarcity. Public affairs and its tools of government relations, lobbying, and negotiation techniques will be called upon to arrive at understandings. Consumer relationship management can help consumers reduce water consumption in the same way utility companies are doing by providing consumers with home energy reports. Eversource, for example, tells consumers how their consumption compares with "efficient neighbors" and "average neighbors."

Recycling has been another response to shortages.[20] Adam Minter's *Junkyard Planet* describes how the scrap industry has grown, citing such examples as improved shredding machines and methods that by 2007 eliminated the backlog of abandoned cars.[21] The going principle is that no scrap should be left behind. In 2012 nearly half of China's copper supply came from scrap yards, mostly American ones. When buildings are torn down these days, they are taken apart without damaging parts that can be sold and reused.

14.2.2 Greater Attention to Supplier Relations

The sustainability issue changes the focus of minimizing damage to the environment to that of preserving and improving natural resources by instituting conserving supplier relations programs. From this perspective, the factor of production called "land" includes natural resources. This factor requires that supplier relations be included in "land" as one of a firm's stakeholders. Supplier relations is concerned with obtaining a reliable and sustainable flow of natural resources. It depends not only on the marketplace for dependable supplies – made more abundant through globalization – but deliberate efforts to achieve a sustainable flow of natural resources.

Sustainability is achieved by implementing the four principles of *Natural Capitalism*:

1) Radically increase resource productivity and use resources more effectively.
2) Reduce the wasteful throughput of materials and indeed eliminate the very idea of waste.
3) Shift from an economy of goods and purchases to one of service and flow, entailing a new perception of value, from acquisition of goods as a measure of affluence to any economy where the continuous receipt of quality, utility, and performance promotes well-being.
4) Reinvest in sustaining, restoring, and expanding stocks of natural capital, i.e. natural resources, thus enabling the biosphere to produce more abundant ecosystem services and natural resources.[22]

These principles are demonstrated in several approaches to sustainability. One is recognition of the dangers of the "commons" approach to resources. The other is the willingness of a company not to deplete the water resource in a given area, as exemplified by Pepsi and Coca-Cola in India.

14.2.2.1 Concept of the Commons and its Effect on Fishing

The meaning of "the commons" was displayed in the early days of Boston in 1634 when the Boston Common was established for local resident use as a grazing area for their cattle. The inevitable happened as residents took advantage of this free resource by increasing the number of cattle to a point where the cattle were starving. That put an end to the original idea of the Common and it became a public park. The same scenario applies to the seafood industry.

The seafood industry accounts for 40% of all protein (of both plant and animal origin) consumed in the developing world and is the main animal protein source for over a billion Asians. It now faces an existential threat, says Jared Diamond.[23] The main reason for the collapse of fisheries is the "tragedy of the commons," which occurs when a resource like ocean fish is seen as belonging to everyone, but nobody takes responsibility for limiting fishing catches or maintaining the areas. Each country tries to exploit the free fishing. The fishing ships have become larger, the nets longer and wider, and the practices more damaging. Some fishermen selfishly net the seabed with trawlers and others damage coral reefs by dynamite and cyanide fishing. Waters controlled by multiple nations have been the earliest to collapse. Some of the most threatened fish are the Atlantic halibut, Atlantic bluefin tuna, Atlantic swordfish, North Sea herring, Grand Banks cod, Argentinian hake, and Australian Murray River cod.[24]

14.2.2.2 Eco-Labeling

Some businesses with economic power, however, have taken encouraging action. Unilever, which is one of the world's largest buyers of frozen fish, teamed up with the WWF to found the Marine Stewardship Council (MSC). Its goal was to offer credible eco-labeling to consumers and to enable fishermen to solve their commons problem through the positive incentive of market appeal. MSC's criteria were developed in consultation between fishermen, fisheries managers, seafood processors, retailers, fishery scientists, and environmental groups. The essence of MSC is independent third-party certification.[25]

Other companies have joined the MSC effort or decided to buy certified seafood products. They include Young's Bluecrest Seafood Company, Britain's largest seafood company; Sainsbury's, Britain's second largest fresh food supplier; and the supermarket chains Marks and Spencer and Safeway. In the US, supporters include Whole Foods, Shaw's supermarkets, and Trader Joe's markets.

Diamond is hopeful that the tragedy of the commons can be averted. But he realistically recognizes that a business can really maximize its profits, at least in the short term, by damaging the environment and hurting people. Hopefully, he says, "But when government regulation is effective, and when the public is environmentally aware, environmentally clean big businesses may outcompete dirty ones . . . ."[26] Ultimately, he says, the public has responsibility. They can take several measures: They can sue business for harming them, as happened after the Exxon Valdez, Piper Alpha, and Bhopal disasters. Or they can prefer buying sustainably harvested products by making employees in companies with poor track records feel ashamed of their company and complaining to their own management.

Diamond recognizes that with all of these alternatives, "Invocation of moral principles is a necessary first step for eliciting virtuous behavior, but that alone is not a sufficient step." Restrictions must be placed on destructive practices such as killing between 26 and 73 million sharks globally just to supply fins for soup.[27]

14.2.2.3 Pepsi and Coca-Cola Address the Water Issue in India

A well-known activist, Suita Narain, charged Pepsi with consuming excessive groundwater in often parched communities in India and allowing pesticide residue from groundwater to get into locally made soda.[28] She was a formidable foe. She was born into a family of freedom fighters who supported Mahatma Gandhi in his push for independence in 1947. Through her research organization, she tested the brands of Pepsi and other soft drinks and found that the residue level of Pepsi was 36 times higher than the stringent European Economic Commission standards. Protesters in Mumbai and Kolkata defaced Pepsi and Coca-Cola ads and burned placards depicting soda bottles. The state of Kerala banned the manufacture and sale of all Coca-Cola and Pepsi products, and other states cut soft drink sales in schools colleges and hospitals.

To rebuild Pepsi's reputation and sales, Indra K. Nooyi, chief executive officer (CEO) of Pepsi Co. Inc., headquartered in Purchase, NY, tried several strategies. One was diplomacy as shown when Abhiram Seth, executive director of exports and external affairs and native of India, visited Narain. His version of the meeting is that he wanted "to understand the data and see if we could work together to address the issues." But Narain's version is that Seth bullied her and "gave me a huge lecture about nationalism or some rubbish . . . . He was clearly trying to get me to back off."[29]

A second strategy was "give them the facts," a favorite business tactic associated with public information and publicity. Ignoring Narain, Pepsi went straight to the Indian media. Pepsi met with editorial boards to present its own data in press conferences, one that was held jointly with Coca-Cola (which was also implicated). They showed that the level of pesticides in soda was far lower than what Indians put up with in most other foods. It was well known that India has one of the worst qualities of water in the world, because of poor sewage treatment, heavy pesticide use, and industrial pollution. Also, water has sacrificial aspects and bathing in rivers can be a sacred act. Shortage of water is an increasingly large problem in India as well as China and several other countries.

A third, better and more sustainable strategy emerged: do something about the water shortage and pollution. Pepsi announced it would reduce water usage in its plants to 8.6 l for every case of two dozen 8-oz bottles, down from the former 3 l. CEO Nooyi announced: "We have to invest too in educating communities in how to farm better, collect water, and then work with industry to retrofit plants and recyle." Agreeing with its competitor, E. Neville Isdell, Coca-Cola's chairman and CEO, said "If we do not act responsibly society will not give us the social license to continue to cooperate."[30] Coca-Coca also promised to give $20 million to the WWF(formerly the World Wildlife Fund) over several years to help it run water conservation efforts in several major river basins round the world, including the Yangtze in China, the Mekong in Southwest Asia, the Danube in Europe and the Rio Grand and Rio Bravo in the US and Mexico.

14.2.3 Unilever Launches a Broad-Scale Plan

Unilever has become the leading company advocate of sustainability, exemplified by its Sustainable Living Plan inaugurated by its chief executive Paul Polman. Setting 2020 as a target, the plan aims to halve several elements of sustainability: the GHG impacts of its products across the life cycle, the water associated with the consumer use of its products, and the waste associated with disposal of its products. It also aims to help more than a billion people worldwide improve their hygiene habits, provide safe drinking water to 500 million people, double the proportions of portfolio that meets the highest nutritional standards, and better the livelihoods of more than 500 000 smallholder farmers and small-scale distributors.

A major practice is sustainable sourcing – 50% by 2026 and 100% by 2020.[31] An example is its announcement that it will buy palm oil only from traceable sources by the end of 2014 in order to reduce harm to the environment. It hopes to end the harvesting of palm oil from plantations responsible for mass deforestation in countries such as Malaysia and Indonesia. Palm oil is a cheap and versatile vegetable oil used in everything from washing detergents to lipstick.[32]

14.2.3.1 Supply Chains

Unilever's initiative suggests that companies pay more attention to the often neglected stakeholder group of a firm's suppliers. As supply chains become more important, partly because of concerns about sustainability, companies have paid more attention to supplier relations. For this purpose, Wal-Mart installed a vice president of ethical sourcing, Rajan Kamalanathan.[33] The store warned suppliers about its new "zero tolerance policy," to start on March 1, 2013, and that it would sever ties with anyone who subcontracts work to factories without the retailer's knowledge (which was in response to the Bangladesh apparel factory disaster discussed in Chapter 16). Wal-Mart said it will begin publishing the names of factories that aren't authorized to do business with its suppliers. A problem with such pronouncements, however, is that they conflict with the low prices Wal-Mart pays for the goods it purchases, leading to pressures to evade them. Wal-Mart also seeks to draw the attention of potential suppliers. It placed a full-page ad in the *Wall Street Journal* announcing the "Walmart Open Call Event," which asked, "Are you a U.S. manufacturer that wants to get your product on our shelves?"[34]

Recognizing the importance of global supply chains, companies like Cisco Systems are planning improved supply chain resiliency.[35] It developed the following five-step process:

1) Identify strategic priorities (e.g. whether cost or response times mattered more for a particular product line).
2) Map the vulnerabilities of the supply chain design (based largely on political risk analysis).
3) Integrate risk awareness into the product and the value chain (e.g. building extra supply options, specifying alternate components in a bill of materials, or creating buffer stocks of key components to mitigate risk).
4) Monitor resiliency (Cisco created an index to assess time-to-recover for all capabilities including a supplier, product, or particular supply chain design).
5) Watch for events (e.g. instituting a 24/7 monitoring of worldwide events that may impact the company's value chain. The scheme basically applies to company supply chain management and risk management).

14.2.4 Other Sustainability Measures

14.2.4.1 Innovations

Matt Ridley, author of *The Rational Optimist*, is buoyantly optimistic about the prospects of sustainability, saying that humans are resilient and capable of inventing "new ways of doing more with less."[36] He cites gains in agriculture from the use of fertilizers and genetically modified seeds produced by Monsanto, DuPont, and others. Furthermore, the use of aircraft radar to map the geology of remote areas and the use of drones to survey crops increase the availability and productivity of farm land. Where water becomes scarce, drip irrigation methods can be used in agriculture and desalination technologies to produce drinking water from salty sea water.

Finding ways of becoming greener contributes to sustainability. An outstanding example is Wal-Mart, the world's largest retailer, which over the decade leading up to 2015 saved as much as $1 billion annually by changing the routes of its American vehicle fleet.[37]

As stated by Benoit Faucon, a *Wall Street Journal* senior reporter, "scarcity induces some sort of innovation."[38] When the world was worried about a looming oil shortage, deepwater drilling – drilling 500 ft or more below the surface of the sea – became the next big frontier for oil and natural gas production. Then came the shale boom with technology of hydraulic fracturing or fracking – injecting air and other materials into the earth to unlock oil and natural gas. And as more communities face water shortages, "New Tech Tools Aim to Reduce Water Use," as one article describes it.[39] WaterSmart Software has developed a system that tells households how much water they consume compared with others. It relies heavily on peer pressure, together with conservation tips, and rewards, to motivate households to reduce water consumption.

Another type of innovation is the transition from an ownership society to a rental and "sharing" society.[40] Zip cars, which routinely are rented on an hourly basis, are an early notable example. A newer one is Uber's use of smart phones to connect people who seek rides with those who want to provide them (see Case 4). The same system is used to rent rooms on a hotel-like basis. The related concept of privatization may also produce efficiencies that increase sustainability. An example is the privatizing of the UK's Severn Trent plc water supply in 1989, a system that services more than 4.2 million household in England's Midlands regions and parts of Wales.

The importance of the sustainability issue is confirmed by new university programs. Arizona State University started the nation's first degree-granting program in sustainability research. It founded the School of Sustainability, along with the Global Institute of Sustainability. The cofounder of these programs, Julie Ann Wrigley, has invested more than $50 million in them since 2004.[41] The university states that it offers 500 courses university-wide that address sustainability and has received funding by external awards exceeding $70 million annually.

Furthermore, recognizing the growing importance of supply chain management, more than half a dozen universities have introduced undergraduate majors, MBA concentrations, and even entire degree programs dealing with procurement, inventory management, global supply chain strategy, and social responsibility in the supply chain. Among the schools are Bryant University in Smithfield, Rhode Island, Rutger University's Business School, Arizona State, Texas Christian University's Neeley School of Business, University of North Carolina's Kenan–Flagler Business School, Michigan State University's Broad College of Business, Portland State University's School of Business Administration, and University of Southern California's Marshall School of Business.[42]

14.2.4.2 Assisting Farmers in the Cocoa Supply Chain

Ghana, the world's number two grower of cocoa beans, saw a huge drop in crop yields in recent years, because of numerous factors including rough weather and old, diseased cacao trees. With the drop in supply, cocoa prices jumped nearly 40% since the start of 2012. Cocoa farmers in the Ivory Coast work on smallholdings of as little as 2 acres of land. Because they use traditional farming techniques, their tiny businesses trap them in a life of poverty. Most are unable to earn enough to make a sustainable living for themselves and their families. Meanwhile, some of world's wealthiest confectionery companies make huge profits on the back of insufficient wages.

Responding to this unsustainable situation, the top 10 chocolate-producing companies have pledged to share "a wide swath of private data on farming practices and crop yields." Mondelez, which makes Oreo and Cadbury, has committed $400 million, a quarter of its sustainability budget, to fueling a cocoa sustainability program through 2022. Employees on the ground in Ghana will give cocoa farmers advice on better ways to space seedlings, apply fertilizer, and prune trees.

Another company, Mars, the $33 billion foods giant, decided to share the benefits of its global success with 150 000 of the impoverished growers in its supply chain. Along with Tata Trusts, India's oldest philanthropic organization, it will invest in Ghana's agri-food sector. Working together, the two will address agriculture development, malnutrition reduction, and food safety improvement. "Given Mars global leadership in nutritive foods and sustainable agriculture, the Tata Trusts believe this collaboration will have lasting, meaningful benefits for Indian communities," said Ratan Tata, chairman, Tata Trusts.[43] Chocolate companies say farmers could easily triple a hectare's output from the current 500 kg.[44]

After these and other companies invested in new technology for farmers, the average cocoa yield has tripled and raised average farmer incomes along with it. More of their children will remain on the farms. Mars benefits by having more access to cocoa. This pilot project is just one part of a 5-year research project between Mars and the University of Oxford's Saïd Business School, exploring the concept of mutuality in business – the notion that the benefits of a company should not just be benefits that accrue to the shareholders but to include suppliers, customers, communities, future generations – and even the planet as a producer.[45]

14.3 Climate Change: The Ultimate Sustainability Challenge

Climate change deals with sustainability on a vastly larger geographical scale and time horizon than concerns about supply chains. It is truly an existential issue that affects the continuity of the economic system and the health, and possibly survival, of people on the planet. Businesses, environmental groups, and government are paying increasing attention to climate change. Warming in the Arctic has been occurring at twice the rate of the rest of the world for decades. Greenland is particularly vulnerable; it has lost an average of 375 billion metric tons of ice per year between 2011 and 2014. The eight countries surrounding the Arctic have interests in shipping, fishing, and drilling in the region, raising the possibility of conflicts. Mining firms are eyeing the Arctic for metals. No wonder that the Arctic has received renewed attention from world leaders.[46]

Several communication practices are being employed with the climate change issue. Public relations is used by environmental groups, such as Greenpeace, to attract attention by business to their current reliance on fossil fuels, and by government to obtain compliance with its climate change regulations. Public affairs is employed by environmental groups to seek government regulations such as the reduction of pollution by electricity-producing plants, and by businesses to question such regulations. Marketing has been used by environmental groups to encourage the use of alternative energy sources and by power companies to engage in "demarketing" to reduce power consumption so as to avoid the need for peak power production. Social marketing seeks to influence consumer behavior and the behavior of the general public to cooperate with efforts to reduce global warming.

Despite these efforts, several authorities have expressed serious doubts about whether the problem of sustainable growth can be solved in time to prevent the consequences of climate change.[47] The issue is much talked about but accorded a low priority because radical changes in production and consumption would be required. Furthermore, the widely held belief that the global environment is getting progressively worse is challenged by groups such as the Copenhagen Consensus Center, organized by Bjorn Lomborg, the author of *The Skeptical Environmentalist.*[48] He argues that attempts to phase out fossil fuels immediately may be misguided because of the urgency of other problems. One of the world's most pressing health problems, he states, is indoor air pollution, whose annual death toll is more than 4 million people. This is because so many of the world's poor lack access to affordable fossil fuel-generated electricity that they cook over burning wood or dung.[49]

An encouraging development is that US businesses – wanting clarity – are increasingly not resisting a carbon tax or cap-and-trade system. A carbon tax requires a company to pay for every ton of carbon it emits; in a cap-and-trade program a company must buy from a fixed pool of permits to emit carbon, which they can then trade with other companies on a market. Despite President Trump's intention to dismantle the current climate change agenda, many companies, including American Electric Power Co., Wal-Mart Stores, and Google, are planning to stay the course.[50] The argument that such climate policies would disadvantage the US economy against other countries like China is challenged because China announced its intention at the World Economic Forum to launch a nationwide cap-and-trade carbon-pricing market.[51] This move might help China promote its already strong clean-tech industry.

14.3.1 Global Warming and Human Activity Argument

Climate change is attributed to the greenhouse effect: the way the gases in the Earth's atmosphere, such as water vapor, carbon dioxide, methane, and nitrous oxide, act like a greenhouse and trap some of the sun's heat. The result of these GHGs is global warming. Al Gore's 2006 documentary film, *An Inconvenient Truth*, dramatizes the effects of GHGs by showing retreating glaciers in the Arctic, the breaking up of the Antarctic ice sheet, and the rising incidence of hurricanes and droughts. Others warn of the dangers of rising ocean water levels. A 3-ft rise would flood much of Bangladesh and threaten the national survival of The Netherlands, Shanghai, and Hong Kong. A 4-in. rise would imperil parts of coastal Florida and the Carolinas. Hurricane Sandy – also known as Superstorm Sandy – in late October 2012 flooded much of the subway system in lower Manhattan, New York. It was a reminder of the devastation that changing weather patterns could cause. It can't be ignored that the ocean level of the Eastern Seaboard of the US is roughly one-third of a meter higher than a century earlier.[52]

The human activity argument largely refers to the use of fossil fuels, especially coal, which fueled the Industrial Revolution. These resources made the huge growth in gross domestic product (GDP) and people's living standards possible, and they are still the power behind the growth in our economy. Not only business, but the general public is aware of this dependence.

There is strong evidence that the concentration of GHGs has increased significantly since the Industrial Revolution, thus refuting the argument that climate change simply reflects cycles in the Earth's temperature, which a few scientists still believe. A July 2015 report from the Pew Research Center found that 72% of American adults say there is "solid evidence" of global warming, and of those respondents, 46% said the warming trend is "mostly due to human activity" compared to 22% who blamed it mostly on "natural patterns." Most scientists agree that GHGs are the result of human activity, among which are:

- deforestation, especially in the Amazon and Indonesia;
- heating of buildings;
- driving of vehicles fueled by gasoline;
- electricity production by coal;
- use of electricity.

14.3.1.1 ExxonMobil's Stance

The issue of whether human activity causes global warming should be a question of science; instead it has become controversial. A notable industry voice was that of Lee Raymond, former CEO of ExxonMobil, who categorically declared global warming did not exist. In a speech at the 15th World Petroleum Congress in Beijing in October 1997, Raymond argued that climate change was an "illusion" and that there was no need for cuts in CO_2.[53] To provide ammunition in the battle for public opinion, the company financed research by scientists to support his stand. It had the resources, for as Sachs points out, the large oil and gas companies are generally among the world's largest companies by revenue.[54] Seven of the 10 largest companies in the world in 2013, as ranked by Global Fortune 500, are Royal Dutch Shell, Exxon Mobil, Sinopec Group, China National Petroleum, BP, State Grid Corp. of China, and Total.

Explaining Raymond's comment, Ken Cohen, vice president of ExxonMobil's public and government affairs, explained, "Honesty and directness are virtues . . . . But they can also lead to scrutiny and attack."[55] Dozens of demonstrations around the world, such as the "Stop Esso" campaign in Britain, protested the company's stance on climate change. Realizing that it was criticized for its intransigence, ExxonMobil announced it will contribute $100 million over 10 years to a global energy and climate research project at Stanford University. Peter Altman, national coordinator of Campaign ExxonMobil, a shareholder group, characterized the latest company action as "We're seeing Exxon Mobil trying to soften its villainous image on climate change." In response, Frank Sprow, the company's vice president for safety, health and environment asked, "We've said all along that there are uncertainties in climate science . . . . Is the responsible thing to ignore the risks or take strong and aggressive moves to mitigate them?"[56]

In November 2015, New York Attorney General Eric Schneiderman launched an investigation into whether ExxonMobil intentionally clouded public debate about science and hid from investors the risks that climate change could pose to its business. *The Los Angeles Times* and the online publication *Inside Climate News* published articles charging that although ExxonMobil researchers were concerned about climate change from fossil fuel emissions decades ago, the company for long periods publicly raised doubts about the science and its executives contradicted the warnings of its own scientists. Kert Davies, executive director of the Climate Investigations Center and formerly with Greenpeace, said, "We have watched Exxon sow doubt on climate science and delay action on climate change for nearly a generation,"[57]

When PBS Newshour aired a segment on "Has Exxon Mobil mislead the public about its climate change research?," Ken Cohen accepted the invitation to respond to critics. He skillfully separated the question of the science of climate change – which he repeatedly said was a "very complex subject" – from policy deliberations. He chose to focus on Exxon's opposition to the Kyoto accord in 1997, which would have exempted most developing nations. He also mentioned the company's opposition to the "cap and trade" policy because it would have exempted coal companies. Using a fear tactic, he said that the estimated cost of shifting to renewal energy by the turn of the century would cost a family 44% of its income.[58]

14.3.1.2 More Reporting on Human Activity

Pressure on business by investors to disclose the environmental impact of their companies and vulnerability to green regulation is intensifying. Investors are being aided by groups like Carbon Disclosure Project (CDP), which collect environmental data on their behalf. The CDP sends out questionnaires to 5000 firms asking about such things as "Does your company have emissions reduction targets?" and "If you do not have any emissions reduction initiatives, please explain why not?." Investors are demanding standardized, comprehensive information that is consistent over time.[59]

In the US, the Securities and Exchange Commission (SEC) requires all firms that file standardized annual reports to include details of climate change risks that are "material" to investors. Further pressure comes from the Sustainable Accounting Standards Board, which is a non-profit that tries to make firms fulfill their legal SEC obligations to disclose material environmental risks to their business. Joining the board on May 1, 2014, was Michael Bloomberg, previously New York City's mayor, and Mary Schapiro, the ex-chairman of the SEC.[60]

Among the voices giving support to the global warming argument is Pope Francis. He contends in his encyclical on the environment, *Laudato Si*, published on June 15, 2015, that global warming is due mainly to human activity and calls it an urgent matter.[61] He blames the current global system "where priority tends to be given to speculation and the pursuit of financial gain." He furthermore states, "As a result, whatever is fragile, like the environment, is defenseless before the interests of the deified market, which becomes the only rule."[62]

14.3.2 Application of Communication Practices

14.3.2.1 Public Relations Role in Climate Change Debate

Public relations has been playing an increasing role in the climate change controversy. On the one hand, Kert Davies, the founder of Climate Investigations, disparagingly states:

> The PR industry is a major component of the influence peddling industry that stretches across Washington and the world, and they are making large sums of money from energy companies and other important players that have businesses connected to fossil fuels and energy policy . . . . For the majority of them, they would rather remain neutral on any issue . . . . They don't want to have positions on anything because they like to keep options open to take on any client who walks in the door. They pretend they are above the fray and they are not involved, and yet they are the ones designing ad campaigns, designing lobbying campaigns, and designing the messages their clients want to convey around climate change.[63]

On the other hand, a survey by *The Guardian* reports that many public relations firms – including WPP, Waggener Edstrom (WE) Worldwide, Weber Shandwick, Text 100, and Finn Partners – would no longer do business with an entity that rejects the existence of climate change, or take on campaigns with the goal of blocking carbon pollution regulations. The survey described firms as having major power in shaping public conversation.

Public opinion polls support the finding that public will is lacking to tackle the global warming issue. Polls show that in 2014 only 29% of respondents said that dealing with global warming should be a top priority, which changed little from 2009 when 30% thought so. When it comes to the public's willingness to pay to do something about climate change, a nationally representative poll found that 43% of Americans were unwilling to pay an additional $1 a month in their electricity bill to combat climate change.[64] Most Americans see climate change as a collective threat but not as a threat to them personally.

Business attitudes toward climate change are reflected in the *Sloan Management Review's* fifth annual survey in 2013, which shows that climate change has yet to become a very urgent issue for most companies. Only 8% consider it very urgent, 15% quite urgent, 27% fairly urgent, 20% slightly urgent, and 26% not at all urgent.[65] President Obama, who wanted to pressure Congress to act on climate change, had little success. Framing the issue as a public health issue, which resonates more with people, had not altered public opinion.[66]

Some advocacy advertising campaigns have been used in the climate change debate. A notable one is "The tck tck tck campaign for Climate Justice" created by Havas Worldwide as a pro bono favor requested by Kofi Annan, former head of the United Nations.[67] The British government officially supported the campaign and asked the country's top 100 businesses and media personalities to give it their backing. The combined total of "tck tck tck" actions reached more than 1 million, and the movement was taken around the world – from Oxfam's stunts in Central Park to Brazil Young & Rubicam's production of a TV ad. Moreover, international TV and press coverage has been extensive.

A counter group, Friends of Science, a Calgary-based non-profit group, ran a national radio advertising campaign that mocked the whole idea of climate change. Green groups claimed that the oil and gas industry funded these efforts and that the group was one of several "industry front groups" trying to create uncertainty about the existence of climate change.[68]

14.3.2.2 Social Marketing Needed

Drastic changes in business practices and the habits of individuals are necessary to address the issue of global warming, which calls for social marketing. Dire consequences are often predicted if no preventive action is taken. One of the hypothesized scenarios is: "If humankind doesn't reduce immediately its use of carbon-based technologies then the scenarios for humankind's future are not only exceedingly grim but downright apocalyptic."[69] Although global warming would affect the entire planet, northern climes would still be able to produce food, but southern climes would be "devastated altogether."[70] Political will is lacking because "when presented with policy choices that favor preserving the environment at the expense of future economic development and jobs the economy consistently wins out over the environment."[71]

14.3.3 International Actions and Agreements

14.3.3.1 The EU, China, and the USA

The European Commission announced its ambitious "20-20-20" goal in 2008 – to cut emissions by 20%, boost renewable energy use by 20%, and increase renewable energy use by 20%. Europe's 28 governments, industry, and environmentalists are resisting those goals. Most countries don't want binding agreements on renewal power.[72]

Efforts to build renewable energy sources are continuing. Individual countries are exploring new renewable energy sources, as demonstrated by Scotland. It positions itself as a world leader in tidal and wave power research, plans to install the world's first commercial tidal turbine array, and hopes to produce all of its energy from sustainable low-carbon sources by 2020. The tidal currents are so strong in that part of Scotland that the waters there can be moving from 4 to 5 meters per second.

Its financing is international. The private company Atlantis Resource, originally from Singapore but now based in Scotland, put together £50 million (about $80 million), for this very first phase, which was built during 2014 and 2015. In 2016, environmental monitoring was conducted to make sure there is no adverse impact on the environment. By the end of this decade in 2020, 60 turbines will have been built.[73] Scotland currently has about 11 000 people employed directly in the renewables industry – more than in its famous scotch whisky industry.

China has a major air pollution problem, as embarrassingly revealed by the smog in Beijing during the 2010 Olympics. It has now declared "war on pollution," particularly targeting state enterprises. One measure is to overhaul resources taxes on coal and introduce a tiered pricing model for electricity that will make power more expensive for big users, such as cement and aluminum companies.[74] An encouraging sign is that in September 2015, President Barack Obama and Chinese President Xi Jinping fortified earlier pledges to cut GHG emissions with specific goals that exceed those pledged in 2014. The US said it would reduce carbon dioxide emissions by between 26% and 28% by 2025, compared with 2005 levels, while China said it would make sure its emissions peak by 2030 or earlier.[75]

In the US Obama mostly concentrated on executive action. He directed the Environmental Protection Agency (EPA) to limit the amount of carbon dioxide that power plants may produce, ordered the strengthening of fuel economy standards for trucks and buses, and offered $8 billion in loan guarantees for the deployment of technologies, such as carbon capture that make fossil fuels less harmful to the climate. He also planned to tighten energy efficiency standards for federal buildings and urge mortgage lenders to take more account of energy efficiency in home sales.[76] President Trump threatens to undo some of these actions.

14.3.3.2 The Paris Agreement

Climate change is truly a global issue that requires agreement among all emitters of GHGs. Efforts have been undertaken as evidenced by the Kyoto Protocol of 1995, the Copenhagen Climate Change Conference in 2009, and the UN Climate Summit in Durban, South Africa in 2011.[77] UN negotiations are underway to develop a new international climate change agreement that will cover all countries. A new agreement was adopted at the Paris climate conference in December 2015.

The Paris agreement reached by 195 countries on December 12, 2015, has been heralded by country leaders as a great accomplishment. It is a step in the right direction to end the era of fossil fuels. They agreed on the goal of keeping the increase in the global average temperature to below 2°C above pre-industrial levels, and making efforts to limit the temperature increase to 1.5°C above pre-industrial levels. By the second half of the century they will also pursue a goal of zero net emissions – removing as much GHG from the atmosphere as is being added to it. But countries signed on for what they think they can do, not for what they will do.[78]

Compared to the Kyoto agreement and previous ones, the Paris agreement was a relief. It succeeded because fixed goals were replaced by intentions, and developing nations, such as China, were no longer exempt from the fight to curb climate change. Moreover, the "rich" developed countries promised a flow of $100 billion a year to developing ones by 2020, much of it to be spent on adapting to climate change rather than attempting to stop it.[79]

The fact that an agreement, and not a treaty, was reached in Paris, is important, says David Shorr, a wealth management advisor. He believes that agreements have a better chance of addressing climate change than a treaty. He states: "There is no substitute for high-level diplomacy in getting everyone to do their utmost and in keeping track of their efforts."[80] Agreeing with Shorr, the State Department's special envoy for climate change Todd Stern states:

> An agreement that is animated by the progressive development of norms and expectations rather than by the hard edge of law compliance, and penalty has a much better chance of working. Stern believes in applying a healthy measure of realism in the demand that can be made of countries. Diplomats must identify what government and other actors, like the private sector, are willing to do to combat global warming and develop mechanism to choreograph, incentivize, and monitor them as they do it.[81]

The Economist was critical of many aspects of the Paris agreement. It considers the 2°C target "as unrealistic as it is arbitrary." Furthermore, technological changes deserve more attention; it says, "radical innovation is the key to reducing emissions over the medium and long terms." Examples are research into crops that can survive extreme weather, and research into cooling the Earth artificially through "geoengineering." In the meanwhile, says *The Economist*, realism is needed: many people will have to adapt to a hotter Earth.[82]

The Trump administration's stance on climate change is worrisome. Promises to bring jobs back to West Virginia coal miners are misguided, efforts to undermine the EPA may undo Obama's actions, and talk of removing the US from the Paris agreement undermines the US's previous determination to control climate change. At the same time, public concern about global warming is rising in the US: 64% of Americans say they are worried "a great deal" or "a fair amount" about it, and 71% say America should not withdraw from the Paris accord.[83]

Of special importance is that notable corporate leaders have spoken up on the issue of the Paris agreement. Anheuser-Busch InBev's CEO Carlos Brito said, "Cutting back on fossil fuels is good for the environment and good for business." He is committed to getting 100% of its global electricity from renewable sources by 2025. ExxonMobil Corp.'s CEO Darren Woods said that "climate risks warrant action" and called the Paris deal "an effective framework" for dealing with rising emissions. Another company, Mars Inc., was most direct. It stated that it was "disappointed the administration has decided to roll back climate regulation" and that "The science is clear and unambiguous: Climate change is real and human activity is a factor." In a post to employees, General Electric's CEO Jeffrey Immelt referred to the Trump administration's move and said climate change "should be addressed on a global basis through multinational agreements" such as the 2015 Paris agreement.[84]

On May 12, 2017, the CEOs of 31 companies supported a paid advertisement to "express our strong support for the United States remaining in the Paris Climate Agreement."[85] Among the CEOs were General Electric's Jeffrey Immelt, JP Morgan Chase's Jamie Dimon, Procter & Gamble's Daid Taylor, and DuPont's Edward Breen. Addressed to "Mr. President," the ad ended by saying, "We appreciate the opportunity to share our views and would welcome the opportunity to provide further input as the Administration continues to shape its policies."

14.4 Conclusions

Sustainability is a broad issue that encompasses environmental concerns, adequacy of supply chains of resources, and long-term effects on climate change. Each industry and company must examine its own situation and choose effective and acceptable responses. Whether the mechanism of the free market and the ideology of maximizing profits for stockholders are still adequate justifications for inaction is increasingly questioned, and corporate communication professionals should be able to help inform management of growing public concern and suggest ways of responding.

Public relations and public affairs have been deeply involved on all sides of the sustainability issue. Economic interests typically want to go slow on these efforts because they cost money and jeopardize current operations. But environmentalists seek changes in corporate behavior to avert future dangers. Corporate communicators face the challenge of reconciling opposing views.

Jeffrey Sachs's principles of good governance for sustainable development serve as a suitable conclusions statement. After discussing the traditional dimensions of sustainable development, which are economic development, social inclusion, and environmental sustainability, Sachs says they need to be underpinned by a fourth dimension of good governance. He defines it as the rules of behavior, encompassing both the public sector and private sector. The latter refers especially to major organizations, especially large multi-national corporations (MNCs).Good governance follows five principles:

- *Accountability*. Businesses are mainly accountable to the free market system, but also to the court of law and the court of public opinion.
- *Transparency*. To hold government and businesses accountable, their actions and behaviors must be known. Tax havens and "secrecy havens" must be resisted.
- *Participation*. The ability to participate in public deliberations and hearings on regulations is important. Organizations need to engage with all of their stakeholders, including suppliers and consumers.

- *Assumption of social costs.* Sachs calls it the "polluter pays principle, which says we all need to clean up after ourselves."
- A clear affirmative commitment to a universal commitment and universal participation in sustainable development.[86]

Discussion Questions

14.1. Do you agree that when a company and environmental group meet to resolve an issue, the goal is to win?

14.2. What's the meaning and significance of such terms as "social costs" and "externalities?"

14.3. What is the triple bottom line?

14.4. How does "green marketing" work?

14.5. What's the relationship between sustainability and the adequacy of natural resources?

14.6. What's the connection between the price system of our economy and sustainability?

14.7. What is the concept of "the commons" and how does it affect concerns about sustainability?

14.8. What problem did Pepsi create in India and how was it resolved?

14.9. In what ways have companies developed the stakeholder relationship known as supplier relations?

14.10. What is the "greenhouse effect" and how is the problem addressed?

14.11. How should companies respond to climate change proposals?

Endnotes

1 Rachel Carson, *Silent Spring* (1962); Paul Ehrlich, *The Population Bomb* (1968), and Barry Commoner *The Closing Circle* (1971). Curt Stager, *Deep Future, The Next 100,000 Years of Life On Earth* (New York: St. Martin's Press, 2011).

2 Bob Willard, *The New Sustainability Wave: Building Boardroom Buy In* (Gabriola Island, B.C., Canada: New Society Publishers, 2005).

3 See Kenneth D. Kearns and Anna L. West, "Innovations in Public Affairs Programming: Collaborative Planning and Beyond," in Lloyd B. Dennis, *Practical Public Affairs in an Era of Change* (New York: PRSA, 1995), chapter 25, pp. 355–370. Patrick Jackson, a former president of PRSA, often made this point.

4 GE Sustainability Highlights 2014, pdf.

5 Tibbett L. Speer, *American Demographics*, Vol. 19, No. 8, August 1997.

6 Jacquelyn A. Ottman, *The New Rules of Green Marketing: Strategies, Tools, and Inspiration for Sustainable Branding* (Abingdon: Greenleaf Publishing and Berrett-Koehler Publishers, February 2011), p. xiii
7 Ibid., pp. 23–25, 196.
8 Diamond, op. cit., p. 443.
9 Ibid., p. 449.
10 D.H. Meadows, D.L. Randers, and W. Behrens, *The Limits to Growth: A Report for the Club of Rome's Project on the Predicament of Mankind* (New York: Universe Books).
11 Curt Stager, *Deep Future: The Next 100 000 Years of Life on Earth* (New York: St. Martin's Press, 2011).
12 Jeffrey D. Sachs, *The Age of Sustainable Development.* (New York: Columbia University Press, 2015), p. xiii.
13 Paul Hawken, Amory Lovins, and L. Hunter Lovins, *Natural Capitalism: Creating the Next Industrial Revolution* (Boston, MA: Little, Brown and Company, 1999), p. 3.
14 Adam Werbach, *Strategy for Sustainability: A Business Manifesto* (Boston, MA: Harvard Business Press, 2009), p. 8.
15 Paul Hawken, *Natural Capitalism Solutions*, 2002–2013. www.natcapsolutionsorg/about/sustainability.
16 Patrick Barta and John W. Miller, "Innovation and Investment Top Commodity Bubble," *WSJ*, December 9, 2013, pp. A1 and A14.
17 Cassandra Sweet, "Large U.S. Utilities Take Greener Route," *WSJ*, May 10, 2016, p. B6.
18 "Water: The Dry Facts," *The Economist*, November 5, 2016, p. 8.
19 "Liquidity Crisis," *The Economist*, November 5, 2016, pp. 17–19.
20 James R. Hagerty, "Wrecking the Place – One Piece at a Time," *WSJ*, December 22–23, 2012, C11.
21 Erica Grieder, "One Man's Trash Is Another's Trade," *WSJ*, December 21–22, 2014, p. C3.
22 Hawken, Lovins, and Lovins, op. cit. pp. 10–11.
23 Jared Diamond, *Collapse: How Societies Choose to Fail or Succeed* (New York: Penguin Books, 2011), p. 479. Diamond is the author of the Pulitzer Prize-wining *Guns Germs, and Steel.*
24 Ibid., p. 480.
25 Ibid., pp. 480–481.
26 Ibid., p. 483.
27 "Shark-Fin Bans Hard to Police," *WSJ*, February 15, 2014, p. A3.
28 Diane Brady, "Pepsi: Repairing a Poisoned Reputation in India," *Bloomberg BusinessWeek*, June 11, 2007, pp. 46–55.
29 Ibid.
30 Andrew Batson, "Coke Aims to Improve Water Recycling," *WSJ*, June 6, 2007, p. A1.
31 "The HBR Interview: Unilever CEO Paul Polman," *Harvard Business Review*, Vol. 90, June 2012, p. 112.
32 Peter Evans, "Unilever to Verify Palm-Oil Suppliers," *WSJ*, February 13, 2013, p. B7.
33 Shelly Banjo, "Wal-Mart Toughens Supplier Policies," *WSJ*, January 22, 2013, p. B1.
34 May 27, 2014, p. A5.
35 Maria Jesus Saenz and Elena Revilla, "Creating More Resilient Supply Chains," *Sloan Management Review*, Summer 2014, Vol. 55, No. 4, pp. 22–24.
36 Matt Ridley, "The Scarcity Fallacy," *WSJ*, April 26–17, 2014, p. C1.
37 "Unsustainability," The World in 2017, *The Economist*. www.theworldin.com/edition/2017/article/12584/unsustainability
38 Benoit Faucon, "Oil Companies Go Deep," *WSJ*, December 12–13, p. A14.
39 Article by Ucilia Wang, *WSJ*, May 19, 2014, p. R5.
40 Ibid, pp. 144, 168, 217.

41 See full-page ad of the announcement, "Sustainability at Arizona State University," *WSJ*, May 12, 2014, p. A5.

42 Melissa Korn, "Hot New MBA: Supply-Chain Management," *WSJ*, June 6, 2013, p. B6.

43 Reeba Zachariah, "Tata Trusts, Mars Join Hands to boost Agriculture Productivity, Reduce Malnutrition," *The Times of India*, January 7, 2016.

44 Alexandra Wexler, "Chocolate Makers Fight Melting Supply," *WSJ*, January 14, 2016, p. A1.

45 Hannah Fearn, "Mars Tries to Share Benefits of Business without Parting with Profits," *The Guardian*, November 4, 2014.

46 "Briefing the Arctic: Skating on Thin Ice," *The Economist*, April 29, 2017, pp. 14–18.

47 Sachs, who mentioned this literature, lists Jane Jacobs and her book *Dark Age Ahead*; Lord Martin Rees's *Our Final Century: Will the Human Race Survive the Twenty-First Century?*; and James Lovelock, *The Revenge of Gaia: Earth's Climate Crisis and The Fate of Humanity* (Oxford: Oxford University Press, 2000), p. 505.

48 Bjorm Lomborg, *The Skeptical Environmentalist: Measuring the Real State of the World.* (Cambridge: Cambridge University Press, 2001).

49 Matt Ridley, "Smart Aid for the World's Poor," *WSJ*, July 26–27, 2014, p. C2.

50 Bradley Olso and Cassandra Sweet, "Companies Stay Course on Emissions," *WSJ*, December 9, 2016, p. B1.

51 Ms. Jaffe, "The Coming Price on Carbon," *WSJ*, September 14, 2015, p. B1.

52 Sachs, op. cit., p. 35.

53 "Exxon's 5 Year "Drop Dead" Denial Campaign," *Oil Change International*, April 24, 2015.

54 Sachs, op. cit., p. 396.

55 Thaddeus Herrick, "CEO's Controversial Views Lead to Tough Summer for Exxon Mobil," *WSJ*, August 29, 2001, p. B1. Also see: "An Age of Abundance?" Based on Daniel Gilbert, "Exxon Presses for Exports," *WSJ*, December 12, 2013, p. B1.

56 Thaddeus Herrick, "Exxon Contributes $100 Million to Research on Energy, Climate," *WSJ*, November 21, 2002, p. B2.

57 Chris Mooney, "Exxon investigated over climate change research," *Washington Post*, November 6, 2015, p. A01.

58 PBS Newshour, November 10, 2015.

59 "Schumpeter; A Green Light," *The Economist*, March 29, 2014, p. 74.

60 "Climate Change and Business: Nobody's Fuels," *The Economist*, June 17, 2014, p. 32.

61 Francis C. Rocca, "Pope Calls Global Warming a Threat and Urges Action," *WSJ*, June 16, 2015, p. A9.

62 Francis X. Rocca, "Pope Blames Markets for Environment's Ills," *WSJ*, June 19, 2015, p. A7.

63 "Top P.R. Firms Will No Longer Represent Climate Deniers," *The Guardian*, August 4, 2014. The survey included the top 25 public relations firms on climate change, together with the Climate Investigations Center [sic], a Washington-based group that conducts research on climate disinformation campaigns.

64 Sam Ori, "Few Will Pay for Climate Change Fight," in "Insights on Climate Change and Carbon Pricing," *WSJ*, November 14, 2016, p. R8. The poll was conducted by the Energy Policy Institute at the University of Chicago and the Associated Press-NORC Center for Public Affairs Research at the University of Chicago.

65 David Kiron, Nina Kruschwitz, Knut Haanaes, and Sonja-Katrin Fuisz-Kehrbach, "How Serious is Climate Change to Business?," *MIT Sloan Management Review*, Vol. 55, No. 1, Fall 2013, p. 76.

66 Colleen McCain Nelson, "Obama Climate Push Faces a Lukewarm Public," *WSJ*, May 8, 2014 p. A4.

67 "Giving the UN's Climate Justice a Sense of Time," *Campaign*, October 9, 2009, p. 10.

68 Martine Mittelstaedt, "Skeptical Ads Anger Green Groups," *The Globe and Mail* (Canada), November 18, 2009, p. A12.
69 Ian I. Mitroff and Can M. Alpasian, *The Crisis-Prone Society: A Brief Guide to Managing the Beliefs That Drive Risk in Business* (New York: Palgrave Macmillan, 2014), Mitroff, p. 68.
70 Ibid., pp. 68–69.
71 Ibid., p. 71.
72 Vanessa Mock, "Climate Goals to Fall Short of Europe Ambitions," *WSJ*, January 18–19, 2014, p. A7.
73 "Scotland Launches the World's Largest Tidal Wave Project," Living on Earth, Host Steve Curwood spoke with Calum Davidson, director of Energy and Low Carbon with Scotland's Highlands and Islands Enterprise, August 29, 2014.
74 Wayne Ma and Chuin-Wei Yap, "Chinas 'War on Pollution' to Hit Big Firms," *WSJ*, March 7, 2014, A8.
75 William Mauldin and Colleen McCain Nelson, "Obama, Xi Advance Climate Deal," *WSJ*, September 16, 2015, p. A10.
76 "Climate Change: While Congress Sleeps," *The Economist*, June 29, 2013, p. 31.
77 For a review of these treaties, see Otto Lerbinger, *The Global Manager: Contemporary Issues and Corporate Responses* (Basingstoke: Palgrave Macmillan, 2014), pp. 179–182.
78 "The Paris Agreement on Climate Change: Green Light," *The Economist*, December 19, 2015, p. 89.
79 Ibid.
80 David Shorr, "Think Again: Climate Treaties," *Foreign Policy*, March/April 2014, p. 43.
81 Ibid., p. 39.
82 "Clearing Thinking Needed," *The Economist*, November 28, 2015, p. 11.
83 "Climate Policy: Up in Smoke?," *The Economist*, November 26, 2016, p. 56.
84 Thomas Gryta and Bradley Olson, "GE's Immelt Says Climate Change is Real," *WSJ*, March 31, 2017, p. B3.
85 Ad appeared in the *WSJ*, p. A7.
86 Sachs, op. cit., pp. 502–505.

15

Technology and Innovation: New Risks and Issues

Technology has revolutionized the way people and organizations communicate, and has created four new challenges for communications. One is now well known: the implications of the technologies of the internet, the Web, and digital technologies that have enabled senders to instantaneous connect with a wide range of people and organizations throughout the globe with vast types and quantities of information.[1] The growth of social media has particularly affected marketing because it broke the monopoly of the mass media as the outlets for publicity and the origins of news.

A second aspect of technology is that multi-national corporations (MNCs) are building up knowledge networks as well as production networks, many of them abroad. An annual survey of the world's 1000 most innovative companies found that in 2015 those that deployed 60% or more of their research and development (R&D) spending abroad benefited from significantly higher operating margins and return on assets, as well as faster growth in operating income. Global companies are doing their research in cheaper places and take advantage of local innovation resources. General Electric (GE), for example, develops more than a quarter of its new healthcare products in India. And in China, half the staff of 150 000 of Huawei, which makes networking and telecommunications equipment, work in the research department.[2] Such efforts encourage Huawei to push for a 5G Edge. This technology allows for faster speed and smoother interaction between connected objects.[3]

A third aspect of technology is that because innovations are valuable they are protected by patent laws, which allow inventors to benefit from their discoveries. But so-called "intellectual property (IP) rights" are constantly challenged by competitors. A notable example is Apple's suit against Samsung for allegedly wrongly using its patents in the development of its smart phones. In 2012 Apple was awarded $399 million for Samsung's infringement of Apple's design patents. In 2016, however, the case went to the Supreme Court for reconsideration of the penalty.[4] Drug companies are major defenders of their patents, as illustrated by France's Sanofi SA's suit against Merck & Co. to prevent it from launching a rival version of its best-selling diabetes treatment Lantus.[5]

Another kind of threat to patents is from patent trolls who engage in abusive patent litigation based on patent rights they have solely acquired for this purpose. They do not make products or sell services based on them; they make money by filing often meritless or overblown lawsuits against technology manufacturers and against small businesses. Trolls account for more than 6% of patent litigation in the US.[6] Another threat to IP is from outright theft. Both lawyers and public relations people are hired to defend IP rights. When a case appears in court, the specialty of litigation public relations provides an advantage.

A fourth aspect of technology is that it often entails risks, some of which may escalate into crises. These have been dramatized by the nuclear disasters of Chernobyl and Fukushima, as well as the environmental damage caused by the BP oil rig explosion in the Gulf of Mexico. Although

Corporate Communication: An International and Management Perspective, First Edition. Otto Lerbinger.

the latter disaster was mainly due to mismanagement, it was also a technological crisis caused by deficiency of deep sea drilling technology and insufficient pre-existing technology to cap the well.[7] BP made a number of faulty tradeoffs between safety and cost. As of February 2013, criminal and civil settlements and payments to a trust fund have cost the company $42.2 billion.[8]

Another kind of risk is the threat to jobs from robots and the fast-moving technology of artificial intelligence (AI) that enables machines to perform tasks which could previously be done only by humans. According to the McKinsey Global Institute, AI is "happening 10 times faster and at 300 times the scale, of roughly 3000 times the impact" of the Industrial Revolution.[9] In medicine AI jeopardizes the jobs of radiologists because AI can effectively analyze images such as X-rays and computerized tomography (CT) scans. In other fields, information workers may feel threatened in that ever smarter machines can perform tasks done by them. One study examining the probability of computerization for 702 occupations found that 47% of workers in America had jobs at high risk of potential automation.[10] With many jobs at risk, firms promoting AI face potential public opposition, making the process of adaptation to technological change more difficult. Fortunately for occupations such as public relations that involve empathy and human interaction, members are less likely to be endangered by AI.

But the penetration of technology in many organizations has provided new challenges for public relations professionals, especially in healthcare and scientific organizations. Public relations professionals need to expand their knowledge of the special features of these organizations and develop new skills, such as science writing. And because innovations often lead to patent disputes, the specialized area of litigation public relations has become increasingly applicable. Public relations' repertoire is expanding.

As reported in the 2015 Edelman Trust Barometer Annual Global Survey, the rapid implementation of technology carries the additional risk that it may depress trust in business. About half (51%) of the respondents thought the pace of innovation was too fast vs. 19% saying "just right" and 28% saying "too slow." Regarding the food industry, only a third trust it to do what's right. And with fracking, only 48% trust industry with it. Not surprisingly, the survey found that a ratio of four to one respondents want more government regulation. Public affairs attention is therefore required.[11]

Risk communication and crisis management, which are specialized area of corporate communications, are often needed. Organizations that are particularly active in scientific research often have public relations offices that specialize in dealing with scientific media and organizations concerned with science and research. An example is Esso Research & Engineering.

15.1 Gaining Acceptance for New Technologies

An objective of public relations and marketing activities is to publicize the products and services of new technologies and gain consumer acceptance for them. Public affairs efforts are also required when regulatory authorities intervene. Some technologies, such as nanotechnology, 3-D printers, and new uses of robots have been relatively non-controversial. Nanotechnology, which deals with materials that are extremely small – 1 nm is a billionth of a meter – mainly concerns manufacturers rather than consumers. An exception was when a nano-face cream was marketed and an article warned that the nano-particles might penetrate the skin and reach organs.[12] 3-D printers have been benign and robots are selectively accepted despite their threat to jobs. McKinsey & Co. finds that 45% of "the activities individuals are paid to perform can be automated" using existing technology. And Morgan Stanley predicts that nearly half of US jobs will be replaced by robots over the next two decades.

China says that its workers shouldn't fear robots because the coming demand for manufactured goods is expected to be so high.[13] Based on this assumption, Chinese companies are targeting German companies with advanced technologies. For example, the Chinese appliance maker Midea Group Co. bid £4.4 billion for the German robotics specialist Kuka AG. German shareholder associations and labor unions have expressed concerns. As voiced by Roland Klose, a professor at FOM Institute of Strategic Finance in Essen, Germany, "Automation and Industrie 4.0 are supposed to be of long-term, strategic importance for Germany industry, [and] the L4.4 billion for Kuka isn't much money for access to key technologies."[14]

15.1.1 The Diffusion/Adoption Process

With companies producing a never-ending stream of product innovations that need to be introduced to potential users, marketing efforts must apply the communicators models of the diffusion/adoption process and the hierarchy of effects discussed in the introduction to Part II. Everett M. Rogers' diffusion process explains how an innovation spreads within a group and his adoption process describes how an individual acquires it. He lists five stages of an individual's mental process in making a decision:

- Knowledge – exposure to an innovation and some understand of its function.
- Persuasion – formation of an attitude toward the innovation.
- Decision – activity resulting in a choice to adopt or reject the innovation.
- Implementation – putting the innovation into use.
- Confirmation – reinforcement or reversal of the innovation decision.[15]

The resultant adoption process is divided into five stages: awareness, interest, evaluation, trial, and adoption.[16] The individuals of the adoption process are divided into the five adopter categories: innovators, early adopters, early majority, late majority, and laggards.[17] These categories are also used to rank the innovativeness of countries: early adopters are associated with Canada, Denmark, Sweden, Switzerland, and Germany; early majority with Australia, France, Italy, Korea, and the UK; late majority with Argentina, Brazil, Venezuela, Hungary, and Malaysia; and laggards with Algeria, China, India, and Zambia.[18]

The diffusion/adoption process has been used by pharmaceutical companies to introduce new drugs and by Monsanto and DuPont to gain acceptance for genetically modified organisms. Public relations and marketing play a major role in these campaigns.

15.1.2 Controversial Technologies

Driverless cars, drones, Uber's car service, and fracking have become controversial and therefore invoke regulatory scrutiny.[19] Such government intervention makes the application of public affairs by innovators necessary. Driverless cars, also called autonomous vehicles, sense their surroundings with such techniques as radar, GPS, and computer vision. Advanced control systems interpret sensory information to identify appropriate navigation paths, as well as obstacles and relevant signage. Some autonomous vehicles update their maps based on sensory input, allowing the vehicles to keep track of their position even when conditions change or when they enter uncharted environments. Driverless cars will test people's tolerance for risk and their trust in their manufacturers.

15.1.2.1 Drones

Small drones are another product innovation that is receiving regulatory attention. Their advantages are numerous. They have been helpful to farmers to survey their crops, to sheep herders to replace sheepdogs, to city officials to check road conditions and the extent of flooding, and to photojournalists, who can access new areas.[20] In addition, Amazon and other sellers envision delivering packages directly to consumers within 30 minutes, which may be critical for emergency medications. US law enforcement is also greatly expanding its use of domestic drones for surveillance, and drone manufacturers are considering offering police the option of arming these remote-controlled aircraft with (non-lethal for now) weapons like rubber bullets, Tasers, and tear gas.

But opposition to drones is growing. Pilots fear interference with their aircraft, pilots of small aircraft complain of unfair competition, and people see danger in drones circling above them and creating noise. No wonder that Jeff Bezos, the founder and chief executive officer (CEO) of Amazon, said at a Business Insider conference: "Technology is not going to be the long pole. The long pole is going to be regulatory."[21]

The long pole is evident in the Federal Aviation Administration's assertion that it has authority to regulate "the airspace from the ground up" and that all flying devices are subject to its regulations.[22] A critic of drones is the American Civil Liberties Union, which warns that routine aerial surveillance would profoundly change the character of public life in America. Rules must be put in place to ensure that people can enjoy the benefits of this new technology without bringing them closer to a "surveillance society" in which our every move is monitored, tracked, recorded, and scrutinized by the government.

15.1.2.2 Uber

A new marketing trend associated with digital technology is the renting of things instead of owning them, a trend that is compatible with the values of sustainability.[23] Major examples are Uber, (which is a short-time version of zipcars), Lyft, AirBnb,[24] Couchsurfing, TaskRabbit, BlaBlaCar, Girl Meets Dress, SideCar, SnapGoods, and Zipcar. These innovations have gone global. Uber, for example, has spread to Europe, China, and Asia.

Uber, which is the outstanding example of the sharing economy, applies the innovation of connecting persons who need a car ride with persons who offer their own vehicles to provide rides to designated places for agreed-upon prices. It says it is an online service provider rather than a transportation provider.[25] Uber makes the arrangements for rides and charges a 20% fee. The advantages of Uber to society are that more vehicles are available for transportation, including vehicles that might not otherwise be used, lower fares, and often improved service. Both full-time and part-time jobs are created. Uber has gone global, operating in 277 cities around the world by early 2015. It was valued at $50 billion by the end of July 2015, making it the world's most highly valued private company.

A spirit of innovation and entrepreneurship created Uber. Its service was made possible by the smart phone and GSP, demonstrating that technology refers to new ideas as well new equipment and industrial processes. Travis Kalanick, who co-founded the ride-hailing company, credits his success to a culture valued at Uber which he calls "the champion's mind-set." It isn't always about winning, he say, "It's about putting everything you have on the field, every ounce of passion and energy you have. And if you get knocked down, overcoming adversity."[26] However, Uber has learned that having an innovative idea and marketing it can encounter enormous opposition by those who are hurt. Experience is showing that public affairs and legal efforts are needed in order for it to defend itself.

Uber has already replaced its defiant and aggressive entry into new markets with a willingness to seek compromises with government officials in the cities and countries where it operates. Uber executives say they are aiming to make Uber explicitly legal everywhere it operates. Demonstrating the importance assigned to public affairs, Uber originally named David Plouffe, a strategist behind Barack Obama's two presidential wins, as senior vice president of policy and strategy. He oversaw global policy, communications and branding and headed the approach that Uber's first chief executive Travis Kalanick called "principled confrontation" (see Case 4).

15.2 Intellectual Property Rights

Corporate communicators must be concerned about IP. As stated by Barbara Berschler, who specializes in IP law, "Because your job as a public relations professional necessitates your work product incorporating creative, original material, you are constantly dealing with IP."[27] Dennis Wilcox et al. point out, "Knowledge of copyright law is important from two perspectives: (1) what organizational material should be copyrighted and (2) how correctly to utilize the copyrighted materials of others."[28] Both deal with the concept of what an "idea" is. Interestingly, it is the central theme of Edward L. Bernay's *Biography of an Idea*.[29]

15.2.1 Patent Disputes and Theft of IP

Patent disputes and theft of IP are perennial problems for inventors and creators. They arise from patent laws that protect the IP rights of their creators. In the US, the Constitution gives Congress the power "to promote the progress of science and useful arts by securing for limited times to authors and inventors the exclusive right to their respective writing and discoveries."[30] Patents are treated as property rights that can be sold, licensed, and otherwise treated by the inventors. Not all innovations may be patented: abstract ideas that are available to all cannot be, such as patents on DNA.[31]

Trade secrets, of great concern to marketers and public relations practitioners, are distinguished from patents. They are considered confidential or proprietary information that can cover a variety of materials that may be encountered and used. For example, while working with clients, access may be gained to their business plans, lists of customers, vendors or contractors, and price lists. To better protect the secrecy of this type of information, clients may require consultants to enter into a confidentiality agreement. In turn, consultants involved with outside contractors should consider having them sign confidentiality agreements to protect their own secrets as well as those of their clients.

15.2.1.1 Rights of Privacy and Publicity

An important area of IP concerns the "right of privacy" and the "right of publicity." The right of privacy belongs to most people and means that someone else cannot take your likeness and use it for commercial purposes without your permission. The legal reasoning is that a private person has a right to maintain his or her privacy.

The right of publicity is more often associated with celebrities. In such cases, someone else uses the image or voice of the famous person in association with their business enterprise, suggesting that there is some kind of endorsement by the celebrity. Such an unauthorized use would result in an infringement of the celebrity's right of publicity. Only the celebrity can exploit his or her famous status. Public relations communicators should consider these rights whenever using material that can identify another person, such as incorporating photographs or voice recordings. It is always therefore important to know under what authority a third party has given access to such materials.

15.2.1.2 Theft of IP

IP theft is rampant and occurs in many forms: when consumers download the music and software of others, when competitors seek trade secrets and challenge patent rights, and when some nations routinely engage in industrial espionage. The Commission on the Theft of American Intellectual Property estimates that the cost of theft exceeds $225 billion and could be as high as

$600 billion.[32] An article in *MIT Sloan Management Review* in 2014 claimed that Chinese theft of IP alone costs American firms $300 billion a year.

15.2.1.3 Sinovel Wind Group Case

A notorious IP theft is by Sinovel Wind Group Ltd., one of China's biggest makers of wind turbines, against which the US filed criminal charges. The company was accused of inducing Dejan Karabesevic, an employee of American Superconductor (AMSC), a Massachusetts-based engineering firm, to leave the firm and provide the source code for software that controls the way wind turbines connect to the electricity grid. Sinovel was previously the firm's largest customer.[33]

This case confirms the view of the consultancy Kent Kedl of Control Risks that "The easiest way to get intellectual property from a firm is by buying or renting an employee inside it."[34] Peter Humphrey of ChinaWhys, a fraud investigation consultancy, adds that the most dangerous local thieves are "PhD pirates" who may work quietly for years inside multi-nationals, especially in research-intensive industries like pharmaceuticals and chemicals, before striking. The implications for recruitment and employment of scientists are troubling.

Some defend IP theft with the socialist view that IP is a social asset owned by the state because it is created out of the accumulated knowledge of society and should therefore not be the property of any one individual or entity. They see IP theft as an economic development tool. Recognizing these dangers, the chief technology officer of a Western chip-making giant says that although his firm has a research center in China, it "would never bring the crown jewels into the country." He orders his team to smash (not wipe) laptops and mobile phones after visits.[35]

15.2.2 Litigation Public Relations

The specialized field of litigation public relations deals with publicity and other communications to influence the outcome of a legal dispute by a client or itself, or when a public relations firm is a party in a lawsuit. The goal of litigation public relations is to reinforce a case's legal strategy to ensure a win and to reduce damage to an organization's credibility.[36] The idea of winning and surviving can be found in the 2500-year-old Chinese masterpiece, *The Art of War*. The author, General Sun Tzu, was an extraordinary philosopher and military strategist during the reign of the king of Wu in China. His compelling and detailed advice on tactics, maneuvering, and the politics of war is considered as valuable to twenty-first-century business owners and litigants today.

Litigation public relations is conducted mainly through one-way, asymmetrical communication on the basis that the law is adversarial in nature, creating a win–lose situation. The use of public relations in litigation is becoming more and more prevalent in today's world. This is evident from the increased media coverage of court cases. Legal documents are difficult to communicate to the public, so public relations is valued because it can translate "legalese" into "common" English for the media and the public.[37] Lawyers are therefore advised to work closely with their public relations consultants. The firm Jaffe Public Relations describes itself thus: "litigation communications specialists have helped law firms and their clients deal with the constant flow of information inherent to these lawsuits, serving as a centralized resource for reporters and bloggers through all of the lawsuit's milestones, and working with the client to achieve favorable media and blog coverage during and after the litigation."[38]

Two cases in the appendix – BP and Chevron – illustrate the high stakes involved in some legal cases and the role played by public relations.

15.2.2.1 Alternatives to Litigation

The high cost of litigation has led many organizations to opt for alternative dispute resolution (ADR). Contending parties agree on either arbitration or mediation. In arbitration the parties sit in a courtroom-like setting with lawyers on both sides presenting their case to a neutral decision maker. Mediation encourages the two parties to talk to each other in an effort to achieve an agreement. Several bodies exist to help in these resolution efforts. One of Europe's largest mediation bodies is the London-based Centre for Effective Dispute Resolution (CEDR). Of the 3000 or so commercial disputes that have used mediation, around 70–80% reach a settlement within 1–2 days, and a further 10–15% a few weeks later.[39] The US's main mediation and arbitration organization is Judicial Arbitration and Mediation Services, Inc. (JAMS), which was set up nearly three decades ago. It handles about 10 000 cases a year worldwide.

15.3 Technology Creates Risks

Technology has always created new kinds of risks. Machines in the early days of the Industrial Revolution became a new source of employee accidents. Automobiles continue to cause accidents, resulting in 35 200 deaths and 3.8 million injuries in 2013. The power created by the first steam engines has been multiplied a 1000-fold by nuclear power, so when rare accidents occur, as the accidents in Chernobyl and Fukushima demonstrated, they cause thousands of deaths and injuries and widespread environmental damage. Developing countries encounter risks partly because the industrial culture and associated skills are not yet adequately established. The chemical disaster in Bhopal, India, was attributed to a native worker who lacked this kind of socialization and training.[40]

Industries with dangerous technologies, such as the chemical, energy, and nuclear industries, are concerned about public attitudes toward science and technology. Public reactions to technological crises suggest that "the public has lost all perspective and reason on the subject of accepting the normal risks of a technological society."[41] Some people want to enjoy the fruits of an industrial society and seem to believe that they can live in a zero defect, no risk society.

Nuclear power has been a contentious issue. Some have argued that the technology is too dangerous and goes too far in seeking to satisfy energy needs at the expense of nature and human safety. They point to the US's Three Mile Island incident, the Soviet Union's Chernobyl accident, and, most recently, the disaster at Japan's Fukushima Daiichi nuclear facility on March 11, 2011.[42] The World Bank estimated that it was the costliest "natural disaster" in history, estimated by the World Bank as costing at least $235 billion. In addition, there were 1883 deaths, 6150 injuries, 2651 people missing, 129 225 buildings totally collapsed, and 254 204 buildings "half collapsed."[43] Ian I. Mitroff and Can M. Alpasian call it a "human-caused disaster" because there were crucial vulnerabilities in the initial design of the reactors.

The main issue about dangerous technologies is whether they should be used at all. This is basically a top management decision. The view of Mitroff and Alpasian, both of whom addressed the issue, is that the risk should be taken provided that technology is not separated from "ethical management." They state that "both must be done together at every step from the initial design of a technology to its operation, maintenance, and eventual disposal."[44]

Risk perception is a specialized field of study that deserves attention. For example, it identifies so called "dread risks" as the most feared. These are risks with the properties of "perceived lack of control, dread, catastrophic potential, fatal consequences, and the inequitable distribution of risks and benefits."[45] Several additional risk principles are important:

- People do not perceive danger in the familiar, such as driving cars and smoking cigarettes.
- A favorable cost–benefit calculation makes risks more acceptable, e.g. people in less developed countries have less fear of nuclear power plants.[46]

15.4 The Science and Healthcare Settings of Technology

An implication of the growing role of technology and innovations is that public relations is practiced in a wider variety of organizational settings. This need has traditionally been recognized in public relations in terms of the differences in public relations practice in different types of organizations and industries. Thus university public relations programs typically offer specialized courses in the three sectors of society: corporate public relations, non-profit organizations, and government. These courses familiarize students with their differences in terms of their function in society, their organizational structure, their goals, government regulations, specialized language, values, and issues faced.

Technology has introduced a further form of specialization by recognizing two settings: the science setting and the healthcare setting. They are international in scope because both are based on a universal scientific culture. To be really effective in research, "scientists must be totally convinced of the great importance of truth."[47] This feature has an important advantage internationally as more multi-national corporations (MNCs) decentralize their research activities abroad.[48] The common culture helps science communicators when they face the difficult task of interacting with scientists whose daily experiences and value system differ markedly from their own. Fortunately, scientists have become cooperative in efforts to increase public understanding of science.

The subject of organizational culture covers these differences and reminds us that corporate communications professionals must be aware of them and acclimate themselves to the dominant internal culture. At the German firm Siemens, for example, the culture of science and engineering predominates and communicators must not alienate themselves by going overboard with humanistic references. In an industrial relations class at the Massachusetts Institute of Technology (MIT), for example, students challenged the concept of a "logic of sentiments" for they could see no logic to sentiments.[49] Carly Fiorina is said to have failed as CEO of Hewlett-Packard "because she tried to impose a sales-driven culture on an engineering-dominated organization."[50]

15.4.1 Science Settings at the Whitehead Institute and Brookhaven National Lab

The Office of Communications and Public Affairs at MIT exemplifies the challenges of science communication. The routine task continues to be the writing of articles about scientific research conducted at the Institute. This requires that writers have familiarity with biological terms. For example, an article in its quarterly magazine *Paradigm*, "Bearing Witness to the Phenomenon of Symmetric Cell Division" referred to the process of *mitosis*, which would have been learned in a college biology course.[51]

When Rick Borchelt became the Institute's director for public affairs and communication, he set his goal to move beyond publicity activities aimed at a "general amorphous audience" to one of identifying and communicating with key stakeholders for the purpose of establishing relationships of mutual benefit, commitment, and trust. Stakeholders included policy makers in DC, scientists in universities and corporations (especially pharmaceutical companies), science-savvy donors, literate members of the public, their own alumni of post-docs and graduate students, and, most recently, scientists in the European Community. Borchelt became a member of the top management team, which allowed him to participate in strategic planning. By a 1982 agreement with MIT, the faculty of the Institute became tenured members of its Department of Biology.

At the Brookhaven National Laboratory on Long Island, New York, the science culture prevails. The lab conducts research "from physics, to life sciences to nanotechnology supercomputing, and alternative energy."[52] The lab is known in public relations circles for its highly professional communications staff that brought communications, community involvement, and government affairs under one manager, Marge Lynch, who carries the title of assistant laboratory director of community, education, government, and public affairs. She sits at the policy making table and reports directly to the Lab's director.[53] Her staff consists of about 25 employees, seven of whom are in media and communication, and four in lab-wide community relations. Its chief mission is to promote Brookhaven's international reputation as a center for scientific excellence and innovation, using media coverage as the primary vehicle to achieve national recognition. For many years, the staff's performance was reviewed by a Communications and Trust Advisory Panel (C-TAP) consisting of public relations educators and counselors.

The staff is familiar with scientific terms and media. Feature stories have appeared in the prime media of *Scientific American, Newsweek, New York Times, Nature, and Science.* To reach a popular audience, some stories were designed to relate science to topics of general interest. One was a story of "Chinese Flutes," which appeared on the Science and Technology News Network and fed to 150 TV stations nationwide, as well as CNN Science and Technology Week, AP, NPR, and Science Times for the *New York Times, Washington Post, Philadelphia Inquirer*, BBC, and Discovery Channel.

15.4.1.1 How Brookhaven Dealt with Community Fears

At Brookhaven, the surrounding communities at one time opposed many of its research projects because the citizens felt endangered by its nuclear research and experiments on its Relativistic Heavy Ion Collider (RHIC).[54]

It collides two beams of gold ions head-on when they're traveling at nearly the speed of light in opposite directions around a 2.4-mile, two-lane "racetrack." to explore some of nature's most basic and intriguing ingredients known as quarks and gluons, which existed at the beginning of the universe. Some citizens feared that RHIC, which would simulate what happened in the fraction of a second after the Big Bang that formed the Earth, would cause the world to be blown up. Making it difficult for the public relations staff to allay fears is the tradition that scientists avoid making absolute statements. They always state their conclusions in terms of probability, so they would not say that it absolutely wouldn't happen.

In response, Brookhaven's public relations staff established a formidable community relations program. It included a Community Advisory Council consisting of representatives from more than 30 local civic, health, environmental, and business organizations. It also formed three other groups: a 15-person Stakeholder Relations Team that held face-to-face interviews with 60 Long Island opinion leaders and covered 20 issues; an Ambassador program, which involves employee in community activities; and an Envoy program that builds on the relationships employees already have with community organizations; outreach and community programs; and a speakers bureau.

15.4.2 Healthcare Settings

Healthcare public relations covers a number of sectors, including healthcare facilities, biotech, pharmaceuticals, animal health, vaccines, medical technology (device/diagnostics), and healthcare providers. Bliss Integrated Communications, one of the firms listed in *O'Dwyer's Magazine* as specializing in healthcare and medical public relations, describes itself as a "strategic communications partner to pharmaceutical, biotech and medical device/diagnostics companies, advocacy and professional groups, and healthcare data companies." According to the Public Relations Council, healthcare is one of public relations' biggest growth areas, generating over 15% of member firms' revenues.

At individual hospitals, public relations people "interact with physicians, nurses, managers, administrators and patients, and therefore require excellent communication skills."[55] They must be aware that doctors are notorious for their poor patient relations and their arrogance. "Public relations responsibilities include writing for internal publications and handling media calls, as well as writing and creating various materials that promote services offered at that facility."

Hospitals have received the attention of a sociologist, Erving Goffman, who calls them "total institutions," similar to the military and prisons, because:

> First, all aspects of life are conducted in the same place and under the same central authority. Second, each phase of the member's daily activity is carried on in the immediate company of a large batch of others, all of whom are treated alike and required to do the same thing together. Third, all phases of the day's activities are tightly scheduled, with one activity leading at a prearranged time into the next, the whole sequence of activities being imposed from above by a system of explicit formal rulings and a body of officials. Finally, the various enforced activities are brought together into a single plan purportedly designed to fulfill the official aims of the institution.[56]

Beth Boswell, former managing director, Southeast Asia at the counseling firm of Fleischman-Hillard in Hong Kong, describes healthcare public relations more broadly as involving "device work, Rx (prescription) work, OTC (aka consumer work), BTC (behind the counter work), and nutrition work." She believes that the work provides considerable personal satisfaction, "At the end of the day you're helping people in a fundamental way. The product you work on could help alleviate a medical symptom, keep someone alive longer, and diagnose what's wrong. You can't say that about a can of Coke."[57]

The tactical skills in healthcare public relations, as listed by Boswell, include:

- writing (adapting the news release to the local market, writing speeches);
- infographic development;
- video development;
- news conference or briefing logistics;
- influencer outreach program;
- partnerships with non-governmental organizations (NGOs) and disease awareness organizations;
- media relations;
- social media outreach and website writing.

Healthcare professionals must "develop insight and the big idea," a challenge which Boswell says is not in skills but the regulatory mandate. For example, "you can't publicize or advertise the name of a Rx product. Instead, you try to create disease awareness in the market, create demand and then launch the product as a public education/information effort."

Product launches of Rx products usually happen in the US first and then spread to other countries, with Asia being last. Because of regulatory requirements, most Asian countries are taking their lead from the EU or the US's Food and Drug Administration (FDA), says Boswell. This saves pharma companies from having to do clinical trials in Asia. The downside, however, is that "when launches are planned there's no local data that the media or influencers want." Aside from regulatory approval, market conditions in different markets vary. Older people, for example, who have the ability to purchase products live in developed markets. The focus in developing countries such as Pakistan, India, Laos, and Myanmar is on primary health, such as stopping measles, stopping dengue fever, getting kids vaccinated, getting basic nutrition and hygiene right.

15.4.2.1 Continuing Health Concerns: Outbreak of Ebola and Zika

As with the 2002 spread of severe acute respiratory syndrome (SARS) in China, the outbreak of Ebola in the West African nations of Liberia, Sierra Leone, and Guinea, which affected over

20 000 people in a few months, demonstrated the health dangers of a globalized world. Aside from the thousands in West Africa who would die from the disease, the fear was that it would spread to other nations. The World Health Organization (WHO) only for the third time declared the outbreak a "public health emergency of international concern"[58] It did not, however, call it a pandemic, which is when an infectious disease is spread to other countries and different regions. WHO was criticized in the scientific journal *The Lancet* for its "bungled" response because it waited too long to sound the alarm. Countries are urged to build stronger outbreak detection and response systems and mechanisms to track progress.[59]

The Ebola crisis, which interrupted foreign trade and travel, was a major challenge to health authorities and required some public relations and social science insight. To stop the spread of Ebola, persons with the disease had to be found and those around them isolated. This was a difficult task because of lack of personnel and facilities and such cultural mores as cleaning and kissing the dead. Some of the isolation tactics used in the mad cow epidemic of the late 1980s were applicable, but obviously diseased persons could not be slaughtered the way whole herds of cows were.

Governments considered travel bans to and from West Africa, but rejected them because the transportation of vital personnel and supplies would be hindered. Instead, health checks were conducted at destination airports. Ebola mainly caused an interruption of international trade and economic development projects. Responses by companies located in the afflicted areas varied: A British company withdrew its "non-essential" employees from the afflicted areas. Some Chinese companies that had a strong presence announced they would stay; others, such as China Civil Engineering Construction Co. imposed a self-quarantine in their compounds. Companies announced careful warnings, such as not shaking hands. Some companies, however, wanted to offer encouragement for the future. Coca-Cola sent a "solidarity" team to its Liberian company and announced that it would build a new plant that would provide more jobs. Pharmaceutical companies made donations, in some cases for research on new drugs.[60]

A more recent health concern is Zika, spread by mosquitoes. The virus, which is believed to have originated in Uganda, has spread across South America, and arrived in Brazil in May 2016.[61] In February 2016, the WHO declared it to be a global health problem, saying that the disease was "spreading explosively" in the Americas and that as many as 4 million people could be infected by the end of the year. It was a reminder that epidemics move faster than global institutions. It happened as the Brazilian business world was ensnared in the country's worst ever corruption scandal, involving billions of dollars of kickbacks to politicians from inflated contracts for public works. The International Monetary Fund (IMF) said Zika posed a serious economic threat.[62]

One question was about travel restrictions. The first case in the US was a Liberian man who flew to Dallas, Texas, to be reunited with his family. His case was so advanced that he soon died. Decisions then had to be made about restrictions on nurses who attended him. One of them, Ms. Amber Joy Vinson, flew to Cleveland, Ohio, to plan for her wedding. She flew before it was known that another nurse, Ms. Pam was sick and had been put under surveillance by health authorities.[63]

The Texas Health Presbyterian Hospital Dallas where the nurses were employed declined to comment on whether workers were instructed not to fly. Lawrence Gostin, director of the O'Neill Institute for National and Global Health Law at Georgetown University, thought that after the first health worker was diagnosed with Ebola, her colleagues "should have been under close supervision . . . and the health department should have been monitoring their symptoms." He said individuals being monitored should "not be in congregate settings, such as close theaters, the metro and certainly not airplanes."[64] Such views threatened the reputation and bottom line of Texas Health Presbyterian Hospital in Dallas. "The *Dallas Morning News* cited a 'deep loss of public trust' in a facility once known as one of the city's most prestigious," said Kathleen Lewton, a hospital and healthcare consultant and author of *Health Care: A Guide for Professionals*.[65] She advises: "If people have obviously made mistakes then apologize early on to those affected and to the community – even if you're still investigating what happened."[66]

Tom Frieden, former director of the Centers for Disease Control and Prevention (CDC), was criticized for over-confidently trying to assuage public fears by prematurely claiming "We're stopping this in its tracks in this country." He repeated the "in its tracks" statement at least six times. He also claimed, "One of the things we want to emphasize is virtually any hospital in the country that can do isolation, can do isolation for Ebola."[67] But nurses reported otherwise, and, as public relations counselor Richard Nicolazzo states, "When nurses – the people in the front lines – complain that training is lacking and they don't have adequate protective gear something is clearly wrong."[68] Spokespersons should make 100% sure that the facts they state are accurate.

15.5 Conclusions

The impact of technology and innovation on public relations is expected to grow, as predicted by Walter Isaacson's *The Innovators: How a Group of Hackers, Geniuses, and Geeks Created the Digital Revolution*. He states: "The next phase of the Digital Revolution will bring even more new methods of marrying technology with the creative industries, such as media, fashion, music, entertainment, education, literature, and the arts."[69] He adds, "This interplay between technology and the arts will eventually result in completely new forms of expression and formats of media." Isaacson echoes the theme of C.P. Snow's books about the unity of the cultures of science and the humanities.[70] Steve Jobs also endorsed this unity. He would conclude his product launches by declaring: "It's in Apple's DNA that technology alone is not enough – that its technology is married with liberal arts, married with the humanities, that yields us the result that makes our heart sing."[71,72] Public relations people can identify with these views insofar as their journalistic training included the reading of good literature and a liberal arts background was part of their degree program.

Technology and innovation stimulate economic growth and improve the well-being of people. But Joseph Schumpeter's recognition of "destructive capitalism" also applies as some technologies become obsolete or inadequate and threaten existing businesses and jobs.[73] Public relations must deal with these problems, including the risk of crises. But the main implication for public relations is that it must learn to apply such communication theory concepts as the diffusion/adoption process and become familiar with the new settings of science and healthcare organizations. Attention must be given to the sub-specialities of science writing and litigation public relations. Advances in technology will challenge the reputation of public relations people as being creative and welcoming change.

Discussion Questions

15.1. What new communications challenges are created by technology?

15.2. What technologies represent the greatest challenges? Discuss an example.

15.3. Why is the diffusion/adoption process relevant?

15.4. How has Uber applied technology to its ride-sharing service?

15.5. What attitudes and behaviors of Uber create the need for the application of public affairs?

15.6. Why are IP rights of concern to corporate communications?

15.7. What is the role of litigation public relations?

15.8. What risks have new technologies caused? Discuss one example.

15.9. What are the special features of health and science settings that relate to public relations? What special attitudes and knowledge are needed?

15.10. What public relations problems did Brookhaven National Lab encounter? How did it manage them?

15.11. What public relations problems attended the Ebola crisis?

Appendix

Science Writing

Science and healthcare settings require skill in science writing, which is a specialized area of journalism represented by the National Association of Science Writers (NASW). It was created in 1934 by a dozen science journalists and reporters in New York City. Its aim is to improve the craft of science journalism and to promote good science reportage. As of September 29, 2007, the organization reported having 2549 members and claimed to be the largest organization of science writers in the world. To help science writers with the necessary vocabulary and ways of thinking of scientists and engineers, some knowledge of one or more physical sciences, such as physics, chemistry, biology, and geology, is helpful.

The counterpart of NASW on the international level is the International Science Writers Association (ISWA). It was formed in 1967 in response to the increasingly international scope of science popularization and technical communications. ISWA states that today's science writer may need to cover stories originating abroad by means of telephoned and written inquiries, to commission reports by science writers abroad, or simply to be aware of developments elsewhere. The growing role of science and technology in economic development has meant that science communicators in both the industrialized and emerging nations now share many common goals, which necessitates an ever wider circle of contacts. Special directories have been organized to assist science writers. One is Writing Assistance, Inc. (WAI), which provides technical writers. Another is Technical Writers on-Site or Remote, which is a guide to thousands of technical writers across the country, in Canada and around the globe.[74]

Two Litigation Cases

BP's Campaign to Reform the Gulf Settlement

In the aftermath of the April 2010 explosion in BP's Deepwater Horizon oil rig in the Gulf of Mexico, the British firm BP paid billions of dollars in damages. A Gulf Settlement Program was established to pay claimants who suffered economic losses as a result of the accident. Unfortunately, BP agreed to pay for any losses, even if not connected to the accident. This led to many questionable requests for payments by people who claimed losses. Examples of fraudulent claims included a $662 000 payment to a Louisiana nursing home that was actually shut down the year before the spill and a $173 000 payout to an adult escort service that was filed with unsigned and undated financial documents.[75]

BP consented to these payments but gradually became aware that the legal system was allowing for "payment of fictitious or artificially inflated losses." BP argued in federal court that the oil spill settlement it signed in 2012 should be scrapped. It placed high-profile issue ads in major newspapers, such as the *Wall Street Journal*, that exposed these claims. The key paragraph in one ad read: "BP has announced that it will ask the Supreme Court to review the lower court decisions that have affirmed this process. We cannot sit idly by while the Gulf Settlement Program pays claimants that were never harmed by the spill. It's not what we agreed to when we signed the settlement agreement – it's not what any company would ever agree to – and it's against the law."[76]

Other ad themes were that "thousands of undeserving claims totaling over half a billion dollars had already been awarded,"[77] and that the process of paying people who never were victims "flies in the face of established law, basic principles of justice, and the US Constitution." Some ads dealt with BP's image intended to garner public favor. One ad declared that BP had not changed its "commitment to the Gulf" and that "BP employs more than 2300 people in its Gulf of Mexico business and supports tens of thousands of additional jobs in the region."[78] In addition to advocacy ads, upon the advice of Ogilvy Worldwide, BP learned in the aftermath of the disaster how to use the social media to advance its views. It used Facebook and Twitter, worked with Mindshare, a WPP Group, and opened a website, "BP Oil spill Response."[79]

Unfortunately for BP, the issue of unjustified claims was dwarfed by a federal judge ruling a few months later that the company was "grossly negligent" in the 2010 Deepwater Horizon disaster, making it liable for as much as $18 billion in pollution fines. The ruling describes repeated instances when BP took measures to cut costs despite safety risks.[80] BP had erroneously reckoned that it would be charged for "simple negligence" and accordingly set aside only $3.5 billion for such penalties. The company's shares closed 5.9% lower after the announcement.

Chevron and Ecuador

When Chevron acquired Texaco Inc. in 2001, it inherited a lawsuit accusing it of sickening Ecuadorians through environmental neglect. The plaintiffs succeeded in convincing an Ecuadorian court to find the company guilty, and in 2011 the court imposed a huge $18.2 environmental judgment against it. But rather than bow to the usual pressure to minimize bad publicity, Chevron decided to fight back against the 20-year old litigation. The company claimed that Texaco met its cleanup obligations and was released by Ecuador from further liability in 1998. Furthermore, it claimed that environmental claims had been settled by Texaco and that the case against it was "obtained by corrupt means."[81]

Chevron lambasted Steven Donziger, the prominent New York lawyer who had brought the case against the company.[82] An American federal judge, Lewis Kaplan, agreed with Chevron. In its case against Donzier, Chevron convinced two firms that had helped bankroll the plaintiffs' legal fight, and another that conducted the research, to side with Chevron instead.[83] Furthermore, one of the law firms, Patton Boggs LLP, which stood to gain nearly half a billion dollars from its share of the judgment, agreed to pay Chevron $15 million to settle its feud over the matter and to cooperate with discovery efforts by Chevron related to its remaining fight with plaintiffs' attempts to seize its assets in Canada, Brazil, and Argentina.[84]

In the latest episode of this case, New York federal judge Lewis Kaplan ruled that he may "conduct discovery"[85] regarding a $6.4 million contract between the government of Ecuador and MC Squared, a Brooklyn NY public relations firm. The firm was reported as paying protesters $85 per person to attend an anti-Chevron demonstration held at the company's annual shareholder meeting.[86]

Case 7 Reputational Crisis Faced by Samsung in Faulty Galaxy Note 7 Recall

On August 19, 2016, Samsung Electronics put its new Galaxy Note series 7 smart phone on the market, hopeful that its advanced features would successfully compete against Apple's 7 and China's Huawei Technologies phones. But, as the news media reported, an increasing number of consumers found that their phones smoked, caught on fire, or combusted, including one on a Southwest Airlines flight before takeoff.

Samsung, the world's second biggest technology company (by revenues), immediately stopped the sale of its new smart phones and asked all telecom carriers and retailers that sold the Note 7 to do the same. It rushed to get replacements. But it botched the recall, for the problem had not been fixed, as shown by at least 92 reports of fires and combustion by the end of September. It again recalled the phones, now reaching 2.5 million. It would have to lose out to its competitors Apple and China's Huawei Technologies Co.[87]

On October 14, US authorities banned carrying phones in the passenger cabin or aircraft hold, including check baggage. Samsung's shares dropped 8% on September 11. It faced an earnings hit of about $2.3 billion for the third quarter ending September 30. Analysts said it was likely to cost it $4 billion or more in recall expenses and lost sales, but the crisis was not likely to affect its A1 credit rating, thanks to its $70 billion cash pile.

Faced by a reputational crisis caused by mismanagement, Samsung said it would "move quickly to investigate the reported case to determine the cause and would share findings as soon as possible." It added, "Samsung understands the concern our carriers and consumers must be feeling after recent reports raised questions about our newly released replacement Note 7 Device." To retain its customers, Samsung offered a $100 credit for a carrier or retail outlet to customers who turned in their Galaxy Note 7 device for another Samsung smart phone.[88] Samsung was also working with such authorities as the US Consumer Product Safety Commission (CPSC) to investigate new incidents.[89] But CPSC chairman said that federal laws restrict the agency's powers in product recalls.[90] The CPSC itself was criticized in Washington for its lack of action in the recall.

Samsung in its haste had not sufficiently tested the Note 7 phone's safety, misjudging the risk that lithium-ion batteries are prone to combustion. It should have remembered Sony's 2006 crisis when bloggers reported instances when its batteries in Dell computers caught fire. And Samsung should have noted that fires occurred in airplanes when lithium-ion batteries were first used. The problem was at the time fixed by placing protective covers over the batteries. Samsung assumed that its problem might have been that the batteries had been too tightly packed, leaving no room for them to expand when charged or heavily used.

The company's big mistake was to use its in-house battery-testing facilities for its Note 7 batteries.[91] In the US, phone makes such as Apple are required to test phone batteries at one of the 28 labs certified by the US wireless industry's trade group, the CTIA. Letting manufacturers test their own phones creates the potential for conflict of interest. The CTIA tests labs to ensure personnel are qualified, that they comply with standards, and that there is no undue influence from manufacturers. Test labs are usually separate facilities and under separate control. Belatedly, Samsung now plans to make "significant changes in its quality-assurance processes."

After switching from Samsung SDI, its own affiliate battery supplier, to an outside one, Samsung quickly began handing out millions of new Galaxy Note 7 phones. But it soon discovered that its initial diagnosis was incorrect. After the replacement phones also failed, Lee Jae-Yong, Samsung's heir apparent, on October 11 ordered the newly appointed mobile chief D.J. Koh to discontinue the smart phone.[92]

Lee said the crisis was "one of the toughest challenges we have ever faced." Indeed, the recall was expected to cost $5 billion or more, including lost sales. Investors lost roughly $20 billion in Samsung's market value. In the third quarter ending September 30, Samsung took an earnings hit of about $2.3 billion.[93] Samsung announced it would "move quickly to investigate the reported case to determine the cause and will share findings as soon as possible . . . . Samsung understands the concern our carriers and consumers must be feeling after recent report have raised questions about our newly released replacement Note 7 devices."[94] On October 14, US authorities banned carrying phones in the passenger cabin or aircraft hold, including check baggage. Lowell McAdam, CEO of Verizon Communications, Inc., called the recall "a major black eye" for Samsung.[95]

Moreover, Samsung faced an additional public affairs problem by failing soon enough to notify the US CPSC, which oversees product recalls. It thereby prevented regulators from figuring out more about the root cause of phone failures. Public relations spokespersons, already busy responding to the recalls, now had to explain why it hadn't notified the CPSC. Although its regulations generally require companies to report potential product hazards within 24 hours, Samsung hadn't notified the agency until the day the recall was announced.[96]

Appearing unhappy with Koh's recall announcement, the CPSC took the unusual step of warning consumers not to use the phones while it did more research. It said it would work to determine whether Samsung's plan to issue replacement phones was "an acceptable remedy." A formal joint recall was consequently announced a few days later. Explaining the lack of notification, a Samsung spokeswoman explained, "We recognized that we did not correctly identify the issue the first time and remain committed to finding the root cause. Our top priority remains the safety of our customers and retrieving 100% of the Galaxy Note 7 devices in the market."[97] Samsung added, "We remain committed to working diligently with appropriate regulatory authorities to take all necessary steps to resolve the situation."[98]

Stuart Statler, a former CPSC commissioner, stated, "What Samsung should have done, very early on, was to share even its preliminary findings or thoughts" with US regulators rather than pushing its own recall. Furthermore, Samsung should have realized that a conflict of interest exists when testing is done internally. Samsung now plans to make significant changes in its quality-assurance processes.[99]

As part of its public relations effort to maintain customer loyalty, Samsung employed institutional advertising. It placed a full-page ad in the *Wall Street Journal* on November 7 addressed "To our valued customers." After praising itself for its innovations "to deliver breakthrough technologies that enrich people's lives," it acknowledged that it "fell short on this promise." It said, "We know you expect more from Samsung, and that your loyalty is earned, not given."[100] The ad was signed by Gregory Lee, president and CEO – Samsung Electronics North America.

Fortunately, by June 2017 Samsung delivered its biggest-ever net profit, which was boosted by strong sales of its new Galaxy S8, which won strong reviews. Samsung shares traded near all-time highs and rose more than 60% over the past year.[101] Taking necessary corrective action, even if painful, paid off.

Discussion Questions

1 In what way was this crisis self-inflicted? Explain.

2 In what ways did the crisis harm Samsung?

3 Why was it a big mistake for Samsung to use its in-house testing facilities?

4 What are the public affairs dimensions of this case?

5 Was institutional advertising used effectively in this crisis? Explain.

6 Do you know of any other situations where competitive pressures or the desire to be No. 1 in the industry have caused a crisis?

Endnotes

1 This aspect of technology is typically discussed in introductory public relations texts. The new technologies refer to such topics as uses of the computer, teleconferencing, and fiber optics.

2 "The Rise of the Superstars," *The Economist*, September 17, 2006, p. 8. The number of research staff is listed as 80 000 by the *WSJ*, which is still a formidable number. Matthias Verbergt, "Huawei Pushes for 5G Edge," *WSJ*, February 27, 2017, p. B6.

3 Ibid.

4 Brent Kendall, "Samsung Award to Apple Set For Review," *WSJ* December 7, 2016, p. B6.

5 "Drugmaker Sues Merck Over Patents," *WSJ*, September 20, 2016, p. B5.

6 John Chambers and Myron E. Ullman, "Stopping the Economy - Sapping Patent Trolls," *WSJ*, February 17, 2015, p. A9.

7 For technological aspects, see Otto Lerbinger, *The Crisis Manager: Facing Disasters, Conflicts, and Failures*, 2nd ed. (New York: Routledge, 2012), pp. 134–139.

8 Ian I. Mitroff and Can M. Alpasian, *The Crisis Prone Society A Brief Guide to Managing the Beliefs That Drive Risk in Business* (New York: Palgrave Macmillan, 2014), pp. 4–5.

9 "The Return of the Machinery Question," *The Economist*, Special Report on Artificial Intelligence, June 25, 2016, p. 3.

10 Ibid, p. 8. Study by Carl Benedikt Frey and Michael Osborne published in 2003.

11 2015 Edelman Trust Barometer Annual Global Survey.

12 Friends of the Earth Report – "Nanomaterials, Sunscreens and Cosmetics: Small Ingredients Big Risks." Available from: www.nano.foe.org.au

13 Andy Kessler, "The Robots Are Coming. Welcome Them," *WSJ*, August 23, 2016, p. A11.

14 William Wilkes, "China's Buyers Eye Germany," *WSJ*, June 9, 2016, p. A1.

15 Everett Rogers, *Diffusion of Innovations*, 3rd ed. (New York: Free Press, 1983), chapter 5. Summarized in Werner J. Severin and James W. Tankard, Jr., 3rd ed., *Communication Theories: Origins, Methods, and Uses in the Mass Media* (New York: Longman, 1992), p. 199.

16 The adoption process is outlined in Dennis Wilcox, Phillip H. Ault, and Warren K. Agee, *Public Relations: Strategies and Tactics*, 3rd ed. (New York: HarperCollins Publishers, 1992), p. 193.

17 Rogers, op. cit., chapter 7.

18 Jean-Pierre Jeannet and Hubert D. Hennessey, *Global Marketing Strategies*, 2nd ed. (Boston, MA: Houghton Mifflin Company, 1992), p. 195.

19 Jill Richardson, "Sharing is Caring," a PowerPoint presentation in fulfillment of an MS degree at Boston University's College of Communication. Douglas MacMillan and Lisa Fleisher, "U-Turn: Hard-Driving Uber Gives Compromise a Try," *WSJ*, January 30, 2015, p. A1. Douglas Macmillan and Telis Demos, "Uber Valued at more Than $50 Billion," *WSJ*, July 31, 2015.

20 Jack Nicas, "Watch Out Sheepdogs, You May Be Replaced by a Drone," *WSJ*, April 18 2015, p. A1.

21 L. Gordon Crovitz, "The Grinch Who Stole . . . Drones," *WSJ*, December 29, 2014.

22 Jack Nicas, "Is It a Toy Plane? A Drone? FAA Weighs In," *WSJ* Abstract, June 9, 2014, p. 1.

23 See Brad Stone, *The Upstarts: How Uber, Airbnb, and the Killer Companies of the New Silicon Valley Are Changing the World* (New York: Little Brown and Company, 2017).

24 In Barcelona where the hotel industry received the backing of the city when it fined AirBnb for violating regional bans.

25 Sam Schechner, "Uber Takes Its Battle to Court in Europe," *WSJ*, November 30, 2016, p. B3.

26 "The Mind-Set at Uber," an Interview by Rebecca Blumenstein with Travis Kalanick, *WSJ*, October 27, 2015, p. R5.

27 Barbara Berschler, "What PR Pros Should Know About Intellectual Property," *PR News*, October 21, 2011.

28 Dennis Wilcox, Phillip H. Ault, and Warren K. Agee, op. cit., p. 303.

29 Edward L. Bernays, *Biography of An Idea: Memoirs of Public Relations Counsel* (New York: Simon and Schuster, 1965).

30 https://ladas.com/education-center/a-brief-history-of-the-patent-law-of-the-united-states-2. Ladas and Parry, "A Brief History of the Patent Law of the United States."

31 Jess Bravin, "Justices Skeptical on Patents," *WSJ*, April 1, 2014, p. B4.

32 *Update to the IP Commission Report*, May 2017. www.ipcommission.org/report/IP_Commission_Report_Update_2017.pdf

33 Keith Johnson, "China Turbine Maker Indicted," *WSJ*, June 28, 2013, p. B2.

34 "Corporate Espionage: Who Needs Cyber-Spying," *The Economist*, February 23, 2013, p. 44.

35 Ibid.

36 B.H. Reber, K.K. Gower, and J.A. Robinson (2006). Also see "The Internet and Litigation PR," *Journal of PR Research*, 18(1), pp. 23–44.

37 www.prweb.com/releases/2013/11/prweb11378437.htm, "Jaffe PR Ranked Top Social Media Consultant by Best of Legal Times Agency."

38 Jaffe PR.

39 "Mediation: Knocking Heads Together," *The Economis*t, February 3, 2007, p. 62.

40 For a discussion of this case, see Padmini Patwardhan and Nilanjana Bardhan, "The Bhopal Carbide Disaster: A Lesson in International Crisis Communication," in Michael G. Parkinson and Daradirek Ekachai, *International and Intercultural PR* (Boston, MA: Pearson Education, 2006), pp. 220–238.

41 James Lindheim, "Distress Signals; Business Crises," *Management Today*, April 1989, p. 101.

42 The 9.0 magnitude earthquake some 100 miles off Japan's north-eastern coast and 150 miles north of Tokyo, overwhelmed the Fukushima facility. Its designers did not reckon with the one-in-a-thousand-year event that the earthquake would be followed by a tsunami with 30-ft waves. The onrush of water damaged the nuclear structure and flooded the plant's cooling system and backup diesel generators. The emergency planning systems failed completely. Furthermore, the owner of the plant, Tokyo Electric Power Co. (Tepco), waited a few crucial hours too long to pour water on Reactor 1, the most damaged of the three. In the downstream phase, the company was indecisive in deciding on the evacuation zone necessitated by radiation. Both Tepco and the government withheld information and were slow in public communication, behavior that is associated with Japan's cultural feature of high power distance.

43 Ian I. Mitroff and Can M. Alpasian, *The Crisis Prone Society: A Brief Guide to Managing the Beliefs That Drive Risk in Business*. (New York: Palgrave Macmillan, 2014), p. 22.

44 Mitroff, op. cit., pp. 26–27.

45 Paul Slovic, "Perception of Risk," *Science*, No. 236, April 17, 1987, pp. 280–285.

46 For a summary, see Otto Lerbinger, *The Crisis Manager: Facing Disasters, Conflicts, and Failures*, 2nd ed. (New York: Routledge, 2012), pp. 276–279.

47 "Communicating with the Publics," *Science*, Vol. 194, November 5, 1976, p. 5.

48 Jack N. Behman and William A. Fischer, "Overseas R&D Activities of Transnational Companies," *Thunderbird International Business Review*, Vol. 22, Issue 3, Fall 1980, pp. 15–17.

49 The author's personal experience.

50 "Corporate Culture; Learning the Lingo," *The Economist*, January 11, 2014, p. 73.

51 *Paradigm*, Spring 2014, pp. 4–5.

52 "Looking Ahead: A Message" from the Laboratory Director (Samuel Aronson) in "Sixty Years of Discovery 1947–2007."

53 Ibid. p. 56.

54 The largest and powerful particle accelerator is Europe's Large Hadron Collider run by the European Organization for Nuclear Research, known as CERN. Gautam Naik, "Hadron Collider Scientists Stumble Upon 'Pentaquark' Particle," *WSJ*, July 14, 2015.

55 As described by Public Relations Society of America.
56 Erving Goffman, *Asylums: Essays on the Social Situation of Mental Patients and Other Inmates* (New York, Anchor Books, 1961).
57 Personal communication.
58 "Ebola: Fever Rising," *The Economist*, August 16, 2014, p. 48.
59 Betsy McKay, "Ebola Failures Spark Calls for Changes," *WSJ*, November 23, 201, p. A13.
60 Peter Wonacott, "Fearful Chinese Firms Rethink Africa," *WSJ*, October 22, 2014, p. A7.
61 James Hider, "Mosquitoes That Shrink Heads of the Unborn Spark Olympic Alert," *The Times* (London), January 19, 2016, p. 31.
62 "IMF Warns G20 That World Economy 'Highly Vulnerable,'" *Zee News*, February 25, 2016. Alexandra Sifferlin,"Do I Still Need toWorry About Zika?," *Time*, April 17, 2018.
63 Jack Nicas, Ana Campoy, and Betsy McKay, "New Push to Check Spread of Ebola," *WSJ*, October 16, 2014, p. A1.
64 Ibid., pp. A8.
65 Kathleen Larey Lewton, *PR in Health Care: A Guide for Professionals* (Chicago, IL: American Hospital Association, 1995). She spent 23 years in hospital and science communications.
66 Kathleen Larey Lewton "'Reputation Recovery': The Ebola Patient Crisis in Dallas," *The Strategist*, Vol. 20, Winter 2014, pp. 22–23.
67 Stephanie Armour, "Upbeat Tone on Ebola Threat Questioned," October 17, 2014, p. A4.
68 Richard Nicolazzo, "Ebola: Caught in an Information Vortex," "*O'Dwyers: The Inside News of PR and Marketing Communications,*" October 17, 2014. www.odwyerpr.com/story/public/3354/2014-10-17/ebola-caught-an-information-vortex.html
69 Walter Isaacson, *The Innovators: How a Group of Hackers, Geniuses, and Geeks Created the Digital Revolution* (New York: Simon & Schuster, 2014), p. 287.
70 One of the books is C.P. Snow, *Two Cultures* (Cambridge: Cambridge University Press, 2001).
71 Ibid., pp. 286–488.
72 Walter Isaacson, *The Innovators* (New York: Simon & Schuster, 2014), p. 486.
73 Joseph A. Schumpeter, *Capitalism Socialism, and Democracy*, 6th ed. (London, Boston, MA: Unwin Paperbacks, 1987).
74 See Deborah Blum, Mary Knudson, and Robi Marantz Henig, eds., *A Field Guide for Science Writers: The Official Guide of the National Association of Science Writers* (New York: Oxford University Press).
75 Tom Fowler, "BP Payments May Continue to Flow," *WSJ*, January 13, 2014, p. A3.
76 *WSJ*, May 30, 2014, p. A7.
77 *WSJ*, March 6, 2014, p. A9.
78 *WSJ*, April 10, 2014, p. A13.
79 Jeff Casale, "BP Spill Response Tars Reputation," *Business Insurance*, May 31, 2010, p. 1.
80 Daniel Gilbert and Justin Scheck, "Judge Hammers BP for Gulf Disaster," *WSJ*, September 15, 2014, p. B1.
81 www.chevron.com/ecuador
82 "Chevron and Ecuador: Courtroom Drama," *The Economist*, March 8, 2014, p. 68.
83 Daniel Gilbert, "Chevron's $19 Billion Case," *WSJ*, April 22, 2013, p. B5.
84 Jennifer Smith, "Patton Boggs Agrees to Pay Chevron $15 Million," *WSJ*, May 8, 2014, p. B3.
85 Discovery refers to the formal process of exchanging information between the parties about the witnesses and the evidence they will present.
86 Mary Anastasia O'Grady, "Chevron Takes Ecuador's Government to Court," *WSJ*, December 1, 2014, p. A15.
87 Jonathan Cheng, "Crisis Tests Samsung Heir Apparent," *WSJ*, October 12, 2016, p. B1.

88 Eun-Young Jeong and Jonathan Cheng, "Samsung Offers Pay to Stay," *WSJ*, October 14, 2016, p. B5.
89 Jonathan Cheng, et al., "Samsung Hits Galaxy Note 7," *WSJ*, October 10, 2016, p. B1.
90 John D. McKinnon, "Safety Panel's Role Draws New Scrutiny," *WSJ*, October 13, 2016, p. B5.
91 Ryan Knutson and Eun-Young Jeong, "Samsung Self-Tested Its Note 7 Batteries," *WSJ*, October 17, 2016, p. B3.
92 Jonathan Cheng, "Crisis Tests Samsung Heir Apparent," *WSJ*, October 12, 2016, p. B1.
93 Eun-Young Jeong and Jonathan Cheng, "Samsung Offers Pay to Stay," *WSJ*, October 14, 2016, p. B5.
94 Jonathan Cheng, Eun-Young, and Georgia Wells, op. cit.
95 Jonathan Cheng and John D. McKinnon, "Samsung Recall's Fatal Flaw," *WSJ*, October 24, 2016, p. A1.
96 John D. McKinnon, "Safety Panel's Role Draws New Scrutiny," *WSJ*, October 13, 2016, p. B5.
97 Cheng and McKinnon, op. cit., p. A12.
98 Jonathan Cheng, Eun-Young Jeong, and Georgia Wells, "Samsung Shaken by Galaxy Woes," *WSJ*, October 11, 2016,p. A1.
99 Ryan Knutson and Eun-Young Jeong, "Samsung Self-Tested Its Note 7 Batteries," *WSJ*, October 17, 2016, p. B3.
100 Ad appeared November 7, 2016, p. A9.
101 Timothy W. Martin and Eun-Young Jeong, "Samsung Soars After Rough Year," *WSJ*, July 27, 2017, p. B1.

Part V

Corporate Communication Contribution to Management

In dealing with the management perspective of corporate communication, the corporate communication officer (CCO) should be able to contribute to management decision making. Here he or she draws on the larger scope and intrinsic meaning of public relations. It is concerned with how an organization relates to society and its stakeholders – whether its behavior is acceptable enough to maintain its legitimacy and reputation. The public opinion and publicity aspects of public relations discussed in Part II are subordinate to this overarching management function of public relations. CCOs must extend their competence to this larger scope of public relations to be able to contribute to management decision making.

This contribution is vitally important in the international arena where the challenges to corporate reputation are most pronounced. Google and Uber know this because their operations in Europe and China are questioned by powerful interest groups and governments. General Electric knows this from the difficulties encountered in France in acquiring Alstom SA. Companies have had their reputations damaged by accusations of deliberate or negligent behavior in product quality, environmental harm, perceptions of greed, and disregard for the interests of others. Simply engaging in defensive communications is not enough when a company's license to operate is jeopardized. CCOs must examine a company's policies and behavior and recommend changes in order to restore trust and goodwill. Ideally, they should be a member of a company's top management team and board of directors.

Management must make key decisions in the international arena about expanding operations abroad, acquiring foreign companies, and accepting changes demanded by non-governmental organizations (NGOs). Furthermore, responses to some of the antitrust charges by foreign governments and supranational organizations, such as the European Union (EU), are the responsibility of top management. But broader aspects of public relations and public affairs are intricately involved. Their role cannot be limited to communications.

Yet even within the communication function, a basic knowledge of management helps a CCO by giving an insight into an organization's or client's organizational goals and ways of operating. For a company, this means knowing what products and services produce revenue, what its supply chains are, and challenges it faces in making a profit. A chronic complaint of employers of communication students is that they "don't know anything about business."

It is also important to know how an organization is structured, e.g. its specialization by departments and the scalar system of levels of authority. A CCO needs a "map" showing where to find people within an organization whose knowledge and views might help in understanding a current issue or an emerging crisis. And a CCO must know how he or she can interact with and support other functions, such as human resources, finance, law, and supplier relations. In this capacity, the CCO's role is to serve as a generalist to make sure

Corporate Communication: An International and Management Perspective, First Edition. Otto Lerbinger.

that there is coherence in how the specialized functions affect a company's stakeholders and its organizational integrity.

The broadest connection of a CCO to management is to help it find an equitable and sustainable balance between its drive to maximize profits for stockholders and a concern for other stakeholders and society at large. How far the latter concern should go remains controversial because some see incompatibility with the free market system. To address this issue, Part V examines two management aspects of corporate communications: whether a company acts as a good corporate citizen by exercising social responsibility, and how it can contribute to corporate governance. The latter is receiving increasing attention since the demise of Enron, the 2008 banking crises, and the recent resignations of the chief executive officer (CEO) and board members at Toshiba and Volkswagen.

Management Systems of International Coordination

Companies face the management problem of maintaining coordination and control among a company's subsidiary offices as they exercise their corporate affairs responsibilities. Local managers must make decisions based on local conditions, but must also conform to headquarters policies and help advance its corporate goals. The problem is essentially one of centralization and decentralization. How are headquarters and country-level corporate communication activities coordinated? How much control should headquarters exercise? What matters should best be decentralized?

Princeton's Study of Centralization and Decentralization

Princeton University's study of *Centralization and Decentralization in Industrial Relations* made an important contribution to management decision making and control.[1] The study's major finding is that decision making is a diffuse process whereby a single decision typically involves several managers and organizational levels.

For example, in a decision at DuPont's Buffalo plant about whether a recently hired employee who lied about having a dependent child for tax purposes should be fired, his supervisor initiated the decision. A meeting was then held that was attended by the factory superintendent, the personnel manager, the local union leader, and the plant manager. They were guided by the policies and procedures of DuPont's company-wide employee relations manual. The group made a recommendation to the plant manager who then exercised his formal authority and decided to discharge the employee. The decision was subsequently reviewed by the Industrial Relations Department in Wilmington, Delaware. The key aspect of the decision making process is that no single person made the decision and that the influence of headquarters guided the local decision.

Exxon's International Public Affairs Department

Decision-making by Exxon Corporation's international public affairs department follows a similar process. James A. Morakis, who headed the department, described the various methods used by his department to coordinate the activities of managers in Europe, Africa, South America, Central America, the Middle East, and the Asia-Pacific region. Morakis said that local affiliates were given "considerable freedom and flexibility to make decisions on their own." However, overall objectives were centrally determined and local managers were aware of corporate policies. Furthermore, local managers sent frequent local status reports to headquarters and were in constant communication with it and visited headquarters periodically. They would check with headquarters "when something was going on that was over their heads."

Morakis and other members at headquarters would frequently visit local affiliates and listen to presentations by the public affairs staff. These visits included meetings with local company CEOs to learn what was going on and what their evaluation was of how well the local public affairs people were doing. A further sharing of information and ideas occurred at an important 1-week annual public affairs seminar at Boston University College of Communication attended by public affairs staff members from more than a dozen countries. They learned what was new in public affairs and they jointly participated in case studies prepared by individual members that illustrated the situations they encountered. It was a way for them better to know one another and to develop a unified approach and culture. Morakis stressed that it was important that each country's public affairs office be familiar not only with their local situations and issues but what was going on worldwide. "There aren't too many decisions that affect other parts of the world, but more than you think." He repeated, "They affect you more than you think, because repercussions occur on a worldwide basis."

These methods of coordination are included and expanded upon by Juan-Carlos Molleda, former chairman of the Department of Public Relations at the University of Florida and now dean of the School of Journalism and Communication at the University of Oregon. He lists corporate culture reports; visits to subsidiaries; management performance evaluation; cost and accounting comparability; evaluative measurement; information systems; global, cross-functional, and virtual teams; advisory personnel; management rotation and socialization; training programs; assemblies and special global or regional meetings; and keeping international and domestic personnel in closer proximity. He states that media relations, government relations, and consumer relations show a medium level of centralization compared with internal communication or employee relations, which had low levels of centralization. Investor relations appears to be the most centralized function and community relations the most decentralized practice. To achieve a *glocal* balance, integrative communication devices are used, such as annual reports, websites, intranets, conferences, teleconferences, videoconferences, newsletters and bulletins, and codes of conducts and ethics.[2]

Coke in Belgium[3]

The need for careful coordination is illustrated by a crisis faced by Coca-Cola, the number one world brand, in Belgium. With its visibility and a reputation for progressive policies, it was particularly vulnerable to rumors and news stories.

In June 1999, Belgian newspapers reported that some people in Belgium became ill after drinking Coke. Upon making normal inquires, Coke managers in Belgium decided there was no justification for any action. But a second incident occurred soon afterwards when school children in the town of Bornem felt dizziness, nausea, and other symptoms after drinking Coca-Cola at school. Forty-two were hospitalized over the next 24 hours.

Coca-Cola remained silent, although it should have realized that it was facing a crisis. Local managers should have engaged in a local recall, but didn't until a third incident, also in early June, when eight children were hospitalized in Bruges after drinking Coke. After the Belgian health minister received 200 calls, he summoned Coke officials to a meeting and ordered all Coca-Cola products off the market and production to be halted in two bottling plants. Coke had forfeited its opportunity to be seen as taking the initiative. Further reports of contamination were received from Luxembourg, France, the Netherlands, and Germany. Instead of taking the lead, Coke was seen as reacting to government orders.

Finally, on June 15, Coke held a press conference and issued its first press release that acknowledged that bottles sold mainly in the Belgian market had been tainted from a shipping pallet. The situation then received the attention of its CEO Douglas Ivester. In an open letter to the public he issued the company's first apology to European consumers, saying that it was "taking all necessary steps" to ensure quality. The next day, 10 days after the first incidence of sick school children, he flew to Brussels. The lack of immediacy harmed the effectiveness of the apology and his visit. After only 2 years as CEO, Ivester resigned.

Coke headquarters had apparently followed a decentralization policy of allowing its Belgian office to handle the contamination problem. But the personnel there seemed to know little about crisis management, and the headquarters office in Atlanta should have interceded. The company was facing a serious threat to its brand name and the tenure of its CEO.

Endnotes

1 Helen Baker and Robert R. France, *Centralization and Decentralization in Industrial Relations* (Princeton, NJ: Industrial Relations Section, Department of Economics and Sociology, 1954. The author participated in this project.

2 Juan-Carlos Molleda and A. Laskin, "Coordination and Control of Global Public Relations to Manage Cross-Cultural Conflict Shifts," in Guy Golan, Thomas J. Johnson and Wayne Wanta, eds., *International Media Communications in a Global Age* (New York: Routledge, 2010), pp. 319–344.

3 See "Tainted Coke in Europe," in Otto Lerbinger, *The Crisis Manager: Facing Disasters, Conflicts, and Failures*, 2nd ed. (New York: Routledge, 2012), pp. 223–225.

16

Global Corporate Social Responsibility

When corporate social responsibility (CSR) is applied globally new challenges are faced. The laws and regulations of the home country, as well as the understandings with stakeholders and the general public, are no longer adequate. In the international arena, new relationships are formed that increase the burden of CSR and require new insights. Multi-national corporations (MNCs) must overcome the temptation to take advantage of weak governments and ineffective public sanctions in developing countries. Non-governmental organizations (NGOs) often compensate for these inadequacies by confronting MNCs with a variety of demands, especially regarding the treatment of employees and protection of the environment.

Rather than be reactive, corporate communicators have an opportunity to apply CSR abroad.

16.1 Corporate Irresponsibility Abroad

16.1.1 Poor Working Conditions: The Bangladesh Disaster

The failure of global corporate responsibility was dramatically demonstrated when a disaster in the apparel factory building in Dhaka, Bangladesh, killed over 1100 people on April 24, 2013.[1] It exposed the dark side of globalization and raised questions about company business practices abroad. The eight-story Rana Plaza building, which housed five garment factories producing clothing for name apparel companies, collapsed the day after its owner told complaining workers who noticed cracks in the wall that the building would last another 100 years. Perhaps because the threshold of 1000 deaths was reached, the news media reported the tragedy. Corporate brands and reputations were at stake, in addition to the economic viability of continuing to do business with Bangladesh apparel exporters.

The Raza Plaza disaster revealed some of the worst side-effects of globalization when companies operate at zero or low levels of CSR. Working conditions were grossly deficient as shown in the use of child labor, lack of fire doors and outside staircases, long work weeks, and harsh supervision (e.g. not being allowed to go to a rest room until an output quota is reached).

The immediate and conventional response of the apparel companies whose garments were manufactured there was to say that they bore no responsibility because their Bangladesh suppliers were independent companies who employed the affected workers. Furthermore, the garment companies argued that they provided badly needed jobs in areas of severe poverty.

This reaction was reminiscent of Nike's exposure in 1992 by *Harper's Magazine* and *The New York Times* for child labor abuses by its Indonesian suppliers.[2] It subsequently suffered loss of sales, declining stock market prices, and other consequences of reputational damage. The main impact, however, was to refute the denial of responsibility. Others could no longer be blamed for Nike's shortcomings. By 1998 it accepted responsibility and switched to a cooperative approach.

Corporate Communication: An International and Management Perspective, First Edition. Otto Lerbinger.

In Bangladesh, Nike publicly acknowledged its negligence and engaged with its suppliers to improve the treatment of the nearly 650 000 workers employed in their factories.

16.1.2 Sales of Dangerous Products Abroad

Many products that endanger the health and safety of millions of people in the world's most vulnerable nations are being sold overseas – and by some of the largest and most respected companies. The headlines of Christopher Scanlan's article in *The Seattle Times* states the problem dramatically: "America's Deadly Exports – Trade of Toxic Products Abroad is a Windfall for U.S. Companies."[3] One of his examples is that while the Environmental Protection Agency wouldn't let Dow-Elanco sell its weed-killer Galant to US farmers because it might cause cancer, it allowed the sale in Costa Rica.

Cigarettes are an oft-mentioned example. While the US surgeon general tells Americans that cigarettes kill, the US government, at the behest of the tobacco industry, has since 1985 repeatedly promoted the sale of cigarettes in Asian countries. For example, US negotiators threatened to retaliate against Taiwan unless it dropped barriers to American cigarettes. Although Taiwan had aimed to prevent their import, Philip Morris, R.J. Reynolds Tobacco, and Brown & Williamson sold 3.7 billion cigarettes a year.[4]

William Shaw's *Business Ethics: A Textbook with Cases* cites other examples of selling dangerous products abroad.[5] One case was "Made in the U.S.A. – Dumped in Brazil, Africa, Iraq." Another was the dumping on developing world countries of millions of children's pajamas treated with TRIS, a suspected cancer-causing chemical. They had been banned from sale in the US. Among other examples are the sale of 450 000 baby pacifiers of a type known to have caused choking deaths, and the sale of wheat and barley treated with a US-banned organic mercury fungicide Winstrol. Four hundred Iraqis died and 500 were hospitalized after eating wheat and barley treated with this fungicide.

Akin to selling dangerous products abroad is the "export" of environmental waste to foreign countries that accept such imports. For example, Formosa Plastics Group in Taiwan planned to export nearly 3000 metric tons of toxic waste to Cambodia in 1998.[6] Similarly, a company may locate environmentally harmful manufacturing facilities abroad. Natural resources companies in the copper industry, for example, find it advantageous to process raw materials in countries where the ore is extracted.

16.1.3 Foreign Purchases of Agricultural Land

Agricultural land is becoming such a scarce resource in many developed countries that some are buying agricultural land in Africa and elsewhere. South Korea, Saudi Arabia, and China are among those who have done so in Africa with the intent of growing agricultural products.[7] They plan to use modern farming techniques to make the land as productive as possible, which includes the use of farm equipment and fertilizer. Existing farmers used century-old methods that were inefficient and produced low yields. Because they typically don't have proof of legal ownership, these farmers were evicted. Only a few, if any, would be employed by the new owners. The new foreign farming companies face a formidable CSR issue of how to deal fairly with former farmers.

Some companies that deal with existing farmers have applied CSR policies to improve their output. In Afghanistan, Fullwell Mill, a British food producer, together with Mercy Corps, a humanitarian NGO, worked with the Parwan Raisin Producers Cooperative, a network of local farmers, to grow and export fair trade raisins to Britain. The venture also received funding support from the US Agency for International Development (USAID), the US government funding agency.[8]

Some governments are resisting land purchases by foreign countries. For example, Australia's Prime Minister Malcolm Turnbull blocked the sale of one of the world's biggest cattle farms, the Kidman property, to Chinese and other foreign investors on national security grounds. Takeovers, particularly in agriculture, are a sensitive matter in Australia.[9]

16.1.4 Offensive Banking and Insurance Practices

Banks and insurance companies, where trust should be high, have unfortunately engaged in irresponsible behavior. Some banks seek to increase profits through stiff overdraft fines, which average about $30. Their calculation method further harms consumers. Those who incur multiple overdrafts in a single day are penalized on a "high to low" basis whereby a bank deducts the largest withdrawal before the smaller ones, making it more likely that multiple overdrafts will bounce. As regulators have stepped up criticism, most giant banks, such as the Bank of America Corp. and Wells Fargo & Co., have dropped the practice, but small and regional banks have not.[10]

The marketing of credit cards to risky borrowers is another questionable banking practice. The *Wall Street Journal* reported that in the first quarter of 2014 banks and other lenders issued 3.7 million credit cards to so-called subprime borrowers. They were considered a growth opportunity after the high-quality market became saturated. The average interest rate for overdrafts by such customers was 21.1% in the first quarter of 2014.[11]

Even reputable insurance companies fell down on CSR. MetLife paid death benefits on life insurance policies only when policy holders' beneficiaries filed claims. It took prodding by multi-state regulators for MetLife to agree to cross-check its life-insurance policy holder base against death databases to identify if payments were due. Subsequent payments to heirs could lead to payments of more than $400 million. It includes hundreds of thousands of older people with small policies, mostly less than $1000 in face value, dating back as early as the 1900s.[12]

Some banks make so-called payday loans, charging exorbitant interest. For example, a $100 14-day payday loan might be charged $15, which amounts to about $390 interest per year. These banks argue that the alternative would force people in need of money to go to pawn brokers and others who charge usurious interest rates.

16.2 Foundations of Global Corporate Social Responsibility

CSR means that business should not just seek to maximize profits but also recognize the interests of society in general. CSR requires that the narrow view of the free market system, which only represents the legal rights of investors, must be replaced by recognition that the interests of at least the key stakeholders of workers, customers, and the community must be served. The basic idea of CSR is to achieve an equilibrium between the economic system and society. Furthermore, sociologists remind economists that the purpose of an economy is to serve society – not the other way around.

16.2.1 A Common Code of Ethics and Professional Standards

CSR is rooted in a common code of ethics.[13] Ethics basically deals with judgments about what is right and wrong, good and bad, virtuous, and evil. On another level, ethics deals with the abstract ideals of fairness, justice, and due process. Some aspects of ethics are embodied in law, but others transcend the law. Some rules of moral common sense include:

- Avoid and prevent harm to others.
- Respect the rights of others.

- Be fair.
- Keep promises and contracts.

Bentley University's well-known Center for Business Ethics considers ethics a key concept in the management of a business organization. Ethics are a fundamental part of an organization's value system and a form of corporate self-regulation integrated into a business model. CSR serves that purpose, for it ensures an organization's active compliance with the spirit of the law, ethical standards, and international norms.

The standards of professional organizations are another framework for safeguarding the public interest. A prominent example is the American Institute of Certified Public Accountants, which sets the ethical standards and auditing standards for the industry. Unfortunately, there has been a decline of professional standards among this important category of accountants who vouch for the transparency and accuracy of company financial reports. They are no longer accorded people's trust, which is also true for bankers, lawyers, and politicians. Accountants are put under enormous pressure by their employers or clients to come up with numbers that seem to comply with standards but paint a picture that is not wholly truthful. Private companies are said to do it all the time, either to depress profits and avoid paying profit-related income to others, or to paint a rosy picture when they need someone else's money. Public companies are usually under pressure to maintain growth for share value and to prevent falling profits, which are seen as a sign of weakness.

The Public Relations Society of America's (PRSA) Code of Ethics seeks mostly to preserve the integrity of the process of communication. It states, "A member shall not engage in any practice which tends to corrupt the integrity of channels of communication or the processes of government." Also, "A member shall adhere to truth and accuracy and to generally accepted standards of good taste." The code asks a member to conduct "his or her professional life in accord with the public interest."[14]

Fair dealings with clients or employers and with fellow practitioners and the general public are also demanded. Confidences are to be upheld, but "A member shall be prepared to identify publicly the name of the client or employer on whose behalf any public communication is made."

16.2.2 Observing Global Declarations

Global CSR has been widely expanded in the international arena through several universal declarations that required MNCs to recognize their responsibilities in every location where they do business. An important endorsement of global corporate citizenship was made by Klaus Schwab, executive chair of the World Economic Forum. He views it as an extension of the stakeholder concept applied on a global scale, whereby the corporation itself acts as a stakeholder in a global society, together with government and civil society.[15] To gain trust and legitimacy, which are the outcomes of CSR, companies must be responsible citizens wherever they operate.

Among the important declarations are the Universal Declaration of Human Rights, the Millennium Development Goals, and the Global Compact, which outline some goals of CSR. After the Millennium Development Goals expired in 2015,they were succeeded in 2016 by a new framework, the Sustainable Development Goals.. So-called LEAD companies who have signed up with the Global Compact have developed Issue Priority Areas for the new Development Agenda, which they portray on a pyramid with four levels:

1) Prosperity and equity.
2) Human needs and capacities: education, women's empowerment and gender equality, and health.
3) The resource triad: food and agriculture, water and sanitation, and energy and climate.

4) Enabling environment: peace and stability, infrastructure and technology, and good governance and human rights.

The Global Compact is particularly relevant to MNCs because it summarizes the aspirations of leaders in the UN and civil society that serve as goals of responsible behavior for global businesses. First presented in July 2000, it contained nine "millennium" principles, with a tenth adopted later. They were organized into four categories:

- *Broad expectations of the business community*: (i) business should support and respect the protection of internationally proclaimed human rights; and (ii) make sure that they are not complicit in human rights violations.
- *Protecting labor and the exploitation of labor*: (iii) business should uphold the freedom of association and the effective recognition of the right to collective bargaining; (iv) elimination of all forms of forced and compulsory labor; (v) effective abolition of child labor; and (vi) elimination of discrimination with respect to employment and occupation.
- *Environmental protection*: (vii) business should support a precautionary approach to environmental challenges; (viii) undertake initiatives to promote greater environmental responsibility; and (ix) encourage the development and diffusion of environmentally friendly technologies.
- *Anticorruption*: (x) business should work against corruption in all its forms including extortion and bribery.[16]

  By 2007, 1700 companies had signed the compact. From 40 who signed up in 2000, 8000 did so by 2013.[17] All of the declarations associated with the UN resemble the pluses and minuses of codes of ethics in that they state desirable moral behavior, but provide for no enforcement. The compact simply requires publication in a company's annual or other report about what they did to support the goals.

Except for scattered anecdotes, little is known about the extent to which corporate behavior has been affected. The goals are abstract and intended to become a part of a company's culture. Like some codes of ethics, they make a company look good. A global corporate communication professional would urge his or her company to join the compact, hoping perhaps that the action would encourage the company to be socially responsible. Some companies that signed the compact were later "delisted" when they failed to comply with the annual reporting requirement. As of 2013, over 4000 corporate participants were dropped. The reason given by one of the small companies is that it couldn't afford the "bureaucracy."

Like many lofty statements, their value must be measured over the long term. Often it takes a crisis to remind a company that it's a good idea to take the principles seriously. Talisman Energy, discussed in Chapter 10, learned this in its operations in Sudan.

16.3 Management Approaches to Corporate Social Responsibility

When a company accepts the doctrine of social responsibility, it concomitantly changes its business practices. One approach is to engage in social bookkeeping by going beyond the strict boundaries of accountancy. Another approach is to expand on its business goals by including social as well as financial and economic criteria.

16.3.1 A Compensatory Approach to CSR: Social Bookkeeping

Business is at the center of the free market system where sellers and buyers trade goods and services at prices set by the interaction of supply and demand. The public interest is safeguarded by the well-known "invisible" hand portrayed by Adam Smith, which works when competition exists. "Society" was somewhere out there taking care of itself. But in the real world, business needs to examine its relationship with society very closely, especially in the international context where there are significant societal differences. Corporate communication professionals are given the responsibility to mediate between business and society.

Under the free enterprise system, organizations individually keep their own bookkeeping system. It shows receipt from sales, expenses of operations, fixed expenses of buildings and equipment, and the resulting profit or loss. But such bookkeeping records only transactions that bear prices mediated through the market system. Many inequities arise from this system because some things of value received by an organization and many costs created by it do not pass through market channels. They are therefore not recorded in an organization's books. They are generally known as social benefits or social costs.

Business sometimes argues that "the books are balanced" with society because it makes tax payments. But these taxes do not completely discharge a company's debt to society. Many social problems and other social costs are attended to by society's non-profit organizations (NPOs), such as the United Way and the America Red Cross. Corporate philanthropic contributions help to compensate for their services, but they are typically insufficient and create their own problems of "free-loader" companies that benefit from non-profit services but don't make any or make only meager contributions.

The purpose of social bookkeeping is to account for these non-market items by going beyond company bookkeeping systems and trying to measure broader rights and obligations to society as a whole. Air and water pollution, noise, and environmental damage are typically not recorded. The corporate communication function is to serve as a social bookkeeper of society by keeping track of these social costs.[18]

Public relations people were among the first to recognize the value of publishing social reports. They refer to what a company does that is beneficial to employees, the community, and the larger society. Some reports also recognize the criticisms of a company about environmental and other social costs and how the company addresses those issues. These reports, variously called social reports or sustainability reports, provide a solid basis for the public relations bookkeeping function.

The larger context of how a company balances its books with society has been studied by sociologists specializing in the relationship between the economy and society. They consider the economy to be a sub-system of society and therefore subordinate to it. Economists use the term *externalities* to refer to the consequences of business activities on society.[19]

16.3.1.1 Corporate Giving in Developed Nations

In developed nations, companies benefit from the existing infrastructure of the communities where they are located. Public utilities, roads, skilled labor, and schools illustrate such infrastructure. Some socially responsible companies acknowledge these "social overhead" benefits by allocating a percentage of profits, e.g. 3% to philanthropic giving. Day-Hudson in Minneapolis was known for giving 5% to a variety of community NPOs in the fields of education, health, welfare, and the arts.

Companies may aim some contributions at specific agencies, such as Family Services of Boston, that particularly help their employees with such problems as alcoholism or drug addiction. The main motivation for giving, however, is to improve livability in the communities where a company is located and thereby make it a more attractive place for employees to work. Recruitment of engineers, managers, and other high-level employees is thereby enhanced.

Policies must be drafted to guide corporate giving to avoid such undesirable practices as letting a chief executive officer's (CEO) spouse decide on a gift to a favorite museum. Corporate giving may be motivated by a company's desire to compensate for past "sins" or to create a favorable image that is appealing to opinion leaders and consumers. As one executive quipped, "It's a lot cheaper than taking out ads saying how great you are."

Following the 2008 banking crisis, Goldman Sachs's motive for giving was driven by a concern for its reputation with ordinary Americans and politicians in Washington. Realizing that it was known by many as a symbol of Wall Street greed and excess, it wanted to show its charitable side. It became one of the nation's leading corporate philanthropists, reporting in 2013 that it had given away more than $1.6 billion since 2008.[20]

A trend in corporate giving has been to devote more money to fewer causes and organizations. For example, from 2009 to 2010, 33% of US companies, compared to 23% during the previous year, devoted more than half of their giving to one cause, with healthcare and education topping the list.[21] In helping to prepare a qualified workforce, some companies lend scientists to teach science courses at local schools and routinely make speakers available for university classes. They also sponsor internships, offer career counseling, and provide employee tutors to reduce adult illiteracy.

US companies are donating more money to foreign charities. The Council on Foundations found that the total of international grants awarded in the United States grew to about $5 billion in 2006 from $4 billion in 2004. Chevron gave nearly $275 million to the Niger Delta Partnership Initiative Foundation in 2014.[22] India showed interest in philanthropy by holding a meeting of Conference Board executives of 20 major corporations to produce a "report on global corporate philanthropy." It said: "But our work was animated by the ongoing, worldwide transformation of philanthropy from a peripheral expense to a strategic investment aligning the interests of companies, shareholders, employees, and communities."[23]

16.3.2 The Global CSR Pyramid

The CSR pyramid, which has long been used as a frame of reference in thinking about CSR, is adaptable to the global arena. Beginning at the bottom of the pyramid, which shows the satisfaction of basic human needs, it reaches higher levels of corporate responsibility. A company should strive to climb the pyramid. As developed by Archie B. Carroll, the pyramid consists of five levels.[24]

1) Performing the basic economic functions of providing society with goods and services and, concomitantly, creating jobs. This goal is the foundation of the free market system. Common measures are a company's contribution to gross domestic product (GDP) and employment. For developing nations, the provision of employment opportunities is a major contribution.

   The extent to which this function is fulfilled, however, must be considered. With employee relations, for example, the various levels are described by Abraham Maslow's "hierarchy of needs" (see Chapter 3). For consumer relations, transactions may be supplanted with the concept of consumer relationship management (CRM), which includes such additional dimensions as disclosure of information, complaint systems, and participation opportunities (see Chapter 2).
2) Minimizing social costs. These are costs that are not recognized in the bookkeeping system of an organization and therefore do not affect its profits. These costs include harm to the health and safety of employees; burdens placed on local communities, such as increased traffic and noise; despoliation of the environment by water and air pollution; and destruction of natural resources.
3) Helping solve social problems that burden employees, their families, and the wider community. These are problems typically left to government or shifted to NPOs. Typical problems are

occupational safety and health hazards, equal opportunity, protection of personal privacy, consumer protection, legal and ethical behavior, community needs for public services and education, and broad national questions such as unemployment, inflation, and international trade.

Some social problems may be attributed to company activities. When work creates high stress, workers may resort to drinking and abuse to family members. Conversely, crime in a community may affect a company and the security of its employees. Michael Porter advises: "Each company can identify the particular set of societal problems that it is best equipped to help resolve and from which it can gain the greatest competitive benefit."[25] This is often called strategic philanthropy

4) Making social investments. Governments usually undertake the building of physical infrastructure such as the construction or improvement of roads, the construction of schools and hiring of teachers, and support of community amenities. But companies can also make social investments, sometimes in the form of public/private partnerships. This level is a feature in developing nations, for many require huge infrastructure investments.
5) Improving the quality of life of employees and community citizens. This level is now often equated with happiness.[26] What counts is the subjective well-being of people. The small country of Bhutan, for example, counts happiness in its national economic statistics. In France, although its GDP per capita is smaller than the US's, less time is spent at work and government programs help in caring for mothers and their children. Furthermore, economists have long pointed out the illogicality that a country's GDP counts the destruction of forests as a plus because the timber is counted as an economic output.[27]

Politicians and people in developing countries may be less dissatisfied with their low per capita GDPs when polls show that their people report high levels of happiness. A poll by Lipso Systems Inc., a transcontinental company that delivers mobile solutions, shows over 50% of Indonesians and about 42% of people in India and Mexico consider themselves "very happy." But caution must be exercised in interpreting such statistics, because of varying measurements used by different polls; for example, Gallup asks about "well-being" and the World Values survey about "life satisfaction."[28]

16.3.2.1 Focus on Infrastructure Investments

Of these five levels, social investment has received the most attention in the global CSR pyramid because it not only relates to the need of companies for supportive infrastructure from the communities where they are located but also to the willingness of companies to supplement infrastructure. A community relations manager must take an inventory of existing community resources and determine what must be done to maintain them. Especially in developing countries with deficits in labor and infrastructure, a company may find it necessary to make social investments.

Labor force deficit is most extreme in countries with an agrarian base because workers hired by entering companies lack the necessary habits and attitudes associated with industrialization. Such companies must investment in extra human resource training to bring employees up to necessary standards. This was reportedly the problem in Bhopal, India, when lethal gas escaped from a Union Carbide plant, killing over 3700 people in the local community.[29] A company exercises CSR in worker training when it exceeds the absolute minimum needed by a worker and helps to more thoroughly prepare the worker for future jobs.

A feature of developing countries is the paucity of physical infrastructure of roads, water supply, and electricity. More expansive infrastructure associated with a developed nation would include housing, education, medical facilities, social agencies, and social and cultural amenities.

Government is the usual provider of infrastructure because of its high capital requirements, the length of time construction takes, and because the beneficiaries exceed those of a particular company.

Even some companies that are in the business of building infrastructure may find that it must compensate for some missing aspects. For example, among United Arab Emirates (UAE)-based companies, telecom service provider Etisalat has been engaged in a number of its CSR-related projects in Tanzania, Nigeria, Egypt, and Sri Lanka, including ensuring available drinking water to villagers. Ahmad Bin Ali, group senior vice president of corporate communications at Etisalat, reports a "good return on investment."[30]

Among developed nations, when a company in one country seeks to build a plant in another country, public relations is employed to gain local approval. An example is the German chemical company BASF when it sought to build a plant near Charleston, South Carolina. It was opposed by several affected communities, even though it had the endorsement of state officials. Harm to the ecosystem and local fishing and recreational interests were paramount issues.[31]

A company has several choices when faced with infrastructure inadequacies. It may decide not to market goods or build facilities there. But if prospects look good, it may decide to provide infrastructure for itself. Cadbury did this when it entered Nigeria and found the water supply lacking.[32] Oil and mining companies have no choice but to build necessary infrastructure in locations where deposits are found.

When General Electric (GE) undertook a healthcare initiative in Africa, its CEO Jeffrey Immelt recognized the relevance of GE's capabilities to the problem of healthcare in Arica. Beyond medicines and doctors, the local healthcare infrastructure depended on clean water, reliable energy, and state of-the art medical technology. GE had substantial expertise in all of these areas. After consulting with experts from UNICEF, Africare, the European Union (EU), USAID, and the US Department of State, GE ultimately selected Ghana to apply its scheme. It realized that any solution required local ownership and participation. Thus, after selecting one of Ghana's 110 districts, GE developed a cross-sector partnership that included the state health ministry, local members of parliament, the mayor, tribal leaders, and NPOs working in the region. Each partner contributed to the project.[33]

16.3.3 Corporate Citizenship

Some companies prefer to speak of corporate citizenship rather than CSR. The latter refers to actions taken by a company – when it explores how it could do some "good" for society through philanthropy, environmental stewardship, and meeting other expectations in accordance with society's values. These actions exceed those required by law and regulatory requirements. These ways are summarized in the CSR pyramid.

Rather than actions, corporate citizenship is a broader commitment to society. It is a status a company acquires when it applies the values of social responsibility to its relationship with society. It states in what ways the interests of all stakeholders and not only those of stockholders could better be satisfied. Boston College's Carroll School of Management's Center for Corporate Citizenship describes corporate citizenship as follows[34]:

> At its core, corporate citizenship is about the role business plays in 21st century society. It encompasses corporate activities related to community involvement, philanthropy, environmental, and governance issues. Companies that embrace it seek to strengthen their relationship with communities and build sustainable strategies for addressing large societal issues.

> A common thread among those companies that experience success with their efforts is a commitment to integrate a corporate responsibility strategy with the overall business strategy in a way that makes it part of a firm's DNA. Firms that integrate corporate citizenship with business goals have at their disposal a more robust set of tools for serving customers, shareholders, and communities.[35]

Both corporate citizenship and CSR may also have a larger purpose of transforming a company's business model to specifically address social and sustainability challenges. IKEA's People and Planet initiative, for example, calls for its entire supply chain to be 100% sustainable by 2020.[36] Such goals constitute a business discipline so that every initiative delivers business results.

However CSR and corporate citizenship are explained, it is the basis to obtain society's *license to operate*. The term was coined in the mining industry whose requirements for specific pieces of land conflicted with communities, but is now used extensively by all industries and governments as a key driver for CSR and community relationships. Communities seek increased involvement in decisions that affect them and demand a greater share of benefits.

Companies realize that they need ongoing approval from local communities to earn their trust. The license to operate is a form of self-regulation whereby a business monitors and ensures its active compliance with the spirit of the law, ethical standards, and international norms. It requires timely and effective communication, meaningful dialogue, and ethical and responsible behavior. Rosabeth Moss Kanter, Harvard Business School professor and author of *SuperCorp*, believes that companies must forge a new with society. To gain trust and legitimacy – values that are associated with CSR – companies must be responsible citizens wherever they operation. Global companies will behave more and more alike, says Kanter: "they will be globally connected, technologically enabled, humanly diverse and socially accountable."[37]

16.3.4 New Business Models

New business models are appearing. In one type, the values of CSR predominate. This approach is embodied in David Bornstein's book, *How to Change the World: Social Entrepreneurs and the Power of New Ideas*.[38] It's about people who have "powerful ideas to improve people's lives and they have implemented them across cities, countries, and, in some cases, the world."[39] Muhammad Yunus, who founded the Grameen Bank, is a notable example.

Another business model is the formation of "the benefit corporation" whose double bottom line is both profit and social benefit.[40] Legislatures in 19 states and the District of Columbia have ratified the new corporate structure. It is for firms that want to do good while making a profit. Most of these are small companies such as Big Bad Woof, a pet store that wants to support local suppliers, and Blue Plant, a diving company that wants to attract investors who support its commitments to ocean conservation.

A large company that became a benefit corporation is Patagonia Inc., a privately owned company whose mission is to "build the best product, cause no unnecessary harm, and use business to inspire and implement solutions to the environmental crisis."[41] Its mantra is Reduce, Repair, Reuse, Recycle. Similarly, Ben & Jerry's, although sold to Unilever after poor stock market performance, was allowed to form a benefit corporation.[42] Benefit corporation statues require companies to fairly compensate their employees and include all stakeholders – not just shareholders – in the governance of the company.

16.4 Forging International Agreements – the Case of Bangladesh

In the aftermath of the Bangladesh disaster, companies whose products were manufactured in its factories recognized the need to take corrective action to reduce or eliminate future occurrences. Other than shifting production elsewhere, it was the only way to avoid reputational damage. Apparel companies therefore initiated joint agreements that put teeth and some money into its inspection system.

One group, consisting mainly of European companies, drafted The Accord on Fire and Building Safety in Bangladesh. It was signed by 30 of the world's leading apparel companies – including Benetton, PVH, Abercrombie & Fitch, H&M, Inditex (Zara), Marks & Spencer, and Tesco. A key feature is that the accord includes a legally binding 5-year commitment to establish a monitoring regime in which workers and their unions will participate. Numbering 72 by mid-July 2013, the companies pledged "to ensure that sufficient funds are available to pay for renovations and other safety improvements." All the factories used by the companies would be inspected within 9 months and would have remediation plans developed for those with safety problems. The companies would pay for safety improvements in factories and the safety audit would be made public. In effect, the fourth level of the CSR pyramid was addressed: making some "social investments" in the factories.[43]

But most American retailers, notably Gap and Wal-Mart, were unwilling to commit to a binding agreement, fearing that legal enforcement would lead to costly and frivolous litigation. They point to vulnerabilities in the US legal system that allow class action suits and contingency fees, and encourage suits because losing plaintiffs are not required to pay legal fees. These dissenting retailers instead formed the Alliance for Bangladesh Worker Safety. It requires inspection within a year of all Bangladeshi factories used by the retailers and the signatories agree to provide grants between $42 million and $100 million in low-interest loans to upgrade factories. Gap proposed that expulsion from the program be the sole remedy for non-compliance in most cases.[44] The government drafted a third plan, the National Tripartite Action Plan, which seeks common standards for plant inspections. The plan was tentatively agreed upon by all parties in November 2013.

Despite these agreements, for the ideals of CSR to be fully achieved, codes of conduct and systems of inspection must be taken seriously. As the proposed government compact requires, inspections must be carried out by competent safety engineers, and brands and retailers must be willing to fund necessary factory renovations. To monitor this arrangement, the formation of worker representation is recommended.

16.4.1 Nike Shows the Way

Nike, which has encountered supplier problems in the past, serves as a model for the Bangladesh reforms. It requires Silver Star, its main contractor in Bangladesh, to consolidate production in one big factory and to establish a system of elected worker representatives to speak up about safety problems, wage violations, and other issues.[45] Nike's chief spokesman, Greg Rossiter, said, "We've learned that monitoring alone isn't enough."[46] And Auret van Heerden, president and chief executive of the Fair Labor Association, said. "You can never visit facilities often enough to make sure they stay compliant – you'll never have enough inspectors to do that. What really keeps factories compliant is when workers have a voice and they can speak out when something isn't right."[47]

Nike learned from its past experience.[48] After being targeted for labor abuses by its Indonesian suppliers, it went through several stages of response. The first was defensive, saying that it bore no responsibility because its suppliers were independent companies and Nike offered badly needed jobs in areas of severe poverty. When the issue didn't go away, in 1998 it switched to a cooperative approach. It publicly acknowledged the problem and engaged with its suppliers to improve the treatment of the nearly 650 000 workers employed in their factories.

Moreover, Nike became more proactive by seeking to improve its supply chain labor practices. It established a comprehensive set of environmental, health, safety, and labor practices, which every new factory was required to meet. That the standards were tough was evidenced by the 43% of the factories reviewed in its 2004 report that failed the test. Nike went a step further by helping suppliers reach the standards by working with factory managers to develop a remediation plan and monitor its implementation. By 2006, it had more than 75 full-time employees who inspected factories and worked with suppliers. It also cooperated with the Fair Labor Association, an independent monitoring organization, to conduct unannounced audits.

16.4.2 Some CSR Lessons Learned

The Bangladesh disaster provides a useful summary of some key CSR lessons:

- Managers who operate in the international arena must agree that the building of sound, enduring relationships with other international players must be the goal of MNCs that expect to operate profitably in the long run. In other words, the transaction mentality must be replaced with a relationship concept that seeks mutual benefit.
- The narrow view of the free market system as maximizing profits for owners and investors must be replaced by recognition that the interests of at least the key stakeholders of workers, customers, and the community must be served. Some call the latter the managerial creed in contrast to the classical creed.
- Codes of conduct and systems of inspection must be taken seriously. As the proposed government compact requires, inspections must be carried out by competent safety engineers, and brands and retailers must be willing to fund necessary factory renovations. To monitor this arrangement, the formation of worker representation is recommended.
- The issue of sustainability must be addressed. As stated by Sir Martin Sorrell, former CEO of the marketing conglomerate WPP Group plc, our challenge now is how best to change people's behavior to mitigate the worst effects of our over-consumption. He asserts that the social and environmental effects of consumption are not properly accounted for by cheap consumer goods. He might point to teenagers who no longer wash their clothes but buy new ones instead. Business managers must recognize that globalization requires new learning.
- A superficial review of simply learning about the cultural patterns of another country is inadequate. The more thorough scrutiny exercised by foreign diplomats in studying the particulars of the country to which they are assigned should serve as a model for managers who work in the international arena. They must recognize that they operate as private sector diplomats and must accordingly study the players and institutional arrangements in the selected areas of the international sphere.
- Knowing only that Bangladesh paid low wages to its workers but neglecting to investigate the woefully dangerous factories and Dickensian conditions in which they worked inevitably led to the Rana Plaza disaster. For globalization to further succeed, managers must learn more about the countries with which they do business and consciously seek to achieve more equitable mutual benefits.

16.5 Conclusions

CSR values are represented in the corporate world across a wide range. A company can decide what form of CSR to practice – focusing on philanthropy, improving operational effectiveness, or transforming the business model.[49] A company can apply a compensatory approach by examining the social costs it creates and, in effect, paying for them. Or it can determine what level on the CSR pyramid it can realistically attain. A few companies are changing their business models to more fully accommodate CSR.

The discussion of some questionable corporate behavior exposes the excesses and deficiencies of the free enterprise system against the growing public attitude that companies should act in a socially responsible manner. The ideology of the classical creed of maximizing stockholder returns is challenged by the ideology of the managerial creed whereby the interests of a company's stakeholders are recognized. In the broadest sense, CSR raises the question of how far a company should go to advance the public interest.[50]

Discussion Questions

16.1. What is the meaning of CSR? Is there any advantage in calling it corporate citizenship?

16.2. What are some examples of violations of CSR abroad? Discuss one.

16.3. Why are PRSA's guidelines important?

16.4. What are some major global declarations and why do they matter for a corporation?

16.5. Explain the compensatory approach to CSR.

16.6. How does a company benefit from corporate giving in developing countries?

16.7. What are the five levels of the CSR pyramid? What considerations should guide a company in deciding which level to achieve?

16.8. What CSR lessons are learned from the Bangladesh tragedy?

16.9. What are the ways of doing business that provide alternatives to profit maximization by corporations?

Endnotes

1 Julfikar Alimanik and Nida Najarjune, "Bangladesh Police Charge 41 With Murder Over Rana Plaza Collapse," *New York Times*, June 1, 2015.
2 Steven Greenhouse, "Accord to Combat Sweatshop Labor Faces Obstacles," *New York Times*, April 13, 1997, p. A1.
3 Christopher Scanlan, "America's Deadly Exports – Trade of Toxic Products Abroad is a Windfall for U.S. Companies," *The Seattle Times*, September 15, 2015.

4 Lairold M. Street, "U.S. Exports Banned for Domestic Use, But Exported to Third World Countries," *Maryland Journal of International Law*, Vol. 6, Issue 1, Article 10.
5 William Shaw, *Business Ethics: A Textbook with Cases*, 8th ed. (Boston, MA: Cengage Learning, 2014).
6 William Cheng, "CSR and New Corporate Social Realities," *The Straits Times* (Singapore), April 17, 2013.
7 "Agribusiness: Feeding the Dragon," *The Economist*, February 6, 2016, p. 58.
8 Gayle Tzemach Lemmon, "New Hope for Afghan Raisin Farm," *New York Times*, October 9, 2010, p. B1.
9 Rob Taylor and David Winning, "Australia Blocks Huge Land Sale," *WSJ*, November 25, 2015, p. A13.
10 Robin Sidel, "Payments Puzzle Persists at Banks," *WSJ*, July 29, 2014, p. C1.
11 Anna Maria Andriotis and Robin Sidel, "Credit Cards for Riskiest Customers Roar Back," *WSJ*, June 27, 2014, p. A1.
12 Leslie Scism, "MetLife Vows to Track Deaths," *WSJ*, April 24, 2012, p. C1.
13 This concept is explored by Thomas Donaldson, *The Ethics of International Business* (New York: Oxford University Press, 1989).
14 Shown and discussed in basic public relations texts such as Scott M. Cutlip, Allen H. Center, and Glen M. Broom, *Effective Public Relation*, 6th ed. (Englewood Cliffs, NJ: Prentice-Hall, 1985), pp. 457–461.
15 "Global Corporate Citizenship. Remarks by Klaus Schwab," Foreign Policy Association, April 17, 2008.
16 David Atkinson and Richard Pierre Claude, "Human Rights and Multinational Corporations: The Global Compact and Continuing Evolution," in Gabriele G.S. Suder, ed., *International Business Under Adversity* (Northampton, MA: Edward Elgar, 2008), p. 12.
17 Georg Kell, "The UN Global Compact and Business: Creating the Architecture of a Better World," Raytheon Lectureship in Business Ethics, November 5, 2013, Bentley University Center for Business Ethics, p. 8.
18 Otto Lerbinger, "The Social Function of PR," in Otto Lerbinger and Albert J. Sullivan, eds., *Information, Influence, and Communication* (New York: Basic Books, 1965), p. 59.
19 In his *Principles of Economics: An Introductory Volume*, 8th ed. (London: Macmillan and Co., 1947). Alfred Marshall also defined externalities as knowledge and resources that are commonly available to all businesses, pp. 284–285.
20 Susanne Craig, "Symbol of Excess Tries to Give Billions Back," *International New York Times*, October 28, 2013, 15.
21 Alissa Gulin, "Corporations Take a Strategic Approach to Philanthropy," *The Daily Record* (Baltimore, MD), March 6, 2013. Also see "Corporate Giving 2014, *The Chronicle of Philanthropy*, July 13, 2014, which reports that companies are favoring bigger commitments to causes that are closer to their expertise.
22 "10 Companies That Gave the Most Cash in 2013," *Chronicle of Philanthropy*, ibid.
23 Sue Asci, "More Money Being Donated to Foreign Charities," *Investment News*, September 29, 2008, p. 21.
24 Archie B. Carroll, "The Pyramid of Corporate Social Responsibility: Toward the Moral Management of Organizational Stakeholders," *Business Horizons*, Vol. 34, July–August 1991, pp. 39–48.
25 Michael E. Porter and Mark R. Kramer, "The Competitive Advantage of Corporate Philanthropy," *Harvard Business Review*, Vol. 80, December 2002, pp. 56–68.
26 See Nick Powdthavee, an economist at the University of York, *The Happiness Equation: The Surprising Economics of Our Most Valuable Asset* (London: Icon Books, 2014).
27 "Economics Focus: Measuring What Matters," *The Economist*, September 19, 2009, p. 88.

28 "Measures of Well-Being Chilled Out," *The Economist*, February 2, 2012.
29 See Otto Lerbinger, *The Crisis Manager: Facing Risk and Responsibility* (Mahwah, NJ: Lawrence Erlhaum Associates, 1997), pp. 92–93, 104.
30 Sarah Algethami, "Corporate Social Responsibility Programmes Can Offer More Than a Good Reputation," *Gulf News* (United Arab Emirates), May 24, 2013.
31 William D. Bryan, "Poverty, Industry, and Environmental Quality: Weighing Paths to Economic Development at the Dawn of the Environmental Era," *Environmental History*, Vol. 16, Issue 3, pp. 492–522.
32 Nigeria's water shortage is discussed in Yinka Ibukun and Chris Kay, "Nigerian Water Shortage is Bigger Killer than Boko Haran," *Bloomberg*, January 25, 2015.
33 Mark Kramer and John Kania, "Changing the Game," *Stanford Social Innovation Review*, Spring 2006, Vol. 4, No. 1, pp. 20–28.
34 Some writers add "global" to corporate citizenship, e.g. Anuradha Dayal-Gulati and Mark W. Finn eds., *Global Corporate Citizenship* (Evanston, IL: Northwestern University Press, 2007). They refer to the Ford Motor Company Center for Global Citizenship of the Kellogg School of Management, p. ix.
35 Boston College, Center for Corporate Citizenship, Carroll School of Management.
36 Kasturi Rangen, Lisa Chase, and Sohel Karim, "The Truth about CSR," *Harvard Business Review*, Vol. 93, No. 2, January–February 2015, p. 43. The World Economic Forum provides another definition: "the contribution a company makes to society through its core business activities, its social investment and philanthropy programmes, and its engagement in public policy. The manner in which a company manages its economic, social and environmental relationships, as well as those with different stakeholders, in particular shareholders, employees, customers, business partners, governments and communities determines its impact." See Naomi A. Gardberg and Charles J. Fombrun, "Corporate Citizenship: Creating Intangible Assets across Institutional Environments," *Academy of Management Review*, Vol. 31, No. 2, 2006, p. 329.
37 Rosabeth Kanter, "Why Global Companies Will Behave More and More Alike," *WSJ*, July 8, 2014, p. R8. See her *SuperCorp: How Vanguard Companies Create Innovation, Profits, Growth, and Social Good* (New York: Random House, 2009).
38 David Bornstein, *How to Change the World: Social Entrepreneurs and the Power of New Ideas* (Oxford and New York: Oxford University, 2004).
39 Ibid., p. 1.
40 Kathleen Wilburn and Ralph Wilburn, "The Double Bottom Line: Profit and Social Benefit," *Business Horizons*, Vol. 57, 2014, pp. 11–20.
41 Philip Kotler, David Hessekiel, and Nancy R. Lee, *Good Works: Marketing and Corporate Initiatives to Build a Better World* (Hoboken, NJ: John Wiley & Sons, Inc., 2012), p. 171.
42 Ibid., p. 14.
43 "Clothing Firms in Bangladesh: Accord, Alliance or Disunity," *The Economist*, July 13, 2013, p. 57.
44 Steven Greenhouse and Stephanie Clifford, "US Retailers Offer Plan for Safety Standards in Bangladesh," *International Herald Tribune*, July 11, 2013.
45 Stephanie Clifford and Steven Greenhouse, "Fast and Flawed Inspections of Factories Abroad," *New York Times*, September 2, 2013, A1.
46 Greg Rossiter, in Clifford and Greenhouse, op. cit.
47 Ibid.
48 Kramer and Kania, op. cit.
49 These are the three "theaters" of CSR named by Kasturi Rangen et al., ibid., p. 43.
50 See Walton H. Hamilton, "Affectation with Public Interest" (1930). Faculty Scholarship Series. Paper 4669. http://digitalcommons.law.yale.edu/fss_papers/4669.

17

Corporate Governance: The Corporate Communication Role

Corporate governance refers to how corporations are controlled and directed. Responsibility for corporate governance resides with a corporation's board of directors, which guides and oversees the corporation's activities. The board is the highest decision making body of a corporation, with ultimate power of direction and control. The top officers are the chairman and the chief executive officer (CEO), positions that are sometimes combined.[1] Especially relevant to corporate communication, the board relates the corporation to the larger society. This comprises the general public, its stakeholders, and government on all levels – including the international – and civil society. In addition to its major responsibility for financial security and profitability, the board is concerned about the corporation's legitimacy and reputation in the eyes of these players, raising the importance of the management roles of corporate affairs.

17.1 Maintaining Corporate Legitimacy

In his landmark book, *Management: Tasks, Responsibilities, Practices*, the celebrated management guru Peter Drucker includes a section on the legitimacy of management. In it he states, "a leadership group needs not only to function. It needs not only to perform. It also has to have legitimacy. It has to be accepted by the community as 'right.'"[2] Drucker acknowledged that the board has a public relations role by saying that the board fulfills an enterprise's need for "public and community relations."[3] He elaborated on this role in a *Wall Street Journal* editorial, "The Real Duties of a Director," in which he said: "The board is responsible for making sure that a company has adequate policies for its key outside relationships – with government, with the labor union, with the public in general; and that it have adequate policies with respect to its legal and regulatory responsibilities."[4] Drucker's comments invite a larger role of public relations, along with public affairs, in corporate governance.

Similarly, Ian H. Wilson, a member of the strategic planning committee of General Electric (GE), once connected a company's concern with public relations as follows: "The crucial role of the board in the corporate decision process is one of oversight – oversight with respect to those actions which a potential for a material impact on the corporation's economic results, its legal position, or its public reputation."[5]

The prestigious Arthur Page Society, whose members represent senior public relations professionals, similarly describes the object of public relations' work as "not the management of a situation, but of an institution." He or she must establish authenticity for an institution by activating the corporate character, defined as "some deep seated characteristics" that make an enterprise unique and define its very nature – "the things that it can't not be and still be itself." In

Corporate Communication: An International and Management Perspective, First Edition. Otto Lerbinger.

Abraham Lincoln's words, "Character is like a tree and reputation like its shadow. The shadow is what we think of it; the tree is the real thing."[6]

17.1.1 Uncertainty of Public Support for Business

The need for corporate communication participation in management is reinforced by public opinion surveys that show that continuing public support for large corporations – and its CEOs – cannot be taken for granted. Management may have become too complacent in ignoring the implications of corporate failures. This shortcoming was noticed by Linda Ferrell and O. C. Ferrell in their examination of 20 "integrity" failures in business and other organizations. They defined integrity as "being whole or complete in adhering to ethics responsibility and stakeholder concerns."[7] Their list of failures is formidable and sobering. The top 10 of 20 are:

1) Exxon's negligence leads to massive oil spill.
2) Nike recovers from reputational disaster.
3) Columbia/Hospital Corporation of America engages in healthcare fraud.
4) Firestone plagued by recall problems.
5) Sunbeam's bad apple: Chainsaw Al.
6) Enron's toxic corporate culture led to its demise.
7) Arthur Andersen's accounting failures lead to demise.
8) WorldCom: the largest bankruptcy of its time.
9) The American Red Cross: mismanagement at the top.
10) Tyco experiences integrity failure but rises again.

The collapse of Enron revealed how corporate codes of ethics are often mere journalistic exercises. Although it had a well-stated code of ethics, its precepts were ignored. Another problem was ineffective corporate governance. Chairman Ken Lay and CEO Jeffrey Skilling claimed ignorance about the financial fraud, saying they relied on approval of attorneys and accountants about the technicality of such arrangements as off-the-balance-sheet partnerships. Yet Lay ignored a letter by Sherron Watkins, an Enron vice president, which expressed concern about potential conflicts of interest and accounting practices. This was a serious lapse in leadership responsibility. As the Ferrells state, "Managers must make a proactive effort to know what is going on within their companies."[8]

In the UK an example of failure is Tesco, which some media described as "a saga of poor corporate governance." Tesco was criticized on three counts. One was the quality of senior management itself, as reflected in the forced departure of five very senior executives. Critics say that Tesco's CEO, Philip Clarke, had struggled to find a strategy that works. His "Big Price Drop" didn't go far enough, and his plan to extend into the US and Japan failed. Many top executives and board members left, and the new board members lacked the experience to stand up to Clarke. The other two criticisms pertained to the internal audit and the audit committee and the external audit. The external audit, which plays a major role in the UK, highlighted the potential problems with supplier accounting and noted it as an "area of focus." There is a long gestation period for a corporation to become aware of loss of public support.

Toshiba became another recent failure of corporate governance when its president Hisao Tanaka resigned on July 21, 2015, taking half of its 16-member board with him. He took responsibility for an accounting scandal amounting to about $1.6 billion. Lax controls and a culture of "high power distance" are blamed. The new president, Masashi Muromachi, apologized at a news conference, saying, "I am strongly feeling the social responsibility of alarming and causing trouble to our 400 000 shareholders, including domestic and international investors, as well as our clients and the authorities concerned." He added: "We will devote ourselves wholeheartedly to regain your trust and revive Toshiba under the new management." Shares consequently rose 1.8%.

17.1.2 Protecting the Free Market System

The public relations aspect of corporate communication is very much concerned not only with the reputation of a company but with the accompanying free market system. At the end of World War II, when some countries in Europe moved toward communism and socialism, US corporations recognized the value of public relations in defending the free market system. This defense became explicit in the many programs and campaigns. One of them, "The How Our Business System Operates" (HOBSO), was conducted for employees at many companies. Today, public relations faces the similar challenge of helping businesses preserve the free market system. Corporate communication professionals are challenged by non-governmental organizations NGOs and the general public, who point to corporate abuses that they feel need correction. There may be future "Occupy Wall Street" movements that are better organized and more dangerous. The issue of income and wealth inequality, which has entered the political arena, may require renewed attention to how our business system operates.

A corporate communication task is to help explain how the "invisible hand" described by Adam Smith protects the public interest. Adam Smith asserted that when a business person acts completely selfishly the business system automatically produces a common good. The underlying assumption is that competitive forces limit private gain. But the history of antitrust legislation shows that business does all it can to limit competition. Mergers and acquisitions are constantly announced.

Marketing and public relations assist a seller to escape competitive forces through advertising and promotion that differentiate its product from others and thereby allow the product not to be subject to the market price set by supply and demand forces. Many megamergers of major multinational corporations (MNCs) across national boundaries raise concern about global monopolistic entities. Furthermore, a culture of materialism is maintained that is often at odds with the goal of sustainability. As described in the previous chapter, businesses are only slowly accepting the second level of the pyramid of social responsibility of addressing social costs, such as the externalities of environmental harm, poor work conditions, and human rights abuses.

17.2 The Business–Society Relationship

In applying the larger meaning of public relations, chief communications officers (CCOs) should view themselves as custodians of the business–society relationship. It is a relationship that has been closely studied by sociologists. From their viewpoint the economy is a sub-system of society and must therefore be subordinate to society and not the other way around, as advocates of the free market system often imply.

Talcott Parsons, who formerly headed Harvard University's Social Relations Department, and Neil J. Smelser explained this relationship in their book, *Economy and Society: A Study in the Integration of Economic and Social Theory*. They advocate that the two fields reestablish interest in borderline relations. They sought to dispel the belief that economics is "a science sufficient unto itself," and that economics should instead "lean on the other social sciences." The psychology of consumer behavior illustrates this need by helping explain consumers' tastes and the forces that influence their "marginal propensity to consume" (which is an integral concept of Keynesian economics). In summary, sociological theory supports the view that business should not be viewed in isolation from society nor as superior to it.

The board's role in overseeing relationships with all kinds of publics and constituencies was recognized by the Fifty-Fourth American Assembly on Corporate Governance in America. It concluded: "Boards of directors have a primary role in interpreting society's expectations and standards for management." To accommodate this function, some corporations established public issues committees that keep track of regulatory, economic, and political issues that have an impact on business. General Electric formed such a committee with twofold tasks: "to provide an independent checkpoint on the issues – present or potential – that affect General Electric; and to apprize the effectiveness of management's response." In the absence of such committees, CCOs who are engaged in issues management can serve this function.

17.2.1 Widening the Composition of the Board

To accommodate views of society, some have recommended the broadening of the composition of the board. In an advertisement called "Commonsense Corporate Governance Principles," 13 leaders of some of America's largest corporations and investment managers state, "Diverse boards make better decisions, so every board should have members with complementary and diverse skills, backgrounds and experiences."[9] At present its members almost exclusively have a business background and orientation.

Some countries in Europe have boards with labor representation. A conspicuous example is Germany. where a system of codetermination in many large companies includes labor representatives on its supervisory board (which is the equivalent of a board of directors). The supervisory board is supplemented by a smaller management board that makes operational decisions.

The idea of broadening representation on company boards appears intermittently in the US. In 1992, *Business Week's* "Special Edition on Reinventing America," predicted that the twenty-first-century corporation would be "governed by an independent board with a broad view of the company's constituents, would include not just shareholders, but also employees, suppliers, customers, and the local community."[10]

In the US, however, the inclusion of directors representing special interests has occurred only under special circumstances. Early examples are General Motors' appointment in 1971 of Reverend Leon Sullivan, a black urban affairs leader, in response to Ralph Nader's Campaign GM proxy resolution, and Chrysler's CEO Lee Iococca's invitation in 1980 to Douglas A. Fraser, the president of the United Automobile Workers (UAW) union, to join the board. This was done at a time when the company was in financial trouble, for labor support was needed to obtain a needed federal loan guarantee of $1.2 billion and to persuade union members to accept a wage cut.

A later instance was Exxon Corporation's appointment of Dr. John M. Steele, a scientist from the Woods Hole Oceanographic Institute, on Cape Cod, Massachusetts, to represent environmental interests in response to stockholder demands at its annual meeting after the Prince Williams Sound oil spill in 1989. The most extreme proposal to invite public directors to the board was that of Robert Townsend, former head of Avis Corporation. In 1973 he proposed that all manufacturing companies with more than $11 billion in assets should be required to have public directors.

Recognizing the importance of environmental issues, some companies, such as Integrys Energy Group Inc., Quicksilver Resources Inc., and Tesoro Corp., created separate environmental panels of the board of directors, following long-established ones at DuPont Co., Occidental Petroleum Corp., and Rohm & Haas Co. Other companies assigned environmental issues to existing board committees. Lester A. Hudson, chairman of American Electric Power Co.'s (AEP) governance committee observed that the issue of the Earth's sustainability "has become a much more important part of every board's activities."[11] AEP planned to invest $3.5 billion in cleaner coal-burning technologies. As a result, Ceres, an investor advocacy group, gave AEP the highest US ranking for board involvement in climate change, among 100 global businesses studied.

17.2.2 Boards Face Activists

Boards face conflicting groups of activists. One group consists of investor activists who seek to maximize profits and stockholder wealth. Their source of power is in ownership of a company's stock and the voting power that this ownership legally bestows. The second group, which is of greater concern to CCOs, consists of social activists who represent the broad range of interests associated with corporate social responsibility (CSR). Their power resides in the ability to cause reputational damage by negative publicity, protests, and participation at corporate annual meetings.

The wide range of causes associated with social activists is more annoying for a company CEO and board of directors than investor activists because they produce media headlines – and sometimes crises – that damage a company's reputation and net worth. Social media have increased the vulnerability of CEOs when they dare present their personal views on highly controversial social and political issues. As stated in *The Economist*, "Thanks to the digital revolution, chief executives now live in glass houses. An ill-judged remark can be broadcast to the world in an instant."[12]

Brendan Eich, CEO of the prominent Silicon Valley company Mozilla (which supports the Firefox Web browser) was blasted in social media over his 6-year old $1000 donation in support of a 2008 California ballot initiative to ban gay marriage. He publicly stated that he was opposed to gay marriage. By so doing, he made the mistake of dealing with "highly arousing" content that evokes anger or anxiety. Such content is more likely to make the "most e-mailed" list, for stories about evil CEOs make perfect click-bait. He decided to resign, saying, "I have decided to resign as CEO effective today, and leave Mozilla. Our mission is bigger than any one of us, and under the present circumstances, I cannot be an effective leader."[13]

Social media also latched on to Target Corp.'s donation of $150 000 to a group that funded ads for an antigay candidate for governor in Minnesota. But the issue subsided after CEO Greg Steinhafel wrote a letter of apology to employees followed by friendly company gestures of support for gays and lesbians. Both events demonstrate that gay rights have become a bedrock civil rights issue for many.

A call for greater activism is epitomized by Robert A.G. Monks, a Boston Brahmin who has been a corporate lawyer, venture capitalist, energy company executive, corporate director, and Reagan administration official. He has an elite background that might have made him a consummate corporate insider. Instead, in his latest book, *Citizens DisUnited: Passive Investors, Drone CEOs and the Corporate Capture of the American Dream*,[14] he issued what he describes as "a call to arms." Monks has been battling for decades to make corporations more transparent and more democratic. He has lobbied institutional investors to influence the behavior of companies in which they invest. Monks believes that corporate governance centers on several main issues: executive pay, corporate compatibility with the public interest, and management's responsiveness to shareholders.

Monks contends that others among the nation's biggest investors, such as charitable funds and endowments, need to play more active roles. He argues that if excessive executive pay is to be curbed, it it important that the trustees of the top dozen endowments and charitable funds, accounting for $200 billion in collective assets, actively take a stand. Monks has also pleaded for the direct involvement of millions of individual corporate shareholders. He said "Democracy isn't going to work without involved citizens and corporations won't work without involved owners."[15]

17.3 Shareholder Resolutions

Annual meetings provide an opportunity for investors and social activists to pressure a company's board of directors. An important feature of these meetings is the right of shareholders to submit proxy resolutions for consideration at the annual meeting. To qualify, some advocacy groups purchase a minimum number of shares for the deliberate purpose of seeking a change in corporate policies such as environmental issues and climate change. Shareholders vote on each resolution, providing a good index of how much support each issue receives.

At an annual meeting, the chairman of the board, the CEO, and other officers of a corporation report to the assembled stockholders on the company's performance. Attendance at these meetings, however, is notoriously low, but is compensated by media coverage of major companies. Coverage is stimulated by sharp questions raised by activists and occasional dramatic encounters. Further publicity is achieved when activists stage protests in front of buildings where meetings are held. Post-meeting reports and corporate annual reports provide details of corporate activities. Corporate annual reports, which are required for public corporations by the Securities and Exchange Commission SEC and stock exchanges, are intended to review financial performance.

Major advocacy groups announce the issues they plan to include in their stockholder resolutions. Two leading advocacy groups are the Interfaith Center on Corporate Responsibility (ICCR) and Ceres. ICCR seeks to promote environmentally and socially responsible practices. Its 2013 Guide describes 180 resolutions filed at 127 companies, mostly on lobbying and political spending. Other proposals addressed concerns about climate-related issues, human rights and supply chain accountability, financial practices, access to healthcare, food and water sustainability, and environmental health. The single most broadly supported ICCR resolution in 2013 called for ExxonMobil to reduce its greenhouse gas emissions. The other major advocacy group, Ceres, describes itself as a national network of investors, environmental organizations, and other public interest groups working with companies and investors to address sustainability challenges.

Some of the nation's largest public pension funds play a major role in filing shareholder resolutions. The California Public Employees' Retirement System (CalPERS), representing 1.6 million public employees, is especially prominent. It publishes an annual comprehensive report that covers both corporate governance and corporate social responsibility issues.

Few resolutions receive a majority vote. Moreover, companies are not legally required to follow through on stockholder resolution votes and investor advocates recognize the limits of their power. Overall, the average voter support for environmental and social shareholder proposals more than doubled from 2005 to 2011, increasing from 10% in 2005 to 21% in 2011, according to a study released by the Investor Responsibility Research Center Institute.[16] Another measure of effectiveness of stockholder resolutions is when investors withdraw resolutions after companies respond affirmatively to their specific requests, which Ceres reported happened in 2013 with more than 40 of the 110 resolutions. Sometimes companies respond to resolutions by making specific changes before their annual meetings.

17.4 Role of Corporate Communication in Corporate Governance

CCOs aspiring to become members of a corporation's top management group, the so-called "dominant coalition," must apply the larger meaning of public relations, which is concerned with business–society relations. The five major contributions are:

17.4.1 Protect Company Reputation and Legitimacy

A company's reputation has been a major concern of company CEOs, as a finding of a PRWeek/Burson-Marsteller CEO survey in 2003 showed: 81% of CEOs were concerned about their company's reputation, with 34% "very concerned" and 47% "somewhat concerned."[17] CEOs want their companies to be well-known and respected. A good reputation is an intangible asset reflected in the Goodwill account on the balance sheet and therefore increases the financial value of a company. Relationships with other players become smoother and more productive when a company has a good reputation.

Legitimacy, however, has a deeper meaning for corporate governance. It deals with whether the general public and specific publics consider the company lawful and genuine and whether its goals and activities conform to society's values, norms, and standards. For example, when the heads of companies in South Korea's *chaebols* faced hostile public reactions to their owners' embezzlement, tax evasions, performance malpractices, and other wrongdoings, their legitimacy was threatened. As stated by the Public Relations Society of America (PRSA), "public relations is essential not just to reputation, but to an organization's very legitimacy . . . intelligent organizations advised by skilled public relations professionals will enjoy not just a new edge – but also new legitimacy."[18]

17.4.1.1 Wal-Mart's Mexican Bribery Crisis

Wal-Mart, the world's biggest retailer, faced a reputational crisis after a *New York Times* article in April 2012 reported on insiders' accounts of bribery by its Mexican arm, Walmex. Stock prices consequently declined 4.7% one day and 3% the following day. Its reason for bribery is that when it sought to expand in Mexico, it encountered bureaucratic officials notorious for their corruption and slowness. It consequently resorted to paying bribes itself, thereby risking prosecution for violating the US Federal Corrupt Practices Act. After the article appeared, Wal-Mart defensively said: "If these allegations are true, it is not a reflection of who we are or what we stand for."[19] In 2017, US authorities asked Wal-Mart to pay $300 million to settle the 5-year investigation.[20]

Another investigation of potential foreign bribery by Wal-Mart arose in Brazil. US federal prosecutors have examined $500 000 in payments believed to have gone to a woman, believed to have previously held a government position, who was hired to obtain government permits to build two stores in Brazil's capital, Brasilia. As Wal-Mart was concerned about delays in getting other store permits, indirect payments to other contractors are also suspected.[21]

The costs of compliance by business have grown as companies spend millions of dollars probing allegations of bribery. A wide range of industries have added compliance committees to corporate boards and created compliance and ethics departments headed by former government officials. Many companies have raised the rank of their compliance officers. Surveys in 2013 by Price-WaterhouseCoopers LLP and Deloitte found that about 50% of chief compliance officers report directly to their company's CEO or board. Regulatory settlements, such as with Johnson & Johnson, sometimes stipulate that a chief compliance officer should not be subordinate to the chief legal officers or chief financial officer. A healthy compliance program can often insulate a company from criminal prosecution, even if employees cross the line.

17.4.1.2 Corporate Mission Statements

A company's reputation and legitimacy are reflected in public perceptions of corporate values. These are seen in company mission statements that indicate their direction and the values that guide them. Although they often end up as a framed document on a wall or filed away, the following examples illustrate important attributes:

Customer satisfaction, team member happiness.
Environmental improvement.
Help our employees fulfill their family responsibilities.
Growing our business and delivering competitive financial results.

Never compromise on quality and business ethics.
Offer opportunities for our people to realize their potential.
Commitment to sustainable development and good governance.
Safety in our operations, and transparency and accountability in our dealings.
Act with integrity, trust, and respect.

Because corporate communication is so closely associated with the maintenance of a company's reputation and legitimacy, 2its contribution to corporate governance is acknowledged by CEOs.

17.4.2 Engage in Issues Management and Direct Crisis Management

Corporate communication professionals are an organization's chief boundary spanners. They alert management of any actual or potential conflicts with stakeholders and other players that might affect the company. They examine its external environment, much as a journalist covers a beat. Locally, they make it their business to know what's going on in their organizations and the communities where their offices and operations are located. They talk with human resources heads, trade associations to which they belong, and, increasingly, monitor social media, using the analytics of big data to become aware of new "communities" and issues.

They also head a company's issues management process. They scan for emerging issues and trends and prioritize them in terms of potential impact on the company. They then analyze the key issues and formulate strategies to cope with them. They constantly study public opinion and appraise the standing of their organization by the general public and its publics. Applying the research technique of gap analysis, they know whether a company should alter its policies or seek to influence public opinion. This process is facilitated when the CCO is a member of the top management group.

In his *Strategic Issues Management*, Robert L. Heath discusses the importance of issues analysis: examining "the facts, premises, conclusions, and policy recommendations that are employed by discussants of the topic."[22] Those engaged in such analysis should examine five aspects of an issue: its nature, its life cycle stage, identification of political participants, importance of public opinion, amount and kind of media coverage (both conventional media and social media), and its legal, regulatory, and constitutional context. Regarding the nature of an issue, four types should be differentiated:

1) *Universal.* Those that affect the general public in a direct and personal manner, e.g. inflation or energy crisis.
2) *Advocacy.* Those initiated by social activists who claim to represent the public interest.
3) *Selective.* Matters of concern to special interest groups, e.g. tariff protection which would motivate a special constituency rather than the grassroots.
4) *Technical.* Issues the public is willing to leave to experts, e.g. regulatory issues such as regulation of drones.[23]

The life cycle stage of an issue determines how it should be treated. It makes a difference if an issue is at the emerging, public involvement, legislative, or regulatory/litigation stage. The latter would receive urgent attention, whereas an emerging issue would simply be monitored. Public opinion surveys would specify the importance of an issue to the general public and segments of it. An analysis of how an issue is treated by the media would reflect the kind of arguments used by different groups of people and organizations.

An MNC should also examine its vulnerability that an issue might escalate into a crisis. Some past problems and issues that have not been resolved might be "simmering crises" – problems that continue to grow in severity until they erupt in crises. Furthermore, a CCO is aware of company characteristics that make it more vulnerable to certain issues and external pressures. Some of them are:

- High company visibility and prominence. The leading company in an industry is typically the one targeted by the media and activists. Companies producing consumer goods and services, such as toys and pharmaceutical are more vulnerable than producer goods companies that sell to other companies. Products that involve safety especially attract attention. Companies with highly advertised brand names are more visible to the public.
- A foreign company that exploits a country's natural resources.
- Uses technologies perceived as dangerous, e.g. nuclear or chemical.
- A company management that is authoritarian, bureaucratic, and averse to ambiguous situations and in high "power distance" situations where subordinates are discouraged from speaking.

Some companies have established advisory boards that provide the board of directors with information and counsel on timely issues pertaining to non-fiduciary matters. A company's issues management process provides information on current issues and trends that affect it.

Public relations is closely associated with crisis management. Public relations consulting firms like Burson-Marsteller specialize in it. They know how to handle crisis communications: how to inform the victims and relevant publics about a crisis in order to minimize secondary effects of media exposure and public reaction to it. Corporate communication contributes to management when it engages in contingency planning that reduces the likelihood of a crisis and enables a quicker and more effective response when a crisis does occur.

17.4.3 Factor Public Opinion into Corporate Decision Making

Companies vulnerable to public, government, and media criticism must factor public opinion into many decisions. Corporate communication adds a "public philosophy" component. This is a term introduced by the influential journalist Walter Lippmann in his book *The Public Philosophy*. Although intended for government public policy deliberations, it answers the question: What is the proper role of public opinion in deciding upon policies that affect the public? Political leaders know they must follow one of the universal laws of politics: no government can long endure unless the governors consider the reactions of those who are governed? Many companies believe likewise, although some feel immune to public opinion because of their monopolistic power.

Corporate communication examines at least three factors that influence a company's public philosophy: (i) whether people care about an issue, (ii) whether the public is well-informed, and (iii) whether the public is willing to translate their interest into political action. Answers to these questions have an antecedent in the early days of the Industrial Revolution, as summarized by Walt Rostow. He found that during intervals of "high social tension," better known as symptoms of unrest, important legislation was passed and anti-industry activities by the Luddites, the Chartists, and other groups grew. During intervals of "low social tension" these movements fade from sight.

17.4.3.1 Personal, Scientific, or Moral Issues

The nature of an issues influences whether the public becomes involved. When seen as a matter of personal taste, people believe they have a right to their opinion. Food producers sometimes take advantage of this attitude by arguing that the amount of fat in a product should not be dictated by government nor set by a company. Let the consumer decide! However, activist groups concerned with the fat issue, see it as a scientific matter. On the issue of genetically modified organism (GMO) foods, Monsanto, and other producers have demonstrated that scientific studies show no ill effects of such foods and use this fact to oppose GMO labeling.

Proponents of an issue sometimes seek to convert a scientific issue into a moral one, thereby making scientific evidence irrelevant. When a community's fluoridate water supply was an issue, the opposition argued that no human agency had the right to "fool with God's water" and that no government had the right to determine "what goes into a person's body." The issue of stem cell research has also been framed as a moral issue.

17.4.3.2 Elitist and Populist Philosophies

The role of public opinion is strongly influenced by whether one supports an elitist or a populist philosophy. Elitism is based on the philosophy of Thomas Carlyle, who said that in the ideal society the "naturally superior" would rule and do so righteously. To him, there was a basic law of nature which sets people in a hierarchy of leader and led. The elite support their right to govern on the basis of legal rights, personal superiority, and social necessity because they carry major responsibility in their organizations. Organizational heads may unwittingly subscribe to this belief.

The populist philosophy is represented by Walt Whitman. He said that what the elite claim for themselves, populists claim for every man, as reflected in his poem "Song of Myself":

> I celebrate myself, and sing myself,
>
> And what I assume you shall assume,
>
> For every atom belonging to me as good belongs to you.

The populist approach to public opinion is that everybody's opinion counts on all matters that have public significance. The way to decide any public issue, therefore, is to find out what the public wants rather than what only leaders want. The Lockian view of human nature is accepted that human beings are born with reason and certain truths are self-evident to every person. There is a belief that there is a primordial wisdom in people: they may make mistakes in the short run but in the long run they seem to have an innate sense for making the right decisions.

Walter Lippmann's warning to government about the limits to public opinion, however, applies equally to company managements. He states:

> I am far from implying that the voters are not entitled to the representation of their particular opinion and interest. But their opinions and interests should be taken for what they are and for no more. They are not – as such – propositions in the public interest. Beyond their being, if they are genuine, a true report of what various groups of voters are thinking, they have no intrinsic authority.[24]

The Gallup polls are reports of what people are thinking. But that a plurality of the people sampled in the poll think one way has no bearing upon whether it is sound public policy.

17.4.4 Help Managers Engage with Stakeholders

By overseeing and participating in stakeholder relations, corporate communicators are familiar with the thinking and attitudes of a company's various stakeholders. They can identify conflicts if the interests of a particular group are neglected. And they can recommend when a CEO should engage with specific stakeholders. This idea was reflected in the 2015 Edelman Trust Barometer's advice that CEOs become chief engagement officers.[25] The report states that interaction with stakeholders is facilitated through a several-fold process: by providing economic benefits, by listening and keeping promises, and having an enduring regard for stakeholder interests. The objective is to provide real participation.

Engagement with stakeholders must be authentic. A useful guide in determining authenticity is Sherry Arnstein's "ladder of public participation," which shows eight levels. She rejects the lower rungs of "manipulation," and "therapy" as sham participation. She also rejects the third rung of "one-way communication" because it excludes listening, and the fourth rung of "consultation" when management cedes no authority. She more positively sees the fifth rung, "placation," as providing a voice. The highest level of participation is achieved in the top three rungs of "partnership," "delegated power," and "citizen control."[26]

Although Arnstein was dealing with government officials in a community setting, the last two rungs would be inappropriate for most corporate situations. But Arnstein's model shows the direction that "engagement" should take. Stakeholders must have meaningful participation with management for engagement to be claimed. There must be two-way communication that allows stakeholders and managers to achieve mutual benefits.

The 2015 Edelman Trust Barometer optimistically shows that public trust in business has grown and surpasses trust in government. "Now it is business's turn to ascend the 'bully pulpit,'" says the report, "and for the CEO to become the Chief Engagement Officer."[27] The CEO should go to the broader publics to "make the macro case for forward progress not just the micro case for a given product or new factory." However, more details are needed to know what "forward progress" and "innovation in industry" mean. Moreover, the report sounds propagandistic when the CEO is advised to tell how "change will improve lives of customers, as well as your bottom line."

17.4.5 Address the Public Interest

Business is expected to address public interest concerns Public interest, however, is an ambiguous concept with both legal and populist definitions. In the legal arena corporations have historically been held to the criterion of acting in the public interest. For example, in the 1934 case of Nebbia vs. New York, the court held that government could regulate prices or control terms of service if businesses are "affected with a public interest." This criterion was especially applied to banks, for lawyers, and economists often ascribe them as being "clothed with the public interest."

Reference to the public interest is frequently made in public policy disputes, each party claiming that its position is in the public interest while that of the opposition is not. Ultimately, no single private entity can claim to represent the public interest, for that is the function of representative government. Corporations, non-profit organizations, and other groups engage in the public policy process to argue for their positions.

The public relations industry broadly and loosely refers to the public interest. PRSA's Code of Ethics simply asks a member to conduct "his or her professional life in accord with the public interest." Furthermore, the interplay of competing messages by public relations people representing diverse views suffices as a manner of addressing the public interest. The usual stance of public relations is expressed by Burson-Marsteller, which believes that public relations serves as an advocate for a person or organization, similar to a lawyer.

An early popular definition of public relations by *PR News* was more explicit about the public interest. It stated: "Public relations is the management function which evaluates public attitudes, identifies the policies and procedures of an individual or an organization with the public interest and executes a program of action to earn public understanding and acceptance."[28] Stated more strongly, J. Carroll Bateman, former president of the Insurance Information Institute and later a professor of public relations, expressed his personal credo as: "I believe that the public interest takes precedence of the interests of those I represent; and I conceive my function as being to assist in conforming the interests of those I represent to the interests of the public when the two do not coincide."[29]

17.4.5.1 Should CEOs Voice Their Views on Public Issues?

An aspect of serving the public interest is the readiness of CEOs to speak out on important public issues that affect their companies. In the US, President Trump's "America First" doctrine announces "Build It Here, Sell It Here, Buy It Here." Shouldn't this be an issue that would arouse CEOs whose business depends on global markets? Yet, as Bill Lane, recently the director of global government affairs at Caterpillar Inc., sadly observed, there's been nary a word about global markets, international supply chains, or the value of all employees worldwide. He asks, "Why the charade" by those visiting the White House? "Why so little push-back?" Even though executives know the dangers of protectionism and isolationism, "they remain in the balcony if not center stage," says Lane. He declares, "Now it's time for corporate America collectively to speak out."[30]

An exception to not speaking out is GE's CEO Jeffrey Immelt. In his 2017 annual letter to investors he said that its transformation over the last decade had enabled it to profit from increasingly important international markets for its jet engines and power turbines, while withstanding a growing political movement against the economic effects of free trade. "In this period of nationalization," he said, "GE's competitive advantages will grow. We don't need trade deals, because we have a superior global footprint. We see many giving up on globalization; that means more for us." He did not confront Trump, however, saying "Over the past generation, the US has done very little to help our manufacturers or workers" and "We are hopeful the new administration will level the playing field."

Some CEOs have been speaking out on specific issues that concern their companies or industries. When President Trump attempted temporarily to ban nationals to the US from seven countries, Apple's Tim Cooke stated that immigration was vital to his company. Leaders from across the technology industry similarly criticized the ban. The industry relies on skilled foreigners to create new startups and fill engineering roles. In addition, more than 150 biotechnology executives and venture capitalists voiced opposition to the immigration order in a letter to the editor of *Nature Biotechnology*, a scientific journal. They pointed out that 52% of US biomedical researchers are foreign-born.

Known for making political statements, Charles Koch of the Koch brothers decided to go public to defend his support for conservative causes. He is chief executive of Koch Industries, one of the nation's largest privately owned companies. He and his brother head a network of conservative donors who planned to spend roughly $750 million to influence the 2016 political races. They seek reduced taxes and regulations, overhauling the criminal justice system, making it easier for low-income Americans to start businesses, and ending subsidies and tax breaks for corporations. On the issue of renewal of the Export–Import Bank, as reported in *USA Today*, he stated his opposition on the ground that those subsidies aiding US companies amount to corporate welfare. On the issue of climate change, he said, "You can plausibly say that CO_2 has contributed" to the planet's warming; however he sees "no evidence" in support of "this theory that it's going to be catastrophic."[31]

Unlike Koch, CEOs have traditionally remained quiet. When David Wessel, *Wall Street Journal*'s economics columnist, asked Peter G. Peterson, former secretary of commerce under President Richard Nixon, "Where have all the corporate managers gone?" his answer was that they seemed to have disappeared. Business consolidation has eliminated some lone voices and, with increased responsibility for managing their enterprises, has lowered the priority for public speaking. Several rules seem to govern:

- Never speak out in support of a particular political candidate. (Some employees and customers might be offended.)

- Support social issues that have general public acceptance, e.g. racial equality and gay rights are of concern to employees.
- Support issues that affect the vital interests of a company and its employees; e.g. a company dependent on foreign trade should oppose trade restriction.
- Oppose socialism and other threats to the free market system.

Randall Stephenson, CEO of AT&T, addressed several hundred company employees on the topic, "Black Lives Matter." He noted that "our communities are being destroyed by racial tension." Going beyond his own views, he urged employees to confront the issue rather than being "too polite to talk about it." He added, "Tolerance and inaction is what keeps prejudice and resentment alive . . . tolerance is for cowards."[32]

CEOs prefer to speak out through their trade associations, as Ben van Deurden did. In the US, the favorite ones are the Business Roundtable, the National Association of Manufacturers (NAM), and the US Chamber of Commerce. The Business Roundtable, organized to influence economic policy, has previously addressed issues of concern to all businesses. Among them are reductions in the federal support of trade agreements (e.g. clearing the way for China's admission to the World Trade Organization); uniting with Europeans against protectionism; and overhauling and elevating the teaching profession. Recent statements have been about opposition to Federal Communications Commission (FCC) internet regulation, support for providing cross-border data flow, and defending the sharing of cybersecurity information among competitors. NAM president Alexander Trowbridge also spoke on the issue of the federal budget, saying the NAM favored a freeze in Pentagon budget authority as well as a freeze in cost-of-living adjustments for Social Security.

In preparation for the UN's Climate Change Conference in Paris in December 2015, van Deurden, CEO of Royal Dutch Shell, urged his fellow executives to make their voices heard. His speech at the intellectual property (IP) Week Dinner in London on February 12, 2015, was appropriately titled "Less Aloof More Assertive." He asked that those fighting climate change to balance their view with the "moral obligation" of providing energy access to all. Oil in advanced economies and the issue of the price of oil throughout the year were important, he said. Speaking more broadly about energy as the "lifeblood of human existence," he urged that people should focus to lower their carbon emissions rather than rule out the use of fossil fuels. "To make our voices heard," he said, "our sector needs to enter into the public climate debate alongside other credible parties."[33]

These business associations choose issues of concern to them and express their views of what is in the public interest. Not surprisingly, their statements have been criticized for being self-serving. Smith Cullen of *The Press* in Christchurch, New Zealand, accused the Business Roundtable of believing in the narrow philosophy that the business of business is just business – that business people should not feel any moral obligation to get involved in the social issues of the country.

In contrast, Starbucks' CEO Howard Schultz believes speaking out on social issues is part of Starbucks' core identity. He is known as a prominent social activist driven by a genuine desire to achieve change on important issues, among which are death-penalty injustices, chronic unemployment, veterans' needs, and the college aspirations of his baristas. This was evidenced in a full-page ad of five paragraphs in bold type on the theme of America as a nation. Part of the first paragraph reads: "You could easily mistake America as a nation, lost. A people who have severed the common bonds that hold us together – compassion, respect, shared responsibility, a belief in service, a willingness to unite despite our differences."[34] Schultz believes that his company could be a force for good.

But Schultz learned that getting involved with social issues can be hazardous when carried too far. He took the initiative on a broad debate about race relation in America, instructing his baristas to write "Race Together" or stick similar stickers on cups given to customers. This led to a huge backlash on social media resulting in the temporary closing of the Twitter account of senior vice president of global communications, Corey duBrowa. This element of the campaign was promptly discontinued, which Schultz said was the intention anyway. Critics suggest it was a mistake to involve its employees on this delicate topic and that they are not trained to facilitate such conversations with customers. It's one thing for a CEO to speak out on issues, but another to ask employees to do so.[35]

Keven Johnson, who replaced Schultz as CEO, has also never been shy about voicing his opinion on social issues. After getting backlash on his pledge to hire refugees, he defended his stand by saying "it's driven by our principles."[36] He said many of the company's veterans had worked with interpreters in Iraq and Afghanistan who are now refugees and have been hired by Starbucks. He thought this stand helped the company and showed that it cared about helping create opportunities for people. In answer to "Why not just sell coffee?" he said, "One of the reasons people come to work at Starbucks is because we stand for something. It's about human connection and having a sense of humanity We think that's part of what makes Starbucks a special place that both partners and customers want to be associated with."

Even when CEOs are not directly involved, a survey by the public affairs agency Global Strategy Group found that Americans overwhelmingly believe that companies should take action to address important issues facing society. For example, companies such as Dow Chemical Co., Alcoa Inc., and Northrop Grumman Corp. have publicly condemned measures in North Carolina, Tennessee, Mississippi, and Georgia over the issue of gay and transgender rights. These measures were seen as discriminatory and hampering the companies' ability to recruit and retain bright young workers. Howard Ugerleider, Dow's vice chairman and chief financial officer, pushed the company's public affairs team to lobby the Missouri legislature over bills seen as discriminatory to lesbian, gay, bisexual, and transgender people. Walt Disney Co. threatened to exit the state over these bills. Thanks partly to social media outlets such as Twitter, chief executives seem to being having more impact now, said Aaron Chatterji, an associate professor at Duke University.

A study by the Public Affairs Council of 92 businesses found that pressure from employees may be mounting on corporate senior management to take a public stand on social issues such as the environment, discrimination based on gender and race, improved access to quality education, and human rights abroad. The study, called "Who's Behind Corporate Advocacy on Social Issues? Employees," states that the motive is not mainly to pacify external critics. A strong majority of companies believe that higher expectations for engagement on social issues are here to stay, with 74% of respondents saying they expect pressure on firms to get involved will increase over the next 3 years. The most common strategies used in such social issue advocacy have been joining a coalition and lobbying at the state or local level.

In other parts of the world, some corporate heads are more active in voicing their opinions. Responding to Russia's annexation of Crimea and incursions into the Ukraine, the US mobilized sanctions against it. But Joe Kaeser, CEO of Siemens, voiced outright opposition, as did some other European CEOs. The British oil giant BP warned that further international sanctions on Russia could have a "material adverse impact" on the company. It owns a 19.75% stake in Rosneft, the Russian oil firm, which is subject to sanctions, preventing it from using US financial institutions for new loans over a period longer than 90 days.

In China, corporate heads appear to be outspoken on the issues of the one-child policy (now lifted), curbs on new-car sales in several cities, release of more accurate air pollution data, and gay rights. Jack Ma, chairman of Alibaba Group Holding Ltd., China's e-commerce giant, went even further by awarding 10 same-sex couples with all-expense-paid trips to the US. Executives fear that China's aging population may not have enough workers in coming decades.

The argument in favor of business's speaking out on public issues is that negative public opinion about business's lack of concern about public welfare might be softened. But the risk to individual CEOs of negative reactions to them stating their views is high. Furthermore, as Milton Friedman stated, their competence to judge social issues could be questioned. When they adhere to matters involving their own companies and industries, they possess competence and legitimacy to do so. The need for CEOs to influence public opinion on given issues is usually unnecessary, for lobbying legislative and executive bodies is generally a more direct and effective way to achieve desired public policy. Speaking within business and industry circles allows CEOs to voice their opinions and at the same time rally lobbying support.

17.5 Conclusions

The above list of five contributions of corporate communication to corporate governance is ambitious. Yet they are indirectly assumed when CCOs assert that they should be members of a company's dominant coalition. Although a CCO's role in strategic communications is critical to company success, a knowledge of management structure and behavior helps to identify the problems that require attention. Furthermore, a CCO can contribute to the quality of management decision making. When in a career track study of the former New England Chapter of PRSA members were asked how they could improve their status in their organizations, the foremost priority was to learn more about management.

In the era of globalization, CEOs must also become corporate diplomats and receive support from their CCOs if they are broadly trained in global affairs. But competence must combine his or her communication roles with the management roles. This combination is the qualification needed to participate in top management decision making.

A goal of CCOs working for MNCs should be to help their CEOs become global managers. The term global manager is derived from Christopher S. Bartlett and S. Ghoshal's *Harvard Business Review* article "What is a Global Manager?" They explain that a global manager may be (i) global business or product division managers who must build worldwide efficiency and competitiveness, (ii) country managers whose unit is the building block for worldwide operations, or (iii) worldwide function specialists. The common denominator is that a global manager is any manager who has a significant role in relating to players in the international arena.[37]

Their key features of global managers are familiarity with other cultures, an appreciation of diversity of views and people, and possession of relationship skills, such as recognizing emotions in others. Because these are attributes of diplomats, Clyde Pestowitz, former counselor to the secretary of commerce in the Reagan administration noted, many CEOs have metamorphosed into something resembling heads of state. Some CEOs such as Bill Gates, find it easier to arrange meetings with President Hu Jintao of China than do the prime ministers of some of their allies. Global managers see the world not just s a collection of national marketplaces, but also as a source of scarce information, knowledge, and expertise.

Discussion Questions

17.1. Why is legitimacy such an important top management consideration? What does it mean? How does it relate to ethics and "integrity"?

17.2. Choose one of the 20 "integrity" failures listed by Linda Ferrell and O.C. Ferrell and discuss what went wrong.

17.3. How have CCOs become involved in defending the free market system?

17.4. Would you agree with those who believe that the board of directors should subordinate the interests of society to those of business? Discuss.

17.5. Is it a good idea to broaden representation on the board of directors to include other than business interests? Why or why not?

17.6. What types of advocacy groups confront corporations? What are their objectives?

17.7. What are stockholder proxy resolutions? Why are they important? What are some common demands? Are they effective?

17.8. For what kinds of management decisions should public opinion be an important consideration?

17.9. How much weight should the board of directors give to proxy resolutions?

17.10. To what extent is the public interest a consideration in management decision making?

17.11. What advice would you give a CEO who wants to speak out on a public issue?

Case 8 VW's Crisis of Corporate Governance

Volkswagen AG faced a reputational scandal when on Monday, September 21, 2015, Michael Horn, the boss of Volkswagen US, disclosed that his company had falsified emissions tests of its diesel autos. On the previous Friday, the Environmental Protection Agency (EPA), had announced its finding that VWs and Audis had software that concealed NOX – nitrogen oxides – pollutants during emissions testing. Not to be confused with carbon dioxide, NOX is a pollutant that causes smog and potentially fatal respiratory illnesses. On-the-road tests showed that the cars were producing as much as 40 times the acceptable levels of NOX. The environment was one casualty of VW's deception.

Making his statement at a company event to launch the new VW Passat, Horn said that "defeat devices" were installed in auto electronic systems. VW diesel engines could detect when they were being tested and change their performance accordingly. With the favorable results, VW could then advertise "Clean Diesels," an appeal that was central to penetrating the American market. Horn candidly admitted, "Our company was dishonest with the EPA, and with the California Air Resources Board (CARB) and with all of you, and in my German words: We have totally screwed up . . . . This kind of behavior is totally inconsistent with our qualities . . . . We will pay what we have to pay."[38] The economic and financial impact was huge, for VW is Germany's biggest company with nearly £203 billion in sales, 300 000 employees, and 29 plants across the country.[39] Stock prices plunged 35% as its vaunted reputation was punctured.

VW could not wiggle out of the problem by saying discrepancies were caused by "technical glitches," which for more than a year it told American regulators caused tailpipe emissions to soar on the road.[40] VW, which includes the Audi, Porsche, and Lamborghini brands, faced a crisis that traversed the globe – a crisis that exposed its dysfunctional corporate governance. Whether VW would recognize the full significance of the crisis and how it would handle it would determine the impact on its reputation and financial welfare.

Background

Knowledge of the deception can be traced back to at least 2012 when EPA officials and California regulators were in touch with European counterparts about high emissions in diesel vehicles. In spring 2014, EPA officials discovered that a 2012 Jetta and 2013 Passat had significantly higher NOX emissions during normal driving conditions. This finding was confirmed by emissions experts at West Virginia University, who reported in April 2014 that they had discovered a discrepancy between test emissions results and actual emissions during driving. The findings were shared with the CARB. VW disingenuously said its engineers in the US were at a loss to explain the problem.[41]

Belatedly, on March 2, 2016, VW disclosed the chronology of events in its online newsroom. It stated that CEO Martin Winterkorn, a metals scientist and engineer, received a memo about the diesel issue in November 2014 – a year before the public disclosure – when VW was negotiating with the EPA about how to bring its cars' emissions into compliance. Surprisingly, he and others in top management did not recognize the gravity of the situation. The diesel issue was treated simply as only one of many product issues facing the company, and "did not initially receive particular attention at the management levels of Volkswagen."[42] The issue was also discussed at a July 2015 meeting, but only on the periphery of a meeting about product issues in the presence of Winterkorn and Herbert Diess, the executive in charge of Volkswagen brand cars.

The company said it was not clear whether the two executives understood that Volkswagen software had been illegally modified.[43] The following month, however, Volkswagen technicians provided information to a member of the management board, who was not identified, indicating that the diesel cars were equipped with illegal software. Subsequently on January 2017 German prosecutors named Winterkorn as a suspect in its fraud investigation, saying he may have known about the issue earlier than he acknowledged.[44]

Who knew what and when is further described in various news reports. The German newspaper *Bild am Sonntag* on February 14, 2016, stated that Bernd Gottweis, a quality control executive and troubleshooter known internally as "the fireman," sent a memo to CEO Winterkorn in May 2014 warning about an impending investigation by US environmental authorities. The memo was included in a package of documents Winterkorn took home with him. VW states that it is not known whether he read the memo. Nevertheless, Jack Ewing of *The International New York Times* believes senior Volkswagen management did not realize the gravity of the diesel emissions problem and the potential financial impact until much later. This amazing insensitivity to an impending crisis suggests a serious flaw in VW's top management and an absence of information and advice from its corporate communications officer.

What Winterkorn knew and the role he played in the diesel emission deception will become evident following a US indictment against him announced on May 3, 2018. He was charged with conspiracy and wire fraud related to the criminal investigation into the company's efforts to cheat on the diesel-emissions testing. Federal prosecutor allege that in a July 2015 meeting, Winterkorn "approved the continued concealment of the cheating software from U.S. regulators." He faces up to 5 years in prison and a $250 000 fine for the conspiracy count.[45]

Crisis Analysis

VW's emissions scandal is best described in terms of crisis management and failure of corporate governance. It constitutes a serious blindness to corporate ethics and specifically about VW's sense of social responsibility. The crisis can be classified as a serious management failure, a crisis category that contains three elements: skewed values, deception, and gross misconduct.[46]

Skewed Values

Skewed values were evident when VW exclusively focused on the bottom line and became obsessed with becoming the world's number one auto producer. By doing so it neglected the interests of its consumer, dealer, and investor stakeholders – as well as harm to the environment. To address skewed values, these interests would promptly have to be addressed.

VW did address car owners' concerns on November 9, 2015, when it announced a "good will program" for owners of diesel-powered cars with 2.0 l engines under investigation by the US's EPA. It offered $500 on a prepaid Visa card, $500 in dealership credits, and 3 years of free roadside assistance. In the US, this offer was announced in a full-page issue ad in major newspapers such as the *Wall Street Journal* in November 2015, which was headlined, "We're working to make things right."[47] It asked loyal customers for "your continued patience," adding that it was working "tirelessly to develop a remedy." Reflecting VW's poor judgment, some US lawmakers called VW's offer "insultingly inadequate."[48] As CNN's *Money* program put it, "Lots of VW car owners are mad as hell." The value of their diesel cars dropped, as well as the expectation that they were helping the environment.

It wasn't until mid-January 2016 that VW announced it would begin repairing vehicles in the US. But customers and car dealers were still largely uninformed about how and when their vehicles would be repaired. The German newspaper *Sueddeutsche Zeitung*, however, reported that VW was considering buying back up to 115 000 vehicles in the US. An article in *The Guardian* subsequently stated in April 2016 that VW would buy back or repair nearly 600 000 vehicles, including a fund for corrective efforts over excess pollution and to commit other money to promote green auto technology. Volkswagen public relations\spokesperson Kurt McGuiness explained, "It's a process and that's why we are moving through the cars model by model."[49]

Ultimately, VW bought back, or terminated the leases of 125 000 diesel vehicles from affected owners.[50] The total cost of the diesel emissions scandal was estimated to be at least $23 billion. It agreed to pay up to $17.5 billion to compensate consumers, regulators, dealer, and state attorneys general in the US. It also agreed to pay a criminal fine of $4.3 billion and at least $1.2 billion in compensation to owners of about 80 000 3.0-l diesel vehicles.[51]

Dealer concerns were addressed at an annual VW conference on April 2, 2016, in Las Vegas where hundreds of dealers were told during a 90-minute meeting with Herbert Diess, head of the VW passenger car brand. He vowed to "redefine" the company's tarnished image and "relaunch" the Volkswagen brand. He devoted much attention to new products, such as an Alltrack wagon and a sport utility vehicle. But he failed to provide details on the legal, financial, and commercial ramifications. Although some dealers were ready to file a lawsuit, they generally agreed they would continue to work with VW and be patient for financial settlements and other reparations.[52] A settlement was reached in August that expected VW to pay a collective $1.2 billion and to buy back unfixable diesel vehicles on dealers' lots.[53]

Investors, another aggrieved party, decided to take legal action. Attorneys representing almost 300 institutions filed a lawsuit for $3.67 billion on March 14, 2016, for losses resulting from the cheating scandal. CalPERS is part of the lawsuit. Their claim is that VW failed to inform the financial markets in a timely fashion about the risks associated with investigations by US environmental authorities.[54]

In Germany, prosecutors opened an investigation in June 2016 of former CEO Winterkorn and Herbert Diess for allegedly not informing investors enough about potential losses in connection with the emissions cheating scandal.[55] In May 2017 the charge was extended to include Matthias Mueller, the current CEO, and other key board members.[56] They were briefed months before US environmental regulators raised questions about diesel emissions levels. In Germany individual investors (class action suits are not allowed in Europe) have filed lawsuits seeking up to $4.4 billion in damages for the plunge in VW shares.[57] New claims filed in January 2017 with the Braunschweig district court that has jurisdiction have raised the amount demanded by investors to around $9.1 billion.[58]

Further repercussions were mounting. The pension fund in the German state of Bavaria planned to file a lawsuit against VW. And in South Korea, 80 models of VW cars, including its Audi and Bentley, affecting more than 80 000 vehicles, were banned. Furthermore, the chief executive of VW's Korean unit was indicted on charges of fraud linked to the diesel scandal.[59]

Deception

The second aspect of management failure, deception, most accurately characterizes the form of this crisis. Deception refers to the deliberate communication of false information or providing no information. Environmental quality was the worst casualty of the deception. That cannot be undone, to the dismay of some auto owners whose motive in buying a diesel was in part to protect the environment. Just as BP was sued for billions of dollars for pollution in the Gulf of Mexico, VW faces civil lawsuits, and criminal and regulatory probes in the US, Europe and elsewhere related to damage to the atmosphere caused by its emissions cheating.

In the US alone, the Justice Department sued VW seeking billions of dollars in penalties for violating the Clean Air Act. It also accused the company of obstructing efforts by the government to "learn the truth about the emissions exceedances and other irregularities."[60] VW faces fines of as much as $18 billion from US environmental regulators alone, and it faces an additional barrage of US litigation for billions of dollars of damages.[61] Joining the fray, the Federal Trade Commission planned to file a complaint for false advertising that the diesels were environmentally friendly.[62] Eleven million vehicles worldwide are affected, not only the 2.0 engines but also, as later disclosed,

3.0-l diesel engines used in luxury sedans and sport utility vehicles of the Audi and Porsche units.[63] On the state level, New Jersey's acting attorney general sued VW over the emissions scandal.[64]

Deception seriously damaged VW's reputation, as shown by a Harris poll of Americans' attitudes toward the 100 most visible companies, which ranked VW dead last. Volkswagen was seen as particularly brazen. Although the public tends to show "a little more tolerance" for recalls and labor issues, said Wendy Salomon, a vice president at Nielsen, which conducted the poll, respondents were "least tolerant" of lying and misrepresentation and intentional wrongdoing.[65] VW's reputation at the European Investment Bank (EIB) was also damaged. Its president, Werner Hoyer, commented, "I am somewhat astonished about the communication behavior in Wolfsburg [headquarters of VW], not only toward us but also toward the public."[66]

Germany's nation brand was also at stake. Sigmar Gabriel, the vice-chancellor and economics minister, hoped the export brand of Germany as a whole would not be tarnished. As stated by *The Economist*, "Germany's economic strength rests in large part on the idea that anything stamped 'Made in Germany' will offer a high level of reliability, trustworthiness, and engineering prowess."[67] VW is large enough to cause such damage for it directly or indirectly employs one in seven of the country's workers. Its brands include Porsche and Audi. An environmental ethic seems to have been lacking in VW's top management and in its engineers. Ironically, Germany has been a leader in addressing climate change issues by shifting energy sources to the renewal energy of wind power and solar energy, and by gradually dismantling its nuclear energy plants. VW management was out of sync with its own government's environmental goals.

The solution to deception is full disclosure of all pertinent information. EPA findings should have been made public earlier. Although the new CEO Matthias Mueller promised to cooperate fully and cooperatively with US officials, he has refused to turn over documents, including emails, from its US files, citing German privacy laws.[68] Germany has some of the world's toughest privacy laws because of its past when surveillance was both dreaded and commonplace.[69] When interviewed by NPR during a visit to the US, Matthias dismissively said, "It was a technical problem. We had not the right interpretation of the American law . . . we didn't lie."[70] He quickly withdrew that statement. But a stance of pretending not to have known about the emissions deception and the deliberate belittling of the diesel issue by board of director members fortifies the impression of deception and a faulty culture. As suggested by some, car makers, particularly in Europe, "are used to getting away with a great deal in such matters. Their trickery is an open secret within the industry . . ."[71]

Misconduct

The third kind of management failure, and most severe, is misconduct. Winterkorn himself called the scandal one of "misconduct." He might not have been aware that the standard crisis response to misconduct almost always calls for the resignation of the CEO. Speculation that VW's Winterkorn would have to resign quickly materialized after the disclosure was made. It followed a meeting of the company's supervisory board on the Wednesday after the September 17, 2015, disclosure.

Other conspicuous resignations were also announced. Two top Volkswagen engineers, Ulrich Hackenberg and Wolfgang Hatz, were suspended. Both are viewed as two of the best and brightest engineers in German industry. Hackenberg is credited with developing VW's modular manufacturing.[72] He and Hatz were put in charge of research and development at the VW group shortly after Winterkorn became CEO in January 2007 and were known to be confidantes with him.[73] Winterkorn announced that he would "accept responsibility" for the "irregularities that have been found in diesel engines" and tendered his resignation to the board. Feigning innocence, he said, "I am stunned that misconduct on such a scale was possible in the Volkswagen

Group."[74] In a video message he lamented, "Millions of people in the world trust our brand, our cars, and our technology. I am endlessly sorry that we have betrayed their trust."[75]

VW further suspended nine managers suspected of being involved. Prosecutors must investigate individual employees suspected of being responsible. These include employees of one of VW's suppliers, Robert Bosch GmbH, who assisted in installing engine control software as part of a routine contract.[76] This auto parts supplier was later sued by car owners for supplying the software and working "hand-in-glove" with the car maker.[77] VW's internal audit found no evidence of involvement by the executive board or supervisory board. No mention was made of individual executive culpability and nothing was said about Gottweis's memo to CEO Winterkorn. Email of executives cannot be examined in Germany because of privacy protection. Furthermore, under German law, companies cannot be held liable for criminal wrongdoing.

Seemingly to further support the claim that no one on top levels was involved in the deception, Herbert Diess theatrically sent a memo to employees on November 12 enlisting their help to get to the bottom of the emissions scandal, giving them until November 30 to provide "complete and truthful" information. He said, "We depend on the cooperation and knowledge from you our employees, to carry out a complete resolution of all events connected to the diesel and [carbon dioxide] issues."[78]

Nearly 2 months after the disclosure, VW said it said its internal probe hadn't been able to produce a clear explanation of how the deception happened or identify those in the company responsible. Diess promised that employees who came forward before the deadline would "have nothing to fear from the company in the way of repercussions on the job such as being fired or held liable for damages." Even this safeguard was qualified because it would apply only to workers covered by collective bargaining pacts and VW reserved the right to transfer employees or change their responsibilities if they incriminated themselves. The inability, or unwillingness, of VW to identify who was responsible for the installation of defeater software remains troublesome. A crisis requires greater openness.

VW's Ethics and Culture

A basic response to misconduct is to change an organization's culture, which begins with ethics. A code of ethics must be applied that is agreed upon by all managers and employees. As stated by Dan Neil in the *Wall Street Journal*, VW must send a clear message that integrity is vital at every level in a company. The danger in an engineering-oriented organization like VW is that a "scientific" culture prevails. Hard facts and measurable things dominate thinking. Engineers resist the idea that public attitudes and societal values are valid considerations. When this author spoke of the "logic of sentiments" in an industrial relations class at the Massachusetts Institute of Technology (MIT), a student yelled out "there's no such thing as logic in sentiments." Engineering and science professionals may be blind to some aspects of ethics because the focus is on problem-solving and achievement of goals. VW must foster a common culture that encourages open discussion of ethics, even if uncomfortable.[79]

Chairman Hans Dieter Poetsch and CEO Matthias Mueller blamed VW's "culture of tolerance" for rule-breaking during a 2-hour news conference on December 10, 2015, in the VW headquarters city of Wolfsburg, Germany. They referred to the "chain of mistakes" that started with VW's push into the US in 2005. Poetsch believed that a small group of employees carried out the deception and that the roots of the deception were the "misconduct and shortcomings of individual employees."[80]

James Womack, an expert on the international auto industry, and others expressed doubts about Poetsch's explanation. Womack questions whether a handful of engineers "could do this under the radar [and] have it last for years," and that there would be no knowledge of management's running of VW's regulatory and business wings. Joan Claybrook, former administrator of the National Highway Traffic Safety Administration, said, "There are not rogue engineers who unilaterally decide to initiate the greatest vehicle emission fraud in history. They don't act unilaterally . . . . They have teams that put these vehicles together. They have a review process for the design, testing and development of the vehicles." The German weekly *Der Spiegel* thought that at least 33 engineers were involved in the deception.[81] In short, the honesty and credibility of top management were questioned.

A quick way to change an organization's culture is to replace its CEO. When another German company, Siemens, faced a bribery scandal, it hired an outsider as the new CEO. But VW chose Mueller, an insider, as the new CEO, explaining that it thereby made clear that shareholders and labor representatives "want a CEO who is at home in the company's culture, one that values reaching consensus between management and labor above simply maximizing profits."[82] Mueller stated, "We don't need any yes men . . . . The future belongs to the courageous. I am appealing to the curious, to the nonconformists, to the pioneers." Whether an insider CEO can change a culture that accepts ethical values and responsibilities to customers and society remains to be seen. VW's culture has been described in mostly negative terms. Geoffrey Smith and Roger Parloff called it "confident, cutthroat and insular." It was a "ruthless, overweening culture" in which the organization was run like an empire, with overwhelming control vested in a few hands, and particularly with the founding families of Ferdinand Porsche and Hans Dieter Poetsch.

Most of Mueller's early reforms have focused on structural changes aimed at decentralizing decision making. He promised to restructure and streamline what has been called VW's unwieldy decision making process. Shortly after being appointed Mueller hired Thomas Sedran, a former consultant who had also served as the interim CEO at General Motors' Opel unit, as strategy chief – a newly created position.[83] Part of his job was to eliminate inefficiencies and the other was to examine the direction of the huge VW enterprise. This effort was in line with an editorial in the weekly *Der Spiegel* that recommended that VW be broken up into several units. About a dozen board-level executives have been removed "from the bottleneck in the CEO's office" and replaced by several of its core brands and a number of outsiders. The number of executives reporting to the CEO himself was halved to 17, which, however, is still, in organizational lingo, a wide span of control.[84]

Mueller vowed to get to the bottom of the scandal by launching an internal investigation. To do so he hired US law firm Jones Day to conduct an "independent investigation," which is another action common to a crisis of management failure. The firm is one of the tenth largest in the world and best known for its litigation practice. It has been granted unhindered access to more than a decade of documents, including emails. Even in the US, however, VW has been slow to produce documents from its US files.[85]

Concerned about its image, VW also hired an international team of public relations firms and recruited an "Integrity Officer."[86] Reflecting the international dimensions of the crisis, the firms are based in three different countries – Gershon Kekst in the US, Finsbury in Britain, and Hering Schuppener in Germany – to join Edelman, an American firm already on retainer. To handle anticipated owner lawsuits, VW hired Kenneth Feinberg, who previously set up funds for victims of the BP Deepwater Horizon oil disasters and victims of defective General Motors Co. cars. Feinberg's program would address US owners of nearly 500 000 cars with 2-l diesel engines and about 85 000 vehicles with 3-l diesel engines. The affected brands include Volkswagen, Audi, and Porsche.[87]

Implications for Corporate Governance

The scandal raises the question of VW's corporate governance. Smith and Parloff say, "One has to wonder how the brass could have been blind to conduct that was so central to achieving the company's goal." How could the managers of one of Germany's largest and most successful companies fail to know about the deception and realize that it constituted a major crisis? One explanation is VW's dysfunctional organizational culture, which led to a mindset that blinded engineers and executives to happenings in the socio-political environment. The company repeatedly claims that no one in the chain of command was aware of the deception and its formidable consequences. As stated in *Der Spiegel*, they shielded themselves and didn't want to see what the general public knew.[88] Consistent with this claim, VW's executive pay packages remained untouched by the emissions scandal, but the board accepted management's offer to withhold 30% of performance-related pay.[89]

A Misguided Board of Directors

VW's board of directors was misguided. They focused on car sales and were obsessed with becoming the number one world producer of autos. As *Der Spiegel* stated, they wanted to be known as "the Biggest, the Best, and most successful."[90] The operating slogan was "Mach 18," meaning achieving both 2018 targets and moving at 18 times the speed of sound.[91] VW sales topped 10 million units in 2014, with an operating profit of $14.2 billion.[92] Their sales goal minimized or ignored the question of the effect on air quality on car emissions; only bottom line results counted. The climate of "angst" at VW was such that no one dared to object. An organizational culture of high power distance prevailed.

Articles by journalists and others confirm deficiencies in corporate governance.[93] The German daily *Süddeutsche Zeitung* compared VW's governance to that of North Korea, adding that its "autocratic leadership style has long been out of date." It said "functioning corporate governance is missing."[94] Germany has a two-tier corporate governance system with a 10-person supervisory board (equivalent of a board of directors) that oversees a 5–7-person management board responsible for day-to-day operations.[95] A key feature of the supervisory board is that labor representatives occupy 10 of the 20 seats, a requirement of a codetermination law that applies to major industries. The nation's most powerful union, IG Metall, which controls the labor seats, is chiefly interested in jobs for its members. One of the five management members represents the state of Lower Saxony, which owns 20% of VW and is also interested in the bottom line and employment. Most of the remaining power of the board rests with the heirs of the original Beetle designer Ferdinand Porsche and members of the Piëch family, who own over 50% of the voting stocks and control the company. Such centralized power discourages dissenting voices. Piëch's influence was reported to be seen everywhere at VW. Such centralized power discourages dissenting voices.[96]

The board lacks a wider diversity of members who represent other viewpoints and the interests of the larger society The board is thus very insular, reflecting its "famously clubby" culture where "success depends on being well-connected in Wolfsburg and striking a balance between boosting profit margins and maintaining strong ties to labor."[97] The shortcomings of codetermination are exposed, for the labor unions and the state of Lower Saxony are chiefly, if not wholly, interested in preserving jobs.

Given Volkswagen's history, culture, and structure, the real mystery may be why something like this didn't happen sooner, says reporter James Steward. He quotes Charles Elson, professor of finance and director of the John L.Weinberg Center for Corporate Governance at the University of Delaware, as saying, "The governance of Volkswagen was a breeding ground for scandal. It was an accident waiting to happen." Even by German standards, "Volkswagen stands apart," said Markus Roth, a professor at Phillips-University Marburg and an expert in European corporate governance. "It's been a soap opera ever since it started."[98]

The scandal revealed a failure of politics too, as demonstrated by the government's seeming inability to regulate the auto industry. Ties have been too cozy. For example, Matthias Wissmann, who runs the country's powerful VDA auto-industry lobbying group, is a former lawmaker and transport minister. Another example is Thomas Steg, a former deputy government spokesman who stepped down in 2009 and just a few years later became VW's head of external and government relations reporting directly to CEO Winterkorn.[99] One environmental group, *Deutsche Umwelthilfe*, lamented that the government hadn't been more vigilant about the diesel engine emissions of nitrogen oxides. Dorothee Saar, who heads up the group's transport and air control unit, said it "was no secret that there were significant discrepancies between laboratory tests and real driving conditions."[100]

Needed: A Corporate Communication Presence

VW has a CCO position, which was occupied by Stephan Grühsem, who reported to the management board. But his function was limited to publicity and media relations. On one occasion he appeared with Winterkorn to receive an "Image-Award" conferred by DPRG (Germany's equivalent of PRSA) in 2011. Another occasion was a news release about shareholder lawsuits which claimed that VW fulfilled disclosure requirements under the German capital market law.[101] VW optimistically considers that the approximately 500 000 affected vehicles would be manageable and could be contained by "effective technical solutions." The press release blamed the crisis on the fixation on the 2005 major diesel campaign in the US, saying that "a group of persons – whose identity is still being determined – at levels below the Groups Management Board . . . decided to modify the engine management software." It said there was no need to involve superior levels because changes were "within budget," implying that this was the chief or sole criterion.

Hans-Gerd Bode is Volkswagen's new CCO, appointed in September 2015. But his job seems to have been limited to cleaning up the mess caused by the crisis. He commented: "A crisis like this, the company was not prepared for." His reference was to the "thousands of calls and emails coming in at the same time," which he likened to "something like a tsunami."[102] Bode's background is not commensurate with the needed qualifications of a professional CCO. He had been top spokesman for Volkswagen's Porsche division, hosting media events featuring vintage sports cars and the glamorous tennis star Maria Sharapova. Could he now lead the damage control in a globe-spanning public relations crisis? A CCO with more than a publicity background is needed.

It's the job of a CCO to make management aware of "what's going on." This is more likely to happen when the CCO plays a management as well as a communication role and is a member of the top management group. Such a person is a "boundary-spanner" who connects management with society and ideally should have a strong voice in all matters affecting a company's reputation. A CCO is responsible for issues management, which monitors the socio-political environment to identify relevant issues affecting the company.[103] He or she would also be qualified to direct a crisis response.

But as the failures at VW suggest, formal structures do not necessarily indicate actual behavior. As stated by Sasja Beslik, head of responsible investments at the Swedish fund group Nordea Asset Management, "Volkswagen's communications have been totally reactive."[104] Both the issues management process and upward communication system must be examined to ensure that there is continual monitoring of the news media, opinion leaders, and public opinion and that findings are reported to top management. Instead of scheming to falsify emissions, the CCO should have been educating managers about the importance of the environment issue in all of its activities.

Discussion Questions

1 Why is this case of scandal associated with corporate governance? What aspects of corporate governance pertain to corporate communication and reputation management?

2 "VW has misapplied its technological and engineering prowess." Explain what VW did.

3 What categories of a crisis of management failure apply to this case? How does recognition of these categories help decide on appropriate responses to the VW crisis?

4 What stakeholders were affected by this crisis? Has VW adequately responded to their concerns?

5 What should VW have immediately done when the crisis erupted?

6 In what way is VW's culture the cause of the crisis?

7 What should the qualifications of a CCO be?

8 Can VW repair its reputation? How? What must it do?

Endnotes

1 The annual survey of the world's biggest public companies by Booz & Company found that firms now routinely separate the jobs of chairman and chief executive. "Schumpeter: Corporate Constitutions," *The Economist*, October 30, 2010.
2 Peter Drucker. *Management: Tasks, Responsibilities, Practices* (New York: Harper & Row, 1974), p. 809.
3 Ibid., pp. 631–632
4 Peter Drucker, "The Real Duties of a Director," Editorial, *WSJ*, June 1, 1978, p. 20.
5 Ian Wilson "One Company's Experience with Restructuring the Governing Board", *Journal of Contemporary Business*, Vol. 8, No. 1, 1979, p. 73.
6 John C. Iwata, chairman, Arthur W. Page Society, "Building Belief: A New Model for Activating Corporate Character and Authentic Advocacy," Arthur W. Page Society, Monograph 2012. For a list of Arthur W. Page Principles, see Don K.·Wright, "The Organization of the Corporate Communication Function," in Rossella Gambetti and Stephen Quigley, eds, *Managing Corporate Communication: A Cross-Cultural Approach* (Basingstoke: Palgrave Macmillan, 2013), p. 77.
7 Linda Ferrell and O.C. Ferrell, "Examining Organizational Integrity Failures," in Robert C. Chandler, ed., *Business and Corporate Integrity: Sustaining Organizational Company Ethics and Trust* (Santa Barbara, CA: Praeger, 2014), p. 182.
8 Ibid.
9 See paid advertisement, *WSJ*, July 21, 2016, p. A14. Also https://corpgov.law.harvard.edu/.../commonsense-principles-of-corporate-governance, July 22, 2016.
10 *Business Week*, Special Issue, Reinventing America: Meeting the New Challenges of a Global Economy, 1992.
11 Joann S. Lublin, "Environmentalism Sprouts up on Corporate Boards," *WSJ*, August 11, 2008.
12 "Chief executives now live in glass houses", *The Economist*, October 10, 2014.

13 John Swaine, "Mozilla CEO Brendan Eich resigns in wake of backlash to Prop 8," *The Guardian*, April 3, 2014.
14 Robert A.G. Monks, *Citizens DisUnited: Passive Investors, Drone CEOs, and the Corporate Capture of the American Dream* (Miniver Press, 2013).
15 Robert A.G. Monks, ibid.
16 https://www.iccr.org/reports-and-publications
17 *PR Week*/Burson-Marsteller survey in 2003.
18 Daniel Tisch, "#PRin2013: PR to give organizations a new legitimacy", PRSA, January 23, 2013. http://prsay.prsa.org/2013/01/23/prin2013-pr-to-give-organizations-a-new-legitimacy
19 "Walmart's Mexican Morass," *The Economist*, April 28, 2012, pp. 71–72.
20 http://fortune.com/2017/05/10/walmart-bribery-investigation-settlement
21 Aruna Viswanatha and Sarah Nassauer, "U.S. Probes Possible Wal-Mart Misconduct in Brazil," *WSJ*, November 24, 2015. https://www.wsj.com/articles/u-s-probe-of-wal-mart-finds-possible-misconduct-in-brazil-1448401190
22 Robert L. Health, *Strategic Issues Management: Organizations and Public Policy Challenges* (Thousand Oaks, CA: Sage Publications, 1997), pp. 104–105.
23 Peter F. Bartha, "Managing Corporate External Issues: An Analytical Framework," *Business Quarterly*, Vol. 47, October 1982, pp. 78–90.
24 Walter Lippmann, *Essays in the Public Philosophy* (Boston, MA: Little, Brown and Co., 1955), pp. 41–42.
25 2015 Edelman Trust Barometer, www.edelman.com
26 Sherry Arnstein, "A Ladder of Citizen Participation," *Journal of the American Institute for Planners*,, Vol. 35., No. 4, July 1969, pp. 216–220.
27 The statement appears in the Edelman Trust Barometer, see www.edelman.com
28 Scott M. Cutlip and Allen H. Center, *Effective Public Relations* (Englewood Cliffs, NJ: Prentice-Hall, 1958), p. 5.
29 J. Carroll Bateman, "A World-Wide Profession," *PR Journal*, October 1976, p. 15.
30 Bill Lane, "Confessions of a Free-Trade Lobbyist," *WSJ*, February 24, 2017, p. 17.
31 Patrick O'Connor, "A Frustrated Koch Brother Decides It's Time to 'Spout Off,'" *WSJ*, October 27, 2015, p. A1.
32 Brian Fung, "Watch AT&T's CEO give a forceful defense of Black Lives Matter," *The Washington Post*, September 30, 2016. https://www.washingtonpost.com/news/the-switch/wp/2016/09/30/watch-atts-ceo-give-a-forceful-defense-of-black-lives-matter/?noredirect=on&utm_term=.8fe5d81918c3
33 James Gerken, "Shell CEO Says Industry Needs to be Less Aloof in Climate Change Conversation," *Huffington Post*, December 2, 2015. https://www.huffingtonpost.co.uk/entry/shell-ceo-climate-change_n_6671800
34 The five-paragraph ad appeared in the *WSJ* on March 24, 2016, p. A9. Julie Jargon, "Starbucks CEO Faces U.S. Challenge," *WSJ*, April 3, 2017, p. B3.
35 George Anders, "The President of Coffee Nation," *Forbes*, March 21, 2016, p. 44. See entire article, pp. 41–52.
36 Julie Jargon, "Starblucks CEO Faces U.S. Challenge," *WSJ*, April 3, 2017, p. B3.
37 Christopher Bartlett and S. Ghoshal, "What is a Global Manager?," *Harvard Business Review*, Volume 70, No. 5, September–October 1992, pp. 124–132.
38 For background on the case, see "Testimony of Michael Horn, President and CEO of Volkswagen Group of America, Inc". Before the House Committee on Energy and Commerce Subcommittee on Oversight and Investigations, October 8, 2015. media.vw.com/release/1087.
39 William Boston, "VW Tries to Stem Growing Scandal," *WSJ*, September 24, 2015, p. A1.

40 Oliver Balch, "Don't Brand Your Business with the Label 'Ethical,'" *The Guardian*, March 26, 2015.
41 William Boston, "2014 VW Memo Warned of Probe," *WSJ*, February 16, 2016, p. B3.
42 Jack Ewing, "Former VW chief Got Report on Diesels in 2014," *International New York Times*, March 3, 2016, p. 16.
43 Jack Ewing, "Former VW Chief Got Report on Diesels in 2014," *International New York Times*, March 3, 2016, p. 16.
44 William Brown, "Former CEO Named in VW Probe," *WSJ*, January 28–29, 2017, p. B5.
45 "U.S. Indicts VW's Former Chief," *WSJ*, May 4, 2018, p. A1.
46 See Otto Lerbinger, *The Crisis Manager: Facing Disasters, Conflicts, and Failures*, 2nd ed. (New York: Routledge, 2012), pp. 253ff.
47 On November 21–22, 2015, p. A5.
48 William Boston and Mike Spector, "VW Draws Regulators' Ire," *WSJ*, November 19, 2015, p. B1.
49 Jana Kasperkevic, "Volkswagen to Buy Back or Repair Nearly 600,000 Vehicles in Emissions Scandal," *The Guardian*, April 21, 2016.
50 Adrienne Roberts, "Diesel Buybacks Aid VW's Sales," *WSJ*, February 23, 2017, p. B3.
51 William Wilkes, "Volkswagen Adds to Scandal Cost," *WSJ*, February 2, 2017, p. B3.
52 John C. Stoll, "VW Meets U.S. Dealers, Vows to Repair Image," *WSJ*, April 4, 2016, p. B1.
53 Sara Randazzo and Jonathan Bach, "VW Car Dealers Applaud Settlement," *WSJ*, August 17–18, 2016, p. B5.
54 William Boston, "Investors Take Aim at VW in Suit," *WSJ*, March 16, 2016, p. C4.
55 William Boston and William Wilkes, "Former VW Leader Faces Probe," *WSJ*, June 21, 2016, p. B3.
56 William Boston, "Inquiry Targets Volkswagen CEO," *WSJ*, May 18, 2017, p. B1.
57 William Boston, "VW Investors to Get Their Day in German Court," *WSJ*, August 9, 2016, p. B3.
58 William Boston, "Investor Claims Against VW Jump," *WSJ*, September 29, 2016, p. B3.
59 William Boston, "Volkswagen's Legal Battles Heat up Around the Globe," *WSJ*, August 24, 2016, pp. B1, B2.
60 Aruna Viswanatha and Mike Spector, "U.S. Suit Seeks Billions from VW," *WSJ*, January 5, 2016, p. B1.
61 Kimberly S. Johnson and James Willhite, "Volkswagen CFO is in the Hot Seat," *WSJ*, September 29, 2015, p. B4.
62 Sara Randazzo, "FTC Sues Volkswagen Over Its 'Clean Diesel' Vehicle Advertising", *WSJ*, March 30, 2016, p. B3.
63 Eyk Henning and Hendrik Varnholt, "VW Weights Scandal's Impact on Finances," *WSJ*, October 5, 2015, p. B3.
64 Mike Spector, "New Jersey Sues VW Over Emissions," *WSJ*, February 8, 2016, p. B3.
65 Oliver Balch, "Don't Brand Your Business with the Label 'Ethical,'" *The Guardian*, March 26, 2015.
66 Garbriele Steinhauser, "Volkswagen is Chastised by EU Bank for its Response to Scandal," *WSJ*, January 14, 2016.
67 "Briefing – The Volkswagen Scandal: A Mucky Business," *The Economist*, September 26, 2015, p. 23.
68 William Boston, "Sales Slide at VW Continues Globally," *WSJ*, January 9–10, 2016, p. B3.
69 Zeke Turner, "Germans Rethinks Stringent Privacy Laws," *WSJ*, August 20–21, 2016, p. A4.
70 Geoffrey Smith and Roger Parloff, "Hoaxwagen," *Fortune*, March 15, 2016; Danny Hakim, "VW's Crisis Strategy: Forward, Reverse, U-turn; Carmaker Made Mistakes in its Public Response to the Uproar Over Cheating," *International New York Times*, February 27, 2016, p. 11.
71 "A Mucky Business," *The Economist*, September 26, 2015, p. 25.
72 William Boston, "VW Probe Targets Engineers," *WSJ*, October 5, 2015, p. A1.

73 Ibid., pp. A1, A4.
74 William Boston, "VW Tries to Stem Growing Scandal," *WSJ*, September 24, 2015, p. A1.
75 William Boston et al., "VW Scandal Threatens to Upend CEO," September 23, 2015, p. A1–2.
76 William Boston and Ulrike Dauer, "Germany Examines Bosch in VW Emissions Scandal," *WSJ*, December 17, 2015, p. B3.
77 William Boston, "Suit Claims Bosch Aided VW's Cheating," *WSJ*, August 19, 2016, p. B3.
78 William Boston, "VW Seeks Whistleblowers," *WSJ*, November 13, 2015, p. B3.
79 Dan Neil, "VW Lost its Moral Compass in Quest for Growth," *WSJ*, September 26–27, 2015, p. D10.
80 William Boston, HenrikVarnholt, and Sarah Sloat, "VW Says 'Culture' Flaw Led to Crisis," *WSJ*, December 11, 2015, p. B1.
81 Paul Kedrusky, "An Engineering Theory of the Volkswagen Scandal," *The New Yorker*, October 16, 2015.
82 Ibid.
83 "Reinventing These Wheels," *Bloomberg Businessweek*, December 19–28, 2016, pp. 19–20.
84 William Boston, "VW Still a Work in Progress," *WSJ*, February 24, 2016, p. B7.
85 William Boston, "Sales Slide at VW Continues Globally," *WSJ*, January 9–10, 2016, p. B3.
86 William Boston and Mike Spector, "VW Draws Regulators' Ire," *WSJ*, November 19, 2015, p. B1.
87 Mike Spector, "VW Setting up Program for Diesel-Owner Claims," *WSJ*, December 18, 2015, p. B2.
88 "Per Du Mit Dem Chef," *Der Spiegel*, April 2, 2016, pp. 74–78.
89 Nils Pratley, "Volkswagen's Executive Pay Packages Remain Untroubled by Emissions Scandal," *The Guardian*, April 28, 2016.
90 "Äyerschlagt Diesen Konyern!," *Der Spiegel*, Vol. 46, 2015.
91 William Boston, "Recall Costs Hit VW, Fiat," *WSJ*, October 29, 2015, p. B3.
92 Dan Neil, "VW Lost Its Moral Compass in Quest for Growth," *WSJ*, September 26–27, 2015, p. D10.
93 For example, see James B. Steward, "Problems at VW Start at the Boardroom," *New York Times*, September 25, 2015.
94 William Boston, Mike Spector, and Amy Harder, "VW Scandal Threatens to Upend CEO," *WSJ*, September 23, 2015, pp. A1–A2.
95 Eyk Henning, "Activists Hit Block on German Boards," *WSJ*, October 27, 2015, p. B8.
96 Charles M. Elson, Craig K. Ferrere, and Nicholas J. Goossen, "The Bug at Volkswagen: Lessons in Codetermination, Ownership and Board Structure," *Journal of Applied Corporate Finance*, Vol. 27, No. 4, 2015.
97 William Boston, "VW Tries to Stem Growing Scandal," op. cit.
98 James B. Steward, "Culture at VW Made Scandal More Likely; Common Sense," *International New York Times*, September 25, 2015, p. 18.
99 Ruth Bender, "Scandal Tests Auto Ties," *WSJ*, September 26–27, 2015, p. B4.
100 Ibid.
101 "Volkswagen Considers Shareholder Lawsuit to Be Without Merit," *WSJ*, March 2, 2016.
102 Danny Kakim, op. cit. Geoffrey Smith and Roger Parloff.
103 Based on a study by Ansgar Zerfass of the University of Leipzig and Joachim Klewes of Ketchum Pleon in Duesseldorf, "The Future of Organizing Corporate Communications: Implications of a Benchmarking Study in Global Companies," *Harvard Business Manager*, Vol. 34, No. 4, April 2012.
104 William Boston and Mike Spector, "VW to Meet with Regulator as Patience Frays," *WSJ*, November 9, 2015.

Index

Corporate Communication: An International and Management Perspective, First Edition. Otto Lerbinger.

q

r